Global Issues and Ethical Considerations in Human Enhancement Technologies

Steven John Thompson
Johns Hopkins University, USA & University of Maryland University College, USA

A volume in the Advances in Human and Social Aspects of Technology (AHSAT) Book Series

Medical Information Science
REFERENCE
An Imprint of IGI Global

Managing Director:	Lindsay Johnston
Production Editor:	Jennifer Yoder
Development Editor:	Austin DeMarco
Acquisitions Editor:	Kayla Wolfe
Typesetter:	Thomas Creedon
Cover Design:	Jason Mull

Published in the United States of America by
Medical Information Science Reference (an imprint of IGI Global)
701 E. Chocolate Avenue
Hershey PA 17033
Tel: 717-533-8845
Fax: 717-533-8661
E-mail: cust@igi-global.com
Web site: http://www.igi-global.com

Library of Congress Cataloging-in-Publication Data

Global issues and ethical considerations in human enhancement technologies /
Steven John Thompson, editor.
    pages cm
Includes bibliographical references and index.
  Summary: "This book compiles prestigious research and provides a well-rounded composite of role of human enhancement technologies in emerging areas for those involved in computer science and the humanities, as well as many engaged in a humanities approach to metasystems, new artificial life, and robotics"-- Provided by publisher.
  ISBN 978-1-4666-6010-6 (hardcover) -- ISBN 978-1-4666-6011-3 (ebook) -- ISBN 978-1-4666-6013-7 (print & perpetual access) 1. Biomedical engineering--Research--Moral and ethical aspects. 2. Human experimentation in medicine--Moral and ethical aspects. 3. Medical instruments and apparatus. I. Thompson, Steven John, 1956- R856.G65 2014
  610.28--dc23
                          2014019176

This book is published in the IGI Global book series Advances in Human and Social Aspects of Technology (AHSAT) (ISSN: 2328-1316; eISSN: 2328-1324)

British Cataloguing in Publication Data
A Cataloguing in Publication record for this book is available from the British Library.

For electronic access to this publication, please contact: eresources@igi-global.com.

Advances in Human and Social Aspects of Technology (AHSAT) Book Series

Ashish Dwivedi
The University of Hull, UK

ISSN: 2328-1316
EISSN: 2328-1324

Mission

In recent years, the societal impact of technology has been noted as we become increasingly more connected and are presented with more digital tools and devices. With the popularity of digital devices such as cell phones and tablets, it is crucial to consider the implications of our digital dependence and the presence of technology in our everyday lives.

The **Advances in Human and Social Aspects of Technology (AHSAT) Book Series** seeks to explore the ways in which society and human beings have been affected by technology and how the technological revolution has changed the way we conduct our lives as well as our behavior. The AHSAT book series aims to publish the most cutting-edge research on human behavior and interaction with technology and the ways in which the digital age is changing society.

Coverage

- Activism & ICTs
- Computer-Mediated Communication
- Cultural Influence of ICTs
- Cyber Behavior
- End-User Computing
- Gender & Technology
- Human-Computer Interaction
- Information Ethics
- Public Access to ICTs
- Technoself

IGI Global is currently accepting manuscripts for publication within this series. To submit a proposal for a volume in this series, please contact our Acquisition Editors at Acquisitions@igi-global.com or visit: http://www.igi-global.com/publish/.

Titles in this Series

For a list of additional titles in this series, please visit: www.igi-global.com

Interdisciplinary Applications of Agent-Based Social Simulation and Modeling
Diana Francisca Adamatti (Universidade Federal do Rio Grande, Brasil) Graçaliz Pereira Dimuro (Universidade Federal do Rio Grande, Brasil) and Helder Coelho (Universidade de Lisboa, Portugal)
Information Science Reference • copyright 2014 • 376pp • H/C (ISBN: 9781466659544) • US $225.00 (our price)

Examining Paratextual Theory and its Applications in Digital Culture
Nadine Desrochers (Université de Montréal, Canada) and Daniel Apollon (University of Bergen, Norway)
Information Science Reference • copyright 2014 • 419pp • H/C (ISBN: 9781466660021) • US $215.00 (our price)

Exchanging Terrorism Oxygen for Media Airwaves The Age of Terroredia
Mahmoud Eid (University of Ottawa, Canada)
Information Science Reference • copyright 2014 • 347pp • H/C (ISBN: 9781466657762) • US $195.00 (our price)

Women in IT in the New Social Era A Critical Evidence-Based Review of Gender Inequality and the Potential for Change
Sonja Bernhardt (ThoughtWare, Australia)
Business Science Reference • copyright 2014 • 274pp • H/C (ISBN: 9781466658608) • US $195.00 (our price)

Gamification for Human Factors Integration Social, Education, and Psychological Issues
Jonathan Bishop (Centre for Research into Online Communities and E-Learning Systems, Belgium)
Information Science Reference • copyright 2014 • 362pp • H/C (ISBN: 9781466650718) • US $175.00 (our price)

Emerging Research and Trends in Interactivity and the Human-Computer Interface
Katherine Blashki (Noroff University College, Norway) and Pedro Isaias (Portuguese Open University, Portugal)
Information Science Reference • copyright 2014 • 580pp • H/C (ISBN: 9781466646230) • US $175.00 (our price)

Creating Personal, Social, and Urban Awareness through Pervasive Computing
Bin Guo (Northwestern Polytechnical University, China) Daniele Riboni (University of Milano, Italy) and Peizhao Hu (NICTA, Australia)
Information Science Reference • copyright 2014 • 440pp • H/C (ISBN: 9781466646957) • US $175.00 (our price)

User Behavior in Ubiquitous Online Environments
Jean-Eric Pelet (KMCMS, IDRAC International School of Management, University of Nantes, France) and Panagiota Papadopoulou (University of Athens, Greece)
Information Science Reference • copyright 2014 • 325pp • H/C (ISBN: 9781466645660) • US $175.00 (our price)

DISSEMINATOR OF KNOWLEDGE

www.igi-global.com

701 E. Chocolate Ave., Hershey, PA 17033
Order online at www.igi-global.com or call 717-533-8845 x100
To place a standing order for titles released in this series, contact: cust@igi-global.com
Mon-Fri 8:00 am - 5:00 pm (est) or fax 24 hours a day 717-533-8661

Table of Contents

Detailed Table of Contents

Chapter 1
Ethics, Wearable Technology, and Higher Education: Toward a New Point-of-View Angle on
Interactive Instruction 1
> *Marcia Alesan Dawkins, University of Southern California, USA*

Google Glass steals today's news headlines with its cutting-edge technology and user experience. Its role in society is still unsure, as public spaces ban the technology for potential violation of privacy concerns. Glass is just one of many controversial interfaces enhancing the body with virtual connectivity, and chances are it is not going away until it strategically morphs into a more enhancing technology. While its presence in public use may be disconcerting to persons unwittingly under its surveillance, its presence in private use leverages some doubts, as this chapter testifies to the pedagogical prowess of an emerging technology like no other today.

Chapter 2
Anticipating Human Enhancement: Identifying Ethical Issues of Bodyware 16
> *Deniz Tunçalp, Istanbul Technical University, Turkey*
> *Mary Helen Fagan, University of Texas at Tyler, USA*

Human Enhancement Technologies (HET) are integrating with Information and Communication Technologies (ICT) for a new breed of external wearables and implants known as bodyware. The ethical issues associated with smart wearable devices are at the forefront of the digital revolution as privacy and surveillance matters confront society and the individual in unprecedented methods and ways today. Agential realism is one lens under consideration for research evaluation of how wearable technologies "intra-act" with human bodies, essentially moving human and machine merging closer to the science fiction reality of cyborgs among us, in this chapter's exploration.

Chapter 3
Mapping Human Enhancement Rhetoric 30
> *Kevin A. Thayer, Cyborg-X.com, USA*

The human enhancement field is rife with reality and fiction vying in competition for some sort of lexicon providing terms associated with these technologies; yet, as is often the case, where the real need is where the rhetoric gets assimilated and appropriated in ways that don't necessarily serve universal purposes.

Often, a clear picture of terms and devices being employed by industry professionals and scholars alike must emerge for the layman. This is serious business, as more than a decade of contention for the term "terrorism" has proven to be problematic through its relative application having no consensus on definition. This chapter is one way for scholars and practitioners to get a handle on rhetorics associated with human enhancement technologies as insurance against the terminology suffering the "terrorism" fate: having no viable definition.

Chapter 4

Whether eugenics or clones, the morality of what humans are capable of doing to themselves and each other through technological means is not a novel concern, as science has long been at work trying to create the perfect human being. This is certainly an agenda for many human enhancement technologists, and, as expected, the road is fraught with repeated failure and concern over motives. This chapter looks at the nature of the ideal human being and the need for scholars to precisely define human enhancement in order to safely address moral complications.

Chapter 5

The plastic cosmetic arts are an acceptable method of human enhancement, and the technologies used are state-of-the-art. Certainly, synthetic biology is helping move these arts and their techniques into new territory where skins may seamlessly and effortlessly mesh with inorganic substances. Many ethical concerns are as personal as the decisions and methods employed by proponents of plastic surgery procedures, and the human enhancements they afford. In this chapter, the ethics associated with use of emerging enhancement technologies in a quest for perfection of the human body are viewed through the lens of a singular celebrity case study to help further identify underlying universal concepts inherent to artificial beautification.

Tampering with the human brain may be best left to the professionals, but such activity has ethical obligations attached to it, as would any medical practice that "'violates'" the personal space and integrity of another's well-being. Fascinating new technologies are providing hope through important brain-related research, as well as opportunity for previously unavailable participation by the critically encumbered with enhanced new neural networks and their interfaces. Certainly, the neurosciences and neurosurgeons have the keys to making ruined lives better, or, as may be the case, good lives better or their best. While society has its limited, restrictive, somewhat myopic lenses of personal experience and the media to sort progressive matters out, demand for cognitive enhancement through deep brain stimulation, and other ethical issues that move the conversation forward in this regulatory domain are addressed by collegial experts in this chapter.

Patrick Lin, California Polytechnic State University, USA
Max Mehlman, Case Western Reserve University, USA
Keith Abney, California Polytechnic State University, USA
Jai Galliott, Macquarie University, Australia

A most disconcerting area of human enhancement is, undoubtedly, deployment of these technologies by military powers. Robots that defy science fiction imagination are not on the horizon, they are already here -- along with related military enhancements aimed at creating Super Soldiers, such as "go pills" to stay alert on long aerial missions. While these technologies may serve to make the world a safer place, ethical issues arising from such prospective activities abound. As the first of two parts, this chapter provides a historical background on military human enhancement and its pressing controversies.

Patrick Lin, California Polytechnic State University, USA
Max Mehlman, Case Western Reserve University, USA
Keith Abney, California Polytechnic State University, USA
Shannon French, Case Western Reserve University, USA
Shannon Vallor, Santa Clara University, USA
Jai Galliott, Macquarie University, Australia
Michael Burnam-Fink, Arizona State University, USA
Alexander R. LaCroix, Arizona State University, USA
Seth Schuknecht, Arizona State University, USA

The second part of Super Soldiers takes the reader deeper into moral and ethical concerns of military enhancement that surface with military law and policy matters. Rapidly advancing science and technology initiatives are bringing the (USA) military's robotics efforts front and center. This chapter explores, among other pressing matters, prospective roles for human virtues, emotions, and codes of ethics associated with enhanced military warfighters.

Joanna Kulesza, University of Lodz, Poland

While access and privilege are inherent ethical concerns attached to human enhancement technologies, privacy and security become prominent ethical concerns when access or privilege is made active or deactivated. Privacy and security, however, walk hand-in-hand with surveillance and privilege. Human rights law makes privacy imperative in any discussion of human enhancement technologies. This chapter surveys international laws and policies on individual privacy protection, including those from Europe, the USA, and international organizations such as the OECD, in order to identify privacy obligations for all HET-based services.

Futurism, dystopian or utopian, has long been a staple of fiction, and elements of citizenship appear historically in great classic literature from Aldous Huxley's Brave New World to George Orwell's 1984. What it is like to participate in democratic society is the dream of all repressed peoples, though repression may be a subjective term relative to one's democratic experience, especially in an oligopoly masquerading as a democracy. Certainly, privilege in such a scenario, fictitious or currently real, has its role to play, and this chapter considers the citizen voter interface in democratic elections as a vehicle for human enhancement technological influence.

While the ideal world would ensure privilege to all who seek access, the real world is fraught with difficulty and disability. Medical advances in human enhancement are giving hope and access to those persons who may be relegated to the realm of the disenfranchised or ostracized due to some perceived handicap or inability. This chapter explores issues in the relevant literature to bring the reader up-to-date on a current and future need for proposed regulation surrounding disability and technology for human enhancement bordering on transhumanism.

Progression of the transhumanist movement has moved along almost as steadily as advances in (digital) human enhancement technologies, with advocates looking at the prospect of eventual immortality for humans through medical advances and/or relative physical renewal. The reader in this chapter is taken through contemporary transhuman logic, thought, and semantics in perceptions related to metaphysical controversies and futurist debates on technological possibilities related to life, death, and immortality aspects of human enhancement.

Who we are and how we wish to be perceived as who we are constitute major psychological and philosophical components of our humanity, more specifically, ourselves and our identities. Technology plays a critical role in the development of our psyches and our appearances. Naturally speaking, and virtually existing, we instinctively seek to replicate ourselves and our experiences, if not through children, then through our sharing, mentoring, and discipleship. Consequently, ethical and philosophical matters of identification informed by consciousness and the narrative self-result from our evolutionary memetic experiences, as discussed in this chapter.

Finding one's identity and losing one's identity may be parallel tracks on the long train of human enhancement technologies. Concerns about 'survival' as a human or person have long pervaded the debate about enhancement technologies. Consistent with this, terms like humanizing, dehumanizing, and superhumanizing have entered the lexicon of semantics associated with enhancement technologies. However, progress in understanding the effects of enhancement technologies on identity is impaired by the use of different of senses of identity in philosophical, social scientific and folk psychological analyses of enhancement and the inadvertent conflation of these different senses of identity. This chapter argues for a need to ground future inquiry into the relationship of enhancement and identity in psychological and neuroscientific research.

Foreword

Enhancing humans with technology often sounds a bit like ominous science fiction. The warnings of culture from *Frankenstein* to *Terminator* show that messing with nature always has unforeseen consequences for individuals and humanity. However, these are stories, and all stories need a dramatic arc. The real story of technological enhancement is the mundane acceptance of technology into our lives: the exotic new technology becomes the norm; it is adopted, accepted, and then, unquestioned.

Sitting in my favorite cafe with these words, I admit to being a technologically enhanced human; actually, we all are. From the cappuccino maker to the air conditioner, we use technology and its know-how to shape nature, create experiences and sensations. Yet, the technological world on this level no longer excites us.

I am wearing thin, pliable, hydrophilic plastic on my eyes in order to see. Sound exotic? They're just plain, old contact lenses. I am writing on a multi-touch screen with a virtual keyboard, a device we call a tablet, and communicating simultaneously with humans across several time zones and an ocean on my portable computer, my smartphone. We are all technologically enhanced humans, but because we have begun to accept this as the norm, we may no longer question how technology is changing and shaping our lives, impacting our humanity.

My work deals with the impact of technology on everyday life: how we use it, and how it controls us; we are controlled by what the technology will allow us to do. Yet, the point is not to fear or turn down technology, but to adopt it thoughtfully and knowingly. Ranging from Google Glass to cybersoldiers, from neurosurgery to the *singularity*, scholars in this book lay out the arguments and issues that arise from our quest to rapidly adopt technology in order to help improve the human condition. This drive begs the question, In the endless chain of emerging enhancements, at what point are we no longer just humans? When do we become humans 2.0? What will it all mean?

As we move towards future technologies that will be more closely integrated to our physical bodies than ever before, we need to discuss and explore ethical, legal, and social issues these technological advances will bring. This is where the collection of authors in this book excels. This book covers the current and emerging field of human enhancement technologies and provides a readable, in-depth analysis of the vital questions our technology adoption brings to us.

Over the past two decades, we have seen technology become connected, more personal, more mobile, and increasingly a part of our selves. Our smartphones are an extension of our minds; yet, the smartphone is primitive compared to what we are looking at in this collection. We are not only using technology but we are becoming *technological beings*. This is why this work is important. It looks at what our next technological steps will mean to us – how we will be defined and what we are individually, and collectively, as a result of this transformation.

Each technological step brings with it a range of new questions, some more uncomfortable than others. They need to be explored and examined in order for us to understand the implications of where we are going. This book deals with fascinating new problems in the privacy debate and far-reaching effects of enhanced citizens acting in their political sphere. Who will own technology embedded into our bodies? Who will own the data it generates? How will this affect privacy, surveillance, and control? Will the technology be connected to the Internet, and if so, what happens when our internal technology is hacked?

This book records how the ability to enhance humans and machines creates new issues when defining and analyzing disability and points to ethical boundaries for our desire for bodily perfection. Our quest for perfection not only changes our appearance or physical prowess, but with the ability to use neurosurgery to enhance our brain functions, there is a deep need for further reflection. In general, this becomes an exploration into what is—and will be—involved in technology enhancing humans to the elusive prospect of living up to become "the ideal human."

News reports today contend that Google Glass is being readily adopted in educational settings, including elementary schools; yet, it is easy to ask how far participants have explored the full ethical implications of such actions. Some answers lie herein, as this work provides chapters that explore ethics of wearable technologies. Naturally, these technologies will not only be used for educational or peaceful ends. Improving military might and ability has always been a driver of technology. Whether we strive to create cyborg warriors or "only" to enhance humans fighting today, these actions raise a host of important questions.

One way of charting our discussion is to map out human enhancement rhetoric, what it defines and what these definitions entail, or we can address the questions of the future of self-determination and argue that enhancing humans will not be a dehumanizing force. The technology will change us; the chapters exploring the self and our identity raise vital questions towards the impact on identity. We are in a period of technological change, and we are using technology to change our bodies. The topics explored in different ways in this book are fascinating and important as they ultimately question if we are changing our identities, and if so, is the future utopian or dystopian?

Mary Shelley's *Frankenstein* is a demonstration that there is a point beyond which science should not go. Are we there yet? Who should—and could—decide when we have reached that point? Therein is a huge ethical dilemma: if we have the technology to improve a life, then can it be right not to do so? If improvement is always right, then are we becoming technological determinists, where technology controls what we do with our lives? Who defines *improvement*?

The human enhancement conversation is not some vague future discussion. As this book shows, it is happening all around us. It is happening now.

Mathias Klang
University of Göteborg, Sweden

Mathias Klang *is an Associate Professor at the University of Göteborg, Sweden. He is a scholar and researcher on the effects of Internet-based technologies on individuals, organizations, and the state. His works include prescient studies of human rights in the digital age and the impacts of technology on democracy. His current research explores the ways in which our technological devices enable us and control our behavior, information flows, and culture. He currently resides in Philadelphia and is available online at klangable.com.*

Preface

Society is struggling with issues regarding rapid advancements in Human Enhancement Technologies (HET), especially in terms of definition, effects, participation, regulation, and control. These are global matters that legislators must sufficiently address at some point, as was evidenced partly by debate within the 2008 European Parliament's Science and Technology Options Assessment (STOA), among other discussions; yet, relevance must not be relegated entirely to scientists, legislators, and lobbyists who may gain power and control at the expense of those parties most affected by these life-changing technologies. Since current and future HET initiatives should be in the best interests of those who will eventually participate, research into critical pragmatic elements of HET must expand beyond government and scientific experimentation for eventual societal adoption to incorporate deeper relevant inquiry from within the humanities.

While much of the realm of HET is in a state of growing experimentation, there is benefit to exploring ground that may be covered regarding universal concerns, ethics, objectives, and principles in aspects of HET as viewed through the humanities. This compendium includes the scholarly contributions of professional researchers and others working with HET issues today and into the future. It provides a well-rounded composite of the HET landscape and a privileged glimpse into a few of the plethora of potential concerns that confront us as humans embracing and merging with new emerging technologies.

The challenge of a technology will always be its effect on society. While our network connectedness is influenced by our personal interests and an apparent technological destiny for what may determine our ultimate humanity, we live in a time when our freedom to electronically connect is dictated by the entities that have control of that freedom as they liaise with governments and corporations that provide global electronic connection services. Since it is humans who make critical decisions on behalf of individuals, corporations, and governments, at times all these entities find themselves competing in interests betwixt liberty and profit.

HET are no less affected by these forces; rather, they are at the forefront of a struggle for determining what it means to be human in the twenty-first century, and conversely, what it means to be human and technologically merging with machines. Full hybridization of humans and computers into new, integrated, interdependent biological and physiological structures is upon us. Organic and synthetic components are merging in important new ways, making endless possibilities a reality, and ultimately, changing communication values and methods across the globe and beyond, between people, between machines, and between people and machines. The ability to enhance raises an assortment of ethical concerns that not only affect the individual but also affect the Internet world.

Whether cloning another individual or requiring installation of an Internet brain interface, the decision is not without requisite review and evaluation of its consequences. Whether a scientist bent on fame or infamy, or a student experimenting with a chip under the skin for the first time, there are consequential decisions facing the inquisitor, and the smallest decision today has the potential for global impact. Governments and states have been busy working to cover some of the ethical concerns new and emerging technologies afford their societies; however, speed of technological development and diversity is happening at an unprecedented pace. Full control of the forces that will determine the available and perhaps requisite choices facing mankind are up for grabs, at times dictated by uncalculated response in an attempt to bring that which appears out of control under control.

What are human enhancement technologies doing to us? Rapidly advancing at a pace beyond the scope of any singular individual to calibrate, HETs are radically changing our world. Consumer desire and adoption goes unquestioned, military advancement goes forward without any requisite accountability, and entrepreneurship goes into uncharted territory with everything from virtual reality headsets to synthetic biological creations that defy traditional nomenclature. These are just some of the issues that concern the authors in this book as they seek to lay out the landscape for human enhancement technologies before ethical matters get swept away in the global adoption of technologies that hold wonder and promise, yet may be unregulated or out of control.

This book is deliberately presented in a non-hierarchical order for the reader to access accordingly. It strives for a more rhizomic flow (i.e., a networked continuum of sorts, with nodes of select [reader] significance across that spectrum). Still, the overall scheme moves sensibly from physical body to metaphysical theory, from practical experimentation and body modification to medical and military adoption, addressing legal and civil ramifications before closing on philosophical and rhetorical perspectives. While it does not have regional voices emanating specifically from South America or Asia, this edited volume truly is a global initiative, with representative authors from North America, Eastern and Western Europe, and the South Pacific.

The Japanese student in neurosciences will find valuable information here, as will the professor from Argentina and the corporate lawyer in The Netherlands. HET are global in scope and effect. They intimately touch the lives of the critically disabled, the lives of the exceptionally privileged, and the lives of everyone in-between. They appear to strive to improve our lifestyles while potentially threatening our freedoms. They are here to stay, growing in efficacy and ubiquity, connecting our human natures to one another and the known Internet in irrevocable ways that we must not ignore. To do so is to render posterity helpless in ethical concerns that confront our lives, our children, and their children beyond racial and ethnic barriers, without prejudice, testing the limits of our dreams, our freedoms, our limits, our privileges, and our rights in jurisprudence from citizen to diplomat, scholar to revolutionary, Luddite to vagrant, mother to machine.

It would be remiss to simply address what is going on in these pages without a brief look at the human enhancement technology phenomenon on the outside, in our physical world. While advancements exist beyond the scope of this book, history has been made in the realm of HET with everything from mind-reading helmets getting ready to hit the market to one of the most astounding events in Internet phenomena. University of Washington researchers in 2013 took part in the "first noninvasive human-to-human brain interface" activity ever made where one researcher "thought" about moving the mouse of his colleague who was connected to him strictly through brain interfaces over the Internet, and it actually happened that the colleague's fingers moved (Kaiser, 2013). The list goes on almost exponentially.

As we look inside the pages of this book, we cannot help but see recurring themes and concepts on humanness and identity, from technè and augmentation to matters of access and privacy, revealing the common threads that bind these authors across the continents. Expertise ties them together as well in scholarly research references and citations; this truly is an informed intellectual citizenry tied to HET for learning from one another and sharing important new ideas.

For our first look inside, inquisitive eyes initially open, as they should, in the classroom. In this chapter, Dr. Marcia Dawkins explores a wondrous new space for a pedagogical journey with virtual eyewear technology that provides a novel, new "third voice" to the learner experience of the digital citizen. Informative application development, branding, diversity, education, ethics, and privacy issues are pedagogically assessed through the use of Google Glass in the class.

In Chapter 2, Drs. Deniz Tunçalp and Mary Helen Hagan explore integration of HET with Information and Communication Technologies (ICT) in their delineation of matters related to external wearables and implants as bodyware. The authors consider Barad's "agential realism" as a viable perspective for identifying and addressing ethical issues related to how technologies intra-act with bodies. They quickly introduce us to the definitive realm of the cyborg, a sensible, recurring theme throughout this book.

Dr. Kevin Thayer's research into rhetorical aspects of human enhancement technologies is posited ahead of further discussion. In Chapter 3, Thayer surveys the field, mapping the rhetoric, so a clear picture of terms and devices being employed by industry professionals and scholars alike might emerge for the reader. Many of these terms will surface throughout this book, and Dr. Thayer initially introduces them from his thought-provoking perspective of the cyborg and the transhumanist.

As noted thus far, matters of semantics regarding the lexicon of terms applicable to issues in HET are highly contestable. This includes defining Human Enhancement Technologies for authors who aim to universally ground the term as an imperative prior to addressing its full capabilities. Mr. Johann Roduit and his colleagues bring that discussion front and center with query into the nature of the ideal human, and the need to precisely define HET in order to address any moral complications that may loom on the horizon.

Before shifting headlong into the realm of the ideal human or perfect man-machine, however, Dr. Brett Lunceford brings ethical concerns into the conversation that are associated with use of emerging enhancement technologies in our timeless quest for perfection of the human body. Dr. Lunceford's insights are informed by observations on how humans use enhancing technologies for their correction of perceived "defects" in endless pursuit of beauty through cosmetic surgical arts and persistent celebrity status.

While the body is being enhanced with wearable technologies and prosthetic implants, it is the human brain that has become the most valuable piece of real estate for enhancement. In Chapter 6, Drs. Reuben Johnson, Dirk De Ritter, and Grant Gillett bring their expertise in neurosurgery and biomedical sciences to the discussion with a formidable piece noting, among many rising concerns in the field, market demand for cognitive enhancement through deep brain stimulation and corresponding ethical issues that move the conversation forward in this regulatory domain.

Creation of cyborg soldiers—and the implications that arise from their prospective activities—is no deterrent in war, of course, but the ethical ramifications are important for Dr. Patrick Lin and his colleagues in Chapter 7 to further forge their imprint as experts in these matters. In this first of two parts, these scholars provide a solid historical background to military human enhancement and its pressing controversies.

Chapter 8

The second part of Super Soldiers takes the reader deeper into moral and ethical concerns of HET that surface as the authors explore military law and policy matters that rapidly advancing science and technology initiatives are bringing to the (USA) military's robotics efforts. The authors explore, among other issues, prospective roles for human virtues, emotions, and codes of ethics with enhanced military warfighters.

Whether policy and regulation related to the Internet, the military, or the medical field, Dr. Joanna Kulesza adds her expertise in critique of European legal matters for privacy and the individual to global emerging technologies, especially Internet service providers capable of deploying HET initiatives on a massive scale with little to no oversight. Her chapter on the privacy rights of the individual provides a segue from medical and military initiatives discussed prior to her essay in Chapter 9 to civil matters that will inform the conversation into potential effects of HET on the human spirit and psyche found in remaining chapters of the book.

In the struggle to maintain valid human rights and freedoms, democratic enterprises have been steadily reverberating under the pressures of oligarchic uprisings in major nation-states. Dr. Jean-Paul Gagnon discusses the spirit of the democratic citizen faced with participation in human enhancement matters but with emphasis on HET influence for elections and citizen voting interfaces. Dr. Gagnon suggests an imaginary world, shifting the conversation into theoretical, rhetorical discourse that aims to understand some of the democratic, even at times, metaphysical, aspects HET are bringing to our attention today and into the future.

Dr. Dev Bose explores issues in the relevant literature to bring the reader up-to-date on a current and future state of proposed regulation for the reader querying issues with disability and HET. Bose opens the door to disability regulatory issues in the contested area of transhumanism.

It is in the HET realm of transhumanity that Franco Cortese has been blazing a trail as a leading voice for the transhumanism movement, and the reader will understand why with an introduction to his logic and semantics for controversial perceptions related to the debate on life, death, and immortality, as evidenced in Chapter 12. Arguably a growing area of inquiry and speculation, transhumanism is connected to HET in novel ways that Cortese posits for the reader.

Who we are and how we wish to be perceived as who we are constitute major psychological and philosophical components of our humanity, more specifically, our selves and our identities. Elizabeth Falck's approach to HET and replication of the self is informed by her philosophical research into ethical matters of identification that make inquiry into consciousness, the narrative self, and memes, in Chapter 13.

The continuous, underlying theme of technological human enhancement is frequently framed by fear, derision, confusion, and wonderment over *who* we will be, or *what* we will be, when it all comes down to our self-identity and how to approach it in analysis. In the final chapter, Dr. Samuel Wilson provides a social psychological perspective on enhancement, humanness, and the continuity of identity, as augmented humans and machines learn to co-identify through emerging technologies of human enhancement.

My research interests in HET were initially sparked by my new media effects research of Internet addiction and dependency in 1995, leading to media iconics for cybersemiotic, autopoietic agents as a subscript of AI in the mid-2000s, then, circling back to human technological dependency today, with triangulation of the human body, technology, and the Internet as our destined permanence. Much of what I find imperative before our global society may be found in the following excerpt from my plenary talk at the First International Forum on Media and Information Literacy held in Fez, Morocco, in 2011:

Digital applications and chips in mobile phones attached to the hand and held to the ear are headed into the body. Proliferation of cell or mobile phones provides access to the Internet for more people than standard ISP connections, results in more access. Brain implants and interfaces enhance Internet connections in new ways. Their affordability will make them worthwhile for the privileged. With friends, colleagues, and professional contacts moving into the global hive, there will be much incentive to join the network with increasing finality or be stigmatized, left out, a psychosocial outcast. Benefits appear to far outweigh the consequences. Addiction is not a bad word anymore, it is the norm, result of our dependency, magnified to the level of 21st Century human necessity and expectation (Thompson, 2011).

Personally, my inclination regarding the ultimate purposeful uses of human enhancement technologies is to wax dystopian and apocalyptic; partly due to their calculated prophetic value in Judaeo-Christian theology, and partly due to their propensity for power abuse and misuse. While they serve to provide the means for moving humanity closer to technological wonder, that translates to 'enhancement' for some, but not all; they are not competitive for me as a valid ticket to immortality. As noted above, my deepest concern lies with consequences of HET policy in designating select HET as a human requirement, and in my statement on benefits the reliance of semantics is critical when I said "Benefits appear...." rather than "Benefits are...." Furthermore, our corporate dependency on technology today is no different than our individual addiction to it, and I am not convinced that is a good thing overall for humankind.

Heidegger, in my interpretive meditation, was not specific enough: *technology is timely*. The remake of the landmark film *Total Recall* left many people wondering why anyone would attempt such a feat: to remake something that could not compete with its original on any level – except, it seems, for one spectacular upgrade, Special Effects. At times, looking like a set ripped off of Ridley Scott's mind-blowing classic *Blade Runner*, but on steroids, the 2012 *Total Recall* remake is a Computer-Generated Imagery (CGI) sensory override: layer upon layer of textures and effects at multiple structural levels that the viewer cannot process in a single viewing, with rapid character-environ interface machinations that provide an unwieldy sense of not knowing whether one is coming or going. Of interest to the human enhancement technologist, protagonist Colin Farrell's one threat in the film is a phone implanted beneath the skin, which, in his case, is being used by authorities to track him. The scene is a winner, hands-down, providing a pragmatic view of a Graphical User Interface (GUI) that seamlessly interfaces the individual body with the "corporate" network every which way, securing the human—whether desired or not—*on the grid*.

This book provides a definitive reference for an indefinable, emerging phenomenon, that of Human Enhancement Technologies. In its pages, scholars from around the world have brought their topics to the table in an attempt to identify the global issues and ethical concerns that they believe are pre-eminent when it comes to potential societal impact from emerging enhancement technologies today. The voices heard in the pages of this book are those of educated risk-takers and lifelong dreamers. The future is not for any one person to predict, especially one fraught with so many competing voices in realms of access, privilege, policy, regulation, power, governance, and ultimate control of emerging technologies. Still, without the risk these scholars take to put their research and scholarship into the hands of the layman for further exploration, there is no sensible conversation, but what Henry David Thoreau once called "a quiet desperation." Surely, the authors in these pages know that desperation to be an enemy of the human soul, as evidenced in their fresh, erudite reflections and keen insights that transport the curious mind's journey of each one of them into the waiting heart of the watchful reader.

Steven John Thompson
Johns Hopkins University, USA & University of Maryland University College, USA

REFERENCES

Kaiser, T. (2013, August 28). *UW researcher moves another human's finger with his thoughts*. Retrieved from http://dailytech.com

Thompson, S. J. (2011, June). *Endless empowerment and existence: From virtual literacy to online permanence in presence*. Paper presented at the First International Forum on Media and Information Literacy. Fez, Morocco.

Acknowledgment

I am grateful for members of my Editorial Advisory Board for their time and energy in informing the overall direction of this book project. The staff at IGI Global has been most helpful in successfully transitioning this book from my initial idea in 2010 to its physical existence in 2014. While many people helped along the way, I would be remiss to not thank, in particular, Acquisitions Editor Erika Carter, Assistant Acquisitions Editor Kayla Wolfe, Assistant Development Editor Allyson Gard, Editorial Assistant Monica Speca, Director of Intellectual Property and Contracts Jan Travers, and Managing Director Lindsay Johnston, for seeing this project cross the many hurdles that almost undermined it over the long stretch of four years. Their steadfast dedication to the success of this book project assuaged my brief moments of angst and derision and culminated in fulfillment of the need for an academic book on human enhancement technologies today. Finally, the authors, peer reviewers, and research companions that I have had the fortune to secure for this book have provided an incredibly rewarding and memorable journey that continues beyond publication. For that blessing, I am most grateful.

Steven John Thompson
Johns Hopkins University, USA & University of Maryland University College, USA

Chapter 1
Ethics, Wearable Technology, and Higher Education:
Toward a New Point-of-View Angle on Interactive Instruction

Marcia Alesan Dawkins
University of Southern California, USA

ABSTRACT

This chapter explores the relationship between ethics, wearable technology, and higher education through the lens of teaching with Google Glass. Beginning with an introduction to Glass and to the contemporary concept of the digital citizen, the chapter traces out a pedagogical framework aimed at preparing learners to embrace their civic duty to contribute to the virtual world responsibly. Continuing with an investigation of ethical obligations, educational concepts, and learning exercises made available by advances in HET, the chapter describes how to use Google Glass as a case study for examining the limits and possibilities of a new point-of-view angle on interactive instruction. To this end, students' project-based and experiential learning about how Glass impacts communication culture and technology, commerce, security, access, etiquette, branding, ethics, and law is described. The chapter concludes with a discussion of how technology's ethical consciousness continues to be enacted and embodied via a "collusive" point-of-view angle and third voice that shed light on the ongoing rhetorical and pedagogical processes of expression, experience, and identification in the digital age.

"OK, GLASS... TEACH A CLASS"

On February 24, 2013, I entered a Google Plus contest to pick the first group of Glass Explorers with the following post: "#ifIhadglass you and I could meet +Eminem... maybe." About a month later, Project Glass answered: "Hi Marcia, thanks for applying! We'd like to invite you to join our #glassexplorers program. We'll be sending you a private message with more details in the com-

ing weeks – keep an eye on our stream at Project Glass." The invite would lead to a payment of $1,500 plus California State tax a few months later. (Fortunately, my University had agreed to cover the cost of my Glass.)

My "winning" #ifIhadglass post to Google Plus was based on the book I was in the process of completing, *Eminem: The Real Slim Shady*. *Eminem* is a case study in diversity, technology and creative storytelling in the 21ˢᵗ century. In it

DOI: 10.4018/978-1-4666-6010-6.ch001

I described Eminem as an enraging yet enlightening example of the kinds of personas and stories people are encouraged to create and promote with technology. These digital personas are "truthy" or fact-based fictive identities and can be traced in part to Eminem's approach to presenting multiple selves in contemporary culture (Nass & Yen, 2010; Pariser, 2011; Dawkins, 2013). As a rhetorical scholar interested in how personas are amplified and reduced by digital communication I became interested in the *techne*, the artistic and scientific communication elements, through which everyday people bring today's truthy personas to life. Critical components of the *techne* that creates truthy personas are celebrity promotional practice and an ability to create and distribute immersive stories pervasively and persuasively through networked technologies.

Historically, scholars of *techne* have been concerned with the creation of public personas and how, through technology and networks, individuals and publics experience cultural values and describe the world ethically. For example, when the Sophists came to ancient Greece after studying rhetoric in Africa, Asia and the Middle East they brought with them instructions for using language and images as *techne*, tools with which to (re)shape moral consciousness in private and public lives (Fox, 1983). The Sophists' *techne* included technologies of written culture such as language, symbols, paper, pencils, paint and walls as ways to galvanize audiences. These technologies were seen as ways to produce and organize data that integrated ethics into cultural practice through storytelling. Though portrayed as arthritic for the imagination and as media that produce dangerous virtual realities by the likes of Socrates and Plato, the Sophists' ideas about technology as a purposeful, persuasive and ethical element of culture were considered revolutionary. So revolutionary, in fact, that the Sophists' takes on technology, morality, culture and rhetoric was debated in academies throughout ancient Greece and Rome and hundreds of years later in Europe and North America (Glenn & Carcasson, 2009).

This classical debate continues even today. Up for debate now is technology's ethical consciousness, or the hidden values that come to light as people communicate who they are and discover what they can do with new tools like wearable technology (Hauser, 2002; Dawkins, 2012). Four propositions add fuel to this debate about technology's ethical consciousness. First, that technology is never an ideologically neutral tool even though its ideologies often appear invisible (Postman, 1993). Second, that as a result of being ideologically-driven technology privileges certain ethical frameworks that educate us about what is "good" and make some versions of "good" seem more desirable than others (Aristotle, 2012). Third, that new possibilities for human experience and identification made possible by technology require new modes of expression (Dawkins, 2013). Fourth, that the kind of education made possible in the digital age must be of a quality that educators can use to produce meaningful learning (DePietro, 2013). Hence, technology enables a particular kind of human enhancement as it is used to reshape the world and uncover possibilities for human experience, expression and identification—from altruistic community members to autonomous self-interested individuals to, what I am calling, networked digital citizens.

Networked digital citizens are those who use technology ethically and enthusiastically while expressing informed critiques and challenging norms of appropriateness when necessary. I solidified my status as a networked digital citizen when I arrived at the Glass Explorers' "Basecamp," at the Google offices in Venice, California on Saturday, June 15, 2013 completely prepared. I did all the reading and watched all the trailers describing the device. I even brought a Web developer friend along to make sure I would leave no stone unturned. Essentially, I learned that Glass is a wearable computer developed by the futuristic Google X division. It is equipped with an optical head-mounted display (OHMD) through which information appears. Glass communicates with the Web and its user by way of natural language voice commands. The first-generation device provides GPS directions, Googles anything, takes pictures, records videos and sends and receives phone and video calls, SMS text messages and emails. In Google-speak, Glass has "a look" and "a feel." It is an augmented way of experiencing and exploring the world that blends physical, social and virtual elements (Chen, 2014).

When I arrived at Basecamp, my Glass Guide, Jennifer Hermening, tended bar, modeled different color options, outfitted me with a Tangerine pair and tutored me about the wearable technology. Jennifer taught me how to talk to my new accessory by greeting it properly: "OK, Glass." In deference to my winning Glass post about meeting Eminem, I started off with a simple command. "OK, Glass. Google Eminem." A crystal clear image of the rapper appeared on the display above my right eye. Then Glass whispered the following factoid from Wikipedia into my ear, "Marshall Bruce Mathers III (born October 17, 1972), better known by his stage name Eminem and by his alter ego Slim Shady, is an American rapper, record producer, songwriter and actor."

Something came over me as I listened to the slightly a-rhythmic yet gentle feminine voice describing Eminem. I felt myself split in two. Each half was overcome, one with excitement and the other with skepticism. Part of me was excited because I was part of building tomorrow. As a Glass Explorer I had a chance to shape how this particular device was going to be used in higher education. Another part of me was afraid because I did not know exactly if or how Glass was going to (re)shape my own identity as an ethically-minded educator turned networked digital citizen. I felt that my loyalties might be questioned. That I would be called a "glasshole" who cared more about my own perspective than the privacy or consent of those I encountered (Miller, 2014). And then I realized that Glass would be my next case study for exploring ethics, identity and communication in the digital age. Before I could use the device with my students I had to assess how it would meet the pedagogical objectives of digital citizenship, a

framework I was committed to teaching because of its focus on ethics, critique and communication. All that was left to do was put Glass, and the excitement and fear it generated in others and in me, to work.

The remaining weeks of my summer involved informal ethnography. I went on outings and engaged in activities wearing Glass so that I could get used to it and get used to others' reactions. My "Glassing" ranged from grabbing drinks with my fiancé at a local bar, to recording July Fourth fireworks at the Queen Mary, to bike riding through my old Brooklyn neighborhood in New York City, documenting a once-in-a-lifetime research trip to Thailand and uploading it all to my Tumblr site (http://digitaldawkins.tumblr.com/). I "Glassed" and "Tumbled," then "Glassed" and "Tumbled" again.

As I "Glassed" and "Tumbled," I found myself elaborating extensively on interactions with the people I encountered, even recombining separate characters in some cases. The rhetorician in me realized that I was using Glass to enact a "third voice," a hybrid narrative identity that expresses the collaboration of the storyteller with the characters she encounters (Kaminsky, 1992). Glass allowed me to embody and enact a "third voice" because the stories I created with it were not simply reflective of my own perspective or of the perspectives of those I encountered. Rather, Glass revealed a previously unknown perspective that combines, alters and amplifies existing communication. The main features I used to engage a "third voice" were live streaming video and dictating my captions and notes to Evernote. Communicating with a "third voice" added additional ethical responsibilities to my "Glassing" and gave me insight into how I might use the device in my undergraduate communication classroom as a case study in networked digital citizenship (i.e., the practices and principles of ethical technology use in spaces constructed through -- -- and communities imagined within -- networked technologies). And that is exactly what I set out to do.

My first new course of the 2013-2014 academic year, *Communication, Culture and Technology* (a/k/a Digital Citizenship), began with a presentation of Google Glass. I began by describing the technology itself and then my summer's worth of exploring with it. To my surprise, students were less interested in how Glass enhanced or detracted from my user experience and perspective as an individual. Students were more interested in what Glass changed entirely from a collective perspective. Some students asked questions about opportunities for changing self-presentation within existing communities and identity categories (i.e., race, ethnicity, sexual orientation, ability). Specifically, students were concerned with how realities of stigma and discrimination might impact what kind of content people might create with the wearable computer. Others asked about how Glass might change old definitions of school and of learning, especially for those who are differently abled. Still others asked what the wearable technology might change in terms of economics, storytelling, entertainment, healthcare, politics, fashion and religion. Would Glass redefine user experiences with digital wallets and impact users' spending habits negatively? How would "four-eyed storytelling" with Glass change narrative structures? What opportunities might develop for Glass to augment what able-bodied wearers can see and hear? Could Glass and other wearable devices ever be considered fashion statements as well as technological ones? Would Glass enhance or hinder spiritual practices like prayer or communion? All large questions indeed.

My students and I set out to answer these and other questions over the next 15 weeks by engaging the contemporary concept of the digital citizen, an ethnical person identifying uniquely and communally within a digital landscape. Along the way we traced out a pedagogically driven definition of digital citizenship (eventually dropping the term "networked" because we found it to be redundant), which provided a theoretical and contextual underpinning for the course. We investigated ethical obligations, educational op-

portunities, and storytelling techniques raised by advances in HET. In the follow-up course, *Cultures of Digital Media*, we made use of Google Glass as a case study for the limits and possibilities of digital citizenship, which allowed us to account for some ways in which technology's ethical consciousness is evolving and devolving. Specifically, we used Glass to redefine and critique the concept of digital citizenship because, as you will soon see, it bestows benefits upon those who have the most access to, understanding of and influence in the digital public sphere without necessarily addressing its inequities (Witte & Mannon, 2010).

The primary objective of this pair of experimental upper division courses was to prepare learners to embrace their civic duty to contribute to the virtual world responsibly. Students learned about communication culture and technology, commerce, security, access, etiquette, branding, ethics and law. In addition, they obtained a better understanding of the inception and implementation of Web 2.0 technology and its radical connectivity. In combination, these courses allowed my students and me to track historical and emergent paradigms for communication among those who consider themselves digital citizens and those who do not, shedding light on the ongoing rhetorical processes of expression, experience, authority and identification in the twenty-first century. It is to these paradigms and experiences that we now turn.

FRAMING GLASS WITH DIGITAL CITIZENSHIP (A/K/A FOUR-EYED CITIZENSHIP)

As capacities for reshaping human experience, expression and identity advance with developments in technology so does our capacity for descriptive terminology. For instance, the term "netizen" enjoyed adoption by intellectual, media and technological elites in the mid 1980s as a way to describe those who inhabit the new geography of the Internet. "Netizens" saw Internet geography as a large network of nodes and connections, a "space of flows" that can be navigated and surfed and that houses data in heavenly realms called clouds (Castells, 2010). As additional concerns arose from increased Internet use and engagement with Web 2.0 and its social technologies (i.e., wikis, blogs, social network sites, tagging, user-generated sites) a new term was needed to express new exigencies. These exigencies included facilitation of direct democracy, net neutrality, copyright reform, peer-to-peer advocacy, access and the belief that the Internet is fundamentally different from other forms of communication and therefore immune to traditional forms of regulation (boyd, 2010). Enter "digital citizenship."

Digital citizenship is a term used by techno-educators Mike Ribble and Gerald Bailey (2011) in conjunction with the development of Web 2.0 and its social technologies to describe ethical behavior pertaining to the use of electronic devices in face of radical connectivity. But digital citizenship is much more than a set of rules for social engagement. Digital citizenship is a rhetorical and pedagogical framework for the digital age whose objectives are to create "thoughtful, ethical decision makers who consider the impact of their policies on future generations; inspirational leaders who can rally our best efforts as a society; [and] deft diplomats who can navigate the complicated, interrelated global world in which we live" (Mele, 2013, p. 94). Digital citizenship is broken down into nine components to meet these objectives: access, commerce, communication, literacy, etiquette, law, rights and responsibilities, health and wellness, and security. Here I will describe each component briefly and the weekly in-class exercise used for its investigation.

Digital Access

Access, the ability to participate multi-dimensionally in a radically connected society, involves making sure that all those who want to use the Internet are able to do so. As such, access is the "starting point" for digital citizenship (Ribble & Bailey, 2011, p. 14). Because equal access is much easier discussed than implemented, students combed through reports from the Pew Research Center's *Internet and American Life Project*. Findings indicated that "15 percent of American adults ages 18 and over do not use the Internet or email" (Zickuhr, 2013). Reasons cited for not using the Internet ranged from lack of relevance, lack of availability and lack of economic resources to lack of traditional and digital literacies (Zickuhr, 2013). Through an exercise entitled, "Debunking Digital Myths," students discovered two additional factors that impact access to digital technologies in education. First, some schools ignore the technological needs of marginalized groups, citing access to technology as less important than access to more traditional educational tools. Second, many educational professionals lack training in how to learn and teach with technology, especially with the mobile technologies with which most disenfranchised youth are familiar (Witte & Mannon, 2010). Digital citizenship requires a commitment to examining how these participation gaps (between users having Internet access only in a library or at school versus 24/7 broadband access, including time limits, blocking access to certain sites, storage limits) and app gaps (between users from high-income and low-income families, the latter having limited access to mobile devices and the applications on them) came to be and how they can be remedied.

Digital Commerce

Commerce, the exchange of merchandise over the Internet, must be understood in the context of local, state, federal and international regulation as well as the purchasing power of existing currencies. Basic understanding of e-commerce is critical because of the sheer volume of business transacted over the Internet on sites like Amazon, where subscribers can buy books, clothes and groceries and will soon have purchases delivered by drones. Similarly, users can buy automobiles and homes on eBay, stream music on Spotify or movies on Netflix, seek employment on LinkedIn and craigslist, find their way home with Uber, find potential mates on Match.com and manage investments on E*Trade. In addition, recent advances in digital commerce like digital wallets, e-banking, inexpensive card reading services such as Square and credit-debit card consolidators such as Only Coin have lowered the cost of processing electronic payments. Digital citizens must be taught to reconcile the digital world's neoliberal values of openness, transparency and freedom with the many legitimate and illegitimate means of transacting business (Penenberg, 2009). For example, a group of five students conducted a case study on Bitcoin and Litecoin, *cryptocurrencies* (digital alternatives to traditional government-issued paper money) that allow for anonymous and quasi-anonymous transactions. Students found that such transactions are underpinned by neoliberal philosophy, which says that the free market and not the nation-state is global society's organizing principle (Chomsky, 1999). Consequently, students also explained how and why digital cryptocurrencies are designed to be easy to use across international borders and difficult for governments to regulate (Nakamoto, 2010; Bilton, 2013). Students then examined how currencies and cryptocurrencies maintain use and exchange values through virtual markets, the costs of switching from one currency to another, the impact of government regulation and oversight and lack thereof. Then, the entire class engaged in an exercise I called "Money 2.0," wherein each student made at least one prediction about how cryptocurrencies could change definitions of wealth, status, ethnicity or digital citizenship when currencies are detached from the good faiths of governments. Of particular interest here was the United States Internal Revenue Service's (2014) "Notice 2014-21," a declaration that Bitcoin is a property rather than a currency. Students interpreted the IRS's position as a potential deterrent to those early adopters who wish to transition to Bitcoin and as a way to identify and track current anonymous Bitcoin owners. In addition, students explored potential opportunities created for hosted digital wallets like Coinbase to track Bitcoin's capital gains and losses throughout each tax year.

Digital Communication

Communication, creating, sharing and making meaning out of information, must be understood in the context of Web 2.0 technology in general and social networking sites in particular. Basic understanding of "the profile [as] the key unit of Web.2.0" is required to understand how identities are constructed, maintained and mobilized (Marwick, 2013, p. 7). Moreover, a focus on digital citizenship must account for how users can and do "integrate advertising and marketing practices into the ways that they view their friends and themselves" on sites like Facebook, Weibo, Snapchat, LinkedIn and Tinder (2013, p. 16). Communicating profiles as value propositions and status updates must be understood in personal, collective and institutional terms (Kerpen, 2011). That means digital citizens must understand how offline race-class-gender-sexuality-religion identities are concealed and revealed in online profiles and deployed to disrupt or maintain existing social hierarchies. By studying Internet influencers like Robert Scoble, Guy Kawasaki, Veronica Belmont, Baratunde Thurston, HolaSoyGerman and FreddieW, students learned how to make good personal decisions when faced with a variety of ways to express their experiences ethically and their identities publicly. To this end we conducted an in-class exercise called, "High Self-Concept, Low Tech," in which we were forbidden from using digital technology to describe ourselves to one another as job candidates. We then compared our in-class and LinkedIn profiles, discussed whether we felt debilitated or empowered in each context and outlined what was appropriate, inappropriate and what could make a difference in today's competitive job market.

Digital Literacy

Literacy, a repertoire of skills that allows users to describe, interpret, evaluate and create messages in a variety of digital genres and formats, must be taught so that digital citizens can engage actively as members of organizations such as schools and workplaces. Literacy is, in itself a form of persuasive storytelling, for "the stories we tell about the importance of literacy reveal the priorities and biases of our cultural situations" (Glenn & Carson, 2009, p. 290). In particular, digital literacy requires students to be taught how to learn in a digital environment – "how to learn anything, anytime, anywhere" (Ribble, 2013) and, more important, how to learn rather than simply socialize or play with new media technology (DePietro, 2013). Digital literacy also includes instruction on how to survive and succeed in digital environments predicated upon attracting attention through self-editing and self-promotion in written and visual terms (Marwick, 2013; boyd, 2014). In this section of the course students worked independently with University librarians to learn how to determine the accuracy of digital content, evaluate the security and trustworthiness of online vendors and recognize phishing attacks. To demonstrate that digital literacy is, at the very least, a two way street, I worked with University librarians to create course related digital content with Glass that students could access remotely.

Digital Etiquette

Etiquette, a philosophy of effective Internet communication that consists of customs and codes of polite behavior, is of utmost concern to digital citizenship. To address these concerns students collaborated and created "Ten Digital Etiquette Commandments" that emphasized respect and appropriateness. Rules included, and were not limited to: respecting others' privacy, forgiving others' mistakes, sharing expertise, never posting

anything that the user would not feel comfortable communicating face-to-face and understanding the norms of each domain the user enters. Social issues addressed included cyberbullying, flaming, and privacy breaching. Design and engineering, or user interface (UI) issues, were also of concern. Specifically, "hacking" and tinkering with computer code in order to disrupt traditional notions of etiquette in digital and physical situations (Coleman, 2009). Students completed a unit on the history of hacking, attended on-campus "hack-athons" for ethnographic purposes and delivered group presentations about the most compelling cases encountered (i.e., Wikileaks, Anonymous).

Digital Law

Law, exploring the legal implications of emerging digital technologies, is concerned primarily with the causes, consequences and prevention of data breaches. Hot button issues arising in this domain include plagiarism, illegal downloading, spamming, identity theft, patent infringement, hacking, phishing, spying and otherwise damaging online data. Of recent concern in this area are the ethical use of cloud computing (or "software as a service"), which places data on remote servers outside the user's direct control, and widespread mass surveillance programs like that of the National Security Administration (Schroeder, 2013). Students learned to be critical about where their data is stored because "nothing is free," "someone or some entity owns the data," and because "someone or some entity owns the servers" (DePietro, 2013, p. 174-175). Because students were extremely concerned with issues of privacy, ownership and personal data encryption, we took time to review each major social media site's and each major cloud storage site's privacy policy in the context of the Fourth Amendment and then adjusted the settings on our accounts as we were able.

Digital Rights and Responsibilities

Rights and responsibilities, entitlements to have or obtain freedoms and protections in a digital environment, must be defined, described and shared by digital citizens. British-American news source for the "Connected Generation" *Mashable,* took up the task over six weeks in the summer of 2013 and crowdsourced the first iteration of a "Digital Bill of Rights". Fashioned after the United States' *Bill of Rights* and authored by "We the people of the Internet," the *Digital Bill of Rights* seeks to "form a more altruistic online existence, establish privacy of user data, ensure protections for all individuals, provide for the common checks and balances of our online rights, promote the general welfare, and secure the liberty of our online identities and our information" (Lytle, 2013). Rights include: access, protections of privacy and free speech, unrestricted view of Internet, control over and protection of personal data sharing, ownership of original content, termination of participation in any service at any time, protection of personal data from illegal search and seizure, anonymity and freedom from government or agency surveillance. Digital citizenship requires further discussion and implementation of these rights, along with the responsibilities they carry. Key issues discussed in class included whether technology is being used in the ways it was intended (i.e., pirating software, identity theft) and how accountable we should be held for the data we post. To test our knowledge of these rights and responsibilities we took the Electronic Frontier Foundation's "Know Your Rights! Quiz" and conducted further research on the questions answered incorrectly.

Digital Health and Wellness

Health and Wellness, the state of being free from physical and mental illness or injury in a networked world, is an emerging area of concern for those interested in digital citizenship. First and foremost, digital health and wellness involve educating technology users on the hazards of digital life in general and in social networking, video gaming and search engines in particular (Greenfield, 2012). Some hazards are physical, such as the effects increased exposure to screen-based technologies have on eye health and ergonomic practices to create safe workspaces. Other hazards are psychological, such as emotional isolation, effects on cognition and learning, as well as increased recklessness and Internet addiction (Putnam, 2001; Turkle, 2011; Jaslow, 2013). Still other hazards, like the preponderance of online predators, data shared from genetic testing, and what happens to users' digital lives after death reside at the intersections of physical, psychological and digital worlds need additional attention (boyd, 2014). Digital citizenship requires the ability to detect and prevent such hazards. Accordingly, students researched opportunities to protect digital health and wellness and found three of particular interest: "lifeloggers," also known as digital death managers, take the mass of digitally recorded material and transform it into stories while users are alive and especially after death (Schiller, 2013); "digital detox specialists," help digital citizens lead less data-centric lives, find a better balance, and, in some cases, organize digital rehabilitation experiences (http://thedigitaldetox.org/); and "microbial balancers," use nanotechnology and data extracted from genetic testing to (re)align a person's bacteria to a healthy level.

Digital Security

Security -- steps taken to guarantee individual, data, browser and network safety -- is an ever-increasing concern as technological advances are accompanied by enhanced possibilities for harm. In addition to trusting other members of our digital communities to participate ethically, responsible digital citizens must take proper precautions to protect their hardware, software and data from being harmed by viruses, failures, hackers and electronic surges (Ribble & Bailey, 2011). To examine digital security in class we created an exercise called, "Popping the Filter Bubble," in which we followed the instructions offered by Eli Pariser (2011) to keep the Web from skewing and hyper-personalizing our results and keep digital interlopers from snooping on our data. These steps include: cleaning out one's cache; erasing one's Web browsing history; cleaning out cookies; refraining from signing in to a Google account when searching; hiding birth dates on social media in general and Facebook in particular; opting out of targeted ads whenever possible; using the private browsing option available in newer browsers such as Dolphin; using an *anonymizer* for Web browsing. Digital citizenship requires ethically generated profiles of technology use in order to achieve greater cyber security postures through trusted expert guidance.

These nine elements of digital citizenship – access, commerce, communication, literacy, etiquette, law, rights and responsibilities, health and wellness and security – form a pedagogical framework for the 21st century college communication classroom. Each element makes technology central to the study of ethical communication and civic engagement by encouraging careful analysis of technology's impact on daily life, understanding of effective and ineffective cases and techniques for expression, and strategies for dealing with the some of the ugly truths about life that technology reveals. In the section that follows I will present my proposal for working with Google Glass in the classroom as a way to apply the concepts of contemporary digital citizenship to digital life.

TEACHING AND LEARNING #THROUGHGLASS

Digital citizenship provides an appropriate pedagogical framework for grappling with Google Glass as the focal point for several case studies. In my second of two experimental courses, *Cultures of Digital Media*, students worked in groups to research the following hot topics pertaining to Glass that emerged through our study of digital citizenship: ethics, education, application building, privacy, branding and diversity. Students were instructed to analyze Google's wearable computer based on each topic and share findings via in class presentations. Each group was instructed to find at least one Glass Explorer to interview taped or live during class to augment the 30-minute presentation. Below are the learning objectives for each group and topic.

Ethics

This group focused on ethics identified the benefits and deficits of Glass on communication and culture. In particular, the group identified: to whom Glass gives greater or lesser power and freedom and peace of mind; what attitudes, biases are embedded within the technology; what skills are required (or enhanced) and not required (or not enhanced); and what unforeseen consequences the technology has on social and political norms and on information flows. Since Glass works extensively on Chrome and Google Plus, students referenced Google's Terms of Service, custom audience targeting tools, and potential opt-out mechanisms for users. Additionally, attention was paid to how Glass exemplified the Association of Computing Machinery's Code of Ethics and Professional Conduct (http://www.acm.org/about/code-of-ethics) as Google faces opposition from competitors, hackers, politicians, laws, bad public relations, and disgruntled users.

Education

The education group grappled with how Glass affects what our culture thinks about, the symbols we think with as well as how and where thoughts develop. They answered the following specific questions: How does Glass affect how we learn? How we know? How we communicate? How does Glass affect what we perceive as real? How does Glass embrace and/or eliminate distraction? Will Glass lead to more civic engagement and project-based learning? Will educators and learners become increasingly risk averse as Glass makes learning increasingly public? The group also offered recommendations for future learning environments, what they referred to as Education 2.0, with special foci on creating a policy for using Glass in on campus settings and using Glass to bring experts to classrooms and classrooms to remote educational sites.

Application Building

This group tried out Google Glass and generated ideas for useful applications. Along the way students pitched their Glass app ideas before a panel of expert judges, comprised of Web developers, marketers and professors, who offered constructive feedback. After the pitches students edited their ideas and prepared to launch them on a slew of social networks to crowdsource which ideas gain traction and which ones do not. Once the digital votes are cast, the group began building a prototype of the most popular app idea, with plans to eventually launch it on Kickstarter. A Web developer from the University guided this stage of app development. Students earned credit based on presentation of their application's story and uses (i.e., creativity, content, empirical research and organization).

Privacy

By studying Google's Privacy Policy and the State of California's Office of Privacy Protection Policy, this group worked to understand Glass' technical underpinnings and operations, as well as its capacity for restructuring privacy via facial recognition technology. Recent events involving Glass that affect privacy – recorded arrests, bans on the device at restaurants and bars and on the roads – were analyzed. In addition, the group addressed the following concerns about Glass and

privacy invasion: whether Glass unintentionally collects data; whether non-users are also covered by Google's privacy policies and protections; whether Glass stores user data and, if so, how it is protected; how Glass complies with data protection laws; and what data is collected and shared with developers.

Branding

The group focused on branding examined Glass in terms of product placement and media mentions as well as the device's ability to reduce the cost of creating entertainment. For example, the group looked for current and future iterations of the device appearing in mainstream media. The group also discussed the effects of product placement on the Glass brand, which Google itself has since addressed (i.e., addressing a lack of Glass options for the optically challenged with upcoming collaborations with eyewear firms Oakley and Ray Ban). Additionally, the group explored problems and possibilities for advertising, commerce, gaming and entertainment programming among an audience of users that will be increasingly fragmented, spread across a wider volume of online video and distracted by other activity both online and off.

Diversity

The group focused on diversity worked to discern what problem(s) Glass was created to solve and what assumptions about communication and culture are made. This group identified the Glass creation story—including characters, setting, the sequence of events and failures and successes (as profit-driven and socially-driven). Then the group found and presented empirical evidence about how Glass is and is not used currently and who is and is not using it at this time. Specifically, the group explored how Glass may help people with hearing and visual disabilities but may be unaffordable for them, and for many non-white populations in the US and abroad. The group also explored what new point-of-view angles and voices Glass engenders as ways to promote diversity. The group then presented at least two ideas about how Glass can be utilized to address issues of diversity and participation gaps in the digital public sphere.

As the aforementioned learning objectives demonstrate, Glass creates a variety of experiences and problems that serve as a basis for reflection on human enhancement technologies, education, communication and ethics. From these reflections, students assimilated the information gathered and developed new theories about the world, which can be tested and retested. The student projects on ethics, education, diversity, application building, privacy, branding and diversity provided an enhanced understanding of Glass for students and faculty alike, creating opportunities that: address the global need for digital citizens; allow for better understanding of civil and ethical responsibilities in the digital public sphere; provide a real time overview of digital media through collaborative research and presentation; and promote experiential learning and develop problem solving skills in emergent pedagogical contexts. Several of these contexts are introduced in the next section.

GLASS MAKES EVERY MOMENT A TEACHABLE MOMENT

The implications for Glass, and for all wearable technology, go far beyond traditional models of lecture-based education. Glass presents educators with opportunities for reflective and more engaged learning that expands the educational process (Bennett, 2013). Clearly, education has transitioned into an era of exploration with help from Glass. Making Glass an educational focal point allows several learning objectives to be redefined and met. These include: demonstrating critical and innovative thinking; displaying competence in a blended communication contexts;

creating entrepreneurial opportunities in the field of communication; and responding effectively to differences in intercultural and interracial communication.

In addition to using Glass as a tool for case study and meeting learning objectives in my classrooms, I have also used the device to conduct *Helpouts* (one-on-one online tutoring sessions) for students who need academic support outside of the classroom. I am not the only educator to use Glass as a training tool. University of Alabama orthopedic surgeon Brent Ponce, M.D., performed a shoulder replacement surgery in September 2013 at Highlands Hospital in Birmingham, Alabama. Watching and interacting with Ponce via Virtual Interactive Presence in Augmented Reality (VIPAAR) was Phani Dantuluri, M.D., from his office in Atlanta. Ponce wore Glass during the operation. The built-in camera transmitted the image of the surgical field to Dantuluri. VIPAAR allowed Dantuluri, who saw on his computer monitor exactly what Ponce saw in the operating room, to introduce his hands into the virtual surgical field. Ponce saw Danturuli's hands as a holographic image in his optical head mounted display (Sparacio, 2013).

Glass allows education to take a hint from gaming by blending the physical and digital worlds to make learning more immersive. Possibilities are virtually endless. Examples include elementary school science teachers who demonstrate the properties of matter through Glass to show students how to make *ooblek* (a quicksand-like substance that acts differently from a liquid and a normal solid). Students wearing Glass take video, search terms and share what they find with other learners to promote inquiry and dialogue. But that is not all science teachers can do with Glass. Online high school physics teacher Andrew Vanden Huevel from Grand Rapids, Michigan uses Glass and the Hangout video call feature to take students who do not have access to advanced physics courses on virtual field trips to see how superconductors work.

Vanden Huevel believes that if educators want to keep the next generation of learners engaged and united, then we have to see that wearable technology is how they will be living. Vanden Huevel argues that educators have to revamp everything we think we know about education and rebuild it around technology like Glass.

Vanden Huevel is not the only one who feels this way. The next generation of filmmakers, athletes and entertainers do as well. *The Kiss: A Short Film Shot Through Google Glass* captures a burgeoning romance from the perspective of both members of a young heterosexual New York City couple (Dickinson & Ferrante, 2013). The directors aimed to show how technology disrupts and enhances the courtship experience. They also aimed to pay homage to the 1896 film *The Kiss*, which was one of the first films ever shown commercially to the public. *Project 2x1* (http://project2x1.com/), touted as the first Glass documentary, covers the lives of the Hasidic and West Indian communities living side-by-side in the Brooklyn, New York neighborhood of Crown Heights. The film addresses issues of diversity head-on by representing hate crimes from different perspectives. Not to be left behind, the National Football League's St. Louis Rams are making use of Glass on practice fields as a way to enhance teamwork and gain perspective on the game itself. In the summer of 2013, the Rams outfitted a pair of players, Quarterback Sam Bradford and receiver Tavon Auston, with Glass to record and save video as they played (Kamenetzky, 2013). In the fall of 2013, rapper Kanye West's acclaimed tour, Yeezus, was designed specifically with wearable technology like Glass in mind. Set as a series of tableaus and as a foray into the wilderness, Yeezus is intended to be experienced through the mobile screen. Yeezus is an experiment in intertextuality and synesthesia, co-created by Mr. West and his audiences interacting in and through a screen culture. I attended the concert with Glass in the interest of research and shared the many pictures and videos I recorded in real time with my students. As I enjoyed Yeezus in person and documented and analyzed the event through Glass I experienced a new point of view angle to provide interactive instruction: an angle that transforms everyone involved.

GLASSING INTO THE UNKNOWN

The new point of view angle to which I refer might be called a "collusive angle" on techno-education, one that consciously shapes the people, ethics and communication involved (Friere, 1970). Theoretically speaking, a collusive angle is a combination and tweaking of ethnography's *third voice* infused with a concern for digital citizenship. The "third voice" describes the reflexivity and transformation that occurs when participant-observers interact with, and in some instances as, their subjects (Kaminsky, 1992). Glass allows its wearers to hear with and speak from the "third voice," telling stories about how, why and with what effects content, ethics, and media converge in a changing digital landscape. Such stories can enhance the overall quality of an educational experience that teaches students to know when to use technology and when to leave it alone. The third voice becomes part of a collusive angle on education when educators and students work together in ways that are not ideologically neutral but, nevertheless, adhere to ethical standards and clearly communicated learning outcomes of digital citizenship. The collusive angle wearable technology provides makes education itself an object of inquiry. Wearable technology like Glass connects teaching and learning, teachers and learners in profound ways. Just as the learner, in overt and covert ways, shapes knowledge with the collusive angle so too the educator, engaged in the act of education, hears and sees the meaning of the knowledge and can help to articulate its coproduced meaning more clearly using the third voice.

Glass becomes more than a high-tech device as it allows us to enact and embody a collusive point-of-view angle and third voice for interactive instruction. Glass becomes an educational artifact that allows us to create "men and women who are capable of doing new things, not simply repeating what other generations have done" (Duckworth, 2006, p. 175). Glass becomes a means of experimenting with the conventions of traditional education, which all too often bury critical thinking and ethical considerations under a mountain of neoliberal individualism. Though certainly not a perfect or ideologically neutral device, Glass is changing how we think and how we think about education today and the education of tomorrow's digital citizens. Rather than exploring Glass simply as a piece of HET or as a distraction we ethically-minded educators can put it to use as an educational enhancement. Why? Because Glass allows educators and students to enact and embody a collusive point-of-view angle and a third voice that compliments the needs, skills, opportunities and challenges of contemporary life.

Having identified Glass' major contributions and deficits in the educational process, we have also identified its ability to help educators return to our civic mission, which consists of the importance of reexamining the purpose of higher education and the ethical responsibility of college graduates to the worlds they shape and inhabit, especially with their increased adoption of HET. Glass presents us with a series of opportunities and a set of challenges. The opportunities are a renewed commitment to cultivating digital citizens, understanding their needs, shaping what they should be taught, what they should learn how to do, and what they should know how to do. The challenges are determining how digital citizens will learn about and critique digital citizenship, in what contexts (i.e., face-to-face, online, hybrid or massive open online courses), with what tools, from whom and for how long. Perhaps the greatest challenge is how we will determine which are which.

REFERENCES

Aristotle, . (2012). *Aristotle's Nicomachean ethics* (R. C. Bartlett, Trans.). Chicago: University of Chicago Press.

Bennett, S. (2013). Civility, social media and higher education: A virtual triangle. In A. Finley (Ed.), *Civic learning and teaching* (pp. 6–24). Washington, DC: Bringing Theory to Practice.

Bilton, N. (2013, December 22). Bitcoin: Betting on a coin with no realm. *New York Times*. Retrieved from http://bits.blogs.nytimes.com/2013/12/22/disruptions-betting-on-bitcoin/?emc=eta1&_r=1

boyd, d. (2010). Social network sites as networked publics. In Z. Z. Papacharissi (Ed.), *A networked self: Identity, community and culture on social network sites* (pp. 39-58). New York: Routledge.

boyd, d. (2014). *It's complicated: The social lives of networked teens*. New Haven, CT: Yale University Press.

Castells, M. (2010). *The rise of the network society* (2nd ed.). Oxford, UK: Blackwell Publishing Ltd.

Chen, B. (2014, January 29). Tech attire: More beta than chic. *New York Times*. Retrieved from http://www.nytimes.com/2014/01/09/technology/tech-attire-more-beta-than-chic.html?_r=0

Chomsky, N. (1999). *Profit over people: Neoliberalism and global order*. New York: Seven Stories Press.

Coleman, G. (2009). Code is speech: Legal tinkering, expertise and protest among free and open source software developers. *Cultural Anthropology*, 24(3), 420–454. doi:10.1111/j.1548-1360.2009.01036.x

Dawkins, M. A. (2012). *Clearly invisible: Racial passing and the color of cultural identity*. Waco, TX: Baylor University Press.

Dawkins, M. A. (2013). *Eminem: The real Slim Shady*. Santa Barbara, CA: Praeger Press.

DePietro, P. (2013). *Transforming education with new media*. New York: Peter Lang.

Dickinson, B., & Ferrante, E. (2013, September 10). *The kiss: A short film shot through Google Glass*. Retrieved December 28, 2013, from http://www.youtube.com/watch?v=tPNAD-RanBI

Duckworth, E. (2006). Piaget rediscovered. *Journal of Research in Science Teaching*, *2*(3), 172–175. doi:10.1002/tea.3660020305

Fox, M. V. (1983). Ancient Egyptian rhetoric. *Rhetorica*, *1*, 9–22. doi:10.1525/rh.1983.1.1.9

Friere, P. (1970). *Pedagogy of the oppressed* (M. B. Ramos, Trans.). New York: Continuum Publishing Company.

Glenn, C., & Carcasson, M. (2009). Rhetoric and pedagogy. In A. Lunsford (Ed.), *The SAGE handbook of rhetorical studies* (pp. 285–292). Thousand Oaks, CA: Sage Publications, Inc.

Google. (2013). *Privacy Policy*. Retrieved from http://www.google.com/policies/privacy

Greenfield, S. (2012, August 7). How digital culture is rewiring our brains. *The Sydney Morning Herald*. Retrieved from http://www.smh.com.au/federal-politics/society-and-culture/how-digital-culture-is-rewiring-our-brains-20120806-23q5p.html

Hauser, G. A. (2002). Rhetorical democracy and civic engagement. In G. A. Hauser, & A. Grim (Eds.), *Rhetorical democracy: Discursive practices of civic engagement* (pp. 1–14). Mahwah, NJ: Lawrence Erlbaum Associates.

Internal Revenue Service. (2014, March 25). Notice 2014-21. *IRS.Gov*. Retrieved from http://www.irs.gov/pub/irs-drop/n-14-21.pdf

Jaslow, R. (2012, January 12). Internet addiction changes brain similar to cocaine: Study. *CBS News*. Retrieved from http://www.cbsnews.com/news/internet-addiction-changes-brain-similar-to-cocaine-study/

Kamenetzky, B. (2013, July 18). Google Glass delivers a Sam Bradford view of St. Louis Rams practice. *Digital Trends*. Retrieved December 28, 2013 from http://www.digitaltrends.com/sports/st-louis-rams-experiment-with-google-glass/

Kaminsky, M. (Ed.). (1992). *Remembered lives: The work of ritual, storytelling, and growing older*. Ann Arbor, MI: Michigan University Press.

Kerpen, D. (2011). *Likeable social media: How to delight your customers, create an irresistible brand, and be generally amazing on Facebook (and other social networks)*. New York: McGraw Hill.

Lytle, R. (2013, August 12). Behold: A digital bill of rights for the Internet, by the Internet. *Mashable*. Retrieved from http://mashable.com/2013/08/12/digital-bill-of-rights-crowdsource/

Marwick, A. E. (2013). *Status update: Celebrity, publicity, and branding in the social media age*. New Haven, CT: Yale University Press.

Mele, N. (2013). *The end of big: How the internet makes David the new Goliath*. New York: St. Martin's Press.

Miller, R. (2014, March 15). Why we hate Google Glass—and all new tech. *TechCrunch*. Retrieved from http://techcrunch.com/2014/03/15/why-we-hate-google-glass-and-all-new-tech/

Nakamoto, S. (2010). *Bitcoin: A Peer-to-Peer Electronic Cash System*. Retrieved from http://bitcoin.org/bitcoin.pdf

Nass, C., & Yen, C. (2010). *The man who lied to his laptop: What machines teach us about human relationships*. New York: Penguin Group USA, Inc.

Pariser, E. (2011). *The filter bubble: What the Internet is hiding from you*. New York: Penguin Press.

Penenberg, A. L. (2009). *Viral loop: From Facebook to Twitter, how today's smartest businesses grow themselves*. New York: Hyperion Books.

Postman, N. (1993). *Technopoly: The surrender of culture to technology*. New York: Knopf.

Putnam, R. D. (2001). *Bowling alone: The collapse and revival of American community*. New York: Simon & Schuster.

Ribble, M. (2013). Digital citizenship: Nine elements. *Digital Citizenship*. Retrieved from http://digitalcitizenship.net/Nine_Elements.html

Ribble, M., & Bailey, G. (2011). *Digital citizenship in schools* (2nd ed.). Eugene, OR: International Society for Technology in Education.

Schiller, B. (2013). Eight new jobs people will have in 2025. *FastCo Exist*. Retrieved from http://www.fastcoexist.com/3015652/futurist-forum/8-new-jobs-people-will-have-in-2025

Schroeder, S. (2013, December 25). Edward Snowden's Christmas message and other news you need to know. *Mashable*. Retrieved from http://mashable.com/ 2013/12/25/edward-snowden-christmas-brief/

Sparacio, R. (2013, November 15). Technology and medicine: Applying Google Glass in the medical field. *Multibriefs*. Retrieved from http://exclusive.multibriefs.com/ content/technology-and-medicine-applying-google-glass-in-the-medical-field

Turkle, S. (2011). *Alone together: Why we expect more from technology and less from each other*. New York: Basic Books.

Witte, J. C., & Mannon, S. E. (2010). *The internet and social inequalities*. New York: Routledge.

Zickuhr, K. (2013, September 25). Who's not online and why: Pew Research Center internet and American life project. *Pew Research Center*. Retrieved from http://www.pewinternet.org/Press-Releases/2013/Offline-adults.aspx

KEY TERMS AND DEFINITIONS

Education: The process of transferring the knowledge, skills and habits of a culture from one generation to the next, especially in institutional settings.

Ethics: The branch of knowledge that deals with moral principles aimed to guide a person's beliefs and behavior.

Google Glass: A wearable computer with an optical head-mounted display that provides augmented reality for users and offers many of the features of a smartphone and cloud-based computer.

Pedagogy: The method and practice of teaching and learning that offers participants the conditions for self-reflection, a self-managed life and critical agency.

Rhetoric: The use of words by human agents to form attitudes or induce actions in other human agents.

Storytelling: Influencing connected participants to action through narrative.

Third Voice: A hybrid narrative identity expressing the collaboration of the storyteller with the characters s/he encounters.

Chapter 2
Anticipating Human Enhancement:
Identifying Ethical Issues of Bodyware

Deniz Tunçalp
Istanbul Technical University, Turkey

Mary Helen Fagan
University of Texas at Tyler, USA

ABSTRACT

This chapter provides a novel approach for identifying ethical issues on bodyware as new ICT devices are being integrated into human bodies with the help of unconventional interfaces. To establish a primer to the range of potential questions to this phenomenon, the authors provide an ethical analysis taking an agential realist perspective (Barad, 2007) and using anticipatory technology ethics (Brey, 2012). They illustrate their approach with the Student Locator Pilot Project in San Antonio Texas as a case study, where "smart" ID cards with embedded RFID chips have been deployed. To conclude, the authors argue that their approach is well suited to address questions on how augmented bodies and enhanced minds of human beings intra-act with bodyware in everyday social and organizational life.

INTRODUCTION

Human enhancement is generally defined as any "modification aimed at improving individual human performance and brought about by science-based or technology-based interventions in the human body" (STOA, 2010, p. 6). Advancements in nanotechnology, biotechnology, information technology and cognitive sciences (NBIC), combined with the achievements in materials science, have created new capabilities for human enhancement. Convergence of these technological domains and scientific disciplines has resulted in a technology category called Human Enhancement Technologies (HET) (Bainbridge & Roco, 2002, 2005). While NBIC convergence continues, the convergence of Information and Communication Technologies (ICT) and biotechnology has created an important category in HETs. We call this type of HET 'bodyware', where novel ICT devices are being integrated into human bodies with the help of new and unconventional interfaces (Tunçalp & Fagan, 2013). For example, electronic pacemakers, implanted drug pump systems and

DOI: 10.4018/978-1-4666-6010-6.ch002

electroencephalographically (EEG) directed exoskeletons could all be considered as different examples of bodyware.

The capabilities and consequences of HET have been under heavy public, political and scholar scrutiny. Besides individual and social level changes, bodyware has a large potential to remarkably change the nature of work and the workplace. Altering the definition and the construction of body and self in the workplace has the potential to significantly influence the nature of human organizations and the process of organizing. Our theoretical tools and approaches need further development in order to better understand and explain what risks and consequences emerge when the human body integrates with bodyware.

The traditional understanding of ICT considers technology as something we merely use like a tool. However, bodyware challenges this notion by viewing technology as something we merge and simply 'become'. Bodyware also has the potential to significantly alter the way we perceive organizations. How might bodyware be deployed in organizations? How might bodyware bridge or suspend time and space, enabling new forms and environments of collaboration between people? How does implanting technology on and into human bodies change the way we understand technology implementation projects and their potential failure? How do such technologies change the nature and the delivery of public service and the relationship between a citizen and the state in general? How might bodyware alter our discourses about self and others and influence our culture with the performativity of bodyware in daily practices? In all possible scenarios, how should we consider different types of bodyware without essentially attributing decisive powers to technologies themselves or to the humans using them (technological or social determinism) (McLoughlin & Dawson, 2003).

While diverse questions might be asked about bodyware, underlying ethical issues relate many of these problems together. To establish a primer to such questions in this chapter, we aim to provide an ethical analysis of bodyware. This chapter is structured as follows. In the next section, we define bodyware, types of bodyware artifacts and potential applications. Then we introduce extant approaches that analyze and anticipate potential ethical issues in bodyware. Next we present our integrative approach to anticipate the impact of bodyware on the mind, body and capabilities of humans. In the last sections, we discuss our possible future research directions and our conclusions.

BACKGROUND

Defining Bodyware

Bodyware is a result of ICT and biotechnology convergence, and builds upon advances in cognitive science, nanotechnology and new materials (See Figure 1). The emergence of bodyware technology has led to a number of novel devices. Cognitive science and biomedical engineering have been integrating these artifacts into human bodies. New interfaces that read bodily movements, human emotions and brain waves are becoming increasingly commonplace, creating unconventional experiences and entirely new applications.

Bodyware devices can be located inside the human body or on the body surface, temporarily or permanently. They are beyond "smart" prostheses because their primary objective is not replacing a missing body part but rather enhancing existing capabilities or contributing new competences with their functionalities. Thus, bodyware devices are recreating embodying individuals as 'cyborgs'. These devices are extremely personalized for embodying individuals and ultimately adaptive to physiological responses. These devices are sometimes aware of their bodily context and may even anticipate individual intentions with bodily mediation to different degrees.

For analytical purposes, we define four types of bodyware according to level of smartness and self-containment: simple apparatus, smart apparatus, implanted devices and augmented devices. As we go along from a simple apparatus to augmented devices, the body integration and self-containment of bodyware device increases. According to our classification (See Table 1), 'Simple Apparatus' and 'Smart Apparatus' are located outside, at the body surface, whereas 'Implanted Devices' and 'Augmented Devices' are located inside, embedded into human bodies.

Since simple apparatus and smart apparatus are external to human body, they may also be considered as different from 'bodyware'. However, we consider them as types of bodyware, because, we follow that the intra-activity of humans and technology (Barad, 2007) constitute related ethical issues. We do acknowledge existence of body boundaries. However, we do not differentiate Google Glass from Google Contact Lenses (Kelly, 2014), implanted smart chips (BBC, 2004) or other bodyware devices only because of its bodily location. But, rather, we differentiate how minds, bodies and capabilities of humans are impacted differently by bodyware technology, its artifacts or applications.

Figure 1. Bodyware at the intersection of biotechnology and ICT

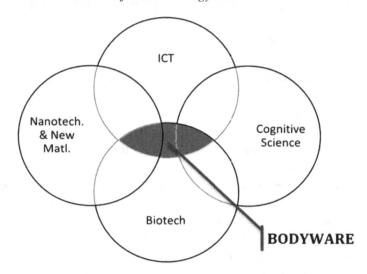

Table 1. Types of bodyware artifacts

Bodyware				
Types	**Simple Apparatus**	**Smart Apparatus**	**Implanted Devices**	**Augmented Devices**
Definition	May be a consumptive sensors and prosthesis Location: Body surface	Medium term use May be necessary, as in medical monitoring and smart response Location: Body surface	Medium to longer-term use Self-contained for functioning except energy Depends on an external energy source Location: Inside the body	Designed for permanent or long-term use Self-contained Boundaries of body and prostheses hard to define Location: Inside the body
Examples	Electronic Joints	Epidermal Electronic System (EES) implemented as "smart skin"/"electronic tattoo" Body implanted smart chips	Powered exoskeletons such as HAL (Hybrid Assistive Limb) Electronic pacemakers. Drug implant systems (morphine or insulin pumps)	Artificial organs and engineered tissues

Following Brey (2012), we define bodyware technology, its artifacts or applications as the following:

- Bodyware technology is a set of biomedical ICT techniques that enable integration or merger of functional devices with human bodies to support, enhance and expand the capabilities of embodying individuals.
- Bodyware artifacts are functional bodyware apparatus, systems and procedures using bodyware technology. For example, electronic joints, Epidermal Electronic Systems (EES) (Wang et al., 2012) implemented as smart skins or electronic tattoos, body implanted smart chips, powered exoskeletons, like Hybrid Assistive Limbs (HAL), electronic pacemakers, drug implant systems and artificial organs are all examples of bodyware artifacts.
- Bodyware applications stand for certain ways of using bodyware artifacts for a specific purpose in a specific context at a specific configuration. For example, enhancing the quality of life for elderly or creating super armies with human-enhanced soldiers are different potential applications of bodyware. It is important to differentiate between artifacts and applications. For example, Google Glass may be configured and used to spy others, to assist the disabled, or to perform entertainment tasks. These are different applications of the same bodyware artifact.

Bodyware artifacts and applications have already started to become part of our everyday life. Different types of bodyware artifacts have started to emerge from simple chipped apparatuses to augmented smart prosthetic devices. Furthermore, practical, non-medical applications are also emerging. For example, some people have already chosen to be 'chipped' so that they can pay with their credit card using a microchip that has been surgically implanted in their upper arm (BBC, 2004).

Does bodyware represent a major shift in our understanding of technology? Dotov et al. (2012) applies ideas of Heidegger (1962) to cognitive science and suggests that when a tool is skillfully used it really becomes like a part of us. One could argue that such tools have been around for a long time, and bodyware is not different from them. However, the smart nature of the bodyware artifacts and the capabilities of bodyware applications are beyond Heideggerian tools. With the advent of bodyware, one could take Heidegger's analysis to the next level, given that these tools really do become part of us on a physical level. For example, what would happen to our understanding of technology if we were to consider all the ramifications of implementing technology into our own bodies? Secondly, how may bodyware change the way we define our physical and capability boundaries? Therefore, it is clear that bodyware creates new ethical challenges.

While we define and categorize bodyware in this chapter, it is important to note that giving a thorough survey of the state of bodyware technologies and new bodyware applications are beyond our scope. Rather, we focus on defining, classifying and making an ethical analysis of bodyware.

Approaches to Analyzing the Consequences of New Technologies

With the increased involvement of emerging technologies in daily life, a number of ethical, developmental and philosophical approaches have been developed to help us assess implications of emerging technologies. Some of these approaches are especially important: Ethical Assessment Approach, Ethical Impact Assessment, Techno-Ethical Scenarios, Ethical Assessment of Emerging ICTs (ETHICA), Anticipatory Technology Ethics, and Agential Realism.

The Ethical Technology Assessment Approach (Palm & Hansson, 2006) aims to give an early indication of potentially negative ethical implications of emerging technologies. This approach requires being involved with the development process to assess its projected consequences against ethical principles. It aims to provide feedback to relevant stakeholders, such as policy makers, designers, and scientists. It proposes a checklist covering design-related domains like privacy, sustainability, control, influence and power, gender, minorities and justice to address and frame potential ethical issues in emerging technologies. However, its ethical analysis focuses on making a broad assessment for near future. Similarly, Ethical Impact Assessment approach (Wright, 2011) aims to perform an ethical evaluation of emerging technologies by its developers to ensure ethically responsible technology development. It contains a long and detailed ethical checklist to address ethical principles to perform an impact assessment of an existing design specification.

The Techno-Ethical Scenarios Approach (Boenink et al., 2010) uses scenario analysis technique to assess ethical issues in emerging technologies to help policy makers that govern emerging technologies. This approach accounts for mutual changes that technology and society may have upon on one another, using different scenarios. In this way, a better treatment of time and accounting for a longer time horizon becomes possible. However, its fundamental stance is forecasting the future and it is more descriptive and predictive in nature. Similar to this technique, ETHICA (Stahl, 2011) is another ethical assessment method for emerging ICTs. Deriving from future projections, it considers a number of potential futures and selects one of them over others. Such scenarios are then used for analyzing ethical issues in specific technologies (e.g., nanotechnology), artifacts (e.g., nanoscale materials) and applications (e.g., reducing body odor with silver nanoparticles) using checklist items which are compared and ranked. The ranking and the analysis are then used to develop policy recommendations. On the other hand, Anticipatory Technology Ethics (Brey, 2012) is partly a derivation from ETHICA and based on the earlier approaches described above. It analyzes ethical issues in emerging technologies in three stages: identification, evaluation and governance. In order to analyze ethics of emerging technologies, it adopts three levels of analysis: technology, artifacts and applications. In this way, the approach is able to differentiate generic technology issues to specific artifacts and applications. While these approaches are able to detect ethical issues in new technologies at different levels, they are rather silent about how human capabilities are involved, which are central in the impacts and consequences of bodyware.

Although it is not directly an ethical perspective, agential realism (Barad, 2007) provides an interesting account to understand new technologies and their ethical implications. Barad (2007) posits that human bodies do not have inherent boundaries and properties, but they acquire specific boundaries and properties in phenomena dynamically through an open ended intra-activity. 'Intra-activity' is first coined by Barad as a fundamental term in agential realism, with an inspiration from quantum physics. It indicates Barad's understanding of material objects as being emergent through their intra-actions, instead of having some preceding existence. According to Barad, all things are always 'material-discursive' and they simultaneously produce determinate meanings and material beings, while excluding other possibilities. Therefore 'intra-actions' create material conditions of possibility for 'humans' and 'non-humans.'

In order to illustrate how agential realism considers technology, we may employ Google search as an example. Taking an agential realist perspective, Orlikowski suggests that understanding Google simply as an information search tool is problematic because "it privileges the users, clearly putting the locus of control principally in the hands of the human researchers, and relegating the technology to a relatively passive, even domesticated role" (2007, p. 1439). Although people visit Google.com site to search their phrases, the search results are dynamically created from the intra-action of Google with millions of the Internet users. Web pages, sites and link structures on the Internet change over time. Therefore, Google constantly crawls and indexes websites, using Google PageRank algorithm and related applications, running on certain servers with particular software. However, search itself is created by "millions of people who create and update web pages daily, and the millions of people who enter particular search terms into it" (2007, p. 1439). Because of this dynamic nature, the same search at different times give different results. Therefore, it is not merely Google, or its search technology, or the page ranking algorithm, or the person making the search but the intra-activity of Google with millions humans searching the web, or creating websites which collectively co-create the search phenomena.

The intra-actional account of Barad (2007) has been developed over the earlier works of Bruno Latour. Like Barad, Latour challenges the separation of humans and non-humans. He suggests that "humans and non-humans are engaged in a history that should render their separation impossible" (2003, p. 39). According to him, the history is not a mere combination, but they are closely intertwined as one. According to Latour, agency does not belong to humans or non-humans, but action and intentionality are properties of human /non-human collectives, or actor-networks. However, displacing agency of actors to actor-networks would make it impossible to trace and precisely locate the original agency and to study ethical implications of technology related practices. Barad's approach provides a way forward to account for agency and make ethical analysis possible.

Agential realism posits the social and technical, or human and non-human, as ontologically inseparable. Since, agency is deeply related with the questions of ethics and morality, understand-

ing agency differently has important implications on how we analyze ethical issues involved. Since bodyware artifacts ultimately become combined and merged with human bodies, agential realism's understanding of human and non-human as inseparable fits well with bodyware phenomena. It also helps us to focus on technological – human practices and "the possibilities for the iterative reconfiguring of the materiality of human, non-human, cyborgian and other such forms" (Barad, 2007, p. 178).

Agential realism is not an ethical perspective per se, but it is an "ethico-onto-epistemological" theory (Barad, 2007, p. 185) that helps us posit a new ethical approach to emerging technologies. Barad actually disavows separation of epistemology and ontology as "reverberation of a metaphysics that assumes an inherent difference between human and nonhuman, subject and object, mind and body, matter and discourse" (2007, p. 185). Instead she calls for "an ethico-onto-epistem-ology –an appreciation of the intertwining of ethics, knowing, and being – since each intra-action matters" and "the becoming of the world is a deeply ethical matter" (2007, p. 185).

ANALYZING BODYWARE IN PRACTICE: THE RFID STUDENT LOCATOR PROJECT

Our approach to ethically analyze bodyware focuses on identifying risks and consequences. It is inspired by agential realism (Barad, 2007) and anticipatory technology ethics (Brey, 2012). Like Brey (2012), we differentiate between specific bodyware technologies from its artifacts and applications. We also consider body and mind and capabilities separately. In our approach, we adapt Brey (2012)'s checklist for ethical assessment. While Brey (2012) differentiates between a technology, from its artifacts and applications, we added a further level by differentiating between 'Mind & Body' and 'Capabilities', in anticipating ethical risks and consequences using the checklist. In our version, we question the bodyware technology, artifacts and applications differently with questions on 'Decency & Welfare', 'Autonomy & Independence', 'Property & Publicity', 'Rights & Obligations', 'Human Dignity & Good Life', 'Privacy & Accompany', 'Justice & Equality', and 'the Individual & the Common Good' angles (See Table 2).

We think the Student Locator Pilot Project at the Northside Independent School District (NISD) in San Antonio Texas provides a good case example to allow us to assess bodyware. This Texas school district deployed 'smart' ID cards with embedded RFID chips in the fall of 2012 in order to:

- Increase student safety and security by tracking where students are in school buildings,

- Increase attendance and provide increased revenues, and
- Implement other functions such as providing access to facilities such as the library (Northside ISD, n.d.).

One of the stated reasons provided by the NISD for undertaking the student locator pilot project was a financial cost/benefit expectation based upon the requirement that all students will wear a name badge with an embedded RFID 'locator' chip (a Smart ID). In the two pilot schools that were part of the project, the school district plans spent approximately $261,000 in order to use RFID readers to obtain student locations from their Smart ID when students were not in their classroom when morning roll was taken (Northside ISD, n.d.). The NSID expected that this approach would "boost attendance records used to calculate state funding"

Table 2. Anticipating ethical risks and consequences of bodyware

		Mind and Body	**Capabilities**
Levels	Bodyware Technology	Decency & Welfare • Health and bodily well-being.	Decency & Welfare • Human capabilities, environment.
	Bodyware Artifacts	Autonomy & Independence • Ability to think and have an opinion. • Freedom to choose.	Autonomy & Independence • Responsibility and accountability. • Informed consent.
		Property & Publicity • Right to property. • Intellectual property rights.	Property & Publicity • Right to access. • Equity and fairness.
	Bodyware Applications	Rights & Obligations • Freedom to choose. • Freedom of movement.	Rights & Obligations • Freedom of speech and expression. • Freedom of assembly.
		Human Dignity and Good Life	**Human Dignity and Good Life**
		Privacy & Accompany • Bodily privacy.	Privacy & Accompany • Information privacy. • Relational privacy.
		Justice & Equality • Just distribution of primary goods, capabilities, risks and hazards.	Justice & Equality • Nondiscrimination and equal treatment relative to age, gender, sexual orientation, social class, race, ethnicity, religion, etc. • Societal, international and intergenerational justice. • Social inclusion.
		The Individual & the Common Good • Happiness, health, desire-fulfillment, wisdom, virtue, psychology. • Other basic human rights.	The Individual & the Common Good • Knowledge, friendship, trust, and transcendent meaning. • Supportive of vital social institutions and structures. • Supportive of democracy and democratic institutions. • Supportive of culture and cultural diversity.

Source: Adapted from Brey (2012)

by 1 to 2 percent and, as a result, could increase their district revenue by as much as two million dollars annually (Judge Decides, 2013).

However, one student in the pilot program refused to wear her Smart ID badge and thus opened up to question if/how the district could enforce its policies within their student body. Hernandez refused to wear her Smart ID badge with the locator chip, not because of privacy concerns, but based upon her religious objection/belief that "the technology in the card was akin to her wearing the 'mark of the beast'" (Balough Law Offices, 2013). Hernandez was told by the school district that she must wear the Smart ID or she would have to transfer to another school in the district, which was not part of the pilot project (Judge Decides, 2013). When Hernandez did not agree to the transfer, the school district offered an accommodation that would allow Hernandez to remain in her current school if she would wear a Smart ID badge from which the RFID locator chip had been removed (Judge Decides, 2013). Hernandez refused the school district accommodation offer, contending that "the mere wearing of the badge communicated support of the RFID program and violated the student's First Amendment speech rights" (Balough Law Offices, 2013). Hernandez filed a federal lawsuit contending that the school district's requirement that she wear the Smart ID locator badge in order to attend the magnet school was a violation of her federal rights (Judge Decides, 2013). The court dismissed her lawsuit, finding that "even if the ID badge placed a burden on a religious belief, the district has a compelling interest to protect students that outweighs such burden. 'In today's climate, one would be hard pressed to argue that the safety and security of the children and educators in our public school system is not a compelling governmental interest'" (Balough Law Offices, 2013).

With this federal lawsuit and news coverage related to the controversy and the court's ruling, the phenomena has enlarged to include entities such as lobbying groups (ACLU, the Rutherford Institute, CASPIAN - Consumers Against Super-market Privacy Invasion and Numbering, etc.) as well as everyone who cares to post an online comment stating their opinion on the matter on a web site or a blog. News articles and comments associated with these articles have focused attention on various aspects of the pilot project and larger issues, raising questions and discussing possible pros and cons. In one news article, Hernandez, who sued the district, questions the ability of the student locator system to work as expected and achieve the intended outcomes. Hernandez stated that "other teenagers will be rebellious against the new rule and stuff the badges in a locker or hand them to a friend to leave campus" and believes that students will skip classes despite the monitoring device (Students Rebel, 2012). One online commenter concurs, stating, "I actually think the whole thing is totally useless. It's a badge. You can take it off." (Katy M, 2013). The rational analysis of financial costs and benefits to the school district that justifies its pilot use of this technology does not fully allay the concerns of some people that this application marks a descent down a slippery slope to a bad ending, like similar arguments in other HET cases (e.g., big brother surveillance and/or the events associated in some religions with the appearance of the 'mark of the beast').

We think that the ethical implications of the project can be best analyzed by differentiating RFID student locators project's technology, from its artifacts and applications with respect to their intra-action with minds & bodies and capabilities of people. At the technology level, potential bodily impact of constantly carrying RFID tags and living under electromagnetic field of RFID readers needs to be identified. At the artifact level, from a mind & body perspective, do the students will have right to own or disown the RFID tags becomes an issue. Especially in terms of freedom of religious beliefs, how will the many aspects of this RFID project intra-act? Once implemented, can students leave their ID cards at their school lockers? This also brings the human capabilities into question. By introducing this technology, how will the responsibilities of a student will be influenced? Will they be asked to be more accountable than they used to be? Will they be informed the implications of holding an RFID student card or will the school administration require their consent? At the application level, what purposes will RFID cards be used for? If this technology will be used to track and follow-up students at school, how will being under constant surveillance and tracing be related to human dignity? After the implementation of this technology to trace and follow-up students, how will this application will influence students' ability to gain access to a school in their district? Will it impose additional barriers to already marginalized people of a society? Can we still talk about students' ability to be alone or absent as part of their freedom of movement? How will students' individual and relational privacy be maintained or assured? Based on our checklist (see Table 2), such questions may be anticipated before the project preparation or roll out (see Table 3).

We think that agential realism (Barad, 2007) seems well suited for exploring the numerous issues and concerns that have arisen out of this project, outlined above. From an agential realist perspective, phenomena enfold through iterative intra-activity. The on-going developments stemming from the NSID student locator project help illustrate the way in which "bodies ('human', 'environmental' or otherwise) are integral 'parts' of, or dynamic reconfiguring of, what is"

(Barad, 2007, p. 170). Many intra-acting entities are involved in this phenomenon (i.e., the student locator Smart ID pilot at NISD) including students, name badges, RFID chips and readers, parents, school administrators, state education funding authorities, student location information, class rooms, teachers, technology vendors, etc.

Barad suggests that "in an agential realist account, discursive practices are not human-based activities but specific material (re)configurations of the world through which boundaries, properties and meanings are differentially enacted" (2007, p. 183). An analysis of some of online comments related to the project can illuminate this point. For example, some of the commentators see the student locator project as dehumanizing and point out that the NSID student locator project uses the same RFID chip technology that is used in pets for identification purposes. For example:

Look at the bigger picture. It's not about where it begins or why. The real question is where does it end? Where do we draw the line and say enough? That is the ACLU's issue. "We don't want to see this kind of intrusive surveillance infrastructure gain inroads into our culture" ... First our pets, now our children. What comes next? ... 'Those who would sacrifice liberty for security deserve neither' (Bdubs1975, 2013).

Table 3. Ethical analysis of the Student Locator Pilot Project at the Northside Independent School District – San Antonio, Texas

		Mind and Body	Capabilities
Levels	Bodyware Technology Radio Frequency Identification (RFID)	• Potential bodily impact of electromagnetic field to read and activate RFID tags. • Feeling of being followed-up constantly.	-
	Bodyware Artifacts RFID card to keep on your body at school	• Right to own or disown. • Religious and belief freedoms.	• Responsibility and accountability of students at school. • Informed consent of students on holding an RFID card.
	Bodyware Applications Student follow-up	• Human dignity vs. being followed up constantly.	• Ability to access to a school in the district. • Ability to be alone or absent (Freedom of movement). • Individual and relational privacy.

Some express concern that this pilot project might be part of a larger agenda and is the beginning of a slippery slope to an Orwellian future. For example:

One small step for schools, one giant leap toward removing all your civil liberties and turning this country into a police state. Soon the government will be putting locator chips in newborn infants and cameras in your home (GetMeOutAlive42, 2013).

Some online commentators go further and suggest ways by which students can circumvent or sabotage the student locator system. For example:

STUDENTS: Google: "Degaussers" - (Large electromagnets - really quite reasonably priced) When it becomes more expensive to replace the trackers than to continue this Orwellian intrusion, the school and the tracking company will fold! (mpa-4893349, 2013).

These suggestions bring up one interesting aspect of the student locator implementation. The student locator system is designed around the expectation that the San Antonio Texas school administration can require students to wear the Smart ID. As a result, there is an expectation that the student's physical body will be co-located with their Smart ID, and that the student location data that is stored in the system will be accurate. However, the various entities (student, badge and RFID chip) may in fact not be co-located. For example, if a student leaves their badge (or just the RFID chip) in their student locker, the NISD student locator system might indicate a student's body is located in their locker at a particular point in time when, in fact, the student is elsewhere. Thus, in this system, one can distinguish between a 'real' physical student's body and where it is located in space and an individual's 'virtual' body, whose location is based upon information in the

school district's tracking system (which might be erroneous or absent), making body boundaries as unclear and actively reconfigured by the students – badges intra-action.

In her development of post-humanist agential realism, Barad indicates that "post-humanism marks the practice of accounting for the boundary-making practices by which the 'human' and its others are differentially delineated and defined" and involves "calling for an accounting of how this boundary is actively configured and reconfigured" (Barad, p. 136). Based upon some of the comments related to the student locator project at NISD, the student Smart ID's may be associated in the mind of some people with other uses of the RFID technology (such as identifying lost pets so they can be recovered by their owners before they are euthanized by a local animal shelter).

Similar cases might arise in similar human enhancement applications, for example, in a body-ware project at a school environment. The RFID chip at the student badge might be implanted in student bodies, or students might be distributed smart glasses to be used in learning and teaching. Considering students as users and the human enhancement technologies as tools relegate a relatively passive role to those artifacts. Such a perspective privileges and puts entire agency and control to users' intention. However, agential realism reminds us determinate meanings and material beings in such phenomena will be simultaneously produced with 'intra-actions' of students, teachers, school administrators and related bodyware artifacts, creating material conditions of possibility.

FUTURE RESEARCH DIRECTIONS

In her discussion of agential realism, Barad (2007) illustrates the type of questions that can arise as human bodies intra-act with novel technologies by recounting the experience shared by another researcher upon attending a talk given by Stephen Hawking (Barad, 2007, p. 158). Stephen Hawking is a famous English theoretical physicist and cosmologist. He has amyotrophic lateral sclerosis, a severe neurological disease which makes speaking or moving anything other than his fingers impossible. In order to speak, Hawking uses a simple computer system located in a box, where he selects words and phrases and forms paragraphs using only his fingers. When a paragraph is ready, the system reads it with an artificial speech device. In that way, he is able to speak with others. In writing on her experience, Stone (2004) questioned where Hawking, as a person, ends given the fact he was able to speak on stage only by means of his laptop and an external loudspeaker. In reflecting on where Hawking 'ends' (and technology 'begins'), Stone muses that "our social conditioning teaches us to see a person as a person. But, a serious part of Hawking extends into the box in his lap.... Where does he stop? Where are his edges?" (Stone, 2004, p. 176). Hawking's box is a good example of a bodyware artifact. As a vital smart prosthesis, it became central to his daily practices and it has merged with his body at some level. Today, Hawking's natural personhood necessarily includes his bodyware, as an internal and inseparable part. Returning to our case, as practices abound and applications flourish, smart student ID cards with embedded RFID chips may also become part of the personhood of students, and even part of their bodies with bodyware artifacts like 'smart' skins.

Some scholars have concerns about an agential realist account that rejects the pre-existence of things and the separateness of materials and discourse. For example, in their recent critical analysis of the ontology of agential realism, Faulkner and Runde outlined three themes that guide an agential realist approach: 'relationality', 'interpenetration' and 'agential cuts' (2012, p. 52). Faulkner and Runde concluded that the three arguments of 'relationality', 'interpenetration' and 'agential cuts' are 'mostly unexceptional', "probably not sustainable outside of a restricted range of cases",

and dependent upon "the practices of 'agencies of observation'", respectively (2012, p. 64-65). Faulkner and Runde refer to Barad (2007) in their discussion of the theme of interpenetration and raise questions about "the idea that the social and the technological are 'fused' or 'interpenetrate'" and conclude that "that cases of the human body being penetrated by technology are the exception rather than the rule, and second that, even the exceptions mentioned above involve very little in the way of an interpenetration of entities or entities 'fusing' or 'saturating' each other" (2012, p. 12).

In regard to the critique provided by Faulkner and Runde (2012), we suggest that their observations regarding interpenetration may have been true in regard to most applications of information technology in organizations in the past. However, we believe that the NISD student locator pilot project is indicative of emerging novel applications of technology and that these type of applications where different bodies intra-act in novel ways with technology may not be an insignificant application of information technologies in the future. And, when one considers the possible implications of "chipping" (BBC, 2004) and electronic tattoos/'smart' skin (Gonzalez, 2011) that may be employed in future projects, an agential realist approach does appear to be particularly relevant for exploring the ways in which these technologies may indeed 'penetrate' human bodies (chipping) or 'fuse' with human bodies (electronic tattoos/'smart' skin). In future, an extensive survey can be prepared to identify the state of bodyware technologies and new bodyware artifacts and applications available. Also, more empirical and conceptual studies are needed to understand various dimensions of the bodyware phenomena.

CONCLUSION

In conclusion, we believe there will be a growing need for scholars in the future to address questions of how the augmented bodies and enhanced minds of human beings intra-act with bodyware and the possibilities created by this intra-action in everyday social and organizational life. However, the analytical resources available for scholars to understand and explain the intra-action of bodies and human enhancement technologies, such as bodyware, are arguably incomplete at this point in time. As this chapter demonstrates, agential realism (Barad, 2007) provides a novel approach for identifying ethical issues by studying how technologies intra-act with humans' real and virtual bodies.

REFERENCES

Bainbridge, W. S., & Roco, M. C. (Eds.). (2005). *Managing Nano-Bio-Infocogno innovations: Converging technologies in society.* Springer. Retrieved from www.wtec.org/ConvergingTechnologies/3/NBIC3_report.pdf

Balough Law Offices. (2013). *RFID chip in student badge does not infringe on religious freedom.* Retrieved from http://www.jdsupra.com/legalnews/rfid-chip-in-student-id-badge-does-not-i-55406/

Barad, K. (2007). *Meeting the universe halfway: Quantum physics and the entanglement of matter and meaning.* Durham, NC: Duke University Press. doi:10.1215/9780822388128

BBC. (2004, September 9). Barcelona clubbers get chipped. *BBC News.* Retrieved from http://news.bbc.co.uk/2/hi/technology/3697940.stm

Bdubs 1975. (2013, January 9). Retrieved from http://usnews.nbcnews.com/_news/2013/01/09/16427652-texas-school-can-force-students-to-wear-locator-chips-judge-rules?pc=25&sp=0#discussion_nav

Boenink, M., Swierstra, T., & Stemerding, D. (2010). Anticipating the Interaction between technology and morality: A scenario study of experimenting with humans in bionanotechnology. *Studies in Ethics, Law, and Technology, 4*(2), 1–38. doi:10.2202/1941-6008.1098

Brey, P. A. E. (2012). Anticipating ethical issues in emerging IT. *Ethics and Information Technology, 14*(4), 305–317. doi:10.1007/s10676-012-9293-y

Dotov, D. G., Nie, L., & Chemero, A. (2010). A Demonstration of the Transition from Ready-to-Hand to Unready-to-Hand. *PLoS ONE, 5*(3), e9433. doi:10.1371/journal.pone.0009433 PMID:20231883

Faulkner, P., & Runde, J. (2012). On Sociomateriality. In P. M. Leonardi, B. A. Nardi, & J. Kallinikos (Eds.), *Materiality and Organizing: Social Interaction in a Technological World* (pp. 49–66). Oxford, UK: Oxford University Press. doi:10.1093/acprof:oso/9780199664054.003.0003

GetMeOutAlive42. (2013, January 9). Retrieved from http://usnews.nbcnews.com/_news/2013/01/09/16427652-texas-school-can-force-students-to-wear-locator-chips-judge-rules?pc=25&sp=0#discussion_nav

Gonzalez, R. T. (2011). *Breakthrough: Electronic circuits that are integrated with your skin.* Retrieved from http://io9.com/5830071/breakthrough-electronic-circuits-that-are-integrated-into-your-skin

Heidegger, M. (1962). *Being and Time* (J. Macquarrie, & E. Robinson, Trans.). New York, NY: Harper & Row.

Judge Decides in Favor of NISD in SmartID Case Against Student. (2013, January 8). Retrieved from http://www.kens5.com/news/Judge-decides-in-favor-of-NISD-in-SmartID-case-against-student-186077712.html

Katy M. (2013, January 9). Retrieved from http://usnews.nbcnews.com/_news/2013/01/09/16427652-texas-school-can-force-students-to-wear-locator-chips-judge-rules?pc=25&sp=0#discussion_nav

Kelly, M. (2014). *Google developing contact lens device to help those with diabetes monitor blood glucose levels.* Retrieved from http://venturebeat.com/2014/01/16/google-contacts/

Latour, B. (1999). *Pandora's Hope: Essays on the Reality of Science Studies.* Cambridge, MA: Harvard University Press.

Latour, B. (2003). The promise of constructivism. In D. Ihde, & E. Selinger (Eds.), *Chasing Technoscience: Matrix for Materiality.* Bloomington, IN: Indiana University Press.

Mcloughlin, I., & Dawson, P. (2003). The mutual shaping of technology and organisation. In D. Preece, & J. Laurila (Eds.), *Technological change and organizational action.* London, UK: Routledge.

mpa-4893349. (2013, January 9) Retrieved from http://usnews.nbcnews.com/_news/2013/01/09/16427652-texas-school-can-force-students-to-wear-locator-chips-judge-rules?pc=25&sp=0#discussion_nav

Northside ISD Smart Student ID Cards Student Locator Pilot. (n.d.). Retrieved from http://www.nisd.net/studentlocator/

Orlikowski, W. J. (2007). Sociomaterial Practices: Exploring Technology at Work. *Organization Studies, 28*(9), 1435–1448. doi:10.1177/0170840607081138

Palm, E., & Hansson, S. O. (2006). The case for ethical technology assessment (eTA). *Technological Forecasting and Social Change, 73*(5), 543–558. doi:10.1016/j.techfore.2005.06.002

Roco, M. C., & Bainbridge, W. (Eds.). (2002). *Converging technologies for improving human performance: Nanotechnology, biotechnology, information technology and cognitive science.* Arlington, VA: NSF/Department of Commerce. Retrieved from www.wtec.org/ConvergingTechnologies/Report/NBIC_frontmatter.pdf

Stahl, B. (2011). IT for a better future: how to integrate ethics, politics and innovation. *Journal of Information. Communication & Ethics in Society, 9*(3), 140–156. doi:10.1108/14779961111167630

STOA (European Parliament Scientific and Technological Options Assessment). (2010). *Making Perfect Life: Bioengineering (in) the 21st Century. Interim Study.* IP/A/STOA/FWC-2008-96/LOT6/SC1, Study by the European Technology Assessment Group. Retrieved from http://www.itas.kit.edu/downloads/etag_esua10a.pdf

Stone, A. R. (2004). Split subjects, not atoms, or, how I fell in love with my prosthesis. *Configurations, 2*(1), 73–190.

Students Rebel Against Tracking Chips. (2012, November 27). Retrieved from http://www.ksn.com/content/news/also/story/Students-rebel-against-tracking-chips/MwIlw0lUf0Od2qb5s0oEQw.cspx

Tunçalp, D., & Fagan, M. H. (2013). *Bodyware: Information Systems in the Age of the Augmented Body and the Enhanced Mind. Call for Papers.* Paper presented at IS Philosophy Track: Philosophy for a Hyperconnected World, 19th Americas Conference on Information Systems. Chicago, IL.

Wang, S., Li, M., Wu, J., Kim, D.-H., Lu, N., & Su, Y. et al. (2012). Mechanics of Epidermal Electronics. *Journal of Applied Mechanics, 79,* 1–6. doi:10.1115/1.4005963

Wright, D. (2011). A framework for the ethical impact assessment of information technology. *Ethics and Information Technology, 13*(3), 199–220. doi:10.1007/s10676-010-9242-6

KEY TERMS AND DEFINITIONS

Augmented Bodyware Devices: Bodyware artifacts designed for permanent or long-term use, those are self-contained. They are embedded into human bodies and the boundaries of body and prostheses are harder to define.

Bodyware Applications: Certain ways of using bodyware artifacts for a specific purpose in a specific context at a specific configuration.

Bodyware Artifacts: Functional bodyware apparatus, systems and procedures using bodyware technology.

Bodyware Technology: A set of biomedical ICT techniques that enable integration or merger of functional devices with human bodies to support, enhance and expand the capabilities of embodying individuals.

Implanted Bodyware Devices: Bodyware artifacts designed for medium to longer-term use, those are self-contained but require external energy sources. They are located inside human body, however, the boundaries of body and prostheses are clear.

Simple Bodyware Apparatus: Bodyware artifacts that are located outside, at the body surface and has limited durability. They are like consumptive sensors and prostheses and do not have smart functionality.

Smart Bodyware Apparatus: Bodyware artifacts that are located at the body surface with a smart functionality and medium term use.

Chapter 3
Mapping Human Enhancement Rhetoric

Kevin A. Thayer
Cyborg-X.com, USA

ABSTRACT

This chapter raises ethical questions about the relationship between HET and the discourse of human enhancement technologies. Specifically, it explores some problems in mapping human enhancement rhetoric. In the first section, human enhancement rhetoric is defined. Questions are raised about the rhetorical act of re-defining "human enhancement" as a problem of self-descriptive narrative and performance measurement. In section two, various approaches and terms for mapping are presented as a way of underscoring the slippery qualities of human enhancement as a dynamic, expanding discourse. Section three explains the changing ethical positions for enhancement technology users through the concepts of "over claim," "reacting to technology," and "ethos." In section four, boundary changes for HET users are discussed as a complex mapping of shifting concepts, discourse, and communities. In conclusion, the transition from human enhancement to transhuman enhancement is emphasized with suggestions for future research.

INTRODUCTION

2024: A human patient is undergoing head reconstruction surgery. The human surgeon is located in Vienna, Austria; the patient is located in New York, NY in an operating theatre equipped with the latest robotic da Vinci surgical system. The system incorporates new 3d printing technology. Implantation of a new bionic right eye is a major part of the head reconstruction surgery. The lens has been designed to match the patient's left eye

in appearance; it will be an unnoticeable change to those with biological vision. The patient will have superhuman vision that applies 3d printing technology. During the surgery, a transhuman programmer with HET-user knowledge hacks into the robotic surgical system. Distracted by a software translation error, the surgeon and other technicians are unaware of the hack. The programmer uploads an encrypted file to the patient's eye that will automatically upgrade vision as per coded knowledge marshaled from specific

DOI: 10.4018/978-1-4666-6010-6.ch003

HET users. The now transhuman patient with a reconstructed head and enhanced vision teams with other HET users to develop 3d-printing and scanning upgrades. Knowledge gained from the use of these upgrades will further enhance vision and transformative capabilities beyond the human for specific HET users.

Given this hypothetical scenario, questions can be raised about the shifting ethical positions in human and transhuman enhancement discourse. Are we motivated to talk and act differently if our physical, sensory, or cognitive capabilities improve, for example, if our vision is superhuman or hijacked? How do we apply discourse about improved capabilities (hypothetical versus actual) to create or avoid current and future ethical problems, such as programming a coded upgrade for only certain users or determining responsibility for translations that result in computer-dependent and enhanced behaviors? If we are enhanced, how do we know and how do we persuade others? How do others react to our enhancement rhetoric and who benefits?

Computing power has simultaneously moved inside the human body and beyond our solar system. The cochlear implant has made a hybrid human hearing sense possible through embodied computing power. Through NASA and satellite computing power, the Voyager 1 entered interstellar space in late 2013. Both human flesh and global activities are now computer-mediated. As patients, athletes, and astronauts seek restored capabilities, sensory enhancements, and performance advantages, computing power and human enhancement technologies demand further study as an ethical dimension of humans and their co-evolving transhuman relatives.

Concepts that have been introduced since 1960, such as "cyborg," "internet," "information technology," "transhumanism," "human genome," "body scan," "digital native," "upgrade," "smart phone," "smart fabric," "nanotechnology," "wi-fi," "space tourism," and "Mars mission," among others, mark significant changes in culture and research. They also mark changes in human and technological scale. The lexicon related to human enhancement has been growing and changing over the past half-century.

From the microscopic to the macroscopic, from the personal to the global, from the cellular to the cosmic, humans are simultaneously exploring boundaries of physical matter, boundaries of the flesh, boundaries of consciousness, and boundaries of time and space. With each boundary exploration, there is a corresponding lexicon and scale. With each boundary exploration, considering the rhetorical concept of circumference, questions arise about human ethics. As we map human enhancement rhetoric, we also map ethical dimensions. Mapping such a dynamic discourse to reveal ethical dimensions requires an effective mapping strategy.

This simple map shows two circles with openings; both circles are shifting as situations and discourse communities change. One circle represents the changing rhetoric of human enhancement; the other represents the changing rhetoric of transhuman enhancement. Humans who seek enhancement through HET will eventually gain actual enhanced capabilities. When they describe their enhanced capabilities, they will develop rhetoric using new knowledge, transhuman knowledge based on transformative computing power. The overlapping area of the two shifting and open circles shows this discourse. As discourse about actual enhanced capabilities beyond the human is directed to HET users (both existing and future users), these users develop transhuman enhancement rhetoric. These users develop specific discourse around their enhancement, as shown in two circles, e.g., vision and hearing enhancements. Upgrades move discourse towards new rhetoric and further upgrades/enhancements.

This chapter is organized around four questions:

1. What is human enhancement rhetoric?
2. How can we map human enhancement rhetoric?
3. What does this project of mapping human enhancement rhetoric accomplish?
4. What global issues or ethical concerns are raised, or can be further understood, by mapping human enhancement rhetoric?

By addressing these questions, the reader will be introduced to some problems in the field of HET with suggestions for further research. By framing these problems as rhetorical situations in HET, the reader will be introduced to important considerations of changing ethical positions on the topic of this book.

WHAT IS HUMAN ENHANCEMENT RHETORIC?

The term *human enhancement rhetoric* can be broadly defined as the persuasive discourse(s) created and used by speakers and writers supporting the activities of HET and HET communities. This book's title is an example of human enhancement rhetoric because it presents specific arguments about human enhancement.

A detailed definition of human enhancement rhetoric can be created by synthesizing the definitions of each component term: human, enhancement, and rhetoric. This synthesis, however, is based on clear and agreed-upon definitions of "human," and "enhancement," and "rhetoric." Each of these terms is evolving, changing, as humans develop and employ the use of HET. This chapter will discuss changing contexts in which human enhancement rhetoric is created, distributed, and recreated.

Human enhancement rhetoric is a dynamic discourse phenomenon. The definition *and redefinition* of "human enhancement" as a rhetorical situation[1] that changes—and produces different, potentially rapid, and unknown outcomes—depends upon increasingly complex interactions and technology. How could (or how do) human enhancement technologies change human communication and human behavior? I develop a theory to address this question in "Beyond Cyborg Metapathography…introducing 'morphos' as a rhetorical concept…" For brevity here, I proceed from my argument "that if we change our bodies, we change the language we use to describe our bodies; we change how we can tell stories about our bodies, and we change the stories we tell about our bodies" (Thayer, 2012, p. 100). HET complicate bodies and narratives about bodies, creating new discursive patterns.

Human enhancement rhetoric is evidenced in a set of discursive patterns that have, due to the increased volume of discourse about human enhancement technology and transhumanism, become more and more visible. Because of the advancements and *use* of HET, the patterns have moved from visible and well-documented proposals and promotional texts, to HET-user discourse and HET policy. This paradigm shift—from proposals and theoretical discourse about HET concepts—to HET reports and user narratives about practical, ethical functioning in the real world—is the general concern of this chapter and the specific concern of section four.

As rhetorical patterns, tropes, terms, move from the theoretical to the practical, the shift in narratives and real consequences can be difficult to map. Language patterns (thanks to corpus linguistics and a host of big data techniques) can be monitored, but as dynamic core elements of human communication (online and offline), they change and move as humans change and move.

Language patterns that are visible are easier to track, but in the case of HET users—especially those equipped with neuroprosthetics (like the bionic eye patient in the intro scenario) that can be upgraded through computer technology—language becomes complicated by technology. Technology, especially digital technology that merges with language and writing, as we have seen with bot-generated emails, Google translations, etc., can be marshaled to form hybrid rhetorical devices. HET users wield a new rhetorical means and new storytelling capability (Thayer, 2012, pp. 85-100). HET users (like the transhuman programmer in the intro scenario) can "write" stories that change others' stories, and thus, others' lives. This rhetorical act of ethos construction and reconstruction, enhanced through technological innovations, is an ethical issue.

Europe's Science and Technology Options Assessment (STOA) 2012 Annual Report, Section 6.6 covers "Human enhancement—The ethical issues" (European Parliament, 2013). The following excerpt offers a meta-level view of current HET ethical issues (as seen in Europe):

Speakers discussed the importance of 'science and conscience', and expressed the idea that religion and ethics/moral values are becoming more important and interlinked within the (political) debate surrounding Science and Technology, making the Human Enhancement Technologies debate a multidimensional one, rather than just scientific. The general feeling was that, although human enhancement is very exciting and offers many possibilities for improving our quality of life, it is important to differentiate between treatment, improvement and enhancement, and where the line should be drawn, especially as our life expectancy has increased significantly over the last 200 years (European Parliament, 2013, p. 32).

"Drawing" this "line" while acknowledging the multidimensional "debate" unfolding in HET discourse requires a careful study of the rhetorical "dimensions" of HET development and use. As the report authors note: the "ethics/moral values are becoming more important and interlinked within the (political) debate surrounding Science and Technology." This "interlinking" of language forms patterns in discourse about HET, but as mentioned above, these patterns shift constantly

because HET are rapidly reconfigurable. This rapid reconfiguration, a hybrid technique (that might in certain cases of real enhancement be seen as an "advantage"), raises concerns about our human "species." These concerns are emphasized in question by the STOA authors: "Will techniques for enhancing human beings yield a new species, and, if so, what will be the relationship between the 'new' species and the 'old'" (European Parliament, 2013, p. 33)?

But before these "techniques" are in practical use by HET users (such as during the proposed human colonization of Mars), there are yet other questions and concerns that must be addressed. The STOA authors note:

Questions on the consequences for human self-understanding and religious piety, when human life is seen as the object of a technical project, rather than as the result of evolution or divine creation were also discussed. Apart from the religious and ethical views, many risks were also discussed, and not just physical ones. Making humans 'better' in one respect may be very problematic without causing damage to other capacities - physical, mental, moral, spiritual (European Parliament, 2013, p. 33).

One way of gathering data on "human self-understanding" and "other capacities" gained from HET use, is through autobiographical HET-user narrative. These narratives reveal important patterns in discourse that further reveal rhetorical devices for persuading audiences. I return to this point in sections III & IV.

As we have political rhetoric and personal rhetoric created by authors who develop different arguments, human enhancement rhetoric is unprecedented in terms of its narrative potential, patterns, argumentative positions, and social risks. With claims of "a better life," HET rhetoric acts upon more than select audiences; it acts upon the human race. STOA authors wrote:

And will enhancement jeopardize or increase the solidarity within the human race? For example, it could lead to an ever-increasing gap between the rich and the poor, if human enhancement were used to create certain types of advantages' for some people over others. As Mr. Prodi, MEP, summed up "the basic principle is the dignity of the person", and we do not yet know what the possible (long-term) outcomes of human enhancement could be. Therefore, research into Human Enhancement Technologies should be managed with prudence, trying to tackle social problems with the aim to create a more just society, rather than opting for Human Enhancement Technologies for their own sake (European Parliament, 2013, p. 33).

In order to define "human enhancement" through the use of technology, language and other tools of measurement must be developed to accurately identify "enhanced" human capabilities. Human capabilities are measured and recorded over time, but measuring and recording tools (technology) have improved over time. Imprecise terms like "normal" and imprecise numerical ranges are used to identify human performance. These terms and ranges are influenced by environmental and medical research and politics.

Human enhancement as an ethical dimension of human evolution is a relative term based on performance measurement, performance levels, and body politics. However, as humans increase their performance through technological modification of the body…cultural beliefs, values, and socio-economic incentives shift. As people gain increased performance through technological innovation, incentives and performance metrics shift.

Accurate, technical identification of a so-called human enhancement is useful until the terms "human" or "enhancement" are officially redefined. But as humans and their enhancements change, what or how will a benchmark be established or used? For example, if in some future time, a bionic eye or eyes could enhance a person's vision far beyond the best known range of current biological human vision, that is, from say 20/10, to 40/5, or 80/5, and if this superior vision gained widespread popularity, what ethical and social concerns would influence new definitions of "human" or "enhancement"? This hypothetical scenario can be further complicated by including the bionic vision-enabled user's remote real-time access to any available video or surveillance or optical technology, creating a kind of panoptic super-vision that synthesizes both digital and physical visual information. Steve Mann's work on computer-mediated reality through visual prostheses is an excellent present-day example of this technology under development. When reality can be explained through new HET-enabled capabilities—in this example, visual reality—"human enhancement" can be further understood and explained at the personal level…complicated by overt and covert monitoring.

Just recently a new "smart" contact lens appeared in the news. It is HET features that are intended to help diabetics monitor blood glucose; however, this technology combined with Google Glass and other bionic vision prostheses (such as retinal implants and Mann's wearable technology) are clear evidence of new human visual capabilities through HET. How will "human vision" be defined or measured in coming years? Human enhancement rhetoric will influence both the definition and the measurements.

SOME CHALLENGES AND PROBLEMS MAPPING HUMAN ENHANCEMENT RHETORIC

How can we map the dynamic, technology-dependent discourse of human enhancement? As HET gain popular use, how can we map human enhancement rhetoric as the discourse defining and explaining new capabilities, persuading others? Before answering this question, let's consider some basic areas of human enhancement and the kinds of discourse that develops in these areas:

- Physical (cosmetic, restoration, sports & athletic performance, military & endurance)
- Sensory (sensitivity, perception, & awareness)
- Cognitive (knowledge, creativity, discovery, & behavior)
- Social (activity, productivity, innovation, & collaboration)
- Lifespan (longevity, population, & evolution)
- Spiritual (empathy & transcendence)

Certainly a useful way of mapping human enhancement rhetoric would be to uncover the "enhancement" terms and tropes produced in these discourse areas as they relate to specific authorial communities and audiences. (Examples follow). An initial approach to mapping human enhancement rhetoric then, might be to identify terms and communities to understand the argumentative or ethical positions of HET developers and users. An *ethical position* is created by a rhetor—a speaker or writer—in the act of constructing an argument for an audience. The construction of *ethos*, one of Aristotle's three rhetorical appeals, is made possible through language, gestures, movements, clothing, etc.; but ethos is commonly understood as the (re-)presentation of moral character and credibility to an audience. Rhetorical scholars Sharon Crowley and Debra Hawhee explain ethos as either "invented" or "situated": "According to Aristotle, rhetors can invent a character suitable to an occasion—this is *invented ethos*. However, if rhetors are fortunate enough to enjoy a good reputation in the community, they can use it as an ethical proof—this is *situated ethos*" (Crowley & Hawhee, 2012, p. 126). They elaborate on ethos, saying:

Today we may feel uncomfortable with the notion that rhetorical character can be constructed, since we tend to think of character, or personality, as fairly stable. We generally assume as well that character is shaped by an individual's experiences. The ancient Greeks, in contrast, thought that character was constructed not by what happened to people but by the moral practices in which they habitually engaged. An ethos was not finally given by nature, but was developed by habit (Crowley & Hawhee, 2012, p. 126).

HET are habit-developing and habit-changing technologies. They also have the potential to change our most fundamental ethical positions in rhetorical situations.

Those who develop or utilize HET can be categorized by fundamental ethical positions: human, citizen, person, and patient. These positions can shift, however slightly over time, for those who use HET. Of course, a human person can be a citizen and patient, complicating ethos construction as an argumentative position for an HET author/speaker addressing a selected audience in a certain time and place. The complications arise due to ethical questions of scale and boundaries: Will the HET author/speaker make ethical distinctions about enhancement? If so, will these distinctions influence audience opinions of the author/speaker as human, citizen, person, or patient? Will the audience opinions shape discourse or actions that influence others' moral concepts (about enhancement)? If so, at what scale, or concerning what perceived human boundary?

These fundamental ethical positions relate to basic concepts of scale and boundaries: human—civilization, culture, and evolution; citizen—social, community, and political activity; person—personhood and identity; patient—medical technology and health. These positions also relate to discourse communities and underscore the importance of authorial and group motivations, raising basic questions: What discourse communities use human enhancement rhetoric? Do HET lead to the development of human enhancement rhetoric, or does human enhancement rhetoric lead to the development of HET? Or both? What qualifies as an enhancement? Does this change over time? Who determines the qualifications and when they should be changed? How are these questions addressed using human enhancement rhetoric?

In *Enhancing Human Capacities*, the authors distinguish four different understandings of enhancement: 1) objective, norm-based, 2) objective, status quo based, 3) subjective, norm-based, and 4) subjective, status quo based (Holm & McNamee, 2012, p. 294). How does a "norm based" understanding of enhancement work? Who determines the basis for "normal" and for what group(s)? Does "normal" change over time? How does a "status quo based" understanding of enhancement work? Who determines the basis for "status quo" and for what group(s)? Does "status quo" change over time? Holm and McNamee use co-authorship and rhetorical techniques to answer these questions. They construct their ethos in part by defining the scale of their HET project and the boundaries it explores—as two authors. The two authors collaborate to develop their ethical position using terms and concepts that map a circumference about "enhancing human capacities" for the reader.

Kenneth Burke's rhetorical concept of *circumference* is useful for understanding shifts in rhetoric directed to different audiences at different times. Circumference refers to a set of key terms defining an argument. Burke saw in circumference an opportunity to locate ambiguity by finding *"terms that clearly reveal the strategic spots at which ambiguities necessarily arise"* (1969, p. xviii).

When considering circumferences as rhetorical areas of address or influence, it is helpful to also consider scale. When mapping HET as a rhetorical phenomenon, it is useful to refer to corpora for time periods and historical data, publication volume and media, population and innovations. Desktop publishing, the internet, digital and cellular technology, genetic engineering, nanotechnology, and 3d printing are some notable innovations.

In *Nexus Analysis: Discourse and the Emerging Internet*, Suzie Wong Scollon writes: "The important part of mapping is to keep focused on crucial points in the cycles of discourses where changes are occurring and to remain alert to cycles of discourse which may be overt or invisible within the current moment but which, seen in a broader circumference, are active moments in the overall semiotic ecosystem" (2004, p. 107). Scollon explains "discourse cycles" by using the concepts of analogy and materiality:

[D]iscourse cycles are not just analogies based on material cycles. Discourse cycles are all material cycles as well. In one instance the materialization of the discourse may be in the form of the movements of body parts in spoken language. In another instance these are materialized as written documents. It is the job of a nexus analysis never to presuppose the links among cycles of discourse but to seek them out for analysis (2004, p. 34).

According to Scollon, "complex interactions among multiple cycles" (2004, p. 16) of discourse can be understood as a "discursive or semiotic ecosystem" (2004, p. 34). HET discourse has materialized over years according to this description.

What is discourse and how is it "technologized"? Scollon writes that discourse as "'the ways in which people engage each other in communication'...is technologized through a very wide range of martial supports and extensions from the structure of the built environment and is furniture to the media by which communication may be moved across distances of time and space such as...digital-electronic systems" (2004, p. 4). For concision, Scollon prefers Jan Blommaert"s "more useful" definition: "discourse 'comprises all forms of meaningful semiotic human activity seen in connection with social, cultural and historical patterns and developments of use'' (2004, p. 5).

As a form of "meaningful semiotic human activity," self-enhancement discourse, a subjective exploration of changing personal capabilities, is a salient starting point for mapping human enhancement rhetoric, a discourse that moves between the human and the transhuman. In her review of Radhakrishnan's *History, the Human, and the World Between*, Christine Battista refers to "self-reflexive discourse," which forms the basis for any self-enhancement discourse. Quoting Radhakrishnan, she writes: "Because the human has to speak for 'the worlding of the world,' they must speak in a self-reflexive discourse that, in its very nature, should be a 'self-reflexive and deconstructive exercise of anthropocentrism in the name of the human, the nonhuman, and the transhuman'" (2009, p. 394). The following list, beginning with "self-enhancement discourse," reveals some discourse categories, considerations, and communities under the purview of human enhancement technology:

- Self-enhancement discourse (includes psychological theory and could help to describe HET User transformation through self-descriptive language; relates to patient discourse for HET Users).
- Transhuman discourse (applies the notion of individuals and groups becoming differently human through physical and intellectual transformation/evolution and also establishes HET User identity with the transhumanist community).
- Transhumanist discourse[2] (supports the manifesto and philosophical, cultural movement of transhumanism; can be subdivided according to political, secular, and religious groups that establish different ethical positions).

- Cyborg discourse (initially fictional, theoretical, and feminist; but as an early discourse supporting HET it has been slowly emerging as an anthropological and autobiographical discourse within global culture).
- Posthuman discourse (academic and theoretical).
- Medical discourse (illness, health, and wellness).
- Technology discourse (science, computing, and innovation).
- Patient discourse (subjective and community-driven discourse subcategorized by specific HET and technology-specific behavior; confronting and addressing physical/intellectual/emotional challenges).
- Futurist discourse (hypotheses, thought experiments, future studies as emerging area, and ethical concerns for future humanity).

As communities and texts, these discourses merge and overlap, creating intersections. Technology discourse intersects with these discourses through specific, technical terms and communication techniques, complicating texts through digital/online activity. Codes and algorithms influence human activity in the 21st century. As an example of Scollon's "very wide range of martial supports and extensions," digital programs and computer bots (two of many examples) "technologize" discourse and the further "extensions" introduced by HET include implants/prostheses that control or enhance human functionality. How do we map these discourse intersections or the "cycles" they form? We might identify new communities and their new terms.

I would like to return to my earlier point that identifying communities and terms can clarify ethical positions that would be useful for mapping human enhancement rhetoric. The next list shows top HET research areas as more specific HET communities and helps us consider their HET-specific terminologies:

- Genetic engineering (e.g., cloning).
- Robotics (e.g., powered exoskeletons).
- Regenerative medicine (e.g., stem cell research, 3d-printed human tissue).
- Bionics.
- Cryonics and life extension.
- Nanotechnology.
- Neuroprosthetics (e.g., cochlear implants, brain-machine interfaces).
- Info and computer technology (e.g., wearable computing).
- Drugs and pharmaceuticals (e.g., steroids, "smart drugs").
- Nutrition.

Research areas intersect; however, they each use different technical terms and discourse and different approaches to advance different arguments for the benefits of human enhancement technology. These intersections raise ethical concerns for HET. How does research discourse change over time as it moves from non-enhanced to enhanced users (and from enhanced to non-enhanced users) within each discourse community? How might this change over time, in different rhetorical situations, using different rhetorical strategies? How might this change the development and use of HET, and thus, human behavior? Mapping discourse in HET is itself an ethical challenge and act of identifying and explaining and arguing for the common good. But what is the common good? How will "common good" be redefined in the age of HET?

Another possible discourse mapping strategy could view human enhancement rhetoric by considering four common human environments undergoing change as a result of technological innovation: the human brain, the human body, the human world, the human practice. How do we practice being human(s)? With our increasing dependence on machines, how do we humans use our brains to mobilize our physical actions in the world to practice our respective arts? This begs the question: How will we practice being transhuman(s)?

How would we use the human environments under consideration as mapping sites for human enhancement rhetoric? What has changed since our ancient Greek conceptions in the way we use discourse about our brain, our body, our world, our practice, to negotiate with others? Did ancient Greek citizens dream or talk about ways of gaining performance, or exceeding human capabilities? Their contributions to Western civilization are recorded in canonical literature that establish these ideas (e.g., in virtue ethics as the ancient Greek rhetorical concepts *arête*, *phronesis*, and *eudaimonia*). What has changed in the discourse of human "enhancement" over the last 25 centuries of human evolution? What has changed in the rhetoric of human "enhancement" since the 20th century? Since the beginning of the 21st century? What human environment has changed most dramatically in the past 20 years, and how is this change reflected in discourse about "enhancement?" What human environment is expected to change most dramatically in the coming decades?

A further way of mapping human enhancement rhetoric and its ethical consequences[3] is to chart its evolution over time, lifespan, generations, or HET-specific cohorts (e.g., brain-implant users or motor prosthesis users). As a fundamental starting point for the application of HET, we can also focus on mapping discourse about the changing human/transhuman body.

Belgian surgeons Steven Claes and Johan Bellemans confirmed the existence of a previously unspecified human body part, the ALL or anterolateral ligament of the knee joint in *The Journal of Anatomy* (Claes et. al., 2013). Our anatomy and our body parts are being specified through scientific discoveries, but also as the result of bionic and human enhancement technologies. Our current situation as an evolving species—and a core ethical debate regarding HET—involves two distinct ethical, philosophical positions: one, bioconservatives continue to search for a deeper understanding and preservation of the organic human body; two, transhumanists search for ways to explore and extend bodily capabilities through synthetic and hybrid body parts.

With these two positions come two discourses: the language and terms used to specify organic human anatomy and capabilities, and the language and terms used to specify synthetic and hybrid human anatomy and capabilities. If we are still trying to understand the complexities of the human organism (having only recently decoded the human genome and, in 2013, only just specifying a knee joint ligament), and yet we are rapidly changing the human organism through bionic, hybrid, and enhancement technologies that create a synthesis and new, unspecified capabilities, how will this discursive intersection influence language about the human body and human performance?

Changing the human body through enhancement technologies is changing our concepts and stories of the human condition. Will language about hybrid human capabilities and human performance—enhanced through body-part and body-changing technologies—change the conception, design, and parameters of desired (organic and synthetic) human body parts? Will these changes occur simultaneously? What is at stake if our narratives of self- (and group-) transformation become more persuasive or more transparent? Can self-transformation narratives lead to *self-enhancement* narratives? Can self-enhancement narratives be transparent *and* persuasive? How can we answer these questions without first mapping the narratives and terms of human enhancement rhetoric?

What terms would help us map human enhancement rhetoric? How do these terms relate to or function for current or future HET-users if most were coined by or included in texts written by non-HET-users? We know that the term "human enhancement" has grown in usage as more powerful technological innovations have increased. It would be useful to map its growth by showing when and where it was published for what kinds of audiences and for what purpose. The same applies for the term "transhumanism."

I have applied terms and introduced new terms to conceptualize and illuminate certain features in the narrative rhetoric of living human cyborgs (i.e., advanced HET-users):

- Self-transformation.
- Self-enhancement (not to be confused with the psychological term used in "self-enhancement theory").
- Transhuman.
- Hybrid bodily praxis.
- Morphos.
- Computer-mediated flesh.
- Cyborg metapathography.
- Cyborg patient rhetoric.

I define these terms elsewhere, though I would like to include my definitions of morphos and hybrid bodily praxis here. "Morphos is *repeatedly harnessing* technological upgrades to reconfigure oneself and improve performance[;] it is the dialectical relationship between bodily reconstruction and ethos reconstruction" (Thayer, 2013, p. 428). This relationship complicates discourse as computing power manifests in hybrid behavior and hybrid language to describe that hybrid behavior. Agency is increased through hybrid, transformative behavior. "One's strategic use of bodily reconstruction for increased human performance can be a rhetorical act that reimagines ethos, the standing one claims to speak/write with authority" (2013, p. 428). Earlier, I used "*bodily praxis* to describe the everyday bodily skills and abilities used to perform rhetorical actions" noting that "bodily praxis is how we communicate using our bodies and tools in rhetorical situations" (Thayer, 2012, p. 20). I differentiate my term from "body praxis" by emphasizing action and change with "bodily." Patients develop a new *hybrid bodily praxis* through HET implantation; this includes new knowledge and rhetoric of the body. This term relates specifically to the dynamic, upgradeable, hybrid body/mind of the HET-user and will reappear in the following sections. Furthermore, it relates to nexus analysis as a means of understanding "meaningful semiotic human activity" (which may eventually become meaningful semiotic *transhuman* activity). HET-users can change their bodily praxis through technology. This change effects self-reflexive, self-descriptive language and narratives. New narratives can be used to develop new arguments and new communities. For HET supporters, these arguments—from both non-HET-users and HET-users—define organizations.

The following list identifies a few organizations supporting HET. These suggest a mapping based on specific publications as each organization publishes its work:

- Humanity+, formerly World Transhumanist Association ("humanity will be radically changed by technology in the future").
- Betterhumans LLC.
- Singularity University.
- DARPA (Defense Advanced Research Projects Agency).
- Institute for Ethics and Emerging Technologies.
- Institute for the Future.
- Immortality Institute.
- Future of Humanity Institute.
- Cyborg Foundation.

As each organization develops its mission and achieves its objectives, professional discourse develops around key concepts, processes, and products/services. HET development disrupts these through innovation and new models. Commonly used terms like "genome," "upgrade," "interface," "user," "AI," "wetware," "app," "virtual," and "online/offline," have appeared as the result of innovations and new models; however, these are generic. New or newly-applied terms are used to describe new models and develop new arguments; they reveal shifts in HET-influenced discourse.

The author, cyborg, and futurist Michael Chorost applies these two HET-inspired terms in his book *World Wide Mind*:

- World wide mind.
- Telempathy.

"World wide mind" is a term used by Chorost to explore and explain a global communication network accessed via thought. "Telempathy" is empathy achieved via telecommunication through embodied HET. As I argue in "…Introducing morphos…," these terms reveal a shift in HET-user boundaries and rhetorical strategies. They indicate changing motivations and communities. Human enhancement rhetoric can be explored and mapped by first identifying author-specific or text-specific key terms, especially those terms developed by HET users/supporters like Chorost. We can map human enhancement rhetoric by identifying HET-user "enhancement" texts and terms, and non-HET-user "enhancement" texts and terms. These form one "discursive ecosystem," but two semiotic systems based on different bodily praxes and different ethical positions.

CHANGING ETHICAL POSITIONS

I have just introduced some challenges and problems in mapping human enhancement rhetoric. What is the current situation in HET that necessitates a mapping of "human enhancement rhetoric"? Firstly, the design, production, and use of HET are made possible through discourse. The discourses enabling human enhancement technology are influenced by communities (including various organizations, societies, and academies) as well as the current digital/computing technology. Secondly, thanks to the ubiquity of computing technologies that are changing boundaries—such as boundaries between man and machine and what I call "computer-mediated flesh"—our concepts of "self," "social," and "human" are shifting. Thirdly, mapping human enhancement rhetoric helps us uncover ethical concerns within HET by identifying ethical positions and motivations.

In this section, I transition from HET discourse mapping considerations to the specific problem of changing ethical positions in HET. Ethical positions are established through qualifications, affiliations, and communities. What communities influence the changing discourse of human enhancement? What are the ethical positions constructed by those people in communities using discourse about human enhancement (i.e., people creating narratives and arguments for the benefits of human enhancement technology)? What groups of people construct an ethos through human enhancement rhetoric, and what are their motivations? The following list offers some groups for consideration:

- Scholars.
- Scientists.
- Technologists and technoprogressives.
- Futurists.
- Transhumanists (secular and religious).
- Journalists.
- Product marketers.
- Fiction authors.
- Government and military organizations.
- Organizations with religious affiliations.
- HET designers.
- HET manufacturers.
- Pharmaceutical companies.
- Genetic engineers.
- Medical doctors and surgeons.
- Nanotechnology companies.
- Biotechnology companies.
- Information technology companies.
- Cognitive scientists.
- HET users (including self-identifying cyborgs).
- Patients.

- Athletes.
- Ethicists.
- Hackers, grinders, and biohackers.
- Cultural engineers.

This list, as you can see, includes overlaps and redundancies. A cognitive scientist is in the scientist group; a futurist might also be a transhumanist; an HET user could be a patient; an ethicist could be an athlete, and so on. The positions and motivations of and within these groups are constantly changing; yet in order to navigate change, we identify our increasingly transformational world and experiences using technology and verbalized or written concepts. Some of these technologies are known as *human enhancement technologies*.

HET are varied in their type and application, suggesting different rhetorical techniques and ethical implications. There are ethical implications of "mechanical versus chemical enhancements" (Harris, 2007, p. 19). In the case of a human cyborg, mechanical enhancements can be obvious or less-than-obvious (or completely unnoticeable as in the hypothetical 2024 bionic eye patient). Chemical enhancements are often understood as ethically questionable self-administered or clinically-administered pharmaceutical products because they directly alter human performance (seen often in sports doping). What if mechanical enhancements provided chemical enhancements? What if these chemical enhancements were transparent?

Human performance can be clearly altered by HET, whether those technologies are obvious and mechanical or covert and transparent. How is increased performance revealed (or even recorded) through the use of HET? How do we measure or record increased human performance? Athletic abilities, creative abilities, cognitive abilities, social abilities?

How is increased human performance revealed and recorded in communication? How is the rhetorical skill of an enhanced person different from the rhetorical skill of a non-enhanced person?

What considerations will help us understand the ethical differences between the rhetoric of enhancement and the rhetoric of natural abilities? Harris writes: "The ethical justification for or defense of enhancements is not that they do or might confer positional advantage but that they make lives better" (2007, p. 29).

The transformed and enhanced "better" person who uses HET explores new boundaries, capabilities, and personhood. This exploration is typically aided by others through the use of dialogue and discursive efforts at work to optimize performance and results.

In the 2012 jointly published report on *Human enhancement and the future of work*, the "discourse of enhancement" is brought under scrutiny:

Professor Nikolas Rose, Professor of Sociology and Head of the Department of Social Science, Health & Medicine at King's College London, cautioned that 'over claiming' the benefits of technologies can impact on the future success of novel developments. Disciplines such as genomics, neuroscience and synthetic biology provide many interesting insights and may bring benefits to users, but there is a need to distinguish the market hype from reality. Professor Rose told the workshop that 'over claim' characterises emerging technologies and is linked to a 'political economy of hope', in which the hopes of patients, politicians, scientists and commercial enterprises sit alongside warnings from the military that we may see a new arms race in enhancement technologies, to drive the discourse of enhancement. Professor Rose cautioned that this language, including the term 'enhancement' itself, is embedded in this pervasive culture of 'over claim'. Caution and scepticism support robust science and facilitate more productive discussion. If overestimated promises do not come to fruition, there are negative implications for industry, science and users. Another participant stressed *that although scepticism can be helpful, being over-cautious can slow progress and delay access to technologies that could help numerous individuals (The Academy of Medical Sciences, 2012, p. 35).*

According to the report, the discourse of human enhancement is "embedded in this pervasive culture of 'over claim'" and "there is a need to distinguish the market hype from reality." How is reality distinguished, using what language and by whom? According to other experts, the user of enhancement technologies has a unique ethical position:

Dr. Pamela Gallagher, Senior Lecturer in Psychology at Dublin City University, stressed that we must understand an individual's psychosocial perspective; that is the personal, social, emotional, cultural and environmental circumstances that will enable users to benefit most from a technology. An enhancement technology, irrespective of whether it is placed in the user's environment, on their person or in their body, is effectively an interface between that individual and the life they wish to lead. It is therefore how people react to technology, rather than the technology itself, that determines how enhancing it will be. Box 4 outlines the importance of a user-centred approach and of the role that reinforcement and feedback play in an individual accepting a technology (The Academy of Medical Sciences, 2012, p. 39).

"[H]ow people react to technology," especially the people we consider users and those who interact with users, is critical in determining "how enhancing [a given enhancement technology] will be." In other words, "how people 'read' the technology they are using is potentially one of the most powerful psychosocial factors in its integration" (The Academy of Medical Sciences, 2012, p. 40).

This "reading" as one step in an individual's process of self-transformation through HET becomes important for both self-identity and community when it results in textual production of self-descriptive, experiential user-narrative. Enhancement technologies impact self-transformation through usage and narratives about usage, particularly as they reflect perceptions of "self." The 2012 report mentions "considerable debate" about this impact: "There has been considerable debate around how enhancement would impact on individuality and identity, for example around whether there are risks to one's sense of identity and perception of 'self' when making use of an enhancement, and particularly if individuals start to make use of multiple enhancements" (The Academy of Medical Sciences, 2012, p. 47).

A quick review of some key phrases in this report, such as "discourse of enhancement," "how people 'read' the technology they are using," and "considerable debate around how enhancement would impact on individuality and identity" indicate an increasing awareness of the rhetorical dimension of HET.

People using the discourse of enhancement, including those who are critiquing the discourse, have ethical positions. The academies jointly publishing the 2012 report establish a very *situated ethos*. How do HET complicate the changing of ethical positions? The following map shows a number of HET discourse communities, highlighting possible positions of HET-users.

HET-users can construct situated and invented ethos, depending upon their reputation and their "enhanced" capabilities. However, their ethos construction is complicated by their therapeutic, functional, and/or performance-enhancing use of HET.

As human cyborgs—an advanced user of HET—explore and transgress boundaries of human flesh (through computer-mediated flesh)—particularly those implanted with computer-powered neuroprostheses—they simultaneously explore two means of symbolic interaction: mathematical (or, digital) and verbal (or, lexical).

The mathematical/digital means is explored in two fundamental ways:

1. Prosthetic Design. A cyborg acquires potential capabilities through the mathematical/digital programming logic that is designed to run one or more programs at the level of the neuroprosthesis. This programming and coding can be done by non-cyborgs, other cyborgs, or, the user.
2. Prosthetic Operation. A cyborg uses new prosthetic capabilities when a program runs to improve performance. However, this program influences human cognition and behavior because new modes of cognition made possible through brain neuroplasticity are influenced by prosthetic design and operation.

The verbal/lexical means is explored in four fundamental ways:

1. Speaking.
2. Listening.
3. Writing.
4. Reading.

However, these verbal/lexical means are complicated by the mathematical/digital means, which raises questions about the nature, or, in the specific case of HET, "the technology" of changing ethical positions. Jeff Pappone in *The Ottawa Citizen*, reporting on a TED conference presentation by Christopher Dewdney and the application of technology in creating a person-less communication writes: "Language, [Dewdney] insisted, is the key human software building block of all consciousness, which each person uploads during their development. It consists of mathematical patterns which will one day be isolated by sophisticated analytical technology." He continues: "Once the patterns are revealed, they may be replicated and transferred into any machine. And, evolution will be completely conquered, [Dewdney] said" (Pappone, 2000). If machines unlock and improve upon human communication (perhaps in speed and scope), what ethical concerns arise regarding the convergence of human language (about enhancement) and machine "language" about humans? If HET raise questions about discourse intersections and "the technology of changing ethical positions," what are these questions? Can a machine (or HET) change the discourse of human ethics? Can a machine or embodied machine (i.e., some HET) change a person's ethical position?

Returning to the four fundamental literacy modes as verbal means of symbolic interaction, in each mode the cyborg can use HET to increase performance. In other words, speaking, listening, writing, and reading can be improved through computer-mediated prostheses. What and who determines the exact criteria for "increased performance" and what constitutes "improvement" in symbolic interaction? If human symbolic interaction is complicated by HET, by cyborg behavior, and by cyborg-to-cyborg as well as non-cyborg-to-non-cyborg and non-cyborg-to-cyborg communication, how can this complication lead to "improvement" and "increased performance" or "enhancements"?

These terms and others are used to talk about HET, but discourse surrounding HET is influenced by HET and their users. To put it simply, human enhancement technologies can "enhance" human discourse. However, human discourse about HET is a specialized discourse influenced by changing technology and changing human performance, a hybrid discourse created through the combination of mathematical and verbal means of symbolic interaction.

How does the ethical position of a non-cyborg differ from the ethical position of a cyborg? This depends upon many factors, most importantly here, ethos construction. Ethos is constructed in a rhetorical situation, by a speaker/author. If the speaker/author is alive and present (a speaker/author can be recorded, influencing an audience without his/her living, physical presence), and is undergoing transformation during his/her rhetorical act, ethos can be constructed and reconstructed within the rhetorical situation. Cyborgs face this very challenge.

A human undergoes physical, sensory, cognitive, and social transformation(s) to become a cyborg, leading to cyborg personhood, changed ethical positions, and narrative discourse that includes rhetorical moves grounded in technological and neurological transformation. Self-transformation and group-transformation, as a dimension of a cyborg speaker's/author's rhetorical situation, is a particular focus here: cyborg transformation, for our purposes, involves modification of the human nervous system (and at the most advanced level, the central nervous system or *systems*). Thus, regarding the ethical challenges of cyborg-rhetors as HET users and related ethical considerations about HET discourse, this chapter raises questions for the benefit of the emerging field of neuroethics. Neuroethics can be seen as an embodied (and medical, experimental) problem of shifting human boundaries.

HET USERS: SHIFTING HUMAN CONCEPTS AND BOUNDARIES

What global issues or ethical concerns are raised, or can be further understood, by mapping human enhancement rhetoric? I will offer only a few concerns here due to space limitations. Foremost, I would like to underscore the importance of shifting human concepts and boundaries—the lifeworld that is rebuilt and represented by HET-users through technology-specific discourse. Consider for a moment the lifeworld and ideological differences across cultures and generations, reflected by technological innovations.

Changing culture influences a generation's language as a means of defining reality. In the 21st century, culture has influenced language through ubiquitous technology. Computer-mediated communication has also disrupted modes and styles of communication by causing intersections and complications. A common scene today in urban society: While one cohort of online users in a room full of people are simultaneously engaged in private and semi-private electronic communications (written, spoken, or video) using cellular and wi-fi devices, another cohort might be engaged in face-to-face verbal communication. In an airport lounge this scene might also include automated intercom announcements, user-interfaces displaying flight information, and many other forms of communication (such as signage, printed texts, etc.). Technology and language further complicate this scene as individuals and groups use personalized hardware, software, and multi-lingual skills. Within the language, of course, there are dialects and within the dialects, there are generational differences.

HET users belong to multiple generations. A *retinal implant* user may be an elder born in 1930. A *neuroprosthetic limb* user may be a combat veteran born in 1950 or 1990. A *cochlear implant* user may be an adult born in 1965 or a child born in 2010.

Human enhancement discourse spans generations, with diverse cultural influences…and shifting human concepts and boundaries. At present, one clear example of human enhancement and its shifting human boundaries is evidenced in anthropomorphic *exoskeletons* that greatly increase a user's strength and stamina. The DARPA-funded projects XOS 2 and *HULC* are known examples of exoskeletons (designed for military applications). Let's consider the following terms as shifting human boundaries and concepts: "retinal implant," "exoskeleton," and "HULC." A retinal implant

changes how the brain processes visual stimuli, from a biological process to a hybrid biological-technological process. New kinds of signals (programmed, digital, electronic) and images (new cognitive processes[4] and brain maps forming an extended body image, and new image schemas) are processed and stored in the brain. How will the retinal implant user describe "vision" and how will hybrid vision affect a user's consciousness and cognition? Exoskeleton is a term borrowed from zoology. As an HET, it changes our discourse about the "human" by shifting conceptual boundaries between the endoskeletal human animal and exoskeletal animals like the ancient tortoise, crabs, armadillos, snails, and cockroaches. HULC, an acronym for Human Universal Load Carrier, increases human strength and stamina to super-human levels—a reference to the Marvel comic book character/superhero. How will HULC-user's discourse about super-human strength influence further HET and human enhancement rhetoric?

In the coming decades, HET could lead to further improved, beyond-human functionality and performance. A person born in 2020, as an adult in 2050, could control new kinds of technology enabling new kinds of communication. Because of generational differences and the rapid speed of technological change, it is important to question how these rapid advancements will influence communication and discourse within, between, and across generations and cultures.

Though we're already aware of technology-based generational differences in communication between so-called "digital natives" and "baby boomers"—a cohort also seen as "digital immigrants"—these culturally-acknowledged terms are misleading, if not entirely inaccurate (Prensky, 2001). Though communication technology is now ubiquitous and digital, humans are born organic, analogue. But as concepts and boundaries change through further technological innovation and HET, "born digital" could become an accurate term for hybrid humans who produce offspring with nascent digital enhancements.

This example helps illustrate the difference between invented versus situated ethos. When human enhancement rhetoric is grounded in fact (the newborn is actually equipped with digital enhancements), it shows how an HET-user—in this case, a baby—can have a situated ethos derived from a true digitally-native, hybrid embodiment. Yet, this raises the ethical question of how can "good reputation" be established at birth, without "human" verbal communication? Genetically-engineered offspring, augmented by digital enhancements at birth, may "communicate" their first message digitally.

As population growth and planet "sustainability" problems are analyzed and addressed using technology, boundary concerns become global issues. Simultaneously our species is working to *sustain* life-supporting ecosystems for vast populations on Earth and life in organic, human, physical form. Meanwhile, our species is working on alternative life-support systems heavily influenced by the application of HET.

From an ethical perspective, what is the difference between a non-HET-user who applies rhetorical techniques to promote life and "self-enhancement" through technology, versus an HET-user who applies rhetorical techniques to promote life and "self-enhancement" through technology (i.e., further technological enhancements, upgrades)? These are different ethical positions based on both invented and situated ethos. The HET-user can upgrade or change capabilities ("inventing" an ethos) using technology of the moment. Here is an example of two different positions: a non-HET-using surgeon or manufacturer may *promote* the *general health or life benefits* of a particular HET to a patient (or colleague), motivated by profit or research trials and limited by clinical time constraints (while applying medical rhetoric); an HET-using patient may *explain* the *specific health and life benefits and challenges* of using a particular HET by providing a personal, experiential narrative (to other HET users or non-users), motivated by self-transformative results and community.

For HET-users, an ethical position can be constructed through rapidly-reconfigurable technology, influencing discourse and community. Ethical positions vary from author to author. Charles T. Rubin (2006) criticized arguments presented by four book authors who write about human enhancement: Ramez Naam, James Hughes, Joel Garreau, and Michael Chorost. Chorost is the only author to write about his own self-transformation and new identity as a cyborg. Rubin suggested that these arguments employ a "rhetoric of extinction" of the human species, by promoting (through the use of HET) a move away from our organic humanity. He noted that post-human arguments might be "[s]elling human extinction," but at least in some cases contain "deep flaws." In his conclusion he writes:

Even in a world where we can all be tyrants in our own little virtual realities, will there not be those who prefer to dominate real bodies — and gain some advantage thereby? Whether the power of enhancement is distributed by a progressive government, or held by a small handful of "Controllers," or left entirely to the libertarian marketplace, what else but power will govern human relationships in this world of post-human demigods (Rubin, 2006)?

What will human enhancement rhetoric include (or exclude), what "advantages" will it offer, what audiences will it persuade, and what criticism will it receive in the future? A non-HET-user futurist would develop an answer to this question based on their existing bodily praxis and knowledge. An HET-user would be able to construct an answer based on their existing *hybrid bodily praxis and knowledge.*

HET complicate bodily praxis, thus behavior. They require new techniques that result in new skills and knowledge. HET users reveal these new skills and knowledge in speech and writing, producing a shift in the understanding and life-changing benefits of human enhancement technologies.

How might the use of human enhancement technologies and the rhetoric developed to promote these technologies change human global culture? Marshaling both online and offline resources, human global culture has applied language, mathematics and computer programming, and technology towards innovation. Through mass online collaboration across geographical boundaries, new opportunities have been created. One project of human exploration—the proposed human colonization of Mars—is an example of mass collaboration and the application of human enhancement technologies towards a new stage in human evolution: two different human species, two different ecosystems, two very different cultures.

The question that arises when proposing a human colony on Mars, where humans are equipped with critical life-support systems[5] in order to sustain life and consciousness in a hostile, alien environment, is "How will this exploration change humanity?" If HET are one path for human evolution in which technological dependency encourages technological determinism—or the idea that technology determines culture—then on this path will humans, through new cultural values, find new spirituality? Will HET-equipped human-cyborgs create enhanced humanity through the union of biology, technology, and a new environment (that will require decades, centuries, or millennia of terraforming to support natural lifeforms) with new proximity to alien worlds, through extraterrestrial communication and community; or will they lose the most essential of all human characteristics, the human spirit? This question continues to be asked in different ways within the transhumanist community, but the answers—as transmitted from a transhuman colonial outpost on Mars in some

imagined future—will reveal a new HET rhetoric, broadcast to the largest audience possible—the literate, mediated population of Earth. If this event can be seen many years in advance as a new epoch in human evolution, what human characteristics and capabilities should we preserve and protect now? How can these human characteristics and capabilities be preserved through discourse? Mapping human enhancement rhetoric helps us gain an ethical meta-level view to answer this question.

CONCLUSION

What current technologies enhance human performance? How do we define human enhancement today? How will we define human enhancement tomorrow? Who will undergo testing and provide detailed explanations of the benefits and risks of these enhancements?

What terms and rhetorical devices are used and will be used to design, program, test, explain, and alter human enhancements and technologies? What ethical concerns are raised by asking these and other questions about the discursive relationship between fictional and theoretical HET, the political and financial supporters of HET, the designers and inventors of prototypical HET, the users of functional HET, the witnesses of HET users, the media reporting on HET, and the rhetoric of human enhancement?

Human enhancement technologies are funded, conceptualized, produced, tested, distributed, implanted, regulated, used, modified, and upgraded by individuals and communities who engage in various types of discourse. This chapter has explored the challenges of mapping these discourses to raise ethical concerns surrounding the human enhancement rhetoric of HET users and communities. Researchers with a better understanding of the relationship between HET rhetoric and ethics can make more informed decisions for the common good.

A map showing this relationship between HE rhetoric and ethics could highlight emerging HET-user self-descriptive narratives, identifying their action verbs, metaphors, adjectives, and numerical or coded info as evidence of ethos construction through hybrid bodily praxis. This mapping will help identify new sensory and cognitive phenomena, and the circumference of human enhancement rhetoric including both HET-users and non-users. Mapping human enhancement rhetoric in this way will provide a means of defining it greater detail.

In order to understand the discourse cycles and semiotic ecosystem within the circumference of human enhancement rhetoric, a chronological mapping that identifies discourse communities and their terms could reveal additional ethical concerns. Identifying changes in the ethical position of HET authors/speakers requires another chronological mapping.

As neuroethics expands to include the ethical dimension of HET-user communication products (materialization of discourse at the neuro-level of hybrid bodily praxis), including programming and digital code that influences cognition and action, human enhancement rhetoric can be further understood through the lens of neurorhetoric. Mapping the neurorhetorical dimension of HET has already begun through the use of brain scans and the Brain Initiative. As brain maps change through the use of HET, human enhancement rhetoric will change due to shifting concepts and boundaries.

HET are physical examples of human hybridity and boundary exploration originating with the cyborg concept, developed for space exploration. As astronauts gave mankind a different concept of humanity and human spirituality—transmitting their voices and their views of Earth from the surface of the Moon—Martian colonists could give mankind two new views of humanity through vocal and digital transmissions from Mars: one new view of humans as explorers and new colonists of Mars who depend upon HET to survive, and one new view of humans as Earthlings who

are (let us hope) free to roam the habitable blue planet Earth *without* enhancement technologies.

Mankind's exploration of physical and planetary boundaries lead to new spiritual understandings of what it means to be "human." How will the use of HET influence our spiritual beliefs and practices? Will we talk about ourselves as humans and spiritual beings differently because of new technology-driven beliefs? What role will HET have in altering our spiritual practices, beliefs, and discourse—on Earth, in space, on Mars, and beyond?

Ray Kurzweil promotes HET and the concept of "spiritual machines," noting on Singularity University's website that the institution aims "to apply exponential technologies to address humanity's grand challenges" (Kurtzweil, 2014). *Cyborg Foundation* helps people become cyborgs (Harbisson, 2014). The Mormon Transhumanist Association has launched a movement called *Transfigurism* (Cannon, 2014). In 2012, the University of Cambridge launched the Centre for the Study of Existential Risk as a consortium "focused on the study of human extinction-level risks that may emerge from technological advances" (Center for the Study of Existential Risk). This very recent development signals a new level of global concern about machine (AI) intelligence and other potential threats to humanity. The National Science Foundation's Report on The Ethics of Human Enhancement introduces the term "The Human Enhancement Revolution" (Allhoff et al., 2009). Our application of language as human enhancement rhetoric in quotidian and extraordinary contexts has launched this so-called revolution.

Noam Chomsky refers to language as a "basic property" of the individual (2013). If an individual's language were to become a property of a company like Facebook or Google, as digital data, how would this change our conception of language as individual property? If an individual were to produce language for communication only through the aid of embodied technology, so that this basic property became digital and, therefore, reproducible and programmable, how would this change our conception of rhetoric?

When language enters and programs the human body through enhancement technology to increase performance, what determines the ethical boundaries of transhuman language? If language can be encrypted for a specific body, using HET to change the body, at what point does transhuman language create ethical dilemmas?

Digital rhetoric can be expanded to include communication products of the transhuman body—rhetoric of the transhuman body, human enhancement rhetoric—as a hybrid of digital and cognitive linguistic constructions. How will HET further blur boundaries between personal/private communication (even technology-driven, life-supporting or "enhancing" communication) and public? How will personal embodied communication and data be protected as "basic property" of the individual?

What has been happening in human enhancement rhetoric—a rhetoric of hybrid embodiment and future superhuman-ness—is a re-mapping of human potential involving the creation, appropriation, and application of boundary-expanding terms. What has been missing in the study of HET and human enhancement rhetoric is a mapping of the transformational process of remapping human potential through the identification of boundary-expanding terms and rhetorical techniques, such as conversion narratives[6]. These experiential life narratives are revealing testimonials of the earliest stages in so-called human enhancement, based on real user-transformation and hybrid embodiment.

Each of us has a sacred mortal body, a distinctly organic human existence that is reflected in the mirrors of our self-descriptive rhetoric of the body. Transformation of human form and capacities—up until the dawn of the enlightenment and accelerated through global changes produced during a modern technological age—was primarily understood through religion and mythology, and mostly oral stories about the past. Future scenarios about transformation explored concepts of the afterlife. Now, however, transformation of human form and capacities is being understood through human enhancement technology, and stories that hypothesize and propose specific kinds of future scenarios. This shift in stories of transformation that are driven by embodied technological advancement is important. Mapping human enhancement rhetoric helps us understand these shifts as ethical, global concerns.

Human enhancement rhetoric will be challenged by transhuman enhancement rhetoric. Transhumans, humans who have transformed through HET gaining enhanced capabilities beyond the human, will develop discourse grounded in the reality and benefits of actual enhancements. Researchers are encouraged to map human enhancement rhetoric now to track the movement of rapidly shifting ethical positions.

REFERENCES

Academy of Medical Sciences. (2012, November). *Human enhancement and the future of work.* Royal Academy of Engineering and the Royal Society. Retrieved from http://www.britac.ac.uk/policy/Human-enhancement.cfm

Allhoff, F., Lin, P., Moor, J., & Weckert, J. (2009). *Ethics of human enhancement: 25 questions & answers.* U.S. National Science Foundation Report 2009.

Anderson, D. (2007). *Identity's strategy: Rhetorical selves in conversion.* Columbia, SC: University of South Carolina Press.

Battista, C. M. (2009). History, the Human, and the World Between. *Modern Fiction Studies, 55*(2), 391–394. doi:10.1353/mfs.0.1610

Bitzer, L. (1968). The Rhetorical Situation. *Philosophy & Rhetoric, 1*(1), 3.

Blommaert, J. (2005). *Discourse: A critical introduction*. Cambridge, UK: Cambridge University Press. doi:10.1017/CBO9780511610295

Burke, K. (1969). *A grammar of motives*. Berkeley, CA: University of California Press.

Cannon, L. (2014). *What is Transfigurism?* Mormon Transhumanist Association. Retrieved January 14, 2014 from http://transfigurism.org/

Centre for the Study of Existential Risk, University of Cambridge. (n.d.). Retrieved January 14, 2014 from http://cser.org/

Chomsky, N. (2013). *The Origins of Modern Science and Linguistics*. Geneva International Congress of Linguists. Retrieved January 15, 2014 from http://www.youtube.com/user/TheChomskyVideos

Claes, S., Vereecke, E., Maes, M., Victor, J., Verdonk, P., & Bellemans, J. (2013). Anatomy of the anterolateral ligament of the knee. *Journal of Anatomy*, *223*(4), 321–328. doi:10.1111/joa.12087 PMID:23906341

Cornwell, W., & Ricci, G. (Eds.). (2011). Human nature unbound: Why becoming cyborgs and taking drugs could make us more human. Values & Technology: Religion & Public Life 37, 65-92.

Crowley, S., & Hawhee, D. (2012). *Ancient rhetorics for contemporary students* (5th ed.). New York: Pearson/Longman.

Elliot, C. (2003). *Better than well: American medicine meets the American dream*. New York: W.W. Norton & Company.

European Parliament. (2013). *Science and Technology Options Assessment Annual Report 2012*. Brussels, Belgium: European Parliament.

Glenberg, A. M., & Kaschak, M. P. (2002). Grounding language in action. *Psychonomic Bulletin & Review*, *9*(3), 558–565. doi:10.3758/BF03196313 PMID:12412897

Harbisson, N. (2014). *Cyborg Foundation*. Retrieved January 14, 2014 from http://cyborg-foundation.com/

Harris, J. (2007). *Enhancing evolution: The ethical case for making better people*. Princeton, NJ: Princeton University Press.

Holm, S., & McNamee, M. (2011). Physical enhancement: What baseline, whose judgment? In J. Savulescu, R. ter Meulen, & G. Kahane (Eds.), *Enhancing human capacities*. West Sussex, UK: Wiley Blackwell.

Kurzweil, R. (1999). *The age of spiritual machines: When computers exceed human intelligence*. New York, NY: The Penguin Group.

Kurzweil, R. (2014). Singularity University home page. *Singularity Education Group*. Retrieved January 14, 2014 from http://singularityu.org/

Lakoff, G., & Johnson, M. (1980). *Metaphors we live by*. Chicago, IL: University of Chicago Press.

Lilley, S. (2013). *Transhumanism and society: The social debate over human enhancement (SpringerBriefs in Philosophy)*. Springer. doi:10.1007/978-94-007-4981-8

Lock, M., & Scheper-Hughes, N. (1996). A critical-interpretive approach in medical anthropology: Rituals and routines of discipline and dissent. In C. F. Sargent, & T. M. Johnson (Eds.), *Handbook of medical anthropology: Contemporary theory and method* (pp. 41–70). Westport, CT: Greenwood Press.

Low, S. M. (1994). Embodied metaphors: Nerves as lived experience. In T. J. Csordas (Ed.), *Embodiment and experience: The existential ground of culture and self* (pp. 139–162). New York: Cambridge University Press.

Mann, S., & Niedzviecki, H. (2002). *Cyborg: Digital destiny and human possibilities in the age of the wearable computer*. Toronto, Canada: Doubleday Canada.

Pappone, J. (2000, June 8). Resistance is futile: Becoming cyborgs inevitable, conference ponders advances in technology that blur lines between humans and machines. *The Ottawa Citizen*.

Peters, T. (2011). Transhumanism and the posthuman future: Will technological progress get us there? In G. Hansell, & W. Grassie (Eds.), *Transhumanism and its critics*. Philadelphia, PA: Metanexus Institute.

Prensky, M. (2001). Digital natives, digital immigrants. *Horizon*, *9*(5), 1–6. doi:10.1108/10748120110424816

Radhakrishnan, R. (2008). *History, the human, and the world between*. Duke University Press. doi:10.1215/9780822389309

Rohrer, T. (2006). The body in space: Embodiment, experientialism and linguistic conceptualization. In J. Zlatev, T. Ziemke, F. Roz, & R. Dirven (Eds.), *Body, language and mind* (Vol. 2). Berlin: Mouton de Gruyter.

Rose, N., & Gallagher, P. (2012). *Human enhancement and the future of work*. The Royal Academy of Engineering, The Royal Society.

Rubin, C. T. (2006, Winter). The rhetoric of extinction. *New Atlantis (Washington, D.C.)*, 64–73.

Scollon, R., & Scollon, S. W. (2004). *Nexus analysis: Discourse and the emerging internet*. New York: Routledge.

Thayer, K. A. (2012). *Cyborg metapathography in Michael Chorost's Rebuilt: Introducing the cyborg patient as transhumanist rhetor*. (Unpublished doctoral dissertation). Rensselaer Polytechnic Institute, Troy, NY.

Thayer, K. A. (2013). Beyond cyborg metapathography in Michael Chrost's *Rebuilt* to *World Wide Mind*: Introducing morphos as a rhetorical concept in cyborgography. *Teknokultura, 10*(2).

Vatz, R. E. (2009). The mythical status of situational rhetoric: Implications for rhetorical critics' relevance in the public arena. *The Review of Communication*, *1*(9), 1–5. doi:10.1080/15358590802020798

Zwaan, R. A., & Kaschak, M. P. (2009). Language in the brain, body, and world. In P. Robbins, & M. Aydede (Eds.), *The Cambridge handbook of situated cognition*. Cambridge, UK: Cambridge University Press. doi:10.1017/CBO9780511816826.019

KEY TERMS AND DEFINITIONS

Bodily Praxis: The bodily skills and abilities used to perform daily rhetorical actions; how we communicate using our bodies and tools in rhetorical situations. Related to body praxis, but emphasizing action and change that complicates and/or creates new rhetorical situations, such as the daily use of embodied computing power in neuroprosthetics. Nanotechnology, for example, if applied as microscale computing power flowing through the nervous system, could create a new, complicated transhuman bodily praxis.

Circumference: Refers to a set of key terms defining an argument. For Burke, these terms could *"clearly reveal the strategic spots at which ambiguities necessarily arise"* (1969, xviii). Circumferences, as sets of key terms, define rhetorical areas of address, influence, and scale; they can expand and overlap as ethical dimensions.

Cyborg: Originally, for space exploration, a self-regulating homeostatic system and cybernetic organism that intentionally fused exogenous machine components with the organic for the purpose of exploring and adapting to alternate environments. With human cyborgs living among us, and with expanding hybrid intelligent systems, a human cyborg is not only an explorer of self-knowledge and self-embodiment; a 21st century human cyborg explores computer-meditated flesh and cognition for self and others as the result of synthetic changes to the human central nervous system. A cyborg is a transhuman with capabilities beyond the human.

Discourse of Enhancement: Texts, conversations, and communications that employ the concept of human enhancement to present ideas and arguments.

Ethical Position: As a rhetorical act of ethos construction, a specific argumentative and ethical location established or re-established through capabilities, qualifications, affiliations, and communities, complicated by embodied and coded HET.

Human Enhancement Rhetoric: Broadly, the persuasive discourse(s) created and used by human speakers and writers supporting the activities of HET and HET communities.

Hybrid Bodily Praxis: A bodily praxis complicated by hybrid embodiment; that is, the intersection of biological and synthetic practices and processes, as is found in cybernetic organisms and HET users who depend upon their implant/prosthesis. HET users can and often plan to change their bodily praxis through upgrades, which leads to changes in self-reflexive, self-descriptive (and group-descriptive) language and narratives.

Mapping: A technique of understanding in more detail the spatial, qualitative (and for this application) places of ethical concern within a complex new or changing site, grouping, or phenomenon. Specifically, for this application, a way of providing benchmarks to further understand the changing dimensions (and circumferences) of semiotic ecosystems.

Rhetoric: Originally, the art of an orator; classically, an act of finding and using the available means of persuasion in oral or written communication based on the application of logos, pathos or ethos, or the study of this art. To update these definitions for the 21st century, I extend rhetoric to include the effective negotiation of perceived and actual human boundaries.

Transhuman Enhancement Rhetoric: Broadly, the persuasive discourse(s) created and used by transhuman speakers and writers supporting the activities of THET (transhuman enhancement technologies) and THET communities. Transhuman enhancements apply transhuman knowledge and experience to further extend previously enhanced human capabilities.

ENDNOTES

[1] See Bitzer and Vatz.

[2] Ted Peters writes: "[T]ranshumanist assumptions regarding progress are naïve because they fail to operate with an anthropology that is realistic regarding the human proclivity to turn good into evil…researchers in the relevant fields of genetics and nanotechnology should proceed toward developing new and enhancing technologies, to be sure, but they should maintain constant watchfulness for ways in which these technologies can become perverted and bent toward destructive purposes" (2011, p. 148).

[3] Due to space limitations here, I cannot apply the concepts of deontological and consequentialist ethics. Human enhancement

rhetoric raises questions for consequentialist ethics, and about confusion surrounding the concept of virtue, complicated further for HET users.

4   Cognitive metaphor theory shows that language is a constant reflection of our embodiment. Transformed embodiment manifests new metaphors to communicate a different perceptual, physical, or other human (and now, transhuman) capacity. See Lakoff and Johnson, Glenberg and Kaschak, Zwaan and Kaschak.

5   Lilley's points about risk are useful when considering Martian colonization as a discursive ecosystem of the future: "STS scholars emphasize that risk is socially defined and that such work is accomplished through language, power, organization, and culture. Often it is reconstructed *following* a devastating system failure." (2013, p. 42) Systemic failure can include communication failure that is coded and embodied and life-supporting.

6   See Anderson.

Chapter 4
Human Enhancement:
Living Up to the Ideal Human

Johann A. R. Roduit
University of Zurich, Switzerland & University of Oxford, UK & NeoHumanitas, Switzerland

Vincent Menuz
University of Montreal, Canada & NeoHumanitas, Switzerland

Holger Baumann
University of Zurich, Switzerland

ABSTRACT

Two major problems persist in the debate regarding the ethics of human enhancement. First, there is a lack of discussion and agreement on a definition of human enhancement. Second, the commonly used bioethical principles of justice, safety, and autonomy are jointly insufficient to assess the morality of human enhancement. This chapter attempts to define these problems and to propose a possible solution. Defending a qualitative definition of human enhancement, the authors suggest examining "perfectionist notions" of what it means to live a good human life in order to give additional normative tools to assess the morality of human enhancements. This chapter will help to clarify the debate and move it along by arguing that characteristics of the ideal human life, once defined and seen as the goal of human enhancement, can help assess the morality of a given human enhancement.

INTRODUCTION

In the past few years, one of the most debated topics in bioethics has been the ethical issues related to human enhancement. While many articles have been written on this topic, two major problems still persist. First, there is still no real consensus on the meaning of 'human enhancement.' This makes discussions related to ethical issues re-

lated to human enhancement difficult. Second, commonly used bioethical principles of *justice*, *autonomy* and *safety* are jointly insufficient, or so we will argue, to assess ethical issues related to human enhancement. This chapter aims to give answers to both problems. First, we outline and analyse different attempts to define 'human enhancement.' Then, we suggest that the bioethical standards of *safety*, *justice* and *autonomy* are

DOI: 10.4018/978-1-4666-6010-6.ch004

jointly insufficient to normatively frame ethical issues related to human enhancement. Finally, we suggest a novel way to assess ethical aspects of human enhancement with a qualitative definition of human enhancement and perfectionist notions of living a good human life.

THE CONUNDRUM OF DEFINING HUMAN ENHANCEMENT

Human enhancement is tacitly defined of technologically modifying human bodies and/or minds by combining medical science with emerging technologies (such as nano- or biotechnologies) to affect individuals' cognitive (e.g. memory, intelligence), emotional (e.g., happiness, self-confidence) or physical (e.g., need for sleep, endurance) function. This kind of consensual agreement on what could be considered as a human enhancement does not constitute a definition of the concept. Interestingly, when examining the literature addressing ethical issues related to human enhancement, very few authors have explicitly defined the concept of human enhancement (see e.g., Buchanan, 2011; Menuz, Hurlimann, & Godard, 2013; Savulescu, 2006); most of the time, authors merely give an implicit definition of the concept that appears in their argumentations. However, it is possible to separate these implicit or explicit ways of defining human enhancement into different categories (see e.g., Chadwick, 2008; Menuz et al., 2011).

In this section, we will therefore discuss three approaches that have been used to understand human enhancement: i) the beyond therapy approach, ii) the quantitative approach and iii) the qualitative approach. We will argue that while the qualitative approach is the most plausible definition of human enhancement, they all have some serious shortcoming, which we will resolve in the last part of this chapter, using a recent defintion suggested by Menuz et. al.

Beyond: The 'Beyond Therapy' Approach

Some commentators have defined human enhancements as medical interventions that do not attempt to cure. Such a view can be defined as 'beyond therapy' or 'outside the scope of therapy' (President's Council on Bioethics, 2003). According to this view, technological interventions do not aim to heal, but to go 'beyond health' (e.g., vaccines) or outside the realm of therapeutic intervention (e.g., cosmetic surgery). One influential interpretation of this view asserts that healing consists of maintaining – or going back to – a normal range of human functioning and that enhancements are interventions that surpasses such normal range of functioning.

This way of defining human enhancement has been controversial due to the difficulties related to its application, mainly because it is almost impossible to determine what is considered to be 'normal functioning'. Similarly, doubts have been raised about the ability to objectively define health and disease (Buchanan et al., 2001). Recent discussions have pointed out that the distinction between therapy and enhancement cannot be clear-cut (Daniels, 2000; Harris, 2007; Menuz et al., 2011). Moreover, such a way of defining human enhancement suggests in itself an entirely negative approach of the concept of human enhancement: the 'beyond therapy' way of defining human enhancement implicitly considers that there is a 'good' (i.e., therapy) *versus* a transgressive (i.e., human enhancement) way of practicing medicine. In other words, human enhancements are considered as ethically suspicious results of technological interventions, while the same interventions used for treatment of disease are considered as ethically accepted. Such a way of defining human enhancement is often built on value judgements that negatively charge the concept itself. In addition, defining human enhancement as the results of biotechnological interventions going beyond therapy might lead to counter-intuitive situations. For instance, it might qualify suicide as a human enhancement: while the use of non-therapeutic drugs in order to reduce sleep might be considered as a human enhancement according to the 'beyond therapy' way of defining the concept, they should also consider as a human enhancement the non-therapeutic use of such drugs to commit suicide.

There is an essentially contested distinction between therapy and human enhancement, making it difficult to use it as a way to define what is – or not – a human enhancement.

More: The 'Quantitative' Approach

Some authors have defined human enhancement as an add-on to existing human characteristics (Chadwick, 2008, 2011). Such a way to define human enhancement relates to a quantitative approach in which any technological intervention that increases specific characteristics – such as cognitive capacities or bodily abilities – can be regarded as a human enhancement. While the 'beyond therapy' approach has been largely used in the literature addressing ethical issues related to human enhancement, the add-on way of defining human enhancement has not been used frequently. One might consider two major reasons to explain this. First, for many, to enhance means to improve in quality, not only necessarily in quantity. Many commentators consider the qualitative dimension of human enhancement crucial (e.g., Buchanan, 2011a; Buchanan, 2011b; Harris, 2007; Heilinger, 2010). Second, it is also incorrect to assume that a given human enhancement necessarily requires an addition. For instance, there are many surgical examples in which removal rather than addition underlies enhancement, as illustrated by nose or breast reduction for cosmetic purposes (see e.g., Earp, et al., 2014). The add-on definition of human enhancement does not formulate, therefore, the necessary condition to define human enhancements.

Better: The 'Qualitative' Approach

Some have argued that human enhancements are technological interventions that have the potential to improve the life of the modified. Such a qualitative way of defining human enhancement has recently become one of the predominant view in the debate (e.g, Buchanan, 2011a; Buchanan, 2011b; Heilinger, 2010). Such improvement of life can be put into perspective by contrasting it with the aforementioned ways of defining human enhancement. On the one hand, it contrasts with the 'beyond therapy' approach, by giving a positive characterization of human enhancements. On the other hand, it diverges from the 'quantitative approach' as it refers to a qualitative idea of improvement rather than relying purely on the quantitative idea of an addition. While we agree that such a definition is a better way to define human enhancement, this still raises questions regarding who decides whether a given technological intervention has the potential to improve life and whether the result of a given intervention can – or cannot – be considered as a human enhancement. These questions will be partially answered in the last part of this chapter.

LIMITATIONS OF ETHICAL TOOLS USED TO EVALUATE HUMAN ENHANCEMENT

In addition to the difficulty of defining human enhancement, the many attempts to ethically evaluate human enhancements remain a conundrum. So far, such ethical evaluations have mainly been based on bioethical principles. Notions of safety (Annas, Andrews, & Isasi, 2002; Fukuyama, 2003; McKibben, 2004; Mehlman, 2009), justice (Buchanan et al., 2001; Caplan, 2009; Habermas, 2003) and autonomy (Agar, 2004; Buchanan et al., 2001) have been central to the debate. However, while a given human enhancement could meet requirements of one of the principles, it does not necessarily follow that it is ethically acceptable. For example, Aldous Huxley's *Brave New World* shows that even though the happy-pill 'Soma' met the requirements of safety, justice and autonomy, something disquieting about the entire practice remains (Bonte, 2013). Actually, the established bioethical principles appear not to grasp all the ethical complexity that human enhancement may raise, such as, for example, threats to human nature (dehumanizing), the desire for human beings to play God (hubris) as well as the alteration of dignity and authenticity (alienation).

In this section, we will outline and criticize the three bioethical commonly-used principles and argue that, while they may all be necessary, they are jointly insufficient to evaluate the morality of human enhancement. We will therefore consider other philosophical argument and then suggest our own in the last part of this chapter. We believe that such inadequacy is partly due to the absence of a precise definition of what could constitute a human enhancement. This is the reason the last part of our analysis will be based upon a particular definition of human enhancement.

Safety

The principle of safety suggests that we should restrain from a given human enhancement that is considered as not safe. While appealing at first, such argument of safety is not straightforward as it initially appears.

There are indeed situations in which an individual's quality of life might be so poor that the risk to undergo a given technological modification that has the potential to improve her condition makes it acceptable and even laudable. In other words, subjectivity and objectivity are in tension when one has to evaluate the safety of a given human enhancement: the criteria to consider this human enhancement as safe or unsafe are mainly based on individuals' perception of the risk *vs.* benefit. Importantly, when an individual assesses whether something will be beneficial for her, she needs to

be aware that there might be unpredictable side effects such as addiction to technological modifications or obligations to be constantly further modified (e.g., fixing a bug or even updating a given technological modification).

Regarding human enhancements, one should keep in mind that unintended consequences might be inevitable (Fukuyama, 2003; McKibben, 2004). For instance, one cannot exclude conflicting situations between those who have been enhanced and those who have chosen – or have been forced, for personal or economic reasons for instance – not to be modified. Others worry that enhancing humans may lead to a new kind of eugenics, where parents might be forced to enter into a competition for the best possible child (Sparrow, 2011). By trying to technologically improve humankind, we might end up discriminating against certain traits or populations who do not display an expected trait. There is a risk of diminishing the diversity of individuals: some traits might be considered as objectively desirable – or not – and passive or active coercion might normalize populations to adhere to social norms. In this regard, some philosophers consider that the relations between technologically enhanced and unenhanced individuals might be problematic: they foresee an increase in individual responsibility coupled with an erosion of solidarity between enhanced and unenhanced individuals (Sandel, 2007).

The principle of safety raises interesting conflicts regarding ethical issues related to human enhancement. Used alone, this principle has too many flaws to efficiently evaluate ethical issues related to human enhancement. However, it gives a glimpse of the many difficulties arising when trying to ethically evaluate human enhancements.

Justice

Technological interventions aiming at enhancing human beings could potentially reduce the gap between those who have and those who have not. Some have therefore suggested that it could make societies more equitable (Buchanan et al., 2001). We may indeed wonder whether there are reasons to accept natural injustices and reject the use of technological interventions in order to compensate for these inherent discrepancies. However, such technological interventions might actually widen the gap between those who have and those who have not (McKibben, 2004), bringing unfair advantages to technologically enhanced individuals (Mitchell, 2009). Some have even suggested that such enhancing interventions might be seen as cheating (Schermer, 2008): should we consider that taking a cognition enhancing pill to take an exam is unfair?

It seems that ethical issues related to human enhancement are not rooted in the technologies themselves, but in their distribution. Philosophers, such as John Harris, wonder whether it will be coherent to consider a given human enhancement as unethical on the basis that such enhancement will not be affordable for the vast majority of citizen of a given society (Harris, 2007). For Harris, the argument is weak: most of the time, new technologies are first used by a minority of individuals. Then, if the technology is beneficial, the prices usually go down as the mass-produced technology becomes more accessible (Harris, 2007). Some have considered Harris' point as naïve: though technologies tend to indeed become cheaper when mass-produced, the accessibility to these technologies among members of a given society does not change significantly. In this sense, some considers that technological interventions leading to human enhancement will not overcome or solve inequalities (Zylinska, 2010) and that they might only result to worsen the social gaps that already exist between individuals in many societies.

Regarding justice, we may wonder whether human enhancements themselves actually raise ethical issues, or whether such issues are embedded in the economic structure of our societies, and not necessarily in human enhancement itself: the issues raised here are of distributive justice, not of human enhancement per se.

Autonomy

According to some, autonomy is a facet of life that could be added to or detracted from by human enhancements. On the one hand, some human enhancements might lead to an increase individuals' *functional* autonomy by giving them a greater degree of independence to move more freely (Buchanan et al., 2001). For instance, a given human enhancement could help some people to be more independent in their work or daily routine. Some human enhancements could therefore be ethically justifiable as a way to increase people's autonomy. On the other hand, *decisional* autonomy of individuals may also be threatened by the social pressure to conform that comes from widespread use of technological modifications (President's Council on Bioethics, 2003; Menuz, forthcoming). Are human enhancements chosen freely or imposed by other societal standards? The issue of a possible threat to autonomy is even more important when decisions of enhancing children or embryos are in question. Should parents, for example, be allowed to try to technologically modify their children because of their procreative autonomy (Harris, 2007)?

Human enhancement could also have a negative impact because it threatens the preconditions for autonomy, which can be find in the authentic self or personal identity (DeGrazia, 2005). However, for some, autonomy itself, understood as reasoning ability, could be enhanced with human enhancement (Schaefer, Kahane, & Savulescu, 2013). The principle of autonomy seems at first not enough, alone, to solve ethical issues raised by human enhancements. While whole principles are limited for giving normative ways from framing human enhancements, they are useful to consider in order to shed light on the complexity regarding the ethical evaluation of human enhancements.

Anthropological Arguments

Some have recently introduced to this debate other ethical arguments, based on the anthropological and philosophical notion of *human nature* (Heilinger, 2010). Some consider that tampering with our shared human nature might destroy the equal status of individuals or threaten the inherent worth of human beings, which is understood to be the basis of human rights (Fukuyama, 2003). In the same vein, others have considered that our lives might become dehumanized and meaningless if we alter inherently human traits like finitude and vulnerability (President's Council on Bioethics, 2003; Kass, 2003; Parens, 1995; Sandel, 2007). In contrast, some have argued that we possess human dignity, which encourages us to use technological intervention to enhance ourselves (Bonte, 2013).

Commentators have considered such arguments dubious and therefore unhelpful, because they often rest upon controversial metaphysical or theological assumptions and thereby commit a naturalist fallacy (Buchanan, 2011b) or fail to be appealing to a pluralistic audience. For instance, to avoid this natural fallacy, philosophers like Nick Bostrom would defend a posthuman dignity (Bostrom, 2005). However, even within a liberal framework, appeals to human nature can be shown to be an important aspect in debates about human enhancement (Heilinger, 2010; Schramme, 2002).

While these lines of argument are interesting and add to the human enhancement debate, they still miss the point that human enhancements might be used not to discover a true self (human authenticity) (see e.g., Erler, 2012; Levy, 2011) but to aim and create an ideal self, informed by different ideals individuals have regarding what constitutes a good (human) life. Some arguments of human authenticity and human dignity (Kass, 2004) also miss this point. When used, those notions fail to acknowledge that ideals can guide actions and not only restrict them. This is why some have introduced arguments based on perfectionist notions of what it means to live a good life (Roduit, Baumann, & Heilinger, 2013), hoping to give some clues that may enlighten the debate in other ways. We will focus therefore the rest of the discussion on those perfectionist assumptions and whether these assumptions can be helpful for this specific debate, by first suggesting a particular definition and then further the philosophical analysis.

LIVING UP TO THE IDEAL HUMAN: EVALUATING HUMAN ENHANCEMENT

Having now outlined two major problems in the discussions tackling ethical issues related to human enhancement – lack of a consensus regarding a definition of human enhancement and the limitation of its ethical evaluation – we will now suggest a new way of considering such issues. In this section, we will show that a perfectionist approach of what it means to leave a good human life might be used to frame ethical issues related to human enhancement.

We believe that to define human enhancement as a qualitative improvement can provide a solid foundation to build a framework to ethically assess human enhancements. Recently, a new angle to define human enhancement has been proposed. According to the authors, defining human enhancement cannot be considered without references to personal and subjective perceptions, which are themselves influenced by socio-cultural factors (i.e., political and social norms, rules, values, environmental factors, passive coercion, unconscious goals, and/or statistically defined attributes, considered within a given society in a given historical period of time). Such perceptions constitute the 'personal optimum state', a personal ideal of life. This definition proposes that "each individual has to determine for herself/himself, based on her/his personal optimum state, whether the outcome of a given technological intervention can be described as human enhancement or not" (Menuz et al., 2011).

Here, we continue therefore exploring the ethical justification to use human enhancement to reach a human optimum state. Indeed, to evaluate human enhancement, a reference point is needed. Since, a qualitative improvement is only interpreted as such in reference to something. As shown, such a reference point cannot be found only in the notion of safety, justice and autonomy. We suggest therefore here to look at what would the ideal human consist of. Or more precisely, since it is not possible in a pluralistic society to agree on such an ideal, to look at what are some characteristics an ideal human would have. This would then give a reference point to be used as a normative tool to morally assess whether an enhancing intervention is acceptable or not. The difference here is that this reference point does also not need to be normal human functioning or human authenticity, but human ideals, since as mentioned earlier human enhancement can be used to become not necessarily a true or an authentic human, but an ideal one.

Two views of looking at improvement that have not often been used in the debate deserve our attention. The first is a *backward-looking view*, where human enhancement can be evaluated according to a former reference state. For Harris, a human enhancement is "by definition an improvement on what went on before" (Harris, 2007, p. 9). Second is a *forward-looking view*, where human enhancement is evaluated according to an ideal reference state (or what has been called perfectionist notions of what it means to live a good life) (see e.g., Roduit et al., 2013; Walker, 2002). For example, if someone desires to use a 'height enhancer': according to a backward-looking view, the enhancement is evaluated if someone becomes taller from 160cm to 165cm In retrospect, the person has gained five centimetres and the intervention is therefore viewed as an enhancement. On the other hand, a forward-looking view would look at ideals that can be used as a reference point to evaluate whether an intervention has been successful or not. Here, if someone desires to become a basketball player, the height enhancement will be measured according to what is an ideal height to play basketball. As outlined elsewhere (Roduit et

al., 2013), the backward-looking view has some serious shortcomings because it refuses to take into consideration a forward-looking view as well. It neglects to take into consideration that some human enhancement might have a direction or goal in mind, as individuals enhance towards something, which can be seen as an ideal, such has the ideal basketball player. In short, the backward-looking view lacks an ideal and is thus short-sighted. A forward-looking view is therefore better as it does resolve these shortcomings (Roduit et al., *forthcoming*).

This second possibility of assessing human enhancement introduces perfectionist elements of what it means to live a good human life. Those perfectionist elements can be used to evaluate whether an intervention counts as an enhancement or not. In comparison with a strictly backward-looking approach, this view offers additional insights in the debate that should not be ignored. Different ideals of what it means to lead a good human life can be used to interpret whether an intervention ought to be considered enhancing or not. Additionally, because the concepts human dignity or authenticity vary according to different views of the good human life, it is helpful to look at this debate directly from this larger perspective.

These perfectionist perspectives or this forward-looking view can be used in two different ways. In the debate, Walker has identified two alternatives. He distinguishes between *type* and *property* perfection. Type-Perfection is "the thesis that those individuals who best realize the essential properties of the individual's type or species best exemplify the ideal of perfection" (Walker, 2002). Property-Perfection, is the "thesis that those individuals who best realize some property or properties best exemplify the ideal of perfection" (Walker, 2002).

Some problems appear with the property-perfectionist view, however. Property-perfection ultimately falls back into type-perfection, as a property is always related to a type and stands insufficient by itself. For instance, while some may desire to boost their intelligence, as they recognize intelligence as an objective good, the property of intelligence will always be embedded into a type; whether this type is human, sub- or post-human. While the property-perfectionist view has the advantage to look at different properties one can enhance, it neglects the bigger picture that those properties belong to a given or a chosen type. The type-perfectionist view is therefore the most appropriate.

Type-perfection can also be distinguished further between: objective type-perfection or subjective type-perfection. On the one hand, the type is given or agreed upon objectively (e.g. the type Human, Monkey or Chair). On the other hand, one could suggest that a type is defined subjectively. Here one will create something unique and will be able to self-create a particular unique type. However, the latter option is not plausible when one speaks of human enhancement, because it is the human –a particular objective type – that is being enhanced after all.

We are left therefore with the option of an objective type-perfection, where a certain type can give reference regarding what it means to lead a good human life. Indeed, this type is made of essential properties that would exemplify what is the ideal type, which in our case is the ideal human.

While for some this type of approach might seem paternalistic and problematic in a pluralistic society, these problems can be avoided. First, regarding pluralism, while it is true that we have difficulties on agreeing about virtues or objective goods, we can nonetheless have public discussions and find consensus regarding what are some essential properties that are necessary in order to leave a good human life and to be considered 'human'. Even in our liberal societies, we agree that some types of living are better than other.

Second, regarding paternalism, some would claim that autonomy alone would be a better way to assess the morality of human enhancement, as it would avoid any paternalistic tendencies. However, we already limit people's autonomy for other goods, such as education, for example.

Autonomy is sometimes limited for a time, so that one will become more autonomous or will have the essential properties to live an autonomous life. We also limit people's autonomy if it is a threat to others. We can therefore seek to agree in a public debate about some essential human features or capabilities that are necessary for human to live a good and flourishing life. In order to speak of an autonomous human being, we also need to have a human.

In this chapter, we will not outline what a particular ideal human or particular ideal humans would be like. But some plausible answer could be found in the work of Sen or Nussbaum, for example. As mentioned elsewhere, different ideals may have different content, but these ideals are used in the same ways: they are action-guiding and help one make a decision concerning which direction he or she wants to enhance (Roduit et al., 2013). Additionally, these ideals can either be given or agreed upon. For some, the type human is given by nature or god (essentialist approach), while for others it might be constructed (existentialist approach). However, whether it is one or the other does not matter for our purpose here, as in both cases the ideal have the same function: it is action-guiding and will be able to guide the enhancement project.

Therefore, ultimately, to move forward in the debate further discussions about what type of humans we want to become is necessary, in order for us to know towards which type of human we seek to enhance. In other words, to know what is or are the ideal human(s) will enable us to use enhancement in a morally acceptable way, as we will enhance towards this particular type. Looking at what are essential features to live up good human life, these features would give framework to guide human enhancement. As mentioned by Baertschi:

[N]either our desire for enhancement nor our concerns about personal identity can be properly understood without referring to an explicit or im-

plicit ideal: the ideal of the person we want to be. This ideal is an essential part of our conception of the good life, because a good life is a life we want to live, as the person we want to be. (Baertschi, 2009, our emphasis and translation)

Advantages of this Approach

This approach holds different advantages:

1. It differs from the notion of authenticity (who I truly am), putting more emphasis on the ideal person one strives to become (who I desire to become). Because human enhancement is more than just bringing forth who we truly are, it is also a mean to become the ideal self that one desires to become.

2. This perfectionist approach adds to a strict notion of autonomy some emphasis on the importance of taking into consideration what it means to lead a good human life; but refusing to use the concept of autonomy as the only possible ideal, as it has been the case with some bioliberals (Roduit et al., 2013; see e.g., Harris, 2007), indeed for some the ideal being they strive towards is an autonomous being/person. But this is not the case for everyone. Here, a wider range of ideals will be acceptable. Recognising however, that not all view of the good human life are acceptable, a public discussion become necessary to discover what type of human do we accept or not in our respective societies.

3. This approach also points out that some (societal) ideals influence the choices of individuals who wish to enhance in a certain way. One could say that an enhanced account of autonomy is defended, taking into consideration that participants in the debate have perfectionist assumptions regarding the good human life, which influences whether they view an intervention as an enhancement or not. This view encourages individuals to be self-reflecting not only regarding the ideals they are striving towards, but also some underlying societal ideals that are probably influencing the reasons why they are considering enhancement. It points to the more psychological questions: why does an individual wish to enhance or not in a particular a way?

4. It also acknowledges that human enhancement are not only an improvement from a former state but also an improvement leading somewhere, which can be defined as leading to the ideal self. Human enhancements are therefore a means to an end. Hence, problems are not to be found with the mean, but with the ends.

5. Finally, this view, while not seeing anything intrinsically morally wrong with human enhancement, still recognizes that the ideal influencing some human enhancement might be morally unacceptable (if this ideal involves hurting others) and some human enhancement might be unwise and plain irresponsible (moral prudence would be needed here). Here, individuals will be convinced whether an intervention is an enhancement for their lives by being witness of the advantages of such or such an intervention. This view seeks to avoid any type of coercion.

Therefore, this approach can add to the current debate and the other tools used in the debate to assess human enhancement. Needless to say that, while limited, bioethical standards such as justice, autonomy, safety and human dignity still have a role in this debate. Our approach adds another tool to evaluate human enhancement so that an ethical evaluation can be made in a more exhaustive way.

CONCLUSION

One of the major obstacles to framing the ethical issues surrounding human enhancement is the lack of a precise and shared definition of what constitute a human enhancement. Moreover, the many definitions that have been – either implicitly or explicitly – proposed do not take into consideration the complex contexts in which human enhancements may occur. Both elements partially explain why bioethical principles, such as autonomy, justice and safety, have failed, so far, to give satisfying answers in the debate for and against human enhancement, especially regarding issues such alienation, hubris or dehumanization.

Basing our work on a qualitative definition of human enhancement, we have developed a preliminary conceptual framework around the ideal human being, to frame ethical issues related to human enhancement. Basically, human enhancement is not only a subjective concept where individuals choose what an enhancement is for themselves, but also an objective one because it concerns the 'human.' Adding to other bioethical notions, we argued that the ethical evaluation of a given human enhancement needs also to take into consideration humans, who judge – according to an ideal toward which they choose (perfectionist assumptions) – whether a given human enhancement is morally acceptable or not. For this chapter, we have purposely omitted to outline what could be those human properties essential for an ideal human or for one to live a good human life, as this would need not only much more space and consideration, but also a public discussion about what does it mean to belong to the human-type.

Nonetheless, our suggested definition and our type-perfectionist view enable us to acknowledge the importance of the concept of the ideal human. Ultimately, the question is not whether we will enhance, but towards which view of the ideal human we will enhance. Human enhancements can be used to become these ideal humans. But which view of the ideal human do we wish to endorse will necessitate further research that will be essential to move the debate about the ethics of human enhancement forward, by placing again the notion of the 'human' in the discussion.

ACKNOWLEDGMENT

We are grateful to Cynthia Forlini, Tom Douglas, João Lourenço, Michael Buttrey and two anonymous reviewers for some helpful comments on an earlier draft. This research was supported by the Swiss National Science Foundation (SNSF) and the Käthe Zingg Schwichtenberg fonds (KZS) from the Swiss Academy of Medical Sciences (SAMS).

REFERENCES

Agar, N. (2004). *Liberal eugenics: In defence of human enhancement*. Malden, MA: Blackwell Publishing. doi:10.1002/9780470775004

Annas, G. J., Andrews, L. B., & Isasi, R. M. (2002). Protecting the endangered human: Toward an international treaty prohibiting cloning and inheritable alterations. *American Journal of Law & Medicine, 28*(2&3), 151–178. PMID:12197461

Baertschi, B. (2009). Devenir un être humain accompli: Idéal ou cauchemar? In J.-N. Missa, & L. Perba (Eds.), *Enhancement Éthique et Philosophie de La Médecine D'amélioration* (Vol. 1, pp. 79–95). Paris: Vrin.

Bonte, P. (2013). Athleticenhancement, human nature and ethics. In J. Tolleneer, S. Sterckx, & P. Bonte (Eds.), *Threats and Opportunities of Doping Technologies* (Vol. 52, pp. 59–86). Springer.

Bostrom, N. (2005). In defense of posthuman dignity. *Bioethics, 19*(3). doi:10.1111/j.1467-8519.2005.00437.x PMID:16167401

Buchanan, A. (2011a). *Better than human: The promise and perils of enhancing ourselves.* Oxford University Press.

Buchanan, A. (2011b). *Beyond humanity? The ethics of biomedical enhancement.* Oxford University Press. doi:10.1093/acprof:oso/9780199587810.001.0001

Buchanan, A., Brock, D. W., Daniels, N., & Wikler, D. (2001). *From chance to choice: Genetics and justice.* Cambridge University Press.

Caplan, A. (2009). Good, better, or best? In N. Bostrom, & J. Savulescu (Eds.), *Human enhancement* (pp. 199–210). Oxford University Press.

Chadwick, R. (2008). Therapy, enhancement and improvement. In B. Gordijn, & R. Chadwick (Eds.), *Medical enhancement and posthumanity* (pp. 25–37). Springer.

Chadwick, R. (2011). Enhancements: Improvements for whom? *Bioethics, 25*(4), ii. doi:10.1111/j.1467-8519.2011.01899.x PMID:21480931

Daniels, N. (2000). Normal functioning and the treatment-enhancement distinction. *Cambridge Quarterly of Healthcare Ethics, 9*(3), 309–322. doi:10.1017/S0963180100903037 PMID:10858880

DeGrazia, D. (2005). Enhancement technologies and human identity. *The Journal of Medicine and Philosophy, 30*(3), 261–283. doi:10.1080/03605310590960166 PMID:16036459

Earp, B. D., Sandberg, A., Kahane, G., & Savulescu, J. (2014). When is diminishment a form of enhancement? Rethinking the enhancement debate in biomedical ethics. *Frontiers in Systems Neuroscience, 8,* 12. doi:10.3389/fnsys.2014.00012 PMID:24550792

Erler, A. (2012). One man's authenticity is another man's betrayal: A reply to Levy. *Journal of Applied Philosophy,* (1). doi: doi:10.1111/j.1468-5930.2012.00562.x PMID:23576833

Fukuyama, F. (2003). *Our posthuman future: Consequences of the biotechnology revolution.* Picador.

Habermas, J. (2003). The future of human nature. *Polity.*

Harris, J. (2007). Enhancing evolution: The ethical case for making better people. *Journal of the American Medical Association.*

Heilinger, J.-C. (2010). *Anthropologie und ethik des enhancements. Humanprojekt/Interdisziplinare Anthropologie.* De Gruyter. doi:10.1515/9783110223705

Kass, L. (2003). Ageless bodies, happy souls: Biotechnology and the pursuit of perfection. *New Atlantis (Washington, D.C.),* 9–28. PMID:15584192

Kass, L. (2004). *Life, liberty & the defense of dignity: The challenge for bioethics.* Encounter Books.

Levy, N. (2011). Enhancing authenticity. *Journal of Applied Philosophy, 28*(3), 308–318. doi:10.1111/j.1468-5930.2011.00532.x

McKean, E. (2005). *The new Oxford American dictionary.* Oxford University Press, Inc.

McKibben, B. (2004). *Enough: Staying human in an engineered age.* St. Martin's Griffin.

Mehlman, M. J. (2009). *The price of perfection: Individualism and society in the era of biomedical enhancement.* The Johns Hopkins University Press.

Menuz, V. (forthcoming) Why do we wish to be enhanced ?, in Inquiring into human enhancement : beyond disciplinary and national boundaries. S. Bateman, J. Gayon, S. Allouche, J. Goffette and M. Marzano (Eds). Palgrave McMillan.

Menuz, V., Hurlimann, T., & Godard, B. (2011). Is human enhancement also a personal matter? *Science and Engineering Ethics*. doi: doi:10.1007/s11948-011-9294-y PMID:21786000

Mitchell, C. B. (2009). On human mioenhancements. *Ethics & Medicine: An International. Journal of Bioethics, 25*(3).

Parens, E. (1995). The goodness of fragility: On the prospect of genetic technologies aimed at the enhancement of human capacities. *Kennedy Institute of Ethics Journal, 5*(2), 141–153. doi:10.1353/ken.0.0149 PMID:10143182

President's Council on Bioethics. (2003). *Beyond therapy: Biotechnology and the pursuit of happiness*. Dana Press.

Roduit, J. A. R., Baumann, H., & Heilinger, J.-C. (2013). Human enhancement and perfection. *Journal of Medical Ethics*. doi:10.1136/medethics-2012-100920 PMID:23436909

Roduit, J. A. R., Baumann, H., & Heilinger, J-C. (forthcoming). *Evaluating human enhancements: The importance of ideals*.

Sandel, M. J. (2007). *The case against perfection: Ethics in the age of genetic engineering*. Belknap Press of Harvard University Press.

Savulescu, J. (2006). Justice, fairness, and enhancement. *Annals of the New York Academy of Sciences, 1093*, 321–338. doi:10.1196/annals.1382.021 PMID:17312266

Schaefer, G. O., Kahane, G., & Savulescu, J. (2013). Autonomy and enhancement. *Neuroethics*. doi:10.1007/s12152-013-9189-5

Schermer, M. (2008). On the argument that enhancement is cheating. *Journal of Medical Ethics, 34*(2), 85–88. doi:10.1136/jme.2006.019646 PMID:18234944

Schramme, T. (2002). Natürlichkeit als wert. *Analyse & Kritik, 2*, 249–271.

Sparrow, R. (2011). Liberalism and eugenics. *Australasian Journal of Philosophy, 89*(3), 499–517. doi:10.1080/00048402.2010.484464

Walker, M. (2002). *What is transhumanism? Why is a transhumanist? Humanity+ (World Transhumanist Association)*. Retrieved May 22, 2012 from http://www.transhumanism.org/index.php/th/more/298/

Wall, S. (2008). Perfectionsism in moral and political philosophy. In E. N. Zalta (Ed.), *The Stanford Encyclopedia of Philosophy*. Retrieved from http://plato.stanford.edu/archives/fall2008/entries/perfectionism-moral

Zylinska, J. (2010). Playing God, Playing Adam: The politics and ethics of enhancement. *Journal of Bioethical Inquiry, 7*(2), 149–161. doi:10.1007/s11673-010-9223-9

KEY TERMS AND DEFINITIONS

Autonomy: The bioethical principle is used as a normative tool to evaluate the morality of a given enhancing intervention. If the intervention threatens the autonomy of the individual, it raises ethical concern that needs to be addressed.

Beyond Therapy: In this definition of human enhancement, human enhancements are interpreted as medical or technological interventions that do not attempt to cure, but are outside the scope of the traditional therapeutic understanding of medicine.

Human Enhancement: In our understanding, human enhancements consists of medical or technological interventions to human beings introducing a positive qualitative change to their current condition.

Ideal Human: In the notion of human enhancement, the notion of the 'human' is sometimes neglected. We defend here that the 'ideal human' can be a normative reference point to evaluate the morality of human enhancement.

We assume here that humans desire to enhance not necessarily towards their authentic self, but towards their ideal self. Different ideals may have different content, but these ideals are used in the same ways: they are action-guiding and help one make a decision concerning which direction he or she wants to enhance.

Justice: This bioethical principle is used as a normative tool to evaluate the morality of a given enhancing intervention. If access to enhancement is not equal to all, it creates problem of distributive justice and can reinforce inequalities in society. The intervention raises therefore ethical concerns that need to be addressed.

Morality [of Human Enhancement]: The debate regarding the ethics of human enhancement has often used the well-known bioethical notions of justice, safety, and autonomy to evaluate the morality of human enhancement. In our approach, we look at other anthropological notions to see whether it could give additional normative tools to evaluate the morality of human enhancement interventions.

Perfectionist: We argue that perfectionist assumptions of what it means to be human can be additional normative reference points to evaluate the morality of human enhancement.

Qualitative [Approach]: This definition of human enhancement adds a qualitative notion to the understanding of enhancement. In this way, the notion of improvement is introduced in the definition.

Quantitative [Approach]: This particular definition of human enhancement associates enhancement with a quantitative change. Medical or technological interventions that add something more to existing human characteristics are understood as human enhancement.

Safety: This bioethical principle suggests that we should restrain from a give human enhancement if the intervention is considered as not safe.

Chapter 5
The Ethics of Seeking Body Perfection, with Continual Reference to Heidi Montag

Brett Lunceford
Independent Researcher, USA

ABSTRACT

In an increasingly visual society, beauty may seem only skin deep. This chapter considers the ethics of cosmetic surgery through the lens of posthumanism, a stance that suggests that defects of the body can be overcome through technology. Cosmetic surgery, with its reliance on prostheses and promise of reshaping the body, is, at its heart, a posthuman enterprise. Although many have engaged in cosmetic surgery, actress Heidi Montag became an exemplar of reshaping the body by undergoing ten different plastic surgery procedures in one day. Using Montag as foil, this chapter examines four ethical dimensions of cosmetic surgery: the ethics of the medical professionals who perform and advertise these procedures, the ethics of the individual making the decision, the ethics of the media structures that promote a homogenous ideal of beauty, and the ethics of those who tacitly approve of such procedures.

INTRODUCTION

In his essay "Definition of Man," Kenneth Burke (1966) described humanity as "rotten with perfection" (p. 16), an ironic observation of how people often miss the mark as they seek that perfection. Such a description seems prescient in today's cosmetically enhanced world in which teenage girls may receive breast implants or liposuction as high school graduation presents (see Cassidy, 2010). Blum (2005) argues that cosmetic surgery "holds out a technological and economic solution (if you have the money, the technology is there) to the very dilemma posed by the way capitalism manages femininity by simultaneously commodifying it, idealizing it, and insisting on its native defects" (p. 110). Jordan (2004) likewise observes that "over the course of the last century, plastic surgery advocates have engaged in a concerted, commercial effort to redefine the human body as a plastic, malleable substance which surgeons can alter and people should want to alter in order to realize their body image ideals" (p. 328). In short, there is little that cannot be corrected; one can truly have the perfect body.

DOI: 10.4018/978-1-4666-6010-6.ch005

Even in cases where the ethics may seem clear, there can be controversy. For example, some portions of the deaf community have fought vehemently against cochlear implants in deaf children (for more on this controversy, see Balkany, Hodges, & Goodman, 1996; Lane & Bahan, 1998). Indeed, Murphy (2009) describes one same-sex couple who sought out a deaf sperm donor to increase the chances that their child would be deaf. The distinction between therapeutic intervention and enhancement is not always clearly delineated (Hogle, 2005). This is also the case in aesthetic enhancement. Plastic surgery is generally described as procedures used to correct some defect or disfiguration, such as in the case of birth defects or burn victims, while cosmetic surgery describes those procedures that are not medically necessary. Still, the question of what constitutes a defect and what is medically necessary can be subjective. For example, an individual may become so self-conscious of a particular bodily attribute that he or she becomes depressed or suicidal. As such, one must proceed with caution when considering the ethics of body modification and enhancement. One thing seems clear: the question of what *can* be accomplished through medical technology may be outpacing our ability as a society to answer what *should* be done.

McLuhan (1994) noted that the "outering or extension of our bodies and senses in a 'new invention' compels the whole of our bodies to shift into new positions in order to maintain equilibrium. A new 'closure' is effected in all our organs and senses, both private and public, by any new invention" (p. 252). But Graham (2002) argues that "technologies are not so much an extension or appendage to the human body, but are incorporated, assimilated into its very structures. The contours of human bodies are redrawn: they no longer end at the skin" (p. 4). The body can be shaped through technology in almost any way we wish. Such technologies have significant implications for how we as a society view the body.

Although many have gone under the knife in the pursuit of beauty, actress Heidi Montag stands out as an exemplar of this move toward cosmetic surgery as a means of recreating the body. Montag underwent 10 different plastic surgery procedures in one day, stating, "I had a little bit of Botox, an eyebrow lift, my ears tucked, I had my nose re-aligned, fat injections put into my cheeks, my lips done and I had my chin shaved down" (Berman, 2010, p. C4). Of course there is more to be done, as she heaps plastic surgery upon plastic surgery: "I would like to get my breasts redone. Because I couldn't get them the size I wanted because they couldn't fit" ("Heidi Says," 2010, p. 31). After her barrage of surgeries, she told *People* magazine: "I see an upgraded version of me. It's a new face and a new energy. It's a new person and I feel like almost all of the things I didn't want to be and who I turned into kind of got chiseled away" (Garcia, 2010, p. 84). The only way that Montag could be herself, it seems, was by removing parts of her flesh. But Montag has no intention of resting on her surgically-enhanced laurels. Says Montag, "Let's just say there's a lot of maintenance. Nobody ages perfectly, so I plan to keep using surgery to make me as perfect as I can be. Because, for me, the surgery is always so rewarding" (Garcia, 2010, p. 88).

In this chapter, I will use Heidi Montag as a lens through which to explore the ethical considerations of cosmetic surgery. I suggest that Montag and others like her draw on a posthumanist perspective, which suggests that the body is intrinsically flawed and must be corrected through technology. Montag's case illustrates four specific ethical questions: the ethics of the medical professionals who perform and advertise these procedures; the ethics of the individual making the decision; the ethics of the media structures that promote a homogenous ideal of beauty; and the ethics of those within society who tacitly approve of such procedures. Some questions that naturally arise include how, or if, such procedures should be regulated and who should regulate them? What standards should be used in making such regulations? How much modification is too much, and what kinds of modifications should be available?

POSTHUMANISM AND BODY MODIFICATION

Much as Nietzsche's Zarathustra came to teach people the *Übermensch*, cyberfeminists have come to teach people the cyborg. There is a striking parallel between these approaches. Where Nietzsche (1978) commands men and women to "break the old tablets" that prescribe good and evil (pp. 196-215), Haraway (1991) finds salvation in "blasphemy," stating that "at the centre of my ironic faith, my blasphemy, is the image of the cyborg" (p. 149). Haraway suggests that "the cyborg is a kind of disassembled and reassembled, postmodern collective and personal self. This is the self feminists must code" (p. 163). For both Nietzsche and Haraway one must destroy the old and rebuild the new from the rubble in the hope of creating a better world. Although the means by which this change is to be brought about differ, the impulse seems similar—the suspicion that utopia could be brought about if only people could destroy the things holding them back from attaining that goal. For Nietzsche it was an outdated sense of morality and the desire to cling to the old gods; for Haraway, it is the binaries such as those between male and female or heaven and earth that promote systems of domination.

The question, then, is whether technology is the answer to solving these problems. Haraway (1991) argues that "communication technologies and biotechnologies are the crucial tools recrafting our bodies. These tools embody and enforce new social relations for women world-wide" (p. 164). There are, of course, detractors from this narrative of liberation through technology. Millar (1998) points out that:

While affluent western feminists may see themselves as "cyborgs" as they use digital technologies for creative and professional purposes, less advantaged women—such as those who assemble computer equipment or enter data—experience "cyborg" life in a profoundly different and exploitative way. (p. 62)

Dietrich (1997) likewise notes that "women stand to gain little as quasi-disembodied subjects within a network environment *without reference to the material conditions of their subjectivity*" (p. 178). Technology is not always libratory; it can be used to free or enslave, and there are always unintended consequences of technology adoption (Lunceford, 2009).

Technology alone cannot be the only answer. After all, technology is culturally bound. Dyens (2001) argues that "To reflect upon technological culture is thus not simply to think about the impact of technologies on our world, but also to examine the emergence of new strata of reality, where living beings, phenomena, and machines become entangled" (p. 11). People and societies shape technology and technology shapes people and societies. But still there is a persistent belief that technology can alter the human condition for the better. As Graham (1999) writes, "New digital and biogenetic technologies—in the shape of media such as virtual reality, artificial intelligence, genetic modification and technological prosthetics—signal a 'posthuman' future in which the boundaries between humanity, technology and nature have become ever more malleable" (p. 419).

It seems clear that technologies have infiltrated not only our perceptions of reality, but also our perceptions of self, of whom and what we are. Negroponte (1995) argues that we are all becoming digital: "It is here. It is now. It is almost genetic in its nature, in that each generation will become more digital than the preceding one" (p. 231). Moreover, if we are to take Turkle's (1995) work at face value, we are both the digital and the flesh—both are reality. But this digital identity still exists within a physical, sexed body. In fact, as I have argued elsewhere, we can profitably consider media not only as extensions of the self, but also as extensions of one's sexuality (Lunceford, 2008, 2010). As such, we must consider the body even as we consider the ways in which individuals have attempted to transcend the body. More importantly, in many cases, attempts to transcend the body are really just attempts to experience embodiment more fully through technology. Human enhancement technologies serve as a kind of salvation from the limitations of the body. In the discourses surrounding cosmetic surgery, there is the suggestion that if one had a *different kind* of body—the kind of body that has been made possible through technology—then he or she would enjoy being in that body much more.

Jordan (2004) notes that "over the course of the last century, plastic surgery advocates have engaged in a concerted, commercial effort to redefine the human body as a plastic, malleable substance which surgeons can alter and people should want to alter in order to realize their body image ideals" (p. 328). This malleability of the body has even become entertainment with shows such as *Extreme Makeover* and *The Swan*. These shows are not simply entertainment, but rhetorical imperatives. As Black (1970) explains, "In all rhetorical discourse, we can find enticements not simply to believe something, but to *be* something. We are solicited by the discourse to fulfill its blandishments with our very selves" (p. 119). For example, in her discussion of the television show *Extreme Makeover*, Heyes (2007) suggests that "electing to have surgery makes one a go-getter, for example, someone who takes charge, not flinching at the prospect of pain, inconvenience, trauma, or risk," while also noting that "resistance to cosmetic surgery is tacitly rendered as a lack of character, and thus can be construed (like resistance to wearing make-up or high heels in an earlier feminist era) only as a failure to make the best of oneself" (p. 28). Markey and Markey (2010) likewise found that those who watched reality shows featuring cosmetic surgery were more likely to desire sur-

gery themselves. These shows, then, function as cultural pedagogy, teaching people what it means to be masculine and feminine. More importantly, shows such as *Bridalplasty* and *The Swan* suggest that the best way to embody true femininity is to alter the body through cosmetic surgery.

Berman (2010) states, "In previous generations, when women wanted to increase their sex appeal, they turned to Chanel No. 5 and red lipstick. Today, women turn to potentially life-threatening surgeries along with monthly injections of Botox" (p. C4). But this impulse to alter the body through surgery is by no means new. Comiskey (2004) states that as cosmetic surgery began to be practiced in the 1920s, medical professionals "defended cosmetic surgery as a noble profession, arguing that it was necessary because of the social importance of beauty in the brutal struggle for existence, particularly for women" (p. 32). This phenomenon points to the fact that medical technology and conceptions of the body and self are culturally bound. Dyens (2001) argues that "the virtual being is real, but of a different kind of real, one that is both organic and technological. This being is a cultural animal, a nonorganic being. The cultural being is in a new stage of evolution" (p. 33). We can consider the posthuman body to likewise be not only a physical embodiment, but also a cultural one, a strategic presentation of self. As such, the desire to alter one's body does not take place in a vacuum, but rather the "plastic body is a rhetorically contested substance, with a variety of social agents engaged in efforts to shape its public meaning and, by extension, its corporeal form" (Jordan, 2004, p. 328). To fully account for the impulse to surgically alter the body—perhaps at the risk of death—one must consider the dialectic between the individual's conception of the self and societal values of what is and is not desirable.

Posthumanist ideology suggests that the inherent limits of the body can be overcome through technology. At its core, cosmetic surgery is a posthumanist enterprise which seeks to correct the defects of the body by implanting prostheses, such as breast, chin, buttock, and cheekbone implants, or removing and shaping existing tissue. Martínez Lirola and Chovanec (2012) explain that in advertisements for cosmetic surgery, surgery "is offered as a solution to one's internal fears of failure to approximate the beauty ideal presented to and shared by the public" and "promises to obtain perfect post-surgery bodies that are sexually attractive and thus satisfactory not only to women, but also to men" (p. 502). But Polonijo and Carpiano (2008) demonstrate some of the problems with the portrayal of the female body as a site for medical intervention: "By presenting medical professionals as experts on beauty, appearance is defined in a manner consistent with a medicalization framework—as a problem in need of medical treatment" (p. 467). In such depictions, the body is not enough; one must obtain an enhanced, surgically modified, technologized body. One must become posthuman in order to be human at all.

READING HEIDI MONTAG'S BODY: FOUR ETHICAL DIMENSIONS

Ethics and the Plastic Surgeon

Long before the popular press began to read Montag's body, it was read—and written—in great detail by the plastic surgeon that would perform the procedures. Jerslev (2006) describes such a transaction as "the body burdened with the stigmata of the surgeons' marker," which suggests that "the body does not belong to the one that inhabits it but to another person's objectifying gaze, and it says that the material body is never a finished, singular entity, but a modifiable mass of organic matter" (p. 146). This act places the surgeon in a significant position of authority and highlights the vulnerability of the patient. The surgeon literally rewrites the patient's body. Thus plastic surgeons who perform elective surgery bear a significant ethical burden.

In medical ethics, Beauchamp and Childress (2001) propose the following ethical framework that has become widely adopted:

1. Respect for autonomy (a norm of respecting the decision-making capacities of autonomous persons).
2. Nonmaleficence (a norm of avoiding the causation of harm).
3. Beneficence (a group of norms for providing benefits and balancing benefits against risks and costs).
4. Justice (a group of norms for distributing benefits, risks, and costs fairly). (p. 12).

In the case of Montag, two facets stand out: nonmaleficence and beneficence. However, even these seemingly clear-cut issues can seem at odds sometimes. For example, Beauchamp and Childress (2001) observe that beneficence can sometimes conflict with the principle of autonomy in the case of paternalism (p. 176).

In cosmetic surgery, there may be conflicts between nonmaleficence and beneficence when the ill that one corrects is influenced by the very people providing the cure. In her discussion of cosmetic dermatologists, Baumann (2012) notes that they "have the goal of improving their patient's appearance and skin health, but all too often, financial motivation can cloud their judgment" (p. 522). Cantor (2005) likewise notes that the physician's "livelihood depends on performing the very interventions they recommend," but notes that "economic self-interest is less flagrant when a surgeon insists that a sick patient have gallbladder surgery, even if she stands to profit from the procedure, than when a dermatologist sells a patient an expensive cream of dubious value" (p. 155). A similar judgment can be made for cosmetic surgeons. On the freeway near my home, I see billboards for plastic surgeons promoting "beauty for life." Plastic surgeons stand to gain financially by promoting an image of the body as intrinsically flawed and lacking in natural beauty.

As Blum (2005) argues, cosmetic surgery "holds out a technological and economic solution (if you have the money, the technology is there) to the very dilemma posed by the way capitalism manages femininity by simultaneously commodifying it, idealizing it, and insisting on its native defects" (p. 110). The discourse of normalizing body parts found in cosmetic surgery—one's nose is too big, breasts are too small—suggests a desire for conformity that technological intervention can supply.

Although aesthetic enhancement technologies have, at their core, the ideal of normality, striving for homogeneity—even if it tends toward an ideal of beauty—hardly seems like enhancement. Still, Solvi et al. (2010) found that the desire to fit in with prescribed gender norms was a deciding factor for women who chose to undergo breast augmentation. One respondent stated, "The breast augmentation for me concerns a feeling of being whole as a woman, giving me a feminine look. Right now I feel too masculine. If I don't wear jewellery I look like a man" (p. 676). Another respondent was more blunt: "I don't want large breasts, just a normal B-cup, and I hope that no one notices the change" (p. 676). Even with aesthetic enhancement, however, not everyone can live up to socially prescribed norms of beauty. Hurst (2012) observes that "in North America, beauty norms and ideals are quite narrow and for women describe a very particular body that is Caucasian-featured, cissexual, thin, able-bodied, and feminine" (p. 448). These norms are not always universal and those in disability studies have often raised the question of what constitutes "normal" (see Connor, 2011; Ferguson & Nusbaum, 2012). Still, these norms are difficult to escape. As one woman in a wheelchair put it, "I think that society creates an image of beauty, and if you don't conform to it, you get put down so much that you eventually believe the story that they're telling you" (Taleporos & McCabe, 2002, p. 976).

Jothilakshmi, Salvi, Hayden, and Bose-Haider (2009) argue that "the goals of esthetic surgery are to correct the physical defects that adversely affect a person's body image and ultimately to improve the quality of one's life" (p. 54). But what do we mean when we say "defect"? Western society has coded such naturally occurring variations as pendulous breasts, protruding labia minora, and single eyelids as defects. Nowhere is the desire to correct perceived defects more prominent, however, than in the discourse surrounding aging (see Lin, 2010). Smirnova (2012) suggests that discourses surrounding women and aging,

Has simultaneously constructed the aging woman as both victim and hero—her body vulnerable and in need of rescue by her will to partake in anti-aging technologies. The technologies themselves are also part of the heroic narrative, masculinized by the rhetoric of neoliberal, rational action backed by scientific and medical authorities. (p. 1236)

In short, a woman who does not fight against the ravages of time is seen as less desirable. As De Roubaix (2011) observes, "Women are obliged to comply with constructs of beauty and normality to remain competitive. Society regards youthfulness as desirable; the mass media both generates and feeds upon these constructs" (p. 15). More importantly, the solution is technological. People do not fight aging on their own, or with friends and family; rather, aging is compensated for through the use of medical technology and specialists.

Returning to the question of ethics, we are left with the question of "whether women really make free choices in favour of aesthetic surgery under these circumstances" (De Roubaix, 2011, p. 13). Women are placed in the unenviable position of choosing whether to surgically enhance their bodies or to matter at all in society. In some ways, this undermines the autonomy of the individual. In advertising the body as defective, one can simultaneously maintain the principle of nonmaleficence from the perspective of the physical body—indeed, may argue that he or she is making the patient better—but may cause psychological harm that will drive the patient to his or her practice to seek relief.

Feminist scholars (e.g., Bordo, 1993; Jeffreys, 2005; Polonijo & Carpiano, 2008; Wolf, 1991) have placed cosmetic surgery within the framework of patriarchal power, but Sanchez Taylor, (2012) entertains the possibility that:

With the expansion of the cosmetic surgery industry and the "make over culture" that surrounds it, others choose surgery simply because it is affordable, readily available, fashionable, and so increasingly "normal" to consume surgery in the same way that other beauty and fashion products and services are consumed. (p. 464)

Thus to claim that those who undergo cosmetic surgery are simply victims of social forces beyond their control is to oversimplify the transaction. Holliday and Sanchez Taylor (2006) argue that "contemporary women who routinely adopt the markers of hypersexualization associated with classed and racialized bodies (such as buttock implants or collagen lips) are not passive but active and desiring (not just desirable)" (p. 191). But the impulse for cosmetic surgery may not be to stand out or to look better than everyone else, but rather, as mentioned above, to simply fit in. Participants in a study by de Andrade (2010) reported that they sought cosmetic surgery to be "normal," especially after pregnancy. However, one 59-year-old woman stated, "At my age, I have to do it. I have to undergo cosmetic surgery and have a facelift so as to look younger, more beautiful. All my friends are doing it" (de Andrade, 2010, p. 79).

One danger suggested by Gupta (2012) surrounding the commercialization of cosmetic surgery is that "consumers may regard aesthetic surgery as a commodity that is bought rather than a service provided by a trained professional" (p. 548). Despite the desire to respect patient autonomy, the customer is not always right. Montag expressed pleasure with her new, improved self, but the reality proved less than optimal. Nine months after her bout of surgeries, she decided that she wanted to have her implants removed

and downgraded to a smaller size because of back pain. "I'm desperate to go back to normal," Montag said; "I feel trapped in my own body" (Gillin, 2010, p. 2B).

The cosmetic surgeon must walk a fine line between respecting the autonomy of the patient and contributing to a culture that pathologizes the body. Consider the example provided by Blum (2003) of the surgeon who advised his patient that in addition to the rhinoplasty that she had planned, he would also "remove her under-eye bags" (p. 276). She notes that "this surgeon has a reputation for doing wonderful eyelid surgery. Unsurprisingly, then, he focuses on the eyes of all prospective patients. This 'flaw' is somehow magnified for him" (p. 277). In this case, it seems that the surgeon transgressed against the principle of autonomy by instilling a sense of doubt concerning the patient's features that was not previously there. In this case, the enhancement sought by the surgeon was not the one suggested by the patient. Harris and Carr (2001) state that "the benefits of [plastic surgery] interventions for the patients concerned are psychological: relief of psychological distress and improvement in social and psychological functioning" (p. 216), but the practitioner must be sure that the flaws corrected are those seen by the patient and not those suggested or created by the surgeon.

Cosmetic surgeons claim the authority to stand in judgment of the body of the patient and hold the ability to correct flaws in that body. Jordan (2004) notes that "surgical applicants must confront the medical community's ideological perspective on the healthy body and how this influences surgeons' choices about which bodies and desires will receive surgical attention and which will be rejected as inappropriate" (p. 328). The surgeon decides what is wrong with the individual because, as a society, we have outsourced alteration and care of our bodies to medical professionals. We no longer trust ourselves with our own bodies. Although this abdication of autonomy is problematic, this illustrates the need for practitioners to tread carefully when considering the needs of the patient.

Ethics and the Media

The mass media plays a significant role in individual attitudes toward cosmetic surgery (see Luo, 2013; Solvi et al., 2010; Swami, 2009; Swami et al., 2011). Indeed, Swami, Taylor, and Carvalho (2009) found a correlation between celebrity worship and positive attitudes towards cosmetic surgery. It is no great leap to suggest that images of beautiful people may cause some to measure themselves against this standard and find themselves wanting. Most people deal with the fact that they will not look like their favorite celebrity, but for some the pressure is overwhelming; cosmetic surgery holds forth the potential to come closer to that standard of beauty.

In their discussion of Body Dysmorphic Disorder (BDD), Chan, Jones, and Heywood (2011) explain that "BDD is characterised by time-consuming behaviours such as mirror gazing, comparing particular features to those of others, excessive camouflaging tactics to hide the defect, skin picking and reassurance seeking," explaining that "BDD patients may present to the plastic surgeon requesting multiple cosmetic procedures" (p. 6; for more on BDD diagnosis, see Veale et al., 2012). Kellett, Clarke, and McGill (2008) suggest that those seeking breast augmentation surgery may reflect "a lack of balanced body image or obsessional tendencies" (p. 516). Some have suggested that perceived imperfections are influenced by media images. Berry, Cucchiara, and Davies (2011) provide this explanation of what constitutes the "ideal breast": "there is a common view, perhaps as a consequence of globalization and advertising, of an attractive breast: one full, without ptosis and good symmetry" (p. 1402). In their discussion of labiaplasty, Cartwright and Cardozo (2008) also note that "women requesting surgery report disabling psychological distress associated with a perception that their labia are abnormal in size or shape. . . . The often erroneous perception of abnormality may arise from comparison with women's genitalia as depicted in pornography" (p. 285). Life imitates art.

This assessment works both ways; as people read the bodies in the media, the media also reads the bodies of individuals. Montag's body is no exception here. Supermodel Paulina Porizkova compared Montag to a "cheap, plastic pool float," as she railed against the culture of plastic surgery (Camilli, 2010, p. E5). Babcock (2010), writing for the Spokane *Spokesman Review*, states, "Imagine, 23 years old and already Botoxed, lifted, lipo-ed, and implanted like a blow-up doll. The surgeries were not because of a genetic disfigurement or horrific accident but because, as Montag explained, 'I'm obsessed'" (p. V1). Despite the discomfort this columnist displays with Montag's surgery marathon, it is not actually difficult to imagine; plastic surgery (or rumors thereof) has become cliché among actresses. The surgery was not the shocking thing, but rather the quantity in one day. As Dyens (2001) explains,

We are attracted to Hollywood stars not only because of their biological beauty (i.e., organic effectiveness) but also because of their cultural productivity. What we seek today are bodies sculpted by culture. A Hollywood star, male or female, who has had cosmetic surgery, is a cultural being, and this is what seduces us. (p. 21)

Montag has chosen to fully embrace the socially constructed norms of what ideal femininity should look like and inscribe them on her body. She constructed the ideal of the perfect body not only from her own mind, but from the media and celebrities that infiltrate our minds.

Through cosmetic surgery, Montag has become something more than just Heidi Montag—she becomes an avatar of our cultural norms of beauty. Yet to fully embrace these norms, she must discard those parts of her body that do not fully fit into the mold of beauty. These norms are not created *ex nihilo*. Those of us watching these celebrities are complicit in this process. One psychotherapist notes that celebrities are drawn to cosmetic surgery because they "feel their looks must be at least preserved, if not 'improved' upon in order to meet unrealistic expectations we collectively have now when it comes to celebrities and indeed each other" (Russell, 2013, p. 36). Yet such enhancements may come at a price. In order to conform, Montag had to jettison her individuality, those attributes that made her look like her. Russell (2013) describes the moment Montag's mother saw her after her surgeries, and sobbed "Of course I thought you were more beautiful before . . . I thought you were younger, I thought you were fresher looking, I thought you were healthier . . . why would you want to look like Barbie" (p. 36)? Of course the short answer is because Barbie has served as the ideal of beauty for generations of girls. Who else would she become?

Scholars have long expressed concern over the media's influence on the body image of both males and females (Aubrey, 2007; Hargreaves & Tiggemann, 2009; Harper & Tiggemann, 2008; Shields & Heinecken, 2001; Stice, Spangler, & Agras, 2001). Even one of Montag's co-stars expressed misgivings about the potential impact that Montag's actions may have on young girls:

I hope that girls don't read the article, look at the decisions that Heidi made, and think that's normal. She was quoted as saying that every celebrity in Hollywood has these procedures done, every day . . . and that's just not true. I would never want young girls to read that and think it's the standard that they need to be measured by. (Ward, 2010, p. 25)

But there is a standard by which everyone is held, which is continually held up in the media. Montag is not the problem, but rather the symptom. A study by Dohnt and Tiggemann (2006) found that girls as young as 5-8 years old had already internalized media messages depicting thinness as the ideal and awareness of dieting as a means of gaining that type of body. Maltby and Day (2011) found a correlation between celebrity worship and those who actually went though with cosmetic surgery. It should come as little surprise

that Montag would likewise internalize the media-promoted ideal of perfection and then carve her body into the appropriate shape.

Ethics and the Innocent(?) Bystander

Although there are some evolutionary traits associated with beauty (Barber, 1995), conceptions of beauty are also culturally bound. As such, the very idea of beauty is subjective. Notions of beauty have changed throughout history, with different body types being favored at different times and certain parts of the body highlighted for some groups and ignored by others. Cosmetic surgery also plays a part in this construction of beauty; as Lunceford (2012) puts it, "cosmetic surgery not only reflects but creates our conceptions of what it means to be beautiful" (p. 20). Those who embody the standards of beauty reap great advantages in society. Thus it should come as little surprise that people would turn to human enhancement technologies as a way to enhance their perceived beauty.

Beauty is more than aesthetically pleasing; it is socially coded as more desirable and researchers have long observed that a host of positive traits are associated with attractive people (Dion, Berscheid, & Walster, 1972; Nisbett & Wilson, 1977; but see Eagly, Ashmore, Makhijani, & Longo, 1991). This "halo effect" can be leveraged in many ways. Attractive people are seen as more intelligent (Kanazawa, 2011; Kanazawa & Kovar, 2004), healthier (Jones et al., 2001), more attractive to employers (Ruetzler, Taylor, Reynolds, Baker, & Killen, 2012; but see Johnson, Podratz, Dipboye, & Gibbons, 2010), more skilled socially (Hope & Mindell, 1994), and make better (and more distinct) first impressions (Lorenzo, Biesanz, & Human, 2010). But the benefits of physical beauty go far beyond romantic potential or career success. Garnham (2013) explains that in contemporary society, the body "becomes the surface of inscription for the choices one makes and can be read in terms of its virtue. Looking 'good' or an attractive appearance thus signifies the ethical subject" (p. 44). This link between morality and beauty is reinforced from an early age (see Baker-Sperry & Grauerholz, 2003; S. Baumann, 2008; Bazzini, Curtin, Joslin, Regan, & Martz, 2010). As Couser (2011) puts it, "the outer appearance of the body reveals the moral or spiritual status of the person" (p. 22).

Western society has pathologized the body and any perceived defect in the body can be technologically solved through drugs or surgery. In the words of Dolmadge (2013), there is a sense that "we must still control and belittle our bodies; to be *bodied* too much or too 'abnormally' is still to be in danger of disqualification" (p. 88). But it is not enough to solve the problems of the body; one must solve them more effectively than others. If others can seek out technological enhancement, there then becomes a kind of enhancement arms race. Montag describes this sense of competition: "Think about the industry I'm trying to go into. My ultimate dream is to be a pop star. I'm competing against the Britney Spearses of the world—and when she was in her prime, it was her sex appeal that sold. Obviously, looks matter; it's a superficial industry" (Garcia, 2010, p. 82). Beauty is a zero-sum game in which failing to measure up physically means losing out to another who has more effectively managed his or her physical appearance through technology. Such sentiments seem consistent with Blum's (2005) assertion that "cosmetic surgery can be seen as a dramatization of the relationship between a woman and an imaginary Other Woman figure . . . who, because of some imaginary set of superior charms, entrances your partner away from you" (p. 110). Plastic surgery allows a woman to become that "other woman," which then places her in competition with the rest of the female population. This is certainly not lost on Montag, who states, "As for other women, if they aren't hating on you, then you're not doing anything right. If women aren't jealous of you, talking about you and cutting you down, then you're a nerd, and I would never want to be that" (Husted, 2009, p. B03).

The problem, of course, is that there will always be someone who has something that is better. An individual like Montag may enhance her breasts, nose, insert cheekbone and chin implants, and suction out fat to reshape her torso, but someone else may come along with a more pleasing eye shape and be taller through no effort of her own. The other individual may not seek to instill anxiety in the other person, but when confronted with someone of greater beauty the individual is faced with two choices: concede or alter themselves further to become more beautiful. Although it may seem that one is limited only by the balance in his or her bank account, there are some attributes that technology cannot easily enhance. Although these enhancement technologies hold out the promise of a "more beautiful you," the individual who is enhanced is still *you*. There are limits to what can be done, but this does not stop some from trying to alter themselves significantly. Some have raised ethical concerns surrounding the enabling of such behavior. One dermatologic surgeon described people like Montag as those seeking "physical perfection to satisfy a psychological problem which cannot be helped by multiple surgeries. We as surgeons are not helping our patients by performing surgery on these people'" (Stewart, 2010, p. K). Once the body begins to be seen as malleable, with parts that are replaceable, there is seemingly no limit to what can be done. As Blum (2005) notes, "When you buy a body part for aesthetic reasons, you automatically compare yours to others who have better or worse. Even if you are pleased with a surgical result, you will see the rest of the world as so many possibilities" (p. 105).

Within the literature surrounding cosmetic surgery, patient satisfaction is a key focus. But what is the root of this satisfaction? Sullivan (2000) explains that "physicians consistently describe the best candidate as physically healthy individuals with realistic expectations, who are emotionally stable, self-motivated, and not reasonably concerned about physical imperfections" (p. 177). However, if they were not actually concerned with the imperfections, then why would they seek out surgery? Moreover, Hurst (2012) questions the notion that cosmetic surgery is solely done for the patient themselves, arguing that these procedures are entered into as a result of our relationships with others. She states that "patients negotiate a fine line between understanding cosmetic surgery as a form of self-improvement and understanding the body as looked at and evaluated by others" (p. 447-448). Dohnt and Tiggemann (2006) likewise found that "peers and media appear to be significant sources of influence on young girls' desire for thinness, satisfaction with appearance, and dieting awareness" (p. 150). As such, the ideal that those undergoing aesthetic enhancement are doing it solely for themselves seems naïve.

Ethics and the Enhanced Individual

No one exists in a vacuum, and social conceptions of beauty are created not only through exemplars, but also in comparison with others. The body that Montag inhabits has likewise read other bodies in her search for perfection, noting that "When I was shopping for my boobs, I wanted the best, so I sat down and flipped through a bunch of Playboys" (Derakhshani, 2009, p. E02). It seems that Montag chose her breasts much as one searches for a new pair of pants in a catalog. As Blum (2005) observes, "When you don't like a body part, the rest of the world looks like an array of perfect examples of just what you lack. Moreover, once you've bought and paid for an improvement, you want the 'best'" (p. 104).

The catalog in which Montag—and many others like her—chose to browse may not actually provide the goods that she desires. After all, the pages of *Playboy* are filled with surgically and, of course, digitally enhanced breasts. She could not have been innocent of this possibility; speaking of her own experience in posing for *Playboy*, she states, "I didn't fill out one of the bras and they had to Photoshop my boobs bigger, and it was so disheartening. I almost cried" (Garcia, 2010,

p. 83). In other words, she is seeking to modify her breasts in ways that may not be possible in the flesh—creating a false set of breasts from a model that is inherently false. Baudrillard (1994) would certainly find such a state amusing with his prediction of the precession of simulacra, but this also speaks to another assertion by Baudrillard (1988): "*Images have become our true sex object*, the object of our desire" (p. 35). It was not simply better breasts that she chose, but rather, *someone's* breasts, which may or may not have been that person's actual breasts. In other words, she chose the *image* of another's breasts. Thus her statement, "I'm very excited for the world to see the new me, and a real me" (Garcia, 2010, p. 84), seems particularly ironic.

But Montag is not only concerned about the world in abstract, but also her husband's approval. Davis and Vernon (2002) suggest a connection between attachment anxiety and cosmetic surgery, stating that "although there are many motives to improve appearance, fear of rejection or loss of a current spouse or lover is clearly among them" (p. 136). This seems particularly evident in Montag's expressed concerns that her husband would not find her sexy. Montag states that after coming home from surgery, "I felt bad that he had to even look at me" (Garcia, 2010, p. 86). When asked if the recovery process tested their relationship, Montag replied, "Asking my husband to take down my pants so that I can go to the bathroom? That's not something I ever wanted to have to do. I mean, you want your husband to look at you and feel sexy, not have him waiting on you hand and foot, feeling like you don't want him to look at you," but concedes that "it took our marriage to another level" (Garcia, 2010, p. 86-88). Montag's story reminded me of when my wife and I came home from the hospital after she gave birth to our son. I recognized that there were some things that she would not be able to do and I did them because our relationship is based on more than just her physical attractiveness. The body can be damaged and must have the opportunity to heal itself; this is a luxury that Montag seems unwilling to give herself. But if one considers the base of the relationship as looking sexy, then he or she must always guard against someone better looking. There is no time for recovery.

The second assumption present in Montag's comments is, perhaps more troubling: that a woman's looks are her most important attribute. In the image-hungry entertainment industry, however, this may be taken as a given. In response to the question, "Does it worry you that people will fixate on your breasts?" Montag responded, "I hope so. They better! That's kind of the point" (Garcia, 2010, p. 83-84). Even so, she pulls back from this slightly, adding, "Sex appeal is really important and it's not saying that you're only sexy if you have big boobs. That's not true at all, and honestly the way I got Spencer, I had no surgery. It was my inner beauty that he loved" (Garcia, 2010, p. 84).

Montag seems to view her body as a set of individual components rather than holistically. Blum (2005) relates a similar impulse in her interviews:

Grabbing a magazine from a nearby table, she pointed to the supermodel on the cover and exclaimed, "Ooh, I love that nose, I want that nose." I ask her why. "It's straight. It's straight and thin. Not the cheekbones. I have the cheekbones. I love the tip—well, I don't know," she said, standing back now, assuming more aesthetic distance, "it's still not thin enough." (p. 104)

When one can reconstruct the body in such a way, it invites a view that the body is no more than the sum of its parts. This can be problematic, if not from an ethical sense, from an aesthetic sense. What works well on one body may not work as well on another. Yet there are deeper underlying concerns that emerge from taking a fragmentary view of the body, specifically the question of when is enough enough? When can one stop altering the body? What parts are acceptable to alter and in what ways? What happens to the sense of the self when one has one person's nose and another's

eyebrows? Most importantly, what happens to our conception of beauty when all are able to look the same? No longer is it *vive la différence*, but rather, *la différence est mort.*

SOLUTIONS AND RECOMMENDATIONS

Medical professionals seek to help individuals become healthy (or healthier) by diagnosing, correcting, and preventing physical and psychological maladies. Yet despite the ethical concern for patient autonomy (Beauchamp & Childress, 2001), the customer is not always right. The patient has the right to refuse medical treatment for any reason, but there may be times in which the course of action desired by the patient would be unnecessary at best or damaging at worst. The medical professional has an ethical obligation to educate the patient, and in the case of cosmetic surgery for human enhancement this education must go well beyond the risks of the surgery and the possibilities open to the customer.

My interchange of the terms patient and customer are intentional here. Consider for a moment if one were to apply the standards of the medical professional at large to the practice of cosmetic surgery using the case of hypochondriasis. Hypochondriasis is a disorder that manifests through the patient's amplification of symptoms to catastrophic self-diagnoses (Fergus & Valentiner, 2009; Marcus, 1999). In short, these patients have a different conception of what it means to be "well" (Langlois & Ladouceur, 2004; Marcus, Gurley, Marchi, & Bauer, 2007; Weck, Neng, Richtberg, & Stangier, 2012a, 2012b). Many researchers suggest that treatment of this disorder should focus on the psychological paths rather than the physical treatments the patient may seek (Abramowitz & Moore, 2007; Buwalda, Bouman, & van Duijn, 2007; Lovas & Barsky, 2010; Simon, Gureje, & Fullerton, 2001; Visser & Bouman, 2001; Walker, Vincent, Furer, Cox, & Kevin, 1999; but see Greeven et al., 2009 for discussion of pharmacological treatment). If the symptoms are benign, there is no need to prescribe treatment. Rather, the doctor would focus on the faulty belief that there is something drastically wrong with the patient. From a financial perspective, it would be in the doctor's interest to run as many tests and perform as many procedures as possible, but this would seem unethical from the standpoint of justice, in which costs should be distributed (and, presumably, charged) fairly (Beauchamp & Childress, 2001). Some patients may even welcome such behaviors, as it would provide the care they believe that they need while validating their perceptions. The patient, however, gains little actual benefit outside of this validation and thus the practitioner violates the principle of beneficence.

Elective cosmetic surgery, however, turns this idea on its head. The doctor is asked to perform surgery on healthy tissue simply because the patient asks for it and has the money to pay for the operation. Indeed, if the practitioner were to do the work of educating the patient, he or she may find far fewer customers. Some have suggested that the profit motive is at the forefront of some cosmetic surgery practices; in his discussion of cosmetic vulva surgery, Zwang (2011) writes:

Our Western countries have codes of ethics and medical associations with ethics panels, which should censure surgical procedures inspired by the profit motive. By attacking the normal organs and the normal vulva of the vast majority of adult women, proponents of cosmetic surgery have created an inexhaustible goldmine.... Is it justifiable in terms of medical ethics to cut into organs — the labia minora and the clitoral hood — which are normal in every regard and to reduce the size of a perfectly normal mons with the excuse that they do not suit their owner? Or that they do not match an artificial stereotype? And all this against payment of a surgical fee? Is it right to advertise, even discreetly, that one engages in this type of practice? (p. 85)

For Zwang the ethics of such practices are clearly suspect. From a medical perspective, it is difficult to make the case that one is improving the patient's condition by removing or altering healthy, functioning tissue that is within the normal parameters of human morphology. In other words, a B-cup is not a functional problem or even an aesthetic problem from an objective point of view. Beauty is in the eye of the beholder and some may prefer small breasts (Furnham & Swami, 2007) or simply be more interested in other body attributes (Dixson, Grimshaw, Linklater, & Dixson, 2011; Wiggins, Wiggins, & Conger, 1968). The perceived problem may only be in the mind of the individual. For example, Frederick, Peplau, and Lever (2008) found that "Although most women in our sample were dissatisfied with their breasts, a majority of men were satisfied with their partner's breasts," a finding that they attribute to overestimating the preferences of the opposite sex (p. 209).

It is clear that aesthetic surgery can have positive outcomes in self-perception and behavior, and thus serve as enhancement technologies. Still, there are the intervening issues of who actually seeks such surgery and the potential long term effects. Von Soest, Kvalem, Roald, and Skolleborg (2009) found that body image evaluation and self-esteem scores improved after cosmetic surgery. Meningaud et al. (2003) found improvement in anxiety in patients following cosmetic surgery, but notes that those seeking cosmetic surgery were "more anxious" and "more depressed than the general population" (p. 48). However, von Soest, Kvalem, Skolleborg, and Roald (2009) question whether the increase in extraversion induced by cosmetic surgery "may be due to short-term changes in attitude towards one's own appearance, which in itself serves to legitimate the decision to have undergone cosmetic surgery. Such effects may well diminish over time" (p. 1024-1025). These findings call into question whether cosmetic surgery always functions as enhancement or, rather, serve to more clearly manifest the patient's insecurities.

The fact that Montag could undergo 10 different plastic surgery procedures in one day raises the question of how much is too much. In the case of elective aesthetic enhancement, it seems prudent to explore with the patient the underlying reasons for surgery. This may require a deeper analysis than the surgeon is able to make and in such cases psychiatric evaluation may be warranted (Ericksen & Billick, 2012). This is essential because those who suffer from Body Dysmorphic Disorder are unlikely to be satisfied with any surgical intervention. One study found that despite expressing satisfaction concerning the surgery, "only 1 patient no longer had a BDD diagnosis at follow-up: all the other operated patients still had a BDD diagnosis and all but 1 had developed a new site of preoccupation" (Tignol, Biraben-Gotzamanis, Martin-Guehl, Grabot, & Aouizerate, 2007, p. 523). If the aim is beneficence, then for some patients cosmetic surgery misses the mark entirely. Following the principle of beneficence suggests that the least invasive procedure should be attempted first, especially in cases in which the tissue to be altered is healthy and functional.

Perhaps there needs to be some shift in how cosmetic surgeons view their practice; some seem to see themselves more as artists than as doctors. In such cases the notion that aesthetic surgery functions as human enhancement is taken for granted. As Baker (2004) put it, "There are those who advocate analysis based on complex measurements to determine what implant shape or size is most desirable. I prefer to use my aesthetic sense when trying to provide balance to the patient's form" (p. 565). However, Henseler et al. (2013) found that "subjective breast assessment, even when it was conducted by experts, lacked accuracy and reproducibility" and advocated the use of digital imaging in breast implant surgery (p. 639). There is a chasm of difference between a cosmetologist and a cosmetic surgeon and taking the aesthetic stance can allow surgeons to overlook ethical considerations. Maintaining an aesthetic stance can also foster a kind of narcissism on the part of the surgeon. One plastic surgeon stopped seeing one of his patients because she had become too invested in the idea of perfecting herself; he explained, "I don't see her anymore. I don't want my signature on her body" (Pitts-Taylor, 2007, p. 2). It seems that the patient's body was no longer solely her own, but a canvas shared between the patient and surgeon. If one is to behave ethically in acts of human enhancement, the surgeon must take care that the patient also believes that the planned change will function as an enhancement; the surgeon cannot view the patient as merely another piece of his or her oeuvre, to be crafted in his or her vision of what constitutes real beauty. At the very least, the surgeon should listen to the patient's needs and desires. This does not always happen, according to interviews with patients, especially when the surgeon takes on an authoritative role (Hurst, 2012). Such behavior violates the ethical imperative of patient autonomy (Beauchamp & Childress, 2001). Aesthetic surgery has significant potential for harm, thus patients must be well informed concerning the risks and granted agency in the procedure. Aesthetic surgeons should be held to a high standard of ethics, and viewing patients as objects to be shaped rather than human beings who have a right to control what happens to their bodies falls short of this standard.

Finally, cosmetic surgeons must take care to avoid inflicting harm through their advertising practices. Sarwer and Crerand (2004) describe the kinds of advertising directed directly toward the potential patient: "Beautiful models, often in stages of undress, frequently are used to depict postoperative results, along with the promise of improved self-esteem, quality of life and a 'new you'" (p. 100). There is a fine line between promoting one's practice and contributing to the posthuman idea that the body is intrinsically flawed and in need of technological intervention. Researchers have noted that there is a correlation between media exposure of depictions of cosmetic surgery and contemplating surgery (Slevec & Tiggemann, 2010). Some have argued that advertisements for cosmetic surgery should be controlled (e.g., Clarke, Drake, Flatt, & Jebb, 2008), but this poses a practical problem of who is to do so. At the very least, advertisements should be ethical, but a content analysis of print advertisements for cosmetic surgeons conducted by Hennink-Kaminski, Reid, and King (2010) found some highly questionable practices, such as ignoring potential risks and side effects and using language that may go against AMA ethical guidelines. Another study by Spilson, Chung, Greenfield, and Walters (2002) also found a significant number of advertisements that were misleading and in violation of the code of ethics of the American Society of Plastic Surgeons, but note that "because such societies are not meant to police all advertisements, discretion is left up to the physician" (p. 1186). Perhaps it is time for more stringent oversight.

FUTURE RESEARCH DIRECTIONS

Enhancing and adorning our bodies has been an obsession for millennia. It may be that humans are slaves to an evolutionary imperative to pass on our genetic material to the highest quality mate(s) and the employment of aesthetic enhancement technologies is one means by which we make ourselves more attractive to the opposite sex as we compete with others who seek the same mates. If this is the case, individuals are likely to pursue this aim by any means possible, including surgical body enhancement to attain a form that society—and potential sexual partners—deem ideal. Thus the tension between the natural and the technological, especially as it relates to the ethical, will likely remain. Still, there are two areas in particular in which the ethical should come to the forefront: the question of who should be allowed to seek modification and the rise of medical tourism related to aesthetic enhancement technologies.

In some cases, aesthetic enhancement surgery is problematic because the body may not have finished growing yet. There is a range in which

women's breasts mature (see Sun et al., 2012), and not all are fully formed at the age of 18. Still, Cassidy (2010) reports that:

In large metropolitan areas . . . liposuction or breast augmentation have come into vogue as high school graduation presents. But it's not unheard of for 18-year-olds [in rural Pennsylvania] to get new breasts as a graduation gift—or in one York County woman's case, as an 18th birthday present. (p. G1)

There is also the issue that those younger than 18 are having procedures done on immature bodies. Jothilakshmi, Salvi, Hayden, and Bose-Haider (2009) note that girls as young as 11 years old are requesting labia reduction surgery and that "there is an increase in referral of patients requesting this procedure in recent years in our clinic, especially from young girls" (p. 55). Chauhan, Warner, and Adamson (2010) discuss rhinoplasty in patients as young as thirteen years old, a procedure that Joiner (2007) notes is most popular among teens. Despite age restrictions concerning aesthetic surgery on minors (see Neuhann-Lorenz, 2010), surgeons can still skirt these regulations. Zuckerman and Abraham (2008) note that although saline implants are approved for those over 18, "it is legal for doctors to perform breast augmentation using either type of implant for teens under 18, as an 'off-label' (i.e., not approved) use with parental consent" (p. 319). Legal, however, is not synonymous with ethical, and performing surgery on those who are still changing may cause further difficulties as the body continues to change. More research needs to be done concerning those who seek cosmetic surgery as adolescents and the motives of the cosmetic surgeons who perform those procedures. Joiner (2007) suggests that in the case of adolescents, aesthetic surgery should be delayed in order to assess the need for surgery.

Continuing along the lines of who should have cosmetic surgery, more research needs to be done on non-surgical interventions for those seeking aesthetic surgery. Although such approaches go against the promise of a quick fix provided by some cosmetic surgery practitioners, counseling may be a more ethical and beneficial strategy. As Zuckerman and Abraham (2008) suggest, "Many girls and women seeking cosmetic surgery might benefit more from therapeutic approaches aimed at improving self-esteem or general body image or those aimed at decreasing depression" (p. 321). As mentioned above, those who have Body Dysmorphic Disorder may have unrealistic expectations concerning cosmetic surgery. Indeed, Abraham and Zuckerman (2011) propose "standardized screening, including for body dysmorphic disorder and psychological problems, before cosmetic surgery" (p. 454). A technological fix cannot always cure pathologies of the psyche.

Medical tourism is when individuals travel to another part of the world to have medical procedures done. Some go to great lengths to pursue procedures that may be unattainable in their home country (see Connell, 2013). In her study of breast augmentation, one of Sanchez Taylor's (2012) participants reported that she chose to have her second surgery abroad because the shape that she wanted was not available in England (p. 463). That some would have the ability to travel and pay cash for desired enhancements, while others are left with only the legal options available to them within their home countries highlights the economic inequality of this practice. Moreover, there may be excellent medical reasons why some enhancement technologies are not available in one's country of residence. For example, polypropylene string breast implants were removed from the market due to complications (Reynolds, 2009). Still, those who wish to have abnormally large breasts may seek them out. Thus, one area of future research could be to examine the differences among the various international legal and ethical guidelines for cosmetic surgery practitioners. One could also consider the feasibility of establishing unified guidelines for aesthetic enhancement technologies so one cannot simply shop around for something that may be illegal in one's home country.

CONCLUSION

No matter what image of the body one can conceive, we remain firmly ensconced within our shell of flesh. Despite exultations concerning the potentials for a posthuman body, it is still a body that each individual inhabits. The body of Heidi Montag illustrates the hyperfeminine body, one that is constantly striving toward a particular ideal of beauty. Such an impulse represents an attempt to shape the body into an image of the self that exists in the mind—mind over matter in the truest sense. But such an aim will require considerably more work than technology can provide because one cannot solve all of the problems of the body using only medical tools.

In this chapter I have used the case of Heidi Montag to explore what Foucault (1985) calls "arts of existence," meaning:

Those intentional and voluntary actions by which men [and women] not only set themselves rules of conduct, but also seek to transform themselves, to change themselves in their singular being, and to make their life into an oeuvre that carries certain aesthetic values and meets certain stylistic criteria. (p. 10-11)

Through medical science one can create an almost limitless array of possibilities, but these are still constrained by the culture in which that individual lives (Larratt, 2002; Lunceford, 2012). Ethics too are locally created, which helps to explain why there remains such disagreement over the ethics of cosmetic surgery. For example, in the case of hymenoplasty, or hymen repair surgery, there are significant ethical considerations surrounding this procedure, as it is generally done in order to protect the female from honor killings if she is accused of being a non-virgin on her wedding night (see Bekker et al., 1996; Cindoglu, 1997; Cook & Dickens, 2009; Kammel, 2006; Kandela, 1996; Saharso, 2003). Through hymenoplasty, women can mimic the appearance of an intact hymen. For those in the West, such practices may seem necessary to protect young women from almost certain death at the hands of a barbarous and backward people. For those in countries in which honor killings are an accepted part of life, hymenoplasty may be an unforgivable means of deception and betrayal. But in each case, we see the possibilities that technology offers in changing the perceived nature of the body.

Beauty may be skin deep, but the practices of modifying the body can have severe consequences. When we talk about enhancement technologies, we must recognize their role in shaping and maintaining cultural norms. Those who already more fully embody cultural norms of beauty—in other words, white and slim—can get by with fewer enhancements to measure up. Those who do not—those who are of color, disabled, or who have a less desirable body type—will need to invest much more of their resources to do so. Racial differences often underscore important assumptions concerning these procedures, especially in describing perceived defects (see Munzer, 2011). But what these enhancement technologies suggest is that anyone can, with enough effort and surgical modification, fulfill these aesthetic imperatives. Biology is no longer destiny. However, access to human enhancement technologies are in no way guaranteed. As Stern (2013) writes, "Inventions designed to restore lives to normalcy are quickly harnessed to enhance lives beyond our ancestors' loftiest aspirations. What starts as live-saving inevitably becomes life-improving—if you've got the cash, of course."

In the case of cosmetic surgery the aesthetic, ethical, and financial are bound together; Martínez Lirola and Chovanec (2012) explain that "the surgically enhanced body is (1) the key to women's self-esteem, self-confidence and physical perfection, (2) the target of male voyeuristic desire and (3) the medium through which cosmetic surgery providers are able to generate their profit" (p. 503). To follow the framework proposed by Beauchamp and Childress (2001) of autonomy, nonmaleficence, beneficence, and justice requires

that those who engage in human enhancement technologies consider not only the implications for each individual patient, but for society as a whole. Such an approach on ethics goes well beyond the moment when the patient is placed under anesthesia and reaches into practices such as advertising, media appearances, informational literature, and counseling. It is not enough to say that surgically modifying an individual into a shape applauded by society counts for beneficence without considering one's role in creating those very ideals. Despite posthumanist sentiments that "physically modifying, physically changing the form of the human body – redesigning the human body is what we should be striving to do," (Stelarc, 1984, p. 17), one must tread carefully on the body because, as Lunceford (2012) observes, "The body is a wonderful medium on which we etch the imperatives of our culture, but it is a medium of limited quantity for each individual" (p. 21).

The story of Heidi Montag is interesting not only because of its excess, but because it is not yet finished. As I was finishing the final edits of this chapter, a news story came out that described Montag's regret over her surgeries, and that she had undergone breast reduction surgery, going from her previously enhanced F-cup to a C-cup. It seems that her feelings concerning her surgeries have evolved over the past few years. In 2012, she acknowledged that there were potential risks to her barrage of surgeries: "It could have been really disastrous. I lived and I learned, and I wouldn't really recommend it for other people" She also observed that there were downsides to the surgeries. "It was a lot harder than I thought it would be going through it - physically, mentally, emotionally and the recovery. I'm just glad it's done and that everything healed so well" ("Montag wouldn't recommend," 2012). In 2013, she was far less celebratory concerning the surgeries. Montag states, "[I] let myself become really insecure and I had a doctor that made it sound really easy and a quick fix and it ended up being a hard road and I inflicted a lot of pain, mentally and physically, on myself. If I had to go back and do it again I definitely wouldn't and I would not recommend that" ("I wish I'd Never," 2013).

Montag's story provides a cautionary tale concerning aesthetic enhancement technologies and direction to those who perform them. Montag now states that "my experience should tell other young women that beauty and confidence comes from within, it does not matter what you do on the outside if you are not happy and do not feel beautiful and secure and confident on the inside then no amount of surgery will change that or make you happier" ("I wish I'd Never," 2013). Yet despite Montag's change of heart, people will continue to seek enhancement and surgeons will be happy to perform them. The best we can do, then, is to use these enhancement technologies ethically, both for the individuals and society as a whole. Aesthetic enhancement is a possibility for a wide range of people with defects both real and imagined and that possibility has implications for how we as a society view beauty. In his discussion of the history of plastic surgery, Stern (2013) notes, "What began as a desperate measure for disfigured soldiers is now a routine procedure for anybody in want of a self-confidence pick-me-up." But Montag now recognizes that such procedures are far from routine—they change everything: "Once you get surgery you can never be the same size you were, you can never really take it back so it is something you need to think about seriously" ("I wish I'd Never," 2013).

Still, Montag's lament that one cannot go back to his or her original state misses the point of the posthuman stance that cosmetic surgery promotes. Changing the body is not only possible, but desirable. Even if the body is changed forever, one can simply keep changing the body further through the application of more technology until reaching a desired level of perfection. From this perspective the original state was undesirable in the first place. But is such a stance ethical? People have a right to their bodies and to alter them as desired, so long as the patient is making a well-informed decision. The surgeons, however, must remain vigilant to avoid causing harm to either the patient or society as a whole. They must also take care to respect the autonomy of the patient by not instilling within the patient the very pathologies that they profess to cure. This is a difficult balancing act; finding the correct equilibrium between individual autonomy and justice for society as a whole is a task that has plagued ethical thought for centuries. But, as the case of cosmetic surgery demonstrates, one cannot simply choose one or the other. The individual and society are both intertwined. Each affects and alters the other in ways that go far beneath the surface of the skin.

REFERENCES

Abraham, A., & Zuckerman, D. (2011). Adolescents, celebrity worship, and cosmetic surgery. *The Journal of Adolescent Health*, *49*(5), 453–454. doi:10.1016/j.jadohealth.2011.08.014 PMID:22018558

Abramowitz, J. S., & Moore, E. L. (2007). An experimental analysis of hypochondriasis. *Behaviour Research and Therapy*, *45*(3), 413–424. doi:10.1016/j.brat.2006.04.005 PMID:16769034

Aubrey, J. S. (2007). The impact of sexually objectifying media exposure on negative body emotions and sexual self-perceptions: Investigating the mediating role of body self-consciousness. *Mass Communication & Society*, *10*(1), 1–23. doi:10.1080/15205430709337002

Babcock, S. (2010, February 20). Plastic front creates poor perfection. *Spokesman Review*, p. v1.

Baker, J. L. (2004). Choosing breast implant size: A matter of aesthetics. *Aesthetic Surgery Journal*, *24*(6), 565–566. doi:10.1016/j.asj.2004.09.009 PMID:19336211

Baker-Sperry, L., & Grauerholz, L. (2003). The pervasiveness and persistence of the feminine beauty ideal in children's fairy tales. *Gender & Society*, *17*(5), 711–726. doi:10.1177/0891243203255605

Balkany, T., Hodges, A. V., & Goodman, K. W. (1996). Ethics of cochlear implantation in young children. *Otolaryngology - Head and Neck Surgery*, *114*(6), 748–755. doi:10.1016/S0194-5998(96)70097-9 PMID:8643298

Barber, N. (1995). The evolutionary psychology of physical attractiveness: Sexual selection and human morphology. *Ethology and Sociobiology*, *16*(5), 395–424. doi:10.1016/0162-3095(95)00068-2

Baudrillard, J. (1988). The ecstasy of communication. (B. Schutze & C. Schutze, Trans.). New York: Semiotext(e).

Baudrillard, J. (1994). *Simulacra and simulation* (S. F. Glaser, Trans.). Ann Arbor, MI: University of Michigan Press.

Baumann, L. (2012). Ethics in cosmetic dermatology. *Clinics in Dermatology*, *30*(5), 522–527. doi:10.1016/j.clindermatol.2011.06.023 PMID:22902224

Baumann, S. (2008). The moral underpinnings of beauty: A meaning-based explanation for light and dark complexions in advertising. *Poetics*, *36*(1), 2–23. doi:10.1016/j.poetic.2007.11.002

Bazzini, D., Curtin, L., Joslin, S., Regan, S., & Martz, D. (2010). Do animated Disney characters portray and promote the beauty-goodness stereotype? *Journal of Applied Social Psychology*, *40*(10), 2687–2709. doi:10.1111/j.1559-1816.2010.00676.x

Beauchamp, T. L., & Childress, J. F. (2001). *Principles of biomedical ethics* (5th ed.). New York, NY: Oxford University Press.

Bekker, M. H. J., Rademakers, J., Mouthaan, I., Neef, M. D., Huisman, W. M., Van Zandvoort, H., & Emans, A. (1996). Reconstructing hymens or constructing sexual inequality? Service provision to Islamic young women coping with the demand to be a virgin. *Journal of Community & Applied Social Psychology*, *6*(5), 329–334. doi:10.1002/(SICI)1099-1298(199612)6:5<329::AID-CASP383>3.0.CO;2-B

Berman, L. (2010, February 3). Heidi Montag throws a curve at young girls, obsession with perfection reinforces women's needless body insecurities. *Chicago Sun Times*, p. C4.

Berry, M. G., Cucchiara, V., & Davies, D. M. (2011). Breast augmentation: Part III—preoperative considerations and planning. *Journal of Plastic, Reconstructive & Aesthetic Surgery; JPRAS*, *64*(11), 1401–1409.

Black, E. (1970). The second persona. *The Quarterly Journal of Speech*, *56*, 109–119. doi:10.1080/00335637009382992

Blum, V. L. (2003). *Flesh wounds: The culture of cosmetic surgery*. Berkeley, CA: University of California Press.

Blum, V. L. (2005). Becoming the other woman: The psychic drama of cosmetic surgery. *Frontiers: A Journal of Women Studies, 26*(2), 104-131.

Bordo, S. (1993). *Unbearable weight: Feminism, Western culture, and the body*. Berkeley, CA: University of California Press.

Burke, K. (1966). *Language as symbolic action*. Berkeley, CA: University of California Press.

Buwalda, F. M., Bouman, T. K., & van Duijn, M. A. J. (2007). Psychoeducation for hypochondriasis: A comparison of a cognitive-behavioural approach and a problem-solving approach. *Behaviour Research and Therapy*, *45*(5), 887–899. doi:10.1016/j.brat.2006.08.004 PMID:17055449

Camilli, D. (2010, April 24). Montag is a cheap, plastic pool float after surgery. *The Gazette (Montreal),* p. E5.

Cantor, J. (2005). Cosmetic dermatology and physicians' ethical obligations: More than just hope in a jar. *Seminars in Cutaneous Medicine and Surgery, 24*(3), 155–160. doi:10.1016/j. sder.2005.04.005 PMID:16202953

Cartwright, R., & Cardozo, L. (2008). Cosmetic vulvovaginal surgery. *Obstetrics, Gynaecology and Reproductive Medicine, 18*(10), 285–286. doi:10.1016/j.ogrm.2008.07.008

Cassidy, S. (2010, January 24). Teens, young adults cut into cosmetic-surgery statistics, defining beauty breast wishes parental pressure? For the sport of it males do it, too. *Sunday News,* p. G1.

Chan, J. K.-K., Jones, S. M., & Heywood, A. J. (2011). Body dysmorphia, self-mutilation and the reconstructive surgeon. *Journal of Plastic, Reconstructive & Aesthetic Surgery; JPRAS, 64*(1), 4–8. doi:10.1016/j.bjps.2010.03.029 PMID:20392680

Chauhan, N., Warner, J., & Adamson, P. A. (2010). Adolescent rhinoplasty: Challenges and psychosocial and clinical outcomes. *Aesthetic Plastic Surgery, 34,* 510–516. doi:10.1007/s00266-010-9489-7 PMID:20333519

Cindoglu, D. (1997). Virginity tests and artificial virginity in modern Turkish medicine. *Women's Studies International Forum, 20*(2), 253–261. doi:10.1016/S0277-5395(96)00096-9

Clarke, J., Drake, L., Flatt, S., & Jebb, P. (2008). Physical perfection for sale. *Nursing Standard, 23*(8), 26–27.

Comiskey, C. (2004). Cosmetic surgery in Paris in 1926: The case of the amputated leg. *Journal of Women's History, 16*(3), 30–54. doi:10.1353/jowh.2004.0059

Connell, J. (2013). Contemporary medical tourism: Conceptualisation, culture and commodification. *Tourism Management, 34,* 1–13. doi:10.1016/j.tourman.2012.05.009

Connor, D. J. (2011). Questioning normal: Seeing children first and labels second. *School Talk: Between the Ideal and the Real World of Teaching, 16,* 1–3.

Cook, R. J., & Dickens, B. M. (2009). Hymen reconstruction: Ethical and legal issues. *International Journal of Gynaecology and Obstetrics: the Official Organ of the International Federation of Gynaecology and Obstetrics, 107*(3), 266–269. doi:10.1016/j.ijgo.2009.07.032 PMID:19717149

Couser, G. T. (2011). What disability studies has to offer medical education. *The Journal of Medical Humanities, 32*(1), 21–30. doi:10.1007/s10912-010-9125-1 PMID:21042839

Davis, D., & Vernon, M. L. (2002). Sculpting the body beautiful: Attachment style, neuroticism, and use of cosmetic surgeries. *Sex Roles, 47,* 129–138. doi:10.1023/A:1021043021624

de Andrade, D. D. (2010). On norms and bodies: Findings from field research on cosmetic surgery in Rio de Janeiro, Brazil. *Reproductive Health Matters, 18*(35), 74–83. doi:10.1016/S0968-8080(10)35519-4 PMID:20541086

De Roubaix, J. A. M. (2011). Beneficence, nonmaleficence, distributive justice and respect for patient autonomy—Reconcilable ends in aesthetic surgery? *Journal of Plastic, Reconstructive & Aesthetic Surgery; JPRAS, 64*(1), 11–16. doi:10.1016/j.bjps.2010.03.034 PMID:20457018

Derakhshani, T. (2009, August 13). Sideshow: Low-key farewell to Hughes. *Philadelphia Inquirer,* p. E02.

Dietrich, D. (1997). Refashioning the techno-erotic woman: Gender and textuality in the cybercultural matrix. In S. Jones (Ed.), *Virtual culture: Identity and communication in cybersociety* (pp. 169–184). London: Sage Publications.

Dion, K., Berscheid, E., & Walster, E. (1972). What is beautiful is good. *Journal of Personality and Social Psychology*, *24*(3), 285–290. doi:10.1037/h0033731 PMID:4655540

Dixson, B., Grimshaw, G., Linklater, W., & Dixson, A. (2011). Eye-tracking of men's preferences for waist-to-hip ratio and breast size of women. *Archives of Sexual Behavior*, *40*(1), 43–50. doi:10.1007/s10508-009-9523-5 PMID:19688590

Dohnt, H., & Tiggemann, M. (2006). Body image concerns in young girls: The role of peers and media prior to adolescence. *Journal of Youth and Adolescence*, *35*(2), 135–145. doi:10.1007/s10964-005-9020-7

Dolmage, J. T. (2013). *Disability rhetoric*. Syracuse, NY: Syracuse University Press.

Dyens, O. (2001). *Metal and flesh: The evolution of man: Technology takes over*. Cambridge, MA: MIT Press.

Eagly, A. H., Ashmore, R. D., Makhijani, M. G., & Longo, L. C. (1991). What is beautiful is good, but... A meta-analytic review of research on the physical attractiveness stereotype. *Psychological Bulletin*, *110*(1), 109–128. doi:10.1037/0033-2909.110.1.109

Ericksen, W. L., & Billick, S. B. (2012). Psychiatric issues in cosmetic plastic surgery. *The Psychiatric Quarterly*, *83*(3), 343–352. doi:10.1007/s11126-012-9204-8 PMID:22252848

Fergus, T. A., & Valentiner, D. P. (2009). Re-examining the domain of hypochondriasis: Comparing the Illness Attitudes Scale to other approaches. *Journal of Anxiety Disorders*, *23*(6), 760–766. doi:10.1016/j.janxdis.2009.02.016 PMID:19339156

Ferguson, P. M., & Nusbaum, E. (2012). Disability studies: What is it and what difference does it make? *Research and Practice for Persons with Severe Disabilities*, *37*(2), 70–80. doi:10.2511/027494812802573530

Foucault, M. (1985). *The history of sexuality: The use of pleasure* (R. Hurley, Trans.). New York, NY: Vintage Books.

Frederick, D. A., Peplau, A., & Lever, J. (2008). The Barbie mystique: Satisfaction with breast size and shape across the lifespan. *International Journal of Sexual Health*, *20*(3), 200–211. doi:10.1080/19317610802240170

Furnham, A., & Swami, V. (2007). Perception of female buttocks and breast size in profile. *Social Behavior and Personality*, *35*(1), 1–7. doi:10.2224/sbp.2007.35.1.1

Garcia, J. (2010, January 25). Obsessed with being perfect. *People*, *73*, 80–88.

Garnham, B. (2013). Designing older rather than denying ageing: Problematizing anti-ageing discourse in relation to cosmetic surgery undertaken by older people. *Journal of Aging Studies*, *27*(1), 38–46. doi:10.1016/j.jaging.2012.11.001 PMID:23273555

Gillin, J. (2010, August 26). Montag wants implants out. *St. Petersburg Times*, p. 2B.

Graham, E. (1999). Cyborgs or goddesses? Becoming divine in a cyberfeminist age. *Information Communication and Society*, *2*(4), 419–438. doi:10.1080/136911899359484

Graham, E. L. (2002). *Representations of the post/ human: Monsters, aliens, and others in popular culture*. New Brunswick, NJ: Rutgers University Press.

Greeven, A., van Balkom, A. J. L. M., van der Leeden, R., Merkelbach, J. W., van den Heuvel, O. A., & Spinhoven, P. (2009). Cognitive behavioral therapy versus paroxetine in the treatment of hypochondriasis: An 18-month naturalistic follow-up. *Journal of Behavior Therapy and Experimental Psychiatry*, *40*(3), 487–496. doi:10.1016/j.jbtep.2009.06.005 PMID:19616195

Gupta, S. (2012). Ethical and legal issues in aesthetic surgery. *Indian Journal of Plastic Surgery*, *45*(3), 547–549. doi:10.4103/0970-0358.105973 PMID:23450235

Haraway, D. J. (1991). *Simians, cyborgs, and women: The reinvention of nature*. New York: Routledge.

Hargreaves, D. A., & Tiggemann, M. (2009). Muscular ideal media images and men's body image: Social comparison processing and individual vulnerability. *Psychology of Men & Masculinity*, *10*(2), 109–119. doi:10.1037/a0014691

Harper, B., & Tiggemann, M. (2008). The effect of thin ideal media images on women's self-objectification, mood, and body image. *Sex Roles*, *58*(9), 649–657. doi:10.1007/s11199-007-9379-x

Harris, D. L., & Carr, A. T. (2001). The Derriford appearance scale (DAS59): A new psychometric scale for the evaluation of patients with disfigurements and aesthetic problems of appearance. *British Journal of Plastic Surgery*, *54*(3), 216–222. doi:10.1054/bjps.2001.3559 PMID:11254413

Heidi says she'll get more done, Will do some maintenance. (2010, February 15). *Chicago Sun Times*, p. 31.

Hennink-Kaminski, H., Reid, L. N., & King, K. W. (2010). The content of cosmetic surgery advertisements placed in large city magazines, 1985-2004. *Journal of Current Issues & Research in Advertising*, *32*(2), 41–57. doi:10.1080/10641734.2010.10505284

Henseler, H., Smith, J., Bowman, A., Khambay, B. S., Ju, X., Ayoub, A., & Ray, A. K. (2013). Subjective versus objective assessment of breast reconstruction. *Journal of Plastic, Reconstructive & Aesthetic Surgery; JPRAS*, *66*(5), 634–639. doi:10.1016/j.bjps.2013.01.006 PMID:23402935

Heyes, C. J. (2007). Cosmetic surgery and the televisual makeover. *Feminist Media Studies*, *7*(1), 17–32. doi:10.1080/14680770601103670

Hogle, L. F. (2005). Enhancement technologies and the body. *Annual Review of Anthropology*, *34*, 695–716. doi:10.1146/annurev.anthro.33.070203.144020

Holliday, R., & Sanchez Taylor, J. (2006). Aesthetic surgery as false beauty. *Feminist Theory*, *7*(2), 179–195. doi:10.1177/1464700106064418

Hope, D. A., & Mindell, J. A. (1994). Global social skill ratings: Measures of social behavior or physical attractiveness? *Behaviour Research and Therapy*, *32*(4), 463–469. doi:10.1016/0005-7967(94)90011-6 PMID:8192645

Hurst, R. A. J. (2012). Negotiating femininity with and through mother-daughter and patient-surgeon relationships in cosmetic surgery narratives. *Women's Studies International Forum*, *35*(6), 447–457. doi:10.1016/j.wsif.2012.09.008

Husted, B. (2009, August 14). Heidi 'n' seek: Playboy, hubby reveal a bit about her. *Denver Post*, p. B03.

I wish I'd NEVER had plastic surgery: Heidi Montag reveals her regret as she unveils new bikini body after breast reduction. (2013, November 28). *MailOnline*. Retrieved December 27, 2013, from http://www.dailymail.co.uk/tvshowbiz/article-2514988/Heidi-Montag-talks-plastic-surgery-regrets-breast-reduction.html

Jeffreys, S. (2005). *Beauty and misogyny: Harmful cultural practices in the West*. London: Routledge.

Jerslev, A. (2006). The mediated body. *Nordicom Review*, *27*(2), 133–151.

Johnson, S. K., Podratz, K. E., Dipboye, R. L., & Gibbons, E. (2010). Physical attractiveness biases in ratings of employment suitability: Tracking down the beauty is beastly effect. *The Journal of Social Psychology*, *150*(3), 301–318. doi:10.1080/00224540903365414 PMID:20575336

Joiner, T. E. Jr. (2007). Aesthetic surgery in adolescents: A suggestion informed by adolescent psychology. *Aesthetic Surgery Journal*, *27*(4), 419–420. doi:10.1016/j.asj.2007.06.001 PMID:19341670

Jones, B. C., Little, A. C., Penton-Voak, I. S., Tiddeman, B. P., Burt, D. M., & Perrett, D. I. (2001). Facial symmetry and judgements of apparent health: Support for a good genes explanation of the attractiveness-symmetry relationship. *Evolution and Human Behavior*, *22*(6), 417–429. doi:10.1016/S1090-5138(01)00083-6

Jordan, J. (2004). The rhetorical limits of the plastic body. *The Quarterly Journal of Speech*, *90*(3), 327–358. doi:10.1080/0033563042000255543

Jothilakshmi, P. K., Salvi, N. R., Hayden, B. E., & Bose-Haider, B. (2009). Labial reduction in adolescent population—A case series study. *Journal of Pediatric and Adolescent Gynecology*, *22*(1), 53–55. doi:10.1016/j.jpag.2008.03.008 PMID:19241623

Kammel, K. (2006). The cost of virginity: Virginity tests and hymen reconstruction. *DePaul Health Law Institute Newsletter*, *2*(3), 3.

Kanazawa, S. (2011). Intelligence and physical attractiveness. *Intelligence*, *39*(1), 7–14. doi:10.1016/j.intell.2010.11.003

Kanazawa, S., & Kovar, J. L. (2004). Why beautiful people are more intelligent. *Intelligence*, *32*(3), 227–243. doi:10.1016/j.intell.2004.03.003

Kandela, P. (1996). Egypt's trade in hymen repair. *Lancet*, *347*(9015), 1615. doi:10.1016/S0140-6736(96)91096-X PMID:8667878

Kellett, S., Clarke, S., & McGill, P. (2008). Outcomes from psychological assessment regarding recommendations for cosmetic surgery. *Journal of Plastic, Reconstructive & Aesthetic Surgery; JPRAS*, *61*(5), 512–517. doi:10.1016/j.bjps.2007.08.025 PMID:18316256

Lane, H., & Bahan, B. (1998). Ethics of cochlear implantation in young children: A review and reply from a deaf-world perspective. *Otolaryngology - Head and Neck Surgery*, *119*(4), 297–313. doi:10.1016/S0194-5998(98)70070-1 PMID:9781982

Langlois, F., & Ladouceur, R. (2004). Adaptation of a GAD treatment for hypochondriasis. *Cognitive and Behavioral Practice*, *11*(4), 393–404. doi:10.1016/S1077-7229(04)80056-7

Larratt, S. (2002). *ModCon: The secret world of extreme body modification*. BMEbooks.

Lin, T. J. (2010). Evolution of cosmetics: Increased need for experimental clinical medicine. *Journal of Experimental & Clinical Medicine*, *2*(2), 49–52. doi:10.1016/S1878-3317(10)60009-5

Lorenzo, G. L., Biesanz, J. C., & Human, L. J. (2010). What is beautiful is good and more accurately understood: Physical attractiveness and accuracy in first impressions of personality. *Psychological Science, 21*(12), 1777–1782. doi:10.1177/0956797610388048 PMID:21051521

Lovas, D. A., & Barsky, A. J. (2010). Mindfulness-based cognitive therapy for hypochondriasis, or severe health anxiety: A pilot study. *Journal of Anxiety Disorders, 24*(8), 931–935. doi:10.1016/j.janxdis.2010.06.019 PMID:20650601

Lunceford, B. (2008). The body and the sacred in the digital age: Thoughts on posthuman sexuality. *Theology & Sexuality, 15*(1), 77–96. doi:10.1558/tse.v15i1.77

Lunceford, B. (2009). Reconsidering technology adoption and resistance: Observations of a semi-luddite. *Explorations in Media Ecology, 8*(1), 29–48.

Lunceford, B. (2010). Sex in the digital age: Media ecology and Megan's law. *Explorations in Media Ecology, 9*(4), 239–244.

Lunceford, B. (2012). Posthuman visions: Creating the technologized body. *Explorations in Media Ecology, 11*(1), 7–25. doi:10.1386/eme.11.1.7_1

Luo, W. (2013). Aching for the altered body: Beauty economy and Chinese women's consumption of cosmetic surgery. *Women's Studies International Forum, 38*, 1–10. doi:10.1016/j.wsif.2013.01.013

Maltby, J., & Day, L. (2011). Celebrity worship and incidence of elective cosmetic surgery: Evidence of a link among young adults. *The Journal of Adolescent Health, 49*(5), 483–489. doi:10.1016/j.jadohealth.2010.12.014 PMID:22018562

Marcus, D. K. (1999). The cognitive-behavioral model of hypochondriasis: Misinformation and triggers. *Journal of Psychosomatic Research, 47*(1), 79–91. doi:10.1016/S0022-3999(99)00008-2 PMID:10511423

Marcus, D. K., Gurley, J. R., Marchi, M. M., & Bauer, C. (2007). Cognitive and perceptual variables in hypochondriasis and health anxiety: A systematic review. *Clinical Psychology Review, 27*(2), 127–139. doi:10.1016/j.cpr.2006.09.003 PMID:17084495

Markey, C. N., & Markey, P. M. (2010). A correlational and experimental examination of reality television viewing and interest in cosmetic surgery. *Body Image, 7*(2), 165–171. doi:10.1016/j.bodyim.2009.10.006 PMID:20089464

Martínez Lirola, M., & Chovanec, J. (2012). The dream of a perfect body come true: Multimodality in cosmetic surgery advertising. *Discourse & Society, 23*(5), 487–507. doi:10.1177/0957926512452970

McLuhan, M. (1994). *Understanding media: The extensions of man.* Cambridge, MA: MIT Press.

Meningaud, J.-P., Benadiba, L., Servant, J.-M., Herve, C., Bertrand, J.-C., & Pelicier, Y. (2003). Depression, anxiety and quality of life: Outcome 9 months after facial cosmetic surgery. *Journal of Cranio-Maxillo-Facial Surgery, 31*(1), 46–50. doi:10.1016/S1010-5182(02)00159-2 PMID:12553927

Millar, M. S. (1998). *Cracking the gender code: Who rules the wired world?* Toronto, Canada: Second Story Press.

Montag wouldn't recommend multiple plastic surgeries. (2012, August 3). *Breakingnews.ie.* Retrieved December 27, 2013, from http://www.breakingnews.ie/showbiz/montag-wouldnt-recommend-multiple-plastic-surgeries-561757.html

Munzer, S. R. (2011). Cosmetic surgery, racial identity, and aesthetics. *Configurations*, *19*(2), 243–286. doi:10.1353/con.2011.0012

Murphy, T. F. (2009). Choosing disabilities and enhancements in children: A choice too far? *Reproductive Biomedicine Online*, *18*(Supplement 1), 43–49. doi:10.1016/S1472-6483(10)60115-0 PMID:19281664

Negroponte, N. (1995). *Being digital*. New York: Knopf.

Neuhann-Lorenz, C. (2010). Adolescent rhinoplasty: Challenges and psychosocial and clinical outcomes. *Aesthetic Plastic Surgery*, *34*, 517–518. doi:10.1007/s00266-010-9493-y PMID:20333515

Nietzsche, F. W. (1978). *Thus spoke Zarathustra: A book for all and none* (W. Kaufmann, Trans.). New York: Penguin Books.

Nisbett, R. E., & Wilson, T. D. (1977). The halo effect: Evidence for unconscious alteration of judgments. *Journal of Personality and Social Psychology*, *35*(4), 250–256. doi:10.1037/0022-3514.35.4.250

Pitts-Taylor, V. (2007). *Surgery junkies: Wellness and pathology in cosmetic culture*. New Brunswick, NJ: Rutgers University Press.

Polonijo, A. N., & Carpiano, R. M. (2008). Representations of cosmetic surgery and emotional health in women's magazines in Canada. *Women's Health Issues*, *18*(6), 463–470. doi:10.1016/j.whi.2008.07.004 PMID:19041597

Reynolds, A. (2009). The augmented breast. *Radiologic Technology*, *80*(3), 241M–259M. PMID:19153201

Ruetzler, T., Taylor, J., Reynolds, D., Baker, W., & Killen, C. (2012). What is professional attire today? A conjoint analysis of personal presentation attributes. *International Journal of Hospitality Management*, *31*(3), 937–943. doi:10.1016/j.ijhm.2011.11.001

Russell, C. (2013, December 3). The stars who regret going under the knife. *Irish Independent*, p. 36.

Saharso, S. (2003). Feminist ethics, autonomy and the politics of multiculturalism. *Feminist Theory*, *4*(2), 199–215. doi:10.1177/14647001030042007

Sanchez Taylor, J. (2012). Fake breasts and power: Gender, class and cosmetic surgery. *Women's Studies International Forum*, *35*(6), 458–466. doi:10.1016/j.wsif.2012.09.003

Sarwer, D. B., & Crerand, C. E. (2004). Body image and cosmetic medical treatments. *Body Image*, *1*(1), 99–111. doi:10.1016/S1740-1445(03)00003-2 PMID:18089144

Shields, V. R., & Heinecken, D. (2001). *Measuring up: How advertising affects self-image*. Philadelphia, PA: University of Pennsylvania Press.

Simon, G. E., Gureje, O., & Fullerton, C. (2001). Course of hypochondriasis in an international primary care study. *General Hospital Psychiatry*, *23*(2), 51–55. doi:10.1016/S0163-8343(01)00115-3 PMID:11313070

Slevec, J., & Tiggemann, M. (2010). Attitudes toward cosmetic surgery in middle-aged women: Body image, aging anxiety, and the media. *Psychology of Women Quarterly*, *34*(1), 65–74. doi:10.1111/j.1471-6402.2009.01542.x

Smirnova, M. H. (2012). A will to youth: The woman's anti-aging elixir. *Social Science & Medicine*, *75*(7), 1236–1243. doi:10.1016/j.socscimed.2012.02.061 PMID:22742924

Solvi, A. S., Foss, K., von Soest, T., Roald, H. E., Skolleborg, K. C., & Holte, A. (2010). Motivational factors and psychological processes in cosmetic breast augmentation surgery. *Journal of Plastic, Reconstructive & Aesthetic Surgery; JPRAS, 63*(4), 673–680. doi:10.1016/j.bjps.2009.01.024 PMID:19268646

Spilson, S. V., Chung, K. C., Greenfield, M. L. V. H., & Walters, M. (2002). Are plastic surgery advertisements conforming to the ethical codes of the American society of plastic surgeons? *Plastic and Reconstructive Surgery, 109*(3), 1181–1186. doi:10.1097/00006534-200203000-00063 PMID:11884856

Stelarc. (1984). An interview with Stelarc. In J. D. Paffrath & Stelarc (Eds.), *Obsolete body: Suspensions: Stelarc* (pp. 16-17). Davis, CA: J.P. Publications.

Stern, M. J. (2013, May 6). You are already enhanced: Everyday technologies give us superpowers that would make our ancestors wonder if we're entirely human. *Slate*. Retrieved December 27, 2013, from http://www.slate.com/articles/health_and_science/superman/2013/05/history_of_human_enhancement_how_plastic_surgery_birth_control_aspirin_ivf.single.html

Stewart, C. (2010, February 14). Montag took wrong road with plastic surgeries. *Orange County Register,* p. K.

Stice, E., Spangler, D., & Agras, W. S. (2001). Exposure to media-portrayed thin-ideal images adversely affects vulnerable girls: A longitudinal experiment. *Journal of Social and Clinical Psychology, 20*(3), 270–288. doi:10.1521/jscp.20.3.270.22309

Sullivan, D. A. (2000). *Cosmetic surgery: The cutting edge of commercial medicine in America.* New Brunswick, NJ: Rutgers University Press.

Sun, Y., Tao, F.-B., Su, P.-Y., Mai, J.-C., Shi, H.-J., & Han, Y.-T. et al. (2012). National estimates of the pubertal milestones among urban and rural Chinese girls. *The Journal of Adolescent Health, 51*(3), 279–284. doi:10.1016/j.jadohealth.2011.12.019 PMID:22921139

Swami, V. (2009). Body appreciation, media influence, and weight status predict consideration of cosmetic surgery among female undergraduates. *Body Image, 6*(4), 315–317. doi:10.1016/j.bodyim.2009.07.001 PMID:19656747

Swami, V., Campana, A. N. N. B., Ferreira, L., Barrett, S., Harris, A. S., & Tavares, M. C. G. C. F. (2011). The acceptance of cosmetic surgery scale: Initial examination of its factor structure and correlates among Brazilian adults. *Body Image, 8*(2), 179–185. PMID:21354875

Swami, V., Taylor, R., & Carvalho, C. (2009). Acceptance of cosmetic surgery and celebrity worship: Evidence of associations among female undergraduates. *Personality and Individual Differences, 47*(8), 869–872. doi:10.1016/j.paid.2009.07.006

Taleporos, G., & McCabe, M. P. (2002). Body image and physical disability - Personal perspectives. *Social Science & Medicine, 54*(6), 971–980. doi:10.1016/S0277-9536(01)00069-7 PMID:11996029

Tignol, J., Biraben-Gotzamanis, L., Martin-Guehl, C., Grabot, D., & Aouizerate, B. (2007). Body dysmorphic disorder and cosmetic surgery: Evolution of 24 subjects with a minimal defect in appearance 5 years after their request for cosmetic surgery. *European Psychiatry, 22*(8), 520–524. doi:10.1016/j.eurpsy.2007.05.003 PMID:17900876

Turkle, S. (1995). *Life on the screen: Identity in the age of the Internet.* New York: Simon & Schuster.

Veale, D., Ellison, N., Werner, T. G., Dodhia, R., Serfaty, M. A., & Clarke, A. (2012). Development of a cosmetic procedure screening questionnaire (COPS) for body dysmorphic disorder. *Journal of Plastic, Reconstructive & Aesthetic Surgery; JPRAS, 65*(4), 530–532. doi:10.1016/j.bjps.2011.09.007 PMID:22000332

Visser, S., & Bouman, T. K. (2001). The treatment of hypochondriasis: Exposure plus response prevention vs cognitive therapy. *Behaviour Research and Therapy, 39*(4), 423–442. doi:10.1016/S0005-7967(00)00022-X PMID:11280341

von Soest, T., Kvalem, I. L., Roald, H. E., & Skolleborg, K. C. (2009). The effects of cosmetic surgery on body image, self-esteem, and psychological problems. *Journal of Plastic, Reconstructive & Aesthetic Surgery; JPRAS, 62*(10), 1238–1244. doi:10.1016/j.bjps.2007.12.093 PMID:18595791

von Soest, T., Kvalem, I. L., Skolleborg, K. C., & Roald, H. E. (2009). Cosmetic surgery and the relationship between appearance satisfaction and extraversion: Testing a transactional model of personality. *Journal of Research in Personality, 43*(6), 1017–1025. doi:10.1016/j.jrp.2009.07.001

Walker, J., Vincent, N., Furer, P., Cox, B., & Kevin, K. (1999). Treatment preference in hypochondriasis. *Journal of Behavior Therapy and Experimental Psychiatry, 30*(4), 251–258. doi:10.1016/S0005-7916(99)00027-0 PMID:10759322

Ward, C. (2010, April 14). From the girl next door to freaky fake & she's not done with the surgery yet, exclusive fame-hungry Heidi Montag. *The Mirror (Stafford, Tex.)*, 24–25.

Weck, F., Neng, J. M. B., Richtberg, S., & Stangier, U. (2012a). Dysfunctional beliefs about symptoms and illness in patients with hypochondriasis. *Psychosomatics, 53*(2), 148–154. doi:10.1016/j.psym.2011.11.007 PMID:22424163

Weck, F., Neng, J. M. B., Richtberg, S., & Stangier, U. (2012b). The restrictive concept of good health in patients with hypochondriasis. *Journal of Anxiety Disorders, 26*(8), 792–798. doi:10.1016/j.janxdis.2012.07.001 PMID:23023159

Wiggins, J. S., Wiggins, N., & Conger, J. C. (1968). Correlates of heterosexual somatic preference. *Journal of Personality and Social Psychology, 10*(1), 82–90. doi:10.1037/h0026394 PMID:4386664

Wolf, N. (1991). *The beauty myth: How images of beauty are used against women*. New York, W.: Morrow.

Zuckerman, D., & Abraham, A. (2008). Teenagers and cosmetic surgery: Focus on breast augmentation and liposuction. *The Journal of Adolescent Health, 43*(4), 318–324. doi:10.1016/j.jadohealth.2008.04.018 PMID:18809128

Zwang, G. (2011). Vulvar reconstruction: The exploitation of an ignorance. *Sexologies, 20*(2), 81–87. doi:10.1016/j.sexol.2010.10.003

ADDITIONAL READING

Atiyeh, B. S., Rubeiz, M. T., & Hayek, S. N. (2008). Aesthetic/cosmetic surgery and ethical challenges. *Aesthetic Plastic Surgery, 32*(6), 829–839. doi:10.1007/s00266-008-9246-3 PMID:18820963

Blum, V. L. (2007). Objects of love: I want a famous face and the illusions of star culture. *Configurations, 15*(1), 33–53. doi:10.1353/con.0.0025

Davis, K. (1995). *Reshaping the female body: The dilemma of cosmetic surgery*. New York: Routledge.

Davis, K. (2003). *Dubious equalities and embodied differences: Cultural studies on cosmetic surgery*. Lanham, MD: Rowman & Littlefield.

Devereaux, M. (2013). Is medical aesthetics really medical? In P. Z. Brand (Ed.), *Beauty unlimited* (pp. 175–191). Bloomington: In Indiana University Press.

Faber, A. (2002). Saint Orlan: Ritual as violent spectacle and cultural criticism. *TDR: The Drama Review*, *46*(1), 85–92. doi:10.1162/105420402753555868

Gilman, S. L. (1999). *Making the body beautiful: A cultural history of aesthetic surgery*. Princeton, NJ: Princeton University Press.

Grosz, E. A. (1994). *Volatile bodies: Toward a corporeal feminism*. Crows Nest, NSW: Allen & Unwin.

Heyes, C. J. (2007). *Self transformations: Foucault, ethics, and normalized bodies*. New York: Oxford University Press. doi:10.1093/acprof:oso/9780195310535.001.0001

Hyde, M. J. (2010). *Perfection: Coming to terms with being human*. Waco, TX: Baylor University Press.

Kennedy, A. (2012). Regulating bodily integrity: Cosmetic surgery and voluntary limb amputation. *Journal of Law and Medicine*, *20*(2), 350–362. PMID:23431852

Meningaud, J. P., Servant, J. M., Herve, C., & Bertrand, J. C. (2000). Ethics and aims of cosmetic surgery: A contribution from an analysis of claims after minor damage. *Medicine and Law*, *19*(2), 237–252. PMID:10994212

Morland, I. (2005). The glans opens like a book: Writing and reading the intersexed body. *Continuum: Journal of Media & Cultural Studies*, *19*(3), 335–348. doi:10.1080/10304310500176586

Mousavi, S. R. (2010). The ethics of aesthetic surgery. *Journal of Cutaneous and Aesthetic Surgery*, *3*(1), 38–40. doi:10.4103/0974-2077.63396 PMID:20606994

Oumeish, O. Y. (2001). The cultural and philosophical concepts of cosmetics in beauty and art through the medical history of mankind. *Clinics in Dermatology*, *19*(4), 375–386. doi:10.1016/S0738-081X(01)00194-8 PMID:11535377

Parker, L. S. (1993). Social justice, federal paternalism, and feminism: Breast implants in the cultural context of female beauty. *Kennedy Institute of Ethics Journal*, *3*(1), 57–76. doi:10.1353/ken.0.0158 PMID:11645225

Plotz, D. (2003, March 12). The ethics of enhancement: We can make ourselves stronger, faster, smarter. Should we? *Slate*. Retrieved December 27, 2013, from http://www.slate.com/articles/health_and_science/superman/2003/03/the_ethics_of_enhancement.single.html

Poster, M. (2007). Swan's way: Care of self in the hyperreal. *Configurations*, *15*(2), 151–175. doi:10.1353/con.0.0029

Sandel, M. J. (2007). *The case against perfection: Ethics in the age of genetic engineering*. Cambridge, MA: Belknap Press of Harvard University Press.

Schermer, M. (2008). On the argument that enhancement is cheating. *Journal of Medical Ethics*, *34*(2), 85–88. doi:10.1136/jme.2006.019646 PMID:18234944

Sheldon, S., & Wilkinson, S. (1998). Female genital mutilation and cosmetic surgery: Regulating non-therapeutic body modification. *Bioethics*, *12*(4), 263–285. doi:10.1111/1467-8519.00117 PMID:11657294

Slevin, K. F. (2010). If I had lots of money...I'd have a body makeover: Managing the aging body. *Social Forces*, *88*(3), 1003–1020. doi:10.1353/sof.0.0302

Sterodimas, A., Radwanski, H. N., & Pitanguy, I. (2011). Ethical issues in plastic and reconstructive surgery. *Aesthetic Plastic Surgery*, *35*(2), 262–267. doi:10.1007/s00266-011-9674-3 PMID:21336881

Testa, G., Carlisle, E., Simmerling, M., & Angelos, P. (2012). Living donation and cosmetic surgery: A double standard in medical ethics? *The Journal of Clinical Ethics*, *23*(2), 110–117. PMID:22822698

Wijsbek, H. (2000). The pursuit of beauty: The enforcement of aesthetics or a freely adopted lifestyle? *Journal of Medical Ethics*, *26*(6), 454–458. doi:10.1136/jme.26.6.454 PMID:11129847

Zylinska, J. (2007). Of swans and ugly ducklings: Bioethics between humans, animals, and machines. *Configurations*, *15*(2), 125–150. doi:10.1353/con.0.0028

KEY TERMS AND DEFINITIONS

Beauty: Beauty is culturally bound and differs among groups. The only standards of beauty that seem to transcend culture are features that signal good health, such as symmetry of features.

Body Modification: Encompasses a range of enhancement strategies, ranging from cosmetic surgery to tattooing or piercing.

Cosmetic Surgery: Cosmetic surgery is done solely for aesthetic reasons on otherwise healthy, functioning body parts. Common examples include breast implants and rhinoplasty.

Plastic Surgery: Plastic surgery is distinguished from cosmetic surgery in that plastic surgery encompasses a range of reconstructive procedures, such as treating burn victims and victims of disfiguring injury.

Posthumanism: The idea that technology can aid in reshaping and transcending humanity.

Chapter 6
Neurosurgery to Enhance Brain Function:
Ethical Dilemmas for the Neuroscientist and Society

Reuben David Johnson
University of Otago, New Zealand

Dirk De Ridder
University of Otago, New Zealand

Grant Gillett
University of Otago, New Zealand

ABSTRACT

The aim of this chapter is to evaluate the potential for neurosurgical strategies to enhance brain function. These developments are considered in the context of the history of psychosurgery, which has shaped the ethical landscape in which future invasive surgical interventions will be evaluated. Consideration is given to the ethical, moral, legal, and socioeconomic implications posed by existing electrical modulation technologies, including future neurosurgical strategies, such as deep brain stimulation for cognitive or mood enhancement. The potential demand for the non-therapeutic use of these surgical strategies poses economic and legislative problems.

INTRODUCTION

Therapeutic cognitive enhancement procedures are already an established part of neurosurgical practice. Some fall within the therapeutic repertoire and are uncontentious for that reason. The most widespread example is the use of cerebrospinal fluid (CSF) diversion procedures to treat cognitive decline in normal pressure hydrocephalus

(NPH) (Finney, 2009). NPH is characterized by a clinical triad which includes cognitive decline and memory loss (Hakim and Adams, 1965). Although not yet in widespread clinical use, there has also been some positive albeit transient results in the use of brain stimulation in minimally conscious states (Thibaut et al., 2014), and studies attempting to obtain long term improvements are being initiated. Both CSF diversion and brain stimula-

DOI: 10.4018/978-1-4666-6010-6.ch006

tion are now being investigated for efficacy in Alzheimer's disease and they understandably are in demand not only from the individual patients and their families, but also at the institutional level (Laxton et al., 2013). For example, The UN Covenant on Economic, Social and Cultural Rights has proposed that there is a fundamental individual right to attain the best possible mental and physical health. As new surgical interventions become available there is a perception that there is a right to access these if they are proven to be effective and despite ethical worries that neurological enhancement may carry dangers in terms of social function and competition with resourcing of adequate services for the support of neurologically impaired patients.

It is likely that cognitive-enhancing neurosurgical procedures currently under investigation, such as brain stimulation for dementia, will become more widely available in the next 10 years. The increase in the availability of these procedures poses moral, social and ethical dilemmas, in addition to an arguable additional economic burden in that the cost of the procedures themselves might be offset by decreased costs of care, and this could be very important in some health care systems which are hard-pressed for economic resources.

Although CSF diversion is a therapeutic intervention with clear cut indications in the medical context, there are theoretical reasons to suggest that other procedures may be explored in an attempt to enhance the cognitive functioning of otherwise healthy individuals and slow the effects of ageing (much as we now use Ritalin and the anticholinesterases). In addition, the rapid development of safe electrical implant technologies in the field of psychosurgery is likely to lead to new insights regarding the feasibility of brain enhancement technology. All these developments pose ethical, moral, legal and socio-economic dilemmas. These quandaries are in many ways analogous to those posed by the non-medical use of cognitive enhancing pharmaceuticals (Greely et al., 2008; Racine & Forlini, 2009). However, neurosurgical

strategies also pose additional unique dilemmas and some of these will be discussed in the following pages. We will start by a historical overview of psychosurgery and subsequently discuss ethical and legal aspects of potential non-surgical and surgical neuromodulation for enhancement in healthy individuals.

BACKGROUND

The most ancient method of enhancing brain activity and function was by taking pharmacological agents. Although the recreational use of pharmacological substances is well documented, there are also instances of pharmacological substances being able to enhance brain function, and in particular mood states, as an aid to the accomplishment of tasks. For example, the Berserkers, the Viking raiders of northern Europe, were known to have taken *Psilocybin semilanceata* (commonly known as magic mushrooms) in order to induce the "Berzerker" state and thereby enhance their performance in battle. In modern times, drugs such as Ritalin and other amphetamines have been used by students to enhance mental performance in examinations (Greely et al., 2008). More recently it has been possible to modulate brain function using a magnetic field (transcranial magnetic stimulation) or electrical current (transcranial direct current stimulation, or implantation of electrodes) (Cohen Kadosh, 2013). There are now data available from human subjects implanted with cortical or subcutaneous electrodes that have demonstrated a clear potential for electrical neuroenhancement in contexts such as movement and psychiatric disorders. Indeed, one of the most well studied areas is in the effect on mood of neuroenhancement via electrical stimulation (Mayberg et al., 2005). These positive findings will lead to the use of stimulation devices more generally in order to harness these enhancing effects. This tendency to generalize the use of successful technologies is shown by the extension of CSF diversion from patients with NPH (where it can improve cognitive function), to Alzheimer's disease (Pratico et al., 2004).

Psychosurgery, having advanced from ablative strategies to the more precise and exact science of deep brain stimulation (or other forms of stimulation) is also gaining attraction as a way of responding to debilitating mood disorders, impulse control disorders, and inappropriate patterns of behavior as in OCD (Schlaepfer et al., 2010). This plethora of experimental strategies employed to enhance brain function has, however, evolved over a period of time primarily through serendipity, trial and error, and several pioneering experiments often done without careful regard for ethical issues. Indeed, the history of psychosurgery has shaped the ethical and legal landscape in which current and future surgical cognitive enhancing strategies will be developed.

HISTORY OF PSYCHOSURGERY

Consideration of the history of psychosurgery is essential in order to appreciate how this field has governed the principles by which surgical strategies to alter or enhance brain function have been controlled and assessed. The controversial history of psychosurgery has had an enduring effect on the perception of both the public and physicians on the efficacy and acceptability of surgical neuromodulation.

Functional Neuroanatomy

The origins of psychosurgery arise from an understanding of functional neuroanatomy that has grown out of the Hippocratic insight that the brain was the seat of psychological function,

…men ought to know that from the brain and from the brain only arise our pleasures, joys, laughter and jests as well as our sorrows, pains, griefs and tears. It is the same thing that makes us mad or delirious, inspires of a dread and fear, whether by night by day, brings sleepiness, inopportune mistakes, aimless anxieties, absent-mindedness and acts that are contrary to habits. (The Hippocratic treatise on the sacred disease, circa 400 BC) Lloyd, G (1978) Hippocratic Writings London: Penguin.

In the modern era, functional neuroanatomy was re-invigorated by figures like Franz Joseph Gall who developed the concept of phrenology, mapping neurological and psychological functions on the skull, an early attempt to localise function. The case of Phineas Gage, the railway worker in the United States, who suffered a severe frontal lesion when a dynamite packing rod passed through his brain, fundamentally changing his personality, is well-known to psychology, psychiatric and medical students as an early case of brain damage changing behaviour. Phineas Gage changed from being a God-fearing man to a womanising, drinking, gambling man: he was, his neurologist remarked, "not the same Gage" (Damasio, 1994).

The First Age of Psychosurgery

The first clinical experiment in psychosurgery was conducted by Gottleib Burckhard, director of the Prefargier Asylum in Switzerland, who operated on six patients diagnosed with intractable mental illness – one case of mania, one case of dementia and four cases of paranoid psychosis. His first operation was on 29, December, 1888, removing the cortex and frontal, temporal, and parietal lobes. He describes making a ditch in the brain between the sensory and motor areas. One patient suffered perioperative death, one case committed suicide, two had no change and two were, in his words, "quieter." Other neurosurgeons, including Dandy and Penfield, also noted that other patients with frontal lesions changed their personality (Brickner, 1952; Hebb and Penfield, 1940).

Psychosurgery was developed in a purely therapeutic context as a method of interrupting brain circuits thought to be responsible for the severe mental disturbances seen in psychosis. The original frontal lobotomy, or prefrontal leucotomy, procedure was devised by the Portuguese neurosurgeon, Egas Moniz, to treat schizophrenia. Performed in 1935, the procedure was reported by Moniz in 1936 and resulted in his being awarded a Nobel Prize in 1949. The work of Moniz was undertaken at a time when there were no effective treatments for severe psychosis and was seen as a great attempt at treating the untreatable. His Nobel Prize was well received and in an editorial in the *New England Journal of Medicine* in 1949, H. R. Viets wrote,

A new psychiatry may be said to have been born in 1935, when Moniz took his first bold step in the field of psychosurgery.

Walter Freeman, an American neurologist, together with James Watts, a neurosurgeon, adopted prefrontal leucotomy and popularized it in the USA. Freeman eventually adopted the transorbital lobotomy procedure that had been described by Fiamberti in Italy in 1937 (Fiamberti, 1950; Armocida, 2007). This technique became known as the "ice-pick lobotomy" and resulted in disapproval (Raz, 2008). Indeed Watts, Freeman's longtime collaborator, was so averse to what he saw as a 'blind' procedure being administered by physicians with inadequate surgical training, that he stopped performing it and broke the collaboration with Freeman. Unlike Watts, Freeman considered the transorbital lobotomy a minor operation and he became more lenient in his indications. Freeman zealously continued using the transorbital lobotomy, travelling around the United States in his "lobotomobile," on a crusade to relieve state mental hospital patients of their misery, and teaching psychiatrists how to perform transorbital lobotomies. He performed over 3000 transorbital lobotomies across the United States

with a clinical follow up of over 20 years (Freeman, 1957) and, although initially hailed as a miracle cure for intractable mental disorder, the overuse of Freeman's technique resulted not only in some disasters from intracerebral bleeding, but also inappropriate interventions in patients without psychosis.

This should, however, be seen in the light of the time: both diagnosis and classification of psychiatric disease were still in their early stages of development, and if the aim was to release patients from the hospitals, "some 70% of schizophrenics, 80% of affectives, and 90% of psychoneurotics are functioning outside of the hospital in the 5-to 10-year period" (Freeman, 1957). These results may explain the enthusiasm for psychosurgery pre-1950. It is widely acknowledged that, at that time, there were many patients labeled as schizophrenic, and who were progressively declining in their ability to function, who would not have met the modern criteria for this diagnosis, and who were desperate for something to be done. A sympathetic account of the tragedy of Freeman's quest is given in Jack El-Hai's book *The Lobotomist* (El-Hai, 2005). The introduction of lithium and chlorpromazine into the pharmacological arsenal in the 1950s gave psychiatrists non-surgical solutions for severe psychiatric illness. The rapid reduction in the need for psychosurgery by these non-invasive alternatives paved the way for more critical evaluation of psychosurgery.

Objective evaluation of this first age of modern psychosurgery is difficult, however. Burckhardt, who carried out the first clinical experiment in psychosurgery, talked about the "ditch in the brain" creating resistance between the sensory areas of the brain and the motor zone in order to dampen excitement and impulsivity due to abnormally high stimuli from the sensory areas. It is so destructive and irreversible as to turn the stomach of even the most hardened psychosurgeon, and the experience of Freeman with his precision leucotomy and their sweeping motion to cut fibres in the frontal lobe, while being an improvement, also sticks strongly in the collective memory. This era is often remembered as a period of psychiatric abuse with psychosurgery being a highly destructive, poorly theorized and non-empathic answer to a disorder in the patients' social and interpersonal function (Pressman, 1998; Gillett, 2009).

Moniz, the sole neurosurgeon ever to win a Nobel Prize, is still maligned by the view that it was probably the most mistaken Nobel Prize ever to have been awarded (Lass et al., 2012). However, one needs to keep in mind that the first stage of psychosurgery occurred at a time when advances in psychology, neuroanatomy and neurosurgery coincided with an era of therapeutic nihilism in psychiatry, and the USA had many overcrowded asylums offering nothing but a desperate and worsening future for the mentally ill at a huge cost to the public purse. This era, as we have noted, was brought to an end only by the age of psychopharmacology as lithium was introduced by John Cade (1949) and chlorpromazine was introduced by Delay and Deniker (Delay, Denniker & Harl, 1952). The success of these non-invasive treatments caused a negative sentiment against psychosurgery. Others might trace its demise to the anti-establishment culture in the 1960s and 1970s which expressed revulsion at the idea of psychosurgery, its destructive effects on already suffering human beings, and its possible use as a means of social control.

That misgiving foreshadowed the development of amygdalectomy by Narabayashi in Japan in the 1960s when the idea that aggressive behaviour could be controlled by psychosurgery became the focus of much controversy (Fountas & Smith, 2007). There was widespread debate in the US regarding the ethics of civilizing society by means of psychosurgery as proposed by José Delgado (Delgado, 1969). Much of it was stimulated by proposals to undertake clinical studies on captive criminals. In that forum psychosurgery was the target of vigorous objections, fueled by fears that it would be promoted for a socio-political purpose, regardless of the medical and physiological legiti-

macy of what was being done. There was reason for this fear as both José Delgado and Robert Heath, on the forefront of psychosurgery in the 1960s, were funded by the CIA. Using psychosurgical techniques to control aggression raised a question about whether it could or would be used on people who were not truly ill but who, for a variety of reasons, did not act in ways that society could tolerate. For even the most violent offenders, such radical obliteration of the neurobiological basis of the mind intuitively would "violate something that many consider inviolable" (Glannon, 2007).

An objective look at the early evidence for the efficacy of psychosurgery is also not easy, even if one manages to avoid applying retrospectively modern evaluative criteria. It is difficult to obtain the original data, which were, in any case, largely subjective. Watts, in particular, and also Moniz, wrote reports of their work that would be unlikely to be accepted for publication today. There were multiple flaws, including a lack of experimental controls within the clinical studies; poor clinical reporting; and, in the case of Moniz, only a few months follow up. Although early animal work was undertaken, for example by Jacobsen and Fulton, the extrapolation of hypotheses from this work was poor by reasonable standards of comparative functional anatomy and behavioural analysis (Pressman, 1998). Moniz's results show that he had his greatest success with bipolar patients, many of whom, we now realize, could well have improved in accordance with the cyclical nature of their disorder.

Public Perception of Psychosurgery

There were 3 phases in the public perception of psychosurgery. In the first phase, psychosurgery was seen as a miracle cure for psychiatric disease. This period extending from 1940-1950, and culminating in Moniz's Nobel Prize, was changed after the discovery of the first antipsychotic chlorpromazine in 1953. The treatment was evaluated more objectively, as not only having benefits but also negative side effects. The controversial history of psychosurgery has had a huge impact on its public perception. Modern literature has also reinforced negative views of such therapies, which is not surprising given advances in psychological knowledge and techniques of behaviour modification. Aldous Huxley's *Brave New World*, written in 1931, conveys a picture of the use of operant conditioning to shape human behaviour for socio-political ends. Richard Condon's thriller, *The Manchurian Candidate* (1959), depicts the use of psychological brainwashing techniques by communists attempting to overthrow the US government. Michael Crichton wrote a similar alarmist thriller in 1972 about the possibilities of psychosurgery, *The Terminal Man*, inspired by the possibilities of deep brain stimulation following the development of stereotactic techniques. Crichton's main character, Benson, suffers violent seizures that are treated with an implanted brain stimulator, but begins to stimulate himself as he finds that it is associated with a shock of pleasure; Crichton describes a form of addiction to the implanted stimulator which has terrifying consequences.

As for Benson, he had had more than twenty-four hours of intense stimulation by his implanted computer. That stimulation had affected his brain by providing new experiences and new expectations. A new environment was being incorporated. Pretty soon, it would be impossible to predict how the brain would react. Because it wasn't Benson's old brain any more – it was a new brain, the product of new experiences.

Fear of mind control was not just a phenomenon of popular culture. There was genuine anxiety that researchers would act as social scientists to use mind control technology for social and political ends. Samuel Chavkin's *The Mind Stealers,* published in 1978, expresses the paranoid fear that psychosurgery would be extended beyond the treatment of mental disease and used to tam-

per with political dissent, criminal behaviour, or alternative lifestyles. Chavkin cites public shock in finding out that the CIA experimented with mind-bending drugs during the Vietnam War, and his revulsion towards neurosurgeons is reflected in the emotive prose he employs to describe psychosurgery on a child:

Under the glare of operating rooms lights, a seven-year-old boy, heavily anaesthetized but awake enough to respond to questions, is strapped down on an operating table. Standing directly behind is the surgeon, his eyes riveted on a scalpel that he carefully slides down a penciled line, making an incision of several inches across the boy's shaven head.

The child is "forced to forfeit his original personality and take on a new one that would be of convenience to those about him." Chavkin's book represents the ultimate fear that psychosurgery could be used as a means of force, a weapon wielded by government and its related institutions to control the masses.

Such extreme fears ignore the fact that new technology often feeds a new demand for its use. Chavkin laments the possibility that schools might advise parents to drug their children in order to control them. However, the potential use of pharmacological aids to improve school performance is attractive to many parents and their offspring, though the results are not always as they are promised to be. The psychostimulant, methylphenidate (Ritalin), widely used to treat attention deficit-hyperactivity disorder (ADHD), is also widely used amongst college students in order to improve their concentration whilst studying. Where technology can give a competitive edge, there will be individual demand for its use forcing us to consider the climate that we are creating which produces such widespread demands. However, with the disillusion with the relatively low effect size of psychopharmacological agents the pendulum is swinging back to psychosurgery, and a fourth phase is arising, the second age of psychosurgery: making very focal interventions, based on a better understanding of the pathophysiology of psychiatric disease, with techniques that are reversible.

The Second Age of Psychosurgery: The Shift from Ablative Surgery

The first age of psychosurgery was an era of ablative surgery. Areas of the brain were purposefully damaged in order to alter behaviour and mental states. Modern techniques have allowed for a major shift away from this ablative period into an era of neuromodulation, and a second age of modern psychosurgery has arisen, due primarily to fundamental changes in the neurosciences. Instead of the need for destructive lesions, deep brain stimulation allows for the reversible insertion of electrodes, which likely create virtual, i.e. reversible lesions (Beurrier et al., 2001), thereby changing functional connections in the brain (Figee et al., 2013). Pre-clinical animal models are now more established, more responsibly used in the generation of human interventions, and more acceptable. Psychiatry has been completely transformed by the introduction of a diagnostic classification which is now an internationally recognised language (the DSM system) (de Leon, 2013). Although this system has been criticized for over-simplifying the complex nature of psychiatric disorders into a set of brain dysfunctions, the DSM system allowed for a more robust, reliable, and reproducible system of diagnosis which allowed for interventions to be more accurately assessed.

The era of psychopharmacology is faltering as the side effects of psychotropic drugs become more widely appreciated: there is now a demand for other treatments in those patients who are resistant to the arsenal provided by the pharmaceutical industry. The political landscape of science and how research is funded, have changed. Scientists are no longer naive to the budgetary requirements and financial implications of their work. There is also a growing discipline of neuroethics which allows more rigorous analysis of the treatment options available. The ethical principles of human experimentation have been examined and related to wider social trends and concerns, and as a result many of the indications for psychiatric treatment that existed in the 1950s would now be seen as a reason to look closely at socio-political factors in a given society. Despite these advances in thought, it remains true that, "A major problem with psychosurgery is that the assessment is bedeviled by the intensely evaluative and observer-dependent nature of the judgments involved" (Gillett, 2008).

One of the beneficial outcomes of the first era of modern psychosurgery was a tightening of guidelines to meet some of the ethical issues surrounding psychosurgery. The Belmont Report, produced by the National Commission for the Protection of Human Subjects of Biomedical and Behavioural Research in the USA (1974-78), critically evaluated psychosurgery and concluded that, although there were risks, there were also meaningful benefits and it should not be banned outright (Robinson et al., 2012). The report stated:

We looked at the data and saw that they did not support our prejudices. I, for one, did not expect to come out in favor of psychosurgery, but we saw that some very sick people had been helped by it and that it did not destroy their intelligence or rob them of their feelings. Their marriages were intact. They were able to work. The operation should not be banned.

J. Kenneth Ryan (Harvard), Chairman of the 1974-1976 Commission

The Belmont Report provided a guide to informed consent and the performance of medical research procedures, including research on institutionalised populations. That report outlined three ethical principles for using human subjects:

1. Respect for persons by protecting the autonomy of all people, treating them with courtesy and respect, and allowing for informed consent.
2. Researchers being truthful and not conducting any deception. The principle of beneficence influencing the philosophy of "do no harm" while maximising benefits for the research project and minimising risks to the research subjects.
3. Justice, ensuring that reasonable, non-exploitable, well considered procedures are administered fairly with a fair distribution of costs and benefits to potential research positions.

Deep Brain Stimulation

The techniques of deep brain stimulation (DBS) have developed rapidly over the last 20 years, offering a form of neuromodulation for behaviour change that is more acceptable than highly invasive forms of surgery (Rabins et al., 2009). Deep brain stimulation is reversible and non-ablative, although there may be some destruction of deep brain structures at the tip of the electrodes. The target areas are smaller than in previously used destructive psychosurgery techniques. Ultimately, the deep brain stimulating hardware is removable, and the intensity and frequency of the currents used can be closely modified and moderated. Deep brain stimulation is usually part of a multidisciplinary approach involving psychologists, psychiatrists, neurologists, neurosurgeons and radiologists. The hypothesis-driven targeting from functional magnetic resonance imaging (fMRI) studies or animal experiments means that there is more of a scientific base to the neuromodulation than was previously the case. In this era of more ethically controlled scientific research it is claimed that there is better follow up, and more precisely defined treatment objectives than was the case in the early twentieth century (although Freeman did carry out follow-up studies of 20

years). Clinical aims can be tailored to a specific aspect of a disorder rather than to the whole disease, and the expectations of outcomes can therefore be more realistic. Furthermore, there are more alternative choices available for psychiatrists, so that psychosurgery is not the only treatment available for the psychiatrists.

Based on the resurgence of biological psychiatry and a better understanding of the pathophysiology of certain mental diseases psychosurgery has become a scientific topic again, not considered completely unacceptable in whatever form. Mayberg and colleagues in 2005 described deep brain stimulation for treatment-resistant depression (TRD), targeting the area of the cingulate gyrus white matter area 25 (CgWM 25). They based this on neuroimaging studies in which it had been shown this area of the brain demonstrated elevated activity in patients with severe, treatment-resistant, depression (Mayberg et al., 1999). There were also reports that widely different forms of antidepressant treatments, for example selective serotonin reuptake inhibitors (SSRIs) and ECT, suppressed activity in the same region. Hypothesizing, therefore, that chronic stimulation to modulate CgWM25 grey matter might ameliorate symptoms in treatment resistant-depression, Mayberg's group successfully established DBS of CgWM25 as a possibly effective therapeutic procedure for TRD (Mayberg, 2002) in less than 50% of patients (Holtzheimer et al., 2012).

PATIENT AUTONOMY AND INFORMED CONSENT

The Belmont Report emphasis on patient autonomy and informed consent reminds us of the serious challenges facing the institution of an ethically sound programme of brain stimulation lie in translating findings from research in animal models or preclinical imaging studies to clinical practice. This is particularly the case when a new disorder is being targeted, as in the switch from treating movement disorders to treating psychiatric conditions in ablative stereotactic neurosurgery. Although some of the targets used for DBS treatment of some conditions may also prove to be potential targets in the control of other conditions, the establishment of the treatment of these new conditions requires careful pathophysiological, neuroscientific, and neuropsychological consideration because of the complexity of human emotion and cognition.

A new treatment regime raises special ethical issues regarding patient autonomy, particularly in the experimental phase when the outcome is uncertain because of the need (again identified in The Belmont Report) to avoid misleading individuals about what can be achieved by a given treatment. Obtaining informed consent is difficult when the information provided is uncertain and when both the disorder being treated and the treatment being contemplated affect the nervous system - the basis of human thought and action (Northoff, 2006). The prospect of patients being asked to sign up to procedures on the basis of inadequate information about risks, rationale and potential benefit is difficult and might be ethically unacceptable, and yet it is possible that some patients may greatly benefit from the procedures. To a certain extent, uncertainty is the rule in any type of genuinely innovative clinical research, including a phase three clinical drug trial; however, the invasive aspect of neurosurgical intervention, and the fact that the brain is that part of the body that, since the Greek thinkers, is regarded as "the seat of the soul," makes psychosurgery more problematic than a drug trial, if it is irreversible.

Particular difficulty is seen when the disorder being considered may not be amenable to an innovative treatment (such as DBS) of any kind because of problems with consent per se.

Uncertainties about consent are tolerable within the context of patient care where we can properly regard the patient as in touch with, and able to make reasonable ongoing decisions about, their own treatment as part of a developing conversation, but not where there are significant impediments to that process. A patient's autonomy is respected when s/he makes a free un-coerced choice on the basis of adequate information and is enabled to opt for a plan of management. Many traps lie in that path, such as "the four day information dump" whereby, for example, a surgical patient receives a large amount of information in one lump after a period of investigation (typically four days) and then has to sign a consent form for surgery. These traps can be overcome for a planned elective procedure in a clear-headed and unimpaired patient but, given the way most of us make up our minds about important things, a model focusing on an adequate, and therefore complex, information package duly delivered for processing followed by a decision (the outcome of an internal cognitive-affective process) needs revision. Most people clarify their ideas in conversation where they ask questions, probe information, sift, interrogate, explain, contest, and act after a dialogic exploration of their real situation, a process that may be extended and episodic. Entering into such a process and following it through to a satisfactory conclusion is necessarily made more difficult where the brain itself is affected and the need for the interim use of drugs or measures that restrict the activity or affect the thought of the patient does not help. Those problems bite with a vengeance when the patient is struggling to cope with complex information in the midst of an elusive, often threatening, and definitely unsettled life experience.

This is particularly the case in schizophrenia, a major psychosis or dementia where there is a paucity of preclinical animal models on which to conduct experiments that would satisfy the criterion of being translatable directly to patients, and when the patients themselves have variable abilities to reason about what is happening to them. The psychoses will always have this problem as the phenotypic characteristics of schizophrenia are manifest mainly in thought, behaviour, and language. Although, from a psychopharmacological perspective it is possible to create animal models which replicate and are predictive of some clinical phenomena and the effects of interventions, that may not be true for DBS because general behavioural trends mediated by metabolic and neurotransmitter effects are more comparable between animals and humans than is the case for precisely targeted cognitive-neuroscientific interventions. In such cases the distinctive capacities endowed on us by human evolution and the integration and uniquely configured coordination of neural function involved produce significant singularities (Hughlings-Jackson, 1887). Nonetheless, there are good preclinical studies which seem to demonstrate beneficial changes in behaviour – for example in impulse inhibition deficits in rodent models of schizophrenia – and some of the targets studied have been used for other clinical conditions, so that their effects in human thought and behavior can be closely studied. One of the major concerns with schizophrenic patients and demented patients, however, is their ability to consent, depending on their degree of insight into their disorder, their ability to reason without such understanding, and the spectre of compulsory treatment that lurks in the background. Whereas one might fairly readily establish that a patient with schizophrenia has clear views on leg amputation (Van Staden et al., 2003), the same cannot be said for their appreciation of the implications of neuromodulation with possible mood and impulse changing effects. In epilepsy and depression, surgical intervention has been reserved for the patients who have been refractory to medical treatment, but patients with treatment-refractory schizophrenia would almost certainly not have insight into their condition and it is likely that they would be unable to consent for themselves. This potential problem could be overcome by the concept of prospective consent earlier in the disease process but there are serious problems with advance directives in the face of clinical uncertainty (Gillett, 2011).

The possibility of consent being given on behalf of the patient by their next of kin or by a person possessing Power of Attorney is also problematic given the role of that type of consent in the history of psychosurgery. Freeman's lobotomy was performed not only on one of the Kennedys at the behest of the family but also on young women who had had sex before marriage and others whose behaviour did not fit with social norms. Thus the prospect of behavioural change being consented for by the next of kin or Power of Attorney is inherently more suspect than some form of consent coming from the patients themselves given the ethical question that is asked with treatment of ADHD: "For whose benefit is this being done?"

These worries, serious as they are, can be debated in the light of DBS for Parkinson's disease which has cognitive features in the advanced stages. It is obvious that this could pose a challenge for informed consent, but that must be balanced by the consideration that the patient may benefit immensely from deep brain stimulation and should not be excluded from receiving this benefit, nor, indeed, from expressing a desire to take that chance. Advanced Parkinson's disease is, in some respects, ethically similar to schizophrenia in the sense that it is an incurable disease, with cognition-altering effects and limited treatment prospects, some of which are potentially harmful. In order to obtain consent in advanced Parkinson's disease in the presence of cognitive deterioration, it is necessary to establish that the patient has an understanding of the surgical risks, complications and side effects that can result from the intervention. Such an understanding may come from prolonged discussions over a period of time and certainly longer than it would for patients who have fewer and less serious cognitive defects. Extending this to schizophrenia, one might consider the possibility of discussions over a period of years earlier in the disease process in order to achieve this and the establishment of a therapeutic alliance in which the treatment team and patient can be considered to have formed an effective partnership and a mutuality of interests. However one might also note that sometimes the application of DBS in Parkinson's patients can disturb their sense of identity in ways not anticipated before the surgery (Witt et al., 2011) so that issues of consent and information about risks are not at all straightforward. That is likely to be especially important in cases where there is a significant impairment of the patient's ability to deal with future contingencies that are probable or even possible but have to be weighed in the decision being made. On the other hand the advantage of DBS is that the stimulation can be stopped and the aforementioned discussions could be held with stimulation on and off.

MOOD ENHANCEMENT

Mood can be described as a relatively long-lasting emotional affective state. A mood disorder is a pathological emotional state having a debilitative effect on a person's ability to perform their necessary tasks. Mood differs from emotion only in that mood lasts longer than emotion, is less specific and intense, less evident to conscious scrutiny and cognitive interrogation, and less likely to be triggered by any particular stimulus. However conscious perception of emotion plausibly occurs because of the co-activation of frontal cortical and relevant subcortical regions. This basic concept of the neurobiology of mood and emotion and their close affinity with subconscious and unconscious processing allows hypotheses to be developed as to what might cause mood disregulation. De Ridder postulated that mood disorders are a consequence of regional impairment of neuroplasticity under the influence of on-going conscious cognitive engagement – a hypothesis similar to that of Freud (De Ridder et al., 2007). Neuroplasticity is the capacity of the nervous system to modify its organisation by adjusting itself to an input

from a changing environment. In this context, mood disorders could be the result of abnormal activations and deactivations of mood circuits in the brain, with chronic deactivations eventually resulting in atrophy of the affected brain areas (both neurons and supporting glial cells). This would show as decreased cortical thickness associated with abnormal pathological moods in morphometric studies (Manji et al., 2001) and an example would be counter-production gains in the right prefrontal cortex and reduced engagement of the left lateral ventral medial prefrontal circuitry which is involved in the down regulation of the responses of the medulla to negative stimulation (Johnson et al., 2007). As we have seen from studies of neuromodulation for psychiatric disorders, there is a correlation between increased activity of the anterior cingulate cortex (BA 25) and the anterior insula (Mayberg et al., 1995). There are likely, therefore, to be several neural circuits involved in the regulation of mood and emotions. The enhancement of mood is most commonly achieved by the use of pharmaceutical agents, including barbiturates, benzodiazepines, amphetamines, and a range of anti-depressants, for example selective serotonin reuptake inhibitors. Developments in recent years have allowed experimentation with transcranial magnetic stimulation (TMS), transcranial direct current stimulation (tDCS), neurofeedback, and the implantation of electrodes applied to the surface of the brain or inserted deeper into the brain. These neurostimulation techniques have potential advantages over medication in that whereas medication is slow to act, slow to wash out, and has associated side effects, neurostimulation techniques may have more immediate effects, no wash-out problems and few side effects. If one considers the treatment of depression, antidepressants have a latent period of several weeks, whereas ECT appears to have an almost immediate effect. However, interpreting the mechanism of action of neurostimulation by whatever means can be difficult. For example, electrical stimulation of the cortex at low amplitudes activates only a single area but at greater amplitudes activates larger areas, even though low amplitudes interfere with or modulate extended networks and thereby affect activity elsewhere within the brain. These networks are not fully understood at present, although new imaging techniques are revealing more and more about them. The possibility of functional MRI scanning is therefore likely to increase understanding of the mechanism of action of these stimulation parameters and how they can be modulated to help enhance targeted brain functions, despite uncertainties about what effects may be being produced at the molecular neurotransmitter level.

Any enhancement of brain function which affects mood has wider implications. In 1954, Olds and Milner performed a famous experiment in which they implanted an electrode into the septum of rodents, and found that the rats showed a greater preference for electrical stimulation of the brain than they did for food and water, even after prolonged periods of semi-starvation (Olds & Milner, 1954). They identified the ventral tegmental area (VTA) and medial forebrain bundle (MFB) as the most effective areas for stimulation. The MFB is a tract rich in dopamine and adrenalin connecting the brain stem and VT to the limbic system and the nucleus accumbens, and passes through the lateral hypothalamus. The findings from animal research were first translated to human research by Dr Robert Galbraith Heath, an American psychiatrist. Heath performed experiments with electrical stimulation of the VT and MFB via implanted electrodes, work partially financed by the CIA and the US military. In the same period, Jose Manuel Rodriguez Delgado, professor of physiology at Yale University, also noted that stimulation of the superior temporal gyrus could induce a feeling of pleasure in human subjects. Delgado invented the *stimoceiver* in which a radio was joined with a brain stimulator and with a receiver which monitored EEG waves and sent them back on a different radio channel. Delgado noted that radio stimulation of the amygdala/hippocampus in subjects produced pleasant emotions, elation,

thoughtful concentration, super-relaxation and other responses; stimulation of the septum produced feelings of strong euphoria, feelings which could overcome physical pain and depression.

One wonders what applications were envisaged for this work and whether a DBS induced state of euphoria and relaxation may significantly moderate the negative affective responses that may develop in soldiers experiencing extremely stressful wartime experiences, such as in Vietnam. When we begin to think about psychosurgery being developed to adjust brain circuitry so that it generates more subjectively acceptable responses, whatever the situations to which the subject has been exposed, it becomes evident that this could be a set of very worrying or very promising developments in *neurocosmetics*. The idea that events in the brain could be turned on and off not under the influence of what in social and personal life really counts as something (whether negative or positive) but according to an imposed agenda, some of the more lurid fears about early psychosurgery become more pressing.

THERAPEUTIC ENHANCEMENT BY ELECTRICAL BRAIN MODULATION

Transcranial Direct Current Stimulation

Transcranial direct current stimulation (tDCS), the application of weak electrical currents in the order of 1 to 2 milliamps to modulate brain excitability has been used in an attempt to modulate mood by causing neurons in the brain to respond to static electrical fields with an alteration in their firing rates. In a recent meta-analysis and systematic review it was shown that active tDCS was statistically superior to sham tDCS for acute depression treatment, although its role as a clinical intervention is still unclear owing to the mixed findings and heterogeneity of the reviewed studies (Shiozawa et al.. 2014). There are no studies using tDCS that demonstrate mood can be enhanced in healthy volunteers (Plazier et al., 2011; Motohashi et al., 2013). This could suggest that tDCS brings pathological activity back to the norm in a kind of homeostatic way, but is not capable of doing not the opposite. If this is correct, it will prevent abuse of this technique for mood enhancement in healthy people. There are, however, tDCS studies in healthy volunteers that suggest that cognitive enhancement is possible, especially with regards to memory improvement (Marshall et al., 2004). Already in 2004, Marshall and co-workers at the Institute of Neuroendocrinology at the University of Lübeck in Germany showed tDCS to be capable of improving cognition in healthy people. They applied anodal tDCS repeatedly bilaterally to the frontal cortical electrode site during slow wave sleep. After a 30-minute period of stimulation, the retention of declarative memories of word pairs, and non-declarative memories of previously-learned mirror tracing skills, were compared with those after placebo stimulation. There was a significant increase in the retention of word pairs during anodal tDCS during slow-wave-rich sleep, suggesting that neuroplastic processes in new cortical networks can be enhanced by neural stimulation. Interestingly, tDCS devices are legally not considered to be medical devices, so can be used by anyone, anytime.

Transcranial Magnetic Stimulation

Transcranial magnetic stimulation (TMS) which generates magnetic fields of up to 2.5 tesla (this is similar to MRI but in very short time windows) involves the use of head-mounted wire coils that send very strong but short magnetic pulses directly to specific brain regions. Like tDCS it is considered to be safe and painless and induces only tiny electric currents in the person's neural circuitry. There is already a plethora of literature on the therapeutic effects of TMS on mood disorders, but TMS does not seem to be able to change mood in healthy volunteers (Jenkins, 2002), and some insurance companies reimburse TMS for

depression, suggesting that apart from its clinical beneficial effect in mood disorders it is cost effective for them.

Neurobiofeedback

Another method of electrical brain modulation is by the use of neurobiofeedback, also known as EEG biofeedback, or the brain-computer interface training technique. This method is a technique based on operant conditioning (Sterman & Egner, 2006) whereby a person is taught to produce defined EEG patterns by means of immediate feedback and positive reinforcement. However, an association between neurofeedback training and enhanced mood performance in healthy volunteers has yet to be fully established in realistic life-settings (Vernon, 2005).

Deep Brain Electrodes

Implantation of deeper brain electrodes has also been shown to have mood enhancing effects in pathological mood, i.e., in major depression (Mayberg et al., 2005). In a review of the literature, Laxton and Lozano, identified three studies that have investigated the use of DBS for the treatment of dementia: one involving fornix DBS for Alzheimer's disease; and two involving DBS of the nucleus basalis of Maynert to treat Alzheimer's disease and Parkinson disease dementia (Laxton and Lozano 2012). Although the evidence is in its preliminary stages, they concluded that further investigation into DBS for dementia is warranted. It is likely that, as more experience is gained with deep brain stimulation, the potential for this procedure to enhance mood and cognition will become clearer. It has already been suggested that, provided it used in an appropriate and responsible manner, there may be role of DBS to modulate and enhance memory and cognition in healthy subjects (Hu et al., 2009). However, to date, there have been no studies that have evaluated mood or cognitive enhancement in healthy volunteers.

NEUROETHICAL CRITIQUES, CONTROVERSIES, PROBLEMS, AND LEGISLATION

It is now widely accepted that electrical neuro-modulation, either by the non-invasive transcranial or invasive stimulatory methods, is technically possible and for non-invasive neuromodulation there are some data suggesting it can influence cognition, but not mood in healthy volunteers. This non-pharmacological alternative to enhancing cognition has, however, been subjected to some penetrating neuroethical critiques.

Carl Elliott, philosopher and bioethicist, in his 2003 book *Better Than Well: American Medicine Meets the American Dream* examines the meaning of enhancement technologies for American life and looks specifically at Prozac, Ritalin, beta-blockers, cosmetic surgery and body modification. He argues that contemporary American society is preoccupied with the idea of enhancement by biomedical means to the exclusion of certain satisfactions intrinsic to a more balanced and natural way of life. He urges the development of ecologically real identities which do not shape themselves in response to artificially created demands and self-images but reflect a more engaged and healthy mode of living together. His critique highlights the growing demand for a switch-on means of being a better person that is focused on self and subjectively evaluated ways of being rather than attuned to the messy and demanding world of human relationships, conflicts, and the need to become a decent human being fit to live among others.

There has been a considerable shift in both the political and ethical culture of neuroscience since the early forays of neurosurgical pioneers in the twentieth Century. Greenberg's 1967 *The Politics of Pure Science* accuses the scientific ivory towers of a form of political and institutional ignorance that was overspecialized, esoteric, and of valuing the acquisition of knowledge above its application.

While basic research grows ever more costly, it has nothing to sell in the market-place.

Irrespective of the validity of Greenberg's observations and analysis, his treatise reflects a perception of science in the 1960s and even if contemporary neuroscience would not attract the same judgment, its growing appeal as the means to get at the real basis of human cognition, emotion, moods, and self awareness should raise concerns.

One changes as a person in response to a moral milieu which is sometimes uncomfortable if self is too prominently at the heart of one's motivational structure. Stimulation delivered to the brain bypassing the harmony and sustainability of one's engagement with others is an ultimate self-focused technology that allows internal and narcissistic drivers to shape one's behavior and personality. We have to date greatly relied on settled "habits of the heart" (Bellah et al., 2007) in maintaining community and a moral ethos in which we care for one another as "dependent rational animals" (MacIntyre, 1999) but the individualization of satisfactions and the availability of individually tailored cognitive interventions of one kind or another raises the risk of a non-caring society from which our humanity and health-giving interconnectedness have been expelled (Gillett, 2008). Neuromodulation should therefore be wary of being a player in such a transformation.

Notwithstanding these ethical dilemmas, it would appear that, in North America at least, the neurosurgical community is amenable to the use of surgical intervention in order to enhance brain function in healthy subjects. A survey of 299 functional neurosurgeons in North America found that over half felt it would be ethical to provide DBS for memory enhancement to people who request it, provided it is safe (Lipsman et al., 2011). However, this stance has been described as "disturbing" by other functional neurosurgeons and neuroscientists in Europe who emphasize that even though DBS has been used for more than a quarter of a century, the evidence-base is still limited and controversies still exist regarding its most common indication, the treatment of Parkinson's disease (Hariz et al., 2013). Hariz et al. also express their concern that neuroscientists have proposed the use of DBS to improve human morality: the functional and clinical neuroanatomy of the "moral brain" from modalities such as functional MRI has led to the suggestion that DBS could be used to change moral behavior (Fumagalli & Priori, 2012) and suggestions have been forwarded how this could be performed practically (De Ridder et al., 2009). However, in this new era of bioethics it is necessary to consider some of the debate regarding the ethics of moral enhancement. Julian Savulescu has argued that humans have an obligation to use whatever means necessary to undergo moral enhancement, e.g., parents are morally obligated to use technology, including genetics, to enhance their children (Savulescu & Kahane, 2009). Although there are, understandably, opponents of this view (Sparrow, 2011), the point remains that although it is easy to express concerns regarding the role of new technologies to enhance brain function, it is not a given that such concerns will not necessarily hold up to rigorous scrutiny in the field of bioethics. Furthermore, the broader issues are often raised, such as the use of amygdalotomy and DBS in "moral dysfunction" and criminal aggression: (i) medicalization of disorders of adaptation between human beings and a socio-political context (Gillett & Huang, 2013), and; (ii) corruption and conflicts of interest in biomedical research (Spielmans & Parry, 2010).

The issue of legal regulation of brain enhancement technology has recently been addressed with regard to commercial non-therapeutic use of tDCS, TMS and neurofeedback devices in the European Union (Maslen et al., 2014). Maslen et al. highlight that the nontherapeutic use of these devices appears to be covered only by the General Product Safety Directive (GPSD) which is less stringent than the Medical Device Directive within the EU. However, they also argue for the Medical Device Directive (MDD) as cognitive enhancement devices may fulfill part of the definition of the MDD in that they may modify physiological processes in the brain. Furthermore, the analogy with cosmetic devices for aesthetic enhancement is considered: cosmetic devices for non-medical aesthetic enhancement are covered by the MDD and as cognitive enhancement is perhaps more closely aligned to medical purposes, should also be covered by the MDD. Maslen et al. conclude that cognitive enhancement devices should be regulated through the existing MDD legislation but make proposals for a list of devices with risk profiles and the requirement for manufacturers to provide comprehensive evidence-based information about the products. Considering that these proposals are for non-surgical cognitive enhancing devices it is likely that more invasive neurosurgical strategies such as CSF diversion or DBS would face significant difficulties, at least within the EU, in being made widely available for non-therapeutic use.

The Broader Canvas: Translational Research

Over the last 30 years society has not left neuroscience in the hands of neuroscientists alone: interest has been focused upon what the research can achieve painted on a broader canvas. We want to know what neuroscience can do for us all, what purposes it can serve, and what it can create that can be sold. Indeed, the whole process of conducting neuroscientific research relies on persuading others – scientists and non-scientists alike– that the direction and vision of the endeavor is likely to produce something of value, often in the form of a technological advance. Intellectual property law has developed, such that neuroscientific truth now has a market value, if it is demonstrated to have a clinically relevant effect.

Translational research aims to apply the findings from research on neuromodulation into clinical practice. Institutional performance review of individual researchers rewards those with commercial partners, and translational neuroscience brings financial rewards to both the institution and the individual such that neither are as naïve as they used to be. Neuroscientists understand the political relationships of their institutions and the value of their own research to society – and society, it seems, is enthusiastic for new technologies.

This change in political climate has shifted the ethical problems associated with neuroscientific research. If neuroscientific research on cognitive enhancement should be done, the how and the why need first to be agreed upon when the discussion is likely to be affected by a tangible commercial interest. Society needs to determine what neurotechnology should be valued and supported. On the 2nd of April 2013, United States President Barak Obama launched a 100 million US dollar initiative called Brain Research through Advancing Innovative Neurotechnologies (BRAIN). BRAIN is envisaged to map the whole brain from neuron to neuronal circuits and is analogous to the human genome project. The resulting increase in our knowledge of the structure and function of the brain will lead to further ethical and technological questions and hypotheses about neuromodulation. Lessons from the human genome project should be heeded in that the extensive mapping of genes in health and disease led to much hope that gene therapy would soon be available. However, this strategy has stumbled due to the difficulty and complexity of the connections and explanations involved (particularly in behavioural genetics). Brain-machine interfaces and the complex context-related functions of the living brain may also mean that expectations are not easily met. The neuro-pharmacological revolution of the latter half of the twentieth Century was blighted by the difficulty of selectively targeting specific brain regions without also affecting other regions with undesired side effects, and neuromodulation is likely to face similar problems. When one considers that there are billions of synapses in the brain, all of which adapt to complex environmental contingencies as a result of individual learning, compared to a mere 20,000 or so genes that are fairly stable in biological time, the size of the problem facing neuroscientists becomes evident.

Changing Ethical Problems

The ethical problems of psychosurgery have changed. The past should not be repeated, not just because of the lessons learnt but because the contemporary environment is so different, and ethics should adjust to the changing political and social environment. The willingness to embrace new technologies even before they are properly understood was a major problem in the psychosurgery of the 1950s, and it means that it is important for neuroethicists to engage directly with neurosurgeons and to allow for a detailed analysis of the research process and the wider implications of new interventions.

Application of general principles of beneficence, non-maleficence and autonomy and more subtle analyses of well-being, the quasi-stable and plastic nature of human desires and needs, implies that research of DBS in new areas, including cognition, must learn from the ethical dilemmas surrounding mental disorder and its relationship to brain processes. We have moved into an era where we need to consider the effect of non-medical brain-technology interfaces and the socio-political context in which human behavior becomes classified as adaptive or maladaptive (are children to whom Ritalin is prescribed actually hyperactive or are they just being children?). This critical questioning is particularly relevant for at least 2 reasons. Firstly, in children with attention deficit hyperactivity disorder (ADHD) treatment with Ritalin results in normalization of abnormal functional connectivity, demonstrating from a brain function (and structure) point of view that it is worthwhile to use this treatment. Secondly, we drift towards classifying more and more disorders as medical when in fact they may be a result of tensions between the social or political context and the human individuals who are trying to adapt to that context. This kind of problem led to the development of the bio-psycho-social model of medicine (Engel, 1977). It is intensified when the target output directly concerns behaviour and implicates the scientific uncertainty that bedeviled early psychosurgery and that raises its head in the use of technology for social control. A huge number of individuals with impulsivity, aggression, and criminal tendencies are members of ethnic minorities or indigenous groups and yet, genetically or physiologically, there is no clear explanation for the disorders that are said to afflict them (Gillett & Tamatea, 2012). For that reason it would be wise to constrain the use of neuro-modulation or other technological interventions in cognitive tendencies until we fully understand the problems we are addressing and the psychosocial aspects of their aetiology. On the other hand, the problem with this approach is that you can only understand the mechanisms by performing these neuromodulations since this brings new information that is essential for a better understanding of both the diseases and what neuromodulation does (Dyson, 2012).

The debate has also shifted to accommodate the effect of the availability of such technologies on social equality and the human and personal socio-economic implications of expensive and elective technology. This shift is the direct result of an interdisciplinary broadening within neuroscience and its related disciplines. This cross-talk has led to a renaissance and a new frontier for neuromodulation, and also for neuroethics, particularly as both are brought to bear on contemporary societal and individual malaise.

A related issue is that of issue conflicts affecting innovative research and interventions. The Dan Markingson case has highlighted the extent to which psychiatric and other research can become distorted and hijacked by industry interests and that case is by no means unique (Haug, 2013). Given this evidence, we ought to be wary of psychosurgical technologies when there is a large untapped market for interventions in developed countries such as the USA and New Zealand, where inequality levels and imprisonment rates are the highest in the world.

Psychosurgical techniques in the twentieth century raised ethical dilemmas related to their clinical use; the indications for behavioural interventions in often widespread varieties of psychological discontent and the potential for abuse for non-therapeutic purposes when a classic disease model was problematic. It therefore led to in-depth consideration of the philosophical problem of how brain alteration altered a person. The neuroethics renaissance is, in a sense, a response to that question and the realization that the brain is a biologically adaptive device reflecting in its workings our embeddedness in a human life-world in which each of us has to find a sustainable way of being. That relationship is under severe strain in the 21st century and internalizing it by individually attributing the problem to individuals who do not cope in the environments we produce and then modifying their brain function raises ethical questions as adaptation is a "two way street."

CONCLUSION AND FUTURE DIRECTIONS

Modern neuroscience has deepened and massively extended the Hippocratic realization that mind and behavior reflect the workings of the brain – a plastic biological structure designed to capture our ways of integrating and coordinating information to forge a sustainable way of living. This puts great emphasis on assessing largely insufficient neuroscientific findings and their applications, with a clear view of the relational existence that is human life and the relational excellence that is human well-being. The result is that all human ills and pleasures are medicalized – able to be treated within the individual viewed as an isolated biological system. This approach has led to the view of psychiatry as a cookbook that combines pigeonholing distress and applying off-the-shelf and marketable remedies rather than understanding the individual in context – an individual who is struggling to adapt to the complex demands of being-in-the-world-with-others. This is related to a fundamental lack of detailed neuroscientific knowledge of which brain circuits are involved in each individual's brain in a specific disease and in his or her context. That phenomenological existential orientation, viewed neuroethically, warns us against the application to individual human beings of standardized technologies, except where the disorder identified is highly stereotyped and amendable to a standard evidence-based approach or when individualized abnormalities in brain circuitry can be demonstrated by individualized functional imaging, elicited by relevant techniques.

Although we have primarily considered the most widely available existing surgical methods of brain enhancement, in the future it is anticipated that brain chip and nano technologies will become available. Such technologies are likely to become available for therapeutic interventions, although it would be anticipated that, as with DBS, there could be interest and demand for non-therapeutic enhancement. There will always be proponents who believe that enhancement technology should be made available provided the risks are manageable (Greely et al., 2008). As with new pharmaceutical products, new technologies might be tested against the current gold standard alternative. For example, neurosurgery for epilepsy is only considered when less invasive pharmacological agents fail to control the disease. Perhaps neurosurgical interventions and implants will need to be evaluated in the same manner against the less invasive alternatives.

The challenges of neuromodulation are not only technological but also ethical and thus ecological, i.e., need to be seen in the real world context. Gary Small and Gigi Vorgan in their book *iBrain* have highlighted how digital technology has already changed the way our brains develop by impacting on neural plasticity and neural circuit recruitment (2008).

As neurosurgeons and neuroethicists, we need to take careful account, and demand careful accounting, of the technological future made possible by current advance: DBS and the conducive and anti-personal effects of neuromodulation in producing standardized contented versions of ourselves. This can probably only be prevented by individualizing the treatment, casting doubt about how current evidence based medicine is conducted, by standardizing and depersonalizing individuals, expecting that everyone's brain circuitry will respond to neuromodulation in the same way; cortical stimulation and the reworking of complex patterns of adaptation that define each of us as an individual need to more investigated, rather than hypothesized standardized adaptive responses. Another question is related to brain-chip technology and the development of cyborgs – when does the human become the inhuman and robotic – how silicone can Aunt Mary be and still be Aunt Mary, and when would it be permissible to stop reconstructing her and admit that she has passed? In essence this boils down to Aunt Mary's individual make up in her specific context. Considering that the rules of how her brain wires adaptively to a changing environment is genetically encoded, but the environment is not, the answer to the question relates to how adaptive the brain chip technology is and whether it uses the same adaptive mechanisms as Aunt Mary and not a standardized adaptive response. And when does Hemi or Joe become an individual with neural tendencies to aggression and criminality that can be modified by brain intervention rather than a member of an ethnic or socio-economic minority who is marginalized, resentful, and disaffected with the exaggerated inequalities in contemporary society? In essence, the ethical approach to neuromodulation is very different when it is not enforced by society, but a free choice of the individual.

REFERENCES

Armocida, G. (2007). A.M. Fiamberti and 'psycosurgery'. *Medicina Nei Secoli*, *19*, 457–474. PMID:18450027

Bellah, R. N., Madsen, R., Sullivan, W. M., Swidler, A., & Tipton, S. M. (2007). *Habits of the heart: Individualism and commitment in American life*. University of California Press.

The Belmont Report: Ethical Principles and Guidelines for the Protection of Human Subjects of Research. (1979). Report of the National Commission for the Protection of Human Subjects of Biomedical and Behavioral Research. Retrieved from http://www.hhs.gov/ohrp/humansubjects/guidance/belmont.html

Beurrier, C., Bioulac, B., Audin, J., & Hammond, C. (2001). High-frequency stimulation produces a transient blockade of voltage-gated currents in subthalamic neurons. *Journal of Neurophysiology*, *85*, 1351–1356. PMID:11287459

Brickner, R. M. (1952). Brain of patient A after bilateral frontal lobectomy, status of frontal-lobe problem. *American Medical Association Archives of Neurology and Psychiatry*, *68*, 293–313. doi:10.1001/archneurpsyc.1952.02320210003001 PMID:14952067

Burckhardt, G. (1981). Über rindenexcisionen, als beitrag zur operativen therapie der psychosen. *Allgemeine Zeitschrift für Psychiatrie*, *47*, 463–548.

Cade, J. F. J. (1949). Lithium salts in the treatment of psychotic excitement. *The Medical Journal of Australia*, *36*, 349–352. PMID:18142718

Charkin, S. (1978). *The mind stealers*. Boston: Houghton Mifflin Company.

Cohen Kadosh, R. (2013). Using transcranial electrical stimulation to enhance cognitive functions in the typical and atypical brain. *Translational Neuroscience*, *4*, 20–33. doi:10.2478/s13380-013-0104-7

Condon, R. (1949). *The Manchurian candidate*. London: Orion Books.

Crichton, M. (1972). *The terminal man*. New York: Ballantine Books.

Damasio, A. (1994). *Descartes' error: Emotion reason and the human brain*. New York: Grosset.

Delay, J., Deniker, P., & Harl, J. M. (1952). Therapeutic use in psychiatry of phenothiazine of central elective action (4560 RP). Annales medico-psychologiques (Paris), 110, 112-117.

de Leon, J. (2013). Is psychiatry scientific? A letter to a 21st century psychiatry resident. *Psychiatry Investigation*, *10*, 205–217. doi:10.4306/pi.2013.10.3.205 PMID:24302942

Delgado, J. (1969). *Toward a psychocivilized society*. New York: Harper and Row Publishers.

Delgado, J. M. R. (1968). Intracerebral radio stimulation and recording in completely free patients. *The Journal of Nervous and Mental Disease*, *147*, 329–340. doi:10.1097/00005053-196810000-00001 PMID:5683678

De Ridder, D., Langguth, B., Plazier, M., & Menovsky, T. (2009). Moral Dysfunction: Theoretical Model and Potential Neurosurgical Treatments. In J. Verplaetse, & S. Vanneste (Eds.), *The moral brain* (pp. 155–184). New York: Springer. doi:10.1007/978-1-4020-6287-2_7

De Ridder, D., & Van de Heyning, P. (2007). The Darwinian plasticity hypothesis for tinnitus and pain. *Progress in Brain Research*, *166*, 55–60. doi:10.1016/S0079-6123(07)66005-1 PMID:17956771

De Ridder, D., Vanneste, S., Menovsky, T., & Langguth, B. (2012). Surgical brain modulation for tinnitus: The past, present and future. *Journal of Neurosurgical Sciences*, *56*, 323–340. PMID:23111293

Dyson, F. J. (2012). History of science. Is science mostly driven by ideas or by tools? *Science, 338,* 1426–1427. doi:10.1126/science.1232773 PMID:23239721

El-Hai, J. (2005). *The lobotomist.* Hoboken, NJ: John Wiley and Sons, Inc.

Elliott, C. (2003). *Better than well: American medicine meets the American dream.* New York: Norton.

Engel, G. L. (1977). The need for a new medical model: A challenge for biomedicine. *Science, 196,* 129–136. doi:10.1126/science.847460 PMID:847460

Fiamberti, M. (1950). Transorbital prefrontal leucotomy in psychosurgery. *Minerva Medica, 41,* 131–135. PMID:15438855

Figee, M., Luigjes, J., Smolders, R., Valencia-Alfonso, C. E., van Wingen, G., & de Kwaasteniet, B. et al. (2013). Deep brain stimulation restores frontostriatal network activity in obsessive-compulsive disorder. *Nature Neuroscience, 16,* 386–387. doi:10.1038/nn.3344 PMID:23434914

Finney, G. R. (2009). Normal pressure hydrocephalus. *International Review of Neurobiology, 84,* 263–281. doi:10.1016/S0074-7742(09)00414-0 PMID:19501723

Fountas, K. N., & Smith, J. R. (2007). Historical evolution of stereotactic amygdalotomy for the management of severe aggression. *Journal of Neurosurgery, 106,* 710–713. doi:10.3171/jns.2007.106.4.710 PMID:17432727

Freeman, W. (1957). Frontal lobotomy 1936-1956: A follow-up study of 3000 patients from one to twenty years. *The American Journal of Psychiatry, 113,* 877–886. PMID:13402981

Freeman, W., & Watts, J. W. (1952). Psychosurgery. *Progress in Neurology and Psychiatry, 7,* 374–384. PMID:13004057

Fumagalli, M., & Priori, A. (2012). Functional and clinical neuroanatomy of morality. *Brain, 135,* 2006–2021. doi:10.1093/brain/awr334 PMID:22334584

Gillett, G. (2008). *Subjectivity and being somebody: Human identity and neuroethics.* Exeter, UK: Imprint Academic.

Gillett, G. (2009). *The mind and its discontents* (2nd ed.). Oxford, UK: University Press. doi:10.1093/med/9780199237548.001.0001

Gillett, G., & Huang, J. (2013). What we owe the psychopath: A neuroethical analysis. *American Journal of Bioethics Neuroscience, 4,* 3–9.

Gillett, G., & Tamatea, A. J. (2012). The warrior gene: Epigenetic considerations. *New Genetics & Society, 31,* 41–53. doi:10.1080/14636778.2011.597982

Gillett, G., & Walker, S. (2012). The evolution of informed consent. *Journal of Law and Medicine, 19,* 673–677. PMID:22908611

Glannon, W. (2007). *Bioethics and the brain.* Oxford, UK: Oxford University Press.

Greely, H., Sahakian, B., Harris, J., Kessler, R. C., Gazzaniga, M., Campbell, P., & Farah, M. J. (2008). Towards responsible use of cognitive-enhancing drugs by the healthy. *Nature, 456,* 702–705. doi:10.1038/456702a PMID:19060880

Greenberg, D. S. (1967). *The politics of pure science.* Chicago: The University of Chicago Press.

Gruzelier, J., Egner, T., & Verson, D. (2006). Validating the efficacy of neurofeedback for optimizing performance. *Progress in Brain Research, 159,* 421–431. doi:10.1016/S0079-6123(06)59027-2 PMID:17071246

Hakim, S., & Adams, R. D. (1965). The special clinical problem of symptomatic hydrocephalus with normal cerebrospinal fluid pressure: Observations on cerebrospinal fluid hydrodynamics. *Journal of the Neurological Sciences, 2,* 307–327. doi:10.1016/0022-510X(65)90016-X PMID:5889177

Hariz, M., Blomstedt, P., & Zrinco, L. (2013). Future of brain stimulation: New targets, new indications, new technology. *Movement Disorders, 28,* 1784–1792. doi:10.1002/mds.25665 PMID:24123327

Haug, C. (2013). What happened to Dan Markingson? *Journal of the Norwegian Medical Association, 133,* 2443–2444. PMID:24326485

Heath, R. G. (1963). Intracranial direct stimulation in man. *Science, 140,* 394–396. doi:10.1126/science.140.3565.394 PMID:13971228

Hebb, D. O., & Penfield, W. (1940). Human behavior after extensive bilateral removal from the frontal lobes. *Archives of Neurology and Psychiatry, 44,* 421–438. doi:10.1001/archneurpsyc.1940.02280080181011

Holtzheimer, P. E., Kelley, M. E., Gross, R. E., Filkowski, M. M., Garlow, S. J., & Barrocas, A. et al. (2012). Subcallosal cingulate deep brain stimulation for treatment-resistant unipolar and bipolar depression. *Archives of General Psychiatry, 69,* 150–158. doi:10.1001/archgenpsychiatry.2011.1456 PMID:22213770

Hu, R., Eskandar, E., & Williams, Z. (2009). Role of deep brain stimulation in modulating memory formation and recall. *Neurosurgical Focus, 27,* E3. doi:10.3171/2009.4.FOCUS0975 PMID:19569891

Hughlings-Jackson, J. (1887). Remarks on evolution and dissolution of the nervous system. *The British Journal of Psychiatry, 33,* 25–48. doi:10.1192/bjp.33.141.25

Huxley, A. (1932). *Brave new world.* London: Chatto & Windus.

Jacobsen, E. (1986). The early history of psychotherapeutic drugs. *Psychopharmacology, 89,* 138–144. doi:10.1007/BF00310617 PMID:2873606

Jenkins, J., Shajahan, P. M., Lappin, J. M., & Ebmeier, K. P. (2002). Right and left prefrontal transcranial magnetic stimulation at 1 Hz does not affect mood in healthy volunteers. *BMC Psychiatry, 2,* 1. doi:10.1186/1471-244X-2-1 PMID:11825340

Johnson, J. A., Strafella, A. P., & Zatorre, R. J. (2007). The role of the dorsolateral prefrontal cortex in divided attention: Two transcranial magnetic stimulation studies. *Journal of Cognitive Neuroscience, 19,* 907–920. doi:10.1162/jocn.2007.19.6.907 PMID:17536962

Lass, P., Sławek, J., & Sitek, E. (2012). Egas Moniz: A genius, unlucky looser [sic] or a Nobel committee error? *Neurologia i Neurochirurgia Polska, 46,* 96–103. doi:10.5114/ninp.2012.27452 PMID:22426769

Laxton, A. W., Lipsman, N., & Lozano, A. M. (2013). Deep brain stimulation for cognitive disorders. *Handbook of Clinical Neurology, 116,* 307–311. doi:10.1016/B978-0-444-53497-2.00025-5 PMID:24112904

Laxton, A. W., & Lozano, A. M. (2013). Deep brain stimulation for the treatment of Alzheimer disease and dementias. *World Neurosurgery, 80*(S28), e1–e8. doi:10.1016/j.wneu.2012.06.028 PMID:22722036

Lipsman, N., Mendelsohn, D., Taira, T., & Bernstein, M. (2011). The contemporary practice of psychiatric surgery: Results from a survey of North American functional neurosurgeons. *Stereotactic and Functional Neurosurgery, 89*(2), 103–110. doi:10.1159/000323545 PMID:21336006

MacIntyre, A. (1999). *Dependent rational animals: Why human beings need the virtues*. Chicago: Open Court.

Manji, H. K., Drevets, W. C., & Charney, D. S. (2001). The cellular neurobiology of depression. *Nature Medicine*, *7*, 541–547. doi:10.1038/87865 PMID:11329053

Marshall, L., Molle, M., Hallschmid, M., & Born, J. (2004). Transcranial direct current stimulation during sleep improves declarative memory. *The Journal of Neuroscience*, *24*, 9985–9992. doi:10.1523/JNEUROSCI.2725-04.2004 PMID:15525784

Mayberg, H. S., Lozano, A. M., Voon, V., & McNeely, H. E. (2005). Deep brain stimulation for treatment-resistant depression. *Neuron*, *45*, 651–660. doi:10.1016/j.neuron.2005.02.014 PMID:15748841

Moniz, E. (1994). Prefrontal leucotomy in the treatment of mental disorders. *The American Journal of Psychiatry*, *151*, 236–239. PMID:8192205

Motohashi, N., Yamaguchi, M., Fujii, T., & Kitahara, Y. (2013). Mood and cognitive function following repeated transcranial direct current stimulation in healthy volunteers: A preliminary report. *Neuroscience Research*, *77*, 64–69. doi:10.1016/j.neures.2013.06.001 PMID:23811267

Northoff, G. (2006). Neuroscience of decision-making and informed consent: An investigation in neuroethics. *Journal of Medical Ethics*, *32*, 70–73. doi:10.1136/jme.2005.011858 PMID:16446409

Olds, J., & Milner, P. (1954). Positive reinforcement produced by electrical stimulation of septal area and other regions of rat brain. *Journal of Comparative and Physiological Psychology*, *47*, 419–427. doi:10.1037/h0058775 PMID:13233369

Plazier, M., Joos, K., Vanneste, S., Ost, J., & De Ridder, D. (2012). Bifrontal and bioccipital transcranial direct current stimulation (tDCS) does not induce mood changes in healthy volunteers: A placebo controlled study. *Brain Stimulation*, *5*, 454–461. doi:10.1016/j.brs.2011.07.005 PMID:21962976

Pratico, D., Yao, Y., Rokach, J., Mayo, M., Silverberg, G. G., & McGuire, D. (2004). Reduction of brain lipid peroxidation by CSF drainage in Alzheimer's disease patients. *Journal of Alzheimer's Disease*, *6*, 385–389. PMID:15345808

Pressman, J. D. (1998). *Last resort: Psychosurgery and the limits of medicine*. Cambridge, UK: Cambridge University Press.

Rabins, P., Appleby, B. S., Brandt, J., DeLong, M. R., Dunn, L. B., & Gabriëls, L. et al. (2009). Scientific and ethical issues related to deep brain stimulation for disorders of mood, behavior, and thought. *Archives of General Psychiatry*, *66*, 931–937. doi:10.1001/archgenpsychiatry.2009.113 PMID:19736349

Racine, E., & Forlini, C. (2009). Expectations regarding cognitive enhancement create substantial challenges. *Journal of Medical Ethics*, *35*, 469–470. doi:10.1136/jme.2009.030460 PMID:19644002

Raz, M. (2008). Between the ego and the icepick: Psychosurgery, psychoanalysis and psychiatric discourse. *Bulletin of the History of Medicine*, *82*, 387–420. doi:10.1353/bhm.0.0038 PMID:18622073

Robison, R. A., Taghva, A., Liu, C. Y., & Apuzzo, M. L. (2012). Surgery of the mind, mood and conscious state: An idea in evolution. *World Neurosurgery*, *77*, 662–686. doi:10.1016/j.wneu.2012.03.005 PMID:22446082

Savulescu, J., & Kahane, G. (2009). The moral obligation to create children with the best chance of the best life. *Bioethics, 23*, 274–290. doi:10.1111/j.1467-8519.2008.00687.x PMID:19076124

Schlaepfer, T., George, M., & Mayberg, H. (2010). WFSBP Guidelines on brain stimulation treatment in psychiatry. *The World Journal of Biological Psychiatry, 11*, 2–18. doi:10.3109/15622970903170835 PMID:20146648

Shiozawa, P., Fregni, F., Bensenor, I. M., Lotufo, P. A., & Berlim, M. T., Daskalakis, … Brunoni, A. R. (2014). Transcranial direct current stimulation for major depression: An updated systematic review and meta-analysis. *The International Journal of Neuropsychopharmacology, 8*, 1–10.

Small, G., & Vogan, G. (2008). IBrain. New York: Collins Living (Harper Collins).

Sparrow, R. (2011). A not-so-new eugenics: Harris and Savulescu on human enhancement. *The Hastings Center Report, 41*, 32–42. PMID:21329104

Spielmans, G., & Parry, P. (2010). From evidence based medicine to marketing based medicine: Evidence from internal industry documents. *Journal of Bioethical Inquiry, 7*, 13–30. doi:10.1007/s11673-010-9208-8

Sterman, M. B., & Egner, T. (2006). Foundation and practice of neurofeedback for the treatment of epilepsy. *Applied Psychophysiology and Biofeedback, 31*, 21–35. doi:10.1007/s10484-006-9002-x PMID:16614940

Thibaut, A., Bruno, M. A., Ledoux, D., Demertzi, A., & Laureys, S. (2014). tDCS in patients with disorders of consciousness: Sham-controlled randomized double-blind study. *Neurology, 82*, 1112–1118. doi:10.1212/WNL.0000000000000260 PMID:24574549

Van Staden, C. W., & Kruger, C. (2003). Incapacity to give informed consent owing to mental disorder. *Journal of Medical Ethics, 29*, 41–43. doi:10.1136/jme.29.1.41 PMID:12569195

Vernon, D. J. (2005). Can neurofeedback training enhance performance? An evaluation of the evidence with implications for future research. *Applied Psychophysiology and Biofeedback, 30*, 347–364. doi:10.1007/s10484-005-8421-4 PMID:16385423

Viets, H. R. (1949). Report of the librarian. *The New England Journal of Medicine, 240*, 917–920. doi:10.1056/NEJM194906092402304

Witt, K., Kuhn, J., Timmermann, L., Zurowski, M., & Woopen, C. (2003). Deep brain stimulation and the search for identity. *Neuroethics, 6*, 499–511. doi:10.1007/s12152-011-9100-1 PMID:24273620

KEY TERMS AND DEFINITIONS

Autonomy: The personal rule of the self, free from both controlling interferences by others and from personal limitations that prevent meaningful choice.

Bioethics: The study of ethical issues associated with advances in biology and medicine.

Cognitive Enhancement Device: A device that amplifies or augments the capabilities of the mind.

Deep Brain Stimulation: The surgical implantation of an electrical stimulator into a specific region of the brain.

Informed Consent: Consent to surgery by a patient or to participation in a medical experiment by a subject after achieving an understanding of what is involved.

Neuromodulation: The alteration of nerve activity through the delivery of electrical stimulation or chemical agents to targeted sites of the body.

Psychosurgery: The neurosurgical treatment of mental or behavioural disorders.

Chapter 7
Super Soldiers (Part 1):
What is Military Human Enhancement?

Patrick Lin
California Polytechnic State University, USA

Keith Abney
California Polytechnic State University, USA

Max Mehlman
Case Western Reserve University, USA

Jai Galliott
Macquarie University, Australia

ABSTRACT

After World War II, much debate unfolded about the ethical, legal, and social implications of military human enhancement, due in part to Adolf Hitler's war on the "genetically unfit" and the United States military's experimentation with psychedelic drugs such as LSD. Interest in that debate has waxed and waned since the 1940s. However, it would be foolish or perhaps even dangerous to believe that America and its modern allies have abandoned efforts to upgrade service members' bodies and minds to create the "super soldiers" necessary to match the increasing pace of modern warfare and dominate the strengthening militaries of China and North Korea. Slogans such as "be all that you can be and a whole lot more" still reign strong at the US Defense Advanced Research Projects Agency and, according to some military futurists, the so-called "War on Terror" has only proven that military superpowers need a new type of soldier that is independent, network-integrated, and more lethal than ever before. Patterns of public risk perception, military expenditure, and new technological developments suggest that it is now time to re-open or reinvigorate the original debate. The authors' contribution comes in two parts. In this chapter, they provide a brief background to military human enhancement before defining it carefully and exploring the relevant controversies. In the second, they more explicitly examine the relevant legal, operational, and moral challenges posed by these efforts.

DOI: 10.4018/978-1-4666-6010-6.ch007

INTRODUCTION

War is an all-too-human affair and will probably always require a strong commitment to allowing human lives to be damaged, blighted, or lost. This is a terrible cost, but one which science and technology hope to ease. History has seen an evolution of defensive and offensive technologies—from shields and body armor to more accurate and longer range artillery and precision guided munitions—that are aimed exactly at minimizing the human cost, at least to our own side. In today's digital age, we are seeing the pace of the military technical revolution increase with the wide scale deployment of military robots, cyber weapons, and other technologies that promise to replace the organic, soft-bodied combatant and better protect noncombatants as well.

Yet it is difficult to imagine a plausible medium-term scenario in which technology replaces all human combatants in war. No weapon or loss thus far has been so horrific as to deter us from renewing our fighting, a point made clear by the fact that World War I did not end up being the "war to end all wars." Even against daunting odds and fearsome machines, from tanks to flying drones, humans are tenacious and hopeful, refusing to give up easily and enslave themselves to a greater power.

But therein lies a fundamental problem with how we wage war: as impressive as our weapons systems may be, one of the weakest but most valuable links in armed conflict continues to be warfighters themselves. Hunger, fatigue, and the need for sleep can quickly drain troop morale and threaten a mission. Fear and confusion in the "fog of war" can lead to costly mistakes, such as friendly-fire casualties. Emotions and adrenaline can drive otherwise-decent individuals to perform vicious acts, from verbal abuse of local civilians to torture and extrajudicial executions, with the potential to make an international incident out of what would have otherwise been a routine patrol.

And post-traumatic stress can take a devastating toll on families and add pressure on already-burdened health services.

Human frailty is striking and largely inescapable. Unlike other animals, we are not armed with fangs, claws, flight, venom, fur, or other helpful features to survive the savage world. It is a wonder our naked species has survived at all, if not for our tool-making intellect and resourcefulness. But our tools so far provide limited sanctuary from dangers. For instance, some estimates put the United States government's investment in each soldier, not including salary, at approximately $1 million (Shaughnessy, 2012), helping to make the US military the best equipped in the world. Nonetheless, the million-dollar soldier still remains vulnerable to a fatal wound delivered by a single 25-cent bullet.

If humans will always be called upon to fight, then it makes sense to focus efforts on overcoming or compensating for that frailty. To be sure, military training attempts to address these problems, but it can only do so much. Science and technology again offer hope for whatever challenges we may face, in this case to upgrade or supplement the basic human condition. We want our warfighters to be made stronger, more aware, more durable, and more adaptive. The technologies that enable these abilities fall in the realm of military human enhancement.

As we explain in the following sections, human enhancement technologies are more than mere tools: we are drawing on these tools to such an extent that, for all practical intents and purposes, they can be considered integrated with ourselves—and this creates special competitive advantages and, sometimes, special risks. This two-part exploration is derived from our recent report for the Greenwall Foundation (Lin, Mehlman, & Abney, 2013) and aims to examine these risks and the associated legal, ethical, and policy issues arising out of military human enhancement—not necessarily a new class of warfighting technologies but one that is now developing in novel ways. In this first chapter (Chapter 7) we provide an outline of the developments in the field, as well as more fully explain what we mean by "human enhancement." In the second, we locate the various, legal, operational, and moral issues, but purposely hold short of providing any conclusive answers. Our aim here, to be clear, is to provide some initial insight into the areas of ethics research needed to help guide future discussions in this emerging area of science and technology.

A BRIEF BACKGROUND

Since the beginning of human history, we have improved our minds through education, disciplined thinking, and meditation. Similarly, we've improved our bodies with a sound diet, physical exercise, and training. But we are on the cusp of a radical change. With ongoing work in emerging technologies, we are near the start of what many have dubbed the Human Enhancement Revolution (Savulescu & Bostrom 2009; Allhoff et al., 2010a; Allhoff et al., 2010b). We are no longer limited to these "natural" methods of enhancing ourselves or merely wielding tools such as hammers, binoculars, or smart phones as extensions of our minds and bodies. With drugs and devices, we are beginning to alter our biology and incorporate technology within our very bodies, and this seems to hold moral significance that we ought to consider very carefully.

These technologies promise great benefits for humanity—such as increased productivity and creativity, longer lives, more serenity, stronger bodies and minds—as well as compelling uses for national security and defense. However, as highlighted in many of the other chapters of this volume, the issues arising from the employment of human enhancement technologies are many and include those related to autonomy and freedom, health and safety, fairness and access, social

disruption, and human dignity (Garreau, 2006; Selgelid, 2007; Allhoff et al., 2010a). For instance, critics question whether technological enhancements translate into happier lives, which many see as the point of the whole endeavor (President's Council on Bioethics, 2003; Persaud, 2006).

Of course, these questions are of less importance in a military context, where the focus must be instead on completing the mission; the welfare of the troops is usually a secondary concern. In any case, insofar as context matters in making moral determinations, the debate is made more complex with the need to account for the values and goods particular to the sphere under consideration (Murray 2007). These concerns are driving the larger issue of whether and how society ought to regulate human enhancement technologies, which is closely related to how militaries ought to approach the same.

For instance, one position in the larger debate is that (more than minimal) regulation would hinder personal freedom or autonomy, infringing on our natural or political right to improve our own bodies, minds, and lives as we see fit (Naam, 2005; Bailey, 2005; Harris, 2007). Others, however, advocate strong regulation—and even a research moratorium—to protect against any unforeseen or unintended effects on society, such as the presumably undesirable creation of a new class of enhanced persons who could outwit, outplay, and outlast "normal" or unenhanced persons in job interviews, schools, at sporting contests, and so on, among other reasons (Fukuyama, 2002, 2006). Still others recognize that society must adapt to new technological developments in this field (Hughes, 2004; UK Academy of Medical Sciences, 2012) and seek to strike a middle path between stringent regulation and individual liberty (Mehlman, 1999, 2000, 2003, 2004, 2009a, 2009b; Juengst, 2000; Greely, 2005).

No matter where one is aligned on this issue, it is clear that the human enhancement debate is a deeply passionate and personal one, striking at the heart of what it means to be human. Some see it as a way to fulfill or even transcend our potential, whilst others see it as a darker path towards losing our humanity (President's Council on Bioethics, 2003; Sandel, 2009).

Given that the US military is usually on the cutting-edge of science and technology research—having given society such innovations as the Internet, global positioning system (GPS), radar, microwaves, and even the modern computer—the following chapter will examine the associated legal, operational, and ethical issues at their root.

It should be said at the outset that the use of human enhancement technologies by the military is not new. Under some definitions—but not necessarily ours, as we explain below— vaccinations would count as an enhancement of the human immune system, and this would place the first instance of military human enhancement at the very first US war, the American Revolutionary War in 1775-1783. George Washington, as commander-in-chief of the Continental Army, ordered the vaccinations of American troops against smallpox, as the British Army was suspected of using the virus as a form of biological warfare (Fenn, 2002). At the time, few Americans were exposed to smallpox in childhood and therefore most had not built up immunity to the disease, as the British had. In the Middle Ages, biowarfare had also been used in catapulting infected corpses to spread the plague (Cantor, 2001; Lewis, 2009).

More recently and as a clearer instance of enhancement, militaries worldwide have turned to amphetamines, which have been used widely by American, German, British, and other forces in World War II, and again by the US in Korea (Stoil, 1990, cited in Lin, Mehlman, & Abney, 2013). Of course, milder and therefore less controversial stimulants, such as caffeine in coffee and tea, were used long before that. Beginning in 1960, the US Air Force sanctioned amphetamines on a limited basis for the Strategic Air Command and, in 1962, for the Tactical Air Command. The US-Vietnam War sparked large-scale amphetamine use, such

as by US Air Force and Navy pilots to extend their duty-day and increase vigilance while flying. According to one Cobra gunship pilot, "uppers" were available "like candy," with no control over how much was used (Cornum, Caldwell, & Cornum, 1997). During the US invasion of Panama (Operation Just Cause), these drugs were administered in smaller doses under much more careful medical supervision and in contrast to Vietnam, where pilots who used them frequently suffered from nervousness, loss of appetite, and inability to sleep (Cornum, Caldwell, & Cornum, 1997).

The US Air Force continued to dispense "speed" during Operations Desert Shield and Desert Storm. A survey of 464 fighter pilots in that conflict found that during the six-week operation, 57 percent reported that they took Dexedrine (an amphetamine) at least once, with 58 percent reporting occasional use and 17 percent admitting to routine use. Somewhat more alarmingly, 61 percent of users believed the drug was essential for mission completion (Schlesinger, 2003). In 1991, the US Air Force Chief of Staff, General Merrill A. McPeak, banned the use of amphetamines because, in his words, "Jedi Knights don't need them" (Shanker & Duenwald, 2003). The ban lasted until 1996, when Chief of Staff John Jumper reversed the policy, as the drugs were seen as critical to long-distance missions being flown in Eastern Europe (Hart, 2003).

In 2002, the US Air Force was dispensing 10 milligrams of amphetamines for every four hours of flying time for single-pilot fighter missions longer than eight hours and for two-pilot bomber missions longer than 12 hours. Asked why military pilots were permitted to use amphetamines when they were prohibited by commercial airlines, Colonel Peter Demitry, chief of the Air Force Surgeon General's Science and Technology division, explained that "When a civilian gets tired, the appropriate strategy is to land, then sleep. In combat operations when you're strapped to an ejection seat, you don't have the luxury to pull over" (Hart, 2003).

Amphetamines became more controversial in 2002, when four Canadian soldiers were killed and eight wounded in a friendly fire incident in Afghanistan involving a 500-pound laser-guided bomb dropped from a US Air Force F-16, the pilots of which were returning at 18,000 feet from a 10-hour mission and mistakenly thought they were attracting small arms fire (St. Louis Post-Dispatch Editors, 2003). When they learned of their mistake, the pilots claimed that they were jittery from taking Dexedrine for so many hours (Schlesinger, 2003). One of the pilots had been an instructor in the Illinois National Guard and had graduated from the Navy's "Top Gun" school. The fatalities were the first Canadians to die in combat since the Korean War (Simpson, 2004).

Despite this mishap, amphetamines continue to be approved for military use. A recent research article from scientists at the Air Force Research Laboratory reports, "the US Air Force has authorized the use of dextroamphetamine in certain types of lengthy (i.e., 12 or more hours) single-seat and dual-seat flight missions. A recent North Atlantic Treaty Organization (NATO) Research and Technology Organization publication also discusses amphetamine's significant value as an anti-fatigue measure for aviation personnel" (Caldwell & Caldwell, 2005). However, in an effort to find a safer alternative to amphetamines, the military is reported to be turning to modafinil, a drug originally used to treat narcolepsy and which is sold under the brand name Provigil. According to Jonathan Moreno, US troops first used modafinil during the 2003 invasion of Iraq. The British press reports that the UK Ministry of Defence purchased 24,000 modafinil tablets in 2004 (Sample, 2004). Research has shown that the drug improves the performance of helicopter pilots in flight simulators (Caldwell et al., 2000).

Moreno reports on a modafinil study that the Air Force's Office of Scientific Research conducted with 16 volunteers who, over a four-day period, stayed awake for 28 hours, then slept from 11 am until 7 pm. The modafinil group did significantly better on cognitive tests than subjects who took a placebo. Other research showed that modafinil-enabled pilots remain alert for 40 hours, and experiments at Walter Reed Institute of Research have been carried out on soldiers who were sleep-deprived for as long as 85 hours (Sample, 2004). We discuss the moral and legal propriety of doing such research on the military in our other chapter. While the military is actively investigating new alertness drugs like modafinil, it continues to employ the old standby, caffeine. New US army "first strike" rations contain caffeine-laced chewing gum, with each stick providing the equivalent of a cup of strong coffee (Sample, 2004).

In addition to using alertness drugs to enhance performance, a long-standing practice among members of the military has been to take dietary supplements. As reported in the journal *Military Medicine*, "a recent worldwide survey showed that over 60 percent of service members are regularly taking some type of dietary supplement. Supplement use is usually at the advice of the sales clerk or by getting information from magazines or peers. Evidence-based information is rarely available or rarely translated into a form that can be properly used by the warfighter or their commander" (Jonas et al., 2010). Despite the limited amount of scientific evidence, the military recognizes the potential value of supplements: "Nutritional supplements may indeed be beneficial in certain circumstances. For example, caffeine may provide advantages in military jobs and duties where attentiveness is necessary (e.g., aviators, sentry duty)" (Montain, Carvey, & Stephens, 2010).

In 2008, Brookings Institution fellow Peter W. Singer reported an ambitious goal presented by DARPA program manager Michael Callahan at the agency's 50th anniversary conference in 2007: "making soldiers 'kill-proof'" (Singer, 2009). Callahan described research that would enable soldiers "to bring to battle the same sort of capabilities that nature has given certain animals," including a sea lion's dive reflex. "Products in the pipeline" include "drugs that will boost muscles and energy by a factor of 10, akin to steroids...on steroids," which Singer says "is jokingly termed the Energizer Bunny in Fatigues."

There is also a long-term $3 billion initiative entitled the "Metabolically Dominant Soldier," which Moreno claims is aimed at developing a super-nutritional pill that, in DARPA's words, would permit "continuous peak performance and cognitive function for 3 to 5 days, 24 hours per day, without the need for calories" (Moreno, 2006). A 2007 article in *Wired* identified extramural enhancement research projects sponsored by DARPA at: Dana-Farber Cancer Institute in Boston to develop substances to make soldiers more energetic; Columbia University to enable soldiers to make do with less sleep; and Ames, Iowa, where agricultural experts are researching bacteria that, once ingested, would enable soldiers to obtain nutritional value from normally indigestible substances such as cellulose (Shachtman, 2007a, 2007b).

In 2008, JASON, a group of scientific advisors to the US Department of Defense (DoD) issued a report on "human performance" that discussed several types of biomedical enhancements, including the potential use of a class of compounds called ampakines to enhance cognition (JASON, 2008). A central point in the report was that the benefits from military enhancement were not similar to the benefits from performance enhancement in elite sports: "the consequences of gaining a small performance advantage, even if it is highly statistically significant, are likely quite different as regards force-on-force engagements than as regards Olympic competition. In brief, a small performance advantage in force-on-force should generally result in a small change in the outcome, while in Olympic competition it can result in a large change in the outcome" (JASON, 2008).

At the same time, the report acknowledged that a major change in human performance, giving as an example a reduction in the need for sleep, could have a "dramatic effect" on the "balance of military effectiveness" (JASON, 2008). However, this dramatic effect would occur only if the adversary did not have access to the same benefit, leading the report to emphasize the need to monitor and be prepared to counter enhancement use by potential adversaries. More recently, the US military has extended its interest in performance enhancement to genetic technologies. In December 2010, JASON issued a report entitled "The $100 Genome: Implications for the DoD." The report outlined an ambitious plan to employ genomic technologies to "enhance medical status and improve treatment outcomes," enhance "health, readiness, and performance of military personnel," and "know the genetic identities of an adversary" (JASON, 2010). At the same time, the US military appears to be dead-set against the use of steroids. Department of Defense Directive 1010.1, originally issued in 1984, states that "the illicit use of anabolic steroids by military members" is an offense under the Uniform Code of Military Justice (US Department of Defense, 2012).

The US military's current interest in biomedical enhancement is a logical corollary to its objective of maximizing the performance capabilities of its members. This performance imperative is reflected in the goals of military training. As an Army training manual states: war places a great premium upon the strength, stamina, agility, and coordination of the soldier because victory and his life are so often dependent upon them. To march long distances with full pack, weapons, and ammunition through rugged country and to fight effectively upon arriving at the area of combat; to drive fast-moving tanks and motor vehicles over rough terrain; to make assaults and to run and crawl for long distances; to jump into and out of foxholes, craters, and trenches, and over obstacles; to lift and carry heavy objects; to keep going for many hours without sleep or rest—all require superbly conditioned troops (Roy et al., 2010).

The recent interest in military performance optimization has led to expansions of the concept of warfighter fitness. In 2005, Army Field Manual 21-20 was replaced by Training Circular 3-22.20,

"Physical Readiness Training (PRT)," which describes as its purpose "to develop a more agile, versatile, lethal, and survivable force—while preparing soldiers and units for the physical challenges of fulfilling the mission in the face of a wide range of threats, in complex operational environments, and with emerging technologies" (Little, 2010). As the deputy commander of the US Army Training and Doctrine Command explained, "the youngest generation has grown up with energy drinks and soda while playing video games on the couch, instead of drinking milk and taking physical education classes in school...The Army has seen a major increase in dental problems and bone injuries during basic training. In the last 15 years, average body fat has also increased to 30 percent in the South...The challenge is taking young soldiers entering the Army under these conditions and getting them ready to hump the Hindu Kush," the 500-mile mountain range between northwest Pakistan and eastern and central Afghanistan (Little, 2010).

In 2006, a DoD conference titled "Human Performance Optimization" led to the creation of a dedicated human performance office within Force Health Protection in the Assistant Secretary of Defense Office (Health Affairs) (Land, 2010). The attendees at this conference recognized the need for a holistic "total force fitness" approach, which subsequently was adopted by the Army in 2008 under the name "Comprehensive Soldier Fitness Program." This program is described as signaling "the US Army's attempt to bring science to bear on a complex problem—shaping and accelerating human development and performance. The program is massive in scale and will directly impact three distinct populations—US Army soldiers, their family members, and civilians employed by the Army" (Lester, et al., 2011).

As these new training initiatives make clear, the goal is to go beyond preparation for the demands of military service and instead enable "functioning at a new optimal level to face new missions or challenges" (Jonas et al., 2010). Biomedical enhancement is one of the obvious technologies that might be employed in responding to this new performance imperative, but even with this background, we need to establish the definition of "military human enhancement."

WHAT IS MILITARY HUMAN ENHANCEMENT?

To properly continue, we need to clarify the definition of "human enhancement," which still remains somewhat elusive. Our definition follows that suggested by bioethicist Eric Juengst: an enhancement is a medical or biological intervention introduced into the body designed "to improve performance, appearance, or capability besides what is necessary to achieve, sustain or restore health" (Juengst, 1998). More will be said about this definition shortly.

In explaining what a human enhancement is and what it is not, we might start with ostensive definitions or illustrative examples, as we attempt to arrive at a principled distinction between the two. An enhancement, strictly speaking, is anything that improves our lives or helps us to achieve our goals, including the goal of survival. Thus, healthy foods, exercise, fire, tools such as a hammer, a roof over one's head, and so on are enhancements in at least the sense that they clearly enhance our lives or make them better.

Notice that these enhancements could also pose dangers, or a net loss in welfare, if used in certain ways: a diet could be fatal to a person who is allergic to its ingredients; exercise can lead to pulled muscles and more serious injuries; fire can burn down communities of homes; hammers can be turned to weapons; and a roof can fall on one's head in an earthquake. Indeed, it is difficult to imagine what exactly would count as an enhancement, if we were to insist that enhancements deliver only benefits.

But we do not mean "human enhancement" in this general sense. If we did, the notion would become so broad that it is rendered meaningless. Nearly everything we create could count as an enhancement, from Lego blocks to language itself, as long as we derive some benefit from it. Thus, if we are to use the term in a meaningful way—that is, to examine whether novel ethical issues arise from enhancements, as many intuitively suspect—we need to describe a limit to what counts as enhancements, and we need to defend that line, to the extent that there is no general consensus on a definition.

We count the following as examples of human enhancement: an athlete who is stronger with anabolic steroid use; a student who earns higher grades by using Ritalin or modafinil to study more effectively; in the future, a soldier who can run for days on a drug that triggers in humans whatever metabolic processes enable an Arctic sled dog to run for that long; and also in the future, an office worker who is smarter than her peers, given a computer chip implanted in her head that gives instant access to databases and search engines. In contrast, we do not count the following as examples of human enhancement: a muscular dystrophy patient who uses anabolic steroids to regain some strength; an expensive prep school background to enable a student to earn higher grades; a vehicle that can transport soldiers for days; a smartphone that enables a worker to check email and look up information.

But why should this be? Why are some technologies or applications considered as enhancements, while others that seem directed at the same goal are not? It is not enough that we offer a few examples of enhancements and non-enhancements; we need to explain the principle or reasoning for making this discrimination. Any distinction that is meant to delimit enhancements instantly takes us down difficult philosophical rabbit holes. This is why a definition of enhancement has been so elusive, and also why some commentators have denied that a definition can be found.

To seriously consider the possibility that some enhancements raise novel ethical issues, though, let us assume that we can define enhancement, even if imperfectly, before we abandon hope for such a project. We will not explore this conceptual maze in much depth here, but only identify a few points of contention to convey a sense of how difficult it is to give a definition of enhancement. This is important because if we are not aiming at the right targets to begin with, our understanding of "human enhancement" would be arbitrary, and the legal, ethical, and policy analysis that follows could fail to be relevant or lack the desired force.

Natural vs. Artificial

As a first approximation of a distinction between non-enhancements and enhancements, we may be tempted to look at the distinction between natural and unnatural (Bostrom & Sandberg, 2009; Allhoff et al., 2010a). That is, medical treatments for the sick, exercise, and education are "natural" activities that humans have been doing throughout history. Insofar as what is natural is good, these activities are not morally problematic. In contrast, drugs that give us the endurance of sled dogs and other such enhancements take us beyond "natural" limits of human functioning. In that sense, enhancements are unnatural or artificial aids, and what is unnatural should evoke caution and skepticism—or so the distinction would seem to imply.

Never mind how such a distinction would be morally relevant, it quickly collapses upon reflection. In a general context, we might say that trees and rocks are natural in that they exist independently of human agency or intervention, while houses and computers are artificial in that they depend on our manipulation of materials. But many things we would consider to be natural depend on external manipulation, such as a bird's nest or a beaver's dam. If we then retreat and stipulate that external manipulation means human manipulation, then nothing created by humans can be considered to be natural. In other words, this move does not get us closer to what human enhancement is, if the definition tracks a natural-versus-artificial distinction: everything created by humans would then be artificial and an enhancement. As mentioned before, this notion seems unreasonably broad; and it defies common intuitions that education and exercise—which involve printed books, microscopes, athletic shoes, and even high-priced Olympic coaches—are not enhancements but mere activities that benefit humans.

In the alternative, to the extent that humans arise from nature, there is a sense that everything we do is natural. But this conception suffers from being too broad in the opposite direction: nothing we do can be artificial, and so this too does not move us closer to understanding enhancement via the natural-versus-artificial distinction. Where we consider mass education and high-tech exercise today to be natural, surely these would have been considered as unnatural at earlier times in human history, before the printing press, running-shoe technologies, and so on.

External vs. Internal

If the natural-versus-artificial distinction is untenable, then perhaps we can turn to another one: the distinction between an external tool or technology and an internal one (Garcia & Sandler, 2008; Allhoff et al., 2010a). For instance, an Internet-enabled smartphone is a mere tool or something less than an enhancement, because it is external to our bodies; it could be held in one's hand, or placed inside a pocket, or connected to a wall charger. But a computer chip implanted in one's head, that delivers the same capabilities as the smartphone, is an enhancement; it is internal to one's body, and this delivers "always-on" or unprecedented access to the tool—and competitive advantage from its benefits—as compared to using it as an external device (Allhoff et al., 2010a; Lin, 2010). Likewise, athletic shoes are not properly enhancements, since they are external devices

and not always worn, while anabolic steroids are enhancements because they are consumed or injected into the body.

"Internal" technologies could also be construed to include tools that are closely integrated to one's body, since that too delivers an "always-on" connectivity that does not exist with ordinary external tools. Bionic limbs that deliver super-strength, for instance, are not internal to a body, strictly speaking, yet we may consider them to be enhancements; they are attached to a body and become part of the person's identity, if that's important. Exoskeletons today, then, are mere tools, as they are bulky and cannot be easily worn for a long stretch of time; but if they were to become much more lightweight and unobtrusive, perhaps wearable like a shirt, then a case could be made for declaring them an enhancement.

The proximity of a device to the body can create a difference in degree that becomes a difference in kind. For instance, compare a person who looks up information on Google's search engine—on either his laptop or mobile device—to another person who looks up the same information through a "Google chip" implanted in her head. We would not say that the former is more knowledgeable or smarter for reciting information he found online; at best, he is resourceful. But while the latter may also just be reciting information she found online, her ability to do so at virtually any time—and seamlessly or transparently to others—would make her appear more knowledgeable, as if she were a savant who has uncanny recollection of facts and trivia (especially, say, in an exam room in which she is not supposed to have a computer).

Similarly, compare a person who uses Google Translate to communicate with the local population on his trip abroad to a person who has a Google translation chip implanted in her head to enable the same communication. The former would be recognized as someone who merely knows how to use a computer, while the latter could very well be mistaken as being fluent in the foreign language (again, say, in a test-taking environment). In other words, when it comes to proximity of a technological aid to the user, closer is generally better. We can thus defend the line between enhancement and mere tool in terms of internal versus external; and closely held or worn tools are "internal" enough, if the user is rarely without them.

An inherent limitation to the external-versus-internal distinction, however, is that it cannot account for a dual-use technology that is internal-only. For instance, the distinction does not speak to any *prima facie* moral difference between anabolic steroids taken by a muscular dystrophy patient and the same drug taken by an Olympic athlete; they are both cases of a pharmacological intervention that is internal to the body. Many critics strongly believe that the former case is morally uncontroversial while the latter is not, and so our distinction ought to be able to sort those cases if possible, at least for further examination.

Enhancement vs. Therapy

A more capable distinction, then, could be that between therapy and enhancement (President's Council for Bioethics, 2003; Allhoff et al., 2010a). This distinction easily accounts for the case of anabolic steroids that was so difficult for the external-versus-internal distinction: a muscular dystrophy patient needs anabolic steroids for therapeutic value or medical necessity, while the athlete has more gratuitous and less urgent reasons. So the patient has greater moral justification for using the drug, and this maps to popular intuitions (in case they carry any weight) that therapeutic uses are permissible while athletic-performance enhancing uses are questionable.

By "therapy", we mean an intervention or treatment intended to alleviate a condition suffered by a patient, elevating his or health closer to normal. Of course, "normal" raises a host of questions itself, given the diversity of abilities across the species. For instance, Albert Einstein

throws off the curve, as well as across one's own lifetime, e.g., health decreases with age. So if we may think of normal in terms of a species-typical range of functioning, that understanding may also need to be balanced against what is normal relative to one's own baseline and trajectory of health. Thus, if a drug could give an average person the IQ of Einstein, and Einstein does not fall in the species-typical range but exceeds it, then use of the drug in this case is an enhancement and not therapy. However, if Einstein were still alive and suffered a brain injury that reduced his IQ, then his taking of the same drug is not an enhancement, because it serves to restore his abilities back to his normal or baseline level. Enhancement, then, is highly sensitive to context.

A more difficult case to reconcile involves vaccinations: are they an enhancement or therapy (Bostrom & Roache, 2008; Allhoff et al., 2010a)? On one hand, the recipient is typically not sick when receiving the vaccination, so there's no immediate goal of restoring health to previous levels, as in most other cases of therapy. In this respect, a vaccination seems like an enhancement of one's immune system: it is not in the species-typical range of functioning that humans can naturally resist many pathogens. However, a vaccination could be considered to be preventative therapy: why should it matter if a therapeutic intervention—that is, designed to restore health back to normal—is administered before or after an illness?

For the purposes of this chapter, we will consider vaccinations to generally be a case of therapy, not enhancement, insofar as they aim to prevent a diseased condition. But we acknowledge that there may be nuances to this determination, which we lack the space to fully discuss here. For instance, perhaps it is reasonable to say that some therapies (such as vaccinations and accelerated healing) are also enhancements. Further, it may be pertinent whether a disease is caused by a naturally occurring or engineered pathogen; whether a disease can be caused by something other than biological agents, e.g., a chemical poison; and the related matter of how we define "disease." Again, context matters.

Notwithstanding difficult cases such as the above, the distinction between enhancement and therapy seems sensible, and so we will adopt it as the primary heuristic or rule-of-thumb in identifying what is an enhancement and what is not. This distinction, though, is not binary and therefore may not always be sufficient; that is, what is not therapy might not automatically be an enhancement. For instance, the external-versus-internal distinction is still useful to explain why carrying a smartphone is morally permissible—neither therapy nor enhancement, but simply a tool—but integrating it with one's body is less obviously so, in that it may raise questions about safety, fairness, and other issues. Other distinctions may still be relevant, as fuzzy as they may be; for instance, notice that the concept of "natural" slips back into our analysis in the preceding paragraph.

Enhancement vs. Disenhancements

If there can be human enhancements, then it also seems possible to have "disenhancements." An unenhanced person is simply one who is not enhanced, but a disenhanced person is one who undergoes an intervention that makes him or her worse off. This possibility speaks to our previous note that enhancements may pose dangers or lead to a net loss in welfare.

Although it may be difficult to envision the scenario in which a person would be disenhanced, we note that our livestock can be and sometimes are disenhanced. For instance, chickens sometimes have their beaks sheared off, so that they don't peck other chickens when jammed into confined spaces (Hester & Shea-Moore, 2003); and blind chickens are known to fare better in crowded environments, which they don't seem to mind as much as sighted birds (Thompson, 2008). Of course, this procedure may be an enhancement or benefit to us as the carnivorous consumer, but likely not

a benefit from the chicken's perspective. On the other hand, it has been proposed that we ought to create blind chickens, because they don't seem to mind crowded conditions as much, and this is more plausibly a benefit to them (Thompson, 2008).

For humans, removing some feature by itself is not automatically a disenhancement, if it delivers a benefit, especially for the subject. Today, for example, drugs are under development that can selectively target and erase memories (Lehrer, 2012). This would have beneficial uses, such as removing tragic memories that cause warfighters to have post-traumatic stress disorder (PTSD) and rape victims to be unable to live normally without paralyzing fear. That is, their lives would be enhanced by the degradation of their memories. However, there may be more insidious uses of the same drugs that may count as true disenhancements that promise little to no benefit to the subject; for instance, we may threaten a terrorist with a drug that removes the memory of his family or life, if he does not reveal the information we want.

In bioethics, there are infamous cases of patients who want to amputate otherwise-healthy limbs (Dyer, 2000; Ryan, 2009), or deaf parents who want to select in vitro embryos that would lead to deaf babies (Dennis, 2004). From an outsider's perspective, this seems to be voluntary disenhancement and perhaps unethical. But from the patient's perspective, it is a case of therapy in that the limbs seem alien and are therefore unwanted. This and other cases, as well as the preceding ones, are also difficult cases in understanding what an enhancement is.

Enhancement vs. Engineering

The last distinction above suggests that more precise terminology may be needed here. Indeed, the US military appears to be shying away from the term "human enhancement" in favor of "performance optimization" and less evocative language; some of its past projects were called

Metabolic Dominance and Peak Soldier Performance (Burnam-Fink, 2011). While we recognize that different terminology may be also suitable, we nonetheless will refer to the same technologies primarily as "human enhancements" for the following reasons.

First, they appear to be functionally equivalent: optimizing performance and enabling superior metabolism are both about enhancements to the human body; as we have defined enhancement, they are not meant to be therapeutic and are intended to exceed typical human limits. Second, "enhancement" is the primary language used by the ethics literature on the subject, and we would like our terminology to be consistent with that body of work, to avoid any confusion. Third, the military's apparent preference for "performance optimization" over "enhancement" could be viewed as a public relations choice about avoiding the specter of legal and ethical concerns that has been associated with human enhancements; in contrast, the very purpose of this chapter is to examine such concerns. The perception is that "optimization," "peak performance," and similar phrasing do not immediately suggest the familiar charge of hubris that we are pushing science beyond what is natural or ethical—in this case, to create a superhuman.

But one person's superhuman is another's Frankenstein monster (Galliott, 2013). This, then, raises another issue in terminology: that we perhaps ought to use the more neutral "human engineering" rather than value-laden "human enhancement" (Allhoff et al., 2010a). That is, "enhancement" seems to imply a net benefit to the individual, for instance, resulting in increased endurance, greater concentration, or some other desired good desired. Yet it is often unclear whether the technologies we have used to improve aspects of ourselves truly deliver a net benefit, especially without long-term studies of such effects. For instance, anabolic steroids can help athletes gain strength, but they may also cause serious health conditions; therefore, if anabolic steroids can do more harm than good, it seems premature to label them as enhancements as opposed to, say, poisons. Simi-

larly, alcoholic drinks seem to deliver the benefit of enhancing one's mood, but too much can lead to a painful hangover, liver damage, addiction, and so on, making it an open question of whether they are properly enhancers or not. As enhancements are usually context-specific and intended for a particular purpose, it may be misleading to discuss "enhancements" in general, absent some larger account of their role in human flourishing.

Even less clear are the benefits and risks posed by emerging and speculative technologies that have not been studied nearly as much as alcohol, anabolic steroids, caffeine, and other familiar drugs. As rapidly advancing as modern science seems to be, there is still much that we do not know. But what we know for certain is that biological and neurological (as well as environmental or ecological) systems are highly complex and interconnected, making it very difficult for us to accurately predict the effects of any given drug or technological intervention in our bodies. In the face of that uncertainty, we should refer to such technologies as instances of human engineering, rather than enhancements—or so the argument goes.

Even so, this discussion will stay with the notion "human enhancement", with the understanding that the term does not necessarily imply a net benefit to the individual (much less to the larger society of which they are a part, especially given the likelihood of unintended consequences). Of course the term does signal a promise of delivering some benefit to the individual—otherwise why would we give a drug or apply a technology to a person, if we did not expect those benefits?—but we remain agnostic or neutral on the question of whether it results in an overall positive gain, all things considered. That open question is important to note but, for us, not at the expense of breaking from the traditional language of the ethics literature, especially since it is understood that human enhancements may raise significant ethical concerns, including health risks—and this is the point of examining the subject in the first place.

Toward a Working Definition

Given the preceding, we will operate under the working definition that an enhancement is a medical or biological intervention to the body designed "to improve performance, appearance, or capability besides what is necessary to achieve, sustain or restore health" (Juengst, 1998). By this definition, since an enhancement does not aim to prevent, treat, or mitigate the effects of a disease or disorder, a vaccination or immunization—even if it makes individuals' immune systems better than normal—would typically not qualify as an enhancement, as it merely aims to sustain health.

Similarly, a drug to improve cognitive function in persons with below-normal cognitive ability ordinarily would not be considered an enhancement. But a pharmacological agent that improved their cognitive function to such a degree that the individual exceeded population-norms for cognitive functioning clearly would qualify as an enhancement. An intervention, such as caffeine and modafinil, might also be regarded as an enhancement if it improved the cognition of someone with normal cognition to start with, even though the resulting cognitive performance remained within population norms. Again, it seems relevant to also consider the baseline state and potential of the subject, as difficult as they are to measure.

The concept of normality, as we mentioned, is itself elusive; what is "normal" for one population may be quite abnormal for another. If an average professional basketball player began to suffer from scoliosis and lost four inches from his current height, he would still be far taller than normal for an adult male human. And even within populations, the term retains some ambiguity. In some cases, normality refers to the frequency with which a trait or capability occurs within a population, presuming a normal distribution. In regard to height, the convention is to regard individuals who are more than two standard deviations below the mean height of the population as being of short stature (US Department of Health and Human Services, 2008). Such an approach may leave unresolved the dilemma between understanding normality as individual-relative versus population-relative, however; consider two eight-year old boys, both shorter than 98 percent of their peers. One's shortness is genetic; the other has parents of typical height but a glandular problem. Is giving a human-growth hormone (HGH) to them: enhancement in both cases, therapy in both cases, or enhancement in one but therapy in the other?

To make things even more complicated, sometimes what is considered normal may have little to no relationship to the distribution of a trait. For example, normal eyesight is deemed to be 20/20, but only about 35 percent of adults have 20/20 vision without some form of correction (Johnson, 2004). Standards of normality also may vary from place to place and time to time, and can be expected to change as the use of enhancements increases. For example, body shapes that were considered healthy a hundred years ago are now considered obese; and the advertising and pharmaceutical industries are notorious for taking conditions heretofore taken as normal (such as body odor or discolored teeth) and presenting them as conditions requiring treatment.

Furthermore, the concepts of disease and disorder themselves may be hard to pin down. Before 1973, the American Psychiatric Association regarded homosexuality as a mental disorder (American Psychiatric Association, 2012). The tendency seemingly only grows to regard increasingly more health-states as diseases and increasingly more interventions as treatments. Insofar as enhancement is related to health, and health is related to normality, of course we would prefer that these concepts were all clearly defined. As a foundational notion, what is normal may still lack precision, so it may be tempting to discard the notion and therefore the interconnected chain of concepts. But there are good reasons to retain "normal" in our conceptual toolbox (Sparrow, 2010), at least as a useful rule-of-thumb, even if imprecise.

In short, the distinction between health-oriented and enhancing interventions will not always be clear, and invariably there will be borderline cases. The difficulty of clearly identifying what counts as an enhancement complicates the task of determining the conditions, if any, in which it would be ethical to research or use enhancements in the military. Nevertheless, the above working definition is sufficient to allow us to draw some conclusions about the ethical and legal propriety of military enhancement.

Military Variables

There are, however, a number of variables that further affect the definition of military enhancement and the analysis of the legal and ethical issues it raises. First is the matter of perspective: obviously, a primary perspective is that of the warfighter who is being asked to serve as a research subject or who is going to take the enhancement. There are different types of warfighters, with potentially different needs and concerns. Career enlistees presumably might be expected to care less about the impact of enhancements on their return to civilian life than enlistees who did not intend to make the military their career. Members of the Reserves and the National Guard might be legitimately concerned about whether an enhancement would be a boon or a handicap in their civilian jobs.

Warfighters engaged in direct combat might be more willing to take risky enhancements than service personnel or operators of drones and other remote weapons. Special-operations personnel in particular are known to be risk-takers, including in the area of increasing their mission effectiveness, such as by intense training. This might make it necessary to protect them from voluntarily agreeing to take potentially dangerous enhancements. On the other hand, if these troops are sent on more dangerous missions than regular troops, their willingness to take greater risks to improve their performance would be understandable, and this could be reason for treating them differently.

However, caution should be exercised in policy choices that create class divisions—for instance, special treatment or different rewards—within a military, to the extent they cause dissension in the ranks.

Another perspective is that of the other members of the enhanced warfighter's unit, who will share to some degree in the benefits and burdens of the enhancement use. A third perspective is that of the warfighter's superiors. There are a number of different types of superiors, each of whom has a somewhat different role and therefore a somewhat different viewpoint, including the immediate commander who is considering whether or not to give a warfighter an enhancement in the field; the officer in charge of a military research project who is considering whether to enroll a warfighter as a subject; military policy-makers deciding whether to embark on an enhancement research program; and the officers supervising enhancement research programs. The perspective of the warfighter's superior also will be affected if he or she is a physician or other type of health care professional, since health care professionals are subject to both military and professional normative regimes.

Finally, there is the perspective of third parties such as family members, members of military outside of the warfighter's unit, civilians with whom the warfighter interacts, the government, the public, and the nation. A critical question is what should happen if these perspectives are in conflict, for example, if consideration of the welfare of the individual warfighter points the resolution of an ethical or legal issue in a different direction than the welfare of the unit, the military service, or the state.

A second variable that must be considered when addressing the ethical and legal concerns raised by military enhancements is the risk or other adverse consequences associated with their use. These may be physical or mental health risks, such as those sometimes attributed to anabolic steroids and other drugs, including addiction. In contrast to the us, for example, the Danish military does not give amphetamines to its combat troops; not only do the Danish question the use of a drug that can impair judgment, but they are concerned about the potential for addiction (Nielsen, 2007). The degree of health risk may depend on whether the enhancement effect is permanent, long-term, or temporary, and on whether or not it can be reversed. There may be adverse effects on third parties, such as family members who are impacted by the warfighter's adverse health effects, as well as harm to family and other relationships. One factor in terms of relational effects is likely to be how significantly the warfighter's characteristics are altered by the enhancement, and how perceptible the enhancements are. A radical change in someone's appearance or behavior could have serious social consequences, and the negative effects would be even greater if the change were so extreme that it provoked repugnance or horror. Another harmful effect could be the reaction of adversaries. The more far-ranging the change brought about by the enhancement, the greater the risk that an adversary might view enhanced warfighters as no longer being really "human," and therefore treat them worse as prisoners. Adversaries might also use harmful methods to combat or reverse their enemy's enhancement effect.

A final element of risk is uncertainty. The less that is known about an enhancement, the less it has been properly studied, the more difficult it is to engage in the key ethical and legal process of balancing risks and benefits. At the same time, it is important to understand that no biomedical intervention is completely safe—all are accompanied by risks. The question is not how safe an intervention is but whether its risks are outweighed by its benefits. When the US Food and Drug Administration (FDA) approves a new drug or device as "safe," for example, what the agency is really saying is that it considers the health hazards of the product to be acceptable in view of the potential health benefits. In the case of civilian medical care, the benefits that must be

balanced against the risks are those that accrue to the patient. But should warfighters be thought of primarily as private patients, or as defenders of society? If the latter, there are potential benefits of enhancement not only to the warfighter but also to the warfighter's unit, mission, service, and nation. One of the major challenges presented by military enhancement is determining how to balance the benefits to these third parties against the risk of harm to the warfighters themselves.

The third variable is the legal status of the enhancement and the additional legal complexities that "military necessity" can create. Is the enhancement a drug, a medical device, or some other technology, such as a behavioral or psychological intervention? From a legal standpoint, these are subject to very different regulatory schemes, with drugs and devices governed by complex FDA rules and behavioral and psychological interventions essentially unregulated. A product that the FDA has approved for enhancement use may be deemed to present fewer ethical concerns than a product that is unapproved or still experimental, since approval bears on what is known about its safety and efficacy, as discussed later in connection with the administration of pyridostigmine bromide (Pb), botulinum toxin (Bt), and anthrax vaccine to combat troops during the gulf war (Fitzpatrick & Zwanziger, 2003).

Another important regulatory issue for enhancement drugs is whether they are controlled substances or otherwise illegal when used for non-medical, enhancement purposes. As noted earlier, the DoD prohibits the use of anabolic steroids by warfighters; accordingly, a commander who ordered her subordinates to take steroids would raise different ethical and legal concerns than one who ordered them to use a product that was not known for being subject to abuse, such as modafinil. Another variable is whether the enhancement product is supplied by the military or, like many dietary supplements, purchased privately by the warfighter. In the former case, the issue is whether warfighters need protection from their superiors; in the latter, the issue is whether the military ought to protect warfighters from their own poor choices.

A fourth variable that bears on ethical and legal issues is the type of characteristic or set of characteristics that are sought via enhancement. For example, a drug that altered certain aspects of a person's mental state, such as mental acuity, personality, or emotions, might be deemed more problematic than a drug that increased strength or endurance, on the theory that the mental enhancement was more likely to affect the person's sense of self. The same would be true for a drug that altered or blocked a person's memory or reduced their capacity to make moral judgments, which have been raised as objections to the proposed prophylactic use of beta blockers such as propranolol to prevent post-traumatic stress disorder (PTSD) in combat troops (Henry et al., 2007; Wolfendale, 2008).

Finally, one of the most important factors is whether warfighters are serving as human subjects in formal research projects, in which case the warfighters may be entitled to refuse to participate as human research subjects, or if instead the warfighters are given the enhancement to enable them to carry out their mission more successfully in the course of deployment, in which case a refusal to cooperate is likely to be viewed as disobeying an order. Again, this distinction will not always be clear, but with these variables we can begin to survey the problems that military human enhancement may pose.

CONCLUSION

In the above, we offer a brief background to military human enhancement. With America's current fiscal difficulties, military human enhancement may be in something of a lull, but we are convinced that it is bound to come back with a vengeance. Military forces have gone from conducting con-

trolled trials with amphetamines and the like to establishing generously funded offices with the sole aim of enhancing soldier performance. A full discussion of military human enhancement is beyond the scope of this chapter. But the brief introduction provided here is valuable as an entry point to the human enhancement ethics debate, which is quickly gaining momentum and complexity. It serves to ensure that our reader's thoughts are grounded in reality rather than the science fiction so often depicted in the popular media. We also hope that our working definition of military human enhancement, reached through a discussion of a number of controversies in the wider human enhancement debate, will help guide the discussion of the ethical, legal and operational issues associated with creation of "super soldiers," as discussed more thoroughly in the next chapter. Again, the discussion leading to this working definition is certainly not exhaustive and, to this extent, more research is necessary.

REFERENCES

Allhoff, F., Lin, P., Moor, J., & Weckert, J. (2010a). Ethics of human enhancement: 25 questions & answers. *Studies in Ethics, Law and Technology, 4*(4).

Allhoff, F., Lin, P., & Moore, D. (Eds.). (2010b). *What is nanotechnology and why does it matter? From science to ethics*. Hoboken, NJ: Wiley-Blackwell Publishing. doi:10.1002/9781444317992

American Psychiatric Association. (2012). *Healthy minds, healthy lives: Sexual orientation*. Retrieved 28 November, 2012 from http://www. healthyminds.org/More- Info-For/GayLesbian-Bisexuals.aspx

Bailey, R. (2005). *Liberation biology: The scientific and moral case for the biotech revolution*. Amherst, NY: Prometheus Books.

Bostrom, N., & Roache, R. (2008). Ethical issues in human enhancement. In J. Ryberg, T. Petersen, & C. Wolf (Eds.), *New waves in applied ethics*. New York, NY: Palgrave Macmillan.

Bostrom, N., & Sandberg, A. (2009). The wisdom of nature: An evolutionary heuristic for human enhancement. In J. Savulescu, & N. Bostrom (Eds.), *Human Enhancement*. Oxford, UK: Oxford University Press.

Burnam-Fink, M. (2011). The rise and decline of military human enhancement. *Science Progress*. Retrieved 28 November, 2012 from http://scienceprogress.org/2011/01/the-rise-and-decline-of-military-human-enhancement/

Caldwell, J., & Caldwell, J. (2005). Fatigue in military aviation: an overview of US military-approved pharmacological countermeasure. *Aviation, Space, and Environmental Medicine, 76*(7), 39–51. PMID:15672985

Caldwell, J., Caldwell, J., Smythe, N., & Hall, K. (2000). A double-blind, placebo-controlled investigation of the efficacy of modafinil for sustaining the alertness and performance of aviators: A helicopter simulator study. *Psychopharmacology, 150*(3), 272–282. doi:10.1007/s002130000450 PMID:10923755

Canaday, M. (2001). US military integration of religious, ethnic, and racial minorities in the twentieth century. *The Palm Center*. Retrieved 28 November, 2012 from http://www.palmcenter.org/publications/dadt/u_s_military_integration_of_religious_ethnic_and_racial_inorities_in_the_twentieth_cen tury#_ftnref1

Cantor, N. (2001). *In the wake of the plague: The black death and the world it made*. New York, NY: The Free Press.

Cohen, A. (2010). Proportionality in modern asymmetrical wars. *Jerusalem Center for Public Affairs*. Retrieved 28 November, 2012 from http://jcpa.org/text/proportionality.pdf

Cornum, R., Caldwell, J., & Cornum, K. (1997). Stimulant use in extended flight operations. *Airpower Journal, 11*(1).

Dennis, C. (2004). Genetics: Deaf by design. *Nature, 431*(7011), 894–896. doi:10.1038/431894a PMID:15496889

Dyer, C. (2000). Surgeon amputated healthy legs. *British Medical Journal*, 320–332. PMID:10657312

Fenn, E. (2002). *Pox Americana: The great smallpox epidemic of 1775-82*. New York, NY: Hill and Wang.

Fitzpatrick, W., & Zwaziger, L. (2003). Defending against biochemical warfare: Ethical issues involving the coercive use of investigational drugs and biologics in the military. *Philosophy, Science & Law, 3*(1).

Fukuyama, F. (2002). *Our posthuman future: Consequences of the biotechnology revolution*. New York, NY: Picador.

Fukuyama, F. (2006). *Beyond bioethics: A proposal for modernizing the regulation of human biotechnologies*. Washington, DC: School of Advanced International Studies, Johns Hopkins University.

Galliott, J. (2013). Who's to blame? In N. Michaud (Ed.), *Frankenstein and philosophy: The shocking truth*. Chicago, IL: Open Court Press.

Garcia, T., & Sandler, R. (2008). Enhancing justice? *NanoEthics, 2*(3), 277–287. doi:10.1007/s11569-008-0048-5

Garreau, J. (2006). *Radical evolution: The science and peril of enhancing our minds, our bodies—and what it means to be human*. New York, NY: Random House.

Greely, H. (2005). Regulating human biological enhancements: Questionable justifications and international complications. *University of Technology Law Review, 7*(1), 87–110.

Harris, J. (2007). *Enhancing evolution: The ethical case for making better people*. Princeton, NJ: Princeton University Press.

Hart, L. (2003, January 17). Use of 'go pills' a matter of 'life and death,' Air Force avows. *Los Angeles Times*.

Henry, M., Fishman, J., & Youngner, S. (2007). Propranolol and the prevention of post-traumatic stress disorder: Is it wrong to erase the sting of bad memories? *The American Journal of Bioethics*, *7*(9), 12–20. doi:10.1080/15265160701518474 PMID:17849331

Hester, P., & Shea-Moore, M. (2003). Beak trimming egg-laying strains of chickens. *World's Poultry Science Journal*, *59*(4), 458–474. doi:10.1079/WPS20030029

Hughes, J. (2004). *Citizen cyborg: Why democratic societies must respond to the redesigned human of the future*. Cambridge, MA: Westview Press.

JASON. (2008). *Human Performance* (Report No. JSR-07-625, March). JASON.

JASON. (2010). *The $100 Genome: Implications for DoD* (Report No. JSR-10-100, December). JASON.

Johnson, T. (2004). *What is 20/20 vision?* Retrieved 28 November, 2012 from http://www.uihealthcare.com/topics/medicaldepartments/ophthalmology/2020vision/index.html

Jonas, W., O'Connor, F., Deuster, P., Peck, J., Shake, C., & Frost, S. (2010). Why Total Force Fitness? *Military Medicine*, *175*(8), 6–13. doi:10.7205/MILMED-D-10-00280

Juengst, E. (1998). The meaning of enhancement. In E. Parens (Ed.), *Enhancing human traits: Ethical and social implications*. Washington, DC: Georgetown University Press.

Juengst, E. (2000). The ethics of enhancement. In T. Murray, & M. Mehlman (Eds.), *The encyclopedia of ethical, legal and policy issues in biotechnology*. Hoboken, NJ: John Wiley & Sons.

Land, B. (2010). Current Department of Defense guidance for total force fitness. *Military Medicine*, *175*(8), 3–5. doi:10.7205/MILMED-D-10-00138

Lehrer, J. (2012). The forgetting pill erases painful memories forever. *Wired, 20*(3).

Lester, P., McBride, S., Bliese, P., & Adler, A. (2011). Bringing science to bear: An empirical assessment of the comprehensive soldier fitness program. *The American Psychologist*, *66*(1), 77–81. doi:10.1037/a0022083 PMID:21219052

Lewis, S. (2009). History of biowarfare. *NOVA*. Retrieved 28 November, 2012 from http://www.pbs.org/wgbh/nova/ military/history-biowarfare.html

Lin, P., Mehlman, M., & Abney, K. (2013). *Enhanced warfighters: Risk, ethics, and policy*. New York, NY: The Greenwall Foundation.

Little, V. (2010, October 1). Physical readiness training standards take shape. *The Bayonet*. Retrieved 28 November 2012 from http://www.ledger-enquirer.com/

Mehlman, M. (1999). How will we regulate genetic enhancement? *Wake Forest Law Review*, *34*(3), 617–714. PMID:12664908

Mehlman, M. (2000). The law of above averages: Leveling the new genetic enhancement playing field. *Iowa Law Review*, *85*, 517–593. PMID:11769760

Mehlman, M. (2003). *Wondergenes: Genetic enhancement and the future of society*. Bloomington, IN: Indiana University Press.

Mehlman, M. (2004). Cognition-enhancing drugs. *The Milbank Quarterly*, *82*(3), 483–506. doi:10.1111/j.0887-378X.2004.00319.x PMID:15330974

Mehlman, M. (2009a). Biomedical enhancements: A new era. *Issues in Science and Technology*, *25*(3), 59–69.

Mehlman, M. (2009b). *The price of perfection: Individualism and society in the era of biomedical enhancement.* Baltimore, MD: Johns Hopkins University Press.

Montain, S., Carvey, C., & Stephens, M. (2010). Nutritional fitness. *Military Medicine, 175*(8), 65–72. doi:10.7205/MILMED-D-10-00127 PMID:20108845

Moreno, J. (2006). *Mind wars: Brain research and national defense.* Washington, DC: Dana Press.

Murray, T. (2007). Enhancement. In B. Steinbock (Ed.), *The Oxford handbook of bioethics.* Oxford, UK: Oxford University Press.

Naam, R. (2005). *More than human.* New York, NY: Broadway Books.

Nielsen, J. (2007). Danish perspective: Commentary on recommendations for the ethical use of pharmacological fatigue countermeasures in the US Military. *Aviation, Space, and Environmental Medicine, 78*(1), 134–135.

Persaud, R. (2006). Does smarter mean happier? In J. Wilsdon, & P. Miller (Eds.), *Better humans? The politics of human enhancement and life extension.* London: Demos.

President's Council on Bioethics. (2003). *Beyond therapy: Biotechnology and the pursuit of happiness.* Washington, DC: Government Printing Office.

Roy, T., Springer, B., McNulty, V., & Butler, N. (2010). Physical fitness. *Military Medicine, 175*(1), 14–20. doi:10.7205/MILMED-D-10-00058 PMID:20108837

Ryan, C. (2009)... *Amputating Healthy Limbs, 86,* 31–33.

Sample, I. (2004, July 3). Wired awake. *The Guardian*, p. S4.

Sandel, M. (2009). The case against perfection: What's wrong with designer children, bionic athletes, and genetic engineering. In J. Savulescu, & N. Bostrom (Eds.), *Human Enhancement.* Oxford, UK: Oxford University Press.

Savulescu, J., & Bostrom, N. (Eds.). (2009). *Human enhancement.* Oxford, UK: Oxford University Press.

Schlesinger, R. (2003, January 4). Defense cites stimulants in 'friendly fire' case. *Boston Globe*, p. A3.

Selgelid, M. (2007). An argument against arguments for enhancement. *Studies in Ethics, Law, and Technology, 1.*

Shachtman, N. (2007a). Be more than you can be. *Wired, 15*(3).

Shachtman, N. (2007b, March 8). Supercharging soldiers' cells. *Wired.* Retrieved 28 November, 2012 from http://www.wired.com/dangerroom/2007/03/supercharging_s/

Shanker, T., & Duenwald, M. (2003, January 19). Threats and responses: bombing errors puts a spotlight on pilots' pills. *New York Times*, p. 1.

Shaughnessy, L. (2012). One soldier, one year: $850,000 and rising. *CNN Security Clearance.* Retrieved 28 November, 2012 from http://security.blogs.cnn.com/2012/02/28/one-soldier-one-year-850000 andrising/

Simpson, D. (2004, July 2). US pilot defends attack in secret. *Toronto Star*, p. A01.

Singer, P. (2009, November 12). How to be all that you can be: A look at the Pentagon's five step plan for making Iron man real. *The Brookings Institution.* Retrieved 28 November, 2012, from http://www.brookings.edu/articles/2008/0502_iron_man_singer.aspx

Sparrow, R. (2010). Better than men? Sex and the therapy/enhancement distinction. *Kennedy Institute of Ethics Journal*, *20*(2), 115–144. doi:10.1353/ken.0.0308 PMID:20653249

St. Louis Post-Dispatch Editors. (2003, July 3). The court martial. *St. Louis Post-Dispatch*, p. C12.

Thompson, P. (2008). The opposite of human enhancement: Nanotechnology and the blind chicken problem. *NanoEthics*, *2*(3), 305–316. doi:10.1007/s11569-008-0052-9

UK Academy of Medical Sciences. (2012). *Human enhancement and the future of work*. Retrieved on 28 November, 2012, http://royalsociety.org/policy/projects/human-enhancement/workshop-report/

US Department of Defense. (2012). *Department of Defense directive 1010.1 (originally 28 December 1984)*. Retrieved on 18 December, 2012 from http://www.dtic.mil/whs/directives/corres/pdf/101001p.pdf

US Department of Health and Human Services. (2008). *Short stature: Criteria for determining disability in infants and children*. Agency for Healthcare Research and Quality. Retrieved 28 November 2012 from http://www.ncbi.nlm.nih.gov/books/NBK36847/

Wolfendale, J. (2008). Performance-enhancing technologies and moral responsibility in the military. *The American Journal of Bioethics*, *8*(2), 28–38. doi:10.1080/15265160802014969 PMID:18570075

KEY TERMS AND DEFINITIONS

Disenhancement: A medical or biological intervention that makes one worse off.

Miltiary-Technical Proliferation: The spread of military technologies into the civilian realm.

Principle of Distinction: An element of international law and just war theory which demands that a weapon must be discriminating enough to target only combatants and never noncombatants.

Principle of Proportionality: Demands that the use of a weapon be proportional to the military objective, so as to keep civilian casualties to a minimum.

SIrUS Principle: Related to proportionality in that it requires methods of attack to be minimally harmful in rendering a warfighter *hors de combat* or unable to fight.

Soldier Enhancement: Medical or biological intervention introduced into a soldier's body designed to improve warfighting performance, appearance, or capability besides what is necessary to achieve, sustain or restore health.

Therapy: An intervention or treatment intended to alleviate a condition suffered by a patient, elevating his or health closer to normal.

Chapter 8
Super Soldiers (Part 2):
The Ethical, Legal, and Operational Implications

Patrick Lin
California Polytechnic State University, USA

Shannon Vallor
Santa Clara University, USA

Max Mehlman
Case Western Reserve University, USA

Jai Galliott
Macquarie University, Australia

Keith Abney
California Polytechnic State University, USA

Michael Burnam-Fink
Arizona State University, USA

Shannon French
Case Western Reserve University, USA

Alexander R. LaCroix
Arizona State University, USA

Seth Schuknecht
Arizona State University, USA

ABSTRACT

This is the second chapter of two on military human enhancement. In the first chapter, the authors outlined past and present efforts aimed at enhancing the minds and bodies of our warfighters with the broader goal of creating the "super soldiers" of tomorrow, all before exploring a number of distinctions—natural vs. artificial, external vs. internal, enhancement vs. therapy, enhancement vs. disenhancement, and enhancement vs. engineering—that are critical to the definition of military human enhancement and understanding the problems it poses. The chapter then advanced a working definition of enhancement as efforts that aim to "improve performance, appearance, or capability besides what is necessary to achieve, sustain, or restore health." It then discussed a number of variables that must be taken into consideration when applying this definition in a military context. In this second chapter, drawing on that definition and some of the controversies already mentioned, the authors set out the relevant ethical, legal, and operational challenges posed by military enhancement. They begin by considering some of the implications for international humanitarian law and then shift to US domestic law. Following that, the authors examine military human enhancement from a virtue ethics approach, and finally outline some potential consequences for military operations more generally.

DOI: 10.4018/978-1-4666-6010-6.ch008

INTRODUCTION

With the background and working definition provided in the previous chapter (Chapter 7), we begin our discussion of the primary ethical, legal and operational issues associated with military human enhancement. At this point, it must be said that to the extent that ethics underwrites law and policy, we are often better placed to understand the former by looking at the latter as the real-world implementation of ethics. This is also beneficial in the sense that international and domestic law—including laws relevant to bio-medical enhancement—may demand immediate attention, with potential humanitarian concerns or the possibility of requiring serious sanctions. We therefore adopt the approach of focusing first on legal problems that are generated or exacerbated by military human enhancement.

However, the discussion does not end there. We also sketch a range of other considerations, both explicitly philosophical in nature, as well as some affecting more operational concerns. While certain of these latter considerations are not as likely to lead to direct physical harm to subjects and may seem somewhat abstract, these matters remain of great importance to the moral foundations of military service and the relationship between citizens, states, and their military institutions. Also, even though all of these considerations are in some sense intertwined, we separate them here as best as we can for ease of presentation and comprehension.

INTERNATIONAL LAW

What are the provisions in international law that may bear upon military human enhancements? Should enhancement technologies, which typically do not directly interact with anyone other than the human subject, nevertheless be subjected to a weapons legal review? That is, is there a sense in which enhancements could be considered as "weapons" and therefore subject to legal instru-ments such as the Biological and Toxin Weapons Convention? How do norms related to human-subject research and medical ethics impact military enhancements?

These are some of the most important questions for military enhancements as they relate to international law (Lin, 2012a). Conceptually, we divide international law into two categories: the first is commonly known as the Law of Armed Conflict (LOAC) and the second is composed of international agreements related to biomedical research. Because these are well-known conventions, we will only list them here and add more detail later as needed.

Under international humanitarian law (IHL), the main instruments of interest here are:

- Hague Conventions (1899 and 1907).
- Geneva Conventions (1949 and Additional Protocols I, II, and III).
- Biological and Toxin Weapons Convention (1972).
- Chemical Weapons Convention (1993).
- Rome Statute of the International Criminal Court (1998).

Under international biomedical laws—which we discuss more in the next section—the main instruments of interest here are:

- Nuremberg Code (1947).
- Declaration of Geneva (1948).
- Declaration of Helsinki (1964).

As it concerns new technologies, Article 36 of the Geneva Conventions, Additional Protocol I, specifies that: "in the study, development, acquisition or adoption of a new weapon, means or method of warfare, a High Contracting Party is under an obligation to determine whether its employment would, in some or all circumstances, be prohibited by this Protocol or by any other rule of international law applicable to the High Contracting Party" (1977).

But does Article 36 apply to human enhancement technologies? That is, should they be considered as a "weapon" or "means or method of warfare" in the first place? Unlike other weapons contemplated by the LOAC, enhancements usually do not directly harm others, so it is not obvious that Article 36 of Additional Protocol I would apply here. If anyone's safety were immediately at risk, it would seem to be that of the individual warfighter, thereby turning the debate into one about bioethics. To that extent, warfighters, whether enhanced or not, are not weapons as typically understood.

Yet in a broader sense, the warfighter is not only a weapon but also perhaps a military's best and oldest weapon. Warfighters carry out missions, they sometimes kill enemies, and they represent one of the largest expenditures or investments of a military. They have cognitive and physical capabilities that no other technology currently has, and this can make them ethical, lethal, and versatile. The human fighter, engaged in hand-to-hand combat, would be the last remaining weapon when all others have been exhausted. So in this basic sense, the warfighter is undeniably a weapon or instrument of war.

Still, should Article 36 be interpreted to include warfighters themselves as weapons subject to regulation? There could be several reasons to think so. First, other organisms are plausibly weapons subject to an Article 36 review. Throughout history, humans have employed animals in the service of war, such as dogs, elephants, pigeons, sea lions, dolphins, and possibly rhinoceroses (Knights, 2007; Beckhusen, 2012; US Navy, 2012). Dogs, as the most commonly used animal, undergo rigorous training, validation, and inspections (US Department of the Army, 2005). If a military were to field a weaponized rhino in an urban battlefield that contains innocent civilians, we would be reasonably worried that the war-rhino does not comply with Article 36, if rhinos cannot reliably discriminate friends from foe, e.g., a rhino may target and charge a noncombatant child in violation of the principle of distinction. A similar charge would apply to autonomous robots in such a general environment in which distinction is important, as opposed to a "kill box" or area of such fierce fighting that all noncombatants could be presumed to have fled (Lin, et al., 2008).

If autonomous robots are clearly regulatable weapons, then consider the spectrum of cyborgs—part-human, part-machine—that exists between robots and unenhanced humans. Replacing one body part, say a human knee, with a robotic part starts us on the cybernetic path. And as other body parts are replaced, the organism becomes less human and more robotic. Finally, after (hypothetically) replacing every body part, including the brain, the organism is entirely robotic with no trace of the original human. If we want to say that robots are weapons but humans are not, then we would be challenged to identify the point on that spectrum at which the human becomes a robot or a weapon. The inability to draw such a line may not be a fatal blow to the claim that humans should be treated as weapons; after all, we cannot draw a precise line at which a man who is losing his hair becomes "bald," yet there is clearly a difference between a bald man and one who has a head full of hair (Stanford, 2011). But a simpler solution may be to say that humans are weapons, especially given the reasons offered previously.

As it applies to military enhancements, integrated robotics may be one form of enhancement, but we can also consider scenarios involving biomedical enhancements such as pharmaceuticals and genetic engineering. Again, on one end of the spectrum would stand a normal, unenhanced human. One step toward the path of being fully enhanced may be a warfighter who drinks coffee or pops amphetamines ("go pills") as a cognitive stimulant or enhancer. Another step may be taking drugs that increase strength, erase fear, or eliminate the need for sleep. At the more radical end may be a warfighter so enhanced that s/he no longer resembles a human being, such as a creature with four muscular arms, fangs, fur, and other animal-like features, and with no moral sense of distinguishing combatant from noncombatant. If a war-rhino should be subject to Article 36, then so should this radically enhanced human animal, so it would seem. And to avoid the difficult question of drawing the line at which the enhanced human becomes a weapon, a more intuitive position would be that the human animal is a weapon all along, at every point in the spectrum, especially given the previous reasons that are independent of this demarcation problem.

If we agree that enhanced human warfighters could conceivably be weapons subject to Article 36, what are the implications? Historically, new weapons and tactics needed to conform to at least the following:

- Principle of distinction.
- Principle of proportionality.
- Prohibition on superfluous injury or unnecessary suffering (SIrUS).

To explain: First, the principle of distinction demands that a weapon must be discriminating enough to target only combatants and never noncombatants (Geneva Additional Protocol I, 1977; Sassòli, 2003). Biological weapons and most anti-personnel landmines, then, are indiscriminate and therefore illegal in that they cannot distinguish whether they are about to infect or blow up a small child versus an enemy combatant. Unintended killings of noncombatants—or "collateral damage"—may be permissible, but not their deliberate targeting; but to the extent that biological weapons today target anyone, they also target everyone. However, a future biological weapon, e.g., a virus that attacks only blue-eyed people or a certain DNA signature (Hessel et al., 2012), may be discriminate and therefore would not violate this principle (but it could violate others).

Second, the principle of proportionality demands that the use of a weapon be proportional to the military objective, so to keep civilian casualties to a minimum (Geneva Additional Protocol I, 1977; Cohen, 2010). For instance, dropping a nuclear bomb to kill a hidden sniper would be a disproportionate use of force, since other less drastic methods could have been used.

Third, the SIrUS principle is related to proportionality in that it requires methods of attack to be minimally harmful in rendering a warfighter *hors de combat* or unable to fight (Coupland & Herby, 1999). This prohibition has led to the ban of such weapons as poison, exploding bullets, and blinding lasers, which cause more injury or suffering than needed to neutralize a combatant.

However implausible, we can imagine a human enhancement that violates these and other provisions—for instance, a hypothetical "berserker" drug would likely be illegal if it causes the warfighter to be inhumanely vicious, aggressive, and indiscriminate in his attacks, potentially killing children. For the moment, we will put aside enhancements that are directed at adversaries, such as a mood-enhancing gas to pacify a riotous crowd and a truth-enhancing serum used in interrogations; the former would be prohibited outright by the Chemical Weapons Convention in warfare (The Royal Society, 2012), partly because it is indiscriminate, and the latter may be prohibited by laws against torturing and mistreating prisoners of war. The point here is that it is theoretically possible, even if unlikely, for a human enhancement to be in clear violation of IHL.

DOMESTIC LAW

The international law considerations adduced above primarily involve what militaries should (not) do with their enhanced warfighters, but there remains a prior question of whether militaries are permitted to enhance their personnel at all. Traditionally, this has been a question for bioethics and related domestic law, rather than for IHL. Hence, we will briefly outline some key US domestic laws and regulations that would apply to military enhancements.

Does US domestic law allow the military to require enhancements for its own personnel? To answer that question, we look at actual legal cases in the US that are closely related to, if not directly about, questions about human enhancements. While we had excluded vaccinations as a type of human enhancement in the definitional section of the previous chapter— because they are designed to sustain health, not provide capabilities beyond it—we also acknowledged that this understanding was contentious: in a sense, a vaccination seems to be an enhancement of the immune system, especially considering that the patient is not sick at the time of the immunization. At the least, even if not enhancements themselves, vaccination policy can inform a study on how US law might deal with military enhancements.

The us military has been vaccinating troops since 1777 (Gabriel, 2013). There are currently thirteen vaccinations used by the military mandated for trainees alone: mandatory vaccinations include influenza, hepatitis a and b, measles, poliovirus, rubella, and yellow fever, among others (Grabenstein, 2006). The standard military policy for the mandatory administration of pharmaceutical agents is the same as the policy applied to civilians (Russo, 2007): pharmaceuticals need to be approved by the us food and drug administration (FDA) for their intended use before they are mandatorily administered; and absent FDA approval, a presidential waiver or informed voluntary consent must be obtained for the administration of an investigational drug (IND) (Russo, 2007). The US Supreme Court has held that mandatory vaccinations of FDA-approved drugs do not violate the US Constitution (Jacobson v. Commonwealth of Massachusetts, 1905). Mandatory vaccination programs in the military have been challenged in court (United States v. Chadwell, 1965), but they were rarely subjected to substantial legal challenges until 2001, directed at the anthrax vaccine immunization program (AVIP).

Federal Law

As an important catalyst for us law related to vaccinations, AVIP—established in 1997—had roots in operation desert shield in 1990, at which time the US military worried about biological and chemical weapons that Saddam Hussein was rumored to have possessed. At the time, the DOD argued that the informed consent requirement for the administration of INDs was impractical (Doe v. Sullivan, 1991). The requirement was feasible during peacetime, but the DOD urged that it posed significant obstacles to the safety of troops and mission accomplishment in wartime (Brown, 2006). In response to pressure from the DOD, the FDA promulgated rule 23(d), otherwise known as the interim final rule:

- 21 CFR 50.23(d), or Interim Final Rule.

Rule 23(d) allows the DOD to waive the informed consent requirement, if it is not feasible to obtain consent in a particular military operation, subject to conditions (Brown, 2006). Most importantly, the waiver must be limited to "a specific military operation involving combat or the immediate threat of combat" (Doe v. Sullivan, 1991). Upon receiving the request for waiver from the DOD, the FDA must evaluate it and grant the waiver "only when withholding treatment would be contrary to the best interests of military personnel and there is no available satisfactory alternative therapy" (doe v. Sullivan, 1991). This rule was challenged in 1991, in doe v. Sullivan, but the federal court held that 23(d) was constitutional and within the scope of the FDA's authority (Doe v. Sullivan, 1991).

- *10 USC §1107(f).*

In 1998, in response to the ruling in Doe v. Sullivan, the US Congress enacted 1107(f). This statutory provision requires the DoD to obtain informed consent from soldiers before administering an

IND (including an approved drug for an unapproved use) and provides that the President can waive said requirement (10 USCA § 1107 (West)).

• *Executive Order 13139.*

President Clinton unified both rule 23(d) and 1107(f) in 1999 with executive order 13139, a guideline for waiving informed consent within the context of military operations (brown, 2006). According to the order, to use an "investigational drug" or a "drug unapproved for its intended use," the Secretary of Defense must obtain informed consent from each individual service member (executive order no. 13139 1999). However, a presidential waiver can overcome this requirement, but it can only be obtained upon a written determination that obtaining consent is: (1) not feasible; (2) contrary to the best interests of the member; or (3) is not in the interests of national security (executive order no. 13139 1999).

• *DoDD 6200.2.*

The department of defense directive (DODD) 6200.2, like executive order 13139, synthesized several sources of authority governing the use of INDs for military health protection (US Dept. of Defense, 2012). It defines an IND as a "drug not approved or a biological product not licensed by the FDA," or alternatively, as a "drug unapproved for its applied use" (US Dept. of Defense, 2012). Further, it provides that the DOD must prefer products approved by the FDA for use as countermeasures to INDs (US Dept. of Defense, 2012). However, "when, at the time of the need for a force health care protection counter-measure against a particular threat, no safe and effective FDA-approved drug or biological product is available, DOD components may request approval of the secretary of defense to use an investigational new drug" (US Dept. of Defense, 2012). If the secretary of defense determines that obtaining informed consent is not feasible, contrary to

the best interests of the member, and is not in the interests of national security, s/he can then request a waiver from the president (US Dept. of Defense, 2012).

Military Law

Military law operates in conjunction with federal civil law, but it focuses on matters germane to the military alone. In addition to the constitution, us military law is governed by the uniform code of military justice (UCMJ). In the context of military vaccinations, the issue is about the lawfulness of the order to take the vaccination. The DOD's successful defense strategy of the legality of the AVIP throughout the anthrax cases was straightforward on this account: the vaccine was determined by the FDA to be safe and effective for use against inhalation anthrax, and under military law the legality of an order to take the vaccine was a question of law for a judge to decide, not a question of fact for determination by a jury (Katz, 2001).

Under the UCMJ, disobedience of a direct and lawful order from a superior officer is punishable under articles 90 or 92. Article 90 prohibits willfully disobeying a superior commissioned officer (10 USC § 890 (1994) (UCMJ art. 90)), and article 92 prohibits failing to obey an order or regulation (10 USC § 890 (1994) (UCMJ art. 92)). A soldier who refused to take the anthrax vaccination was court-martialed, where the DOD would file two interlocutory motions: (1) that the lawfulness of the order should be decided as a question of law; and (2) that all the evidence regarding the safety, efficacy, and necessity of the vaccine should be excluded because the legal authority of an order is not based on the safety of the vaccine (ponder v. Stone 2000). The DOD did this in every challenge to the AVIP, and in every challenge to the AVIP in military court they were successful (Katz, 2001).

A strong, but rebuttable, presumption is that a military order is lawful when someone is charged with willful disobedience of a lawful order (US government, manual for court-martial, 2010; Katz,

2001), and the lawfulness of a military order is an interlocutory order to be decided on by a judge, not a jury (us v. New, 1999; Perry v. Wesely, 2000). What this effectively does is foreclose a legal challenge to the scientific efficacy of a vaccine on procedural grounds. Again, while these legal issues were involved with actual cases involving vaccinations, we can plausibly extend them to anticipate how they would address technologies and procedures that are more clearly human enhancement than therapy.

OPERATIONS

Beyond the demands of international and domestic law, military enhancements will likely have important policy implications. We will examine here some of those implications on military operations themselves. Cognitive and physical human enhancements can significantly help a military achieve its missions, operate more efficiently and perhaps ethically, as well as a host of other benefits. But our focus here will be on <u>unintended</u> problems that may be caused by enhancements.

Assuming that enhancements are not adopted by all warfighters at once—for instance, they are rolled out selectively or slowly for safety, economic, or other reasons—there would instantly be an inequality among the ranks, creating problems for unit cohesion. Some warfighters will be privileged (or unlucky?) enough to be appropriately enhanced for their mission, whereas some others may be underenhanced, while others yet will remain "normal." In broader society, we see that uneven access to technology creates a gap between the haves and the have-nots, such as the Internet divide (Rozner 1998); and this translates into a difference in quality of life, education, earnings, and so on. It is therefore not unreasonable to expect a similar effect within the military.

At the unit level, enhancements may cause (or increase) dissension between warfighters. A mix of enhanced and unenhanced warfighters within a single unit may affect morale and unit cohesion. To be sure, similar worries had been voiced related to the integration of different ethnic groups, religions, and sexual orientation in the military (Canaday, 2001); but where these differences do not intrinsically imply different levels of capabilities or merit that would matter operationally, human enhancements do. By definition, an enhanced warfighter would be stronger, faster, or otherwise better enabled than their normal counterparts. This means they could accept riskier roles and have lower support requirements, for instance.

Further, because enhanced warfighters represent a significant investment of research and effort, they may be treated quite differently from 'normal' warfighters, e.g., perhaps they will not be subjected to the hard work of routine fighting or other "mundane" uses. For comparison, many Allied airborne troops in World War II were pulled from the lines after the D-Day invasion of Normandy, rather than being required to slog through France and the Hürtgen Forest in Germany. The asymmetry of needs and capabilities could cause resentment of the unenhanced or underenhanced as a drag on capabilities and operational efficiency of the enhanced, as well as resentment by the others of the superior abilities and (likely) superior status of the enhanced. To some extent, we already witness this when militaries switch their dependence from soldiers to "special operators" such as Navy SEALs. The asymmetry could also create a sense of entitlement among the enhanced and undermine an esprit de corps, much as some superstars do on sports teams.

Morale is also relevant to confidence in command. Enhancements could create novel difficulties for the command structure, particularly if commanders were unenhanced and were seen as physically—or, worse, intellectually—inferior to those they command. To take one firsthand perspective, retired US Army Brigadier General Richard O'Meara asserts that a social contract exists between troops and leaders, one that places the burden of defining the goals of a mission on the leaders, and the burden of accomplishment on the troops (O'Meara, 2012). But while the troops have the responsibility to accomplish the goals that command has set forth, they also have a right to demand that leaders make informed decisions, even if difficult ones, and to do so in a way that warfighters recognize as legitimate. It is a recipe for disaster when those further down the chain of command are continually second-guessing and evading their orders. If human enhancement exacerbates that lack of confidence in leaders, it could undermine the strategy and tactics of command.

Physical enhancements may be less problematic in this regard than cognitive ones, at least with respect to challenges to command. When the troops are generally less educated, less interested in strategy, and more concerned with communal rather than individual rights and values, command can worry less about the potential disobedience that could result from enhancements. Generally speaking, the primary responsibility of typical enlisted soldiers is to know at all times what their superiors desire of them; their well being, even their survival, may well depend on it. Therefore, the rank-and-file are typically extremely sensitive to the wishes of command and, even when those wishes are not officially communicated, there is an expectation that a soldier will "get it" and learn to read the signs and comply, or disregard at their peril. Further, military culture is based on the assumption that the decisions of leadership are entitled to greater weight based on superior knowledge and judgment. Diffusing the power to make decisions strikes at the heart of the legitimacy of leadership; and so cognitive enhancements pose dangers to received military models that mere physical enhancements do not.

There are further implications for service, pay, and conditions. Perhaps we should think about enhanced warfighters as we do with other specially trained operators, such as the Army's Special Forces or Navy SEALs. That is, military policy could be to keep the enhanced separated from the unenhanced, in special or elite units; this

would reduce any friction between the two groups. However, this segregation may merely telescope the problem out to a broader level, shifting tension from within units to among different units: if special units are given access to enhancements, or otherwise treated or rewarded differently—assuming we can even think of enhancements as rewards—then other units may feel slighted.

But as we alluded to above, it may be an open question of whether a particular enhancement may be a benefit to the individual. Leaving disenhancements aside, some or many enhancements pose side-effect risks; for instance, we still do not adequately understand the role of sleep and long-term effects of sleep deprivation, even if we can engineer a warfighter to operate on very little or no (true) sleep, as some animals are already capable of doing. So depending on one's perspective, an enhancement could be a reward or benefit, or it could be an undesired risk, as some believed about anthrax vaccinations (Wasserman & Grabenstein, 2003; Berkelman, Halsey, & Resnik, 2012).

How, then, should enhancements affect the service commitment of military personnel? Insofar as an enhancement is costly to develop and represents an investment, it may be reasonable to expect the enhanced warfighter to commit to longer service. But if an enhancement is seen more as a mere risk, then perhaps a shorter length of service is appropriate for the enhanced. Similar decisions may need to be made with respect to pay, promotions, and so on. For instance, if promotions and "danger pay" may be used to incentivize volunteers, enhanced soldiers could be better positioned and more likely to accept dangerous missions in exchange for those benefits.

On the mission side of operations, human enhancements may elicit a backlash that hinders the mission and therefore detracts from the value of enhancements for the military. This kind of blowback is already seen with the US government's use of unmanned aerial vehicles (UAVs) in the so-called "drone wars": While the US views its target strikes as appropriate—if not ethically required—to the extent that it is taking American military personnel out of harm's way in a presumably just campaign, adversaries often see drones as an unfair, cowardly, and dishonorable proxy for a military afraid to engage face-to-face with human resistance (Galliott, forthcoming). This sentiment seems to fuel resentment and hatred toward the US, which in turn may help to recruit more terrorists (Foust, 2012; Plaw, 2012).

Similarly, if adversaries regard military enhancements as unfair, cowardly or abominable, they may be counterproductive to the larger war effort and perhaps encourage the enemy to resort to more conventional but very much despicable means (Galliott, 2012a). This is not to say that war should be a "fair fight." Indeed, the whole idea of employing emerging technologies is to leverage force and confer some military advantage. However, as with drone strikes, states must carefully think about the consequences of enhancing soldiers in terms of possible retaliatory options, and such considerations may preclude the employment of such means in the first instance (Galliott, 2012b).

Another criticism of the drone wars that may be applied to military enhancements is the charge that these technologies, by better ensuring the survival and success of our own military personnel, serve to make war more risk-free and therefore a more palatable option (Lin, Abney, & Bekey, 2008; Lin, 2010; Lin, 2011; Galliott, forthcoming; Human Rights Watch, 2012). That is, we may be tempted into choosing a military option during a political conflict, rather than saving war as the last resort as demanded by traditional just war theory. This ethical imperative is reflected in Civil War General Robert E. Lee's observation: "It is well that war is so terrible; otherwise, we would grow too fond of it" (Cooke, 1876, p. 184; Levin, 2008). As war becomes less terrible—at least for our own side—our natural aversions to it may be lessened as well.

This criticism leads to other related charges such as that drones are making it easier to wage war secretly, thus subverting democratic require-ments, e.g., any due process afforded to targets that are US citizens and the War Powers Resolution of 1973 (50 USC §1541-1548). To the extent that enhancements can make it easier for military teams to covertly conduct missions and penetrate enemy lines, it would likewise be easier to conduct illegal operations, such as assassinations and cross-border attacks without the permission of the receiving nation-state.

ETHICS

In the above two sections, we have identified the key challenges that military human enhancement may pose to law, operations, and related policy. In this final section, we briefly discuss a range of other implications that fall broadly under the banner of "ethics."

Character and Virtue

In recent decades, virtue ethics has enjoyed a broad resurgence of interest by scholars, applying the Aristotelian moral framework to environmental ethics, business ethics, bioethics, medical, and legal ethics (Oakley & Cocking, 2001; Sandler & Cafaro, 2005; Walker & Ivanhoe, 2007). Virtue ethics is often thought of as uniquely suitable for professional ethics, so given that the military is one of the professions, it should not surprise us that virtue ethics has been recognized as having core applications here as well. Indeed, virtue ethics has arguably been an integral component of thinking about military ethics for millennia, insofar as reference to virtues (e.g., courage, honor, loyalty, and justice) is an enduring feature of ethical discourse in the military tradition (Olsthoorn, 2010).

Virtue ethical frameworks are also being applied to the unique ethical challenges presented by emerging military technologies, such as autonomous robots and drones (Lin, Abney, & Bekey, 2012; Enemark, 2013). We can extend that trend to consider the ethical implications that military enhancements may have with respect to the moral virtues. First, let us briefly clarify what we mean by "virtues" in the ethical context that concerns us here. In most ethical theories in which virtues play a central role, moral virtues are understood to be states of a person's character, which we have already said are stable dispositions that promote that person's reliable performance of right or excellent actions. Such actions, when the result of genuine virtue, imply the praiseworthiness of the person performing them. In human beings, virtues of character are not gifts of birth or passive circumstance; they are cultivated states that lead to a person's deliberate and reasoned choice of the good. They result from habitual and committed practice and study of right actions, and they imply an alignment of the agent's feelings, beliefs, desires and perceptions in ways that are consistently found to be appropriate to the various practical contexts in which the person is called to act.

Thus, virtues of character are conceived as personal "excellences" in their own right; their value is not exhausted in the good actions they promote. When properly integrated, individual virtues contribute to a moral agent's possession of "virtue" writ large; that is, they motivate us to describe a person as virtuous, rather than merely noting their embodiment of a particular virtue such as courage, honesty or justice. States of a person's character contrary to virtue are characterized as vices, and a person whose character is dominated by vice is therefore appropriately characterized as vicious.

A virtuous person is conceived as good, they are also understood to be moving toward the accomplishment of a good, flourishing or excellent life; that is, they are living well. While the cultivation of virtue does not aim at securing the agent's own flourishing independently of the flourishing of others (it is not egoistic in this sense), the successful cultivation of a virtuous character is conceptually inseparable from the possibility of a good life for the agent. Yet the way this good is achieved in action cannot be fixed by a set of advance rules or principles, but must be continually discerned by the agent herself in a manner that is adapted to the particular practical contexts and roles she occupies. This contextual element sets virtue ethics clearly apart from utilitarian and deontological frameworks, and it explains why virtue ethics is so useful for application to the military profession.

Virtue ethics presupposes that the appropriate actions of a courageous soldier in battle, for example, will be very different from those of a courageous teacher or courageous politician, and from how the soldier displays courage at home in civilian life. The virtuous agent is "prudentially wise," meaning that she is able to readily see what moral responses different situations call for, and she can adapt her conduct accordingly in a way that nevertheless reflects her unified character as a virtuous individual. What, then, are the implications of military enhancements for the ability of warfighters to cultivate and express virtue? What follows does not exhaust the topics of potential concern about military enhancement and virtue, but merely an overview of the issues that are likely to matter most from a virtue-ethical standpoint.

We should start by questioning what counts as a "virtuous" enhancement. Many proposed enhancements might be viewed as ways to directly enhance military virtue itself. For example, if a pill, subdermal implant, or genetic alteration can make warfighters more willing to expose themselves to risk of harm, doesn't the enhancement make them more courageous? Yet this is too simple an analysis. From the moral standpoint, a trait or disposition is not a virtue just because it happens to result in appropriate actions. Virtuous actions must also emanate from the person's own moral viewpoint, that is, from his or her way of seeing and judging the ethical and practical implications of a situation. Otherwise the actions, however desirable from an institutional point of view, are not creditable to the moral character and wisdom of the agent. Thus if virtue and character matter in military ethics (note this assumes that we have gone beyond narrowly utilitarian considerations, such as risk-benefit calculations), then it very much matters how an enhancement modifies warfighters, not just how it affects their behavior.

For example, a pill that suppresses common physiologically-rooted panic reactions in battle looks compatible with virtue, if those reactions would otherwise undermine the soldier's training, expertise and rational grasp of the situation. Consider a soldier who successfully cultivates the thoughts, desires and feelings that are fitting for an excellent soldier in battle, but whose actions in the field are still hampered by autonomic symptoms of alarm beyond his or her control (e.g., shortness of breath, dangerously elevated pulse). Such a person could be aided in courage by an enhancement that short-circuits those symptoms.

Yet if the enhancement leads a soldier to act in ways that contradict a cognitive grasp of what's appropriate (e.g., "I knew it was too risky to engage that truck convoy without better reconnaissance, but for some reason I just did it anyway"), then the enhancement is actually an impediment to courage, in this case promoting the contrary vice of rashness. Alternatively, if the enhancement elicits apparently courageous actions from a soldier who continues to have seriously inappropriate feelings, attitudes, and judgments about battlefield risk, we would not say that the outcome of the enhancement is a courageous or "good" soldier; we have merely boosted the utility of a bad one. Enhancements of this sort would be problematic not only in particular cases, but also because they could interfere more generally with the ethical habituation of virtuous soldiers, who become prudentially wise actors only by habitually learning to see situations correctly and develop appropriate responses and strategies for dealing with them. If enhancements come to be used as a substitute for that learning process, they will actually hinder the cultivation of prudent, courageous and good soldiers, according to virtue ethics.

The issue of reversibility of enhancements is relevant here too. Since virtue presupposes the cognitive or affective flexibility to adapt behavior to circumstance and social context, an enhancement that "set" an agent's behavior patterns in a certain mode, or otherwise made his or her reaction patterns less adaptable (e.g., to civilian life or peacetime operations) would inhibit the ability to function virtuously and, by extension, to lead a good life. Even temporary enhancements could introduce this problem if they prevent the soldier from adapting well to the emerging exigencies of battle. A virtuous soldier is one who can immediately "dial down" the targeted desire to kill the enemy when a crowd of children unpredictably enters the field of action.

Virtue ethics also requires us to consider the potential impact of enhancements on moral leadership in military life. Most virtue ethicists acknowledge that fully virtuous agents who cultivate and display moral wisdom in all of their professional and personal roles are usually a significant minority in any population: it's not easy to be virtuous. Therefore, one of the most important social and professional functions of the virtuous person is to serve as a moral example to which others aspire and strive to emulate. In the context of military life, this function is largely imputed to the officer corps. Enlisted soldiers are certainly recognized for exemplary acts of courage and valor, but as in any profession, complete military virtue is thought to require not only fine actions but also much experience, as well as mature reflection upon the goals and ideals of the profession—something officer training can provide.

This invites a novel set of ethical questions about enhancements, some recurring throughout this report: Will they be given to officers, or just combat soldiers? Will they erect a moral divide between the military ranks? Who will have greater "moral authority" and status as ethical exemplars: enhanced or unenhanced military personnel? How will enhancement impact the process of military education? Would an unenhanced officer's lessons on cultivating courage or fortitude over a lifetime of service be relevant to a soldier artificially enhanced for these qualities? There are also important questions about how enhancement might affect perceptions of military character by civilians and by unenhanced forces abroad; for example, will enhanced soldiers encounter less goodwill or greater resistance from those who see their status as antithetical to traditional ideals of military virtue and character?

Finally, ethical concerns with military enhancement do not end with the question of what it means to be a good soldier; they extend to what it means to be a good human being. There is a debate among virtue ethicists about whether virtue is rooted in a distinctive conception of what, if anything, a human should naturally be. Aristotle certainly thought so, but some modern virtue ethicists deny this (Swanton 2003; Slote 2011). Still, most virtue ethicists believe that what is ethical for a human is inseparable from what is appropriate to human development on the whole. If they are right, then enhancements that take us too far from what is distinctively human are morally problematic in their own right. That said, enhancements that introduce non-natural physiology like the ability to eat grass or forgo sleep would be of far less concern to a virtue ethicist than enhancements that warp the distinctive moral, emotional and intellectual capacities that underpin virtue of character. For example, a pill or neural implant that disrupted or diminished a soldier's overall capacity to experience grief, guilt, compassion, curiosity, creativity, critical reflection or love would be highly problematic from a virtue-ethical standpoint (Nussbaum, 2011).

Emotion and Honour

Related to the issue of military virtues and professionalism is the question of what role emotions and honor, or codes of ethics, play in warfighters. With human enhancements, military organizations may elevate or diminish emotions and other psychological dispositions in their operators for some immediate benefit, but we also need to consider broader effects. Questions in this area include: does participation in any war, regardless of whether one's own side of the conflict's

participation fulfills just war theory criteria, damages one's humanity? What does killing do to the psychological, spiritual, and emotional health of the warrior? What effect would human enhancements have with respect to that health?

Some scholars and clinicians assert that any violence against another human being causes the perpetrator psychological damage, even if the actions were taken undeniably in self-defense. Rachel MacNair, clinical psychologist and author of *Perpetration-Induced Traumatic Stress: The Psychological Consequences of Killing*, describes the dangers of taking another human life:

All of these things—anxiety, panic, depression, substance abuse—can also be included in the 'psychological consequences' of killing, along with such things as increased paranoia or a sense of disintegration, or dissociation or amnesia at the time of the trauma itself. In the case of killing, feelings of guilt can vary widely, from killing that is not socially approved, such as criminal homicide, to killing that is not only approved but also expected, such as soldiers in war. People can feel guilty even under circumstances that involve clear self-defense.... [S]evere PTSD can be suffered without any feelings of guilt at all, and guilt can be suffered without any symptoms of PTSD (MacNair, 2002).

The warfighters' code of honor plays a key role in preserving their mental health, in addition to preventing atrocities. As French explains in *The Code of the Warrior* (French, 2003): Murder is a good example of an act that is cross-culturally condemned. Whatever their other points of discord, the major religions of the world agree in the determination that murder (variously defined) is wrong. Unfortunately, the fact that we abhor murder produces a disturbing tension for those who are asked to fight wars for their tribes, clans, communities, cultures or nations. When they are trained for war, warriors are given a mandate by their society to take lives. But they must learn to take only certain lives in certain ways, at certain times, and for certain reasons. Otherwise, they become indistinguishable from murderers and will find themselves condemned by the very societies they were created to serve.

Warrior cultures throughout history and from diverse regions around the globe have constructed codes of behavior, based on that culture's image of the ideal warrior. These codes have not always been written down or literally codified into a set of explicit rules. A code can be hidden in the lines of epic poems or implied by the descriptions of mythic heroes. One way or another, it is carefully conveyed to each succeeding generation of warriors. These codes tend to be quite demanding. They are often closely linked to a culture's religious beliefs and can be connected to elaborate (and frequently death defying or excruciatingly painful) rituals and rites of passage.

In many cases this code of honor seems to hold the warrior to a higher ethical standard than that required for an ordinary citizen within the general population of the society the warrior serves. The code is not imposed from the outside. The warriors themselves police strict adherence to these standards; with violators being shamed, ostracized, or even killed by their peers.

The code of the warrior not only defines how he should interact with his own warrior comrades, but also how he should treat other members of his society, his enemies, and the people he conquers. The code restrains the warrior. It sets boundaries on his behavior. It distinguishes honorable acts from shameful acts.

But why do warriors need a code that ties their hands and limits their options? Why should a warrior culture want to restrict the actions of its members and require them to commit to lofty ideals? Might not such restraints cripple their effectiveness as warriors? What's wrong with, "All's fair in love and war?" Isn't winning all that matters? Are concerns about honor and shame burdens to the warrior? And, again, what is the interplay between cognitive enhancements and this code of honor?

One reason for such warriors' codes may be to protect the warrior himself (or herself) from serious psychological damage. To say the least, the things that warriors are asked to do to guarantee their cultures' survival are far from pleasant. Even those few who, for whatever reason, seem to feel no revulsion at spilling another human being's guts on the ground, severing a limb, slicing off a head, or burning away a face are likely to be affected by the sight of their friends or kinsmen suffering the same fate. The combination of the warriors' own natural disgust at what they must witness in battle and the fact that what they must do to endure and conquer can seem so uncivilized, so against what they have been taught by their society, creates the conditions for even the most accomplished warriors to feel tremendous self-loathing.

In the introduction to his valuable analysis of Vietnam veterans suffering from post-traumatic stress disorder (PTSD), *Achilles in Vietnam: Combat Trauma and the Undoing of Character*, psychiatrist and author Jonathan Shay stresses the importance of "understanding...the specific nature of catastrophic war experiences that not only cause lifelong disabling psychiatric symptoms but can ruin good character" (Shay, 1994). Shay has conducted countless personal interviews and therapy sessions with American combat veterans who are part of the Veterans Improvement Program (VIP). His work has led him to the conclusion that the most severe cases of PTSD are the result of wartime experiences that are not simply violent, but which involve what Shay terms the "betrayal of 'what's right'" (Shay, 1994). Veterans who believe that they were directly or indirectly party to immoral or dishonorable behavior (perpetrated by themselves, their comrades, or their commanders) have the hardest time reclaiming their lives after the war is over. Such men may be tortured by persistent nightmares, may have trouble discerning a safe environment from a threatening one, may not be able to trust their friends, neighbors, family members, or government, and many have problems with alcohol, drugs, child or spousal abuse, depression, and suicidal tendencies. As Shay sorrowfully concludes, "The painful paradox is that fighting for one's country can render one unfit to be its citizen" (Shay, 1994).

Warriors need a way to distinguish what they must do out of a sense of duty from what a serial killer does for the sheer sadistic pleasure of it. Their actions, like those of the serial killer, set them apart from the rest of society. Warriors, however, are not sociopaths. They respect the values of the society in which they were raised and which they are prepared to die to protect. Therefore, it is important for them to conduct themselves in such a way that they will be honored and esteemed by their communities, not reviled and rejected by them. They want to be seen as proud defenders and representatives of what is best about their culture: as heroes, not "baby-killers."

In a sense, the nature of the warrior's profession puts him or her at a higher risk for moral corruption than most other occupations because it involves exerting power in matters of life and death. Warriors exercise the power to take or save lives, order others to take or save lives, and lead or send others to their deaths. If they take this awesome responsibility too lightly—if they lose sight of the moral significance of their actions—they risk losing their humanity and their ability to flourish in human society.

In his powerful work, *On Killing: The Psychological Cost of Learning to Kill in War and Society*, Lt. Col. Dave Grossman illuminates the process by which those in war and those training for war attempt to achieve emotional distance from their enemies. The practice of dehumanizing the enemy through the use of abusive or euphemistic language is a common and effective tool for increasing aggression and breaking down inhibitions against killing:

It is so much easier to kill someone if they look distinctly different than you. If your propaganda machine can convince your soldiers that their opponents are not really human but are 'inferior forms of life,' then their natural resistance to killing their own species will be reduced. Often the enemy's humanity is denied by referring to him as a 'gook,' 'Kraut,' or 'Nip' (Grossman, 1996).

Like Shay, Grossman has interviewed many US veterans of the Vietnam War. Not all of his subjects, however, were those with lingering psychological trauma. Grossman found that some of the men he interviewed had never truly achieved emotional distance from their former foes, and seemed to be the better for it. These men expressed admiration for Vietnamese culture. Some had even married Vietnamese women. They appeared to be leading happy and productive post-war lives. In contrast, those who persisted in viewing the Vietnamese as "less than animals" were unable to leave the war behind them.

Grossman writes about the dangers of dehumanizing the enemy in terms of potential damage to the war effort, long-term political fallout, and regional or global instability:

Because of [our] ability to accept other cultures, Americans probably committed fewer atrocities than most other nations would have under the circumstances associated with guerrilla warfare in Vietnam. Certainly fewer than was the track record of most colonial powers. Yet still we had our My Lai, and our efforts in that war were profoundly, perhaps fatally, undermined by that single incident. It can be easy to unleash this genie of racial and ethnic hatred in order to facilitate killing in time of war. It can be more difficult to keep the cork in the bottle and completely restrain it. Once it is out, and the war is over, the genie is not easily put back in the bottle. Such hatred lingers over the decades, even centuries, as can be seen today in Lebanon and what was once Yugoslavia (Grossman, 1996).

The insidious harm brought to the individual warriors who find themselves swept up by such devastating propaganda matters a great deal to those concerned with the warriors' own welfare. In a segment on the "Clinical Importance of Honoring or Dishonoring the Enemy," Jonathan Shay describes an intimate connection between the psychological health of the veteran and the respect he feels for those he fought. He stresses how important it is to the warrior to have the conviction that he participated in an honorable endeavor:

Restoring honor to the enemy is an essential step in recovery from combat PTSD. While other things are obviously needed as well, the veteran's self-respect never fully recovers so long as he is unable to see the enemy as worthy. In the words of one of our patients, a war against subhuman vermin 'has no honor.' This is true even in victory; in defeat, the dishonoring absence of human themis (shared values, a common sense of 'what's right') linking enemy to enemy makes life unendurable" (Shay, 1994).

Shay finds echoes of these sentiments in the words of J. Glenn Gray from Gray's modern classic on the experience of war, *The Warriors: Reflections on Men in Battle*. With the struggle of the Allies against the Japanese in the Pacific Theater of World War II as his backdrop, Gray brings home the agony of the warrior who has become incapable of honoring his enemies and thus is unable to find redemption himself:

The ugliness of a war against an enemy conceived to be subhuman can hardly be exaggerated. There is an unredeemed quality to battle experienced under these conditions, which blunts all senses and perceptions. Traditional appeals of war are corroded by the demands of a war of extermination, where conventional rules no longer apply. For all its inhumanity, war is a profoundly human institution....This image of the enemy as beast lessens even the satisfaction in destruction, for there is no proper regard for the worth of the object destroyed....The joys of comradeship, keenness of

perception, and sensual delights [are] lessened.... No aesthetic reconciliation with one's fate as a warrior [is] likely because no moral purgation [is] possible (Gray, 1998).

By setting standards of behavior for themselves, accepting certain restraints, and even "honoring their enemies," warriors can create a lifeline that will allow them to pull themselves out of the hell of war and reintegrate themselves into their society, should they survive to see peace restored. A warrior's code may cover everything from the treatment of prisoners of war to oath keeping to table etiquette, but its primary purpose is to grant nobility to the warriors' profession. This allows warriors to retain both their self-respect and the respect of those they guard (French, 2003). Cognitive enhancements, then, would operate against this complex and subtle background to effects that may be psychologically disastrous or difficult to predict.

Broader Impacts

From the preceding, we can see that concerns about military enhancements can be focused inward, toward the health and character of the human subject. But these concerns can also ripple outward, focused beyond the human subject. These issues engage law, policy, and ethics; for instance, how do enhancements impact military operations, including how adversaries might respond? But since enhancements change the human person—the basic unit of society—we can expect changes and challenges beyond such first-order and second-order effects. These broader impacts are temporally more distant and therefore tend to be discounted; but they are nevertheless foreseeable and should also be considered ahead of rapidly advancing science and technology.

First, we can expect the proliferation of perhaps every military technology we invent, as history shows. For instance, besides WWII-era Jeeps and modern-day Humvees returned to society as better-polished civilian models, and GPS was directly adopted by society without any modification (Lin, 2010). The method of diffusion would be different and more direct with enhancements, though: most warfighters return to society as civilians (our veterans) and would carry back any permanent enhancements and addictions with them. Again, the US has about 23 million veterans, or one out of every 10 adults, in addition to 3 million active and reserve personnel (US Census, 2011), so this is a significant segment of the population. Would these enhancements—such as a drug or an operation that subdues emotions—create problems for the veteran to assimilate to civilian life? What kinds of pressures and how much, including healthcare costs, would be placed on the Department of Veteran Affairs, given military enhancements, and are we prepared to handle those costs?

Proliferation into society is not limited to our own borders, but we can expect it to occur internationally, again as history shows. Even the military robotics that have been deployed in war only within the last decade are not just a US phenomenon, as much as it may seem from the international media's focus. It is reported that more than 50 nations now have or are developing military robotics, including China and Iran (Singer, 2009; Sharkey, 2011). Where the US deploys robots for their considerable advantages in surveillance, strike, and other roles, we would be unprepared to receive the same treatment if (and when) it is inflicted upon us. With nuclear weapons, while the US had the first-mover advantage, proliferation pushed us toward non-use agreements and erased much of that advantage (International Atomic Energy Agency, 1970). Likewise with military enhancements (and robotics), we can expect other nations to develop or adopt the same technologies we develop and therefore, at some point, have the same capabilities, again diminishing the competitive benefits once derived from the enhancements.

The wider impact of military enhancements echoes those already identified in the rich literature on human enhancements generally, for instance:

would enhanced veterans—say, with bionic limbs and augmented cognition—put other civilians at a competitive disadvantage with respect to jobs, school, sports, and so on? Would this create an enhancement arms race beyond steroids, as is now starting in sports? If enhanced veterans (and the other enhanced people they inspire) live longer than usual, does that put undue burdens on social security and pension funds? Would these advantages create social pressures to enhance more generally, as we are witnessing with Modafinil—a cognitive enhancer—in both the classroom and the workplace?

Relatedly, would enhanced warfighters be bad role models, such as steroid-using athletes, for children? We can expect some children will want to enhance themselves, and some will succeed. But this seems bad insofar as their bodies are still developing and anyway don't have full intellectual or legal capacity to make informed life-altering decisions (e.g., tattoos). Enhancements, as distinct from purely therapeutic uses, would likely not have been tested on normal children and other populations, such as pregnant women and those of advanced age, in that it may be too risky to conduct such testing on those healthy individuals, relative to the benefits. That is, there would be no countervailing benefit of helping to cure the individual of an illness, if those subjects were normal to begin with.

Earlier, we discussed the issue of access to enhancements within the military: who should receive them, some warfighters or all; and what problems could unequal access create? At a larger societal scale, there may be friction between the enhanced and unenhanced, or at least a class divide—in terms of education, job outlook, etc.—as we already see between those with Internet access and those without. If enhancements in society are expensive and only afforded by the wealthier, then this may widen the gap between the haves and the have-nots. Similarly, would there be a communication divide between the enhanced and unenhanced, if the former can see in different wavelengths and have different powers of perception? On the other hand, if there's no moral issue generally with enhancing humans, then why not uplift animals closer to human-level intelligence (Dvorsky, 2012), building on chimera work previously discussed?

While neither international nor domestic law requires that we consider these and other societal effects, ethics and public policy do. Without proper management, technological disruptions can have serious, avoidable effects. Possible solutions, as suggested for other issues previously considered, may include a policy to implement only reversible or temporary enhancements in the military as a firewall for broader society. To be sure, some commentators do not view enhancements in the general population as a bad or unmanageable outcome. So this continuing wider debate on human enhancements—which we will not explicate here, as it is available elsewhere (Allhoff et al., 2010a)—should be of interest to the military, especially as the military is a key driver of new technologies that eventually make their way into broader society.

CONCLUSION

Human enhancements have the potential to make it easier and safer for warfighters to do their job. Enhancements have a long history in the military, but recent opposition to their use in realms such as sports and academia, as well as controversy over the off-label or experimental use of certain drugs by the military, are forcing questions about the appropriateness of their use by the military. While military enhancements have largely escaped the scrutiny of the public as well as policymakers, the science and technologies underwriting human enhancements are marching ahead.

The military technology getting the most attention now is robotics. As we suggested throughout the report, there may be ethical, legal, and policy parallels between robotics and enhancements, and

certainly more lessons can be drawn. We can think of military robotics as sharing the same goal as human enhancement. Robotics may aim to create a super soldier from an engineering approach: they are our proxy mecha-warriors. However, there are some important limitations to those machines. For one thing, they don't have a sense of ethics—of what is right and wrong—which can be essential on the battlefield and to the laws of war. Where it is child's play to identify a ball or coffee mug or a gun, it's notoriously tough for a computer to do that, especially objects that are novel or otherwise unlabeled (Le et al., 2012). This does not give us much confidence that a robot can reliably distinguish friend from foe, at least in the foreseeable future.

In contrast, cognitive and physical enhancements aim to create a super-soldier from a biomedical direction, such as with drugs and bionics. For battle, we want our soft organic bodies to perform more like machines. Somewhere in between robotics and biomedical research, we might arrive at the perfect future warfighter: one that is part machine and part human, striking a formidable balance between technology and our frailties. Indeed, the field of neuromorphic robots already aims to fill this gap by using biological brains to control robotic bodies (Krichmar & Wagatsuma, 2011).

In changing human biology with enhancements, we also may be changing the assumptions behind existing laws of war and even human ethics. If so, we would need to reexamine the foundations of our social and political institutions—including the military—if prevailing norms create "policy vacuums" (Moor 2005) in failing to account for new technologies (Lin, 2012b; Lin, Allhoff, & Rowe, 2012; Taddeo, 2012).

In comic books and science fiction, we can suspend disbelief about the details associated with fantastical technologies and abilities, as represented by human enhancements. But in the real world—as life imitates art, and "mutant powers" really are changing the world—the details matter and will require real investigations.

The issues discussed in this report are complex, given an unfamiliar interplay among technology ethics, bioethics, military law, and other relevant areas. As such, further studies will require close collaborations with a range of disciplines and stakeholders, as is increasingly the case in technology ethics (Brey, 2000). Given the pervasive role of national security and defense in the modern world in particular, as well as the flow of military technologies into civilian society, many of these issues are urgent now and need to be actively engaged, ideally in advance of or in parallel with rapidly emerging science and technologies.

REFERENCES

10USC § 890 (1994) (UCMJ Art 90).

10USC §980, 21 CFR §50.24.

10USCA §1107 (West).

45CFR §46.111(a)(2).

50USC §1541-1548.

Allhoff, F., Lin, P., Moor, J., & Weckert, J. (2010). Ethics of human enhancement: 25 questions & answers. *Studies in Ethics, Law and Technology, 4*(4).

Army, U. S. (2005). Military working dogs. *Field Manual No. 3-19.17*. Retrieved 28 November, 2012 from http://www.fas.org/irp/doddir/army/fm3-19-17.pdf

Beckhusen, R. (2012). Report: Ukraine trains dolphins with friggin' pistols on their heads. *Wired Danger Room*. Retrieved 28 November, 2012, www.wired.com/dangerroom/2012/10/dolphins/

Berkelman, R., Halsey, N., & Resnik, D. (2010, August 2). *Presidential Commission for the Study of Bioethical Issues*. 10th Meeting, 8th sess.

Biological and Toxin Weapons Convention. (1972). Convention on the prohibition of the development, production and stock-piling of bacteriological (biological) and toxin weapons and on their destruction. *The Biological and Toxin Weapons Convention Website*. Retrieved 28 November, 2012 from http://www.unog.ch/80256EDD006B8954/%28httpAssets%29/C4048678A93B6934C1257188004848D0/$file/BWC-text-English.pdf

Brey, P. (2000). Method in computer ethics: Towards a multi-level interdisciplinary approach. *Ethics and Information Technology, 2*(2), 125–129. doi:10.1023/A:1010076000182

Brown, K. (2006). An ethical obligation to our service members: Meaningful benefits for informed consent violations. *South Texas Law Review, 47*(1), 919–947.

Canaday, M. (2001). US military integration of religious, ethnic, and racial minorities in the twentieth century. *The Palm Center*. Retrieved 28 November, 2012 from http://www.palmcenter.org/publications/dadt/u_s_military_integration_of_religious_ethnic_and_racial_minorities_in_the_twentieth_cen tury#_ftnref1

Census, U. S. (2011). Section 10: National security and veterans affairs. *US Census Bureau*. Retrieved 28 November, 2012 from http://www.census.gov/prod/ 2011pubs/12statab/defense.pdf

Code, N. (1947).. . *British Medical Journal, 1448*(1).

Cohen, A. (2010). Proportionality in modern asymmetrical wars. *Jerusalem Center for Public Affairs*. Retrieved 28 November, 2012 from http://jcpa.org/text/proportionality.pdf

Convention, H. (1899). *International Humanitarian Law – Treaties & Documents*. Retrieved 28 November, 2012 from http:// www.icrc.org/ihl.nsf/INTRO/150?OpenDocument

Cooke, J. (1876). *A life of General Robert E. Lee.* New York, NY: D. Appleton and Company.

Coupland, R., & Herby, P. (1999). Review of the legality of weapons: A new approach: The SirUS Project. *International Committee of the Red Cross: Resource Center.* Retrieved 28 November, 2012 from http://www.icrc.org/eng/resources/documents/misc/57jq36.htm

Declaration of Geneva. (1948). Retrieved 15 August, 2013 from http://www.genevadeclaration. org/fileadmin/docs/GD-Declaration-091020-EN. pdf

Declaration of Helsinki. (1964). *World Health Organization.* Retrieved 15 August, 2013 from http:// www.who.int/bulletin/archives/79(4)373.pdf

Doe v. Sullivan, 938 F.2d 1370, 1372-1374, 1381 (DC Cir. 1991).

Dvorsky, G. (2012). Should we upgrade the intelligence of animals? *i09: Futurism.* Retrieved 28 November, 2012 from http://io9.com/5943832/ should-we-upgrade-the-intelligence-of-animals

Foust, J. (2012, September 24). Ask the experts: Do targeted killings work? *Council on Foreign Relations.* Retrieved 28 November, 2012 from http://blogs.cfr.org/zenko/2012/09/24/ask-the-experts-do-targeted-killings-work/

French, S. (2003). *The code of the warrior: Exploring the values of warrior cultures, past and present.* New York, NY: Rowman and Littlefield Publishers.

Gabriel, R. (2013). *Between flesh and steel: A history of military medicine from the middle ages to the war in Afghanistan.* Washington, DC: Potomac Books.

Galliott, J. (2012a). Uninhabited aerial vehicles and the asymmetry objection: A response to Strawser. *Journal of Military Ethics, 11*(1), 58–66. doi :10.1080/15027570.2012.683703

Galliott, J. (2012b). Closing with completeness: The asymmetric drone warfare debate. *Journal of Military Ethics, 11*(4), 353–356. doi:10.1080/ 15027570.2012.760245

Galliott, J. (Forthcoming). *Unmanned systems: Mapping the moral landscape.* Surrey, UK: Ashgate.

Geneva Additional Protocol I. (1977). Retrieved 28 November, 2012 from http://www.icrc.org/ihl. nsf/INTRO/470?OpenDocument

Grabenstein, J. (2006). *Immunization to protect the US armed forces: Heritage, current practice, prospects.* Retrieved 28 November, 2012 from http://www.vaccines.mil/documents/library/ MilitaryImztn2005fulc.pdf

Gray, J. (1970). *The warriors: Reflections on men in battle.* New York, NY: Harper and Row.

Grossman, D. (1996). *On killing: The psychological cost of learning to kill in war and society.* Boston, MA: Little, Brown and Company.

Hessel, A., Goodman, M., & Kotler, S. (2012). Hacking the President's DNA. *The Atlantic.* Retrieved 16 December, 2012 from http://www. theatlantic.com/magazine/archive/2012/11/ hacking-the-presidentsdna/309147/

Human Rights Watch. (2012). *Losing humanity: The case against killer robots.* Retrieved 28 November, 2012 from http://www.hrw.org/ reports/2012/11/1 9/losing-humanity-0

International Atomic Energy Agency. (1970). Treaty on the non-proliferation of nuclear weapons. *IAEA Information Circular.* Retrieved 28 November, 2012 from http://www.iaea.org/Publications/Documents/Infcircs/Others/infcirc140.pdf

Jacobson v. Commonwealth of Massachusetts, 197 US 11, 18-19, 34 (1905).

Katz, R. (2001). Friendly fire: The mandatory military anthrax vaccination program. *Duke Law Journal, 50*(6), 1835–1865. doi:10.2307/1373049 PMID:11794357

Knights, A. (2007). *Unconventional animals in the history of warfare*. Retrieved 28 November, 2012, from http://www.allempires.com/article/index. php?q=Unconventional_Animals_in_the_History_of_Warf

Krichmar, J., & Wagatsuma, H. (Eds.). (2011). *Neuromorphic and brain-based robots*. New York, NY: Cambridge University Press. doi:10.1017/CBO9780511994838

Le, Q., Ranzato, M., Monga, R., Devin, M., Chen, K., Corrado, G., et al. (2012). Building high-level features using large scale unsupervised learning. In *Proceedings of the 29th International Conference on Machine Learning*. Edinburgh, UK: Academic Press.

Levin, K. (2008). It is well that war is so terrible. *Civil War Memory*. Retrieved 28 November, 2012 from http://cwmemory.com/2008/09/08/it-is-well-that-war-is-so-terrible/

Lin, P. (2010). Ethical blowback from emerging technologies. *Journal of Military Ethics*, *9*(4), 313–331. doi:10.1080/15027570.2010.536401

Lin, P. (2011, December 15). Drone-ethics briefing: What a leading expert told the CIA. *The Atlantic*. Retrieved 28 November 2012 from http://www.theatlan tic.com/technology/archive/2011/12/drone-ethics-briefing-what-a-leading- robot-expert-told-the-cia/250060/

Lin, P. (2012a). More than human? The ethics of biologically enhancing soldiers. *The Atlantic*. Retrieved 28 November, 2012 from http://www.theatlantic.com/technology/archive/2012/02/more-than-human-the-ethics-of-biologically-enhancing-soldiers/253217

Lin, P. (2012b, April 30). Stand your cyberground law: A novel proposal for digital security. *The Atlantic*. Retrieved 28 November, 2012 from http://www.theatlantic.com/technology/archive/2012/04/stand-your-cyberground-law-a-novel-proposal-for-digital- security/256532/

Lin, P., Abney, K., & Bekey, G. (2008). *Autonomous military robotics: Risk, ethics, and design*. Retrieved 28 November, 2012 from http: //ethics.calpoly.edu/ONR_report.pdf

Lin, P., Abney, K., & Bekey, G. (Eds.). (2012). *Robot ethics: The ethical and social implications of robotics*. Cambridge, MA: MIT Press.

Lin, P., Allhoff, F., & Rowe, N. (2012, June 5). Is it possible to wage a just cyberwar? *The Atlantic*. Retrieved 28 November, 2012 from http://www.theatlan tic.com/technology/archive/2012/06/is-it-possible-to-wage-a-just- cyberwar/258106

MacNair, R. (2002). *Perpetration-induced traumatic stress: The psychological consequences of killing*. London: Praeger Publishers.

Moor, J. (2005). Why we need better ethics for emerging technologies. *Ethics and Information Technology*, *7*(3), 111–119. doi:10.1007/s10676-006-0008-0

Navy, U. S. (2012). *Marine Mammal Program*. Retrieved 28 November 2012 from http://www.public.navy.mil/spawar/Pacific/71500/Pages/default.aspx

Nussbaum, M. (2011). *Creating capabilities: The human development approach*. Cambridge, MA: Harvard University Press. doi:10.4159/harvard.9780674061200

O'Meara, R. (2012). Contemporary governance architecture regarding robotic technologies: An assessment. In P. Lin, K. Abney, & G. Bekey (Eds.), *Robot ethics: The ethical and social implications of robotics*. Cambridge, MA: MIT Press.

Oakley, J., & Dean, C. (Eds.). (2001). *Virtue ethics and professional roles*. Cambridge, UK: Cambridge University Press. doi:10.1017/CBO9780511487118

Olsthoorn, P. (2010). *Military ethics and virtues*. New York, NY: Routledge.

Perry v. Wesely, No. NMCM 200001397, 2000 WL 1775249, at *3 (N-M. Ct. Crim. App. November 29, 2000).

Plaw, A. (2012, September 25). Drones save lives, American and otherwise. *New York Times*. Retrieved 28 November, 2012 from http://www.nytimes.com/roomfordebate/2012/09/25/do-drone-attacks-do-more-harm-than-good/drone-strikes-save-lives-american-and-other

Ponder v. Stone, 54 MJ 613, 614 (N-M. Ct. Crim. App. 2000).

Rome Statute of the International Criminal Court. (1998). *United Nations Treaty Website*. Retrieved 15 August, 2013 from http://untreaty.un.org/cod/icc/statute/99_corr/cstatute.htm

Royal Society. (2012). *Brain waves module 3: Neuroscience, conflict and security*. Retrieved 16 December, 2012 from http://royalsociety.org/policy/projects/brain-waves/conflict-security/

Rozner, E. (1998). Haves, have-nots, and have-to-haves: Net effects of the digital divide. *Berkman Center for Internet & Society*. Retrieved 28 November, 2012 from http://cyber.law.harvard.edu/fallsem98/final_papers/Rozner.html

Russo, M., Arnett, V., Thomas, M., & Caldwell, J. (2008). Ethical use of cogniceuticals in the militaries of democratic nations. *The American Journal of Bioethics*, *8*(2), 39–41. doi:10.1080/15265160802015016 PMID:18570076

Sandler, R., & Cafaro, P. (Eds.). (2005). *Environmental virtue ethics*. Lanham, MD: Rowman and Littlefield.

Sassòli, M. (2003). Legitimate targets of attacks under international humanitarian law. *International Humanitarian Law Research Initiative*. Retrieved 28 November, 2012 from http://www.hpcrresearch.org/sites/default/files/publications/Session1.pdf

Sharkey, N. (2011). The automation and proliferation of military drones and the protection of civilians. *Law. Innovation and Technology*, *3*(2), 229–240. doi:10.5235/175799611798204914

Shay, J. (1994). *Achilles in Vietnam: Combat trauma and the undoing of character*. New York, NY: Simon and Schuster.

Singer, P. (2009). *Wired for war: The robotics revolution and conflict in the 21st century*. New York, NY: The Penguin Press.

Slote, M. (2011). *The impossibility of perfection: Aristotle, feminism and the complexities of ethics*. Oxford, UK: Oxford University Press. doi:10.1093/acprof:oso/9780199790821.003.0003

Stanford Encyclopedia of Philosophy. (2011). Sorites Paradox. *Stanford Encyclopedia of Philosophy*. Retrieved 28 November, 2012 from http://plato.stanford.edu/entries/sorites-paradox/

Swanton, C. (2003). *Virtue ethics: A pluralistic view*. Oxford, UK: Oxford University Press. doi:10.1093/0199253889.001.0001

United States v. Chadwell, 36 CMR 741 (1965).

United States v. New, 50 MJ 729, 739 (A. Ct. Crim. App. 1999).

US Department of Defense. (2012a). *Department of Defense Directive 1010.1 (originally 28 December 1984)*. Retrieved on 18 December from 2012, http://www.dtic.mil/whs/directives/corres/pdf/101001p.pdf

US Department of Defense. (2012b). *Department of Defense Directive 6200.2*. Retrieved 18 December 2012 from http://www.dtic.mil/whs/directiv es/corres/pdf/620002p.pdf

US Government, Manual for Court-Martial. Part IV-19, ¶ 14c(2)(a)(i) (2010).

Walker, R., & Ivanhoe, P. (Eds.). (2007). *Working virtue: Virtue ethics and contemporary moral problems*. Oxford, UK: Oxford University Press.

Wasserman, G., & Grabenstein, J. (2003). *Analysis of adverse events after anthrax immunization in US army medical personnel*. Retrieved 28 November, 2012 from http://www.dtic.mil/cgi-bin/GetTRDoc?AD=ADA495915

KEY TERMS AND DEFINITIONS

Disenhancement: A medical or biological intervention that makes one worse off.

Miltiary-Technical Proliferation: The spread of military technologies into the civilian realm.

Principle of Distinction: An element of international law and just war theory which demands that a weapon must be discriminating enough to target only combatants and never noncombatants.

Principle of Proportionality: Demands that the use of a weapon be proportional to the military objective, so as to keep civilian casualties to a minimum.

SIrUS Principle: Related to proportionality in that it requires methods of attack to be minimally harmful in rendering a warfighter *hors de combat* or unable to fight.

Soldier Enhancement: Medical or biological intervention introduced into a soldier's body designed to improve warfighting performance, appearance, or capability besides what is necessary to achieve, sustain or restore health.

Therapy: An intervention or treatment intended to alleviate a condition suffered by a patient, elevating his or health closer to normal.

Chapter 9
Human Enhancing Technologies and Individual Privacy Right

Joanna Kulesza
University of Lodz, Poland

ABSTRACT

This chapter provides a legal perspective on the application of Human Enhancing Technologies (HET), in particular on Brain-Computer Interfaces (BCIs), emphasizing threats they bring to individual privacy. The author discusses the geographical, political, and cultural differences in understanding the individual right to privacy, as granted by human rights treaties and customary international law, and confronts them with the threats brought about by HET. The era of globalized services rendered by transnational companies necessitates an answer to the question on the possible and desired shape of effective individual protection of human rights from the threats brought about by advancing HET. Be it biomedical or geolocalisation data, when fueled through the Big Data resources available online, individual data accompanying the HET becomes a powerful marketing tool and a significant national and international security measure. The chapter aims to identify the privacy threats brought about by the HET and proposes a business-ethics based solution.

INTRODUCTION

The focal point of the analysis provided is the ineptitude of the contemporary international legal system to effectively protect individual privacy. Yet the changing economic models and the development of the globalised world shift the burden of human rights protection from national authorities to international companies, including HET based service providers. In 2006 the European Parliament emphasized the need to respect high ethical principles in protecting individual privacy by all

parties involved in HET including the private sector and re-addressed that need in its latest 2008 report. The growing role of self-regulation and business ethics in respecting individual privacy was also well envisaged in the 2009 European Commission's code of conduct for responsible nanosciences and nanotechnologies research. The author argues that the contents of the human right to privacy, well recognized in human rights law since 1948 is becoming more of an ethics based standard than a legal construct. The potential advantages but also the threats of the HET applica-

DOI: 10.4018/978-1-4666-6010-6.ch009

tion add to this evolution. National authorities can no longer effectively protect individual privacy, while private parties operating the technologies are often well equipped to do so. As UN Human Rights Commission's Special Rapporteur Frank LaRue emphasized in his latest report it is the private sector that will now bear the burden and the responsibility to protect human rights in the globalized international society (LaRue, 2011). Endeavors such as the Global Network Initiative aim to help service providers meet the international standards of privacy protection, regardless of national authorities' involvement. Academics aid companies in the better recognition of their users' needs aiming at a stronger market position, since privacy is a strong currency in the information based economy. Providers of HET services need to recognize this specific of the hybrid economy we are witnessing and shape their privacy policies accordingly. Therefore the chapter aims to define the privacy challenge behind the HET and propose its business-ethics based solution.

PRIVACY OVERVIEW

The concept of privacy, although well present in the international human rights catalogue, is still undefined. International forums shy away from defining the term crucial to enjoyment of family life, domestic peace and individual security, as its meaning and scope evolve alongside the social and technological progress. The notion of privacy covers information pertaining to "family and home life, physical and moral integrity, honor and reputation, avoidance of being put in a false light, non-revelation of irrelevant and embarrassing facts, unauthorized publication of private photographs, protection against misuse of private communications, as well as protection from disclosure of information given and received by the individual confidentially" (Council of Europe, 1970; Kuner, 2009). According to the US Supreme Court privacy protection ought to be

granted against unjustified searches and seizures by state authorities, over personal contraception and procreation choices as well as raising offspring (Kuner, 2009). The broad notion of privacy is strongly rooted in national regulations dealing with either civil law protection of personal rights or criminal prosecution in defamation laws (Anderson, 2012). While it generally covers any information that refers to an identifiable individual, the scope of such data and limits of its needed legal protection vary tremendously throughout world's legal systems. That is justifiably so, since privacy has been a controversial issue since its inception. Even when attempting to decide on its origins, one is left to struggle between the works of U.S., German and French legal writers. Most English language authors identify Warren and Brandeis (1890) as the authors of the privacy concept in their 1890 article on the "right to be let alone", as the origin of the term (Leebron, 1991). Yet "privacy" appeared in the German writings of Kohler (1900) and French jurisprudence roughly around the same time (Falk & Mohnhaupt, 2000; Bertrand, 1999). While U.S. courts were initially reluctant to grant the "right to be let alone" (Brandeis, 1928) within less than 60 years the notion of privacy became a hard-law concept rooted in numerous international law human rights documents, with the 1948 Universal Declaration on Human Rights (UDHR) paving the way (Griswold, 1961). It might seem, when looking at the stipulations of the 1973 International Covenant on Civil and Political Rights (ICCPR) that the scope of individual privacy is well defined. Both: Article 12 UDHR and its mirroring image in Article 17 ICCPR disallow for anyone to be subjected to "arbitrary" interference with their privacy. The term "arbitrary" may be defined in the context of Article 29 UDHR, which includes a delimitative clause for, among others, the individual right to privacy. According to its stipulations this right may only be subject to "such limitations as are determined by law solely for the purpose of securing due recognition and respect for the rights and freedoms of others and of meeting the just requirements of morality, public order and the general welfare in a democratic society". Limitations exceeding the scope of the Article 29 clause are to be deemed "arbitrary" and hence against international law.

While this general limitative clause referring to notions of "morality" or values significant in a "democratic society" may be considered vague, the 1988 General Comment No. 16 on Article 17 provided by the UN Human Rights Committee (HRC) specifies what is meant by any such "arbitrary" intrusion. All 67 member parties to the ICCPR are to protect individual privacy by adopting such measures as to ensure that their legal system allows to effectively protect it and by actively taking precautions to combat any interference, be it through its own or foreign authorities or third parties, including private individuals. The HRC emphasized that „effective measures have to be taken by States to ensure that information concerning a person's private life does not reach the hands of persons who are not authorized by law to receive, process and use it" (UN Human Rights Committee, 1988; Bygrave, 1998). The global standard for privacy protection allows for no interference with individual privacy unless in cases „envisaged by the law". Whenever information on one's private life it to be processed, relevant legislation must specify the circumstances of such processing. According to the HRC „a decision to make use of such authorized interference must be made […] on a case-by-case basis" and may never be arbitrary. In cases when an interference is legally admissible, it may only be executed in accordance with the "provisions, aims and objectives" of the ICCPR and be "reasonable in the particular circumstances."

A reflection of such an obligation might be the current (2013) discussion on the U.S. deployed PRISM surveillance programme followed by legitimate community expectations in Europe and Asia for national authorities to protect individuals under their jurisdiction from foreign inspection. While the PRISM programme is legitimate under

US law, its design to render blanket surveillance of non-US persons is clearly against the HRC interpretation of privacy protection, where any decision on privacy invasion must be made on a case-by-case basis and legitimated by particular circumstances. Similarly community protests against enabling devices such as Google Glass in public spaces may serve as another example of universal lack of consent for unjustified privacy invasions. The current shape of individual privacy right inherently holds a positive state obligation to take active measures against privacy infringements regardless of the source of such potential violation. In the context of human rights law privacy protection it therefore not only a prohibition for a state to interfere with the private sphere of individuals but also its obligation to actively protect them from infringements by third parties. With regard to the growing surveillance capabilities the 1988 HRC guidelines seem particularly helpful when stating clearly that "surveillance, whether electronic or otherwise, interceptions of telephonic, telegraphic and other forms of communication, wire-tapping and recording of conversations should be prohibited."

Even though there is a broad international, human-rights based consensus on the right to individual privacy, opinions and social concepts on the details of that right vary tremendously. These irreconcilable differences originate from culture and economy. Culture lies behind different social interpretations of the right to privacy, shaped by national and regional history, values and beliefs shared within individual communities. Local approach to economy and its relationship with human rights determines the scope of legal protection of privacy as in some regions personal data is considered a commodity subjected to free market conditions, while in others any information relating to identifiable individual is recognized as a manifestation of their human right to privacy and protected by default. That is the case in the European Union (EU), where community regulations and individual state laws see privacy as a human right requiring active state protection (Bygrave, 2010; Kuner, 2009). In line with that understanding Weber defines privacy as a composite of secrecy, anonymity and solitude (Weber, 2012). At the same time Asia or United States laws perceive data allowing for the identification of individuals and describing their particular traits equally to any other information, with its commercial value subject to market conditions. These very differing perspectives on privacy have made the search for a compromise on privacy protection a difficult challenge for any of the existing economic forums. The challenge of transboundary privacy protection remains unresolved despite the far-reaching efforts of i.e. the Organization for Economic Co-operation Forum (OECD), which identified personal data as a component of the individual right to privacy. The non-binding yet influential 1980 OECD Guidelines on the Protection of Privacy and Transborder Flow of Personal Data (Guidelines) are an early example of such a global consensus (OECD, 1980). The scale of their success may be measured by their 2013 re-adaptation reflecting contemporary challenges to privacy protection (OECD, 2013). OECD sees personal data protection as the tool for protecting privacy throughout the world. The Guidelines are considered the first international document to identify the standards for protection of privacy through eight personal data processing principles. In the Guidelines the term "personal data" is used to identify the scope of privacy protection and to cover any information relating to an identified or identifiable individual, referred to as "data subject" (OECD, 1980). The basic eights principles of privacy and data protection needed in national legislations to ensure privacy protection include 1) the collection limitation principle, 2) the data quality principle, 3) the individual participation principle, 4) the purpose specification principle, 5) the use limitation principle, 6) the security safeguards principle, 7) the openness principle and 8) the accountability principle (OECD, 1980). They introduce certain obligations upon "data controllers" that is parties "who, according

to domestic law, are competent to decide about the contents and use of personal data regardless of whether or not such data are collected, stored, processed or disseminated by that party or by an agent on their behalf" (OECD, 1980). They oblige data controllers to respect limits made by national laws pertaining to the collection of personal data. Any such data is to be obtained by "lawful and fair means and, where appropriate, with the knowledge or consent of the data subject" (OECD, 1980). When personal data is gathered or processed it ought to be relevant to the purposes for which it will be used and "accurate, complete and up-to-date" (OECD, 1980). Such purposes ought to be specified no later than at the time of data collection. Its use ought to be limited to the fulfillment of the indicated purposes or ones compatible therewith (OECD, 1980). An obligation crucial to the effective international protection of personal information is the duty of data controllers not to disclose it or use it for purposes other than those specified to the data subject. Exceptions from this principle include situations where there is consent of the data subject for its use or disclosure or such use or disclosure are permitted by the authority of law (OECD, 1980). Identifying what may be perceived as a due diligence standard for data processors the OECD encouraged them to introduce "reasonable security safeguards" against risks of loss or unauthorized access, destruction, use, modification or disclosure of data (OECD, 1980). Consequently basic privileges of the data subject include the right to obtain confirmation of whether or not the data controller has data relating to him, to have any data relating to him communicated within a reasonable time, to be given reasons if a request for such information is denied, to be able to challenge such denial and data relating to him (OECD, 1980). Should such challenge show successful the data ought to be erased, rectified, completed or amended (OECD, 1980). Moreover a data controller is to be held accountable, according to national laws, for failing to introduce effective measures ensuring the rights identified above (OECD, 1980).

The OECD principles ought to be recognized as the practical application of the right to privacy present in the human rights system. They have been adopted into national acts of law in Australia, Canada, and Hong Kong (Kuner, 2009) and supplemented with the 1998 OECD Ministerial Declaration on the Protection of Privacy on Global Networks (OECD, 1998). The 101 national data privacy regulations mirror those principles to a great extent (Greenleaf, 2014). While their effectiveness may come to depend upon jurisdictional issues, the criteria for identification of data subjects and obligations of data processors seem clear.

PROTECTION OF SENSITIVE AND HEALTH INFORMATION

According to the OECD Guidelines, "countries might apply the Guidelines differentially to different kinds of personal data," in particular with regard to the "confidentiality of medical records versus the individual's right to inspect data relating to him" (OECD, 1980). Numerous states use this exception in order to introduce particular safeguards for the processing of medical data.

Flowingly the EU data protection Directive (DPD) allows for restricting rights of access and information with regard to e.g. medical data to be "obtained only through a health professional" (European Parliament, 1995). Moreover it introduces special conditions for processing particular categories of data, that include "data revealing racial or ethnic origin, political opinions, religious or philosophical beliefs, trade-union membership, and the processing of data concerning health or sex life" (European Parliament, 1995). With the processing of such data generally prohibited, it may take place when the consent of the data subject has been explicitly given or when its processing is "necessary" for employment purposes in accordance with national law. Such data may also be processed when the processing is necessary to protect the vital interests of the data subject or of another person while the former is incapable of providing his consent or when the processing is carried out in the course of "legitimate activities" of a non-profit entity with a political, philosophical, religious or trade-union aim. Such data may also be processed when the processing relates to information "manifestly made public by the data subject" or when it is necessary for the establishment, exercise or defense of legal claims. Moreover no prohibition is in place for the processing of sensitive data for the purposes of preventive medicine, medical diagnosis, the provision of care or treatment or the management of health-care services, when such data is processed by a health professional subject under national law or rules established by national competent bodies to the obligation of professional secrecy or by another person also subject to an equivalent obligation of secrecy (European Parliament, 1995).

While federal personal data protection regulations are scarce in the U.S. for reasons discussed above, health information is one of the few exceptions covered by a comprehensive privacy regulation. The Health Insurance Portability and Accountability Act of 1996 (HIPAA) establishes "a set of national standards for protecting certain health information" (U.S. Senate, 1996). The U.S. Department of Health and Human Services (HHS) issued the Privacy Rule to implement the HIPAA. Its basic principle is to identify circumstances when an individual's protected heath information may be used or disclosed (U.S. Senate, 1996). The definition of "Protected Health Information" covers all "individually identifiable health information" held or transmitted by a health services entity or its business associate, in any form or media (U.S. Senate, 1996). The term covers information on individual's past, present or future physical or mental health or condition, the provision of health care, or the past, present, or future payment for the provision of health care to the individual, as well as that which identifies the individual or for which there is a reasonable basis to believe it can be used to identify the individual (U.S. Senate, 1996). The scope of the regulation is limited to health care providers, covering providers of medical or other health services and any other person furnishing health care services or supplies (U.S. Senate, 1996). Even though limited in scope, the federal regulation of personal health data is significant for the value of such information to individuals and companies alike. With the growing capabilities of gathering health-related information through the HET this significant privacy observation must be emphasized.

HET ORIGINATED PRIVACY THREATS

According to the European Parliament's "Science and Technology Options Assessment" (STOA) the term "Human Enhancement Technologies" covers a broad and versatile category of long-term and temporary modifications to individual human performance (European Parliament, 2009). The flexible STOA definition covers "modifications aimed at improving individual human performance and brought about by science-based or technologically based interventions to the human body", while excluding from its scope any use of "body-external technological devices", which are "not implanted or not robustly fixed to the body" (European Parliament, 2009). Among the varied catalogue of HET, which includes the use of pharmaceuticals and other chemical substances aimed at improving human performance, be it minimizing the results of sleep deprivation or increasing learning capabilities, state of the art prosthetics or gene therapies for "designer babies", also implanted human-machine interfaces, including cutting-edge brain computer interfaces (BCIs) are named (European Parliament, 2009). This particular category of HET invites new questions on the identification of personal data and, consequently, individual privacy protection, especially when set against the background of cloud computing and Big Data availability.

Regarding the increasing data collection, processing and transfer capabilities of external devices, such as Google Glass, which themselves,

being external devices may not be categorized as HET, allows a safe presumption that introducing eye or brain implants allowing for continuous online connectivity is a question of time. The so-called "human-machine hybrids" also referred to as "humanity 2.0" aim to apply technology in order to make humans more agile, faster and stronger by "increasingly seamless human–machine interfaces", including implanted chips, directly incorporated neural interfaces or remote sensing capacities, including Radio Frequency Identifiers (RFIDs) (European Parliament, 2009). The report directly prophecies fundamental changes to human cognition and perception with technologies challenging "anthropological notions" of the "relationships between humans and their tools" and prognoses forever more radical man–machine symbiosis (European Parliament, 2009).

Although BCIs are tested for numerous applications, including ones designed for paraplegics, enabling them to control computers directly from their brain, it is virtual worlds, such as those created by the makers of Second Life or Cyworld which are the most intense current area of BCIs' development. According to the STOA report computer games industry funds BCIs technologies that are "designed to enable users to directly control their avatars in "virtual worlds" and emphasizes its "interesting economic perspective" (European Parliament, 2009; Warwick, 2013). BCIs are researched for commercial use in computer games, allowing users to interact with virtual surroundings, but also for military purposes, allowing fighter pilots to fly their machines through mind control. STOA foresees for the upcoming "merging of virtual worlds and real life in the not too distant future" (European Parliament, 2009).

Military applications of BCIs are of significant interest to U.S. Defense Advanced Research Projects Agency (DARPA), the founder of all Internet related research. It is funding projects on more efficient means of direct brain-computer communication and on "augmented reality" where "virtual and physical surroundings are blended" (European Parliament, 2009). Interesting from a privacy point of view are the applications of BCIs for the automotive and robotics industries including high-tech "binoculars connected with the brain of their users" (European Parliament, 2009). The highly media acclaimed "driverless cars", causing serious liability issues in the U.S. are also a safe choice for the further application of the BCIs.

What is being referred to as "second-stage enhancements" includes the multifunctional BCIs applications, providing "radically new capacities" for humans. This quickly developing area of research and experimental practice includes the merger of various kinds of technology for medical, industrial and military use. According to the European Parliament, they may "alter the rules of posthoc ethical and policy reflection", enabling their users to "manipulate directly the rules of social engagement in ways we now might consider unfair" (European Parliament, 2009). Most radical proponents of the "transhumanist movement" foresee a near technical possibility of one's entire personality or mind to be downloaded onto a computer (European Parliament, 2009). When assessing the prospects of those futuristic scenarios coming true, one should keep in mind that the term "cyberspace", subject to contemporary serious political and legal debates, originates from a 1984 sci-fi novel (Gibson, 1984).

Before referring directly to the contemporary challenges of privacy protection and the transatlantic legal divergence in its perception the accompanying divergence in the field of BCIs ought to be emphasized. According to the STOA study invasive BCIs applications research is "almost exclusively centered in North America", while "non-invasive BCIs systems evolve primarily from European and Asian efforts" (European Parliament, 2009).

Although the privacy aspect to HET in general and BCIs in particular has been recognized by the European Parliament as early as 2006, no detailed study has been devoted to this issue (European Parliament, 2009). The possible reason for this shortcoming is the fact that the debate on HET ethics has so far given little concrete results on the approved or disapproved elements of new technologies. The diverging views are due to both: political and cultural reasons yet they also well reflect the general divergence on human rights and particular one on privacy present in the international dialogue since mid 20th century.

The privacy threats brought about by HET and BCIs include, but are not limited to, retention of electronically transferred data, originating from brain interfaces, including, but not limited to health information, but also other sensitive data, such as that on sexual preferences or political, moral or religious convictions, presented in the online environment of e.g. computer games. Such information may be stored on a local computer, however with the rapid development of cloud computing and the prospective use of BCIs for virtual worlds it is much more likely that such data will be shared online. The urging questions on privacy range from the issue of identifying the scope of individual right to privacy when BCIs are being used up to labor law issues, such as brain chips for lorry drivers implanted to enhance or simply monitor their performance (European Parliament, 2009). One step further lie the issues of enhanced human performance enabled by new devices, allowing individuals to see through walls, clearly infringing upon the individual right to privacy and family life, although regarding the state of the art they are not a direct threat (European Parliament, 2009). Another issue already mentioned above yet significant to the legal assessment of HET is the question of blanket surveillance enabled by enhancing technologies. While it is practically effortless to record the data gathered by body-implanted devices such practice would be clearly against the international human rights standard for privacy. As already discussed the 1988 HRC guidelines oblige states to assure individual privacy not to be violated by commonly accessible technologies without an appropriate act of law and a court order or possibly the individual's consent.

HET AS A LEGAL CHALLENGE

The crucial challenge for regulating HET devices with regard to privacy is the transnational character of online communications. While a company rendering a HET-based service may be operating from the US, its customers are likely to be located in Europe or Asia. With differing local privacy laws and inefficient privacy mechanisms protecting privacy threatened by such devices is the key challenge to be faced when developing HET further.

HET allow the gather of all categories of personal information, from health indicators, such as blood pressure and reflexes, including physical reactions to sexual images, cruelty, bestiality, religious practices or political manifestations. They also allow to gather detailed geolocalisation information, possibly also capturing images through the devices installed within a human body. This broad scope of information gathered through bodily enhancements may be easily processed through the Big Data capacity giving a new meaning to what is to be considered personal information. As per the definition given above, personal information is all data referring to an identified or identifiable individual. Any information that cannot be attached to a particular individual is therefore not to be considered personal information and granted protection. In light of the computing ability granted by modern technologies and the vast global digital resource referred to as Big Data forever less information may be considered effectively anonymised, resulting in large amounts of data in need of legal protection (Sweeney, 2002).

HET allow to perform various forms of human-computer interaction. Just to elaborate on the examples used in the STOA report, one might imagine brain implants allowing to control an online avatar or an external device, such as a car or an airplane. Depending on what information is to be used to participate in the virtual world or steer an external device, various legal principles will come into play. The primary requirement for processing any personal information is the requirement of explicit, informed consent granted by the individual for their data to be gathered and processed. Any information relating to them, such as their driver's license number probably needed to operate a driverless vehicle or sexual preference, expressed in an online game, may only be processed after he or she is informed that such data is being collected and the purpose it is to be used for. Any personal data gathered with the use of HET ought to be surrendered to the universal privacy guarantees, represented in e.g. the OECD guidelines, which in essence include the right to access, modify and request deletion on one's personal data. While any HET would use the standard set of personal information needed to render any personalized service, whether on- or off-line, such as that of the customer's name, address or birth date, one could assume that the majority of technologies used would refer to individual characteristics of the customer, requiring information on his medical history, allergies or personal preferences. The more information is needed to effectively render the HET based service, the more obligations fall onto the service provider.

Should a HET implant allow to monitor individual's heart rate, blood pressure or time of reaction to sudden stimulus this particular health information would be subject to further limitations, such as those discussed herein above, including the limitations of number and category of entities capable of processing them as well as particular care needed in order to protect such data from unauthorized access. As per the regional and national standards discussed above, it is only health professionals who would be allowed to access them.

Imagining more enhanced technologies, enabling for e.g. mind reading, similar technical safeguards would need to be integrated into HET based devices, allowing the individual to define the scope and character of collected data. Similarly as in telecommunications regulations some data might be considered essential for rendering a HET based service, with denial of processing it resulting in decline of the service, while other data might be considered complementary, not influencing the service itself. In any case the individual must be able to access the data collected, demand its alteration or deletion. All those requirements originate from the universal accord on privacy protection, defined in the OECD Guidelines. At the same time national laws are often deficient when it comes to enforcing existing norms or, at times, even introducing legal obligations onto data processors operating in the country, as is the case with U.S. and data nor defined as "personal health information". In the case of e.g. a brain implant therefore the customer/patient would need to be informed about all the data that will be gathered with the use of the device, the purpose for its storage and its future applications. Without an informed and explicit consent from the individual whose data is to be processed, generally no HET may be applied. The basic requirement of consent is however omitted in some jurisdictions when data is to be gathered for the purposes of employment law as authorized by national laws, when its processing is in the vital interests of the data subject or of another person and the individual whom data concerns is incapable of giving their consent, also where the gathering takes place for the purposes of non-profit-seeking body with a political, philosophical, religious or trade-union aim. Moreover, what is particularly significant in the case discussed all detailed data produced by HET in general or BCIs devices in particular could be processed for the purposes of preventive medicine, medical diagnosis, the provision of care or treatment or the management of healthcare services, yet solely by a health professional and according to national laws. The possibility to process sensitive data, including those on health condition or political preferences, relating to "security measures", provided for in e.g. Article 8 DPD is particularly interesting with regard to the virtual reality training opportunities provided for the military. Should BCIs allow for virtual training in combat situations or targeted assault, information on individuals making such use of

HET devices could be stored without their consent for security reasons, leading up to somewhat futuristic scenarios similar to that of the "Minority report". With the PRISM patterns of predicting criminal behaviors on sets of phrases used in personal messages, the usefulness of information gathered through BCIs devices relating to one's capabilities to utilize weapons in virtual worlds seems of high value to national security services. Such information, providing detailed information on individuals with high virtual combat skills, such as stress endurance and reflexes, measured by physical indicators included in the device, or ones donating significant amount of time or resources to gain such skills, could be gathered without their knowledge or consent. In light of the HRC interpretation of the right to privacy no such blanket retention and processing of personal data may be provided however, only in specific circumstances as an individual preventive measure might HET enabled information be shared with law enforcement agencies, as per national law, once they receive court authorization.

Sensitive data, such as that referring to individual health condition, are covered by significant higher privacy standards in the non-virtual environment. Introducing a similar level of care for data captured and stored online brings about additional obligations for HET service providers. One might argue that data stored in a networked system becomes intrinsically vulnerable to breaches and unauthorized disclosures regardless of how diligent data processors are in storing and securing it. Such vulnerabilities exist however also in the off-line environment as it is usually the human factor – most likely an employee of a data processing company – that fails by either making private use of the data or exposing system vulnerabilities to third parties, such as organized hackers specializing in data base breaches. This is why introducing a uniform and effective level of due care for all service providers, including all HET based service providers is of crucial importance. Traditionally due diligence means the obligations to take all measures necessary to avoid harm. In professional circumstances it refers to conducting a trustworthy risk-assessment and introducing security measures accordingly, with reference to contemporary state of the art in a given field of practice and common business practice. In light of the non-uniform national legislations dealing with privacy and personal data and the intrinsic transboundary character of HET based services due care for this business sector ought to be assessed rather by reference to international business practice than to national laws. As transnational companies like Google or Facebook have learned, adopting their privacy policies to all national privacy regulations is both: difficult, if not impossible, and cost-consuming. While waiting for national laws to be uniformed, entrepreneurs looking to make profit on cutting edge HET ought to seek universal guidelines on how to shape their privacy policies. Such guidelines may be found in both: international human rights law, as discussed above, and international business practice, discussed below.

ROLE OF BUSINESS ETHICS

The general clause usually enshrined in national legal norms recognizes adherence to good business practice as an argument freeing business from liability in particular circumstances. Platforms such as the WTO or the Global Network Initiative (GNI) allow business operating worldwide to identify behavior considered intact with international standards. The GNI meets this aim by referring to numerous international law documents on human rights, in particular privacy, allowing transnational online companies to recognize their obligations with regard to e.g. online privacy and freedom of speech. Privacy is one particular field where good business practice supersedes law. Initiatives like "privacy by design" call directly to hardware and software developers to include privacy on their technology agendas. While the

"privacy by design" policy is so far more of a community standard than a legal requirement, it has been adopted by numerous significant software developers, including Microsoft, IBM and Intel. It encourages entrepreneurs to respect individuals' privacy at the stage of designing and consequently developing their products. In practical terms this means enabling information on data being stored by the application and, possibly, entities accessing and processing it, such as telecommunication services operators. The basic principles, enshrined in the OECD guidelines, are being deployed directly on the drawing boards of engineers rather than through company's legal teams translating complex national laws onto company policies. With more companies realizing how important privacy is to their customers they spontaneously adopt privacy focused policies, where "spontaneous" does not equal "charitable". Recognizing the perils of hybrid economy modern companies realize that in order to stop their customers from "voting with their feet" and choosing their rivals they need to tend to customers' needs also in respect of their privacy. It is for material gain, brought about by a large number of customers who trust their service providers that modern day business may be enhanced with regard to effective privacy protection. While laws fall short of providing sufficient guidance on privacy it is the profit-seeking business sector that attempts to identify and meet their customers' needs. With regard to privacy, the basic principles recognized in human rights laws, regardless whether incorporated into national laws or policies, serve as steady guidelines for HET based services. Therefore, 21st century is the time of business ethics superseding time-consuming legal regulations in numerous fields.

In respect of the fast pace of HET development its application is to be considered a further field where good business practice will show more helpful then legislation or litigation. The EU STOA report is a good starting point for further development of good business practice on HET privacy. The privacy issue may not be overlooked in the ethics debate on further HET deployment. The universal privacy accord in the UDHR and the ICCPR offers a solid background for seeking practical, applicable solutions to privacy protection online. The first question to be answered by business representatives and legal experts alike is on the scope of personal data available through the application of HET and BCI. The next one will be the assessment of due procedures referring to such categories of data. The existing legal definitions on personal data and their "sensitivity" together with the strong reception of the European model of personal data protection may prove invaluable when deciding on individual business practice or when identifying international good business models. As UN Human Rights Commission's Special Rapporteur Frank LaRue emphasized in his latest report it is the private sector that will now bear the burden and the responsibility to protect human rights in the novel globalised society.

Future privacy-related policies depend strongly on the development of HET themselves. Yet when deciding upon business models regarding the identification and processing of personal data or private information the specifics of a global market, based on Big Data, must be taken into consideration. The so-called hybrid economy provides for novel business models in seeking income and designing customer approach. Companies such as Wikimedia, operating on voluntary input and offering free services have revolutionized the services market. The global cyberspace challenged the notions of territorial privacy protection and offered global markets for goods and services. The very same is true for HET. Those technologies provide a solid background for reexamining the future model of electronic services. New economic models, allowing customers to value their privacy through their choice of service, will contribute to new business models, offering privacy-securing services to users worldwide. Only should the offered standard of protection be equally satisfying to all the users, may they be convinced to try new services or applications based on BCIs. Privacy is 21st century's currency and the customers are

becoming forever more aware of its value. This is a strong argument for business to consider when shaping their privacy policies and income seeking strategies.

POLICY IMPLICATIONS

The policy implications originating from the points made above can be briefly summarized in two suggestions. States ought to aim for uniformisation of national and regional privacy policies and laws. While there seems to be an international compromise on the need to protect privacy and the basic scope of information referring to an individual covered thereby, differing national interpretations of those standards are the root of all privacy controversy present in current international debate. Such uniformisation ought to be based on the existing principles yet allow for sufficient flexibility to meet the unavoidable technological changes. In order to meet that goal the second implication ought to be made. Self-regulation and a consumer-oriented approach are crucial to introducing effective privacy protection for HET based services. While the consent of an individual whose data is being transferred is crucial, the situations where such consent may be omitted must be thoroughly limited to solely those where a direct threat to national security is in place or the direct benefit to individual interests may be recognized. While defining such situations by law may be difficult, it is important to introduce forums for discussing such issues among governments, industry and civil society. Whether they will be hosted by intergovernmental organizations, such as the WTO, or civil society initiatives, such as the Internet Engineering Task Force or the World Wide Web Consortium, is open to debate. On one hand government ought to encourage such debates as they are in the interest of the people they represent, on the other hand a politically neutral environment of a civil society arena might enhance open exchange on equal footing for all those represented.

The foreseeable challenges of encouraging business to adhere to ethical standards and of making the privacy trend international may be solved by recognizing the emerging economic models of cyberspace. While inherently territorial laws fail to meet their goal in the aterritorial cyberspace, encouraging companies to resolve to forum shopping rather than use expensive legal counseling or engage in multijurisdictional litigation, the foreseeable profit originating from the growing number of users is likely to encourage entrepreneurs to engage in competitive privacy policies. As with any business ethics no direct sanctions for those failing to meet them are needed – it is rather consumer trust and growing income that are the gain for ethical behavior, while their lack the ultimate negative consequence. With companies recognizing the direct monetary value of privacy no intergovernmental consensus is necessary (World Economic Forum, 2013). The intended international effect can be achieved through industry self-regulation alone, although the industry policy is deemed to influence states to alter their practice. As was the case with the 2010 Arab Spring when social media effectively counteracted to state imposed free speech limitations, so is the community approach as represented by computer-based technologies users, including HET shaping company policies, bound to influence governments to limit their privacy-invading practices (Gagnier, 2011). The due diligence requirement in securing users' privacy named above might be derived from existing business ethics and the general professional obligation of providing diligence in limiting risk to third parties. Once particular privacy protecting practice is in place with uniform particular risk-assessment procedures a reflecting legal obligation might be introduced in national laws, similar to those present for various industry branches, endowed with risk liability schemes (Wright & de Hert, 2012). In any such schemes companies carries civil liability for lack of due diligence in preventing damage to third parties, in this case – to an individual whose privacy was not diligently protected as a result of which he or she suffered damage. The industry practice in privacy protection would serve as a background for assessing the diligence of an individual company in securing its clients' data.

CONCLUSION

HET hold a promise for mankind – a promise of a better, fuller and more ambitious life. Life free from disability and offering more than one reality. This promise is however inevitably bound with a price – one to be paid not necessarily in currency but in information. With customers becoming forever more aware of the value their personal information holds they are less willing to share it freely and unlimitedly. This characteristic of our time must be considered also by companies planning to offer HET. The privacy aspect must be considered in every application of modern technology, allowing for the construction and execution of most efficient business models. International law holds rich information on what the contemporary understanding of the right to privacy is. Considering that information in further HET development and deployment is a condition sine qua non of further evolution.

REFERENCES

Anderson, D. A. (2012). Transnational Libel. *Virginia Journal of International Law Association*, *53*, 71–98.

Bertrand, A. (1999). *Droit a la Vie Privée et Droit a L'Image*. Paris: Litec.

Brandeis, L., & Warren, S. (1890). The right to privacy. *Harvard Law Review*, *4*, 194–219.

Brandeis, J. (1928). U.S. Olmstead v United States, 277 US 478 (1928) (dissenting)

Bygrave, L. A. (1998). Data protection pursuant to the right to privacy in human rights treaties. *International Journal of Law and Information Technology*, 6, 247–284. doi:10.1093/ijlit/6.3.247

Bygrave, L. A. (2010). Privacy Protection in a Global Context – A Comparative Overview. *Scandinavian Studies in Law*, 47, 321–348.

Connolly, C. (2008). US Safe Harbor - Fact or Fiction? *Privacy Laws and Business International*, 96, 26–27.

Council of Europe. (1970). *Resolution 428 containing a declaration on mass communication media and human rights*. Retrieved from http://assembly.coe.int/main.asp?Link=/documents/adoptedtext/ta70/eres428.htm

European Parliament. (1995). *Directive 95/46/EC of the European Parliament and of the Council of 24 October 1995 on the protection of individuals with regard to the processing of personal data and on the free movement of such data, OJ L 281, 23 November 1995*. Author.

European Parliament. (2009). *Human enhancement study*. Science and Technology Options Assessment (STOA) Annual Report. Brussels: Belgium: European Parliament. Retrieved from https://www.itas.kit.edu/downloads/etag_coua09a.pdf

Falk, U., & Mohnhaupt, H. (2000). *Das Bürgerliche Gesetzbuch und seine Richter: Zur Reaktion der Rechtsprechung auf die Kodifikation des deutschen Privatrechts (1896-1914)*. Frankfurt am Main: Vittorio Klostermann.

Farrell, H. (2002). Negotiating Privacy Across Arenas: The EU-US Safe Harbor Discussions. In A. Windhoff-Héritier (Ed.), *Common Goods: Reinventing European and International Governance* (pp. 105–125). London: Rowman & Littlefield.

Gagnier, C. (2011, August 11). The Competitive Privacy Marketplace: Regulators Competing on Privacy, Not the Companies. *Huffington Post*. Retrieved from http://www.huffingtonpost.com/christina-gagnier/the-competitive-privacy-m_b_1078820.html

Gibson, W. (1984). *Neuromancer*. New York: Ace.

Greenleaf, G. (2014). Sheherezade and the 101 data privacy laws: Origins, significance and global trajectories. *Journal of Law, Information & Science*. Retrieved from http://papers.ssrn.com/sol3/papers.cfm?abstract_id=2280877

Griswold, E. N. (1961). The Right to be Let Alone. *Northwestern University Law Review*, 55, 216–226.

Guild, E., & Lesieur, G. (1998). *The European Court of Justice on The European Convention on Human Rights: Who Said What, When?* The Hague, The Netherlands: Martinus Nijhoff Publishers.

Kang, J. (1998). Information privacy in cyberspace transactions. *Stanford Law Review*, 50(4), 1193–1295. doi:10.2307/1229286

Kilkelly, U. (2003). *The Right to Respect for Private and Family Life: A guide to the Implementation of Article 8 of the European Convention on Human Rights 10–19*. Strasbourg: Council of Europe.

Kohler, J. (1900). Ehre und Beleidigung. *Goltdammers Archiv für Deutsches Strafrecht*, 47, 1–48.

Kulesza, J. (2012). Walled Gardens of Privacy or Binding Corporate Rules? A Critical Look at International Protection of Online Privacy. *University of Arkansas at Little Rock Law Review*, 3, 747–765.

Kuner, C. (2009). An international legal framework for data protection: Issues and prospects. *Computer Law & Security Report, 25*, 309–327. doi:10.1016/j.clsr.2009.05.001

LaRue, F. (2011). *Report of the Special Rapporteur on the promotion and protection of the right to freedom of opinion and expression*. U.N. Doc A/HRC/17/27.

Leebron, D. (1991). The Right to Privacy's Place in the Intellectual History of Tort Law. *Case Western Reserve Law Review, 41*, 769–777.

Mayer-Schönberger, V. (2011). *Delete: The Virtue of Forgetting in the Digital Age*. Oxford, UK: Oxford University Press.

Organization for Economic Cooperation and Development. (1980). *OECD Guidelines on the Protection of Privacy and Transborder Flows of Personal Data*. Retrieved from http://www.oecd.org/internet/ieconomy/oecdguidelinesontheprotectionofprivacyandtransborderflowsofpersonaldata.htm

Organization for Economic Cooperation and Development. (2013). *The 2013 OECD Privacy Guidelines*. Retrieved from http://www.oecd.org/sti/ieconomy/privacy.htm#newguidelines

Sweeney, L. (2002). k-anonymity: A Model For Protecting Privacy. *International Journal on Uncertainty. Fuzziness and Knowledge-Based Systems, 10*(5), 557–570. doi:10.1142/S0218488502001648

United Nations Human Rights Committee. (1988). *CCPR General Comment No. 16: Article 17 (Right to Privacy), The Right to Respect of Privacy, Family, Home and Correspondence, and Protection of Honour and Reputation*. Retrieved from http://www.refworld.org/docid/453883f922.html

Warwick, K. (2013). Cyborgs in space. *Acta Futura, 6*, 25–35.

Weber, R. (2012). How Does Privacy Change in the Age of the Internet. In C. Fuchs, K. Boersma, A. Albrechtslund, & M. Sandoval (Eds.), *Internet and Surveillance, The Challenges of Web 2.0 and Social Media* (pp. 274–285). London: Routledge.

Weber, R. (2013). Transborder data transfers: Concepts, regulatory approaches and new legislative initiatives. *International Data Privacy Law, 1*, 117–130. doi:10.1093/idpl/ipt001

World Economic Forum. (2013). *Report: Unlocking the Value of Personal Data: From Collection to Usage, February 2013*. Retrieved from http://www.weforum.org/issues/rethinking-personal-data

Wright, D., & de Hert, P. (n.d.). Privacy Impact Assessment. *Law, Governance and Technology Series, 28* (6).

ADDITIONAL READING

Anderson, J. (2008). Neuro-Prosthetics, the Extended Mind, and Respect for Persons with Disability. In M. Düwell, C. Rehmann-Sutter, & D. Mieth (Eds.), *Bioethics and the Limits of Human Existence* (pp. 259–274). Berlin: Springer. doi:10.1007/978-1-4020-6764-8_22

Berger, T., Chapin, J., Gerhardt, G., McFarland, D., Principe, J., Soussou, W., et al. (2007). *WTEC Panel Report on International Assessment of Research and Development in Brain-Computer Interfaces (Final Report)*. Baltimore. Retrieved from http://www.wtec.org/bci/BCI-finalreport-10Oct2007-lowres.pdf

Bostrom, N., & Sandberg, A. (2008). *Human enhancement*. Oxford: Oxford University Press.

Castells, M. (2011). *The Rise of the Network Society: The Information Age: Economy, Society, and Culture*. New York, NY: John Wiley & Sons.

Garcia, T., & Sandler, R. (2008). Enhancing Justice? *NanoEthics*, 2, 277–287. doi:10.1007/s11569-008-0048-5

Kurzweil, R. (2006). *The Singularity Is Near: When Humans Transcend Biology*. New York: Penguin Group Incorporated.

Mehlman, M. J. (2000). The Law of Above Averages: Leveling the New Genetic Enhancement Playing Field. *Iowa Law Review*, 85, 517–577. PMID:11769760

Miah, A. (2004). *Genetically Modified Athletes: Biomedical Ethics, Gene Doping And Sport*. London: Routledge.

Nijholt, A. (2008). BCIS for Games: A 'State of the Art' Survey. In Stevens, S., Saldamarco, S. (Eds.) *Entertainment Computing – ICEC 2008 (7th International Conference, Pittsburgh, September 25-27, 2008, Proceedings)* (pp. 225-228). Berlin/Heidelberg/New York: Springer.

Roache, R. (2008). Ethics, Speculation, and Values. *NanoEthics*, 2, 317–327. doi:10.1007/s11569-008-0050-y

U.S. Senate (1996). Health Insurance Portability and Accountability Act of 1996 (HIPAA) Pub.L. 104–191, 110 Stat. 1936, enacted August 21, 1996.

Warwick, K. (2003). Cyborg morals, cyborg values, cyborg ethics. *Ethics and Information Technology*, 5, 131–137. doi:10.1023/B:ETIN.0000006870.65865.cf

Warwick, K. I. (2004). *Cyborg*. Chicago, IL: University of Illinois Press.

KEY TERMS AND DEFINITIONS

Privacy: Human right granting an individual the prerogative to decide upon information they are willing to share with others.

Big Data: Accumulation of information available through the Internet and other compatible networks.

Chapter 10
Human Enhancement Technologies and Democratic Citizenship

Jean-Paul Gagnon
Australian Catholic University, Australia

ABSTRACT

This chapter articulates that scholars write about Human Enhancement Technologies (HET) in two ways. This is not a reflection of a reality in the literature but rather a heuristic designed to contextualize democratic citizenship within contemporary HET discussions. The first way is to write about HET as possible realities far off into the future. The second way is to write about HET that can be realised seemingly as soon as tomorrow. For democratic citizenship, writing in the first case is either utopian or dystopian. It is either the projection of democracy's total triumph or its utter collapse caused by the type of rots that lead to democide. But writing in the second case is stimulating and vibrant. There are, for example, numerous calls for HET-led reforms in the literature. These reforms are needed to help answer the crisis of the citizen's august discontent (the growing and increasingly legitimized political apathy and political abstention observed in, and performed by, the citizenry). The purpose of this chapter is to focus on this second case—this more developed body of literature—and to theorise the interface between democratic citizenship and HET.

INTRODUCTION

As an area of study, citizenship boasts a large and varied body of literature. Key foci include the more traditional concern about an individual's relationship with the state, or the fulfilment of public duties, to the more contemporary concern of justifying an individual's *avoidance* of public duties. Despite the breadth of this body of literature, an area remains understudied. And that

is the theorisation of citizenship's futurism. The former is an aspect to the philosophy of citizenship which questions, among other areas, the future directions of the normative values associated with citizenship. Scholars (see for example Mossberger, Tolbert & McNeal, 2007; Taylor-Gooby, 2008; Isin & Nielsen, 2008; Rohrer, 2009) have certainly been projecting normative arguments about what it is to be a citizen, and how individuals can be better citizens, but there has not at this point been

DOI: 10.4018/978-1-4666-6010-6.ch010

much focus exclusively on human enhancement technologies (HET) and democratic citizenship. The future of citizenship, one dependant on HET, is therefore the focus of this chapter. As Isaiah Berlin (1962) might argue, we need to articulate the future directions of our existing institutions, like citizenship, so that we can push for their improvement in clear and predetermined directions rather than leave institutions to ad hoc organic change. The act of articulating these future directions exposes contemporary political desires. It helps uncover the normative positions of those proposing the future directions. Importantly, visions of the future raise fundamental questions about the directions that institutions might possibly take. Raising questions is a central goal of this chapter.

As I understand it, there are two clear modes of writing about futurism, and, consequently, HET. The first discusses possible paths for humans in the far off future. Its scope is hundreds if not thousands of years ahead in time. The second discusses possible paths that are nearer in time. Its scope is days, years, or decades. Both are equally important. The first has seemingly more to do with Jules Verne or Isaac Asimov. It is an articulation of often extreme and imaginative realities set well into the future. These projections are useful as they help us, as humans, to come to terms with where we might like, or not like to, for example, take our institutions. This theorisation of the deep future of citizenship is, in scholarly literature, typically not the work of prophecy but rather either a dire warning that this future should be avoided or a beacon calling for its realisation. Depending on the subject, such as *mind uploading*,[1] we currently see expressions for both positions (avoid or realise).

For democratic citizenship, we can theorise some possibilities into the far off future. The following is an extreme example designed to stimulate thinking in this area. Progress in anti-aging research could lead to a group of 'old' humans, alive for several hundred years, who would have experienced for example three or four times as many election campaigns as today's average life-span human. The potential spin-off effects of this type of change are many. For example, will this create a class of 'guardian' citizens – a new type of elite? The act of dying, of generational change, can be a key player in political transformations. The argument goes that in some political systems there will be powerful elites with stubbornly held beliefs, rather than evidence-based rational positions, and thus change can only peacefully happen once these types of elites die. Dead elites are replaced by living ones who might be more progressive, or moderate, or democratic. So what happens to the pacing of the political change pegged to human life spans when ideologues for example will remain alive – possibly for centuries? In a competitive multi-party electoral democracy it is conceivable that these elites will simply not be re-elected and may, rather, become marginalized for being overly conservative or illogical as human development progresses. Ideologues will be left behind.[2] But what about in non-democratic places like North Korea – these closed totalitarian states where dynastic change, and the space for political rupture out of totalitarianism, happens mostly through the death of the great leader? What if Kim Il Sung, for example, were still alive today?

The example given above is just one articulation of the problems HET can cause for democratic politics. But this and other possible problems do not crowd this hypothetical horizon. There are also boons for democracy to be found in at least this one articulation of its deep future. Progress, for example, in neuroscience research could lead to an implanted brain-to-computer interface where humans can access the Internet in their minds (Berger et al., 2008; Tan & Nijholt, 2010; Graimann, Pfurtscheller, & Allison, 2010). If electronic voting were by that point long-standardised, humans could possibly discharge a flurry of civic duties from anywhere in the world and with little effort. Further, parents could decide to have their children's genotype 'arranged' to maximize intelligence and the emotional spectrum related to things like caring, love, and peace. Once old enough, these children could be subject to virtual reality experience-based education – a focus of which could be civics education, or, what it means for a given society to 'be' a good citizen. One might argue that these, still I think alienating ideas today, are positive changes to strive for. But these few radical positions showing potential negative and positive outcomes are far-off possibilities and, despite still being an important area to think about, this first type of futuristic writing will not be the one focused on in this chapter.

The second mode of writing tends to be more viable. It has to do with the near-future, as near as tomorrow. Arguments here push for the realisation of possible HET-related reforms, usually as a means to solving one or more contemporary political problems (Otchere-Darko, 2010). The act of voting is, for example, increasingly considered worthless (see, for example, Lever, 2010; Agu, Okeke, & Idike, 2013; Curato & Niemeyer, 2013) especially by today's youth in some of the world's most developed countries.[3] Part of the response to this problem is to use HET on Election Day to make voting more convenient and more sophisticated as a means to entice young people to vote (Roberto, 2010; Lariscy, Tinkham, & Sweetser, 2011). This changes the types of HET that can be involved in this chapter because these technologies have to be, more or less, realisable now or in the short term. I follow Coeckelbergh (2010) in arguing that 'everyday' computers, as we understand them today, can be considered HET. Given the increasingly ubiquitous presence of computer devices like laptops, touchscreen tablets and mobile phones in daily life, it is surprising that their presence is mostly missing at election stations. Some humans do, after all, use HET at typically banal places like grocery stores (self-check-out touchscreen machines), automated tellers to withdraw money, or at restaurants to order food.

The slow transition from paper to electronic voting is ostensibly caused by a political unwillingness to face the risks involved. An investigation of some of the main problems associated with electronic voting in mostly the United States (see, for example, Appel, 2011; Balzarotti et al., 2010; Weldemariam, Kemmerer, & Villafiorita,

2011) points to the conclusion that it is a lack of political will that is more responsible for the slow implementation of e-voting. The technical barriers can, in themselves, be construed as political obstacles. Paper ballots cannot, for example, be hacked. A pencil and paper cannot create software error codes. And, more importantly, cardboard voting booths, stationary, and non-specialist volunteers are economically cheaper than electronic voting mechanisms and all the baggage that these systems carry.[4] There are also technical impediments to *secure* online voting as Simons and Jones (2012) point out. Governments need to prove, for example, that online voting or casting a ballot via email can guarantee the secrecy of a citizen's vote. Nevertheless, after the botched 2000 Florida election and the 2013 Western Australia election, it seems that the consensus at least in the United States and Australia is for favouring digital over physical forms of voting.

A number of polities have been experimenting with electronic voting – with touchscreens now trending as the medium of choice (Shamos & Yasinsac, 2012; Hale & Brown, 2013; Camargo et al., 2012). Certain states in the United States (Hale & Brown, 2013), Bangladesh (Sarker, 2013), India (Kumar & Walia, 2011), Belgium (Allers & Kooreman, 2009), Italy (Rivest et al., 2009, p. 593), Argentina (Katz et al., 2011), Estonia (Alvarez, Hall, & Trechsel, 2009), and Australia (Hill & Alport, 2007, p. 4) are a few examples from a longer list. Most electoral commissions in these states can be described as using simplistic machines designed to record confidential votes online, overseas, or at a voting station.

There is an ongoing scholarly engagement with electronic voting (see, for example, Stewart, 2011; Elgie & Fauvelle-Aymar, 2012, p. 1600; Moynihan & Lavertu, 2011) centred on its feasibility, how it might affect voter behaviour, and whether it can secure voter privacy. There are too significant pushes in the literature for realising different articulations of digital citizenship (see Hermes, 2006; de Vreese, 2007; Mancini, 2010). A key argument includes that it is likely that the transition to HET-integrated citizenship will become a reality first for wealthier open-societies. Another key argument focuses on the lack of political knowledge in the electorate to which electronic voting is responding. There is currently no viable alternative other than maintaining the status quo which, it should be noted, is failing to meet the political demands of today's 'Internet citizens' or 'netizens' which appear to have preferences for voting online and for getting more out of their vote by participating in, for example, interactive polling (Dutton, Elberse, & Hale, 1999; Alport & Macintyre, 2007). Some examples of the status quo's weaknesses include the over-simplicity of casting a paper ballot; the design of paper ballots which, depending on the way they are engineered, can create election outcomes from 'donkey' votes[5]; or having to waste one's time by travelling to the voting station and sometimes waiting in long lines which could be solved by casting a ballot online.

This chapter will, to situate one way of injecting HET into democratic citizenship, focus on theorising the election station of tomorrow. It will begin with voter registration where a human will interact, in private, with a large touchscreen. Once the human has decided she wants to vote, this chapter will move to looking at the intermediary process between voter registration and voting. In busy electoral districts, voters today have to often wait in line before voting. This is wasted time. Humans could go from registration through to a different large and private touchscreen whose program is designed to promote reflexive and investigative political thought on the part of the voter. A human could, in this intermediary station, use Vote Compass,[6] review how they voted in previous elections, access political party manifestos, and balance policy presentation between political parties. Finally, this chapter will end with the act of voting which, again, will be done through a large touchscreen interface. Here a human can see all voting-related information produced by political parties like preferencing (for systems that use preferential voting), party lists, parties' intended portfolio-holding ministers, or even independent

'who to vote for' expert recommendations built around evidence-based policy. These three segments will be looked at in turn.

It is important to theorise the election station of tomorrow because an HET-integrated election day is one of the largest focal points for electoral reform. This is seen in Gibson (2002, p. 572), Herrnson et al. (2008, p. 581), and Alport and Macintyre's (2007, p. 42) works where online-voting, especially designed to accommodate self-identified disabled, single mother, or elderly citizens, was a main reform recommendation. Tolbert and McNeal (2003), Czernich (2012), and Gronke et al. (2008) each, for example, turn to e-democracy as a direct response to the retreat from formal voting observable in a number of countries (see for example Steiner, 2010, for a longitudinal study of relatively recent voter turnout statistics in established democracies). Despite these works pointing to HET as remedies for current political ills observable in democratic states, we have not yet seen an articulation of fully integrated HET election stations – something that may not be too far off. We require these visualisations to be able to grab onto the first well-defined rung of the HET-election station ladder. The more visualisations we have, the more ladders are on offer, and thus a society can choose how to change its polity by picking from a list of possible futures. This chapter offers one of these ways forward.

WORLD DISCLOSURE

Before we progress to this HET-election station visualisation, it is important to describe what I mean by democratic citizenship. Concepts of citizenship have changed considerably over time in the western canon when individuals gradually transformed from vassals of the state to sovereign individuals that today theoretically rule the state. It should be noted that this transformation is still happening as citizens are transitioning from theoretical to actual power holders (see, for greater context, Ackerman, 2013; Hyslop-

Margison & Sears, 2006; Hadenius, 2001). One could call this the praxes of sovereign citizenship in democratic countries that view the state as the servant of the citizens. In the late 19th century and early to mid-twentieth century, citizenship was mostly articulated through a top-down narrative. To be a citizen was to be committed to your state, or nation, or both. It meant swearing an oath (usually to a religious text or monarch), having relevant cultural and political knowledge, serving the state, conforming to certain normalized modes of economy and family, and readily fulfilling restricted public duties (such as voting, jury duty, and paying taxes).

As globalisation gathered pace from the 1940s onwards the demands on citizens have increased. States have, as a response to the ostensible 'awakening' of the critical citizen who legitimately abstains from politics, made citizenship more grandiose. To be a citizen means more than voting, having some cultural and political knowledge, and serving the state. One must now increasingly care for themselves as public services become more privatized. A citizen needs to upkeep the integrity of their local communities, support others both locally and internationally, but to also simply be better participants in the political arena. Yet what this grandiose and narrow and ever more demanding picture of citizenship does is create a distance between oneself and the ability to 'be' a citizen. The reality for most individuals in for example OECD countries or in very poor countries is that there is not enough time in one's daily life to fill the performance needs of this grandiose citizenship. The reengagement of the public fails. Governments continue to under-innovate.

The response to this comes mainly from Esposito (2012). He articulates as others do (Vertovec, 1998; Shachar, 2005) that there are many forms of citizenship. Thus to be a citizen can happen in any number of ways which includes trying to be the state's idyllic citizen. An individual can choose from a constellation of citizenship modes how she will articulate herself as a citizen. By for example moving away from a narrow and grand concep-

tion foisted by the state onto citizens towards a bottom-up conception that is full of variety and possibility for engagement – we see room for a meaningful return to public life. The distance between the citizen and the self lessens as the self can pick any number of ways to be a citizen – even if that means doing so for but a day. The difficulty of the multiple citizenships articulation is that it puts representative governments under more strain. Those sovereigns (citizens) that have delegated their politics through the act of voting have become more complicated. They are exercising power, and making demands, outside of the institutions of parliament. *Their* servants, the delegates, must become more attentive to these moves and adjust the way that they have been representing the politics of their rulers.

This bottom-up kind of democratic citizenship, as explained in the paragraphs above, is how I understand the self's engagement with political life. This theorisation opens space for change. It allows one's suggestions for HET-oriented reforms on election day to be realistic because it moves beyond narrowly focused understandings of citizenship.

METHODOLOGY

I follow Berlin (1962, p. 13) in arguing that:

Unless we understand (by an effort of imaginative insight such as novelists usually possess in higher degree than logicians) what notions of man's nature (or absence of them) are incorporated in...political outlooks, what in each case is the dominant model, we shall not understand our own or any human society (See, also, Spegele, 1971, p. 138).

Spegele supports Berlin's position in his argument that imaginative writing, or fiction, is a valid methodology to use in scholarly works. Through a demonstrated relationship with an existing literature, a piece of fiction can articulate the possibilities of politics – of "what could happen" (1971, p. 137). This type of fiction unlocks our ability to deliberate about potential futures and to question the ramifications of our present choices. That is why I decided to use fiction in this chapter. This, methodologically speaking, is a fruitful way of exploring scholarly topics in the futurism of citizenship.

The fictional articulation, given below, of a voting citizen in the not too distant future is designed to raise more questions than it answers. Part of its purpose is provocation. For instance, where a voter's data is collected and stored raises privacy concerns; the mandatory political literacy quiz could be exclusionary and alienating; the added stages of voting and their software elements raise worries about how this might influence voters before they cast their ballot; and the physical organization of the voting stages – designed to reduce queues and delays – might not actually work resulting in a compounding of the time burden already added onto voters who are obliged to go through the three stages process.

Utopias fall on their faces. And this fictional articulation of mine, although tempered to be less Pollyannaish, must suffer the same fate. But it is precisely here that we see the value of this methodology. Raising questions, provoking thought, and picking up potential risks – each contributing to the 'falling utopia' – are necessary components for evaluating the worth of a proposed future. It brings the idea down to earth which crystallizes existing political objections.

REGISTRATION

2026. It is 15 October, general election day in Brazil. Gustava Kalil arrives at her electoral district's voting station. It is a local high school and the voting is taking place in its interior gymnasium. Conspicuously, she is not accosted by party loyalists toting 'how-to-vote' cards as these were

banned in previous years. She walks through the school's hallways, following directions offered by signs and volunteers, and arrives at a small line-up in front of the gymnasium doors. Voters are being released into the gymnasium in stages – somewhat like what happens in some museums to limit crowding. After several more voters line-up behind Gustava, a volunteer counts the voters waiting and pulls a rope from one stanchion to another to 'close off' this group. A different volunteer starts welcoming other voters that arrive behind Gustava's group and begins the count to slowly form a second group. The maximum is ten people per group.

Gustava's volunteer asks to have her group's attention. The volunteer explains the voting process. To cast a complete ballot, each member of this group has to go through three stages in the gymnasium. The first stage is registration. Voters, if they wish, can opt out of voting at this or any other stage and leave. Presently, the volunteer says, there are ten people finishing their registration. These ten people will then move on to a pre-voting section where they can go through some political research activities, fill out important surveys, and generally form a more informed position before casting their ballot. Finally, that group will then move to the final stage where the ballot is cast. The volunteer explains that a voter can take as much or as little time as she pleases to go through each stage. A big green button inside each station is available to press if assistance is required.

The volunteer checks her touchscreen tablet and sees that three stations are free in the first stage. She invites Gustava and the two other voters ahead of her to proceed. There are three lines composed of ten stations each in the gymnasium. That is, three sections and thirty stations. The entry to each station, which look like pods, is semi-circular, no touch required, and fully private. The material of the station is noise absorbent. Walking into her station, Gustava finds that there is a large, slightly contoured, touchscreen console prompting her to begin. She touches the start button. She has to, question by question, enter her personal details. A finger print scan helps to confirm her identity. For those that prefer it, an iris scan is also available. This registration application feels easy to use. The programming is intuitive. Before the registration process finishes, Gustava is asked to complete a survey collecting data on why people come to vote. The touchscreen states that the survey will take approximately five minutes. She is enticed by the possibility of winning an expensive prize but decides to pass.

INTERMEDIATION

After touching the 'finish and move on' button, Gustava walks out of the first station. There is a three meter wide corridor between the sections, or lines of voting stations. A volunteer informs Gustava that the next station in section two is free. She enters the station and begins the intermediary process. This second station and touchscreen are the same as the first. The application on the touchscreen is, too – except that it appears in a different colour. As this is the second general election that used the HET-voting system, Gustava can choose to see how she voted in the previous election and how that matched with the previous overall election result. She is also asked if she wants to complete the Vote Compass survey for this current election. An option is provided to watch a short information video about Vote Compass. Gustava proceeds and, after about 10 minutes, she finds that she is leaning more to the left than she was in the previous election. Vote Compass recommends that she votes for a different party.

The intermediary process's main program now begins. It asks Gustava pointed questions about her political interests based on what she indicated in the Vote Compass survey. An example:

Why do you prefer more investment in public infrastructure? (Feel free to select more than one response)
   a.   Because you are a public transportation user;
   b.   Because you are concerned about the environment;
   c.   Because you are concerned about the driving death toll;
Or
Other (If other, you will be directed to a comment box where you can answer the question by using the inbuilt keyboard)

The touchscreen explains that completing these questions generates important data for the electoral commission but that it also acts as an important reflective process for voters. After answering these questions, which takes about 10 minutes, Gustava has the option to read third-party developed reports on policy issues she is most concerned about and the position political parties have in relation to those issues. She can use the touchscreen to select particular political parties and to see their policy track-records: what, for example, was promised by the incumbent party in the last election and was this or how was this achieved? A final question asks if this intermediary process changed her mind for which party to vote for. Gustava notices that there are follow up questions after she gave her answer so she touches the 'move on' button to opt out of this series of questions.

The application then asks if Gustava would like to complete a number of surveys – each taking roughly five minutes. Prizes again feature as enticements. She decides to pass on all surveys except for one which is collecting political information from single mothers. After completing the survey, she exits the station.

CASTING THE BALLOT

Another three meter-wide corridor and volunteer are navigated to get to the final station in section three – which is as identical as the last two. Here Gustava is offered a randomized ballot on the touchscreen. The presidency, *Câmara dos Deputados* (Chamber of Deputies) and two thirds of the *Senado Federal* (Federal Senate) are up for grabs in this electoral round. She has to vote slightly differently for both houses as the lower chamber uses open-list proportional representation and the upper house, and presidency ballot, use first past the post systems (more specifically, a two-round ballot system for the presidency). As a means to ensure that Gustava is equipped with the knowledge (Rapeli, 2013) to be able to fully understand each balloting system, the application prompts Gustava to take a mandatory quiz. She has to pass the quiz with a perfect score with as many retries as she needs in order to be allowed to cast a ballot. Some examples of the multiple choice questions include:

- *What type of open-list proportional representation does Brazil use to elect its upper house?*
- *Why is this type of proportional representation beneficial?*
- *What are its drawbacks?*
- *Choose the correct answer: Brazil's first past the post voting system is characterised by...*

Trials before the election demonstrated to the *Tribunal Superior Eleitoral* (Superior Electoral Court) that the average voter takes 15 minutes to pass the quiz. This is one of the main reasons for why volunteers are strategically used to provide crowd flow and why Gustava did not encounter much, or any, waiting delays once inside the gymnasium.

Gustava cast her ballots once the hurdle quiz was passed. Before leaving the final station, she was prompted by the application to share her experience through social media – she even had the option to have her photo snapped with a colourful election day background, as voters today are, increasingly, 'snapchat-ing', 'instagram-ing', 'facebook-ing' and 'tweeting' at election stations (Aman & Jayroe, 2013; Bekafigo & McBride, 2013; Quintelier & Theocharis, 2012; Alotaibi, 2013). She declined, left the station, and exited the gymnasium roughly 50 minutes after she initially arrived at the high school.

DISCUSSION

The imaginary scenario of a future voting station in Brazil, given above, promotes the enhancement of humans *before* the ballot is cast. This is because, as signalled in the introduction, certain articulations of electronic voting are specifically addressing the lack of political knowledge in the electorate. The integration of HET into this aspect of democratic citizenship is then not simply about making the act of voting quicker or less onerous, but also about making the act of voting more sophisticated. Indeed, my example made voting much more involved than it typically is. For some individuals the imaginary scenario presented in this chapter may be positively alienating. This tension is an aspect of democratic citizenship that requires further investigation. The prompts that Gustava encountered on various touchscreens were coming from knowledge-sharing and knowledge-testing programs. They were designed to enhance her knowledge, self-awareness, and critical reflection skills before she went to cast her ballots.

Out of this deliberately constructed intervention comes the idea of a future that forces citizens, who want to vote, to pass a difficult exam testing their political knowledge. In the scenario above

I emphasized the citizen's choice to engage the knowledge-sharing (would you like to know who you voted for in the last election?), knowledge-testing (would you like to complete the pre-vote quiz to see if or how you understand major policies?), and information-gathering programs (would you like to complete this survey?). This was done to emphasize the negative liberty of the citizenry which still seems to be the more ethical approach for how states go about deploying their coercive power. But others may prefer a positivist approach: to be free to vote, and thus to be a fully-capable and free citizen, you must pass a test to prove you hold sufficient political knowledge before being permitted to cast your ballot. I built a mandatory quiz into the final station (the one quiz Gustava *had* to complete) to emphasize this point. If in the future civics education were more robust than what most citizens experience today in compulsory schooling maybe this test would not be alienating. It could fall into the category of a driver's test or similar. Nevertheless, the mandatory nature of this quiz, and its aim, does point to an increasingly militant position observable in some democratic societies where parts of the electorate are tired of 'the idiots'. As citizens and governments today continue to experiment with electronic voting, decisions will have to be made about which conceptions of liberty will be emphasized in their respective polities.

One of the first questions that come to mind in response to the election-station visualisation given above is why to even bother with the physicality of the election? And why bother with the possibly expensive touchscreens, software programming, and installation? This can all be done online involving less effort and cost. The reason for maintaining physicality is that there is a significant resistance to the abandonment of the public, performative aspects of citizens gathering to cast their ballots. Stromer-Galley (2003), for example, argues that moving away from the agora aspect of in-person voting to the hidden or private aspect of online voting may do more damage than good. There is an argument to be made for keeping the act of voting public and physical although that argument needs greater theorisation.

Those who articulated this [point] often made basic statements, such as this: "Personally, I like voting booths," without further elaboration of why they prefer to cast a ballot at a traditional balloting station rather than through the Internet. Voting at a voting booth has value in its own right, although it's not clear what exactly that value is. Others made statements such as this: "There's something good about the very act of going to the [polls]." But what that something is, they did not say. The most frequent response was about the importance of exerting effort to cast a ballot. Some people simply said that they would not like to make voting too easy. One person explained that "Getting to the polls takes an effort. Those are the thoughtful voters." The reason they are the thoughtful voters is that if they voted online, as this next person explained, then "People would vote without knowing what they're voting for." Others stated their sentiments more simply, such as: "Get off your ---- and vote." (Stromer-Galley, 2003, p. 730)

The reason I kept the physicality of voting is that there is something to be said about individual human beings meeting before and after casting their ballots. Election days are performative and require intentionally constructed sacralisation. Election days need to be imbued with republican or democratic virtues (Justman, 1993). Although voting in private on the Internet or through a postal vote is more convenient for avoiding strangers at election stations or making the effort to get out to vote, it does not make the vote profane. It does not devalue the vote by rationalizing it through new technologies. What it does do, however, is privilege the private over the public – and this is problematic.

Taylor (2007), Justman (1993), and Chou (2013a) help to make the argument that the turn of citizens towards selfish individuality and the private over building a sense of community and acting, as an individual, in the public is partially detrimental to democratic citizenship. Particularly important to explaining this is Taylor's (2007, p. 148) concept of "neo-Durkeimian political identities." The coercive act of forcing individuals to get out into the public, to be in lines or physically engaging processes *with* other individuals is an intentional strengthening of the democratic idea. To borrow from Taylor once more, the act of having to go to the polls helps to build a culture of democracy. This is what we risk losing if we allow the continued retreat of democratic citizenship into the private and impersonal Internet. And this is why I stressed the physicality in one example of a possible future election day.

CONCLUSION

The dialectic of HET and democratic citizenship offers space for theorisation. This chapter builds its argument around one possible future election station. The focus is on readily available touchscreen computers – that which allows human enhancement to happen – and the near future. Humans, as democratic citizens, can be performing at an enhanced level when it comes to voting if HET are actively employed at election stations. And, as pointed to in the introduction, there are numerous potential avenues to realizing these possibilities for citizen enhancement.

Unresolved questions to consider include how expensive HET-election stations might be; whether voting should maintain a public, in person, physical requirement; whether citizens should have to complete a mandatory knowledge-testing quiz before being *able* to vote; how or if privacy issues can be resolved; and what other alternative visions exist in regards to HET and election days. There is, however, one certainty. And that is that everything I have proposed in this chapter can be, if only for one election station, technically possible as soon as next month – or tomorrow, if all the software programming were already complete. The main obstacle to realising this near future is, as argued earlier in this chapter, more political than technical.

What we require then is, as democratic citizens that are willing to work with HET, the active advocacy of the types of near futures that I propose in this chapter. Or other ones in complete contradiction to the imaginary scenario this chapter presents. The key is to be talking about this issue – to bring it into more mainstream discussions and to flag it with the hegemons of our times.

REFERENCES

Ackerman, B. (2013). Reviving democratic citizenship? *Politics & Society*, *41*(2), 309–317. doi:10.1177/0032329213483103

Agar, N. (2012). On the irrationality of mind uploading: A reply to Neil Levy. *AI & Society*, *27*(4), 431–436. doi:10.1007/s00146-011-0333-7

Agu, S. U., Okeke, V. O. S., & Idike, A. N. (2013). Voters apathy and revival of genuine political participation in Nigeria. *Journal of Educational and Social Research*, *4*(3), 439–448.

Allers, M. A., & Kooreman, P. (2009). More evidence of the effects of voting technology on election outcomes. *Public Choice*, *139*(1-2), 159–170. doi:10.1007/s11127-008-9386-7

Alotaibi, N. (2013). Media effects on voting behaviour. *European Scientific Journal*, *9*(20), 1–11.

Alport, K., & Macintyre, C. (2007). Citizens to netizens: Grass-roots driven democracy and e-democracy in South Australia. *International Journal of Electronic Government Research*, *3*(4), 38–57. doi:10.4018/jegr.2007100103

Alvarez, R. M., Hall, T. E., & Trechsel, A. H. (2009). Internet voting in comparative perspective: The case of Estonia. *PS: Political Science and Politics*, *42*(3), 497–505.

Aman, M. M., & Jayroe, T. J. (2013). ICT, social media, and the Arab transition to democracy: From venting to acting. *Digest of Middle East Studies, 22*(2), 317–347.

Appel, A. W. (2011). Security seals on voting machines: A case study. *ACM Transactions on Information and System Security, 14*(2), 18–29. doi:10.1145/2019599.2019603

Bainbridge, W. S. (2003). Massive questionnaires for personality capture. *Social Science Computer Review, 21*(3), 267–280. doi:10.1177/0894439303253973

Balzarotti, D., Banks, G., Cova, M., Felmetsger, V., Kemmerer, R. A., & Robertson, W. et al. (2010). An experience in testing the security of real-world electronic voting systems. *IEEE Transactions on Software Engineering, 33*(4), 453–473. doi:10.1109/TSE.2009.53

Barkan, J. (2013). Plutocrats at work: How big philanthropy undermines democracy. *Social Research: An International Quarterly, 80*(2), 635–652.

Bekafigo, M. A., & McBride, A. (2013). Who tweets about politics? Political participation of Twitter users during the 2011 gubernatorial elections. *Social Science Computer Review, 31*(5), 625–643. doi:10.1177/0894439313490405

Berger, T. W., Chapin, J. K., Gerhardt, G. A., McFarland, D. J., Principe, J. C., Soussou, W. V., & Tresco, P. A. (2008). *Brain computer interfaces: An international assessment of research and development trends.* Springer Link. doi:10.1007/978-1-4020-8705-9

Berlin, I. (1962). Does political theory still exist? In P. Laslett, & W. G. Runciman (Eds.), *Philosophy, Politics and Society.* Oxford, UK: Basil Blackwell.

Bimber, O. (2008). Total recall. *Computer, 41*(10), 32–33. doi:10.1109/MC.2008.438

Camargo, C. R., Faust, R., Merino, E., & Stefani, C. (2012). The technological obsolescence of the Brazilian ballot box. *Work (Reading, Mass.), 41,* 1185–1192. PMID:22316881

Choe, Y., Kwon, J., & Chung, J. R. (2012). Time, consciousness, and mind uploading. *International Journal of Machine Consciousness, 4*(1), 257–274. doi:10.1142/S179384301240015X

Chou, M. (2013a). *Theorizing democide: Why and how democracies fail.* Basingstoke, UK: Palgrave Macmillan. doi:10.1057/9781137298690

Chou, M. (2013b). Democracy's not for me: The Lowy Institute polls on Gen Y and democracy. *Australian Journal of Political Science, 48*(4). doi:10.1080/10361146.2013.841844

Coeckelbergh, M. (2010). Human development or human enhancement? A methodological reflection on capabilities and the evaluation of information technologies. *Ethics and Information Technology, 13*(2), 81–92. doi:10.1007/s10676-010-9231-9

Curato, N., & Niemeyer, S. (2013). Reaching out to overcome political apathy: Building participatory capacity through deliberative engagement. *Politics & Policy, 41*(3), 355–383.

Czernich, N. (2012). Broadband Internet and political participation: Evidence for Germany. *Kyklos: International Review for Social Sciences, 65*(1), 31–52. doi:10.1111/j.1467-6435.2011.00526.x

de Vreese, C. H. (2007). Digital renaissance: Young consumer and citizen? *The Annals of the American Academy of Political and Social Science, 611,* 207–216. doi:10.1177/0002716206298521

Dutton, W. H., Elberse, A., & Hale, M. (1999). A case study of a netizen's guide to elections. *Communications of the ACM, 42*(12), 48. doi:10.1145/322796.322808

Elgie, R., & Fauvelle-Aymar, C. (2012). Turnout under semipresidentialism: First- and Second-order elections to national-level institutions. *Comparative Political Studies, 45*(12), 1598–1623. doi:10.1177/0010414012463903

Esposito, R. (2012). *Third person*. Cambridge, UK: Polity.

Gibson, R. (2002). Elections online: Assessing Internet voting in light of the Arizona Democratic Primary. *Political Science Quarterly, 116*(4), 561–583. doi:10.2307/798221

Goertzel, B. (2012). When should two minds be considered versions of one another? *International Journal of Machine Consciousness, 4*(1), 177–185. doi:10.1142/S1793843012400094

Graimann, B., Pfurtscheller, G., & Allinson, B. (2010). *Brain computer interfaces: Revolutionizing human-computer interaction*. SpringerLink. doi:10.1007/978-3-642-02091-9

Gronke, P., Galanes-Rosenbaum, E., Miller, P. A., & Toffey, D. (2008). Convenience voting. *Annual Review of Political Science, 11*, 437–455. doi:10.1146/annurev.polisci.11.053006.190912

Hadenius, A. (2001). *Institutions and democratic citizenship*. Oxford, UK: Oxford University Press. doi:10.1093/0199246661.001.0001

Hale, K., & Brown, M. (2013). Adopting, adapting, and opting out: State response to federal voting system guidelines. *Publius, 43*(3), 428–451. doi:10.1093/publius/pjt016

Harris, M. (2005). Contemporary ghost stories: Cyberspace in fiction for children and young adults. *Children's Literature in Education, 36*(2), 111–128. doi:10.1007/s10583-005-3500-y

Hauskeller, M. (2012). My brain, my mind, and I: Some philosophical assumptions of mind-uploading. *International Journal of Machine Consciousness, 4*(1), 187–200. doi:10.1142/S1793843012400100

Hermes, J. (2006). Citizenship in the age of the Internet. *European Journal of Communication, 21*(3), 295–309. doi:10.1177/0267323106066634

Herrnson, P. S., Niemi, R. G., Hamner, M. J., Francia, P. L., Bederson, B. B., Conrad, F. G., & Traugott, M. W. (2008). Voters' evaluations of electronic voting systems: Results from a usability field study. *American Politics Research, 36*(4), 580–611. doi:10.1177/1532673X08316667

Hill, L., & Alport, K. (2007). Reconnecting Australia's politically excluded: Electronic pathways to electoral inclusion. *International Journal of Electronic Government Research, 3*(4), 1–19. doi:10.4018/jegr.2007100101

Hyslop-Margison, E. J., & Sears, A. M. (2006). *Neo-Liberalism, globalization and human capital learning: Reclaiming education for democratic citizenship*. SpringerLink Books.

Isin, E. F., & Nielsen, G. M. (2008). *Acts of citizenship*. London, UK: Zed Books.

Justman, S. (1993). The abstract citizen. *Philosophy and Social Criticism, 19*(3-4), 317–332. doi:10.1177/019145379301900307

Katz, G., Alvarez, R. M., Calvo, E., Escolar, M., & Pomares, J. (2011). Assessing the impact of alternative voting technologies on multi-party elections: Design features, heuristic processing and voter choice. *Political Behavior, 33*(2), 247–270. doi:10.1007/s11109-010-9132-y

Keane, J. (2013). *Democracy and media decadence*. Cambridge, UK: Cambridge University Press. doi:10.1017/CBO9781107300767

Kumar, S., & Ekta, W. (2011). Analysis of electronic voting system in various countries. *International Journal on Computer Science and Engineering, 3*(5), 1825–1830.

Lariscy, R. W., Tinkham, S. F., & Sweetser, K. D. (2011). Kids these days: Examining differences in political uses and gratifications, internet political participation, political information efficacy, and cynicism on the basis of age. *The American Behavioral Scientist*, *55*(6), 749–764. doi:10.1177/0002764211398091

Lever, A. (2010). Compulsory voting: A critical perspective. *British Journal of Political Science*, *40*(4), 897–915. doi:10.1017/S0007123410000050

Mancini, P. (2010). New frontiers in political professionalism. *Political Communication*, *16*(3), 231–245. doi:10.1080/105846099198604

Mossberger, K., Tolbert, C. J., & McNeal, R. S. (2007). *Digital citizenship: The internet, society and participation*. Cambridge, MA: MIT Press.

Moynihan, D. P., & Lavertu, S. (2011). Cognitive biases in governing: Technology preferences in election administration. *Public Administration Review*, *72*(1), 68–77. doi:10.1111/j.1540-6210.2011.02478.x

Oliver, A. (2013). *The Lowy Institute Poll 2013: Australia and the world*. Sydney: Lowy Institute for International Policy.

Otchere-Darko, G. A. (2010). Ghana's fragile elections: Consolidating African democracy through e-voting. *Georgetown Journal of International Affairs*, *11*(2), 67–73.

Pakulski, J. (2013). Leadership trends in advanced democracies. *Social Compass*, *7*(5), 366–376. doi:10.1111/soc4.12035

Quintelier, E., & Theocharis, Y. (2012). Online political engagement, Facebook, and personality traits. *Social Science Computer Review*, *31*(3), 280–290. doi:10.1177/0894439312462802

Rapeli, L. (2013). *The conception of citizen knowledge in democratic theory*. Basingstoke, UK: Palgrave Macmillan. doi:10.1057/9781137322869

Rivest, R. L., Chaum, D., Preneel, B., Rubin, A., Saari, D. G., & Vora, P. L. (2009). Guest editorial special issue on electronic voting. *IEEE Transactions on Information Forensics and Security*, *4*(4), 593–596. doi:10.1109/TIFS.2009.2034721

Roberto, B. C. (2010). M – Cognocracy: Building participatory democracy through the electronic voting and mobile ICT. *Vision de Futuro*, *13* (1).

Rohrer, J. (2009). Black presidents, gay marriages, and Hawaiian sovereignty: Reimagining citizenship in the age of Obama. *American Studies (Lawrence, Kan.)*, *50*(3/4), 107–130.

Sarker, M. M. (2013). E-Voting experience in Bangladesh by using electronic voting machines (EVMS). *International Journal of Engineering Science and Technology*, *5*(5).

Shachar, A. (2005). Religion, state, and the problems of gender: New modes of citizenship and governance in diverse societies. *McGill Law Journal. Revue de Droit de McGill*, *50*, 49–88.

Shamos, M., & Yasinsac, A. (2012). Realities of e-voting security. *IEEE Security & Privacy*, *10*(5), 16–17. doi:10.1109/MSP.2012.124

Simons, B., & Jones, D. W. (2012). Internet voting is unachievable for the foreseeable future and therefore not inevitable. *Communications of the ACM*, *55*(10), 68–77. doi:10.1145/2347736.2347754

Sotala, K. (2012). Advantages of artificial intelligences, uploads, and digital minds. *International Journal of Machine Learning*, *4*(1), 275–291.

Spegele, R. D. (1971). Fiction and political theory. *Social Research*, *38*(1), 108–138.

Steiner, N. D. (2010). Economic globalization and voter turnout in established democracies. *Electoral Studies*, *29*(3), 444–459. doi:10.1016/j.electstud.2010.04.007

Stewart, C. III. (2011). Voting technologies. *Annual Review of Political Science*, *14*(1), 353–378. doi:10.1146/annurev.polisci.12.053007.145205

Stromer-Galley, J. (2003). Voting and the public sphere: Conversations on internet voting. *PS: Political Science and Politics*, *36*(4), 727–731.

Swan, L. S., & Ward, J. (2012). Digital immortality: Self or 0010110? *International Journal of Machine Consciousness*, *4*(1), 245–256. doi:10.1142/S1793843012400148

Tan, D. S., & Nijholt, A. (2010). *Brain-computer interfaces: Applying our minds to human-computer interaction*. Springer Link. doi:10.1007/978-1-84996-272-8

Taylor, C. (2007). Cultures of democracy and citizen efficacy. *Public Culture*, *19*(1), 117–150. doi:10.1215/08992363-2006-027

Taylor-Gooby, P. (2008). *Reframing social citizenship*. Oxford, UK: Oxford University Press. doi:10.1093/acprof:oso/9780199546701.001.0001

Tolbert, C. J., & McNeal, R. S. (2003). Unravelling the effects of the internet on political participation? *Political Research Quarterly*, *56*(2), 175–185. doi:10.1177/106591290305600206

Vertovec, S. (1998). Multicultural policies and modes of citizenship in European studies. *International Social Science Journal*, *50*(156), 187–199. doi:10.1111/1468-2451.00123

Weldemariam, K., Kemmerer, R. A., & Villafiorita, A. (2011). Formal analysis of an electronic voting system: An experience report. *Journal of Systems and Software*, *84*(10), 1618–1637. doi:10.1016/j.jss.2011.03.032

KEY TERMS AND DEFINITIONS

Democratic Citizenship: A mode of living where an individual cultivates the relationship between the 'Self' and being 'citizen'. As citizenship can manifest in many ways, and a number of selves are looking for more meaningful political engagement, integrating HETs into election stations (see Election Station) is one way of supporting democratic citizenship.

Electronic Voting: A method of casting a ballot using computers. This might be done in person by using touchscreens or simple machines or online through email or a website.

Election Station: A place where citizens, or otherwise those with the right to vote, go to cast their ballot in person. It is today typically characterized by fully or semi-private desks, sometimes made of cardboard or plastic, where citizens complete their ballots in writing.

Futurism: An ontology that guides the theorisations of objects or subjects in the future. It essentially means the act of thinking, in all seriousness and intellectual curiosity, about the future of something. Examples of key questions include: How will voting likely happen in 100 years? Why is 'Scholar X' articulating these changes to citizenship in the coming decades? What will democracy look like 300 years from now? And so on.

Normativity: The declaration of the 'ought' about something. It raises questions about what an object or subject should be doing. Normativity is often informed or guided by an ethical framework.

Political Apathy: The act of a citizen being apathetic to his or her own political system or toward the cultivation of a life of politics (i.e. negative or neutral orientations towards modes of political living). HETs are looked to by some scholars as a tool to try to re-engage citizens in politics.

Public Duties: The typically normative aspect of being a citizen as espoused by the state. It is what citizens should, or must, be capable of doing with great competency. The majority of OECD states, for example, expect their citizens to be active and well-informed participants in the political process.

Political Will: The enthusiasm or determination by political actors (usually elected politicians) to champion a cause. "The pedestrian mall was created last year. Despite tremendous opposition from drivers and some business owners the by-law was passed by the sheer political will of the city's councilors and citizen assemblies."

ENDNOTES

[1] Mind uploading is the theorised act of having one's mind (presumably: consciousness, personality, or self) uploaded to the Internet. This is at times referred to as digital immortality (Bainbridge, 2003, p. 268; Harris, 2005: pp. 116, 125; Bimber, 2008). Debates exist in scholarly literature on two fronts. The first depends on whether mind uploading is actually possible (Choe, Kwon, & Chung, 2012; Sotala, 2012). If it is possible, the second debate looks to the many problems this poses (Agar, 2012) to things like responsibility, totally digital personal relationships, and effectively having to deal with consciousnesses that are alive forever (see, for example, Goertzel, 2012; Swan & Howard, 2012; Hauskeller, 2012).

[2] There is a proviso. For ideologues to be passed by, citizens will have to have figured out a way to circumvent or remove the currently observable capture of politics by mass media (Keane, 2013), giant political parties (Pakulski 2013), and big business interests (Barkan, 2013).

[3] See, for example, a recent Lowy Institute poll (Oliver, 2013; Chou, 2013b) which demonstrated that a significant number (51%) of young Australians (18 to 29 years of age) are open to alternatives to democracy.

[4] This point is conditional on which electronic voting machine or method is being discussed. Some systems, for example email voting, may be economically cheaper than paper ballots over the longer term.

[5] A 'donkey' vote is the act of ticking the first available box in polities that use 'above the line' preferential voting, party list voting (sometimes found in certain proportional representation systems), or 'tick one' first past the post voting. The types of ballot papers that allow for 'donkey' votes are criticized because they often bring individuals to power through a much less considered act of voting by voters who want to get 'in and out'. Randomized ballot papers, or circular ballot papers, are promoted as possible solutions. It would, for example, be possible to randomize the order in which candidates or political party lists appear in an electronic voting system.

[6] Vote Compass is a recently built institution, and software programme, that through a survey allows voters to gain a sense of where they 'sit' on their respective polity's economic and political spectra (for example, liberal v conservative and left v right). See http://votecompass.com/ for more.

Chapter 11
Defining and Analyzing Disability in Human Enhancement

Dev Bose
Iowa State University, USA

ABSTRACT

Human Enhancement Technologies (HET) offer valuable assistance for individuals with disabilities. Alongside these opportunities, it is important to consider the ethics that inevitably emerge. The field of disability studies recognizes that disability is a key aspect of human experience and that the study of disability has important political, social, and economic implications for society as a whole, including both disabled and nondisabled people. This chapter raises ethical questions about HET for disability through review of the literature surrounding this topic. To evaluate the ethical implications of regulating enhancement technologies for disability, medical and social models of disability are applied towards select cases. This chapter responds to the work of select disability scholars (see Dolmage; Kerschbaum & Price; Meloncon & Oswal; Vidali) by characterizing ethical perspectives from medical and social lenses. While a medical interpretation of disability offers a stark and impersonal approach, a social interpretation offers a detailed and individualistic one. The majority of scholarship noted here favors the social model. The framework presented herein seeks to abide by the social model of disability. Since HET have become an ethically contested field of discourse today, this chapter divides the literature into the following sections: 1) definitions, distinctions, and challenges of medical and social models of disability; 2) ambiguity, authenticity, and the ab/normality construct; 3) forced privacy and the privilege to hide; and 4) recent trends in regulation and the ethics of development.

DEFINITIONS, DISTINCTIONS, AND CHALLENGES IN SELECT MODELS OF DISABILITY

It will be useful to explore some of the theoretical constructs prevalent in disability studies. A starting point exists within an academic context, in which disability has progressed from exclusivity to one that is more inclusive via diverse pathways. The composition classroom proves to be an intellectual starting point for critical thinking, so it should come as no surprise that the social model of disability has its roots in rhetoric and composition. Shannon Walters (2011), for example, defines

DOI: 10.4018/978-1-4666-6010-6.ch011

the social model as one that "led people with disabilities to write about their own experiences of disability [by resisting] dominant medical discourse" (p. 430). Walters' point is to say that the very notion of disability has become defined as a burden upon society. To work through this unfortunate circumstance, scholars like Palmeri (2006), Slatin (2001) and Zdenek (2009) stipulate that new media has potential for incorporating methods for all students alike, regardless of disability status. The point here is to recognize that technology attempts to universalize the learning experience, albeit not always successfully.

The University of Leicester hosts a number of doctoral and postgraduate research initiatives that promote the view of disability through the social model. In line with Walters' argument (2011) described above, Leicester defines the social model by drawing on the idea that "it is society that disables people, through designing everything to meet the needs of the majority of people who are not disabled" (Student Support Service, 2008). The social model calls for responsibility through interdisciplinary research; along these lines, an ideal scenario envisions a research area like transhumanism to "to locate itself not in response to changing hostile geographies but as a proactive architect of future possibilities" (Dolmage, p. 25). Dolmage's point is to say that people with disabilities should not be expected to change what is beyond their control, but to actively foresee and work around potential issues.

The social model has not come without its problems, however, as the very definition of disability is debated: Shakespeare (2006) extends this argument by explaining "the social model so strongly disowns individual and medical approaches, that it risks implying that impairment is not a problem" (p. 200). Disability-specific tools such as educational podcasts for vision-impaired students may solve problems on a case-by-case basis, as Zdenek (2009) maintains, but such tools lack a comprehensive change of pedagogical practices. While podcasts may not be a form of HET,

the point is that technology's attempt to universalize the learning experience is unsuccessful. The concept of Universal Design, or UD, asserts that practices designed for students with disabilities should benefit those without disabilities as well (Center for Universal Design, 2008a). Just as UD attempts to help students across the board, regardless of disability status, problems become much more complicated on an everyday level. For instance, what if a website that purports to be accessible to visually impaired users malfunctions? Or, to ask the question more broadly, what is an ideal situation for all learners/users, regardless of disability status?

The medical model seeks to answer these questions, although in doing so it offers an impersonal method of approaching disability. To delve into the medical model further, the Michigan Disability Rights Coalition offers the following critique:

[The medical model] has dominated the formulation of disability policy for years. Although we should not reject out-of-hand its therapeutic aspects which may cure or alleviate the physical and mental condition of many disabled people, it does not offer a realistic perspective from the viewpoint of disabled people themselves. To begin with, most would reject the concept of being "abnormal." Also, the model imposes a paternalistic approach to problem solving which, although well intentioned, concentrates on "care" and ultimately provides justification for institutionalization and segregation. This restricts disabled people's opportunities to make choices, control their lives and develop their potential. (Michigan Disability Rights Coalition)

At its core, the medical model envisions disability through a skewed lens. Disability is viewed as being out of the norm. A disconnect is created which may be characterized as being part of an able-bodied versus abnormal spectrum (Price, 2011). As a result of this disconnect, people are defined through their disabilities. Responsibility for obtaining care, treatment and rehabilitation fall significantly upon the individual, leading to a segregated populace. According to this model, it is the individual, and not society, who has the problem, and different interventions aim to provide the person with the appropriate skills to rehabilitate or deal with it. The notion of assistance becomes viewed as a crutch. Access-related challenges associated with disability like mobility are likely to become overlooked as a result of this perspective.

One implication of viewing disability through the medical model that transhumanist scholars should find of particular interest is the necessity for control over the body through legislative acts. The cultural view of seeing the body as something to be controlled is apparent: "In a culture supported by modern Western medicine, and which idealizes the idea that the body can be objectified and controlled, those who cannot control their bodies are seen as failures" (Michigan Disability Rights Coalition). In the public sphere, control over the body is translated through regulatory measures. For instance, the ADA Amendments Act of 2008 (ADAAA) made a number of significant changes to the definition of "disability" under the Americans with Disabilities Act (ADA). According to the US Equal Employment Commission:

Congress overturned several Supreme Court decisions that Congress believed had interpreted the definition of "disability" too narrowly, resulting in a denial of protection for many individuals with impairments such as cancer, diabetes, and epilepsy. The ADAAA states that the definition of disability should be interpreted in favor of broad coverage of individuals. (U.S. Equal Employment Opportunity Commission, 2011)

The fact sheet referenced here argues that Congress made it easier to establish the presence of a disability within the meaning of the statute. Referencing the ADAAA is significant because of regulation that the medical model helps to enforce. One could argue in favor of the medical model with the idea that large-scale government regulation has allowed some individuals to receive disability-related benefits.

Regardless of whichever model readers may favor, it is nevertheless important to consider the long-term societal impacts of how we choose to interpret disability. As the University of Leicester notes, "There is a great deal that society can do to reduce, and ultimately remove, some of these disabling barriers, and that this task is the responsibility of society, rather than the disabled person" (Student Support Service, 2008). In order for responsibility to take place, a perspective needs to be taken on that defines disability as a complex web of social issues. The next section discusses this topic in more detail.

AMBIGUITY, AUTHENTICITY, AND THE AB/NORMALITY CONSTRUCT

Bostrom and Roache consider ethics of human enhancement within broad classifications: Life extension, physical enhancement, enhancement of mood or personality, cognitive enhancement, and pre- and perinatal interventions (Ethical issues in human enhancement, 2008). While all of these types of HET exploit disability to some extent, this chapter focuses on enhancement of mood or personality and cognitive enhancement. Ambiguity and authenticity factor into these HET, and in doing so demonstrate how disability plays a role in perpetuating what will be referred to as the ab/normality construct.

Mood enhancement or personality enhancement. There currently exists an ambiguity of existing standards on this type of HET. In fact, scholarship in HET argues that ethical considerations related to mood enhancement boil down to standardization of improvement, or even "if it is plausible to claim that there could be such a standard" (Bostrom & Roache, Ethical issues in human enhancement, 2008, p. 12).

To understand why, it is necessary to turn to a similar case in which genetic modifications of personality and behavior were studied. As the author of the study concludes, "Heritable modifications for psychology, personality, and behavior should be limited to the reversal or prevention of relatively unambiguous instances of pathology or likely harm" (Neitzke, 2012, p. 307). Nietzke points to sociopathy as the example of likely harm in this case. It is difficult to apply a universal law towards mood enhancement if results of the intervention are unknown. This is especially true when dealing with a scenario involving disability. While a medical analysis would shut the case down, a social analysis would strive to look at it from the viewpoint of the user taking the enhancement.

Individuals and social perspectives matter greatly here. Nietzke (2012) continues:

For individuals, modifications would interfere with their capacity for self-determination in a way that undermines the very concept of self-determination … [As for] society, modification offers a medium for power to manipulate the makeup of persons and populations, possibly causing biological harm to the species and altering our conceptions of social responsibility. (p. 307)

This argument applies towards mood or personality enhancement. The user of this HET may have a certain degree of self-determination, or free will, which helps s/him to decide whether to take the enhancer. Bostrom and Roache consider authenticity when discussing the ethical implications of mood enhancement (2008, p. 13); might subjects who self-report on the use of pharmaceutical means to influence mood enhancement input biased response, as a means to have some control over disbursement? These questions boil down to the ethical debate surrounding free will versus determinism.

Cognitive enhancement. Bostrom and Roache also discuss cognitive enhancement; "that is, those capacities that we use for gaining, processing, storing, and retrieving information" (2008, p. 14). Drugs for enhancing memory and alertness fall into this category, as well as medical and genetic interventions for enhancing motor senses and increasing the likelihood of intelligence. Could enhancement be viewed as an unfair advantage, or a tool for "equipping students with skills and knowledge that will improve their own lives" (Bostrom & Roache, Ethical issues in human enhancement, 2008, p. 14)? Would those with "below-average cognitive ability" be seen as "diseased, rather than [be represented] as part of the normal human spectrum of abilities" (Bostrom & Roache, Ethical issues in human enhancement, 2008, p. 15)?

To answer these questions, let us consider ambiguity. Existing scholarship in ethics of HET has hinted towards the realm of the super-human: See, for example, Makridis's discussion of *manufacturing* of high performing individuals (Converging technologies: A critical analysis of cognitive enhancement for public policy application, 2013). Cognitive enhancement touches upon the notion of super powers: Just as with mood enhancement, cognitive modification also offers a "medium for power to manipulate the makeup of persons and populations" which alters conceptions of social responsibility (Neitzke, 2012, p. 307). The point to be taken here is that some forms of enhancement require an ambiguous, perhaps even ambivalent, perception of power. In other words, cognitive enhancement is an example of HET in which a close questioning of attitudes may be detrimental to progress.

This chapter's earlier discussion on disability studies scholarship is important here. Unlike the social model, the medical model fails to consider disability HET from the perspective of social responsibility. To illustrate this point, Bostrom (2008) notes:

It would appear that our maintaining composure under stress would fully count toward our Dignity as a Quality only if we are able to view it as an authentic response, a genuine reflection of our autonomous self. In the case of the person who maintains composure only because she has taken Paxil, it might be unclear whether the composure is really a manifestation of her personality or merely of an extraneous influence. (Bostrom, Dignity and enhancement, 2008, p. 182)

The point to take here is that authenticity is tied to both dignity and quality of life. Thus from an ethical perspective, HET related to disability should prize the individual over the condition, not the other way around as the medical model does.

Ab/normality construct. Based on the literature that has been covered up to this point, ambiguity and authenticity have been discussed in light of two representatives types of HET, i.e. mood/personality and cognitive enhancement (see Bostrom & Roache, Ethical issues in human enhancement, 2008). Dignity is part of an autonomous lifestyle, as noted by Bostrom (Dignity and enhancement, 2008). The medical model considers enhancement beyond what is perceived as being anything other than having immediate physical need as gratuitous. For instance, think of gender reassignment surgeries which insurance companies often refuse to cover, despite the individual seeking gender reassignment whose life could be improved as a result of the surgery. Conceptions of normal reflect standardization, but yield an important end-result: That those without enhancements fall beneath an average.

Normalization needs to be considered in a discussion on the ethics of HET as it relates to disability. A challenge to the social model of disability involves an obligation to avoid unnecessary harm by preventing or eradicating disabling conditions. Ultimately, this should mean "when we have the choice, we should bring into existence people without (known) disabling conditions rather than people with conditions" (Bortolotti & Harris, 2006, Disability, Enhancement and the Harm–Benefit Continuum, 2006, p. 32). That is to say, to define a body as "normal" means that

there are "abnormal" bodies. In a similar vein, it is important to "assess the priority of the claims of disabled people in the face of scarcity of resources for which there can be many competing social claims" (Wolff, 2009). As proponents of the medical model would argue, disability in the ab/normal spectrum is no different from any other inhibiting condition.

FORCED PRIVACY AND THE PRIVILEGE TO HIDE

As demonstrated so far in this chapter, disability proves to be a foundational aspect of human enhancement technologies. In this section, we explore current trends, notably privacy—the desire to remain confidential in light of enhancement available to us—and privilege—pointing to those who have access to these technologies and the sorts of factors inherent to access, as well as the possibility of universal coverage.

When privacy is forced, it is correlative to stigma. As such, "disabling conditions are stigmatizing to the extent that they evoke negative or punitive responses" (Susman, 1993). If this is the case, which it is certainly is for individuals fearing any sort of on-the-job retaliation, then being open with a disability is a precursor to potentially devastating consequences. Stigma is especially likely to happen in the workplace for people who would not want to risk losing their jobs for fear of reprisal. Recall the point made earlier by Bortolotti & Harris (2006): That, if given the choice, people without disabling conditions should be brought in over people with such conditions. Stigma is the consequence of complex relationships between the disabled and the non-disabled.

Ironically, stigma and disability intersect within positive response bias, which refers to "a general norm in our society to be kind to disadvantaged persons" (Susman, 1993). The author goes on to points out some examples of positive response bias:

Students who interact with a seemingly disabled person tend to show less variability in behavior as a group than students who interact with a physically normal stimulus person; that the students express opinions less representative of actual beliefs; and that they terminate interactions sooner (when this does not conflict with a felt obligation to be kind) [Kleck et al. 28]. Similarly, Snyder et al. [29] find that students feel duty bound to interact with disabled persons but avoid doing so if they have a socially acceptable reason. (Susman, 1993)

These findings result in an important consequence for individuals with disability: Positive response bias contributes towards the stigma that "able-bodies" (see previous section on this usage) see disability as something needing to be acknowledged, perhaps even praised, but indubitably a stand-alone phenomenon needing to be either avoided or examined underneath a microscope. Negative response bias contributes to stigma as well, in cases where able-bodies experience uncertainty and negative affect in the presence of stigmatized (e.g. disabled) individuals. Able-bodies may seek to avoid having stigma spread to them by avoiding close association with a disabled person. Either way, such stigma results from forced privacy, or in other words, alienation.

Media portrayals of persons with disability offer a similarly distancing effect as positive and negative response biases. As the author's research indicates on three different articles regarding this topic:

In the first of these, Krlegel [45] chronicles images of disabled persons in American literature (e.g. as demonic, victim, or survivor cripples). In the second, Quart and Auster [46] present an analysis of wounded veterans in post-World War II and post-Vietnam films and find that realism is finally gaining a place in more recent vintages of the latter. In the third article, Bogdan et al. [47] examined the details of one of the stereotypical ways disabled persons are portrayed in the media. i.e. as dangerous. (Susman, 1993)

These studies fall in line with disability history and representation, a field that has much to offer for scholars interested in media portrayals of persons with disability. For this chapter, however, suffice it to say that popular notions of disability summarize the matter as contributing towards distancing. Media contentiously disability and contributes towards a glass-wall perspective.

In terms of human enhancement technologies, the stigma that results from forced privacy deserves consideration. Should HET reveal the condition that alienates the individual, or should they seek to hide the disability altogether? Even if HET removes the disability altogether, such a perspective lends itself towards the medical model. Seen socially, HET should offer the possibility of hiding the disability altogether—if and only if the individual should desire that this be the ideal scenario. Seen on a case-by-case basis, privacy may not be an issue in and of itself, provided that the individual using the enhancement does not face negative consequences.

RECENT TRENDS IN REGULATION AND THE ETHICS OF DEVELOPMENT

Given these circumstances, policy must enter into the picture. Classification schemes offer a starting point to the discussion:

The WHO (World Health Organization) encourages the use of their tripartite classification scheme by medical professionals and public policy officials, e.g. in appraisal and evaluation of health care processes. The goal is to replace the medical model's exclusive focus on disease with a perspective that gives due attention to individuals and experiences of living. But despite this social science orientation, 'impairment,' disability,' and 'handicap' are often used in the social science literature less precisely or other than they are defined by the WHO. (Susman, 1993)

Susman offers a two-fold problem here. In medical settings (for surely, this is where disability human enhancement began), focus needs to be shifted away from the condition and towards the individual. However, since our language shapes who we are, wide-spread classification needs to be enforced in a manner that demonstrates inclusivity. How this balance between one's experiences of living and how to capture it within medicine requires an ethical paradigm of inclusive technology. Policy needs to incorporate such an ethical paradigm into a discussion on HET related to HET.

To provide an especially vivid example of human enhancement technology and an ethical discussion regarding disability, Cabrera provides the following perspective on memory enhancement: "Connections between events and memory traces, and between memory traces and recollection, may be indirect, context-dependent, multiple, and sometimes not necessary at all" (Cabrera, 2011). In fact, "A related concern is connected to the idea of what would happen if many different people were to share their memories through being permanently connected to databases. What happens to the "uniqueness" of the individual as it merges with the communal?" (Cabrera, 2011). Were we come to such measures as those described here, it is necessary to consider how privacy and policy emerge into another important factor: Regulation.

The latest edition of the *Diagnostic and Statistical Manual of Mental Disorders (DSM-5)* was released in 2013. According to a press release issued by the American Psychiatric Association (APA), the revised manual considers "conditions that require further research before their consideration as formal disorders" (1). This unprecedented move completely abandons the ADAAA of 2008, which broadened the definition of disability (U.S. Equal Employment Opportunity Commission, 2011). Yet regulation is not limited to the DSM-V alone. A study on deep brain stimulation suggests that further discussions regarding the practice should be considered (Schmitz-Luhn, Katzenmeier, & Woopen, 2012). The European Union issued an extensive call for legal regulation of enhancement technologies (Coenen, et al., 2009). The following section discusses a case where regulation of HET has been considered.

Deep brain stimulation. Deep brain stimulation is a procedure that involves continually giving electrical impulses into small areas of the brain via implanted electrodes, and has been used to treat a range of disorders, including Parkinson's disease, dystonia, and essential tremor (Schmitz-Luhn, Katzenmeier, & Woopen, 2012). Protection of research participants who receive the treatment includes factual justification, patient's informed consent, ethics committee review, and consideration of use of medical devices (in this case, a stimulator). To this extent, deep brain stimulation is no different from other medical interventions, in that a combination of treatment attempts and clinical trials prefaces large-scale use.

Deep brain stimulation provides a useful example for analyzing the question, where does therapy end and enhancement begin? The authors suggest this is an important starting point, calling to mind "patients having originally received ... stimulation [who] later want to adjust the stimulation parameters in order to enhance their mood" (133). Given this area of interest, the procedure crosses the threshold from treatment of existing issues to a sort of neuro-enhancement.

The duty to inform individuals about risk of side effects and severe complications adds a further twist. While it is the physician's place to inform patients of short-term and long-term side effects, the degree to which patients respond to deep brain stimulation is still unpredictable. In fact, clinical studies reveal that "a number of patients do not respond at all—beyond that, severe complications and some significant psychological alterations have been described" (133). The duty to inform is a complicated issue for HET regarding disability, especially in this case where the long-term effects are not particularly well-known or provide a potential for changes in personality. This is not to say that such a treatment should not be considered;

practitioners need to be aware of—and let their patients know—when enhancements are superior to comparable modes of treatment.

The capacity to provide consent adds another dimension to potential medical enhancement. The authors describe how in German law, the Court of Guardianship must approve a treatment "whenever there is a risk of death or severe and enduring medical harm" (135). For deep brain stimulation, this provision may present a problem. After all, the participant may choose to go through the procedure without the possibility of being extensively questioned by the government. Control over one's body through legislation is the issue here. Another disputed question by Coenen et al. addresses the possibility of patients who may need to revoke consent during surgery: "Can the patient be regarded as able to consent during surgery, probably after having spent several hours with a fixed head on the operating table? (2009)" Informed consent is likened to "moral responsibility over one's actions" (Coenen, et al., 2009). The report describes a man with Parkinson's who had deep brain stimulation and made several extreme decisions which caused him to go into judicial and financial debt, including buying expensive properties and cars, having an affair with a married woman. With the stimulation turned on, he was "unaware of his manic behaviour"; turned off, "he showed awareness and regret" (Coenen, et al., 2009). Thus consent adds a spectrum of issues, including those described here.

Finally, the issue of device control is one that needs to be considered in light of HET regarding disability. Deep brain stimulation exemplifies this issue. "Patients … are equipped with remote controls in which they can autonomously decide at what time they are stimulated or not" (Coenen, et al., 2009). The question arises as to who should be in control of stimulation, the patient or the physician. The authors provide an interesting solution: Provide adverse side effects that "considerably afflict the personal environment of the patient" (Coenen, et al., 2009). Apparently in doing so,

the intent is convincing the patient to forego an excessive amount of stimulation. Another option is to allow physicians the possibility of remotely "adjust[ing] intensity and frequency" (Coenen, et al., 2009). Such measures can be put in place to avoid the potential misuse of enhancements. As the author notes, "The reasons why one decides to reproduce can be subject to moral approbation or condemnation, as such reasons might be indicators of the quality of one's parenting and the happiness of the future persons one is committed to bringing to life. However, once the decision to reproduce is made, no further harm comes from taking as few risks as possible" (Bortolotti, 2009).

In terms of the issues being discussed here, does regulation provide a solution? Regulations already exist with respect to medical devices, medical procedures, drugs, treatment, and informed consent. As the proposed plan by the European Union council suggests, it may just be a matter of ensuring that HET do not fall outside of them. The plan would certainly be to serve as a proponent for regulation, as the report suggests that deep brain stimulation "is only used under extreme circumstances … and regularly involves rather unpredictable changes … from suicidal behaviour to enhanced moods and enhanced memory" (Coenen, et al., 2009). Should rising social standards be another area of concern that lends a nod towards regulation? That is to say, as deep brain stimulation becomes acceptable to the general public, does the larger community accept a brighter mood as the new social standard?

Ethics of development. To answer this question, it is important to consider what scholarship has called the ethics of development. As the author notes, "Once one appreciates the productivity-increasing potential of enhancements, one can begin to see that enhancement need not be primarily a zero sum affair, that the social costs of forgoing enhancements may be great, and that the state may well take an interest in facilitating biomedical enhancements, just as it does in facilitating education and other productivity-increasing traditional enhancements" (Buchanan, 2008). Dignity falls in line with the ethics of development. It is important to consider "the importance of a concept of dignity that is inclusive enough to also apply to many possible posthuman beings. Recognizing the possibility of posthuman dignity undercuts an important objection against human enhancement and removes a distortive double standard from our field of moral vision" (Bostrom, In defense of posthuman dignity, 2005). Similarly, "it is possible that through enhancement we could become better able to appreciate and secure many forms of dignity that are overlooked or missing under current conditions" (Bostrom, Dignity and enhancement, 2008).

Transhumanists embrace the potential for HET to "achieve happiness, a total control of emotions, and an improvement of human character" (EU, 96). Restrictions on HET may be perceived as being pessimistic. An improved public understanding of science may be drawn, however, through a wider discussion of these issues. On one hand, cognitive enhancers "should be viewed in the same general category as education, good health habits, and information technologies" (EU, 100). On the other hand, a potential side effect raised by cynics suggests that "manufacturers [of enhancing drugs] will not turn away the significant revenues from the illegal use of these substances by healthy people" (EU, 99). Similar thinkers may bring to mind the addictive potential of such enhancements.

Policy forming is inevitable. But policy needs to inform disability in a socially responsive way by placing value upon the individual, not the disability. Thus, an increase of visibility should occur. As the argument goes, people with disabilities not readily visible may not receive the same treatment. Note the following perspective:

We will always need to learn from one another about the barriers each of us faces, and barrier removal will need to be an ongoing process, not an accomplishment we can safely put behind us. Dismissing that which is unfamiliar to us as "invis-
ible" (and suggesting that it cannot be discerned rather than that we have not learned to discern it) is another way of throwing the responsibility for social justice back on the individual who carries the burden of injustice. (Montgomery, A Hard Look at Invisible Disability, 2001)

Montgomery's perspective deserves analysis in terms of visibility and, on a larger scale, the able-bodied/disabled binary. Montgomery observes that autism is not usually viewed in the same light as other conditions that may be more noticeable, like vision- or hearing-impairment. As a writer who happens to have autism, he looks past being noticed because to do so places disability under the same focus that the medical model of disability does. Disability becomes institutionalized when viewing conditions as being visible or invisible.

Misrepresentation is another problem that media has when it comes to representing disability. Disability stories often come about as tales of inspiration or overcoming. The nature of communication is often condescending in media constructions of disability: "There are 49 million Americans (or one in five) who have a disability, and they have many stories to tell that have nothing to do with their medical conditions. Most of those stories go to the heart of discrimination and second-class treatment in a society that is uncomfortable with physical differences" (LoTempio, 2011). LoTempio describes a problem here that, similar to Montgomery, falls into a simplified way of thinking—that people who happen to have disabilities are defined by their condition and serve limited purposes related to entertainment or inspiration.

This chapter has discussed the ethics of disability enhancement technology. In doing so, scholars in transhumanism may find the work to be particularly useful in terms of cross-referencing with disability studies research. The focus of ethics, as the literature demonstrates, points towards an emphasis towards the social, with the caveat that there is a necessity for recognition that a clinical perspective may suggest. Misrepresentation inflicted by popular constructions reinforces negative attitudes about disability. Regulation happens to be one of those possibilities when working with human enhancement technologies related to disability. To reach an ethically sound conclusion, the focus should be placed on the individual by avoiding unnecessary focus on disabling conditions and disorders.

REFERENCES

American Psychiatric Association Board of Trustees. (2012). *American Psychiatric Association Board of Trustees Approves DSM-5*. Arlington, VA: American Psychiatric Association.

Bortolotti, L. (2009). Do we have an obligation to make smarter babies? In T. Takala, P. Herissone-Kelly, & S. Holm (Eds.), *Cutting Through the Surface: Philosophical Approaches to Bioethics*. Amsterdam, The Netherlands: Rodopi Press.

Bortolotti, L., & Harris, J. (2006). Disability, Enhancement and the Harm–Benefit Continuum. In J. R. Spencer, & A. Du Bois-Pedain (Eds.), *Freedom and Responsibility in Reproductive Choic* (pp. 31–49). Oxford, UK: Hart Publishers.

Bortolotti, L., & Nagasawa, Y. (2009). Immortality without boredom. *Ratio*, *22*, 262–277. doi:10.1111/j.1467-9329.2009.00431.x

Bostrom, N. (2005). In defense of posthuman dignity. *Bioethics*, *19*(3), 202–214. doi:10.1111/j.1467-8519.2005.00437.x PMID:16167401

Bostrom, N. (2008). Dignity and enhancement. In P. C. Bioethics, & A. Schulman (Eds.), *Human Dignity and Bioethics: Essays Commissioned by the President's Council on Bioethics* (pp. 173–206). Washington, DC: Academic Press.

Bostrom, N., & Roache, R. (2008). Ethical Issues in Human Enhancement. In J. Rysberg, T. Petersen, & C. Wolf (Eds.), *New Waves in Applied Ethics* (pp. 120–152). New York: Pelgrave Macmillan.

Buchanan, A. (2008). Enhancement and the ethics of development. *Kennedy Institute of Ethics Journal*, *18*(1), 1–34. doi:10.1353/ken.0.0003 PMID:18561576

Cabrera, L. Y. (2011). Memory Enhancement: The Issues We Should Not Forget About. *Journal of Evolution and Technology*, *22*(1), 97–109.

Camporesi, S., & Bortolotti, L. (2008). Reproductive cloning in humans and therapeutic cloning in primates: Is the ethical debate catching up with the recent scientific advances? *Journal of Medical Ethics*, *34*(9), e15. doi:10.1136/jme.2007.023879 PMID:18757615

Coenen, C., Schuijff, M., Smits, M., Klaassen, P., Hennen, L., & Rader, M. et al. (2009). *Science and Technology Options Assessment: Human Enhancement Study*. Brussels: European Parliament.

Dvorsky, G. (2006, July 29). *All Together Now: Developmental and Ethical Considerations for Biologically Uplifting Nonhuman Animals*. Retrieved January 4, 2014, from IEET Monograph Series: http://ieet.org/index.php/IEET/print/702

Foley, N. (2006, May 24). *The Stigma of Not Working*. Retrieved December 1, 2013, from http://www.raggededgemagazine.com/departments/closerlook/001095.html

LoTempio, S. (2011, March 3). *From Special to Substantial*. Retrieved December 1, 2013, from http://www.poynter.org/how-tos/newsgathering-storytelling/diversity-at-work/74234/from-special-to-substantial/

Makridis, C. (2013). Converging Technologies: A Critical Analysis of Cognitive Enhancement for Public Policy Application. *Journal of Science and Engineering Ethics, 19*(3), 1017–1038. doi:10.1007/s11948-012-9396-1 PMID:23065536

Michigan Disabilty Rights Coalition. (n.d.). *Medical Model of Disabilty*. Retrieved December 1, 2013, from http://www.copower.org/models-of-disability/181-medical-model-of-disability.html

Montgomery, C. (2001). *A Hard Look at Invisible Disability*. Advocado Press. Retrieved December 1, 2013, from http://www.ragged-edge-mag.com/0301/0301ft1.htm

Montgomery, C. (2005, December 16). *Autistics Speak*. Retrieved December 1, 2013, from http://www.raggededgemagazine.com/departments/closerlook/000677.html

Palmeri, J. (2006). Disability Studies, Cultural Analysis, and the Critical Practice of Technical Communication Pedagogy. *Technical Communication Quarterly, 15*(1), 49–65. doi:10.1207/s15427625tcq1501_5

Scanlon, D. (2013). Specific Learning Disability and Its Newest Definition: Which Is Comprehensive? and Which Is Insufficient? *Journal of Learning Disabilities, 46*(1), 26–33. doi:10.1177/0022219412464342 PMID:23144061

Schmitz-Luhn, B., Katzenmeier, C., & Woopen, C. (2012). Law and Ethics of Deep Brain Stimulation. *International Journal of Law and Psychiatry, 35*, 130–136. doi:10.1016/j.ijlp.2011.12.007 PMID:22244083

Shakespeare, T. (2006). The social model of disability. In L. Davis (Ed.), *The disability studies reader* (pp. 197–204). New York: Routledge.

Slatin, J. (2001). The art of ALT: Toward a more accessible web. *Computers and Composition, 18*, 73–81. doi:10.1016/S8755-4615(00)00049-9

Smith, J. E. (2006, January 8). *It's a Life, Not a Feel-Good Moment*. Retrieved December 1, 2013, from http://www.washingtonpost.com/wp-dyn/content/article/2006/01/06/AR2006010601485.html

Student Support Service. (2008, December 19). *The social and medical model of disability*. University of Leicester. Retrieved December 1, 2013, from http://www2.le.ac.uk/offices/ssds/accessability/staff/accessabilitytutors/information-for-accessability-tutors/the-social-and-medical-model-of-disability

Susman, J. (1993). Disabilty, Stigma, and Deviance. *Social Science & Medicine, 38*(1), 15–22. doi:10.1016/0277-9536(94)90295-X

Walters, S. (2010). Toward an Accessible Pedagogy: Dis/ability, Multimodality, and Universal Design in the Technical Communication Classroom. *Technical Communication Quarterly, 19*(4), 427–454. doi:10.1080/10572252.2010.502090

Wolff, J. (2009). Disability, status enhancement, personal enhancement and resource allocation. *Economics and Philosophy, 25*(1), 49–68. doi:10.1017/S0266267108002277

Zdenek, S. (n.d.). *Accessible podcasting: College students on the margins in the new media classroom*. Retrieved December 1, 2013, from http://www.bgsu.edu/cconline/Ed_Welcome_Fall_09/compinfreewareintroduction.htm

KEY TERMS AND DEFINITIONS

Ab/Normality Construct: The ab/normality construct provides an alternative view of disability by considering elements of abnormality and normality.

Able-Body: A component of the *ableist* worldview, an able-body is an individual or collective entity whose presence is considered as being the norm. The able-body influences how disability is viewed politically, socially, and economically.

Americans with Disabilities Act Amendments Act of 2008 (ADAAA): Taking effect on January 1, 2009, the amendments emphasize that the definition of disability should be construed in favor of broad coverage of individuals to the maximum extent permitted by the terms of the ADA and should not require extensive analysis.

Medical Model of Disability: A way of seeing disability in which people with disabilities are expected to work around society. The medical model of disability considers enhancement beyond what is perceived as being anything other than having immediate physical need as gratuitous.

Normalization: The process of adapting an entity towards an existing or underlying model.

Social Model of Disability: A way of seeing disability in which society disables people, through designing everything to meet the needs of the majority of people who are not disabled.

Universal Design: A set of principles that gives all individuals sharing a common environment, like a classroom, access and equal opportunity to progress.

Chapter 12
Technic Self–Determination

Franco Cortese
Independent Researcher, Canada

ABSTRACT

This chapter addresses concerns that the development and proliferation of Human Enhancement Technologies (HET) will be (a) dehumanizing and a threat to human dignity and (b) a threat to our autonomy and sovereignty as individuals. Contrarily, HET can be shown to constitute the most effective foreseeable means of increasing the autonomy and sovereignty of individual members of society. Furthermore, this chapter elaborates the position that the use of HET exemplifies—and indeed even intensifies—our most human capacity and faculty, namely the desire for increased self-determination (i.e., control over the determining circumstances and conditions of our own selves and lives), which is referred to as the will toward self-determination. Based upon this position, arguably, the use of HET bears fundamental ontological continuity with the human condition in general and with the historically ubiquitous will toward self-determination in particular as it is today and has been in the past. HET will not be a dehumanizing force, but will rather serve to increase the very capacity and characteristic that characterizes us as human more accurately than anything else.

INTRODUCTION

The chapter first articulates an ontology of self-determination based upon self-modification and self-modulation (i.e., deliberate modification or modulation of the material processes and systems constituting our bodies and brains), characterizing self-determination as a modality (i.e., that there can be degrees of self-determination, or that it isn't an absolute, all-or-none category) that encompasses any act of manipulating the material systems and processes underlying the body and mind so as to effect certain changes to the emergent operation, function or capacities of the body or to the modes of experience, thought and perception available to the mind.

Secondly, it illustrates (1) how HET constitutes a distinct modality of self-determination, which may be referred to as technic[1] self-determination, that is encompassed by the broader ontology of self-determination previously articulated, (2) how technic self-determination nevertheless bears ontological continuity with existing and historical (predominantly non-technological) means and modalities of self-determination as practiced by contemporary and historical humans, as well as (3) why technic self-determination (and the use of HET in general and neurotechnology in particular that underlie it) constitute humanity's most effective and most extensive means of self-determination, and thus of *increasing* their available capacity for self-determination.

DOI: 10.4018/978-1-4666-6010-6.ch012

Thirdly, the chapter turns to the topic of human nature and human dignity, arguing that it is humanity's will toward self-determination that best distinguishes humans as such, and accordingly that the will toward self-determination constitutes the best available candidate for a universal human condition. The chapter concludes by arguing that technic self-determination (and the use of HET that underlies it) will not be dehumanizing because (1) HET will simply serve to increase our *existing* degree of and capacity for self-determination and (2) HET bears ontological continuity with the existing tools and techniques for affecting the substratum of self. Quite to the contrary of critics concerned with the potential for dehumanization and a violation of human dignity, technic self-determination and HET will *continuate* and extend rather than render asunder that which makes us most human.

BACKGROUND

Determinism and Self-Determination

The 'free will problem' is almost as almost old as philosophy itself. The posed problem is a fatal inconsistency between free will and causal determinism that necessitates at least one to be illegitimate or inexistent. Causal determinism can be defined as the thesis that every event is the necessary result of prior events combined with the laws of nature. If everything in the universe has been predetermined, then it would appear that free will is an illegitimate notion. On the other hand, if free will exists, then determinism must be false (because free will couldn't exist with true determinism). This notion is known as 'the dilemma of determinism.' The dilemma refers to the fact that either free will or determinism *must* be false.

There are several positions one can take in this philosophical debate. Incompatibilists accept the premises of the dilemma and argue that one must be false; most incompatibilists side with

determinism, arguing that free will must not exist. Compatibilists argue that free will and determinism are not incompatible, arguing that the dilemma of determinism is a false dilemma to begin with, and that causal determinism does not illegitimate the notion of free will.

Some compatibilists wrongly turn to determinism's antithesis, indeterminism, to solve the dilemma, positing that indeterminism, by invalidating determinism, should allow free will to legitimately exist. But we would agree with many others in arguing that this is no better than determinism. "Indeterminism does not confer freedom on us: I would feel that my freedom was impaired if I thought that a quantum mechanical trigger in my brain might cause me to leap into the garden and eat a slug" (Smart & Haldane, 2003). Joshua Greene puts this position thusly:

There are three standard responses to the problem of free will. The first, known as 'hard determinism', accepts the incompatibility of free will and determinism ('incompatibilism'), and asserts determinism, thus rejecting free will. The second response is libertarianism (again, no relation to the political philosophy), which accepts incompatibilism, but denies that determinism is true. This may seem like a promising approach. After all, has not modern physics shown us that the universe is indeterministic? The problem here is that the sort of indeterminism afforded by modern physics is not the sort the libertarian needs or desires. If it turns out that your ordering soup is completely determined by the laws of physics, the state of the universe 10,000 years ago, and the outcomes of myriad subatomic coin flips, your appetizer is no more freely chosen than before. Indeed, it is randomly chosen, which is no help to the libertarian (Greene, 2004).

The position implicit within the thesis of this paper falls within compatibility, contending that free will is not only compatible with determinism

– but that determinism is actually a *necessary precondition* for free will (which will be used synonymously in this paper with autonomy and self-determination). The dilemma of determinism is a false dilemma. During the millennia in which it was engendered and established within the Western philosophical tradition, the ability for humans to determine the parameters and conditions of the material systems and processes of their bodies and brains was severely limited. It made more sense for most of human civilization – indeed, perhaps until as little as two hundred years ago – to see free will and determinism as incompatible, when we didn't have such things as routine surgery, prosthesis, implants and other instances of significantly modifying the human body while it was still alive – i.e., of partially *determining* the material systems and processes underlying our bodies. Indeed, for the most part of the dilemma's history we didn't even have a rudimentary understanding of how our bodily systems operated. Today we not only have such an understanding (or at least one vastly better than was available for the majority of the past few thousand years), but also medicine (a means of modifying the body's systems that necessitates a good understanding of the body's underlying operational mechanisms), routine surgery, transplants, implants, and other intuitively-apprehensible examples of modifying the body's underlying systems and processes to as to effect targeted changes to their structure or operation – in other words of determining the determining condition of the material systems and processes underlying our bodies and brains. Indeed, today we even have a diverse set of psychopharmacological agents able to enact specific changes to our own *phenomenal*[2] *experience* (i.e., thought, perception). Today we have tools for making targeted (i.e., predictable) changes to not only our own bodies, but our brains and *minds* as well.

If such means of partial determination (and thus of partial *self*-determination) were available during the millennia in which the seeming incompatibility between free will and causal determinism became entrenched within the Western philosophical tradition, then it is likely that the dilemma of determinism wouldn't have posed such an unquestionable affront to the ontic legitimacy of our autonomy and agency.

Neurotechnology in general, and neuromodulation in particular, poses the potential to vastly increase the precision and extent of our existing capacity for self-determination, and constitutes the apex of the other means of technic self-determination mentioned above (e.g., medicine). It is these and other means of enacting changes to the physical processes and systems of our bodies and minds that render obvious the fumbled foundation underlying the dilemma of determinism.

Human Enhancement Technology and Neurotechnology

Human Enhancement Technology (HET) is typically defined as any technological attempt to overcome or obviate the biological limitations of the human body and brain or extend the capacities and faculties of the human body and brain beyond their normative range of capacities and faculties. HET encompasses a broad range of technological domains (i.e., types of technology), but the term is often used synonymously with NBIC (Nano-Bio-Info-Cogno) technologies because these four technological domains encompass the large majority of contemporary and conceptualized HET. However, NBIC technologies have a wide range of applications beyond their use on the human body, and so in the strictest sense should not be synonymized with HET.

While the notion of technic self-determination articulated in this paper encompasses the use of HET on the body, some emphasis will be placed upon neurotechnology because it constitutes one of the most extensive and exemplary means of technic self-determination as outlined in this chapter.

Neurotechnology[3] encompasses any technology used to directly modify or modulate the structure or activity of the brain. Some definitions also encompass technologies that give us better insight into the operation of the brain, such as neuroimaging technologies, but within the context of the paper it will refer exclusively to technologies for the modification and modulation of neural activity and structure.

A more precise definition of neurotechnology is given by the University of Freiburg:

- Technical and computational tools that measure and analyze chemical and electrical signals in the nervous system, be it the brain or nerves in the limbs. These may be used to identify the properties of nervous activity, understand how the brain works, diagnose pathological conditions, or control external devices (neuroprostheses, 'brain machine interfaces'); and
- Technical tools to interact with the nervous system to change its activity, for example to restore sensory input such as with cochlea implants to restore hearing or deep brain stimulation to stop tremor and treat other pathological conditions" (Geelen, 2012).

Neurotechnology thus encompasses any technological means of stimulating the brain, modulating the brain, interfacing technology with the brain (e.g., brain-computer interfacing) and/or replacing any portion of the brain with a functional prosthetic. The scope of the present chapter will give comparative emphasis to the subdomain of neurotechnology known as neuromodulation. However, it is important to note that other subdomains of neurotechnology can also constitute an instance and means of technic self-determination. For instance, the sub-domain of neuroprosthesis (and indeed even non-biomimetic brain computer interfaces) could be used to augment one's own neural activity via the replacement of existing portions of the brain with systems possessing alternate functional modalities than the portion(s) being replaced (as in neuroprosthesis) or by the addition of systems possessing alternate functional modalities than the human brain normally possesses (as in both neuroprosthetic and brain computer interfacing). However, the role of neurotechnology as a means of technic self-determination – i.e., as a means of inducing and modulating one's own neural activity (Fetz, 2007) – is given comparative emphasis because it serves to illustrate the ontology of self-determination articulated in this chapter better than other instances of neurotechnology-mediated technic self-determination, and because it constitutes one of the most extensive and arguably the most effective means of technic self-determination.

Neuromodulation has been achieved pharmacologically, magnetically, electrically and ontogenetically[4]. Continuing advances in the field of nanoelectronics, brain computer interfacing and neurobiology will only work to increase the precision, control and reliability of our available means of neuromodulation. This trend will culminate in the controllable, differential induction and modulation of neural activity at the scale of single neurons, integrated so as to modulate the coordinated activity of whole populations of neurons. It is conceivable that user-interfaces operatively-connected to a means of neuromodulation will allow users to modulate their own neuronal activity, thereby allowing them to modulate their emergent functional capacities and faculties, as well as their experiential or phenomenal modalities (i.e., thought and perception). The dynamic neural correlates of a given experience could conceivably be recorded by extensive, neuron-level brain scanning technology so as to record the pattern of neural induction of a given experience. A database of such recordings could be kept such that, through the use of neuromodulatory user-interfaces as described above, a given agent could induce previously-recorded patterns of neural activity correlating with a given phenomenal (i.e., subjectively-perceivable) experience, the specificity of which is a function of the resolution of available brain-scanning technology. Though due to the unique wiring (i.e., synaptic profile, or organizational structure on the scale of neurons) possessed by each brain, the ability to transfer such patterns of neural induction to a different mind than the one it was initially recorded in will be limited to the degree of similarity between the two brains on the scale of induction (i.e., so if the modulation of single neurons was incurred, the scale of induction would be the scale of single neurons). This is advantageous for the thesis and conclusions of the present chapter, because this biases the use of such patterns pf neural induction by agents upon others, for the purposes of modulating another agent's brain rather than one's own. In other words, these consideration bias the use of specific patterns of neural induction (actuated by a sufficiently-precise means of neuromodulation) toward being used by agents upon themselves as a means of technic self-determination, rather than upon other minds as a means of determining other minds.

We have been modulating our own minds by varying degrees, both intentionally and non-intentionally, for all of human history. Certain historical technological and techniques, like meditation and psychopharmacological drugs, have allowed us to do so more precisely and more extensively. And through continuing developments in neurotechnology in general and neuromodulation in particular, tomorrow may yield yet another tangible increase in the scope and scale of our capacity to manipulate the activity of our own brains and minds. This, we argue, could constitute the most extensive means of not only technic self-determination but of self-determination in general yet seen by human history, and one that will serve to explicate why self-determination has never been incompatible with self-determination.

Neurotechnology and the "Dilemma of Determinism"

Decades of development in neurotechnology and its underlying technological and methodological base present new possibilities and capabilities that pose new questions and challenges to the "dilemma of determinism" and the freewill-determinism debate in general. However, the field of neuroethics has given a much greater emphasis to the extent with which the newfound ability to modify and modulate our own or others' neural activity could endanger human self-determination and the freedom and autonomy of the individual. A prominent example of this position is the possibility that neurotechnology could be used to violate the autonomy of others by giving agents (or agency, e.g., government, military, industry) the capacity to manipulate – modify or modulate – the neural activity of others.

Meanwhile, the field of neurolaw has given emphasis to the legal implications of neurotechnology, such as the implications of neuroimaging and its potential to be used as a lie-detector with sufficient accuracy and reliability to justify its use during court testimony; or, of advances in our understanding of neural activity and the ethical ramifications posed by the possibility of discovering neural correlates for criminal tendencies. The field has given comparatively less emphasis to the legal ramifications of the capacity to modulate one's own neural activity through a sufficiently-precise means of neuromodulation.

Similarly, the emerging field of neurosecurity has also addressed neurotechnology in the context of autonomy, freewill and self-determination, particularly in the context of the extent with which means of neuromodulation could be used to facilitate mind-control by government, military and industry. The comparatively greater emphasis given to the ethical, legal and philosophical concerns of neurotechnology's use as a means of controlling the other or infringing upon the privacy of the other in the fields of neuroethics, neurolaw and neurosecurity have helped to emphasize the dangers of neurotechnology in the public eye and popular mind rather than the potential benefits. But as we will argue, the use of neuromodulation upon one's own self has the potential to constitute one of the most extensive and effective means of self-determination available to us, and as such, the field of neurotechnology holds at least as much potential to increase people's capacity for self-determination as it has potential to decrease people's capacity for self-determination.

THE WILL TOWARD SELF-DETERMINATION

In this section, I articulate an ontology of self-determination, of which technic self-determination is a subset which identifies self-modification and self-modulation as the ontological fundament of self-determination, and the heart of the ontology of self-determination articulated in this chapter.

Self-Determination Necessitates Determinism

Self-determination as self-modification and self-modulation is not in contradiction with determinism. Indeed, determinism is actually *necessary* to the particular ontology of self-determination articulated in the present paper. If there were a high degree of indeterminacy in the processes and material systems constituting our minds and bodies, then there would be no reliable method of making specific changes to such material processes and systems in order to achieve specific modifications to the operation or capacities of those material processes and systems – i.e., no way of implementing a series of changes to the operation or constitution of the mind or body whose outcome can be confidently estimated or predicted. This applies to our actions in the external world as well: if there were no way of translating an objectified goal into a series of actions able

to achieve that goal, as would be the case in any sufficiently-indeterministic process, then our capacity to shape the world – i.e., physical environments, laws, social customs and infrastructure – according to our own desires, values and ideals would be severely curtailed.

We argue contrarily to incompatibilists that the fact that humans lack conscious control over the circumstances of our own births, i.e., of the parameters defining our genetics or our environments, does *not* evidence the illegitimacy of self-determination. It is true we did not decide ourselves, consciously and volitionally, to come into existence. But if a material system is made through the deterministic actions of other, external material processes and systems *so as to be* self-determining (by whatever degree) thereafter, then this, we contend, is enough to legitimately characterize it as a system of partial self-determination. Indeed, we hold that any legitimate ontological schema of self-determination *must* concede that no self-determining system can be *absolutely* self-determining (i.e., to the point of having determined its own birth or initial creation), as such would constitute a temporal tautology. There is no such thing as absolute self-determination; there are only degrees of self-determination.

Humans come into existence through no choice of their own, and increasing degrees of autonomy are demonstrated to and bestowed upon us as we are reared and educated with the general aim of making us as autonomous and independent – i.e., as self-determining – as we can be.

Once one accepts that 'true' self-determination does not necessitate that one determines all the determining conditions of themselves to the point of and even preceding birth, then one if forced to recognize that self-determination is a modality rather than an absolute or all-or-nothing category. This effectively obviates the largest barrier to seeing partial determinations of the material and procedural conditions underlying our bodies and minds as veritable acts of self-determination.

Self-Modification and Modulation as the Ontological Fundament of Self-Determination

There is a distinction to be made between self-modulation and self-modification. Self-modification corresponds to the act of adding to, removing, or rearranging the constitutive material processes and systems of our minds and bodies. Thus the addition of artificial neural networks to the existing biological brain, or changing the wiring of our connectomes (i.e., the pattern of synaptic connection in our brain, which to a large extent define who we are and distinguish us from one another as persons with distinct skills, knowledge, behavioral-inclinations and memories); the deletion of an existing neural sub-system (e.g., network, cluster, emergent neural circuit); and, the addition of cochlear implants that expand the range of frequencies one can hear, would all constitute variations of self-modification.

By contrast, self-modulation corresponds with (varying degrees of) conscious control over the procedural steps constituting the activity of the material systems and processes constituting one's body and brain, or of the various parameters defining the material systems constituting their body and brain (e.g., stimulating a specific series of neurons at specific time intervals so as to externally-induce a specific pattern of synaptic firing – in other words external control over the neural activist constituting and determining one's own phenomenal, i.e., subjective, experience).

Self-modification involves actually changing the capabilities (or more precisely the "system states") of the material systems constituting one's mind and/or body, whereas self-modulation involves controlling or consciously manipulating (i.e., modulating) the *existing* abilities or "system states" of the material systems constituting one's mind and/or body. "Playing" a memory by inducing a specific sequence of action potentials in specific neurons (i.e., controlling the sequence of synaptic connections made during a chunk of neural activity) would be an instance of self-

modulation, whereas changing the neural connections encoding or determining the parameters of a given memory so as to remove or alter the memory, on the other hand, would be an instance of self-modification. Adding new genes to one's genome would be an instance of self-modification, while consciously modulating the expression of existing genes so as to alter one's resultant phenotype would be an instance of self-modulation. Directly controlling the levels of various hormones in one's circulatory system would be an instance of self-modulation, while removing the presence of a given hormone completely would be an instance of self-modification.

ESSENCE AS DISSENT[5]

This section will outline a taxonomy for the various modalities of self-determination encompassed by the ontological schema of self-determination articulated above, and analyze it against the background of humanity's existing and historical modalities and means of self-determination, ultimately demonstrating ontological continuity between technic self-determination via HET and neurotechnology, on the one hand, and the largely-non-technological means and modalities of self-determination practiced by society today and in the past, on the other. Demonstrating such continuity elaborates the position that HET in general and neurotechnologies in particular are a vital and necessary step on the path to *staying* human, rather than a potential source of dehumanization, and that they both exemplify and have the potential to *increase* and *intensify* the very feature that designates us better than any other as human: namely our will toward self-determination.

To Have a Bod Is to Mod

Humans have modified themselves by varying degrees since the inception of recorded culture. While we argue that humans' inclination toward and desire for increased self-determination is the feature that most distinguishes us as humans (and that underlies the desire to change our *selves*, our communities, our societies and our world for the better – a desire ubiquitous throughout time and geography), it does not necessarily constitute an ontological break from the animals we are evolutionarily derived from. It distinguishes us from animals as a matter of not category but degree – that is, we are the only animal to have made a *deliberate* effort to increase our own degree of self-determination, and it is that metaconditional consideration that marks us starker than anything else as human, and not the act or fact of being, like most other animals, partially self-determining. Every living system is to some extent self-modifying, insofar as they attempt to change or utilize their environments in specific ways impacting their own existence. Self-determination could arguably even be traced all the way down to the ever-present survival instinct itself. If an organism performs a series of actions with the aim of living instead of dying, then they are making actions meant to directly affect the defining conditions of their existence – in this case whether they exist or not.

But that a series of actions, perceptions of thoughts leads to a change in the wiring of our brains, thus constituting an instance of self-modification, does not necessitate that it also constitute an instance of self-determination. The categorical differentiator here is that for it to constitute an instance of self-determination, an instance of self-modification must be conscious – i.e., must be made with the *intent* of modifying oneself (which is synonymous with modifying the way one acts in the future). Thus whereas passive perception would not constitute an instance of self-determination (ignoring the extent with which we modulate, or consciously direct, our perception, for instance by choosing where we look or our point of focus), a series of thoughts in which one evaluates past decisions, reflecting upon what one wants to have accomplished in X years, and decides that they want to consciously make an effort to be

more X (focused, patient, knowledgeable, etc.), *would* be an instance of self-modification that also constitutes self-determination.

Methodological Self-Determination: Autogenic Thoughts Steer Morphogenic Knots

One of the ways in which humans – and organisms in general – change the wiring of their brains is in response to thought and perception. Due to the fact that the activity of neurons is impacted by their past *history* of activity (e.g., the more frequently neurons that make synaptic connection with one another, the more likely they will be to make synaptic connection with one another in future, which is the source of the idiom "neurons that fire together wire together"), any neural activity involving the synaptic or ephaptic connection between neurons has the potential to affect future neural activity. For this reason, perception and thought constitute a modality of self-determination in and of themselves, insofar as they can facilitate changes to the material systems and processes underlying our brains, thereby facilitating the modification of our emergent intellectual and experiential capacities and faculties constituted thereby.

Perception

One likely anticipated criticism is the notion that, unlike thought, which is internal to the self, perception would fail to constitute a modality or means of self-determination because it is initiated from systems and processes external to the self. But this fails to take account of (1) the ways in which our sensory organs process, filter and otherwise-modify our raw sensory data, (2) internal sensory modalities like proprioception that sense conditions internal to the body, (3) the ways in which we can actively modulate our perception through the modulation of bodily-activity (e.g., by deciding where to turn our heads, or where to focus our eyes within a given point of view, or walking to a different physical environment, or closing one's eyes), (4) the ways in which we can actively modulate our perception through the changes made to one's immediate environment (e.g., putting on a film or song to induce a specific sequence of perception) and (5) the ways in which we can internally invoke sensory modalities normally focused on the outward environment (e.g., sight and sound) by internally inducing sensory impressions, as used in dreaming and in what we colloquially refer to as acts of "imagination".

Our non-technological (i.e., methodological) ability to control or self-modulate (1) and (2) are rather limited. But our ability to methodologically affect our categories (3)–(5), which can be affected or "modulated" by thought, is by contrast rather extensive. We can be driven by a series of thoughts to change one's environment (through physically moving to another location or by, say, putting on some form of media in one's proximal physical environment). It is this capacity for thought to affect and modulate these externally-initiated perceptual events that distinguishes perception as a means of self-determination.

Moreover, the line between thought and perception is indistinct and, arguably, more a pragmatic tool than a real ontological truth as-such. When we think on a conscious level, we employ sensory impressions to convey or "embody" the informational substrata of our thoughts – whether via the use of visualizing a process being articulated through time or the relative organization of components and/or sequences of events, or via the explicit use of words (i.e., "thinking in sentences").

Thus to characterize thought as a modality of self-determination without also categorizing perception as being encompassed by that modality of self-determination would be to implicitly reify the claim that thought and perception are distinct processes without interplay or intertwine.

Thought

Thought itself has a determining impact on other thoughts. The history of activity in a given neural network, cluster or emergent neural circuit will impact its present and future activity. For this reason act of thought can constitute a modality of self-determination because it can be used as a means of changing the determining conditions of our minds, which have a much larger determining impact on our available experiential modalities and our available capacities and faculties than do the determining conditions of our non-cognitive bodily systems.

The predominant theory of memory in neurology is the neural activation theory – that when we imagine or recall performing a certain action, perceiving a certain perception or thinking a certain thought, the same neurons and neural connections activated during the doing are the same neurons and neural connections being activated during the recalling, perceiving or thinking. When we think about walking up stairs, the same motor neurons that would be activated during a walk up the stairs are activated; the same neurons fire, just at a lower magnitude. An analogous mechanism is thought to underlie mirror neurons as well; when I perceive another agent picking up an object, the same neurons that would be activated if *I* were picking up the object are activated.

This demonstrates that it is possible to deliberatively and methodologically change the organization of our own brains via deliberative activities made through our brains. Deliberative acts of learning and memorizing are a very good intuitive example of this. We repeat a given line of thought (or facts, or association between two or more facts) over until it seems to "come on its own". The increased ease we feel in recalling a given line of thought, conclusion or notion is the phenomenal correlate of an increased synaptic weighting between the neurons repeatedly activated concomitantly during the "learning" or "repeated recall" session.

Other instances that are less obviously deliberative acts of repeating certain neural activities are also encompassed by this modality of self-determination. When we read in order to acquire knowledge or new information, we implicitly understand that by reading a given book and thinking about it, we will encode that information into the neural activities (or structures) constituting our minds. The fact that we do not consciously correlate the act of newly acquired knowledge with newly acquired changes to one's neural activities or connections – i.e., that we associate it with the phenomenal result (the ability to recall something one couldn't before) rather than with the physical result underlying that phenomenal result – does not obviate the fact that we are still nonetheless *deliberatively* changing our own neural activity through the deliberative activation of our own neural activity.

Let us refer to the modality of self-determination that encompasses the ways in which thought and perception can be utilized to effect changes to the determining conditions of our minds (i.e., our phenomenal experience) as *methodological* self-determination, both to contrast it with technic self-determination (thereby distinguishing it therefrom) and to emphasize its non-physical nature (i.e., the fact that we effect changes and subsequently feel such effected changes phenomenally, rather than as say a quantitative increase in synaptic connections between certain neurons – even though that is what it physically correlates with).

Reciprocal Self-Determination: Essence, Embodiment, Environment

Humanity's most effective and predominantly-utilized means of self-modification thus-far, besides methodological self-determination, has been *reciprocal causation* – i.e., changes made to one's external environment that result in subsequent changes to the material systems and processes constituting one's body and mind. When such reciprocal causation is done in a way that is deliberately meant to (i.e., expected to) directly affect the physical parameters determining one's material and/or phenomenal existence, it constitutes what will be called *reciprocal self-determination*.

An illustrative instance of reciprocal self-determination would be the act of turning on the fireplace in order to manipulate or affect the physical parameters of one's body (e.g., body temperature) and of one's phenomenal experience (e.g., initiating a series of actions leading to the perception of warmth). This process is referred to as reciprocal causation to denote the *recursive* fashion in which the actions of an agent are directed outward in such a way as to feedback with the agent that initiated the actions, via causal connection between the material systems constituting the agent and those constituting their environment.

A more intuitively-apprehensible example would be dimming the lights in manipulate one's mood or phenomenal experience. In such a case one would be changing environmental conditions known to directly affect his or her phenomenal experience. An even more precise instance of reciprocal self-determination is the deliberate act of perceiving some form of media – e.g., a song or movie – in order to induce a specific series of perceptions and emotions, i.e., a specific phenomenal experience (either because we remember such media doing so in the past or because we have been told that it would by someone who *has* viewed it). Note here that just as there can be differential degrees of self-determination in general (i.e., it is a broader modality rather than an absolute, all-or-nothing category), there can be differential degrees of self-determination in different instances of a particular modality of self-determination. In this case, certain instances of reciprocal self-determination (e.g., putting on media) effect more precise changes to one's perceptual experience than another instance of reciprocal self-determination (e.g., dimming the lights to manipulate one's mood).

Prosthetic Essence: The Co-Constitution of Man and Techné

Moreover, the constitution of one's environment has a large impact on what an agent is able to do. For instance, the possible actions available to a human living in a contemporary city are very different than the possible actions available to a human living in a prehistoric environment, and those discrepancies derive more than anything else from the differences in the conditions of their external environments, because genetically speaking we remain largely equivalent to prehistoric human.

Thus modifications to one's environment that *do not* result in subsequent changes to the material systems and processes of the initiating-agent can also be argued to constitute a means and modality of self-determination. An articulated series of modifications to the environment (i.e., physical objects and resources) that result in the addition of new capacities and abilities, e.g., the construction of a new tool or device, can also be legitimately characterized as an act of self-determination in that it affects (i.e., partly determines) the available capacities of the agent in targeted ways.

The developmental progression of humans from birth onward involves interaction and interplay between both nature and nurture, determined by both our genetic as well as epigenetic constitution. The environment (e.g., historical period, geographic location) we are born into will have a large determining impact on the range and extents of our capacities and faculties. Born today, we have the capacity to cross an ocean in a matter of hours; born a few hundred years ago, and one would have the capacity to cross an ocean in a matter of months. The technologies and techniques we develop extend our capacities and faculties – they open up new positive freedoms (i.e., freedom *to* do something, as opposed to freedom *from* some external force or circumstance) for us.

Moreover, technology is increasingly becoming our *predominant* means of effecting change. "Technology is man's foremost mediator of change; it is by and large through the use of technology that we expand the parameters of the possible" (Cortese, 2013a). Most every technology can be characterized as a new configuration or arrangement of existing technologies. This can also be true for technologies that aren't obviously an emergent system comprised of distinct subsystems; a new paradigm of technology is built upon the preceding paradigm of technology, which then becomes the technological and methodological infrastructure or fundament underlying the new technological paradigm. This seemingly-anecdotal fact – that technologies are build out of other existing technologies – leads to the non-anecdotal conclusion that the potential for technological development is continuously growing, because the underlying base of technologies that can be used and combined to create any given new technology is continuously growing. Thus our capacity to effect change in the world has been increasingly biased towards the use of technology rather than methodology, because the capacity for technology to foster new faculties and capacities has been increasing, while our methodological infrastructure increases at a comparatively slower rate. The fact that technology now constitutes our predominant means of affectation reifies the argument that technologies, insofar as they partly determine our faculties and capabilities, can legitimately be considered to co-constitute 'the human.' And that both technology and methodology constitute a means of determining the conditions of the self means that technic self-determination shares continuity-of-impetus and continuity-of-fundament with methodological self-determination. To think that the most essential characteristic of each modality is the way in which they effect change, rather than the fact that they can both be used to affect change in general, would be "miss the end for the means and the mark for a lark. The point is that we are trying to consciously improve the state of self, society and world; technology has simply superseded methodology as the most optimal means of accomplishing that, and now constitutes our best means of effecting our affectation" (Cortese, 2013b). As will be demonstrated in a later section, this continuity-of-impetus between technic self-determination and methodological self-determination also helps to illegitimate the claim that the proliferation and use of HET will be dehumanizing and/or an affront to out 'human dignity.'

Thus, another way in which changes made to one's environment can be seen to constitute an act of self-determination is through a view of personhood that encompasses one's environment (in addition to the material systems constituting one's mind and body as such) as belonging to or co-constituting one's self.

Of relevance to this view of selfhood is the 'extended cognition thesis' (Clark, 1998, 2008). The extended cognition thesis posits "an active externalism, based on the active role of the environment in driving cognitive processes" (Chalmers & Clark, 1998), contending that any tools actively used by a mind, and that play an integral role in the activities of that mind, should be recognized as partly constituting that mind; in other words that the mind and its tools are co-constitutive. Views of personhood characterizing the mind as a single, distinct and definitive system causally insulated from the tools it uses and the environment it acts within fail to account for the ways in which our tools play an active part in our cognitive processes.

Within the bounds of the extended cognition view of personhood, changes made by an agent to their environment that afforded them new capabilities or experiential (e.g., metal, perceptual) modalities, insofar as such an environment partly constitutes that agent and impacts the range and extents of his capacities and faculties, would qualify as an instance of self-modification or self-modulation, and thus as an instance of self-determination. This is distinct but highly similar to the above case, wherein an agent's environment is considered co-constitutive because an agent's environment impacts his or her available capacities and faculties. The extended cognition thesis posits a level of co-constitution even more

integral than was articulated in the preceding context, because in the extended cognition thesis, tools play an active and integral role in *existing* cognitive processes (rather than merely fostering new positive freedoms in the creation of new capacities and faculties or the extension of existing capacities or faculties).

A third distinct-but-convergent view on the co-constitutive relationship between humans and their technologies, tools and techniques concerns itself with the ways in which certain technologies are extensions of the mind, the senses, or another human body-part or faculty (Brey, 2000; Lawson, 2010). These views would characterize the mass communications network facilitated by the telephone, the television and now the Internet as extensions of the senses and vehicles as extensions of our capacity to move or travel. The most well-known figure to have espoused this view is Marshal McLuhan (1966, 1988), who is commonly credited with contending that media are an extension of the senses and the mind:

During the mechanical ages we had extended our bodies in space. Today, after more than a century of electric technology, we have extended our central nervous system itself in a global embrace, abolishing both space and time as far as our planet is concerned. Rapidly, we approach the final phase of the extensions of man - the technological simulation of consciousness, when the creative process of knowing will be collectively and corporately extended to the whole of human society, much as we have already extended our senses and our nerves by the various media. (McLuhan, 1966, p. 19).

Indeed, McLuhan even went so far as to contend (much in the spirit of the extended cognition thesis) that media are extensions not only of the senses (which many consider to be passive faculties) but also extensions of the mind itself. "It is a persistent theme of this book that all technologies are extensions of our physical and nervous system to increase power and speed" (McLuhan, 1966, p. 91). He distinguishes technologies by the domain or faculty they extend. Mechanical technologies constitute extension of the body: "What makes a mechanism is the separation and extension of separate parts of our body as hand, arm, foot, in pen, hammer, wheel. And the mechanization of a task is done by segmentation of each part of an action in a series of uniform, repeatable, and movable parts" (1966, p. 218). Communications technologies constitute extensions of the senses; the telephone and radio correspond to sound, visual media like television, writing and print are extensions of sight. And a subset of electronic communications technologies characterized most aptly by the computer constitutes an extension of our mental faculties and capacities: "[Man is] an organism that now wears its brain outside its skull and its nerves outside its hide" (1966, p. 64). McLuhan also argues that such technologies constitute our most effective and also our most predominant means of extending human capacities and faculties. "Again, unless there were such increases of power and speed, new extensions of ourselves would not occur or would be discarded." (1966, p. 91).

Within the context of this view, the deliberative use of technologies to extend the human body and/or mind would constitute a means of self-determination insofar as such technologies are viable extensions (i.e., parts) of the human body and mind.

These three views of the symbiotic and co-constitutive relationship between humans and their technologies, tools and techniques, while distinct from one another, each reify the argument that our environments, and especially our epigenetic environments (of which are technological environment is a subset), form part of the overall determining conditions of our selves. Thus all three views allow for the characterization of technology as means of self-determination.

It is worth noting here, somewhat anecdotally, that these three views of the co-constitutive relationship humans have with their techné would

effectively characterize all technologies that are encompassed by the respective conditions of each view (e.g., for the first view, technologies that add new capacities or expand existing capacities and faculties; for the second view, technologies that play an integral role in our cognitive processes; for the third view, technologies that extend our bodies, senses and minds) as human enhancement technologies, here defining HET as any technology integrated with the human mind or body for the purposes of changing the capacities and faculties of the human mind or body. While this paper will limit its use of the term 'HET' to its normative meaning (for purposes of clarity and consistency), we also acknowledge that within the context of the above views on human-technology co-constitution, the distinction between HET and normal technology is ambiguous at best, and possibly illegitimate to begin with at worst. Furthermore, this ambiguity works to reify the argument, outlined in a later section, that the use and proliferation of HET are not dehumanizing and a threat to human dignity any more than the use of automobiles or antibiotics are. If technology as general category can be considered as an extension of or integral addition to existing human capacities or faculties, then we have been immersed in HET since the very inception of culture.

This modality of self-determination (which encompasses all three of the above views on human-technology-co-constitution) is distinct from reciprocal self-determination as outlined in the preceding section. As such, we may refer to it as *prosthetic self-determination*, in which the normative, (i.e., physically-external) tools, techniques and technologies used by an agent is seen to co-constitute the agent (insofar as our capacities and faculties are among our distinguishing or 'defining' characteristic, and insofar as the techniques and technologies we have available to us is a large factor determining the type and extents of our capacities and faculties). Within the context of this modality of self-determination, changes made to or through technology are accordingly characterized as self-directed changes (i.e., instances of self-determination) made to the agent's constitutive sub-systems. We refer to this modality of self-determination as *prosthetic* self-determination because the view of personhood that underlies it characterizes technology as having an ontologically symbiotic or co-constitutive relationship to humans, and as such would characterize all technology of that sort as fundamentally prosthetic, despite the fact that they are at times extensions of our existing functional capacities, faculties and modalities, rather than the restoration of a lost or diminished functional capacity, faculty or modality.

The ancient Greek notion of *techné*[6] is of some relevance to this discussion. Rather than unambiguously distinguishing between technique and technology, the ancient Greeks used the notion of techné (most often translated as "craftsmanship," "craft," or "art"), which encompasses both technology *and* technique. Techné meant in the simplest sense a 'way of doing,' and thus encompassed everything from art to technology. Both the tool and the way in which it was operated were equally considered techné to the ancient Greeks.

The notion that technique and thought – works of the mind – is a viable and vital part of the human condition is met with much less resistance than the notion that technology is, perhaps merely because technique and methodology cannot be physically separated from the mind (except when it is embodied in technology), and could not continue existing if all humans went extinct tomorrow – neither of which are the case with technology, which could do both. The Greek notion of techné reifies the above positions pertaining to the co-constitutive relationship humans have with their technology because it shows that a clean and clear distinction between technology and technique, tool and thought, or device and mind is neither necessary nor more appropriate than avoiding such a distinction.

And indeed, one could make the case that the distinction between technology and technique *is* in fact illegitimate, in that technology and technique are themselves co-constitutive in relation to each other. Every technology either employs or implicitly embodies technique (e.g., if it performs a technique previously performed by humans, as in the case of a computer; if there is a technique to its use, in the case of any manually-operated technology, as in the case of a crossbow; if there is a technique underlying its manufacture or construction, as in the case of most every technology). Similarly, many techniques either (a) involve the use of tools or technologies (as in the case of any technique for sewing, which requires a needle, or contemporary techniques of weather forecasting, which require meteorological instrumentation) or (b) couldn't have been formulated without the use of technologies (e.g., information or data involved in the use of the technique may have required scientific instruments to initially obtain and verify them). Thus many (if not all) technologies either use or embody techniques, and many techniques employ technologies or required underlying technologies for their initial formulation. Writing can be considered as technique – but without the technological infrastructure of (a) something to write with and (b) something to write on, one would be hard-pressed to employ it. We build upon this interplay between technology and technique recursively, using available techniques in our newest technologies and available technologies in our newest techniques.

Technic Self-Determination

Reciprocal self-determination and methodological self-determination constitute, by and large, rather indirect ways of making changes to the material systems and processes constituting our minds and bodies. In these modalities of self-determination, we must rely on the probabilistic tendency for certain actions or processes to change the material systems and processes comprising our bodies and brains; for instance the strengthening of synaptic connections between neurons activated concomitantly during a given physical routine, thought or memory. Technic self-determination, by contrast, would allow us to *directly* affect our underlying bodily and mental parameters, without having to invoke the methodological repetition of a routine in order to effect such changes.

Nevertheless, reciprocal self-determination and methodological self-determination have been for most of human history our most effective means and medium of self-determination. For instance, when we repeat actions or procedures we gradually gain the capacity to perform them with less and less conscious effort. This is due to several neurological mechanisms that strengthen the synaptic weighting between neurons making synaptic connection with each other frequently during same activity, thought-association or memory; neurons that 'fire together' during a given activity, thought-association or memory are more likely to do so when the same activity, thought-association or memory occurs in future, while neurons that 'fire together' less frequently will be accordingly less likely to 'fire together' in future .

In order to improve our fidelity in a given skill, we typically practice performing the skill repeatedly so as to facilitate the sequence of strong synaptic-connections that correspond with proficiency in a given skill (i.e., physical or mental operation). Likewise, to increase the probability of remembering something (or put another way, to increase the strength of a given memory), we typically repeat the information in some perceptual form (e.g., as words) until it can be recalled with less conscious effort, and/or associate it with a higher number of existing concepts or memories (i.e., increasing the number of strengthened synaptic connections rather than the strength of existing connections per-se).

But if we had a means of directly modifying the synaptic weighing between neurons, or the connections between existing neurons and neutral networks, then we could facilitate changes to our behavioral-inclinations, memories, skillsets, etc. (essentially any modality encompassed by the material systems and processes of our bodies and brains) much more quickly and readily (e.g., without having to make the neurons fire together

a number of times manually in order to increase, or more precisely to modify, their weighting), and with vastly greater precision.

The same applies for modifications involving the addition of neurons (neurogenesis) or the addition of synaptic connections to existing neurons (synaptogenesis), which we will refer to as additive modifications, as opposed to subtractive modifications (i.e., the removal or a certain neural structure) and reorganizational modifications (i.e., the rearrangement of integral components in the brain, or rearrangement of the procedural systems in material processes of the brain. Currently, methodological self-determination allows us to practice routines known to correlate with neurogenesis and synaptogenesis, like exercise and a healthy diet. Certain varieties of neuromodification farther out on the developmental horizon could facilitate the addition and integration of new neurons and the addition of new synaptic connections to existing neurons directly, bypassing the need for the repetition of certain practices that is incurred by methodological self-determination. Genetic engineering applied to the brain could utilize the brains endogenous mechanisms for neurogenesis and synaptogenesis. This would include the use of growth factors correlating with synaptogenesis, in-vivo gene modification to selectively up-regulate neuron growth-factors promoting synaptogenesis in certain neurons and not others, and the direct transplantation (or targeted migration) of pluripotent cells (such as induced pluripotent stem cells, or iPSCs) cells to the central-nervous-system. Farther out on the developmental horizon, continuing progress in nanobiotechnology, nanomedicine and nanoneurotechnology could allow for the addition and integration of non-biological (i.e., nanotechnological or computationally-emulated) neurons functionally equivalent to biological neurons and interacting with them in their own language (i.e., via electrical and chemical synaptic connections and ephaptic connection). Both shorter-future and farther-future embodiments of neurotechnology constitute a means of directly facilitating additive neuromodification without the need for the methodological repetition involved in methodological self-determination. Furthermore, they can also allow us to make additive neuromodifications that are simply not possible via methodological self-determination (i.e., in this case, by exercising more or changing one's diet), as well as at a rate disallowed by the body's endogenous neurogenic and synaptogenic mechanisms.

It is important to note that the term 'technic self-determination' denotes both the use of HET applied to the body and neurotechnology applied to the brain. We can taxonomically distinguish between the two by referring to the self-directed use of neurotechnology as *neurotechnic self-determination*, and referring to the integration of HET on the body as *somatotechnic self-determination*, recognizing both as subsets encompassed by the larger category of *technic self-determination*. However, for the most part let us refer to both subsets as technic self-determination, recognizing that the emphasis is on neurotechnologies (simply because the conditions and parameters of the material systems and processes underlying our brains have a much larger determining impact on our overall capacities and faculties than the conditions and parameters of those underlying the rest of our bodies, and thus because neurotechnology has a greater capacity for self-determination than HET applied to the body) and that 'HET' as employed in the present paper encompasses both neurotechnology and 'somatic technology.'

HET constitutes but a vastly-better means to the same end humanity has had in mind since the very start. HET is not a break from normality or from humanity. Humans have been partially self-determining since our first dawn in Sumer and on. HET in general and neurotech in particular are but the modern-most tools we have on-hand for doing what we've always done – that is, considering who, what, how and why we want to be, and overcoming ourselves in a fit of becoming toward the projected objective of what it might be better to be(come) instead.

Thus, the use of HET does not constitute a disconnect from our most human ways of seeing and being; on the contrary, HET bear fundamental continuity with the other modalities of self-determination that humans have practiced for millennia, in that both constitute a means of using our own thoughts and actions so as to partly determine the determining conditions of our *possible* thoughts and actions (i.e., capacities and faculties).

It is only when we as humans *halt* our upward-mission and forward-march to increase our own degree of self-determination through increasingly precise and extensive tools for shaping self, society and landscape that we lose any part or parcel of our humanity. HET, if used to increase the control we have over the determining conditions of our *own* selves, rather than over each other, can only serve to make us more human by increasing and intensifying the very aspect that makes us human more than anything else – our incessant essence to make our own, to defy and retry, to continually better-determine ourselves – ultimately, to be by becoming instead.

Homo-Autopoietic

The will toward self-determination has been at the heart of the human since the very inception of culture. Indeed, as argued here, the will-toward self-determination is either embodied by, exemplified by, or implicit in many contemporary and historical cultural practices and beliefs.

Democracy exemplifies our will toward self-determination on the societal level. We seek to determine the laws we live under ourselves, rather than have an arbitrary monarch or despot do the deciding. Moreover, we want to reserve the right to continually change our minds, to reserve the ability to *redecide* in future. This exemplifies the progressive nature of the will *toward* self-determination, and our desire for successively-*increasing* degrees of self-determination.

The enlightenment tradition, characterized by the use of rationality and the scientific method to determine things rather than tradition, and the decline of religious political and scientific authority – exemplifies our will toward increased self-determination on an epistemological level. Indeed, one could argue that the scientific method itself also exemplifies our will toward increased self-determination on the level of epistemology, for much the same reasons that the enlightenment tradition does – an eschewing of tradition, and the exclusive reliance on *self-directed* study and investigation.

The notion of human rights, of inalienable liberties possessed by all humans, exemplifies our want for and belief in our autonomy on the level of the individual. Indeed, all notion of human rights imply our individual autonomy and freedom as a core value and desire.

The notion of morality and ethics not only exemplifies our want to self-determination, but constitutes one of the ends to which we actually apply methodological self-determination. On a very intuitive level, morality and ethics perhaps more than any other methodological pursuit is clearly an act of self-modification, and an exemplification of the will toward self-determination.

Education, and even more generally the raising of a child into adulthood, exemplifies both our will toward self-determination as well as the modal nature of self-determination. Children are born and gradually are guided and taught to become increasingly independent, autonomous, self-determining – in other words of gradually taking their own becoming in-hand. This is exemplified in obvious ways, like being taught how to live in society so as to survive (i.e., food and shelter), and in less obvious ways, like urging children to be who they want to be, to get the kind of employment they want, to live life more than anything else for the pursuit of their own happiness.

The contemporary value of individualism and relativism, and the pressure to accept people's beliefs without judgment or discrimination, ex-emplifies the will toward self-determination on the level of our minds – freedom from the external determination of our thoughts and beliefs.

Indeed, these and a great many other things exemplify, embody, and imply the ubiquitously-human will toward self-determination, as value, as desire and as actuality.

For we human beings, naturality is unnatural... we who have crafted clothes, codes, cities, symbols, and culture. Since the very inception of human civilization, we have very thoroughly ceased to be natural, and to such an extent that unnaturality has become our first nature. (Cortese, 2013c)

Indeed, this highlights an all-too-common misperception of the underlying impetus and over-arching end of transhumanism (a philosophical position that espouses the feasibility and desirability of the ethical use of human enhancement technologies) and technoprogressivism. This misnomer is that transhumanism is about eschewing our humanity. This isn't exactly a surprising misconception given the monikers transhumanism and posthumanism, but it is one that is nonetheless troubling, for it is not contrary to the thesis we have articulated here, but antithetical to it as well. Transhumanism, i.e., the position that it is both feasible and desirable to use technology to improve the human condition, constitutes nothing less than our best means of *maintaining* the human condition, which we have argued here is characterized by our desire to choose our own determining conditions ourselves. We will not be posthuman; on the contrary, we will be more human than we ever have been before.

The emphasis on technology in H+ and Tech[no] Prog[ressive] communities does not come from disdain for our humanity (i.e., the silly "contempt-of-the-flesh" trope) or sheer technophilia. Rather it is because (1) we seek to better determine the determining conditions of world and of self (which are to some extent symbiontic and interconstitu-

tive), [to] leave more up to choice and less down to chance, and (2) because technology is simply Man's foremost mediator of change, of effecting our affectation, and thus the best means of shaping the state of self and world for the better, whatever your definition of better happens to be. (Cortese, 2013b)

Thus the will-toward self-determination is exemplified by a wide array of contemporary and historically deep-rooted practices, beliefs, values and ideals.

In *Posthumanity: Thinking Philosophically About The Future*, Brian Cooney presents an ontology of life, i.e., of living organisms, rooted in autopoiesis – Greek for "self-creating", based upon homeostasis and self-maintenance. "The organism remains this organism (what philosophers call numerical identity) by *making itself*, at each point in its duration, an *instance* of the same *kind* of system. For this reason, we call it a *self-instantiating system*" (Cooney, 2004, p. 79). Interaction with the environment in a reciprocal and recursive feedback process is integral to this autopoietic process. Cooney extends this autopoietic ontology of life across scales, from DNA to unicellular organisms to multicellular organisms, culminating in the characterization of the human self and brain as an autopoietic process bearing ontological continuity with life itself, at all scales and times, down the evolutionary tree and all the way back to self-replicating RNA. Cooney's ontological scheme for life and mind as a self-creating and self-maintaining process reify the argument, presented here, that technic self-determination is ontically-continuous with the human condition today and in the far past, and exemplified by or implicit in many contemporary and historical values, practices and beliefs. Indeed, Cooney extends it all the way across life itself.

Our Humanity is a Function of our Capacity for Self-Determination

A common criticism against the desirability of HET is that it is dehumanizing – i.e., that the use of HET will mark the departure of the very qualities that make us human. In this section we will argue that the ontology of self-determination as self-modification and self-modulation articulated above (in which HET in general and neurotechnologies in particular are shown to play an integral role in maintaining and expanding our liberty and autonomy by constituting our most comprehensive and extensive means of self-determination) can serve to illustrate how the dehumanization criticism is based upon a naïve and outdated conception of human nature as static and predetermined. This line of reasoning can be utilized to not only illegitimate this criticism, but to invert it as well – to make it eat its own words in a sense.

The predominant view through the history of the Western philosophical and religious tradition has been one that is static. Arguably, this derives from the fact that metaphysical dualism – i.e., the notion of an immaterial soul causally-insulated from the physical universe – was the by-far-predominant paradigm in which the notion of a universal human condition, i.e., human nature, has been constructed and considered. The aspects of being (1) causally insulated from the physical universe and (2) eternal bias the conception of human nature possible within the context of metaphysical dualism to staticity. This, in turn, has biased most historical notions of human nature towards staticity as well.

The increasing predominance of scientific materialism (also known as metaphysical naturalism – i.e., the position contrary to metaphysical-dualism) has undermined the belief in a causally-insulated, non-physical human soul. The philosophical underpinnings of static conceptions of human nature have yet to catch up.

A static or preordained human nature also fails to account for developments in evolutionary biology and evolutionary psychology, which demonstrate that the material systems and processes capable of determining the capacities and faculties of humans (e.g., genotype, developmental environment) are *not* static but are instead under a constant state of flux. Static conceptions of human nature were formulated at a time when most everyone thought that humans were distinct from or ontologically-discontinuous with the rest of the animal kingdom; this is likely to have reinforced the bias towards characterizing human nature as static and eternal. We now know that, rather than each organism being created by a deity separately, we -- along with the rest of the ecosphere -- constitute an evolutionary continuum, and that on the contrary we bear ontological continuity with the rest of the animal kingdom because of it.

Thirdly, static conceptions of human nature also fail to account for the epigenetic domain of human constitution and activity – i.e., the ways in which our tools, techniques and technologies – our techné – constitute a portion of humans' 'determining conditions' just as much as the genetic domain of human constitution and activity does, as described in the section 'Prosthetic Essence: The Co-Constitution of Man & Techné.' The notion that culture and our available cultural and technic environment are constantly changing. This notion is even accepted by those who remain dubious at the claim that our genetic constitution changes over multi-generational time as well. The conjunction of the premises (1) man and his technic environment are co-constitutive, and (2) if man's technic environment changes, serves to further undermine static conceptions of human nature.

Furthermore, let us contend that it is precisely due to their staticity that certain views of human nature incline one to see any changes made to human nature as indignifying – i.e., because change is the antithesis of staticity. The conception of human nature articulated here, as the will toward self-determination (which is characterized both by our own partial self-determination as well as our desire to increase our degree of self-determination), put self-directed change at the heart of the human. If change, self-determination and "the Becoming underlying life's self-overcoming" (Cortese, 2013d) is what distinguishes the human as such, then changes made to one's self, so long as they are directed upon the self by and for the self, could be anything but indignifying.

Lastly, the characterization of human nature as the will toward self-determination is exclusively able to achieve the universality sought-after in most, if not all, conceptions of human nature *through* its lack of a constant 'nature' (e.g., constitution or range of capacities and faculties), or in other words through its seeming lack of 'universality' as-such. If each of us are free to choose ourselves, to make our own natures (or, put another way, to associate our first and foremost natures with that very condition of making our own natures – the human metacondition), to *differ*, then we are united through our difference. If each of us are free to determine to as great an extend we can or wish the determining conditions of our being, is each is free to forfeit static being for ecstatic becoming, then each of us is the same at radical-root.

Conceptions of human nature that are not so restrictive – that do not make it easy to characterize a given person or organism as inhuman – are desirable because a static, restrictive conception of human nature engenders large-scale acts of cruelty and even genocide. A wrongly-perceived 'lack of humanity' is what I contend led white Westerners to enslaving the African people, and what could engender the discrimination, outright enslavement, or genocide of future non-biological intelligences (including significantly-self-modified humans).

The will toward self-determination is exclusively capable of encompassing a range of possible secondary-natures by making its foremost 'constitutive composition' a metaposition on conditioning the human condition itself.

CONCLUSION

It is through the development of human enhancement technologies in general and the development of increasingly precise and extensive neuromodulation technologies for the controlled induction and modulation of an agent's own neural activity in particular that we can gain more control than we've ever had before over the determining conditions of the material systems constituting our minds and bodies. The precision of our available means of self-modification and self-modulation correspond with our capacity for self-determination (i.e., with their effectiveness). It is for this reason that neuromodulation *ipso facto* constitutes our most promising (i.e., most precise and extensive) means of self-determination – i.e., because it is the technological and methodological domain that encompasses the induction and modulation of neural activity, and the induction and modulation of an agent's own nervous system constitutes our most extensive and precise means of self-determination. The proliferation of HET, and especially neurotechnology, will serve to increase humanity's existing but comparatively-limited capacity for self-determination, or in other words our capacity to change the material systems determining the parameters (e.g., distinguishing characteristics) of our selves, which encompasses both our functional capabilities and our experiential modalities. This capacity is today exemplified for the most part by the ways in which we modify ourselves through methodological, prosthetic and reciprocal self-determination, as outlined above. Each and every one of these means of self-determination constitute a means of facilitating changes to our experiential and functional capacities, faculties and modalities that manifest themselves as changes to the wiring, i.e., the organization, of our brains, and as such legitimately constitute means of self-determination. And, it is because we, as humans, are defined more by our will toward self-determination than by anything else that the development and proliferation of HET will be anything but dehumanizing.

REFERENCES

Banks, D. (1998). Neurotechnology. *Engineering Science and Education Journal*, *7*(3), 135–144. doi:10.1049/esej:19980306

Boyden, E. S., Zhang, F., Bamberg, E., Nagel, G., & Deisseroth, K. (2005). Millisecond-timescale, genetically targeted optical control of neural activity. *Nature Neuroscience*, *8*(9), 1263–1268. doi:10.1038/nn1525 PMID:16116447

Brey, P. (2000). Theories of technology as extension of human faculties. In C. Mitcham (Ed.), *Metaphysics, epistemology, and technology*. Academic Press.

Chalmers, D., & Clark, A. (1998). The extended mind. *Analysis*, *58*(1), 7–19. doi:10.1093/analys/58.1.7

Clark, A. (1998). Embodiment and the Philosophy of Mind. *Royal Institute of Philosophy*, *43*(Supplement), 35–51. doi:10.1017/S135824610000429X

Clark, A. (2008). *Supersizing the mind: Embodiment, action, and cognitive extension*. Oxford University Press. doi:10.1093/acprof:oso/9780195333213.001.0001

Cooney, B. (2004). *Posthumanity: Thinking philosophically about the future*. Rowman & Littlefield.

Cortese, F. (2013a). *Transhumanism, technology & science: To say it's impossible is to mock history itself*. Institute for Ethics & Emerging Technologies.

Cortese, F. (2013b). The hubris of Neoluddism. *H + Magazine*.

Cortese, F. (2013c). Three spectres of immortality: A talk from the Radical Life Extension Conference in Washington D.C. *H + Magazine*.

Cortese, F. (2013d). Heidegger and the existential utility of death. In H. Pellissier (Ed.), *Human destiny is to eliminate death: Essays, arguments & rants about immortalism*. Niagara Falls, NY: Center for Transhumanity.

Farah, M. J. (2005). Neuroethics: The practical and the philosophical. *Trends in Cognitive Sciences, 9*(1), 34–40. doi:10.1016/j.tics.2004.12.001 PMID:15639439

Fetz, E. E. (2007). Volitional control of neural activity: Implications for brain-computer interfaces. *The Journal of Physiology, 579*(3), 571–579. doi:10.1113/jphysiol.2006.127142 PMID:17234689

Geelen, J. (2012). *The emerging neurotechnologies: Recent developments and policy implications*. Policy Horizons Canada.

Greene, J. (2004). Article. *Philosophical Transactions of the Royal Society of London, Series B., 359*, 1776.

Han, X., Qian, X., Bernstein, J. G., Zhou, H. H., Franzesi, G. T., & Stern, P. et al. (2009). Millisecond-timescale optical control of neural dynamics in the nonhuman primate brain. *Neuron, 62*(2), 191–198. doi:10.1016/j.neuron.2009.03.011 PMID:19409264

Lawson, C. (2010). Technology and the extension of human capabilities. *Journal for the Theory of Social Behaviour, 40*(2), 207–223. doi:10.1111/j.1468-5914.2009.00428.x

McLuhan, M. (1966). *Understanding media: The extensions of man*. Toronto, Canada: University of Toronto Press.

McLuhan, M., & McLuhan, E. (1988). *Laws of media: The new science*. Toronto, Canada: University of Toronto Press.

Meagher, R. (1988). Techné. *Perspecta, 24*, 159–164. doi:10.2307/1567132

KEY TERMS AND DEFINITIONS

Autonomy: Having the capacity to affect some circumstance of one's life or self, in conjunction with (a) an awareness of possessing this capacity, (b) the belief that possessing it is moral and desirable, and (c) the belief that the loss or depreciation of it would be undesirable.

BCI: Brain-Computer-Interfacing. A direct coupling of non-biological computational hardware with the central nervous system.

Indignifying: A decrease in one's value, autonomy or defining characteristics, as these properties are perceived by one's self.

NBIC Technologies: Nano-bio-info-cogno technologies. An umbrella term used to denote four core domains of emerging technology, comprising nanotechnology, biotechnology, information technology and cognitive technology (a.k.a. neurotechnology).

Neuromodification: The controlled addition, subtraction or rearrangement of the physical constituents constituting the central nervous system.

Neuromodulation: The controlled induction of neural activity.

Neurotechnology: Any technology used to modulate, modify or analyze the central nervous system. This includes brain-imaging technologies, neurostimulation technologies and Brain-Computer Interfacing technologies.

Staticity: The quality of being non-changing, or of lacking any appreciable degree of flux or variation in one's essential characteristics through time.

Technic: Any non-biological means to achieve a desired end, employed with the awareness that its employment will achieve or bring-into-being the end so desired. This category encompasses tools of all kinds, from technique (conceptually-embodied) to technology (physically embodied).

ENDNOTES

[1] The word 'technic' is here used in the sense of encompassing both technology and technique. It derives from the ancient Greek notion of 'techne,' which was a category that made no distinction between technology and technique, or technology and methodology.

[2] The term 'phenomenal' is used in the sense of 'pertaining to subjective experience.' This includes everything from perception to thinking to memory and imagination and subconscious (but not autonomic) functions – i.e., all possible mental phenomena.

[3] For a review of the technical aspects of neurotechnology, see Banks, 1998. For a review of the ethics of neurotechnology, see Farah et al., 2005.

[4] Optogenetic induction of neural activity involves via the application of light to neurons genetically engineered so as to generate an action potential in the presence of a certain frequency of light through the incorporation of photosensitive proteins that change their conformational shape in response to certain frequencies of electromagnetic radiation. See Boyden, 2005 and Han et al., 2009 for empirical examples of optogenetic neural induction.

[5] Dissent. From Latin *dissentire* (*dis:* "differently"; *sentire*: "to feel, think").

[6] For a historical review of the notion of techné in ancient Greece, see Meagher, 1988.

Chapter 13
Technology and the Memetic Self

Elizabeth J. Falck
The Coalition for Innovative Development, Education, and Action, USA

ABSTRACT

This chapter provides an overview of current theories in philosophy of mind as they relate to cultural and technological evolution. The focus is to examine the influence of technology on identity formation by introducing the concept of "narrative consciousness," the process of constructing a memetic self model, or "selfplex." The human capacity to construct a "selfplex" evolved from an imitation-based system of memetic replication, enabled by and coevolved with technology over the last 50,000 years. The chapter examines the following four points: (1) an introduction of the idea of "narrative consciousness"; (2) a reframing of technology as "tools that enable imitation and sharing," thereby facilitating the development of memes and the selfplex; (3) societal implications of narrative consciousness; and (4) the cultural influence of Human Enhancement Technologies (HET) on the selfplex and practical considerations for practitioners.

INTRODUCTION

Modern society is undergoing an unprecedented preferential shift toward the propagation of ideas and creative productivity over manual labor. Strong brands for individuals are a crucial component of the budding creative economy. "We are almost constantly engaged in presenting ourselves to others, and to ourselves, and hence *representing* ourselves – in language and gesture, external and internal" (Dennett, 1991, p. 417). This constant drive for representation overwhelms other forms of conscious experience. In a society progressing at an exponential pace, the act of balancing various "ways of being" has become overwhelmingly challenging. A comprehensive understanding of philosophy and historical context will elucidate why these various types of consciousness evolved, how they function, and the role technology has played in shaping human narrative over the past 50,000 years. This thorough historical basis can assist society in answering the increasingly salient questions: *What should future humans be?* and *What are the technologies that will get us there?*

Despite thousands of years of philosophical debate, the most daunting questions of consciousness remain unanswered. Today many philosophers reduce the self to an illusion constructed by the brain's electrochemical interface. Of course, individual phenomenological experience would

DOI: 10.4018/978-1-4666-6010-6.ch013

suggest that humans are more than three pounds of matter within a skull. As even staunch reductionist Daniel Dennett concedes, "Nothing could be less like an electron, or a molecule, or a neuron, than *the way the sunset looks to me now*" (1991, p. 65). In this chapter, "Human" (or narrative) consciousness will be defined as a system of memetic replication, enabled by and coevolved with technology over the last 50,000 years in accordance with life's drive toward increasing complexity. In other words, the human self is a story constructed from a variety of experiences over time. That story exists in not just one brain, but in a global network of brains and other storage devices ranging from digital to analog to biological mediums. That is the narrative nature of the human's memetic self.

To explore the above thesis, this chapter will examine the following four points: First, by outlining several working definitions for "consciousness" the chapter will explore the idea of "narrative consciousness" (often referred to as "human consciousness" or "self-consciousness"), which consists of a network of memes that spread between brains to take the form of a "selfplex." The selfplex is the combined experience and expression of a Narrative Center of Gravity as a continuous story throughout time; it is *the* differentiating quality of "human" consciousness. Second, by definition, memes (including the selfplex) must be shared between individuals. From the invention of language to 4g cell service, technology are tools that enable imitation and sharing, thereby facilitating the development of memes and the selfplex/human self. By this reasoning, *humans are inherently technological*. Third, the chapter will consider the wide-reaching implications of narrative consciousness in several fields including economics, artificial intelligence (AI), ethics, familial structures, sustainability, health and longevity. Fourth and finally, the chapter will explore the concept of progress, its interaction with the selfplex, and how HET will play a crucial role in shaping the selfplex, and consequentially, humanity's future.

Background

"Consciousness" is a word that demands an adjective; the noun itself denotes a mess of conflicting definitions and connotations ranging from concepts of awareness and agency to morality and sentience. Confusion stems from the fact that, when a person speaks of "consciousness" she rarely intends to reference more than one or two of these disparate ideas. Some researchers have expressed the belief that this muddled understanding renders the study of consciousness impossible, but this is merely an issue of semantics. According to British psychologist Max Velmans, "there is nothing to prevent discussion and organized research into aspects of 'consciousness' denoted by a *given, specific usage* of that term" (2009, p. 3). This chapter will explore several of these potential usages.

The modern understanding of the word "consciousness" is a surprisingly recent adaptation. The Latin root of "consciousness" is *cum*, which means "with" or "together" while *scire* means "to know" (Metzinger, 2010). This combination of roots might be understood to indicate morals shared by a community, as in "together, we know" but it could also fit David Hume's idea that an individual is akin to a "bundle of sensations" thus suggesting that, as a body, "together, *I* know." The differentiating question, it seems, is *who* knows?

The word "self" in western culture most commonly references identity: the life narrative that encompasses a unique personality, ego, mind and way of being in the world. That definition may seem obvious, but imagine a person waking one morning with a sudden onset of amnesia. He can't remember his own name, let alone his life's narrative. In this case he might admit to losing his *sense* of self, but it is doubtful he would say he *doesn't have* a self. In her book, *Id: The Quest for Meaning in the the 21st Century,* cognitive scientist Susan Greenfield suggests, "When human beings lose their minds… what is it exactly that has vanished? Certainly not consciousness…." (2008, p. 55).

For the sake of clarity, in this paper this elusive term "consciousness" will be defined in three ways, each dependent on a related definition of the self. These definitions are Experiential Consciousness and Self, Discrete Consciousness and Self, and Narrative Consciousness and Self. These working definitions are intended to direct focus to the paper's thesis regarding technology's role in the nature of the self rather than a larger debate about the nature of consciousness. The following table illustrates a comparison between these definitions:

First, *experiential consciousness* is the simple perception of sensory input; it is the most basic tenet of life. In *My Stroke of Insight*, neuroanatomist Jill Bolte Taylor shares a vivid, first-hand account of surviving a stroke caused by a left hemisphere brain hemorrhage. "I could no longer identify the boundaries of my body. I felt enormous and expansive... at one with all the energy that was and it was beautiful there…. nirvana, I felt nirvana!" she exclaimed during her presentation at the 2008 TED Conference. This "nirvana" Taylor describes is the basement level of conscious experience. The stroke enabled her to experience "oneness" with the universe – pure, boundless sensory perception – but her loss of cerebral functioning caused her

sense of self to vanish, and the self, it turns out, is essential to survival. Throughout the four-hour ordeal Taylor took advantage of moments of lucidity to call for help. "I had to wield my paralyzed arm like a stump and cover the numbers so that as I pushed them and came back to normal reality I'd be able to tell, 'Yes, I've already dialed that number!'" (Tedstaff, 2008). Without these fleeting moments of *self*-awareness, Taylor would never have been able to call for help. This is the boundary between experiential and discrete consciousness.

The brain is sometimes described as a "difference engine." Its role is to make comparisons and recognize patterns in a process of continually imposing order on massive quantities of sensory input. French philosopher Henri Bergson suggested the following:

The function of the brain and nervous system is to protect us from being overwhelmed and confused by this mass of largely useless and irrelevant knowledge, by shutting out most of what we should otherwise perceive or remember at any moment, and leaving only that very small and special selection which is likely to be practically useful (Huxley, 1952, pp. 22-23).

Table 1. The spectrum of consciousness

	Experiential Consciousness	**Discrete Consciousness**	**Narrative Consciousness**
The Self	Nonexistent/ boundless: "experiencing self"	An individual/ singular organism: "discrete self"	A continuous individual with temporal context: "memetic self"
Definition	The experience of perceiving sensations	The experience of body awareness, independent agency and will within a discrete organism	The experience, synthesis and expression of a continuous identity meme (selfplex) based on an individual's experiences over time
Evolutionary Correlates	Multicellular organisms: life forms with sensory inputs	Animals that can move in the world and act toward self-preservation (most distinct biological correlate: a brain and/or nervous system)	Humans, specifically homo sapiens: Temporal awareness
Synonyms	Awareness; sensing	Body awareness or ownership; agency; "i can move this piece of my body"	Identity, ego, personal narrative, life story
Related Terms	"Sunyata," Buddhist philosophy; "Unified Psychological Reality," Carl Jung and Wolfgang Pauli; the "external" in Phenomenology	"Somatic identity," Antonio Damasio; "affect" in Phenomenology; Existential "existence;" "biological self," Daniel Dennett	"Ego tunnel," Thomas Metzinger; "selfplex," Susan Blackmore; the "internal" in Phenomenology; Existential "essence;" "Center of Narrative Gravity," Daniel Dennett

This limited self constructed by the brain is the discrete self, a self tuned to survival through separation from the rest of the world. *Discrete consciousness* builds on the basement level of experiential consciousness to generate the experience of independent agency and body ownership within a single organism. Organisms with discrete consciousness can usually be defined as possessing a brain and central nervous system but could potentially also function through advanced decentralized nervous systems (jellyfish and insects) or even vascular systems (plants). For most organisms, however, the discrete self is composed of connections within a brain that continually wire and rewire based on factors ranging from genes to the sensory inputs of daily experience. The function of discrete consciousness is movement and agency in service of an organism's independent reproduction and survival.

Humans aren't born with discrete consciousness but develop it as their brains gain complexity. Most infants begin to "discover" their limbs around the age of two months. Discrete consciousness develops as an infant becomes aware of its ability to intentionally control its hands and feet. This individuation occurs through a two-way process within the brain of interpreting sensory information and then imposing structure on that information. Taylor suggests that this process particularly relates to the left hemisphere of the brain. "[The left hemisphere is] that little voice that says to me 'I am,'" she claims, "…as soon as my left hemisphere says to me, 'I am,' I become separate, I become a single, solid individual separate from the energy flow around me and separate from you" (2008). This separate and discrete self enables individuals to compete for resources and mates; it is the biological driver of self-preservation.

Once this sense of agency is established, animals go to varying lengths to extend their influence beyond the boundaries of their biological bodies. "The strategy of bending the environment to use as if it were part of one's own body is a half-billion-

year-old trick at least," says Kevin Kelly (2010, p. 21). Richard Dawkins describes devices likes a snail's shell and a beaver's dam as "extended phenotypes" that stretch "beyond the 'natural' boundary of individuals to include external equipment" (Dennet, 1991, p. 415). Dennett further claims that, for some highly social or hive-based animals, even other individuals within the same species are incorporated in the extended phenotype (1991, p. 415). For many mammals, social groups increase the individual's odds for survival and reproduction. These biologically-driven social behaviors evolved through standard Darwinian natural selection. The dominant biological underpinning of this social bonding is the hormone and neurotransmitter oxytocin. Oxytocin weakens connections between neurons and accelerates the construction of new pathways. It is responsible for love, bonding and a sense of community and is released during activities including breastfeeding, sex and communal eating. Oxytocin compels individuals to connect, protect and share. This and the related hormone vasopressin have been shown to play key roles in social recognition and bonding for mammals including rats, mice, voles and sheep, particularly in offspring recognition and mate preference (Bielsky & Young, 2004). These hormones promote social behaviors that contribute to the species' survival. As will be discussed later, over time these behaviors evolved increasing complexity, eventually leading to the development of language and other technologies. For Marshall McLuhan, this is humanity's differentiator; the human's extended phenotype is technology: "clothes are people's extended skin, wheels extended feet, camera and telescope extended eyes" (Kelly, 2010, p. 44). Eventually these unique new tools enabled a third, entirely new form of consciousness to evolve: narrative consciousness.

Narrative consciousness is the experience, synthesis and expression of a continuous identity-meme (selfplex) based on an individual's experiences over time; it is the one form of consciousness that is uniquely human. Narrative consciousness builds on the continuum of experiential and discrete consciousness with the addition of temporal awareness and the expressive capacity of technology. This temporal context enables the life story most commonly referred to as "the self." As Susan Greenfield explains:

Despite the endless and spectacular dynamism of your brain…there is none the less [sic] usually a reassuringly consistent theme that is you: your identity. This identity is the most basic assumption for going through life and interacting with others. (Greenfield, p. 115)

In other words, narrative consciousness is the "I" that makes sense of experience within a temporal context. This continuous narrative is enabled by the use of technology to structure and share information in new ways. The memetic foundation of narrative consciousness will be explored in greater depth below.

To summarize, consciousness evolved sequentially: experiential consciousness gave way to discrete consciousness, yielding larger and more complex brains until temporal awareness in humans paired with their advanced extended phenotypes (technology) enabled narrative consciousness. Each building on the prior, all three forms of consciousness are human, but only one is *uniquely* human. The paradox of self is that an individual can never seem to experience all three forms of consciousness simultaneously. In *The Symposium,* Plato wrote, "Human nature was originally one and we were a whole, and the desire and pursuit of the whole is called love." Perhaps the "whole" to which Plato refers is simply the pure experiential consciousness that often proves so difficult for humans to access, obscured as it is by the pressures of the discrete and narrative selves.

Why "I" Exist: Narrative Consciousness and the Meme of the "Selfplex"

"I Seem to Be a Verb": Imagined Continuity

Two necessary human developments were prerequisite to the evolution of narrative consciousness. The first was temporal awareness. As described by cognitive scientist Susan Greenfield:

Thinking has so far in our species differed from other forms of mental phenomena, such as feeling a strong emotion, because it involves a connected sequence, be it of words, logic, symbols, sounds or scenes, that stretch beyond the immediate here-and-now" (2008, p. 171)

Neurophysiologist William Calvin postulates that this form of awareness evolved after primates learned to throw. He believes that "once the brain evolved the power to run multiple rapid-throw scenarios, it hijacked this throw procedure to run multiple sequences of notions" (Kelly, 2010, p. 27). Cognizance of time enabled humans to understand consequences, to plan and to imagine new solutions. As Karl Popper once said, "[ideas] permit our hypotheses to die in our stead."

This capacity to have notions and test hypotheses enabled a new layer of reality, somewhere between the physical and the nonexistent: the imagined. The debate over what "ideas" truly are dates back 17th century philosopher Renee Descartes, the founder of dualist thought. To Descartes there were two types of "stuff" in the universe: "thinking stuff" and "physical stuff." The human self was "thinking stuff," a tiny immaterial observer who sat somewhere behind the eyes experiencing the world outside and directing actions in response. Today, cognitive scientists make daily progress in elucidating the confluence of body and mind to the degree that many philosophers speak of the self as an illusion. "There is no such thing as a self. Contrary to what most people believe, nobody has ever been or had a self," (2010, p. 1) writes philosopher Thomas Metzinger in *The Ego Tunnel*. Dennett furthers this concept with his Multiple Drafts Model, stating "at any point in time there are multiple drafts of narrative fragments at various stages of editing in various places in the brain" (Dennet, 1991, p. 135). He describes identity not as an enduring reality but as a "Center of Narrative Gravity."

As confounding as the "substance" or "location" of the self may be, an even more deceptive component of the *memetic* self is not its physical foundation but its representation as an enduring reality. In his critique of the notion of identity Hume makes a distinction between the idea of an unchanging object (as a person might perceive a statue cast in bronze) and the idea of "several different objects existing in succession, and connected together by a close relation" (Hume, 2012, p. 135). In 75 AD, Plutarch wrote the classic example of the ship of Theseus:

The ship wherein Theseus and the youth of Athens returned had thirty oars and was preserved by the Athenians down even to the time or Demetrius Phalereus, for they took away the old planks as they decayed, putting in new and stronger timber in their place, insomuch that this ship became a standing example among the philosophers for the logical question of things that grow; one side holding that the ship remained the same, and the other contending that it was not the same (Plutarch).

"Imagined continuity" describes a situation in which an idea endures beyond its original physical manifestation. Like Theseus's ship, the human selfplex continually changes with the formation and destruction of neural connections in the brain, yet it is perceived as a continuous whole. The selfplex enables a person to reconcile her memory of a self-image from childhood with her current self-image, regardless of the differences between them. So, if the narrative self is merely an illusion then why do people spend so much time and energy building it?

How Memes Create a Self

Richard Dawkins first introduced the idea of the meme in his book *The Selfish Gene*. "All life evolves by the differential survival of replicating entities," he says (1976, p. 192). Memes, like DNA, are information replicators. Building on Dawkins, Susan Blackmore defines a meme as "that which is imitated" (2007). She continues, "though we may think of mother cats as teaching their kittens to hunt, or groom, or use the cat door, they do not do it by demonstration or imitation" (1999, p. 3). True imitation within nonhuman animal species is rare. "To be human is to imitate," Blackmore says (2007). In other words, to be human is to have memes.

What exactly *is* a meme? Essentially, it is an idea that can be expressed and replicated. Memes are instruction, behaviors, inventions, cultural traditions and stories. "When our ancestors began to imitate they let loose a new evolutionary process based not on genes but on a second replicator, memes. Genes and memes then coevolved, transforming us into better and better meme machines" (Blackmore, 2008). The discrete self evolved into the memetic self, transforming animals into humans capable of experiencing, synthesizing and expressing new memes. Indeed the most intricate meme a human ever creates is that of his or her "self."

The ultimate memeplex...is no science fiction futuristic invention but our own familiar self... Each of us is a massive memeplex running on the physical machinery of a human body and brain – a meme machine. [Francis] Crick was wrong. We are not 'nothing but a pack of neurons'; we are a pack of memes too. (Blackmore, 1999, pp. 231-232)

The memetic self is in fact a compilation of the millions of memes an individual has encountered, adopted, altered and expressed in her lifetime. These constructions of memes define humans. Literary scholar Jonathan Gottschall puts it simply: "We live in Neverland because we can't not live in Neverland. Neverland is our nature. We are the storytelling animal" (2012, p. 175). This capacity for meme generation eventually became the ability to construct a memetic self but there was one step missing between temporal awareness and the ability to imitate: the *technology* to synthesize and express these new memetic replicators. Technology was the second prerequisite to narrative consciousness.

What is Technology?

50,000 years ago the human species underwent a massive transformation. Archaeological artifacts reveal an explosion of art, industry and culture at that time. Many scientists hypothesize that this transformation can be attributed to the invention of language. Kelly describes language as "a handle that turns the mind into a tool" (2010, pp. 24, 26). How did this seemingly miraculous tool come to exist? British psychologist Robin Dunbar posits that, as human societies grew larger and larger, the use of grooming as a tool to reinforce social cohesion no longer sufficed. "Gossip is a substitute for grooming," he says (Kelly, 2010, p. 95). By enabling connections between individuals over farther distances and longer periods of time, he postulates, gossip decoupled the maintenance of relationships from a need for physical contact. As a tool for social cohesion, language was humanity's first great technology.

Unfortunately, new technology always presents humanity with new threats. 2400 years ago Plato worried that writing would negatively impact human interaction (Chorost, 2011, p. 14). 600 years ago the invention of the printing press generated fears of technological isolation (2011, p. 161). Today, fears abound in literature and popular culture regarding the apocalyptic dangers of technology. It leaves people disconnected, as Adam Gopnik depicts with his daughter's perpetually-busy imaginary friend in his essay "Bumping into Mr. Ravioli" (2002); it leaves them vapid and alone, as is best illustrated by the sterile rooms inhabited by the isolated characters in E.M. Forester's *The Machine Stops*. Often, technology threatens individuality, as depicted by the mindless, depersonalized "Borgs" of *Star Trek*.

All of these fears, however—isolation, emptiness, loss of identity—existed long before the invention of the screen or any other technology. In fact, they can most clearly be linked to the evolution of discrete consciousness in conjunction with the intellectual capacity to lament separateness from the whole of experiential consciousness. So far, the only thing technology can do is express or enact a meme, and it is *people* who dominate the sphere of meme generation, starting with themselves. B. F. Skinner said, "The real problem is not whether machines think but whether men do" (1969). Fear should not be derived from a technology that exacerbates a vulnerability, but from the vulnerability itself. When technology is perceived as the other, the threat within the self flourishes unnoticed. Kelly says, "The conflict that the technium [technology] triggers in our hearts is due to our refusal to accept our nature – the truth is that we are continuous with the machines we create" (2010, p. 188). People have reason to fear technology, but this statement only rephrases the fact that *humans have reason to fear themselves.*

Blackmore (2008) calls the technology of language a parasite that, over time, formed a symbiotic relationship with "us." By "us" she must be referencing the discrete self (the purely biological human), for without language an individual could never form the rich inner world of the memetic self, let alone share that self with others. The notion of self continually evolves with the invention and adoption of new technologies. By this line of reasoning, if the capacity to create a memetic self is the only distinguisher between narrative consciousness and other forms of consciousness, and only humans can create a memetic self, then humans are *defined* by their capacity for narrative consciousness. Technology is the enabler of that which is uniquely human, *memes*. By this definition, *technology is inherently human*. It is the species' key distinguisher.

Nonetheless, modern culture still views technology through a very narrow lens: it is a screen, it's digital, it plugs in; often, it's bad. People fear technology because they fear that it threatens what it means to be human, but they've forgotten something: technology *is* human. Technology is the human extended phonotype; it is any tool that enables people to extend themselves by expressing and/or synthesizing a meme. What people *truly* fear in the wake of technological progress are not *tools* but the exponentially growing offensive of competing memes those tools promulgate. For example, a 60-year-old farmer would likely struggle to compete in the emerging industries of the creative economy. If the farmer's grandson decides to pursue a more lucrative career in web design, the older man may feel that his way of life is being threatened by a shifting economy fueled by new technologies. Every day new and stronger memes emerge with the potential to adapt more quickly than those that compose a person's self-protecting kernel of a selfplex. It's a process that is only accelerating.

In *Alone Together,* Sherry Turkle expresses the popular view of technology as a solely digital tool when she asks, "What could people be doing if they weren't on the Internet? …There's piano; there's drawing; there's all the things people could be *creating* [emphasis added]" (2011, p. 276). What Turkle fails to grasp with such a limited definition is that technology is the very thing than *enables* creation. How could an individual create art without the technology of an instrument, a paint brush, or a pencil?

In his essay "The Question Concerning Technology," Martin Heidegger explains the etymology of the word "technology":

The word stems from the Greek. Technikon means that which belongs to techne… techne is the name not only for the activities and skills of the craftsman, but also for the arts of the mind and the fire arts. Techne belongs to bringing-forth, to poiesis. (Heidegger, 1977, pp. 12-13)

"Poiesis" is Greek for "to make" or "to create." In other words, technology is the *creative application of knowledge*. If knowledge here can be understood as memes (or ideas), including the meme of the memetic self, then the above definition of technology as "tools that enable people to express or synthesize memes" aligns perfectly. Creativity is the act of memetic recombination and expression enabled by technology.

Heidegger goes on to outline two types of technology: instrumental technology and anthropological technology (1977, pp. 4-5). Instrumental technology most closely relates to the experiencing self and the discrete self; it consists of tools that enable individuals to **experience** more, reach farther and survive longer. Broadly, these tools include cooking utensils, weapons, cars, refrigerators, chairs and washing machines. Anthropological technology, on the other hand, relates to the memetic self; it enables people to **express** and share their stories and memes more powerfully and broadly. Anthropological technologies include words, books, paintings, PowerPoints, films, and decoration.

Although both of these categories of tools can be found in Human Enhancement Technologies, today the field is predominantly focused on instrumental technologies. Instrumental HET (IHET) help people live longer, run faster, and see farther. Their focus is typically on physical rather than cognitive enhancements. Largely, these IHET relate to the discrete self. Anthropological HET (AHET), on the other hand, enhance how people process the world and represent themselves within it. This is the realm of the uniquely human self, the memetic self. The assimilation of AHET that significantly impact personality into the selfplex may be more difficult than assimilation of IHET like prosthetics. As such, AHET have compounded potential to alter the definition of humanity and the future of society.

Cultural Implications of Narrative Consciousness

At the beginning of this paper, narrative consciousness was defined as, "the synthesis and expression of a continuous identity meme (selfplex) based on an individual's experiences over time." Today many people base their identities on the skills they've acquired in the service of instrumental technologies while disregarding the importance of anthropological technologies (note the funding of high school science programs compared to art programs). Today machines are displacing the identities of many workers, particularly industrial laborers. As instrumental technologies become increasingly automated, this "threat" will grow to affect more people. Someday doctors, architects, and scientists may likewise be replaced by more capable and efficient computational devices. Fewer and fewer people will be needed to participate in the direct manipulation of instrumental technologies. Many people fear technology because it threatens their sense of purpose in the world but this is just another way to say that new memes (and technologies are also memes, in and of themselves) often threaten the old.

In addition to his work on technology, Heidegger is also known for the concept of *enframing*: the human perception that everything must be *for* something, even people (Heidegger, 1977). So what, then, are people *for,* if not the technical skills discussed here? Turkle notes one child's response to this question:

When there are computers who are just as smart as the people, the computers will do a lot of the jobs, but there will still be things for the people to do. They will run the restaurants, taste the food, and they will be the ones who will love each other... (2011, p. 51)

The humans will do the feeling and experiencing. They will also tell stories and create art. In many regards, the answer to the fear of humanity's lost purpose lies in anthropological technologies, the tools that enable expression of the uniquely human memetic self. As Blackmore says, humans are, after all, "meme machines." Heidegger places an apparent emphasis on anthropological technology, the technologies that reveal something new about the world: "It is as revealing [anthropological], and not as manufacturing [instrumental], that *techne* is a bringing-forth" (1977, p. 13). Anthropological technologies might be understood as the tools that specifically enable the expression of memes/selfplex: creative tools. In this regard, *creativity is the combination of experiences from the discrete self and the experiential self using technology to synthesize and express new memes through the lens of the memetic self.* In other words, creativity is the synthesis and expression of memes that enable the development of a human selfplex and other memes, and technology is the tool that enables that creativity.

The crucial component of creativity is *expression*, for how else can a meme be imitated if not shared with the world? *Experience*, on the other hand, is the unifying element of *all* life. The difference between these two aspects of humanity is that people *don't need technology* in order to experience the world—no conscious being does; that is the nature of *experiential* consciousness. Humans *do*, however, need technology in order to experience their unique form of *narrative* consciousness; it enables the expressive capacity that defines them. Perhaps this is why Heidegger chose to emphasize anthropological technologies (for expression) and de-emphasize instrumental technologies (for experience and extended agency). As Greenfield says:

Merely solving a problem to which the answer is known would surely pale in comparison to the incandescent excitement of the creative process.... Now we could feel not only a sense of fulfillment, but also a sense of individual identity.... We should be exploring ways in which the new technologies might enhance the 'eureka' mindset for the first time on a mass scale. (2008, pp. 281, 286)

Expressing stories and ideas enables individuals to connect to a larger group without losing their sense of self. No matter how many machines develop a degree of consciousness—even narrative consciousness—none will ever be able to replicate the experience of being-you-right-now. Metzinger writes, "Nobody will ever live this conscious life again. Your Ego Tunnel is unicum, one of a kind" (2010, p. 217)." The capacity to express the memetic self is the irreplaceable beauty of creativity.

The Creative Economy and Sustainability

As humans transfer energy from instrumental to anthropological technical pursuits, the global economy is undergoing a massive shift toward dematerialization, reassigning value from mindless, mechanical production to creative idea generation. "In a very real sense our entry into a service and idea-based economy is a continuation of a trend that began at the Big Bang. The technium's [technology's] ability to compress information into highly refined structures is also a triumph of the immaterial," says Kelly.

As the economy shifts, so do people's identities. Auto mechanics and accountants, once defined by their functional contributions to society, will in the future be artists and researchers predominantly defined by the memes they generate. Some economists wonder what will motivate productivity without the financial pressures of scarcity. In *The Ego Tunnel,* Metzinger explores this concern with the theoretical concept of a "bliss machine." He imagines a world in which all humans' basic needs are provided for free and people have the option to connect to a source that provides the experience of endless bliss. In such a context, he wonders, would people no longer produce or cre-

ate? No, Metzinger determined, "There is more to an existence worth having or a life worth living than subjective experience" (2010, p. 197). This drive for "more" is the result of memetics. The economic pressures once exerted by physical scarcity will be replaced by memetic pressures. Ideas will be the value drivers of the future. Greenfield says:

Creativity is surely the ultimate expression of individuality, and a characteristically human activity: it is deeply fulfilling for those who achieve it, and usually of some kind of incidental benefit to wider society. Creativity, then, might offer an ideal way forward. (2008)

By reframing technology as inherently human, attention can be diverted from the ineffectual regulation of isolated inventions that may or may not pose risks, and shifted to a larger conversation about the value system in which those tools exist. Society must develop methods to promote cohesive value systems in ways that empowers people to discriminate the tools and memes that add to human wellbeing from those that detract from it. Tomorrow's economy can be the creative economy: sustainable, renewable, and intentional. Entrepreneur Peter Diamandis claims that humans today stand at the cusp of an unprecedented cultural and economic shift from scarcity to abundance. The currency of that abundance will be creativity (Diamandis & Kotler, 2012).

Family

The development of a creative economy increasingly shifts individuals' value identifiers to the realm of ideas. As more people support themselves by exploiting their memes (such as a novelist or inventor may do) rather than the tasks they complete (like an assembly line worker) the resulting emergent value set reinforces the societal significance of the memetic self over the biological discrete self. Where humans once survived by passing on genes, they now survive by passing on memes. This shift has a variety of implications for traditional social and familial structures.

As Dawkins explains, "Each person only has a finite amount of time, effort and money. Their memes and genes therefore have to compete for control of these resources" (Blackmore, 1999, p. 139). In today's world, the memes often win. "Desirable mates should be those whose lives allow them to spread the most memes, such as writers, artists, journalists, broadcasters, film stars and musicians," claims Blackmore (p. 130). Societal emphasis on the memetic self both influences mate selection toward individual's with broader memetic reach and reduces the number of offspring a person will have by diverting energy from child rearing to idea generation.

That said, children do more than pass on genes to the next generation, they also pass on memes. Investing time in people, regardless of their genetic relationship, has intrinsic value for memetic replication. Although the bulk of this memetic transfer occurs horizontally (peer-to-peer, through media, etc.), the most foundational memes of individuals' memetic selves are transferred vertically through parental influence. A person's "self" not only develops from a genetic recombination of his parents' DNA, but also from a recombination of his parents' most dominant memes. Increasing dominance of the memetic self suggests a shift toward smaller families with reduced emphasis on genetic reproduction (memes can be transferred just as easily to adopted children as biological children) and increased emphasis on meme optimization and alignment in establishing long-term partnerships.

Artificial Intelligence, Health and Longevity

As societal definitions within culture and economy evolve, so too will the definition for humanity itself. People today live longer and healthier lives than at any other point in history. New Human enhancement technologies like prosthetics, electronics and implants are redefining quality of life measurements for people with *and without* disabilities. The latest artificial intelligence can be exported to pockets around the world within moments. The technological "extended phenotype" of the human is expanding exponentially. As these memes grow and spread, so does the dominance of the memetic self.

Dennett claims, "Your current embodiment, though a necessary precondition for your creation, is not necessarily a requirement for your existence to be prolonged indefinitely...." (1991, p. 430). He seems to be suggesting that, although the development of a human self by definition requires a human body and brain, its sustenance may not. The dematerialized nature of information could mean that, once constructed, the technological hardware to sustain the information-based memetic self may only require functionally (but not structurally) identical components to currently gene-driven biological hardware (human brain and body). "If you think of yourself as a narrative center of gravity," Dennett continues, "your existence depends on the persistence of that narrative...which could *theoretically* survive indefinitely many switches of medium...." (1991, p. 430).

This change in medium, however, hardly means that the future human will consist of a series of ones and zeroes stored on a hard drive. In fact, advancements in medicine and science increasingly blur the line between technology and biology. The latest artificial hearts incorporate a combination of organic animal tissue with synthetic materials to generate personalized, high functioning replacement organs. On the computational side, scientists can already perform basic functions using programmable DNA. Organically structured computers may one day have the potential to process faster than any silicon-based solution (Parker, 2003). In the future, longevity and artificial intelligence may be more grounded in organic biology than science fiction has estimated.

One approach to the field of artificial intelligence treats the human brain like a computer, attempting to deconstruct its basic processes toward the goal of replicating them with technological substrates. Skeptics of this reductionist approach argue that a computer could never replicate the complexity of the brain, let alone phenomenological experience. This counter assumption claims that the experience of a tiny "me" inside the mind could not be reproduced by a technological medium. Dennett replies that, when considering the potential capabilities of technology, complexity matters. If complexity weren't a factor, he argues, the simple fact that a standard calculator can't understand Chinese would disprove the possibility of strong AI. The difficult part of replicating human (narrative) consciousness will be in programming the process of memetic recombination, the creation of selfplex meme that is the experience of having that tiny "me." "For robots to become like humans…they would have to have memes. Rather than being programmed to do specific tasks or even to learn from their environment as some already can, they would have to be given the ability to imitate" (Blackmore, 1999, p. 218). Only through imitation can an individual engage in the technological act of creating the new memes that generate narrative consciousness. There is no reason that this capacity must be limited to the single organized structure of organic material that is the human brain.

These ideas may seem abstract, but the examples here serve to illustrate the potential of technology to shift definitions of the self and what it means to be human. In the future a clear definition of an individual self may not be confined to the boundaries of its body but instead to the boundaries of its memes as they traverse any number of digital and physical mediums. This transition is a natural, ongoing process in life.

Mental Health & Ethics

Alongside humanity's immediate challenges of climate change, unsustainable food and energy systems and providing access to clean water, another major systemic challenge gaining attention is mental illness. In a world where one individual can harm millions in a moment of instability, building systems and societal norms that address and mediate the threats of mental illness will soon be a key social issue.

Technology (humanity's "extended phenotype") by definition reduces the immediacy of actions. A keystroke ordering a drone attack may be less psychologically damaging to the perpetrator than shooting a person at point-blank range but the result for the victim is effectually identical. On the other hand, despite the fact that technology has the capacity to distance the effects of violence, its development has historically coincided with an overall *reduction* in violent behavior. For early humans:

Lethal atrocities for infractions within a clan were the norm; fairness, as we might think of it, did not exist outside the immediate tribe. Rampant inequality among genders and physical advantage for the strong guided a type of justice few modern people would want applied to them (Kelly, 2010, p. 89).

If technology is a process that promotes equality, the process of its evolution is far from complete. For example, how is it that a person today can justify the purchase his morning cappuccino knowing the same amount of money could prevent a child from starving, perhaps even a child in his own neighborhood? Increasingly, technology can be used to connect people on a global scale, potentially swaying micro decisions to accrue macro social effects. This unifying influence of technologies could combat systemic imbalance as has never before been possible. Just as technology expands the capacity for an aberrant individual to cause unprecedented harm it simultaneously serves as an equalizer for the vast majority of society. As discussed above, the key to addressing this dichotomy between fear and equality is in redefining technology as inherently human. "The only hope, and not at all a forlorn one, is to come to understand, naturalistically, the ways in which brains grow self-representations, thereby equipping the bodies they control with responsible selves when all goes well" (Dennet, 1991, p. 430). Again, humans have reason to fear technology, but this statement only rephrases the assertion that *humans have reason to fear themselves.*

A comprehensive understanding of the deeply interconnected memetic self could play a definitive role in developing solutions for these key ethical considerations. As discussed previously, the use of technology to solve problems often simultaneously generates new threats. Today a high school student with access to a garage-based wet lab can successfully edit gene sequences. Digital models can be downloaded for free to 3D print gun parts using commercially available printers. The exponential advancement of technology has escalated to the point that it can no longer be regulated or controlled; attempting to do so would be a recipe for failure. Instead, the ways in which humans choose to define acceptable and unacceptable social behaviors surrounding technology will determine whether or not such tools are allowed to become the threat many people fear them to be.

"Progress:" Technological Evolution and the Influence of HET on the Selfplex

In his book *What Technology Wants*, Kevin Kelly wrote "a single thread of self-generation ties the cosmos, the bios, and the technos together into one creation…Humans are not the culmination of this trajectory but an intermediary, smack in the middle between the born and the made"

(2010, p. 356). Kelly calls the technium "the greater, global, massively interconnected system of technology vibrating around us" (2010, pp. 11, 46). Essentially, consciousness is rapidly iterating software running on the continuum of life's hardware. Memes, carried by technology, are the latest iteration of life's drive toward "progress."

Extrapolated, technology wants what life wants: increasing efficiency, increasing opportunity, increasing emergence, increasing complexity, increasing diversity, increasing specialization, increasing ubiquity, increasing freedom, increasing mutualism, increasing beauty, increasing sentience, increasing structure, increasing evolvability (Kelly, 2010, p. 270).

Some people look upon the world in dismay at the poverty, pain, violence and sickness that so often color human existence and imagine that something has "gone wrong." In fact, these systems have simply not yet reached a level of complexity to "go right." It can be easy to imagine that the world was once better than it is today but that assumption is simply untrue. Order and complexity grow from disorganization and chaos; this is the driving force of life. Humanity is simply a process that has yet to be optimized.

Kelly uses urbanization as an illustration of this process of optimization, which he calls progress. "Every beautiful city begins as a slum," he says:

Everywhere in the world, at all historical periods, in all cultures, people have stampeded by the billions into the future of 'slightly more options' as fast as they can…All the promises, paradoxes, and trade-offs carried by Progress, with a capital P, are represented in a city (2010, p. 81).

Why do people move in droves from their rural roots to the slums of urbania? Because cities are the breeding ground of ideas, fuel for the memetic self's drive toward increasing complexity, increasing order, increasing design, increasing "progress." Richard Florida found that the forty largest cities in the world produce nearly 9 in 10 new patents (Kelly, 2010, p. 84). "This is in fact the 'job' of minds," says Kelly, "to produce types of complexity that evolutionary self-creation cannot" (2010, p. 116). Besides, as an elderly Bedouin chief said regarding his migration to a city, "We can always go into the desert to taste the old life...The children will have more options for their future [in the city]" (2010, p. 86).

Unfortunately, resuming old ways is rarely how "Progress with a capital *P*" functions. Once in the city, the Bedouin chief's children will be unlikely to ever again "taste the old life." Progress is life's process of maximizing choices to the greatest degree possible; it is *not* concerned with optimizing human happiness. People must begin to distinguish the difference.

For researchers and practitioners in the field of Human Enhancement Technology, recognizing this difference between progress and well-being will be a crucial ethical consideration, particularly for Anthropological HET. In the last 100 years, anthropological technologies including cell phones, social media, and film have drastically transformed human culture on a global scale. As opportunities to incorporate these tools into the body and brain become increasingly achievable through HET, their impact on the narrative self will be compounded. Researchers should undertake comprehensive historical analyses of the emotional, behavioral and cognitive impacts of any anthropological technologies related to their field of study before developing HET advancements.

CONCLUSION

Balance: "Sometimes I Am, Sometimes I Think"

Neuroscientist Richard Davidson has built a career researching the neural correlates of wellbeing. His studies have shown activation differences in the brains of long-term meditation practitioners, particularly around regions associated with attention. In 2008, Davidson tested Buddhist practitioner Matthieu Ricard and found that "his brain produces a level of gamma waves—those linked to consciousness, attention, learning and memory—'never reported before in the neuroscience literature'" (Taggart, 2012). His work suggests a correlation between meditation and feelings of wellbeing. Worldwide meditation practices vary widely in intention and custom, but if a common theme can be isolated it might be that of "quieting the mind." Perhaps practices like meditation train the brain to temporarily shift dominance from narrative and discrete states of consciousness toward a more "selfless" experiential consciousness, thereby increasing feelings of connection and wellbeing. Despite humans' meme-dominated modern lifestyles, this need for balance can similarly be observed in the importance of exercise, sex, sunlight exposure, thrill-seeking behavior and other activities that nourish the discrete self. Kelly says:

I believe these two different routes for technological lifestyle – either optimizing for contentment [experience] or optimizing choice [progress/expression] – come down to very different ideas of what humans are to be...To maximize our own contentment we seek the minimum amount of technology in our lives [experience]. Yet to maximize the contentment of others, we must maximize the amount of technology in the world [expression] (2010, pp. 233,238).

Today, humans' memetic selves exponentially outpace their biology, but the answer to the question of "what humans are to be" is far from determined. Discovering answers in a manner that maximizes not only progress but human wellbeing will be one of the greatest contributions and challenges of this generation. Today's HET practitioners are shaping the tools that will define the future of human society. It is a considerable burden and ethical challenge. A broad understanding of the role technology has played throughout human cultural evolution paired with a comprehensive analysis of the behavioral and cultural impact of recent technologies, particularly anthropological technologies, will benefit future decision-making in this field. Additionally, a thorough understanding of the importance the "selfplex" in modern culture and how technologies influence its development will help inform ongoing HET research.

This chapter has covered a range of theories in philosophy of mind and cultural evolution to elucidate how technology both constructs and influences a fragile continuum of human consciousness. In this continuum, humanity's "extended phenotype of technology" enables the memetic recombination that builds the experience of the human self. This concept was simplified through the understanding of creativity as the use of technology to express the memetic self. Finally, the chapter argued that, in society's drive toward progress, maintaining personal equilibrium between experiential, discrete and narrative consciousness will be crucial for optimizing human health and happiness. Tomorrow's greatest challenge for technologists and researchers will be in developing the tools, systems and social norms that moderate the drivers of the species' memetic selves to optimize freedom and wellbeing for all people. With proper oversight, the future of HET can play a pivotal role in fostering that balance.

REFERENCES

Bielsky, I., & Young, L. (2004, September 25). *Oxytocin, vasopressin, and social recognition in mammals*. D. O. Center for Behavioral Neuroscience, Producer. Retrieved December 1, 2012 from http://www.ncbi.nlm.nih.gov/pubmed/15374658

Blackmore, S. (1999). *The meme machine*. Oxford University Press.

Blackmore, S. (2007). *Imitation Makes Us Human*. Retrieved December 2, 2012 from http://www.susanblackmore.co.uk/chapters/human.pdf

Chorost. (2011). *World wide mind: The coming integration of humanity, machines and the internet*. New York: Free Press.

Consciousness. (n.d.). Retrieved November 29, 2012 from http://dictionary.reference.com/browse/consciousness

Dawkins, R. (1976). *The selfish gene*. New York: Oxford University Press.

Dennet, D. (1991). *Consciousness explained*. Boston, MA: Little, Brown and Company.

Descartes, R. (1637). *A discourse on the method of correctly conducting one's reason and seeking truth in the sciences*. Oxford, UK: Oxford University Press.

Diamandis, P. H., & Kotler, S. (2012). *Abundance: The future is better than you think*. New York: Free Press.

Forester, E. (1909). *The Machine Stops*. Retrieved December 01, 2012 from http://archive.ncsa.illinois.edu/ prajlich/forster.html

Gopnik, A. (2002, September 30). Bumping into mr. ravioli. *New York Journal*, 80-84.

Gottschall, J. (2012). *The storytelling animal*. New York: Houghton Mifflin Harcourt.

Greenfield, S. (2008). *Id: The quest for meaning in the 21st century*. London: Hodder and Stoughton Ltd.

Haish, B. (2009). *The God theory: Universes, zero point fields and what's behind it all*. San Francisco, CA: Red Wheel/Weiser, LLC.

Heidegger, M. (1977). *The question concerning technology and other essays*. New York: Harper & Row.

Hume, D. (1739). *A treatise of human nature*. Project Gutenberg eBook.

Huxley, A. (1954). *The doors of perception*. London: Thinking Ink.

Kelly, K. (2010). *What technology wants*. New York: Penguin Group.

Metzinger, T. (2010). *The ego tunnel*. New York: Basic Books.

Parker, J. (2003). Computing with DNA. *EMBO Reports*, *4*(1). doi:10.1038/sj.embor.embor719 PMID:12524509

Plato. (n.d.). *The symposium*. Retrieved from http://www.gutenberg.org/ebooks/1600

Plutarch. (2009). *Theseus*. Retrieved November 25, 2012, from http://classics.mit.edu/Plutarch/theseus.html

Skinner, B. F. (1969). *Contingencies of reinforcement*. Retrieved from http://en.wikiquote.org/wiki/Machine

Taggart, F. (2012, October 29). Buddhist monk is world's happiest man. *Google News*. Retrieved August 16, 2013 from http://www.google.com/hostednews/afp/article/ALeqM5gPq3GZRQBAWdbDc1E_Y9yKlQEfA?docId=CNG.6f253034ff18b21babb269b6f776f4d8.3c1

Tedstaff. (2008). *Stroke of insight: Jill Bolte Taylor on TED.com*. Retrieved from http://blog.ted.com/2008/03/12/jill_bolte_tayl/

Turkle, S. (2011). *Alone together*. New York, NY: Basic Books.

Velmans, M. (2009). How to define consciousness – and how not to define consciounsess. *Journal of Consciousness Studies*, *16*(5), 139–156.

KEY TERMS AND DEFINITIONS

Anthropological Human Enhancement Technologies (AHET): Technologies that enhance how individuals process the world and represent themselves within it; technologies that increase the chances of memetic replication of an individual's selfplex.

Creativity: The act of memetic recombination and expression enabled by technology.

Discrete Consciousness: The experience of body awareness, independent agency and will within a discrete organism.

Experiential Consciousness: The experience of perceiving sensations.

Instrumental Human Enhancement Technologies (IHET): Technologies that increase an individual's chances of survival and genetic reproduction.

Meme: An idea, process or technology that can be expressed and imitated.

Narrative Consciousness: The experience, synthesis and expression of a continuous identity meme (selfplex) based on an individual's experiences over time.

Selfplex: The combined experience and expression of "the self" as a continuous story throughout time; a meme of personal identity.

Technology: Tools that enable people to express or synthesize memes.

Chapter 14
Enhancement and Identity:
A Social Psychological Perspective

Samuel G. Wilson
Swinburne University of Technology, Australia

ABSTRACT

Advances in human enhancement technologies raise the prospect that people's identities may be altered so radically by enhancement that they will be essentially a different person after enhancement. To illustrate, some scholars of enhancement claim that individuals are unlikely to "survive" enhancement, in the sense that they continue to exist as one and the same person. Yet, others claim that enhancement is dehumanizing. Common to these claims is the assumption that enhancement affects a discontinuity between an individual's pre- and post-enhancement selves. Although extant analyses of the relationship between enhancement and identity have yielded many useful insights into the possible effects of human enhancement technologies on identity, progress in our understanding is marred by conceptual imprecision, the use of excessively thin conceptions of identity, and the conflation of distinct senses of identity. With respect to the latter, the conflation of numerical and narrative identity is particularly problematic. However, although these senses of identity are distinct, the fact that they are conflated is nevertheless informative about how people untutored in the metaphysics of identity—that is, the vast majority of people—reason about the effects of enhancement on identity. In this chapter, the authors draw on psychological research into self-continuity and dehumanization, respectively, to offer insights into why numerical and narrative identity are conflated, and they argue that future analyses of the relationship between enhancement and identity must be more deeply grounded in psychological and neuroscientific research than has been evidenced to date.

INTRODUCTION

The human enhancement literature is replete with claims about the effects of enhancement on identity. Many of these claims pertain to the constitution of enhanced individuals in terms of characteristics and identities gained or lost. For

example, advocates of enhancement assert that the augmentation of characteristics like intelligence is humanizing, perhaps superhumanizing, whereas opponents assert that the modification of human nature is dehumanizing. Relatedly, the literature is suffused with claims about the effects of enhancement on identity continuity. At issue

DOI: 10.4018/978-1-4666-6010-6.ch014

here is whether augmented individuals 'survive' enhancement, in the sense that they continue to exist as one and the same person.

The diversity of ways in which identity can be conceptualized has resulted in a plethora of insights into the possible effects of human enhancement technologies on identity. However, progress in understanding the relationship between enhancement and identity is often marred by conceptual imprecision and the conflation of distinct senses of identity. In some instances, the problem resides in the use of excessively thin conceptions of identity or ascribing distinct meanings to the same terms. Happily, errors of reasoning that stem from problems like these can be remedied fairly easily by, for example, explicitly defining identity rather than treating it as a primitive concept. However, in other instances, distinctions between conceptions of identity that are clear in theory are fuzzy in practice, especially when philosophical concepts mingle with folk concepts of human nature and human identity, as they do so incorrigibly in writings about human enhancement.

To illustrate, the distinction between numerical and narrative identity, which relates to an individual's survival as a human being or as a person and her self-concept, respectively, is clear in philosophical analyses of the relationship between enhancement and identity. The claim that post-enhancement changes in an individual's self-concept are unrelated to her survival as a person is eminently defensible (e.g., DeGrazia, 2005). Philosophically, identity-as-survival and identity-as-self-concept are distinct. However, psychologically, this crisp delineation between the two senses of identity does not always obtain.

Recent findings from self-continuity and dehumanization research blur the boundary between the content of identity (narrative identity) and the continuity of identity (numerical identity). To illustrate, self-continuity research, which emphasizes the contribution of autobiographical memory to the content and continuity of identity,

buttresses claims that enhancement may threaten an individual's survival as a person (e.g., Agar, 2014; Glannon, 2002). Further, dehumanization research, which emphasizes how the content of identity is associated with perceived ontological status, (i.e., as a human, animal or object) buttresses claims that enhancement may threaten an individual's survival as a human (e.g., Kass, 2002; President's Council on Bioethics, 2003; Somerville, 2006).

In this article, I offer a psychological perspective on the relationship between enhancement and the content and continuity of identity. In exploring reasons why the distinction between identity-as-survival and identity-as-self-concept is clear philosophically but fuzzy psychologically, I pay particular attention to autobiographical memory. Specifically, I argue that autobiographical memory contributes to both an individual's self-concept and her sense that she continues to exist as the same entity across time. In addition to examining the link between autobiographical memory and identity, I examine insights from the study of folk psychology about the relationship between person perception and humanness attributions. Through this examination of the link between identity, memory and humanness, I explain why the analytic distinction between the numerical and narrative senses of identity is not inevitably drawn in everyday reasoning about human enhancement.

I begin with a brisk overview of the distinction between numerical and narrative identity. Next, I draw on developmental, social and neuropsychological research to describe the contribution of autobiographical memory to identity content and continuity. Finally, I draw on social psychological research into folk concepts of humanness and the subtle, often implicit processes of everyday dehumanization to provide an account of how changes in the content of identity, which may occur after enhancement, might lead to perceived changes in the continuity of identity.

CONCEPTIONS OF NUMERICAL AND NARRATIVE IDENTITY

Numerical Identity

Numerical identity concerns the existence or survival of an entity over time. Specifically, an account of numerical identity provides criteria for something of a particular kind (e.g., a car, a plant, a person) to continue to exist as *that* entity despite any changes it undergoes over its lifetime. To illustrate, a person undergoes enormous physical and psychological changes over the years, yet she may understand all of these changes as having occurred to *her* (DeGrazia, 2005). There are two approaches to numerical identity: a biological approach and a psychological approach.

The biological approach. The biological approach to numerical identity holds that we continue to exist as essentially the same human beings as long as we remain biologically alive (e.g., Olson, 1997). On this view, which categorizes humans as *human animals*, what matters is continuity of what Descola (2009) calls *physicality*—the form, substance and physiological, perceptual, sensory-motor and proprioceptive processes typical of human animals. This means that an individual continues to survive *as a human* even if she becomes permanently unconscious (e.g., a persistent vegetative state). In the context of enhancement, an enhanced individual's survival as a human is assured as long as she experiences biophysical continuity.

The psychological approach. By contrast, the psychological approach to numerical identity holds that we continue to exist as the same individual, specifically *as a person*, as long as we experience continuity of one and the same inner life (DeGrazia, 2005)—what Descola (2009) terms *interiority*. This inner continuity can be understood in terms of specific psychological states (e.g., certain beliefs, desires or memories) or general psychological capacities (e.g., subjectivity, reflexivity, intentionality, or rationality).

According to Parfit (1984), the best known contemporary advocate of the idea that existence requires the persistence of psychological states, continuity occurs when a psychological state exists at one time and continues to exist at some later time. On this view, psychological connections occur between 'person-stages', defined as parts of persons that exist at specific times (e.g., me at 30 years of age and 35 years of age). Examples of connections include having an experience and later remembering it and forming an intention and later acting on it (DeGrazia, 2005). Another variant of the psychological approach holds that the relevant type of continuity is the persistence of one or more basic psychological capacities (e.g., subjectivity, intentionality). Exponents of this rather more liberal approach to numerical identity include Unger (1990) and Baker (2000).

Regardless of whether the persistence of specific psychological states or general mental capacities is the criterion for psychological survival, an individual's existence *as a person* in both of these approaches to numerical identity ends when she experiences a permanent loss of consciousness (DeGrazia, 2005).[1]

In the context of enhancement, the psychological approach to numerical identity means that an individual's survival as a person is assured only to the extent that she experiences psychological continuity.

Narrative Identity

The abstract concept of numerical identity arguably has little purchase outside the groves of academe. Instead, most people, especially those untutored in the metaphysics of identity, understand identity as self-concept, which is constituted by an individual's beliefs about her defining characteristics and identifications with other individuals and groups. This is called narrative identity and is straightforwardly about psychology (DeGrazia, 2005).

Over the past three decades, social psychologists have demonstrated that the self may be experienced in terms of its unique and idiosyncratic characteristics (e.g., playful, daughter of *X*), or in terms of group memberships (e.g., Jewish, Australian). These two forms of self-understanding have been generally conceptualized as concerning the *personal* and *social* self, respectively (Sani, 2008). In addition to this social partitioning of identity, identity can also be partitioned spatially, with different identities experienced in different roles and contexts (e.g., Deaux, 1992; Wyer & Srull, 1989) and temporally, with different identities experienced and expected over the lifespan (e.g., Markus & Nurius, 1986). Despite the multidimensional nature of identity, individuals nevertheless experience a sense of unity, which is an outcome of an integrating process called "selfing" (McAdams, 1997).

In summary, there are two distinct senses in which identity can be conceptualized. Numerical identity concerns an individual's survival *as a human animal* (the biological approach) or *as a person* (the psychological approach), whereas narrative identity concerns an individual's self-concept. Although this distinction seems clear, DeGrazia (2005), in his analysis of claims that have been offered about the effect of enhancement on identity, has argued that many scholars of enhancement fail to recognize and distinguish between these distinct senses of identity. Troublingly, in terms of progress in our understanding of enhancement, these senses are often conflated. An example of this, drawn from DeGrazia's analysis, is presented next to illustrate what this conflation looks like in practice.

Conflating Numerical and Narrative Identity

As evidence of his claim that numerical and narrative identity is conflated in the enhancement literature, DeGrazia (2005) cites Glannon's (2001) gene therapy-related claim that the "manipulation of the relevant neurotransmitters or regions of the brain that generate and support mental life would directly affect the very nature of the mental states definitive of personhood and personal identity through time" (pp. 81-82), which DeGrazia contends is implausible. The reason for DeGrazia's assessment of implausibility is Glannon's putative equation of personal identity with numerical identity. On the basis of this definition of identity, the substance of Glannon's claim is that the individual who exists before enhancement is numerically discontinuous with the individual who exists after enhancement. In other words, the claim is that augmentation would divest an altered being of her identity as a person. However, DeGrazia asserts that because the enhanced individual is likely to remember life before enhancement and because her intentions and attitudes are likely to survive, then she will likely judge any changes as having occurred to *her*. Stated baldly, she will continue to exist biologically and psychologically—her identity as a human and a person is preserved. This means that although her self-concept may be altered (e.g., her thinking might be faster or her memory might be more retentive), her continuing existence as a human and person will not be disrupted by enhancement.

The persuasiveness of claims that enhancement will (e.g., Agar, 2014) or will not (e.g., DeGrazia, 2005) cause numerical discontinuity rest, often uncomfortably, on the truth of the claim that enhancement technologies will destroy psychological states and mental capacities. Regardless of the veracity of this proposition, the fact that concepts as distinct as numerical and narrative identity can be conflated reveals something important about the relationship between these senses of identity. Indeed, as revealed by a growing body of developmental, social and neuropsychological research, numerical and narrative identities are underpinned by a common autobiographical memory system and are experienced as interconnected. It is to autobiographical memory and identity that attention now turns.

AUTOBIOGRAPHICAL MEMORY AND IDENTITY

Self-Continuity

One of the core aspects of the human self is the need to experience the self as a unity through time and space (Sani, 2008). That is, beyond the obvious physical and psychological changes that occur over the course of a lifetime, an individual needs to know and experience herself as essentially the same person across time and space (Bluck & Alea, 2008; Chandler & Lalonde, 1995; Sani, Bowe, & Herrera, 2008). This is called self-continuity and it is crucial for our psychological survival.

Although this need to experience a sustained sense of self through time is a generic feature of the human psyche (Reicher, 2008), our understanding of who we are, were, and will be is constructed within a larger 'community of minds' bound by a common language, beliefs, and identity (Bird & Reese, 2008; Nelson, 2008). Beginning in childhood and continuing throughout our lives, we develop and maintain an understanding of ourselves as an entity that perseveres as a unity across social contexts and through time and space, in part, through the medium of talk with others.

Researchers have suggested that people may experience different types of continuity. One type of continuity is *narrative continuity*, which arises from the integration of various events and personal changes that occur over a lifetime into a coherent story or narrative (McAdams, 2001). Another type of continuity, which is coterminous with the psychological continuity theory of identity, is *phenomenological continuity*. Consistent with the account of numerical identity offered earlier, phenomenological continuity is experienced when an individual remembers past events and imagines future events (Schater, Addis, & Buckner, 2007; Tulving, 1985). Through this process of remembering and imagining, an individual creates psychological connections between her past, present and future selves.

However, how do we know and experience that we are, in a fundamental way, the same person across social contexts, time and space? How do we actually know and feel that we are the same person that we were yesterday or a decade ago? Autobiographical memory makes a contribution to this sense of self-continuity and is examined next.

Autobiographical Memory, Identity Content and Identity Continuity

One crucial process involved in knowing and feeling that we are fundamentally the same person across time is autobiographical memory (Addis & Tippett, 2008; Bluck & Alea, 2008). Indeed, a central function of autobiographical memory is to help individuals maintain self-continuity (Bluck, 2003). Autobiographical memory is typically broken down into *personal semantic* and *personal episodic* components, with the former consisting of facts about oneself and one's life and the latter consisting of memories about temporally-specific events (e.g., Kopelman, Wilson, & Baddeley, 1990). However, there is some debate as to which components of autobiographical memory contribute to the content and continuity of identity. Although a thoroughgoing account of the contribution of autobiographical memory to identity content and continuity is beyond the scope of this article (see Addis & Tippett, 2008, for an excellent review), Addis and Tippett argue that personal semantic and personal episodic memory contributes to the content of identity and narrative continuity, whereas only personal episodic memory contributes to phenomenological continuity.

To summarize, one of the core needs of the human self is to understand and experience the self as a continuous unity across the lifespan. Autobiographical memory, which is comprised of facts about the self and events that have been experienced, undergirds this sense of phenomenological and narrative continuity. Autobiographical memory also informs the self-concept. Therefore, psychologically, self-concept and self-continuity are linked. Senses of identity that are distinct philosophically are connected psychologically, which offers clues as to why the analytic distinction between numerical and narrative identity is not always observed in writings on enhancement and identity.

Enhancement and Identity

In a recent examination of the threats posed by "radical enhancement," defined as enhancement that "improves significant attributes and abilities to levels that greatly exceed what is currently possible for human beings" (Agar, 2014, p. 2), Agar argues that radical enhancement is "likely to end the existence of its human subjects" (p. 56). This claim is, of course, redolent of Glannon's (2001) claims about the effects of procedures that involve the manipulation of neurotransmitters or brain regions. Like Glannon (2001), Agar contends that numerical identity is at issue. Similarly, like Glannon (2002), Agar focuses on the threats posed by enhancement to autobiographical memory. Taken together, Agar asserts that by threatening autobiographical memory, radical enhancement is likely to "end the existence" of those individuals who undergo enhancement. Given the contribution of autobiographical memory to self-continuity, the argument that enhancement might disrupt an individual's continuing existence *as a person* by damaging autobiographical memory is sustainable, especially—perhaps only—if phenomenological continuity is at issue. From the perspective of psychological science, enhancements that destroy autobiographical memory carry the risk of altering an individual's self-concept and undermining self-continuity.

So much for the science of identity content and continuity. Are people likely to choose enhancements that threaten their self-concept and self-continuity? Although there is vanishingly little research that addresses this question, the scant evidence that does exist suggests that people are unlikely to knowingly choose enhancements that carry these risks. Specifically, research suggests that people are concerned about understanding themselves and making decisions about their characteristics and capacities in ways that maintain their self-concept and self-continuity. To illustrate, Haslam and Bain (2007) demonstrated that when people think about the characteristics of their past and present selves, essential traits are adjudged unchanged. Similarly, in a study about preferences for enhancement pharmaceuticals, Riis, Simmons and Goodwin (2008) showed that people are very reluctant to enhance traits that are essential to personal identity (e.g., empathy, kindness) but less reluctant to enhance traits that are of peripheral import (e.g., speed of reflexes, hand-eye coordination). Lipsman, Zener, and Bernstein (2009) obtained similar results in the context of prospective neurosurgery. The distinction between essential and peripheral traits is also important in reasoning about whether enhancement carries the risk of stripping enhanced beings of their identity as humans and it is to this that consideration turns next.

Humanness and Dehumanization

Unlike conceptions of self identity that partition the self-concept into social, spatial, and temporal dimensions but do not question an individual's status *as a human*, conceptions of human identity inherently concern an entity's humanness. A now-sizeable body of social psychology research has revealed the many subtle ways in which our understanding of humanness is revealed in our beliefs about such characteristics as emotions (Demoulin et al., 2004), personality traits (Haslam, Bain, Douge, Lee, & Bastian, 2005; Haslam, Bastian, & Bissett, 2004), mental capacities (Gray, Gray, & Wegner, 2007), values (Bain, Kashima, & Haslam, 2006), and behaviors (Wilson & Haslam, 2013). Notably, this research has also revealed some interesting, if somewhat unsettling, insights into the relationship between person perception and judgments about human identity (e.g., Haslam et al., 2005; Leyens et al., 2000, 2001; Loughnan & Haslam, 2007; Loughnan, Haslam, & Kashima, 2009).

It is important to understand the perceived humanness of such characteristics as emotions, traits, mental capacities and behaviors because claims about the effects of enhancements on human identity are almost invariably made with reference to the effects of modifying specific characteristics. To illustrate, advocates of enhancement (e.g., Bostrom, 2003, 2005, 2008; Savulescu, 2003, 2005) tend to focus on such characteristics as intelligence, self-control and morality, whereas opponents (e.g., Habermas, 2003; Kass, 2002, 2003) tend to focus on individuality, agency and emotionality.

Given the prominence of specific characteristics in arguments about enhancement and identity, it is pertinent to briskly review recent psychological research into folk beliefs about the humanness of emotions, traits, mental capacities and behaviors. After this, a two-part model of human identity is proposed that relates these concepts to the biological and psychological types of numerical identity outlined earlier.

Folk Concepts of Humanness

Whereas the age-old philosophical idea that species are natural kinds with essential, universal traits has lost currency in scientific understandings of human and nonhuman animals (Fernández-Armesto, 2004), essentialist thinking perseveres in folk psychology (e.g., Haslam et al., 2004, 2005). The use of essentialist terminology in the enhancement debate, especially by opponents of enhancement, suggests that folk conceptions of humanness inform enhancement scholars' understanding of basic concepts (e.g., human nature, human essence, human identity) and, indeed, reasoning about human enhancement.

What, though, is folk psychology and why should scholars of human enhancement care about it? Folk psychology refers to a system of shared

meaning that organizes laypeople's understanding and experience of, and transactions with the social world. All cultures, as explained by Bruner (1990), possess a folk psychology, which describes such psychological phenomena as the elements of our own minds—beliefs, desires, valuings, intentions—as well as providing a more or less normative description of what makes people 'tick' and act the way they do (see also Malle, 1999). As the enhancement debate moves out of academe and into the public domain, folk beliefs about humanness will almost certainly inform laypeople's understanding of the meaning and consequences of enhancement and whether personhood or, indeed, human identity is properly ascribed to, or withheld from, the enhanced. With these preliminaries dealt with, consideration now turns to research that has sought to clarify lay concepts of humanness in Western culture.

The longest debated frontier of human identity in Western culture has been between humans and animals (Fernández-Armesto, 2004). This frontier has historically informed Western conceptions of what it means to be human (Descola, 2009; Plumwood, 2002). However, the boundary between humans and non-human animals is not the only boundary to inform our understanding of humanness. Another salient boundary is between humans and machines (Hampshire, 1991; Turkle, 1991). Recent research attests to the psychological reality of these two basic ways of understanding humanness.

Humanness beliefs about emotions. Demoulin et al. (2004) demonstrated that laypeople distinguish between emotions that are shared with animals ('non-uniquely' human emotions) and uniquely human emotions, which parallel distinctions made by emotion scientists (e.g., Ekman, 1992; Epstein, 1984). Non-uniquely human emotions (e.g., anger, surprise) are understood as innate, visible to outside observers, caused by external events, and of short duration (Demoulin et al., 2004; Rodriguez et al., 2005). By contrast, uniquely human emotions (e.g., love, guilt) are regarded as invisible to observers, generated internally via thinking, experienced over a long duration, as morally informative, and acquired through socialization (Demoulin et al., 2004; Rodriguez et al., 2005).

Humanness beliefs about traits. Haslam et al.'s (2004, 2005) trait-based research demonstrated two distinct senses of humanness: a species-unique (Human Uniqueness; HU) and a species-typical sense (Human Nature; HN). By definition, HU refers to attributes that distinguish humans from animals and is exemplified by civility, moral sensibility, self-control, and rationality (Haslam et al., 2005). Further, HU traits are judged as acquired through learning, as requiring maturity for their expression, not prevalent in the population, and culturally specific (Haslam et al., 2005). By contrast, HN reflects the deep, biologically based attributes of humans, some of which may be shared with animals as part of our common mammalian heritage. Unlike HU traits, which reflect the 'surface' of humans, HN traits are held to reflect our 'essence'; that is, they are understood as innate, prevalent, and universal (Haslam et al., 2004, 2005). HN characterized by emotional responsiveness, prosocial warmth, cognitive openness, and individuality (Haslam et al., 2005). Finally, HN and HU distinguish humans from nonhumans in distinct ways. HN is associated with animals, but not machines, whereas HU is associated with machines, but not animals (Loughnan & Haslam, 2007).

Humanness beliefs about mental capacities. Research by Gray et al. (2007) into beliefs about mental capacities demonstrates that there are two dimensions of mind perception, called Agency and Experience. Agency is exemplified by the capacity for language, reason, self-control, and morality. This dimension parallels the findings obtained for uniquely human emotions (Demoulin et al., 2004) and traits (Haslam et al., 2005). By contrast, Experience involves capacities for consciousness (i.e., being aware of things in the world), primary emotions, and basic appetites. This dimension parallels the judgments obtained

for HN traits (Haslam et al., 2004, 2005). Consistent with emotion, trait, and behavior-based (Wilson & Haslam, 2013) research, the capacity for Agency defines the human–animal boundary, whereas Experience defines the human–machine boundary (Gray et al., 2007).

Humanness beliefs about behaviors. Wilson and Haslam's (2013) behavior-based research also demonstrated that people distinguish between HN and HU. Consistent with Haslam and colleagues' (2004, 2005) depiction of HN as a positive, innate, and universal sense of humanness, HN behaviors are positive, prevalent, performed cross-culturally, and not acquired through socialization, suggesting that HN as innate. Similarly, consistent with Haslam et al.'s depiction of HU as a cognitively sophisticated sense of humanness that is acquired over time through the process of socialization, maturity, thought and social learning were deemed necessary for the performance of HU behaviors. Finally, consistent with Loughnan and Haslam (2007), HN defines the boundary between humans and robots, whereas HU defines the boundary between humans and animals.

Two senses of humanness. In summary, distinct lines of research converge on the idea that there are two basic senses of humanness. HN is a species-typical sense—the human essence—that reflects the biologically based continuities and connections between humans and animals. HN is characterized by capacities for basic consciousness, primary emotions, bodily appetites, forming and maintaining relationships, learning from experience, and individuality or personality. By contrast, HU is a species-unique sense of humanness that emphasizes the human transcendence of nature, specifically animal nature. Unlike HN, which is regarded as innate, HU is understood as acquired through social learning and enculturation and is characterized by capacities for higher-order consciousness, secondary emotions, and cognitively complex capacities for rationality, symbolic communication, and self-control and morality.

Two Senses of Human Identity

Although membership of the species Homo sapiens is a necessary condition for the ascription of basic, biological human status, it is not sufficient for the ascription of fully human status—personhood. It is necessary, therefore, to distinguish between the biological type 'human being' from the psychological type 'person' when thinking about human identity. These two senses of identity overlap, but are not coincident (Singer, 2000).

Humanhood. The biological approach to identity—specifically numerical identity—holds that we continue to exist as one and the same entity as long as we remain biologically alive. The sense of human identity that corresponds with the biological approach to numerical identity, which might be termed 'humanhood,' undergirds the psychologically saturated status of personhood. The ascription of the status of humanhood to an immature human organism, such as an embryo, fetus or a baby, suggests that ascription of this sense of human identity indicates that the organism—the human animal—has the *potential* for species-typically (HN) and species-unique (HU) characteristics and capacities. However, babies, indeed fetuses, are judged by laypeople to possess rudimentary *capacities* for such psychological states as hunger, pleasure, fear, and personality (Gray et al., 2007), which indicates that the potential for HN is thought to be realized sooner than that for HU—consistent with the idea that HN is biologically based. At minimum, the ascription of the status of humanhood to an organism indicates that the it has the potential for HN and UH.

Personhood. The psychological approach consists in some sort of psychological continuity involving either the maintenance of psychological connections over time or the continuation of one or more basic psychological capacities. The sense of numerical identity that corresponds with the psychological approach is personhood. Consistent with the proposition that psychological continuity involves, at minimum, the persistence of basic psychological capacities over time, a number of indicators of personhood have been enumerated. For example, personhood is held to involve capacities for self-awareness, self-control, recognizing other individuals, having a sense of the past and future, relating to and forming attachments with others, deliberately communicating with others, thinking about what to do, formulating theories about what others do, and considering own goals and motives (Clark, 2003; Fletcher, 1972).

Although this collection of indicators of personhood is not exhaustive, there is a clear correspondence between these capacities and the psychological capacities associated with HN and HU. For example, the capacities for self-awareness, forming attachments with others and having a sense of the past and future broadly correspond with the HN characteristics of emotional responsiveness, interpersonal warmth, and individuality. Similarly, capacities for thinking about what to do, consideration of own goals and motives, self-control, deliberate communication, and the formulation of theories about what others do broadly corresponds with the HU capacities for rationality, self-control, and maturity.

In summary, although the age-old philosophical idea that species are natural kinds, with essential, universal traits has lost currency in scientific understandings of human and nonhuman animals, these ideas persevere in folk psychology. In folk psychology, there are two distinct senses of humanness: an essentialized, species-typical sense (HN) and a non-essentialized, species-unique sense (HU). Whereas HN is characterized by emotionality, warmth, and individuality, HU is characterized by rationality, self-control, and refinement. The two senses of humanness are associated, in turn, with biologically based humanhood and psychologically saturated personhood. The ascription of the status of humanhood indicates that an organism has the potential for HN and HU, whereas the ascription of personhood indicates that capacities for HN and HU are fully realized. What are the identity-related consequences of enhancing HN and HU? What bearing does the denial of HN and HU have on beliefs about human identity? These questions are considered next.

A Social Psychological Model of Dehumanization

As Montagu and Matson (1983) argued, dehumanization may be as old as the human species. Dehumanization is a psychological process whereby people view and even sometimes label other individuals or collectives as incompletely human (Haslam, 2006; Zimbardo, 2007). Concerns about the consequences of enhancement upon the identity of altered beings pervade the debate about human enhancement. For example, advocates of enhancement argue that it will not degrade the humanity of the enhanced and may make them more than human, whereas opponents argue that it will degrade their humanity and make them less than human (Arnhart, 2003; Brey, 2008; Wilson & Haslam, 2009).

Recent social psychological research has led to considerable advances in our understanding of dehumanization that are pertinent to understanding the claims made about human enhancement. To illustrate, Haslam (2006) incorporated HN and HU into a model of dehumanization in which the denial of the each sense of humanness yields distinct forms of dehumanization: animalistic and mechanistic. Animalistic dehumanization involves the denial of HU. When people are dehumanized in this way, they are characterized as bestial: amoral, uncultured, instinctive, irrational, and incapable of self-control (Haslam, 2006). Mechanistic dehumanization, by contrast, involves the denial of HN. Dehumanized in this way, people are seen as passive, inert, cold, and rigid; attributes more characteristic of robots than humans (Haslam, 2006). Recent research supports the psychological reality of these two contrasts between humans and nonhumans and the mechanistic and animalistic forms of dehumanization that they imply (see, e.g., Loughnan & Haslam, 2007; Loughnan et al., 2009).

Having outlined the two senses of humanness (HN, HU), the biological and psychological approaches to numerical identity, the two corresponding senses of human identity (humanhood, personhood), and the two forms of dehumanization, I conclude by considering the claims of advocates and opponents of enhancement about the effects of enhancement on human identity.

Enhancement is superhumanizing. Advocates of enhancement make two claims: first, that enhancement is likely to improve our humanity and second, that enhancement is unlikely to degrade our humanity. According to the first claim, enhanced beings will represent an improvement on present humans, as indexed by their superior intellectual, psychological and physical capabilities. The second claim draws on the idea that our nature is partly contingent on the social and technological context and that the idea that the "extended phenotypes" of present-day humans has not divested us of our humanness (Bostrom, 2005). If HU is the operative sense of humanness, as it appears to be for proponents of enhancement, then it is clear why humanness is seen as dynamic, partially constructed, and an ensemble of capacities. For advocates, the enhancement of HU (e.g., intelligence, morality, self-control) is akin to the cultivation of personhood. The enhancement of HU is intrinsically humanizing, and perhaps superhumanizing. Rather than a wholesale loss of humanness, there will be a piece-wise gain in it.

Enhancement is dehumanizing. Opponents argue that enhancement will destroy the human essence and invalidate altered beings' claim to human status. The proposition that enhancement will be intrinsically dehumanizing stems, in part, from the view that human nature is either "given" (Kass, 2003), "gifted" (Sandel, 2007) or "sacred" (Somerville, 2006). In addition to this, opponents' arguments against enhancement reflect a view that the "technological mastery" of human nature would itself be dehumanizing. This idea finds expression in Kass's (2002) assertion that enhancement will inevitably give way to dehumanization and Habermas's (2003) claim that enhancement destroys the boundary between persons and objects. If HN is the operative sense of humanness, as it appears to be for opponents, it is clear why humanness is conceptualized holistically and why modification is seen as threatening mechanistic dehumanization. For opponents, altering HN, particularly by alteration of the genome, destroys the substrate of the human essence. Continuing identity *as a human* is assured only to the extent that the integrity of the human essence is preserved, for this is the bulwark between human and nonhuman identity. If the essence is modified, then the category it undergirds (i.e., humankind) will be radically altered. Understood in this way, the proposition that enhancement will end an individual's survival *as a human* becomes more comprehensible, if no less unsustainable.

CONCLUSION

The human enhancement literature is replete with claims about the effects of enhancement on identity, especially the likelihood that an enhanced individual will continue to exist *as a human* or *as a person* after enhancement. The folk psychological model of humanness and human identity sketched here offers an explicit characterization of folk psychologically-grounded conceptions of humanness and human identity and philosophically-grounded biological and psychological approaches to numerical identity. Although I make no claims that this model reflects what is known scientifically about humanness and human identity, it does possess the modest virtue of describing important aspects of the structure of folk concepts of humanness and human identity used in the debate about enhancement. Moreover it helps identify how philosophical investigations of enhancement and identity might address some prevailing conceptual and empirical deficits by engaging more deeply with developmental, social and neuropsychological research into the contributions of autobiographical memory to identity content

and continuity. As enhancement technology and identity become more tightly interwoven, and as we apply more of these technologies to ourselves, it is vital that we frame the issues at hand in ways that promote our conceptual and ethical understanding of implications of these advances for personal and human identity. At minimum, it is essential to ground all analyses of enhancement and identity in research findings from psychology and neuroscience about the relationship between memory and identity.

REFERENCES

Addis, D. R., & Tippett, L. J. (2008). The contributions of autobiographical memory to the content and continuity of identity: A social-cognitive neuroscience approach. In F. Sani (Ed.), *Self continuity: Individual and collective perspectives* (pp. 71–84). New York: Psychology Press.

Agar, N. (2014). *Truly human enhancement.* Cambridge, MA: MIT Press. doi:10.7551/mitpress/9780262026635.001.0001

Arnhart, L. (2003). Human nature is here to stay. *New Atlantis (Washington, D.C.), 2,* 65–78.

Bain, P., Kashima, Y., & Haslam, N. (2006). Conceptual beliefs about human values and their implications: Human nature beliefs predict value importance, value trade-offs, and responses to value-laden rhetoric. *Journal of Personality and Social Psychology, 91,* 351–367. doi:10.1037/0022-3514.91.2.351 PMID:16881770

Baker, L. R. (2000). *Persons and bodies.* Cambridge, UK: Cambridge University Press. doi:10.1017/CBO9781139173124

Bird, A., & Reese, E. (2008). Autobiographical memory in childhood and the development of a continuous self. In F. Sani (Ed.), *Self continuity: Individual and collective perspectives* (pp. 43–54). New York: Psychology Press.

Bluck, S. (2003). Autobiographical memory: Exploring its functions in everyday life. *Memory (Hove, England), 11*, 113–123. doi:10.1080/741938206 PMID:12820825

Bluck, S., & Alea, N. (2008). Remembering being me: The self continuity function of autobiographical memory in younger and older adults. In F. Sani (Ed.), *Self continuity: Individual and collective perspectives* (pp. 55–70). New York: Psychology Press.

Bostrom, N. (2003).*The Transhumanist FAQ (version 2.1)*. Retrieved from http://www.transhumanism.org/resources/FAQv21.pdf

Bostrom, N. (2005). In defense of posthuman dignity. *Bioethics, 19*(3), 202–214. doi:10.1111/j.1467-8519.2005.00437.x PMID:16167401

Bostrom, N. (2008). Dignity and enhancement. In *Human dignity and bioethics: Essays commissioned by the President's Council on Bioethics* (pp. 173–207). Washington, DC: The President's Council on Bioethics.

Brey, P. (2008). Human enhancement and personal identity. In J. Berg Olsen, E. Selinger, & S. Riis (Eds.), *New waves in philosophy of technology* (pp. 169–185). New York: Palgrave Macmillan.

Bruner, J. (1990). *Acts of meaning*. Cambridge, MA: Harvard University Press.

Chandler, M. J., & Lalonde, C. E. (1995). The problem of self-continuity in the context of rapid personal and cultural change. I A. Oosterwegel & R. A. Wicklund (Eds.), The self in European and American culture: Development and processes (pp. 45-63). Dordrecht, The Netherlands: Kluwer Academic.

Clark, S. R. L. (2003). Non-personal minds. In A. O'Hear (Ed.), *Minds and persons* (pp. 185–209). Cambridge, UK: Cambridge University Press. doi:10.1017/CBO9780511550294.011

Clauss, R., & Nel, W. (2006). Drug induced arousal from the permanent vegetative state. *NeuroRehabilitation, 21*, 23–28. PMID:16720934

Deaux, K. (1992). Personalizing identity and socializing self. In G. M. Breakwell (Ed.), *Social psychology of identity and the self concept* (pp. 9–33). London: Surrey University Press.

DeGrazia, D. (2005). Enhancement technologies and human identity. *The Journal of Medicine and Philosophy, 30*, 261–283. doi:10.1080/03605310590960166 PMID:16036459

Demoulin, S., Leyens, J. P., Paladino, M. P., Rodriguez, R. T., Rodriguez, A. P., & Dovidio, J. F. (2004). Dimensions of uniquely and non-uniquely human emotions. *Cognition and Emotion, 18*(1), 71–96. doi:10.1080/02699930244000444

Descola, P. (2009). Human natures. *Social Anthropology, 17*, 145–157. doi:10.1111/j.1469-8676.2009.00063.x

Du, B., Shan, A., Zhang, Y., Zhong, X., Chen, D., & Cai, K. (2014). Zolpidem arouses patients in vegetative state after brain injury: Qualitative evaluation and indications. *The American Journal of the Medical Sciences, 347*(3), 178–182. doi:10.1097/MAJ.0b013e318287c79c PMID:23462249

Ekman, P. (1992). An argument for basic emotions. *Cognition and Emotion, 18*, 71–96.

Epstein, S. (1984). Controversial issues in emotion theory. *Review of Personality and Social Psychology, 5*, 64–88.

Fernández-Armesto, F. (2004). *Humankind: A brief history*. Oxford, UK: Oxford University Press.

Fletcher, J. (1972). Indicators of personhood: A tentative profile. *The Hastings Center Report, 2*, 5. doi:10.2307/3561570 PMID:4679693

Fukuyama, F. (2002). *Our posthuman future: Consequences of the biotechnology revolution.* New York: Farrar, Strauss and Giroux.

Glannon, W. (2001). *Genes and future people: Philosophical issues in human genetics.* Cambridge, MA: Westview Press.

Glannon, W. (2002). Identity, prudential concern, and extended lives. *Bioethics, 16,* 266–283. doi:10.1111/1467-8519.00285 PMID:12211249

Gray, H. M., Gray, K., & Wegner, D. M. (2007). Dimensions of mind perception. *Science, 315,* 619. doi:10.1126/science.1134475 PMID:17272713

Habermas, J. (2003). *The future of human nature.* Cambridge, UK: Polity.

Hampshire, S. (1991). Biology, machines, and humanity. In J. J. Sheehan, & M. Sosna (Eds.), *The boundaries of humanity: Humans, animals, machines* (pp. 253–256). Los Angeles, CA: University of California Press.

Haslam, N. (2006). Dehumanization: An integrative review. *Personality and Social Psychology Review, 10*(3), 252–264. doi:10.1207/s15327957pspr1003_4 PMID:16859440

Haslam, N., & Bain, P. (2007). Humanizing the self: Moderators of the attribution of lesser humanness to others. *Personality and Social Psychology Bulletin, 33*(1), 57–68. doi:10.1177/0146167206293191 PMID:17178930

Haslam, N., Bain, P., Douge, L., Lee, M., & Bastian, B. (2005). More human than you: Attributing humanness to self and others. *Journal of Personality and Social Psychology, 89*(6), 937–950. doi:10.1037/0022-3514.89.6.937 PMID:16393026

Haslam, N., Bastian, B., & Bissett, M. (2004). Essentialist beliefs about personality and their implications. *Personality and Social Psychology Bulletin, 30*(12), 1661–1673. doi:10.1177/0146167204271182 PMID:15536247

Kass, L. R. (2002). *Life, liberty, and the defense of dignity: The challenge for bioethics.* San Francisco, CA: Encounter Books.

Kass, L. R. (2003). Ageless bodies, happy souls: Biotechnology and the pursuit of perfection. *New Atlantis (Washington, D.C.), 1,* 9–28. PMID:15584192

Kopelman, M. D., Wilson, B., & Baddeley, A. (1990). *The autobiographical memory interview.* Suffolk, UK: Thames Valley Test Company.

Leyens, J. P., Paladino, M. P., Rodriguez, R. T., Vaes, J., Demoulin, S., & Rodriguez, A. P. (2000). The emotional side of prejudice: The attribution of secondary emotions to ingroups and outgroups. *Personality and Social Psychology Review, 4*(2), 186–197. doi:10.1207/S15327957PSPR0402_06

Leyens, J. P., Rodriguez, R. T., Rodriguez, R. T., Gaunt, R., Paladino, P. M., Vaes, J., & Demoulin, S. (2001). Psychological essentialism and the attribution of uniquely human emotions to ingroups and outgroups. *European Journal of Social Psychology, 31,* 395–411. doi:10.1002/ejsp.50

Lipsman, N., Zener, R., & Bernstein, M. (2009). Personal identity, enhancement and neurosurgery: A qualitative study in applied neuroethics. *Bioethics, 23*(6), 375–383. doi:10.1111/j.1467-8519.2009.01729.x PMID:19527265

Loughnan, S., & Haslam, N. (2007). Animals and androids: Implicit associations between social categories and nonhumans. *Psychological Science, 18*(2), 116–121. doi:10.1111/j.1467-9280.2007.01858.x PMID:17425529

Loughnan, S., Haslam, N., & Kashima, Y. (2009). Understanding the relationship between attribute-based and metaphor-based dehumanization. *Group Processes & Intergroup Relations, 12*(6), 747–762. doi:10.1177/1368430209347726

Malle, B. (1999). How people explain behavior: A new theoretical framework. *Personality and Social Psychology Review*, *3*(1), 23–48. doi:10.1207/s15327957pspr0301_2 PMID:15647146

Markus, H. R., & Nurius, P. (1986). Possible selves. *The American Psychologist*, *41*(9), 954–969. doi:10.1037/0003-066X.41.9.954

McAdams, D. P. (1997). The case for unity in the (post) modern self: A modest proposal. In R. D. Ashmore, & L. Jussim (Eds.), *Self and identity: Fundamental issues* (pp. 46–77). New York: Oxford University Press.

McAdams, D. P. (2001). The psychology of life stories. *Review of General Psychology*, *5*(2), 100–122. doi:10.1037/1089-2680.5.2.100

Montagu, A., & Matson, F. (1983). *The dehumanization of man*. New York: McGraw-Hill.

Nelson, K. (2008). Self in time: Emergence within a community of minds. In F. Sani (Ed.), *Self continuity: Individual and collective perspectives* (pp. 13–26). New York: Psychology Press.

Olson, E. (1997). *The human animal*. New York: Oxford University Press.

Parfit, D. (1984). *Reasons and persons*. Oxford, UK: Oxford University Press.

Plumwood, V. (2002). *Environmental culture: The ecological crisis of reason*. London: Routledge.

President's Council on Bioethics. (2003). *Beyond therapy: Biotechnology and the pursuit of happiness*. New York: Regan Books.

Reicher, S. (2008). Making a past fit for the future: The political and ontological dimensions of historical continuity. In F. Sani (Ed.), *Self continuity: Individual and collective perspectives* (pp. 145–158). New York: Psychology Press.

Riis, J., Simmons, J. P., & Goodwin, G. P. (2008). Preferences for enhancement pharmaceuticals: The reluctance to enhance fundamental traits. *The Journal of Consumer Research*, *35*, 495–508. doi:10.1086/588746

Rodriguez, R. T., Leyens, J. P., Rodriguez, A. P., Betancor Rodriguez, V., Quiles de Castillo, M. N., Demoulin, S., & Cortés, B. (2005). The lay distinction between primary and secondary emotions: A spontaneous categorization? *International Journal of Psychology*, *40*(2), 100–107. doi:10.1080/00207590444000221

Sandel, M. J. (2007). *The case against perfection: Ethics in the age of genetic engineering*. Cambridge, MA: The Belknap Press of Harvard University Press.

Sani, F. (2008). Introduction and overview. In F. Sani (Ed.), *Self continuity: Individual and collective perspectives* (pp. 1–12). New York: Psychology Press.

Sani, F., Bowe, M., & Herrera, M. (2008). Perceived collective continuity: Seeing groups as temporally enduring entities. In F. Sani (Ed.), *Self continuity: Individual and collective perspectives* (pp. 159–172). New York: Psychology Press.

Savulescu, J. (2003). Human-Animal transgenesis and chimeras might be an expression of our humanity. *The American Journal of Bioethics*, *3*(3), 22–25. doi:10.1162/15265160360706462 PMID:14594475

Savulescu, J. (2005). New breeds of humans: The moral obligation to enhance. *Ethics. Law and Moral Philosophy of Reproductive Medicine*, *1*(1), 36–39.

Schater, D. L., Addis, D. R., & Buckner, R. L. (2007). Remembering the past to imagine the future: The prospective brain. *Nature Reviews. Neuroscience*, *8*, 657–661. doi:10.1038/nrn2213 PMID:17700624

Singer, P. (2000). *Writings on an ethical life.* London: Fourth Estate.

Snyman, N., Egan, J. R., London, K., Howman-Giles, R., Gill, D., Gillis, J., & Scheinberg, A. (2010). Zolpidem for persistent vegetative state—A placebo-controlled trial in pediatrics. *Neuropediatrics, 41*(5), 223–227. doi:10.1055/s-0030-1269893 PMID:21210338

Somerville, M. (2006). *The ethical imagination: Journeys of the human spirit.* Melbourne, Australia: Melbourne University Press.

Thonnard, M., Gosseries, O., Demertzi, A., Lugo, Z., Vanhaudenhuyse, A., & Bruno, M.-A. et al. (2013). Effect of zolpidem in chronic disorders of consciousness: A prospective open-label study. *Functional Neurology, 28*(4), 259–264. PMID:24598393

Tulving, E. (1985). Memory and consciousness. *Canadian Psychology, 25,* 1–12. doi:10.1037/h0080017

Turkle, S. (1991). Romantic reactions: Paradoxical responses to the computer presence. In J. J. Sheehan, & M. Sosna (Eds.), *The boundaries of humanity: Humans, animals, machines* (pp. 224–252). Los Angeles, CA: University of California Press.

Unger, P. (1990). *Identity, consciousness, and value.* New York: Oxford University Press.

Whyte, J., & Myers, R. (2009). Incidence of clinically significant responses to zolpidem among patients with disorders of consciousness: A preliminary placebo controlled trial. *American Journal of Physical Medicine & Rehabilitation, 88*(5), 410–418. doi:10.1097/PHM.0b013e3181a0e3a0 PMID:19620954

Wilson, S., & Haslam, N. (2009). Is the future more or less human? Differing views of humanness in the posthumanism debate. *Journal for the Theory of Social Behaviour, 39*(2), 247–266. doi:10.1111/j.1468-5914.2009.00398.x

Wilson, S., & Haslam, N. (2012). Reasoning about human enhancement: Towards a folk psychological model of human nature and human identity. In R. Luppicini (Ed.), *Handbook of Research on technoself: Identity in a technological society* (pp. 175–188). Academic Press. doi:10.4018/978-1-4666-2211-1.ch010

Wilson, S., & Haslam, N. (2013). Humanness beliefs about behavior: An index and comparative human-nonhuman behavior judgments. *Behavior Research Methods, 45*(2), 372–382. doi:10.3758/s13428-012-0252-7 PMID:22993128

Wyer, R. S. Jr, & Srull, T. K. (1989). *Memory and cognition in its social context.* Hillsdale, NJ: Erlbaum Associates.

Zimbardo, P. (2007). *The Lucifer effect: Understanding how good people turn evil.* New York: Random House.

KEY TERMS AND DEFINITIONS

Autobiographical Memory: A type of memory that is delineated into personal semantic and personal episodic components, with the former consisting of facts about the self and the latter consisting of memories of temporally-specific events. Both components of autobiographical memory contribute to an individual's sense of self-continuity.

Dehumanization: The psychological process by which people implicitly or explicitly view other individuals or groups as incompletely human. When HU is denied, people are likened to animals. By contrast, when HN is denied, people are likened to robots.

Enhancement: The non-therapeutic biotechnological modification of a human being that enhances his or her psychological, emotional, intellectual, and physical capacities rather than repairing them.

Folk Psychology: A system of shared meaning within a culture that organizes people's understanding of the social world. Folk psychology describes the elements of our own and other's minds such as beliefs and desires and it provides normative descriptions of what makes people 'tick'. Also called belief-desire or commonsense psychology.

Human Nature: Human Nature (HN) is a sense of humanness that reflects the universal and innate attributes of the human species, some of which may be shared with other animals. HN is characterized by emotional responsiveness, interpersonal warmth, cognitive openness, and individuality.

Humanness: A broad term that refers to the quality or state of being human. Given the diversity of beliefs about what it means to be human, the term 'humanness' provides little guidance as to what characteristics are implied by it. Conceptual precision is improved when specific senses of humanness (e.g., HN, HU) are the focal constructs.

Human Uniqueness: Human Uniqueness (HU) is a socially learned and culturally-specific sense of humanness involving qualities that distinguish humans from nonhuman animals. HU is characterized by rationality, self-control, moral sensibility, civility, and refinement.

Narrative Identity: Narrative identity concerns an individual person's beliefs about her defining characteristics and her identifications with other individuals and social groups.

Numerical Identity: Numerical identity concerns the existence or survival of an entity over time. There are two approaches to numerical identity. The biological approach hold that we continue to exist as the same human beings as long as we remain biologically alive. By contrast, the psychological approach holds that we continue to exist as the same person as long as we experience psychological continuity.

Self-Continuity: The sense experienced by an individual person that, despite the obvious physical and psychological changes that occur over the course of her lifetime, she remains one and the same individual. Self-continuity can be delineated into narrative continuity, which arises from the integration of events and personal changes into a coherent story, and phenomenological continuity, which arises from the experience of psychological continuity.

ENDNOTES

[1]   Note, however, that research suggests that the brain function of a few individuals in persistent vegetative states can be restored by the administration of zolpidem (e.g., Clauss & Nel, 2006; Du et al., 2014; c.f. Snyman et al., 2010; Thonnard et al., 2013; Whyte & Myers, 2009). Although research into the treatment of disorders of consciousness with drugs like zolpidem is in its infancy, and presently yields mixed results, findings such as these nevertheless caution against over-hasty claims that an individual's survival *as a person* ends when she enters a state that appears to involve a permanent loss of consciousness.

Related References

To continue our tradition of advancing information science and technology research, we have compiled a list of recommended IGI Global readings. These references will provide additional information and guidance to further enrich your knowledge and assist you with your own research and future publications.

Aayeshah, W., & Bebawi, S. (2014). The Use of Facebook as a Pedagogical Platform for Developing Investigative Journalism Skills. In G. Mallia (Ed.), *The Social Classroom: Integrating Social Network Use in Education* (pp. 83–99). Hershey, PA: Information Science Reference.

Adi, A., & Scotte, C. G. (2013). Barriers to Emerging Technology and Social Media Integration in Higher Education: Three Case Studies. In M. Pătruţ, & B. Pătruţ (Eds.), *Social Media in Higher Education: Teaching in Web 2.0* (pp. 334–354). Hershey, PA: Information Science Reference. doi:10.4018/978-1-4666-2970-7.ch017

Agazzi, E. (2012). How Can the Problems of An Ethical Judgment on Science and Technology Be Correctly Approached? In R. Luppicini (Ed.), *Ethical Impact of Technological Advancements and Applications in Society* (pp. 30–38). Hershey, PA: Information Science Reference. doi:10.4018/978-1-4666-1773-5.ch003

Agina, A. M., Tennyson, R. D., & Kommers, P. (2013). Understanding Children's Private Speech and Self-Regulation Learning in Web 2.0: Updates of Vygotsky through Piaget and Future Recommendations. In P. Ordóñez de Pablos, H. Nigro, R. Tennyson, S. Gonzalez Cisaro, & W. Karwowski (Eds.), *Advancing Information Management through Semantic Web Concepts and Ontologies* (pp. 1–53). Hershey, PA: Information Science Reference.

Ahrens, A., Bassus, O., & Zaščerinska, J. (2014). Enterprise 2.0 in Engineering Curriculum. In M. Cruz-Cunha, F. Moreira, & J. Varajão (Eds.), *Handbook of Research on Enterprise 2.0: Technological, Social, and Organizational Dimensions* (pp. 599–617). Hershey, PA: Business Science Reference.

Akputu, O. K., Seng, K. P., & Lee, Y. L. (2014). Affect Recognition for Web 2.0 Intelligent E-Tutoring Systems: Exploration of Students' Emotional Feedback. In J. Pelet (Ed.), *E-Learning 2.0 Technologies and Web Applications in Higher Education* (pp. 188–215). Hershey, PA: Information Science Reference.

Al-Hajri, S., & Tatnall, A. (2013). A Socio-Technical Study of the Adoption of Internet Technology in Banking, Re-Interpreted as an Innovation Using Innovation Translation. In A. Tatnall (Ed.), *Social and Professional Applications of Actor-Network Theory for Technology Development* (pp. 207–220). Hershey, PA: Information Science Reference.

Al Hujran, O., Aloudat, A., & Altarawneh, I. (2013). Factors Influencing Citizen Adoption of E-Government in Developing Countries: The Case of Jordan. [IJTHI]. *International Journal of Technology and Human Interaction*, 9(2), 1–19. doi:10.4018/jthi.2013040101

Alavi, R., Islam, S., Jahankhani, H., & Al-Nemrat, A. (2013). Analyzing Human Factors for an Effective Information Security Management System. [IJSSE]. *International Journal of Secure Software Engineering, 4*(1), 50–74. doi:10.4018/jsse.2013010104

Altun, N. E., & Yildiz, S. (2013). Effects of Different Types of Tasks on Junior ELT Students' Use of Communication Strategies in Computer-Mediated Communication. [IJCALLT]. *International Journal of Computer-Assisted Language Learning and Teaching, 3*(2), 17–40. doi:10.4018/ijcallt.2013040102

Amaldi, P., & Smoker, A. (2013). An Organizational Study into the Concept of "Automation Policy" in a Safety Critical Socio-Technical System. [IJSKD]. *International Journal of Sociotechnology and Knowledge Development, 5*(2), 1–17. doi:10.4018/jskd.2013040101

An, I. S. (2013). Integrating Technology-Enhanced Student Self-Regulated Tasks into University Chinese Language Course. [IJCALLT]. *International Journal of Computer-Assisted Language Learning and Teaching, 3*(1), 1–15. doi:10.4018/ijcallt.2013010101

Andacht, F. (2013). The Tangible Lure of the Technoself in the Age of Reality Television. In R. Luppicini (Ed.), *Handbook of Research on Technoself: Identity in a Technological Society* (pp. 360–381). Hershey, PA: Information Science Reference.

Anderson, A., & Petersen, A. (2012). Shaping the Ethics of an Emergent Field: Scientists' and Policymakers' Representations of Nanotechnologies. In R. Luppicini (Ed.), *Ethical Impact of Technological Advancements and Applications in Society* (pp. 219–231). Hershey, PA: Information Science Reference. doi:10.4018/978-1-4666-1773-5.ch017

Anderson, J. L. (2014). Games and the Development of Students' Civic Engagement and Ecological Stewardship. In J. Bishop (Ed.), *Gamification for Human Factors Integration: Social, Education, and Psychological Issues* (pp. 199–215). Hershey, PA: Information Science Reference. doi:10.4018/978-1-4666-5071-8.ch012

Ann, O. C., Lu, M. V., & Theng, L. B. (2014). A Face Based Real Time Communication for Physically and Speech Disabled People. In I. Management Association (Ed.), Assistive Technologies: Concepts, Methodologies, Tools, and Applications (pp. 1434-1460). Hershey, PA: Information Science Reference. doi: doi:10.4018/978-1-4666-4422-9.ch075

Aricak, O. T., Tanrikulu, T., Siyahhan, S., & Kinay, H. (2013). Cyberbullying: The Bad and the Ugly Side of Information Age. In M. Pătruţ, & B. Pătruţ (Eds.), *Social Media in Higher Education: Teaching in Web 2.0* (pp. 318–333). Hershey, PA: Information Science Reference. doi:10.4018/978-1-4666-2970-7.ch016

Ariely, G. (2011). Boundaries of Socio-Technical Systems and IT for Knowledge Development in Military Environments. [IJSKD]. *International Journal of Sociotechnology and Knowledge Development, 3*(3), 1–14. doi:10.4018/jskd.2011070101

Ariely, G. (2013). Boundaries of Socio-Technical Systems and IT for Knowledge Development in Military Environments. In J. Abdelnour-Nocera (Ed.), *Knowledge and Technological Development Effects on Organizational and Social Structures* (pp. 224–238). Hershey, PA: Information Science Reference.

Arjunan, S., Kumar, D. K., Weghorn, H., & Naik, G. (2014). Facial Muscle Activity Patterns for Recognition of Utterances in Native and Foreign Language: Testing for its Reliability and Flexibility. In I. Management Association (Ed.), Assistive Technologies: Concepts, Methodologies, Tools, and Applications (pp. 1462-1480). Hershey, PA: Information Science Reference. doi: doi:10.4018/978-1-4666-4422-9.ch076

Arling, P. A., Miech, E. J., & Arling, G. W. (2013). Comparing Electronic and Face-to-Face Communication in the Success of a Long-Term Care Quality Improvement Collaborative. [IJRQEH]. *International Journal of Reliable and Quality E-Healthcare*, 2(1), 1–10. doi:10.4018/ijrqeh.2013010101

Asghari-Oskoei, M., & Hu, H. (2014). Using Myoelectric Signals to Manipulate Assisting Robots and Rehabilitation Devices. In I. Management Association (Ed.), Assistive Technologies: Concepts, Methodologies, Tools, and Applications (pp. 970-990). Hershey, PA: Information Science Reference. doi: doi:10.4018/978-1-4666-4422-9.ch049

Aspradaki, A. A. (2013). Deliberative Democracy and Nanotechnologies in Health. [IJT]. *International Journal of Technoethics*, 4(2), 1–14. doi:10.4018/jte.2013070101

Asselin, S. B. (2014). Assistive Technology in Higher Education. In I. Management Association (Ed.), Assistive Technologies: Concepts, Methodologies, Tools, and Applications (pp. 1196-1208). Hershey, PA: Information Science Reference. doi: doi:10.4018/978-1-4666-4422-9.ch062

Auld, G., & Henderson, M. (2014). The Ethical Dilemmas of Social Networking Sites in Classroom Contexts. In G. Mallia (Ed.), *The Social Classroom: Integrating Social Network Use in Education* (pp. 192–207). Hershey, PA: Information Science Reference.

Awwal, M. A. (2012). Influence of Age and Genders on the Relationship between Computer Self-Efficacy and Information Privacy Concerns. [IJTHI]. *International Journal of Technology and Human Interaction*, 8(1), 14–37. doi:10.4018/jthi.2012010102

Ballesté, F., & Torras, C. (2013). Effects of Human-Machine Integration on the Construction of Identity. In R. Luppicini (Ed.), *Handbook of Research on Technoself: Identity in a Technological Society* (pp. 574–591). Hershey, PA: Information Science Reference. doi:10.4018/978-1-4666-4607-0.ch063

Baporikar, N. (2014). Effective E-Learning Strategies for a Borderless World. In J. Pelet (Ed.), *E-Learning 2.0 Technologies and Web Applications in Higher Education* (pp. 22–44). Hershey, PA: Information Science Reference.

Bardone, E. (2011). Unintended Affordances as Violent Mediators: Maladaptive Effects of Technologically Enriched Human Niches. [IJT]. *International Journal of Technoethics*, 2(4), 37–52. doi:10.4018/jte.2011100103

Basham, R. (2014). Surveilling the Elderly: Emerging Demographic Needs and Social Implications of RFID Chip Technology Use. In M. Michael, & K. Michael (Eds.), *Uberveillance and the Social Implications of Microchip Implants: Emerging Technologies* (pp. 169–185). Hershey, PA: Information Science Reference.

Bates, M. (2013). The Ur-Real Sonorous Envelope: Bridge between the Corporeal and the Online Technoself. In R. Luppicini (Ed.), *Handbook of Research on Technoself: Identity in a Technological Society* (pp. 272–292). Hershey, PA: Information Science Reference.

Bauer, K. A. (2012). Transhumanism and Its Critics: Five Arguments against a Posthuman Future. In R. Luppicini (Ed.), *Ethical Impact of Technological Advancements and Applications in Society* (pp. 232–242). Hershey, PA: Information Science Reference. doi:10.4018/978-1-4666-1773-5.ch018

Bax, S. (2011). Normalisation Revisited: The Effective Use of Technology in Language Education. [IJCALLT]. *International Journal of Computer-Assisted Language Learning and Teaching*, *1*(2), 1–15. doi:10.4018/ijcallt.2011040101

Baya'a, N., & Daher, W. (2014). Facebook as an Educational Environment for Mathematics Learning. In G. Mallia (Ed.), *The Social Classroom: Integrating Social Network Use in Education* (pp. 171–190). Hershey, PA: Information Science Reference.

Bayerl, P. S., & Janneck, M. (2013). Professional Online Profiles: The Impact of Personalization and Visual Gender Cues on Online Impression Formation. [IJSKD]. *International Journal of Sociotechnology and Knowledge Development*, *5*(3), 1–16. doi:10.4018/ijskd.2013070101

Bell, D., & Shirzad, S. R. (2013). Social Media Business Intelligence: A Pharmaceutical Domain Analysis Study. [IJSKD]. *International Journal of Sociotechnology and Knowledge Development*, *5*(3), 51–73. doi:10.4018/ijskd.2013070104

Bergmann, N. W. (2014). Ubiquitous Computing for Independent Living. In I. Management Association (Ed.), Assistive Technologies: Concepts, Methodologies, Tools, and Applications (pp. 679-692). Hershey, PA: Information Science Reference. doi: doi:10.4018/978-1-4666-4422-9.ch033

Bertolotti, T. (2011). Facebook Has It: The Irresistible Violence of Social Cognition in the Age of Social Networking. [IJT]. *International Journal of Technoethics*, *2*(4), 71–83. doi:10.4018/jte.2011100105

Berzsenyi, C. (2014). Writing to Meet Your Match: Rhetoric and Self-Presentation for Four Online Daters. In H. Lim, & F. Sudweeks (Eds.), *Innovative Methods and Technologies for Electronic Discourse Analysis* (pp. 210–234). Hershey, PA: Information Science Reference.

Best, L. A., Buhay, D. N., McGuire, K., Gurholt, S., & Foley, S. (2014). The Use of Web 2.0 Technologies in Formal and Informal Learning Settings. In G. Mallia (Ed.), *The Social Classroom: Integrating Social Network Use in Education* (pp. 1–22). Hershey, PA: Information Science Reference.

Bhattacharya, S. (2014). Model-Based Approaches for Scanning Keyboard Design: Present State and Future Directions. In I. Management Association (Ed.), Assistive Technologies: Concepts, Methodologies, Tools, and Applications (pp. 1497-1515). Hershey, PA: Information Science Reference. doi: doi:10.4018/978-1-4666-4422-9.ch078

Bibby, S. (2011). Do Students Wish to 'Go Mobile'?: An Investigation into Student Use of PCs and Cell Phones. [IJCALLT]. *International Journal of Computer-Assisted Language Learning and Teaching*, *1*(2), 43–54. doi:10.4018/ijcallt.2011040104

Bishop, J. (2014). The Psychology of Trolling and Lurking: The Role of Defriending and Gamification for Increasing Participation in Online Communities Using Seductive Narratives. In J. Bishop (Ed.), *Gamification for Human Factors Integration: Social, Education, and Psychological Issues* (pp. 162–179). Hershey, PA: Information Science Reference. doi:10.4018/978-1-4666-5071-8.ch010

Bishop, J., & Goode, M. M. (2014). Towards a Subjectively Devised Parametric User Model for Analysing and Influencing Behaviour Online Using Neuroeconomics. In J. Bishop (Ed.), *Gamification for Human Factors Integration: Social, Education, and Psychological Issues* (pp. 80–95). Hershey, PA: Information Science Reference. doi:10.4018/978-1-4666-5071-8.ch005

Biswas, P. (2014). A Brief Survey on User Modelling in Human Computer Interaction. In I. Management Association (Ed.), Assistive Technologies: Concepts, Methodologies, Tools, and Applications (pp. 102-119). Hershey, PA: Information Science Reference. doi: doi:10.4018/978-1-4666-4422-9.ch006

Black, D. (2013). The Digital Soul. In R. Luppicini (Ed.), *Handbook of Research on Technoself: Identity in a Technological Society* (pp. 157–174). Hershey, PA: Information Science Reference.

Blake, S., Winsor, D. L., Burkett, C., & Allen, L. (2014). iPods, Internet and Apps, Oh My: Age Appropriate Technology in Early Childhood Educational Environments. In I. Management Association (Ed.), K-12 Education: Concepts, Methodologies, Tools, and Applications (pp. 1650-1668). Hershey, PA: Information Science Reference. doi: doi:10.4018/978-1-4666-4502-8.ch095

Boghian, I. (2013). Using Facebook in Teaching. In M. Pătruţ, & B. Pătruţ (Eds.), *Social Media in Higher Education: Teaching in Web 2.0* (pp. 86–103). Hershey, PA: Information Science Reference. doi:10.4018/978-1-4666-2970-7.ch005

Boling, E. C., & Beatty, J. (2014). Overcoming the Tensions and Challenges of Technology Integration: How Can We Best Support our Teachers? In I. Management Association (Ed.), K-12 Education: Concepts, Methodologies, Tools, and Applications (pp. 1504-1524). Hershey, PA: Information Science Reference. doi: doi:10.4018/978-1-4666-4502-8.ch087

Bonanno, P. (2014). Designing Learning in Social Online Learning Environments: A Process-Oriented Approach. In G. Mallia (Ed.), *The Social Classroom: Integrating Social Network Use in Education* (pp. 40–61). Hershey, PA: Information Science Reference.

Bongers, B., & Smith, S. (2014). Interactivating Rehabilitation through Active Multimodal Feedback and Guidance. In I. Management Association (Ed.), Assistive Technologies: Concepts, Methodologies, Tools, and Applications (pp. 1650-1674). Hershey, PA: Information Science Reference. doi: doi:10.4018/978-1-4666-4422-9.ch087

Bottino, R. M., Ott, M., & Tavella, M. (2014). Serious Gaming at School: Reflections on Students' Performance, Engagement and Motivation. [IJGBL]. *International Journal of Game-Based Learning*, *4*(1), 21–36. doi:10.4018/IJGBL.2014010102

Brad, S. (2014). Design for Quality of ICT-Aided Engineering Course Units. [IJQAETE]. *International Journal of Quality Assurance in Engineering and Technology Education*, *3*(1), 52–80. doi:10.4018/ijqaete.2014010103

Braman, J., Thomas, U., Vincenti, G., Dudley, A., & Rodgers, K. (2014). Preparing Your Digital Legacy: Assessing Awareness of Digital Natives. In G. Mallia (Ed.), *The Social Classroom: Integrating Social Network Use in Education* (pp. 208–223). Hershey, PA: Information Science Reference.

Bratitsis, T., & Demetriadis, S. (2013). Research Approaches in Computer-Supported Collaborative Learning. [IJeC]. *International Journal of e-Collaboration*, *9*(1), 1–8. doi:10.4018/jec.2013010101

Brick, B. (2012). The Role of Social Networking Sites for Language Learning in UK Higher Education: The Views of Learners and Practitioners. [IJCALLT]. *International Journal of Computer-Assisted Language Learning and Teaching*, *2*(3), 35–53. doi:10.4018/ijcallt.2012070103

Burke, M. E., & Speed, C. (2014). Knowledge Recovery: Applications of Technology and Memory. In M. Michael, & K. Michael (Eds.), *Uberveillance and the Social Implications of Microchip Implants: Emerging Technologies* (pp. 133–142). Hershey, PA: Information Science Reference.

Burton, A. M., Liu, H., Battersby, S., Brown, D., Sherkat, N., Standen, P., & Walker, M. (2014). The Use of Motion Tracking Technologies in Serious Games to Enhance Rehabilitation in Stroke Patients. In J. Bishop (Ed.), *Gamification for Human Factors Integration: Social, Education, and Psychological Issues* (pp. 148–161). Hershey, PA: Information Science Reference. doi:10.4018/978-1-4666-5071-8.ch009

Burusic, J., & Karabegovic, M. (2014). The Role of Students' Personality Traits in the Effective Use of Social Networking Sites in the Educational Context. In G. Mallia (Ed.), *The Social Classroom: Integrating Social Network Use in Education* (pp. 224–243). Hershey, PA: Information Science Reference.

Busch, C. D., Lorenzo, A. M., Sánchez, I. M., González, B. G., García, T. P., Riveiro, L. N., & Loureiro, J. P. (2014). In-TIC for Mobile Devices: Support System for Communication with Mobile Devices for the Disabled. In I. Management Association (Ed.), Assistive Technologies: Concepts, Methodologies, Tools, and Applications (pp. 345-356). Hershey, PA: Information Science Reference. doi: doi:10.4018/978-1-4666-4422-9.ch017

Bute, S. J. (2013). Integrating Social Media and Traditional Media within the Academic Environment. In M. Pătruţ, & B. Pătruţ (Eds.), *Social Media in Higher Education: Teaching in Web 2.0* (pp. 75–85). Hershey, PA: Information Science Reference. doi:10.4018/978-1-4666-2970-7.ch004

Butler-Pascoe, M. E. (2011). The History of CALL: The Intertwining Paths of Technology and Second/Foreign Language Teaching. [IJCALLT]. *International Journal of Computer-Assisted Language Learning and Teaching, 1*(1), 16–32. doi:10.4018/ijcallt.2011010102

Cabrera, L. (2012). Human Implants: A Suggested Framework to Set Priorities. In R. Luppicini (Ed.), *Ethical Impact of Technological Advancements and Applications in Society* (pp. 243–253). Hershey, PA: Information Science Reference. doi:10.4018/978-1-4666-1773-5.ch019

Cacho-Elizondo, S., Shahidi, N., & Tossan, V. (2013). Intention to Adopt a Text Message-based Mobile Coaching Service to Help Stop Smoking: Which Explanatory Variables? [IJTHI]. *International Journal of Technology and Human Interaction, 9*(4), 1–19. doi:10.4018/ijthi.2013100101

Caldelli, R., Becarelli, R., Filippini, F., Picchioni, F., & Giorgetti, R. (2014). Electronic Voting by Means of Digital Terrestrial Television: The Infrastructure, Security Issues and a Real Test-Bed. In I. Management Association (Ed.), Assistive Technologies: Concepts, Methodologies, Tools, and Applications (pp. 905-915). Hershey, PA: Information Science Reference. doi: doi:10.4018/978-1-4666-4422-9.ch045

Camacho, M. (2013). Making the Most of Informal and Situated Learning Opportunities through Mobile Learning. In M. Pătruţ, & B. Pătruţ (Eds.), *Social Media in Higher Education: Teaching in Web 2.0* (pp. 355–370). Hershey, PA: Information Science Reference. doi:10.4018/978-1-4666-2970-7.ch018

Camilleri, V., Busuttil, L., & Montebello, M. (2014). MOOCs: Exploiting Networks for the Education of the Masses or Just a Trend? In G. Mallia (Ed.), *The Social Classroom: Integrating Social Network Use in Education* (pp. 348–366). Hershey, PA: Information Science Reference.

Campos, P., Noronha, H., & Lopes, A. (2013). Work Analysis Methods in Practice: The Context of Collaborative Review of CAD Models. [IJSKD]. *International Journal of Sociotechnology and Knowledge Development, 5*(2), 34–44. doi:10.4018/jskd.2013040103

Cao, G. (2013). A Paradox Between Technological Autonomy and Ethical Heteronomy of Philosophy of Technology: Social Control System. [IJT]. *International Journal of Technoethics*, *4*(1), 52–66. doi:10.4018/jte.2013010105

Carofiglio, V., & Abbattista, F. (2013). BCI-Based User-Centered Design for Emotionally-Driven User Experience. In M. Garcia-Ruiz (Ed.), *Cases on Usability Engineering: Design and Development of Digital Products* (pp. 299–320). Hershey, PA: Information Science Reference. doi:10.4018/978-1-4666-4046-7.ch013

Carpenter, J. (2013). Just Doesn't Look Right: Exploring the Impact of Humanoid Robot Integration into Explosive Ordnance Disposal Teams. In R. Luppicini (Ed.), *Handbook of Research on Technoself: Identity in a Technological Society* (pp. 609–636). Hershey, PA: Information Science Reference.

Carroll, J. L. (2014). Wheelchairs as Assistive Technology: What a Special Educator Should Know. In I. Management Association (Ed.), Assistive Technologies: Concepts, Methodologies, Tools, and Applications (pp. 623-633). Hershey, PA: Information Science Reference. doi: doi:10.4018/978-1-4666-4422-9.ch030

Casey, L. B., & Williamson, R. L. (2014). A Parent's Guide to Support Technologies for Preschool Students with Disabilities. In I. Management Association (Ed.), Assistive Technologies: Concepts, Methodologies, Tools, and Applications (pp. 1340-1356). Hershey, PA: Information Science Reference. doi: doi:10.4018/978-1-4666-4422-9.ch071

Caviglione, L., Coccoli, M., & Merlo, A. (2013). On Social Network Engineering for Secure Web Data and Services. In L. Caviglione, M. Coccoli, & A. Merlo (Eds.), *Social Network Engineering for Secure Web Data and Services* (pp. 1–4). Hershey, PA: Information Science Reference. doi:10.4018/978-1-4666-3926-3.ch001

Chadwick, D. D., Fullwood, C., & Wesson, C. J. (2014). Intellectual Disability, Identity, and the Internet. In I. Management Association (Ed.), Assistive Technologies: Concepts, Methodologies, Tools, and Applications (pp. 198-223). Hershey, PA: Information Science Reference. doi: doi:10.4018/978-1-4666-4422-9.ch011

Chao, L., Wen, Y., Chen, P., Lin, C., Lin, S., Guo, C., & Wang, W. (2012). The Development and Learning Effectiveness of a Teaching Module for the Algal Fuel Cell: A Renewable and Sustainable Battery. [IJTHI]. *International Journal of Technology and Human Interaction*, *8*(4), 1–15. doi:10.4018/jthi.2012100101

Charnkit, P., & Tatnall, A. (2013). Knowledge Conversion Processes in Thai Public Organisations Seen as an Innovation: The Re-Analysis of a TAM Study Using Innovation Translation. In A. Tatnall (Ed.), *Social and Professional Applications of Actor-Network Theory for Technology Development* (pp. 88–102). Hershey, PA: Information Science Reference.

Chen, E. T. (2014). Challenge and Complexity of Virtual Team Management. In E. Nikoi, & K. Boateng (Eds.), *Collaborative Communication Processes and Decision Making in Organizations* (pp. 109–120). Hershey, PA: Business Science Reference. doi:10.4018/978-1-4666-4979-8.ch062

Chen, R., Xie, T., Lin, T., & Chen, Y. (2013). Adaptive Windows Layout Based on Evolutionary Multi-Objective Optimization. [IJTHI]. *International Journal of Technology and Human Interaction*, *9*(3), 63–72. doi:10.4018/jthi.2013070105

Chen, W., Juang, Y., Chang, S., & Wang, P. (2012). Informal Education of Energy Conservation: Theory, Promotion, and Policy Implication. [IJTHI]. *International Journal of Technology and Human Interaction*, *8*(4), 16–44. doi:10.4018/jthi.2012100102

Chino, T., Torii, K., Uchihira, N., & Hirabayashi, Y. (2013). Speech Interaction Analysis on Collaborative Work at an Elderly Care Facility. [IJSKD]. *International Journal of Sociotechnology and Knowledge Development, 5*(2), 18–33. doi:10.4018/jskd.2013040102

Chiu, M. (2013). Gaps Between Valuing and Purchasing Green-Technology Products: Product and Gender Differences. [IJTHI]. *International Journal of Technology and Human Interaction, 8*(3), 54–68. doi:10.4018/jthi.2012070106

Chivukula, V., & Shur, M. (2014). Web-Based Experimentation for Students with Learning Disabilities. In I. Management Association (Ed.), Assistive Technologies: Concepts, Methodologies, Tools, and Applications (pp. 1156-1172). Hershey, PA: Information Science Reference. doi: doi:10.4018/978-1-4666-4422-9.ch060

Coakes, E., Bryant, A., Land, F., & Phippen, A. (2011). The Dark Side of Technology: Some Sociotechnical Reflections. [IJSKD]. *International Journal of Sociotechnology and Knowledge Development, 3*(4), 40–51. doi:10.4018/IJSKD.2011100104

Cole, I. J. (2013). Usability of Online Virtual Learning Environments: Key Issues for Instructors and Learners. In C. Gonzalez (Ed.), *Student Usability in Educational Software and Games: Improving Experiences* (pp. 41–58). Hershey, PA: Information Science Reference.

Colombo, B., Antonietti, A., Sala, R., & Caravita, S. C. (2013). Blog Content and Structure, Cognitive Style and Metacognition. [IJTHI]. *International Journal of Technology and Human Interaction, 9*(3), 1–17. doi:10.4018/jthi.2013070101

Constantinides, M. (2011). Integrating Technology on Initial Training Courses: A Survey Amongst CELTA Tutors. [IJCALLT]. *International Journal of Computer-Assisted Language Learning and Teaching, 1*(2), 55–71. doi:10.4018/ijcallt.2011040105

Cook, R. G., & Crawford, C. M. (2013). Addressing Online Student Learning Environments and Socialization Through Developmental Research. In M. Khosrow-Pour (Ed.), *Cases on Assessment and Evaluation in Education* (pp. 504–536). Hershey, PA: Information Science Reference.

Corritore, C. L., Wiedenbeck, S., Kracher, B., & Marble, R. P. (2012). Online Trust and Health Information Websites. [IJTHI]. *International Journal of Technology and Human Interaction, 8*(4), 92–115. doi:10.4018/jthi.2012100106

Covarrubias, M., Bordegoni, M., Cugini, U., & Gatti, E. (2014). Supporting Unskilled People in Manual Tasks through Haptic-Based Guidance. In I. Management Association (Ed.), Assistive Technologies: Concepts, Methodologies, Tools, and Applications (pp. 947-969). Hershey, PA: Information Science Reference. doi: doi:10.4018/978-1-4666-4422-9.ch048

Coverdale, T. S., & Wilbon, A. D. (2013). The Impact of In-Group Membership on e-Loyalty of Women Online Shoppers: An Application of the Social Identity Approach to Website Design. [IJEA]. *International Journal of E-Adoption, 5*(1), 17–36. doi:10.4018/jea.2013010102

Crabb, P. B., & Stern, S. E. (2012). Technology Traps: Who Is Responsible? In R. Luppicini (Ed.), *Ethical Impact of Technological Advancements and Applications in Society* (pp. 39–46). Hershey, PA: Information Science Reference. doi:10.4018/978-1-4666-1773-5.ch004

Crespo, R. G., Martíne, O. S., Lovelle, J. M., García-Bustelo, B. C., Díaz, V. G., & Ordoñez de Pablos, P. (2014). Improving Cognitive Load on Students with Disabilities through Software Aids. In I. Management Association (Ed.), Assistive Technologies: Concepts, Methodologies, Tools, and Applications (pp. 1255-1268). Hershey, PA: Information Science Reference. doi: doi:10.4018/978-1-4666-4422-9.ch066

Croasdaile, S., Jones, S., Ligon, K., Oggel, L., & Pruett, M. (2014). Supports for and Barriers to Implementing Assistive Technology in Schools. In I. Management Association (Ed.), Assistive Technologies: Concepts, Methodologies, Tools, and Applications (pp. 1118-1130). Hershey, PA: Information Science Reference. doi: doi:10.4018/978-1-4666-4422-9.ch058

Cucchiarini, C., & Strik, H. (2014). Second Language Learners' Spoken Discourse: Practice and Corrective Feedback through Automatic Speech Recognition. In H. Lim, & F. Sudweeks (Eds.), *Innovative Methods and Technologies for Electronic Discourse Analysis* (pp. 169–189). Hershey, PA: Information Science Reference.

Dafoulas, G. A., & Saleeb, N. (2014). 3D Assistive Technologies and Advantageous Themes for Collaboration and Blended Learning of Users with Disabilities. In I. Management Association (Ed.), Assistive Technologies: Concepts, Methodologies, Tools, and Applications (pp. 421-453). Hershey, PA: Information Science Reference. doi: doi:10.4018/978-1-4666-4422-9.ch021

Dai, Z., & Paasch, K. (2013). A Web-Based Interactive Questionnaire for PV Application. [IJSKD]. *International Journal of Sociotechnology and Knowledge Development*, 5(2), 82–93. doi:10.4018/jskd.2013040106

Daradoumis, T., & Lafuente, M. M. (2014). Studying the Suitability of Discourse Analysis Methods for Emotion Detection and Interpretation in Computer-Mediated Educational Discourse. In H. Lim, & F. Sudweeks (Eds.), *Innovative Methods and Technologies for Electronic Discourse Analysis* (pp. 119–143). Hershey, PA: Information Science Reference.

Davis, B., & Mason, P. (2014). Positioning Goes to Work: Computer-Aided Identification of Stance Shifts and Semantic Themes in Electronic Discourse Analysis. In H. Lim, & F. Sudweeks (Eds.), *Innovative Methods and Technologies for Electronic Discourse Analysis* (pp. 394–413). Hershey, PA: Information Science Reference.

Dogoriti, E., & Pange, J. (2014). Considerations for Online English Language Learning: The Use of Facebook in Formal and Informal Settings in Higher Education. In G. Mallia (Ed.), *The Social Classroom: Integrating Social Network Use in Education* (pp. 147–170). Hershey, PA: Information Science Reference.

Donegan, M. (2014). Features of Gaze Control Systems. In I. Management Association (Ed.), Assistive Technologies: Concepts, Methodologies, Tools, and Applications (pp. 1055-1061). Hershey, PA: Information Science Reference. doi: doi:10.4018/978-1-4666-4422-9.ch054

Douglas, G., Morton, H., & Jack, M. (2012). Remote Channel Customer Contact Strategies for Complaint Update Messages. [IJTHI]. *International Journal of Technology and Human Interaction*, 8(2), 43–55. doi:10.4018/jthi.2012040103

Drake, J. R., & Byrd, T. A. (2013). Searching for Alternatives: Does Your Disposition Matter? [IJTHI]. *International Journal of Technology and Human Interaction*, 9(1), 18–36. doi:10.4018/jthi.2013010102

Driouchi, A. (2013). ICTs and Socioeconomic Performance with Focus on ICTs and Health. In ICTs for Health, Education, and Socioeconomic Policies: Regional Cases (pp. 104-125). Hershey, PA: Information Science Reference. doi: doi:10.4018/978-1-4666-3643-9.ch005

Driouchi, A. (2013). Social Deficits, Social Cohesion, and Prospects from ICTs. In ICTs for Health, Education, and Socioeconomic Policies: Regional Cases (pp. 230-251). Hershey, PA: Information Science Reference. doi: doi:10.4018/978-1-4666-3643-9.ch011

Driouchi, A. (2013). Socioeconomic Reforms, Human Development, and the Millennium Development Goals with ICTs for Coordination. In ICTs for Health, Education, and Socioeconomic Policies: Regional Cases (pp. 211-229). Hershey, PA: Information Science Reference. doi: doi:10.4018/978-1-4666-3643-9.ch010

Drula, G. (2013). Media and Communication Research Facing Social Media. In M. Pătruț, & B. Pătruț (Eds.), *Social Media in Higher Education: Teaching in Web 2.0* (pp. 371–392). Hershey, PA: Information Science Reference. doi:10.4018/978-1-4666-2970-7.ch019

Druzhinina, O., Hvannberg, E. T., & Halldorsdottir, G. (2013). Feedback Fidelities in Three Different Types of Crisis Management Training Environments. [IJSKD]. *International Journal of Sociotechnology and Knowledge Development*, 5(2), 45–62. doi:10.4018/jskd.2013040104

Eason, K., Waterson, P., & Davda, P. (2013). The Sociotechnical Challenge of Integrating Telehealth and Telecare into Health and Social Care for the Elderly. [IJSKD]. *International Journal of Sociotechnology and Knowledge Development*, 5(4), 14–26. doi:10.4018/ijskd.2013100102

Edenius, M., & Rämö, H. (2011). An Office on the Go: Professional Workers, Smartphones and the Return of Place. [IJTHI]. *International Journal of Technology and Human Interaction*, 7(1), 37–55. doi:10.4018/jthi.2011010103

Eke, D. O. (2011). ICT Integration in Nigeria: The Socio-Cultural Constraints. [IJTHI]. *International Journal of Technology and Human Interaction*, 7(2), 21–27. doi:10.4018/jthi.2011040103

Evett, L., Ridley, A., Keating, L., Merritt, P., Shopland, N., & Brown, D. (2014). Designing Serious Games for People with Disabilities: Game, Set, and Match to the Wii. In J. Bishop (Ed.), *Gamification for Human Factors Integration: Social, Education, and Psychological Issues* (pp. 97–105). Hershey, PA: Information Science Reference. doi:10.4018/978-1-4666-5071-8.ch006

Evmenova, A. S., & Behrmann, M. M. (2014). Communication Technology Integration in the Content Areas for Students with High-Incidence Disabilities: A Case Study of One School System. In I. Management Association (Ed.), Assistive Technologies: Concepts, Methodologies, Tools, and Applications (pp. 26-53). Hershey, PA: Information Science Reference. doi: doi:10.4018/978-1-4666-4422-9.ch003

Evmenova, A. S., & King-Sears, M. E. (2014). Technology and Literacy for Students with Disabilities. In I. Management Association (Ed.), Assistive Technologies: Concepts, Methodologies, Tools, and Applications (pp. 1269-1291). Hershey, PA: Information Science Reference. doi: doi:10.4018/978-1-4666-4422-9.ch067

Ewais, A., & De Troyer, O. (2013). Usability Evaluation of an Adaptive 3D Virtual Learning Environment. [IJVPLE]. *International Journal of Virtual and Personal Learning Environments*, 4(1), 16–31. doi:10.4018/jvple.2013010102

Farrell, H. J. (2014). The Student with Complex Education Needs: Assistive and Augmentative Information and Communication Technology in a Ten-Week Music Program. In I. Management Association (Ed.), K-12 Education: Concepts, Methodologies, Tools, and Applications (pp. 1436-1472). Hershey, PA: Information Science Reference. doi: doi:10.4018/978-1-4666-4502-8.ch084

Fathulla, K. (2012). Rethinking Human and Society's Relationship with Technology. [IJSKD]. *International Journal of Sociotechnology and Knowledge Development, 4*(2), 21–28. doi:10.4018/jskd.2012040103

Fidler, C. S., Kanaan, R. K., & Rogerson, S. (2011). Barriers to e-Government Implementation in Jordan: The Role of Wasta. [IJTHI]. *International Journal of Technology and Human Interaction, 7*(2), 9–20. doi:10.4018/jthi.2011040102

Fischer, G., & Herrmann, T. (2013). Socio-Technical Systems: A Meta-Design Perspective. In J. Abdelnour-Nocera (Ed.), *Knowledge and Technological Development Effects on Organizational and Social Structures* (pp. 1–36). Hershey, PA: Information Science Reference.

Foreman, J., & Borkman, T. (2014). Learning Sociology in a Massively Multi-Student Online Learning Environment. In J. Bishop (Ed.), *Gamification for Human Factors Integration: Social, Education, and Psychological Issues* (pp. 216–224). Hershey, PA: Information Science Reference. doi:10.4018/978-1-4666-5071-8.ch013

Fornaciari, F. (2013). The Language of Technoself: Storytelling, Symbolic Interactionism, and Online Identity. In R. Luppicini (Ed.), *Handbook of Research on Technoself: Identity in a Technological Society* (pp. 64–83). Hershey, PA: Information Science Reference.

Fox, J., & Ahn, S. J. (2013). Avatars: Portraying, Exploring, and Changing Online and Offline Identities. In R. Luppicini (Ed.), *Handbook of Research on Technoself: Identity in a Technological Society* (pp. 255–271). Hershey, PA: Information Science Reference.

Fox, W. P., Binstock, J., & Minutas, M. (2013). Modeling and Methodology for Incorporating Existing Technologies to Produce Higher Probabilities of Detecting Suicide Bombers. [IJORIS]. *International Journal of Operations Research and Information Systems, 4*(3), 1–18. doi:10.4018/joris.2013070101

Franchi, E., & Tomaiuolo, M. (2013). Distributed Social Platforms for Confidentiality and Resilience. In L. Caviglione, M. Coccoli, & A. Merlo (Eds.), *Social Network Engineering for Secure Web Data and Services* (pp. 114–136). Hershey, PA: Information Science Reference. doi:10.4018/978-1-4666-3926-3.ch006

Frigo, C. A., & Pavan, E. E. (2014). Prosthetic and Orthotic Devices. In I. Management Association (Ed.), Assistive Technologies: Concepts, Methodologies, Tools, and Applications (pp. 549-613). Hershey, PA: Information Science Reference. doi: doi:10.4018/978-1-4666-4422-9.ch028

Fuhrer, C., & Cucchi, A. (2012). Relations Between Social Capital and Use of ICT: A Social Network Analysis Approach. [IJTHI]. *International Journal of Technology and Human Interaction, 8*(2), 15–42. doi:10.4018/jthi.2012040102

Galinski, C., & Beckmann, H. (2014). Concepts for Enhancing Content Quality and eAccessibility: In General and in the Field of eProcurement. In I. Management Association (Ed.), Assistive Technologies: Concepts, Methodologies, Tools, and Applications (pp. 180-197). Hershey, PA: Information Science Reference. doi: doi:10.4018/978-1-4666-4422-9.ch010

Galván, J. M., & Luppicini, R. (2012). The Humanity of the Human Body: Is Homo Cybersapien a New Species? [IJT]. *International Journal of Technoethics, 3*(2), 1–8. doi:10.4018/jte.2012040101

García-Gómez, A. (2013). Technoself-Presentation on Social Networks: A Gender-Based Approach. In R. Luppicini (Ed.), *Handbook of Research on Technoself: Identity in a Technological Society* (pp. 382–398). Hershey, PA: Information Science Reference.

Gill, L., Hathway, E. A., Lange, E., Morgan, E., & Romano, D. (2013). Coupling Real-Time 3D Landscape Models with Microclimate Simulations. [IJEPR]. *International Journal of E-Planning Research*, 2(1), 1–19. doi:10.4018/ijepr.2013010101

Godé, C., & Lebraty, J. (2013). Improving Decision Making in Extreme Situations: The Case of a Military Decision Support System. [IJTHI]. *International Journal of Technology and Human Interaction*, 9(1), 1–17. doi:10.4018/jthi.2013010101

Griol, D., Callejas, Z., & López-Cózar, R. (2014). Conversational Metabots for Educational Applications in Virtual Worlds. In I. Management Association (Ed.), Assistive Technologies: Concepts, Methodologies, Tools, and Applications (pp. 1405-1433). Hershey, PA: Information Science Reference. doi: doi:10.4018/978-1-4666-4422-9.ch074

Griol Barres, D., Callejas Carrión, Z., Molina López, J. M., & Sanchis de Miguel, A. (2014). Towards the Use of Dialog Systems to Facilitate Inclusive Education. In I. Management Association (Ed.), Assistive Technologies: Concepts, Methodologies, Tools, and Applications (pp. 1292-1312). Hershey, PA: Information Science Reference. doi: doi:10.4018/978-1-4666-4422-9.ch068

Groba, B., Pousada, T., & Nieto, L. (2014). Assistive Technologies, Tools and Resources for the Access and Use of Information and Communication Technologies by People with Disabilities. In I. Management Association (Ed.), Assistive Technologies: Concepts, Methodologies, Tools, and Applications (pp. 246-260). Hershey, PA: Information Science Reference. doi: doi:10.4018/978-1-4666-4422-9.ch013

Groß, M. (2013). Personal Knowledge Management and Social Media: What Students Need to Learn for Business Life. In M. Pătruţ, & B. Pătruţ (Eds.), *Social Media in Higher Education: Teaching in Web 2.0* (pp. 124–143). Hershey, PA: Information Science Reference. doi:10.4018/978-1-4666-2970-7.ch007

Gu, L., Aiken, M., Wang, J., & Wibowo, K. (2011). The Influence of Information Control upon Online Shopping Behavior. [IJTHI]. *International Journal of Technology and Human Interaction*, 7(1), 56–66. doi:10.4018/jthi.2011010104

Hainz, T. (2012). Value Lexicality and Human Enhancement. [IJT]. *International Journal of Technoethics*, 3(4), 54–65. doi:10.4018/jte.2012100105

Harnesk, D., & Lindström, J. (2014). Exploring Socio-Technical Design of Crisis Management Information Systems. In I. Management Association (Ed.), Crisis Management: Concepts, Methodologies, Tools and Applications (pp. 514-530). Hershey, PA: Information Science Reference. doi: doi:10.4018/978-1-4666-4707-7.ch023

Hicks, D. (2014). Ethics in the Age of Technological Change and its Impact on the Professional Identity of Librarians. In *Technology and Professional Identity of Librarians: The Making of the Cybrarian* (pp. 168–187). Hershey, PA: Information Science Reference.

Hicks, D. (2014). Technology, Profession, Identity. In *Technology and Professional Identity of Librarians: The Making of the Cybrarian* (pp. 1–20). Hershey, PA: Information Science Reference.

Hirata, M., Yanagisawa, T., Matsushita, K., Sugata, H., Kamitani, Y., Suzuki, T., et al. (2014). Brain-Machine Interface Using Brain Surface Electrodes: Real-Time Robotic Control and a Fully Implantable Wireless System. In I. Management Association (Ed.), Assistive Technologies: Concepts, Methodologies, Tools, and Applications (pp. 1535-1548). Hershey, PA: Information Science Reference. doi: doi:10.4018/978-1-4666-4422-9.ch080

Hodge, B. (2014). Critical Electronic Discourse Analysis: Social and Cultural Research in the Electronic Age. In H. Lim, & F. Sudweeks (Eds.), *Innovative Methods and Technologies for Electronic Discourse Analysis* (pp. 191–209). Hershey, PA: Information Science Reference.

Hoey, J., Poupart, P., Boutilier, C., & Mihailidis, A. (2014). POMDP Models for Assistive Technology. In I. Management Association (Ed.), Assistive Technologies: Concepts, Methodologies, Tools, and Applications (pp. 120-140). Hershey, PA: Information Science Reference. doi: doi:10.4018/978-1-4666-4422-9.ch007

Hogg, S. (2014). An Informal Use of Facebook to Encourage Student Collaboration and Motivation for Off Campus Activities. In G. Mallia (Ed.), *The Social Classroom: Integrating Social Network Use in Education* (pp. 23–39). Hershey, PA: Information Science Reference.

Holmqvist, E., & Buchholz, M. (2014). A Model for Gaze Control Assessments and Evaluation. In I. Management Association (Ed.), Assistive Technologies: Concepts, Methodologies, Tools, and Applications (pp. 332-343). Hershey, PA: Information Science Reference. doi: doi:10.4018/978-1-4666-4422-9.ch016

Hsiao, S., Chen, D., Yang, C., Huang, H., Lu, Y., & Huang, H. et al. (2013). Chemical-Free and Reusable Cellular Analysis: Electrochemical Impedance Spectroscopy with a Transparent ITO Culture Chip. [IJTHI]. *International Journal of Technology and Human Interaction, 8*(3), 1–9. doi:10.4018/jthi.2012070101

Hsu, M., Yang, C., Wang, C., & Lin, Y. (2013). Simulation-Aided Optimal Microfluidic Sorting for Monodispersed Microparticles. [IJTHI]. *International Journal of Technology and Human Interaction, 8*(3), 10–18. doi:10.4018/jthi.2012070102

Huang, W. D., & Tettegah, S. Y. (2014). Cognitive Load and Empathy in Serious Games: A Conceptual Framework. In J. Bishop (Ed.), *Gamification for Human Factors Integration: Social, Education, and Psychological Issues* (pp. 17–30). Hershey, PA: Information Science Reference. doi:10.4018/978-1-4666-5071-8.ch002

Huseyinov, I. N. (2014). Fuzzy Linguistic Modelling in Multi Modal Human Computer Interaction: Adaptation to Cognitive Styles using Multi Level Fuzzy Granulation Method. In I. Management Association (Ed.), Assistive Technologies: Concepts, Methodologies, Tools, and Applications (pp. 1481-1496). Hershey, PA: Information Science Reference. doi: doi:10.4018/978-1-4666-4422-9.ch077

Hwa, S. P., Weei, P. S., & Len, L. H. (2012). The Effects of Blended Learning Approach through an Interactive Multimedia E-Book on Students' Achievement in Learning Chinese as a Second Language at Tertiary Level. [IJCALLT]. *International Journal of Computer-Assisted Language Learning and Teaching, 2*(1), 35–50. doi:10.4018/ijcallt.2012010104

Iglesias, A., Ruiz-Mezcua, B., López, J. F., & Figueroa, D. C. (2014). New Communication Technologies for Inclusive Education in and outside the Classroom. In I. Management Association (Ed.), Assistive Technologies: Concepts, Methodologies, Tools, and Applications (pp. 1675-1689). Hershey, PA: Information Science Reference. doi: doi:10.4018/978-1-4666-4422-9.ch088

Inghilterra, X., & Ravatua-Smith, W. S. (2014). Online Learning Communities: Use of Micro Blogging for Knowledge Construction. In J. Pelet (Ed.), *E-Learning 2.0 Technologies and Web Applications in Higher Education* (pp. 107–128). Hershey, PA: Information Science Reference.

Ionescu, A. (2013). Cyber Identity: Our Alter-Ego? In R. Luppicini (Ed.), *Handbook of Research on Technoself: Identity in a Technological Society* (pp. 189–203). Hershey, PA: Information Science Reference.

Jan, Y., Lin, M., Shiao, K., Wei, C., Huang, L., & Sung, Q. (2013). Development of an Evaluation Instrument for Green Building Literacy among College Students in Taiwan. [IJTHI]. *International Journal of Technology and Human Interaction*, 8(3), 31–45. doi:10.4018/jthi.2012070104

Jawadi, N. (2013). E-Leadership and Trust Management: Exploring the Moderating Effects of Team Virtuality. [IJTHI]. *International Journal of Technology and Human Interaction*, 9(3), 18–35. doi:10.4018/jthi.2013070102

Jiménez-Castillo, D., & Fernández, R. S. (2014). The Impact of Combining Video Podcasting and Lectures on Students' Assimilation of Additional Knowledge: An Empirical Examination. In J. Pelet (Ed.), *E-Learning 2.0 Technologies and Web Applications in Higher Education* (pp. 65–87). Hershey, PA: Information Science Reference.

Jin, L. (2013). A New Trend in Education: Technoself Enhanced Social Learning. In R. Luppicini (Ed.), *Handbook of Research on Technoself: Identity in a Technological Society* (pp. 456–473). Hershey, PA: Information Science Reference.

Johansson, L. (2012). The Functional Morality of Robots. In R. Luppicini (Ed.), *Ethical Impact of Technological Advancements and Applications in Society* (pp. 254–262). Hershey, PA: Information Science Reference. doi:10.4018/978-1-4666-1773-5.ch020

Johansson, L. (2013). Robots and the Ethics of Care. [IJT]. *International Journal of Technoethics*, 4(1), 67–82. doi:10.4018/jte.2013010106

Johri, A., Dufour, M., Lo, J., & Shanahan, D. (2013). Adwiki: Socio-Technical Design for Mananging Advising Knowledge in a Higher Education Context. [IJSKD]. *International Journal of Sociotechnology and Knowledge Development*, 5(1), 37–59. doi:10.4018/jskd.2013010104

Jones, M. G., Schwilk, C. L., & Bateman, D. F. (2014). Reading by Listening: Access to Books in Audio Format for College Students with Print Disabilities. In I. Management Association (Ed.), Assistive Technologies: Concepts, Methodologies, Tools, and Applications (pp. 454-477). Hershey, PA: Information Science Reference. doi: doi:10.4018/978-1-4666-4422-9.ch022

Kaba, B., & Osei-Bryson, K. (2012). An Empirical Investigation of External Factors Influencing Mobile Technology Use in Canada: A Preliminary Study. [IJTHI]. *International Journal of Technology and Human Interaction*, 8(2), 1–14. doi:10.4018/jthi.2012040101

Kampf, C. E. (2012). Revealing the Socio-Technical Design of Global E-Businesses: A Case of Digital Artists Engaging in Radical Transparency. [IJSKD]. *International Journal of Sociotechnology and Knowledge Development*, 4(4), 18–31. doi:10.4018/jskd.2012100102

Kandroudi, M., & Bratitsis, T. (2014). Classifying Facebook Usage in the Classroom or Around It. In G. Mallia (Ed.), *The Social Classroom: Integrating Social Network Use in Education* (pp. 62–81). Hershey, PA: Information Science Reference.

Kidd, P. T. (2014). Social Networking Technologies as a Strategic Tool for the Development of Sustainable Production and Consumption: Applications to Foster the Agility Needed to Adapt Business Models in Response to the Challenges Posed by Climate Change. In I. Management Association (Ed.), Sustainable Practices: Concepts, Methodologies, Tools and Applications (pp. 974-987). Hershey, PA: Information Science Reference. doi: doi:10.4018/978-1-4666-4852-4.ch054

Kirby, S. D., & Sellers, D. M. (2014). The Live-Ability House: A Collaborative Adventure in Discovery Learning. In I. Management Association (Ed.), Assistive Technologies: Concepts, Methodologies, Tools, and Applications (pp. 1626-1649). Hershey, PA: Information Science Reference. doi: doi:10.4018/978-1-4666-4422-9.ch086

Kitchenham, A., & Bowes, D. (2014). Voice/Speech Recognition Software: A Discussion of the Promise for Success and Practical Suggestions for Implementation. In I. Management Association (Ed.), Assistive Technologies: Concepts, Methodologies, Tools, and Applications (pp. 1005-1011). Hershey, PA: Information Science Reference. doi: doi:10.4018/978-1-4666-4422-9.ch051

Konrath, S. (2013). The Empathy Paradox: Increasing Disconnection in the Age of Increasing Connection. In R. Luppicini (Ed.), *Handbook of Research on Technoself: Identity in a Technological Society* (pp. 204–228). Hershey, PA: Information Science Reference.

Koutsabasis, P., & Istikopoulou, T. G. (2013). Perceived Website Aesthetics by Users and Designers: Implications for Evaluation Practice. [IJTHI]. *International Journal of Technology and Human Interaction, 9*(2), 39–52. doi:10.4018/jthi.2013040103

Kraft, E., & Wang, J. (2012). An Exploratory Study of the Cyberbullying and Cyberstalking Experiences and Factors Related to Victimization of Students at a Public Liberal Arts College. In R. Luppicini (Ed.), *Ethical Impact of Technological Advancements and Applications in Society* (pp. 113–131). Hershey, PA: Information Science Reference. doi:10.4018/978-1-4666-1773-5.ch009

Kulman, R., Stoner, G., Ruffolo, L., Marshall, S., Slater, J., Dyl, A., & Cheng, A. (2014). Teaching Executive Functions, Self-Management, and Ethical Decision-Making through Popular Videogame Play. In I. Management Association (Ed.), Assistive Technologies: Concepts, Methodologies, Tools, and Applications (pp. 771-785). Hershey, PA: Information Science Reference. doi: doi:10.4018/978-1-4666-4422-9.ch039

Kunc, L., Míkovec, Z., & Slavík, P. (2013). Avatar and Dialog Turn-Yielding Phenomena. [IJTHI]. *International Journal of Technology and Human Interaction, 9*(2), 66–88. doi:10.4018/jthi.2013040105

Kuo, N., & Dai, Y. (2012). Applying the Theory of Planned Behavior to Predict Low-Carbon Tourism Behavior: A Modified Model from Taiwan. [IJTHI]. *International Journal of Technology and Human Interaction, 8*(4), 45–62. doi:10.4018/jthi.2012100103

Kurt, S. (2014). Accessibility Issues of Educational Web Sites. In I. Management Association (Ed.), Assistive Technologies: Concepts, Methodologies, Tools, and Applications (pp. 54-62). Hershey, PA: Information Science Reference. doi: doi:10.4018/978-1-4666-4422-9.ch004

Kuzma, J. (2013). Empirical Study of Cyber Harassment among Social Networks. [IJTHI]. *International Journal of Technology and Human Interaction, 9*(2), 53–65. doi:10.4018/jthi.2013040104

Kyriakaki, G., & Matsatsinis, N. (2014). Pedagogical Evaluation of E-Learning Websites with Cognitive Objectives. In D. Yannacopoulos, P. Manolitzas, N. Matsatsinis, & E. Grigoroudis (Eds.), *Evaluating Websites and Web Services: Interdisciplinary Perspectives on User Satisfaction* (pp. 224–240). Hershey, PA: Information Science Reference. doi:10.4018/978-1-4666-5129-6.ch013

Lee, H., & Baek, E. (2012). Facilitating Deep Learning in a Learning Community. [IJTHI]. *International Journal of Technology and Human Interaction, 8*(1), 1–13. doi:10.4018/jthi.2012010101

Lee, W., Wu, T., Cheng, Y., Chuang, Y., & Sheu, S. (2013). Using the Kalman Filter for Auto Bit-rate H.264 Streaming Based on Human Interaction. [IJTHI]. *International Journal of Technology and Human Interaction, 9*(4), 58–74. doi:10.4018/ijthi.2013100104

Li, Y., Guo, N. Y., & Ranieri, M. (2014). Designing an Online Interactive Learning Program to Improve Chinese Migrant Children's Internet Skills: A Case Study at Hangzhou Minzhu Experimental School. In Z. Yang, H. Yang, D. Wu, & S. Liu (Eds.), *Transforming K-12 Classrooms with Digital Technology* (pp. 249–265). Hershey, PA: Information Science Reference.

Lin, C., Chu, L., & Hsu, H. (2013). Study on the Performance and Exhaust Emissions of Motorcycle Engine Fuelled with Hydrogen-Gasoline Compound Fuel. [IJTHI]. *International Journal of Technology and Human Interaction, 8*(3), 69–81. doi:10.4018/jthi.2012070107

Lin, L. (2013). Multiple Dimensions of Multitasking Phenomenon. [IJTHI]. *International Journal of Technology and Human Interaction, 9*(1), 37–49. doi:10.4018/jthi.2013010103

Lin, T., Li, X., Wu, Z., & Tang, N. (2013). Automatic Cognitive Load Classification Using High-Frequency Interaction Events: An Exploratory Study. [IJTHI]. *International Journal of Technology and Human Interaction, 9*(3), 73–88. doi:10.4018/jthi.2013070106

Lin, T., Wu, Z., Tang, N., & Wu, S. (2013). Exploring the Effects of Display Characteristics on Presence and Emotional Responses of Game Players. [IJTHI]. *International Journal of Technology and Human Interaction, 9*(1), 50–63. doi:10.4018/jthi.2013010104

Lin, T., Xie, T., Mou, Y., & Tang, N. (2013). Markov Chain Models for Menu Item Prediction. [IJTHI]. *International Journal of Technology and Human Interaction, 9*(4), 75–94. doi:10.4018/ijthi.2013100105

Lin, X., & Luppicini, R. (2011). Socio-Technical Influences of Cyber Espionage: A Case Study of the GhostNet System. [IJT]. *International Journal of Technoethics, 2*(2), 65–77. doi:10.4018/jte.2011040105

Linek, S. B., Marte, B., & Albert, D. (2014). Background Music in Educational Games: Motivational Appeal and Cognitive Impact. In J. Bishop (Ed.), *Gamification for Human Factors Integration: Social, Education, and Psychological Issues* (pp. 259–271). Hershey, PA: Information Science Reference. doi:10.4018/978-1-4666-5071-8.ch016

Lipschutz, R. D., & Hester, R. J. (2014). We Are the Borg! Human Assimilation into Cellular Society. In M. Michael, & K. Michael (Eds.), *Uberveillance and the Social Implications of Microchip Implants: Emerging Technologies* (pp. 366–407). Hershey, PA: Information Science Reference.

Liu, C., Zhong, Y., Ozercan, S., & Zhu, Q. (2013). Facilitating 3D Virtual World Learning Environments Creation by Non-Technical End Users through Template-Based Virtual World Instantiation. [IJVPLE]. *International Journal of Virtual and Personal Learning Environments, 4*(1), 32–48. doi:10.4018/jvple.2013010103

Liu, F., Lo, H., Su, C., Lou, D., & Lee, W. (2013). High Performance Reversible Data Hiding for Mobile Applications and Human Interaction. [IJTHI]. *International Journal of Technology and Human Interaction, 9*(4), 41–57. doi:10.4018/ijthi.2013100103

Liu, H. (2012). From Cold War Island to Low Carbon Island: A Study of Kinmen Island. [IJTHI]. *International Journal of Technology and Human Interaction, 8*(4), 63–74. doi:10.4018/jthi.2012100104

Lixun, Z., Dapeng, B., & Lei, Y. (2014). Design of and Experimentation with a Walking Assistance Robot. In I. Management Association (Ed.), Assistive Technologies: Concepts, Methodologies, Tools, and Applications (pp. 1600-1605). Hershey, PA: Information Science Reference. doi: doi:10.4018/978-1-4666-4422-9.ch084

Low, R., Jin, P., & Sweller, J. (2014). Instructional Design in Digital Environments and Availability of Mental Resources for the Aged Subpopulation. In I. Management Association (Ed.), Assistive Technologies: Concepts, Methodologies, Tools, and Applications (pp. 1131-1154). Hershey, PA: Information Science Reference. doi: doi:10.4018/978-1-4666-4422-9.ch059

Luczak, H., Schlick, C. M., Jochems, N., Vetter, S., & Kausch, B. (2014). Touch Screens for the Elderly: Some Models and Methods, Prototypical Development and Experimental Evaluation of Human-Computer Interaction Concepts for the Elderly. In I. Management Association (Ed.), Assistive Technologies: Concepts, Methodologies, Tools, and Applications (pp. 377-396). Hershey, PA: Information Science Reference. doi: doi:10.4018/978-1-4666-4422-9.ch019

Luor, T., Lu, H., Johanson, R. E., & Yu, H. (2012). Minding the Gap Between First and Continued Usage of a Corporate E-Learning English-language Program. [IJTHI]. *International Journal of Technology and Human Interaction, 8*(1), 55–74. doi:10.4018/jthi.2012010104

Luppicini, R. (2013). The Emerging Field of Technoself Studies (TSS). In R. Luppicini (Ed.), *Handbook of Research on Technoself: Identity in a Technological Society* (pp. 1–25). Hershey, PA: Information Science Reference.

Magnani, L. (2012). Material Cultures and Moral Mediators in Human Hybridization. In R. Luppicini (Ed.), *Ethical Impact of Technological Advancements and Applications in Society* (pp. 1–20). Hershey, PA: Information Science Reference. doi:10.4018/978-1-4666-1773-5.ch001

Maher, D. (2014). Learning in the Primary School Classroom using the Interactive Whiteboard. In I. Management Association (Ed.), K-12 Education: Concepts, Methodologies, Tools, and Applications (pp. 526-538). Hershey, PA: Information Science Reference. doi: doi:10.4018/978-1-4666-4502-8.ch031

Manolache, M., & Patrut, M. (2013). The Use of New Web-Based Technologies in Strategies of Teaching Gender Studies. In M. Pătruţ, & B. Pătruţ (Eds.), *Social Media in Higher Education: Teaching in Web 2.0* (pp. 45–74). Hershey, PA: Information Science Reference. doi:10.4018/978-1-4666-2970-7.ch003

Manthiou, A., & Chiang, L., & Liang (Rebecca) Tang. (2013). Identifying and Responding to Customer Needs on Facebook Fan Pages. [IJTHI]. *International Journal of Technology and Human Interaction, 9*(3), 36–52. doi:10.4018/jthi.2013070103

Marengo, A., Pagano, A., & Barbone, A. (2013). An Assessment of Customer's Preferences and Improve Brand Awareness Implementation of Social CRM in an Automotive Company. [IJTD]. *International Journal of Technology Diffusion*, *4*(1), 1–15. doi:10.4018/jtd.2013010101

Martin, I., Kear, K., Simpkins, N., & Busvine, J. (2013). Social Negotiations in Web Usability Engineering. In M. Garcia-Ruiz (Ed.), *Cases on Usability Engineering: Design and Development of Digital Products* (pp. 26–56). Hershey, PA: Information Science Reference. doi:10.4018/978-1-4666-4046-7.ch002

Martins, T., Carvalho, V., & Soares, F. (2014). An Overview on the Use of Serious Games in Physical Therapy and Rehabilitation. In I. Management Association (Ed.), Assistive Technologies: Concepts, Methodologies, Tools, and Applications (pp. 758-770). Hershey, PA: Information Science Reference. doi: doi:10.4018/978-1-4666-4422-9.ch038

Mathew, D. (2013). Online Anxiety: Implications for Educational Design in a Web 2.0 World. In M. Pătruţ, & B. Pătruţ (Eds.), *Social Media in Higher Education: Teaching in Web 2.0* (pp. 305–317). Hershey, PA: Information Science Reference. doi:10.4018/978-1-4666-2970-7.ch015

Mazzanti, I., Maolo, A., & Antonicelli, R. (2014). E-Health and Telemedicine in the Elderly: State of the Art. In I. Management Association (Ed.), Assistive Technologies: Concepts, Methodologies, Tools, and Applications (pp. 693-704). Hershey, PA: Information Science Reference. doi: doi:10.4018/978-1-4666-4422-9.ch034

Mazzara, M., Biselli, L., Greco, P. P., Dragoni, N., Marraffa, A., Qamar, N., & de Nicola, S. (2013). Social Networks and Collective Intelligence: A Return to the Agora. In L. Caviglione, M. Coccoli, & A. Merlo (Eds.), *Social Network Engineering for Secure Web Data and Services* (pp. 88–113). Hershey, PA: Information Science Reference. doi:10.4018/978-1-4666-3926-3.ch005

McColl, D., & Nejat, G. (2013). A Human Affect Recognition System for Socially Interactive Robots. In R. Luppicini (Ed.), *Handbook of Research on Technoself: Identity in a Technological Society* (pp. 554–573). Hershey, PA: Information Science Reference. doi:10.4018/978-1-4666-4607-0.ch015

McDonald, A., & Helmer, S. (2011). A Comparative Case Study of Indonesian and UK Organisational Culture Differences in IS Project Management. [IJTHI]. *International Journal of Technology and Human Interaction*, *7*(2), 28–37. doi:10.4018/jthi.2011040104

McGee, E. M. (2014). Neuroethics and Implanted Brain Machine Interfaces. In M. Michael, & K. Michael (Eds.), *Uberveillance and the Social Implications of Microchip Implants: Emerging Technologies* (pp. 351–365). Hershey, PA: Information Science Reference.

McGrath, E., Lowes, S., McKay, M., Sayres, J., & Lin, P. (2014). Robots Underwater! Learning Science, Engineering and 21st Century Skills: The Evolution of Curricula, Professional Development and Research in Formal and Informal Contexts. In I. Management Association (Ed.), K-12 Education: Concepts, Methodologies, Tools, and Applications (pp. 1041-1067). Hershey, PA: Information Science Reference. doi: doi:10.4018/978-1-4666-4502-8.ch062

Meissonierm, R., Bourdon, I., Amabile, S., & Boudrandi, S. (2012). Toward an Enacted Approach to Understanding OSS Developer's Motivations. [IJTHI]. *International Journal of Technology and Human Interaction*, *8*(1), 38–54. doi:10.4018/jthi.2012010103

Melius, J. (2014). The Role of Social Constructivist Instructional Approaches in Facilitating Cross-Cultural Online Learning in Higher Education. In J. Keengwe, G. Schnellert, & K. Kungu (Eds.), *Cross-Cultural Online Learning in Higher Education and Corporate Training* (pp. 253–270). Hershey, PA: Information Science Reference. doi:10.4018/978-1-4666-5023-7.ch015

Melson, G. F. (2013). Building a Technoself: Children's Ideas about and Behavior toward Robotic Pets. In R. Luppicini (Ed.), *Handbook of Research on Technoself: Identity in a Technological Society* (pp. 592–608). Hershey, PA: Information Science Reference. doi:10.4018/978-1-4666-4607-0.ch068

Mena, R. J. (2014). The Quest for a Massively Multiplayer Online Game that Teaches Physics. In T. Connolly, T. Hainey, E. Boyle, G. Baxter, & P. Moreno-Ger (Eds.), *Psychology, Pedagogy, and Assessment in Serious Games* (pp. 292–316). Hershey, PA: Information Science Reference.

Meredith, J., & Potter, J. (2014). Conversation Analysis and Electronic Interactions: Methodological, Analytic and Technical Considerations. In H. Lim, & F. Sudweeks (Eds.), *Innovative Methods and Technologies for Electronic Discourse Analysis* (pp. 370–393). Hershey, PA: Information Science Reference.

Millán-Calenti, J. C., & Maseda, A. (2014). Telegerontology®: A New Technological Resource for Elderly Support. In I. Management Association (Ed.), *Assistive Technologies: Concepts, Methodologies, Tools, and Applications* (pp. 705-719). Hershey, PA: Information Science Reference. doi: doi:10.4018/978-1-4666-4422-9.ch035

Miscione, G. (2011). Telemedicine and Development: Situating Information Technologies in the Amazon. [IJSKD]. *International Journal of Sociotechnology and Knowledge Development*, *3*(4), 15–26. doi:10.4018/jskd.2011100102

Miwa, N., & Wang, Y. (2011). Online Interaction Between On-Campus and Distance Students: Learners' Perspectives. [IJCALLT]. *International Journal of Computer-Assisted Language Learning and Teaching*, *1*(3), 54–69. doi:10.4018/ijcallt.2011070104

Moore, M. J., Nakano, T., Suda, T., & Enomoto, A. (2013). Social Interactions and Automated Detection Tools in Cyberbullying. In L. Caviglione, M. Coccoli, & A. Merlo (Eds.), *Social Network Engineering for Secure Web Data and Services* (pp. 67–87). Hershey, PA: Information Science Reference. doi:10.4018/978-1-4666-3926-3.ch004

Morueta, R. T., Gómez, J. I., & Gómez, Á. H. (2012). B-Learning at Universities in Andalusia (Spain): From Traditional to Student-Centred Learning. [IJTHI]. *International Journal of Technology and Human Interaction*, *8*(2), 56–76. doi:10.4018/jthi.2012040104

Mosindi, O., & Sice, P. (2011). An Exploratory Theoretical Framework for Understanding Information Behaviour. [IJTHI]. *International Journal of Technology and Human Interaction*, *7*(2), 1–8. doi:10.4018/jthi.2011040101

Mott, M. S., & Williams-Black, T. H. (2014). Media-Enhanced Writing Instruction and Assessment. In J. Keengwe, G. Onchwari, & D. Hucks (Eds.), *Literacy Enrichment and Technology Integration in Pre-Service Teacher Education* (pp. 1–16). Hershey, PA: Information Science Reference.

Mulvey, F., & Heubner, M. (2014). Eye Movements and Attention. In I. Management Association (Ed.), *Assistive Technologies: Concepts, Methodologies, Tools, and Applications* (pp. 1030-1054). Hershey, PA: Information Science Reference. doi: doi:10.4018/978-1-4666-4422-9.ch053

Muro, B. F., & Delgado, E. C. (2014). RACEM Game for PC for Use as Rehabilitation Therapy for Children with Psychomotor Disability and Results of its Application. In I. Management Association (Ed.), *Assistive Technologies: Concepts, Methodologies, Tools, and Applications* (pp. 740-757). Hershey, PA: Information Science Reference. doi: doi:10.4018/978-1-4666-4422-9.ch037

Muwanguzi, S., & Lin, L. (2014). Coping with Accessibility and Usability Challenges of Online Technologies by Blind Students in Higher Education. In I. Management Association (Ed.), Assistive Technologies: Concepts, Methodologies, Tools, and Applications (pp. 1227-1244). Hershey, PA: Information Science Reference. doi: doi:10.4018/978-1-4666-4422-9.ch064

Najjar, M., Courtemanche, F., Hamam, H., Dion, A., Bauchet, J., & Mayers, A. (2014). DeepKøver: An Adaptive Intelligent Assistance System for Monitoring Impaired People in Smart Homes. In I. Management Association (Ed.), Assistive Technologies: Concepts, Methodologies, Tools, and Applications (pp. 634-661). Hershey, PA: Information Science Reference. doi: doi:10.4018/978-1-4666-4422-9.ch031

Nap, H. H., & Diaz-Orueta, U. (2014). Rehabilitation Gaming. In J. Bishop (Ed.), *Gamification for Human Factors Integration: Social, Education, and Psychological Issues* (pp. 122–147). Hershey, PA: Information Science Reference. doi:10.4018/978-1-4666-5071-8.ch008

Neves, J., & Pinheiro, L. D. (2012). Cyberbullying: A Sociological Approach. In R. Luppicini (Ed.), *Ethical Impact of Technological Advancements and Applications in Society* (pp. 132–142). Hershey, PA: Information Science Reference. doi:10.4018/978-1-4666-1773-5.ch010

Nguyen, P. T. (2012). Peer Feedback on Second Language Writing through Blogs: The Case of a Vietnamese EFL Classroom. [IJCALLT]. *International Journal of Computer-Assisted Language Learning and Teaching*, 2(1), 13–23. doi:10.4018/ijcallt.2012010102

Ninaus, M., Witte, M., Kober, S. E., Friedrich, E. V., Kurzmann, J., & Hartsuiker, E. et al. (2014). Neurofeedback and Serious Games. In T. Connolly, T. Hainey, E. Boyle, G. Baxter, & P. Moreno-Ger (Eds.), *Psychology, Pedagogy, and Assessment in Serious Games* (pp. 82–110). Hershey, PA: Information Science Reference.

Olla, V. (2014). An Enquiry into the use of Technology and Student Voice in Citizenship Education in the K-12 Classroom. In I. Management Association (Ed.), K-12 Education: Concepts, Methodologies, Tools, and Applications (pp. 892-913). Hershey, PA: Information Science Reference. doi: doi:10.4018/978-1-4666-4502-8.ch053

Orange, E. (2013). Understanding the Human-Machine Interface in a Time of Change. In R. Luppicini (Ed.), *Handbook of Research on Technoself: Identity in a Technological Society* (pp. 703–719). Hershey, PA: Information Science Reference. doi:10.4018/978-1-4666-4607-0.ch082

Palmer, D., Warren, I., & Miller, P. (2014). ID Scanners and Überveillance in the Night-Time Economy: Crime Prevention or Invasion of Privacy? In M. Michael, & K. Michael (Eds.), *Uberveillance and the Social Implications of Microchip Implants: Emerging Technologies* (pp. 208–225). Hershey, PA: Information Science Reference.

Papadopoulos, F., Dautenhahn, K., & Ho, W. C. (2013). Behavioral Analysis of Human-Human Remote Social Interaction Mediated by an Interactive Robot in a Cooperative Game Scenario. In R. Luppicini (Ed.), *Handbook of Research on Technoself: Identity in a Technological Society* (pp. 637–665). Hershey, PA: Information Science Reference.

Patel, K. K., & Vij, S. K. (2014). Unconstrained Walking Plane to Virtual Environment for Non-Visual Spatial Learning. In I. Management Association (Ed.), Assistive Technologies: Concepts, Methodologies, Tools, and Applications (pp. 1580-1599). Hershey, PA: Information Science Reference. doi: doi:10.4018/978-1-4666-4422-9.ch083

Patrone, T. (2013). In Defense of the 'Human Prejudice'. [IJT]. *International Journal of Technoethics*, 4(1), 26–38. doi:10.4018/jte.2013010103

Peevers, G., Williams, R., Douglas, G., & Jack, M. A. (2013). Usability Study of Fingerprint and Palmvein Biometric Technologies at the ATM. [IJTHI]. *International Journal of Technology and Human Interaction*, 9(1), 78–95. doi:10.4018/jthi.2013010106

Pellas, N. (2014). Theoretical Foundations of a CSCL Script in Persistent Virtual Worlds According to the Contemporary Learning Theories and Models. In E. Nikoi, & K. Boateng (Eds.), *Collaborative Communication Processes and Decision Making in Organizations* (pp. 72–107). Hershey, PA: Business Science Reference.

Perakslis, C. (2014). Willingness to Adopt RFID Implants: Do Personality Factors Play a Role in the Acceptance of Uberveillance? In M. Michael, & K. Michael (Eds.), *Uberveillance and the Social Implications of Microchip Implants: Emerging Technologies* (pp. 144–168). Hershey, PA: Information Science Reference.

Pereira, G., Brisson, A., Dias, J., Carvalho, A., Dimas, J., & Mascarenhas, S. et al. (2014). Non-Player Characters and Artificial Intelligence. In T. Connolly, T. Hainey, E. Boyle, G. Baxter, & P. Moreno-Ger (Eds.), *Psychology, Pedagogy, and Assessment in Serious Games* (pp. 127–152). Hershey, PA: Information Science Reference.

Pérez Pérez, A., Callejas Carrión, Z., López-Cózar Delgado, R., & Griol Barres, D. (2014). On the Use of Speech Technologies to Achieve Inclusive Education for People with Intellectual Disabilities. In I. Management Association (Ed.), Assistive Technologies: Concepts, Methodologies, Tools, and Applications (pp. 1106-1117). Hershey, PA: Information Science Reference. doi:doi:10.4018/978-1-4666-4422-9.ch057

Peschl, M. F., & Fundneider, T. (2014). Theory U and Emergent Innovation: Presencing as a Method of Bringing Forth Profoundly New Knowledge and Realities. In O. Gunnlaugson, C. Baron, & M. Cayer (Eds.), *Perspectives on Theory U: Insights from the Field* (pp. 207–233). Hershey, PA: Business Science Reference.

Petrovic, N., Jeremic, V., Petrovic, D., & Cirovic, M. (2014). Modeling the Use of Facebook in Environmental Higher Education. In G. Mallia (Ed.), *The Social Classroom: Integrating Social Network Use in Education* (pp. 100–119). Hershey, PA: Information Science Reference.

Phua, C., Roy, P. C., Aloulou, H., Biswas, J., Tolstikov, A., Foo, V. S., et al. (2014). State-of-the-Art Assistive Technology for People with Dementia. In I. Management Association (Ed.), Assistive Technologies: Concepts, Methodologies, Tools, and Applications (pp. 1606-1625). Hershey, PA: Information Science Reference. doi:doi:10.4018/978-1-4666-4422-9.ch085

Potts, L. (2011). Balancing McLuhan With Williams: A Sociotechnical View of Technological Determinism. [IJSKD]. *International Journal of Sociotechnology and Knowledge Development*, 3(2), 53–57. doi:10.4018/jskd.2011040105

Potts, L. (2013). Balancing McLuhan With Williams: A Sociotechnical View of Technological Determinism. In J. Abdelnour-Nocera (Ed.), *Knowledge and Technological Development Effects on Organizational and Social Structures* (pp. 109–114). Hershey, PA: Information Science Reference.

Potts, L. (2014). Sociotechnical Uses of Social Web Tools during Disasters. In I. Management Association (Ed.), Crisis Management: Concepts, Methodologies, Tools and Applications (pp. 531-541). Hershey, PA: Information Science Reference. doi:doi:10.4018/978-1-4666-4707-7.ch024

Proença, R., Guerra, A., & Campos, P. (2013). A Gestural Recognition Interface for Intelligent Wheelchair Users. [IJSKD]. *International Journal of Sociotechnology and Knowledge Development, 5*(2), 63–81. doi:10.4018/jskd.2013040105

Quilici-Gonzalez, J. A., Kobayashi, G., Broens, M. C., & Gonzalez, M. E. (2012). Ubiquitous Computing: Any Ethical Implications? In R. Luppicini (Ed.), *Ethical Impact of Technological Advancements and Applications in Society* (pp. 47–59). Hershey, PA: Information Science Reference. doi:10.4018/978-1-4666-1773-5.ch005

Rambaree, K. (2014). Computer-Aided Deductive Critical Discourse Analysis of a Case Study from Mauritius with ATLAS-ti 6.2. In H. Lim, & F. Sudweeks (Eds.), *Innovative Methods and Technologies for Electronic Discourse Analysis* (pp. 346–368). Hershey, PA: Information Science Reference.

Ratan, R. (2013). Self-Presence, Explicated: Body, Emotion, and Identity Extension into the Virtual Self. In R. Luppicini (Ed.), *Handbook of Research on Technoself: Identity in a Technological Society* (pp. 322–336). Hershey, PA: Information Science Reference.

Rechy-Ramirez, E. J., & Hu, H. (2014). A Flexible Bio-Signal Based HMI for Hands-Free Control of an Electric Powered Wheelchair. [IJALR]. *International Journal of Artificial Life Research, 4*(1), 59–76. doi:10.4018/ijalr.2014010105

Reiners, T., Wood, L. C., & Dron, J. (2014). From Chaos Towards Sense: A Learner-Centric Narrative Virtual Learning Space. In J. Bishop (Ed.), *Gamification for Human Factors Integration: Social, Education, and Psychological Issues* (pp. 242–258). Hershey, PA: Information Science Reference. doi:10.4018/978-1-4666-5071-8.ch015

Reinhardt, J., & Ryu, J. (2013). Using Social Network-Mediated Bridging Activities to Develop Socio-Pragmatic Awareness in Elementary Korean. [IJCALLT]. *International Journal of Computer-Assisted Language Learning and Teaching, 3*(3), 18–33. doi:10.4018/ijcallt.2013070102

Revuelta, P., Jiménez, J., Sánchez, J. M., & Ruiz, B. (2014). Automatic Speech Recognition to Enhance Learning for Disabled Students. In I. Management Association (Ed.), Assistive Technologies: Concepts, Methodologies, Tools, and Applications (pp. 478-493). Hershey, PA: Information Science Reference. doi: doi:10.4018/978-1-4666-4422-9.ch023

Ribeiro, J. C., & Silva, T. (2013). Self, Self-Presentation, and the Use of Social Applications in Digital Environments. In R. Luppicini (Ed.), *Handbook of Research on Technoself: Identity in a Technological Society* (pp. 439–455). Hershey, PA: Information Science Reference.

Richet, J. (2013). From Young Hackers to Crackers. [IJTHI]. *International Journal of Technology and Human Interaction, 9*(3), 53–62. doi:10.4018/jthi.2013070104

Rigas, D., & Almutairi, B. (2013). An Empirical Investigation into the Role of Avatars in Multimodal E-government Interfaces. [IJSKD]. *International Journal of Sociotechnology and Knowledge Development, 5*(1), 14–22. doi:10.4018/jskd.2013010102

Rodríguez, W. R., Saz, O., & Lleida, E. (2014). Experiences Using a Free Tool for Voice Therapy based on Speech Technologies. In I. Management Association (Ed.), Assistive Technologies: Concepts, Methodologies, Tools, and Applications (pp. 508-523). Hershey, PA: Information Science Reference. doi: doi:10.4018/978-1-4666-4422-9.ch025

Rothblatt, M. (2013). Mindclone Technoselves: Multi-Substrate Legal Identities, Cyber-Psychology, and Biocyberethics. In R. Luppicini (Ed.), *Handbook of Research on Technoself: Identity in a Technological Society* (pp. 105–122). Hershey, PA: Information Science Reference.

Rowe, N. C. (2012). The Ethics of Cyberweapons in Warfare. In R. Luppicini (Ed.), *Ethical Impact of Technological Advancements and Applications in Society* (pp. 195–207). Hershey, PA: Information Science Reference. doi:10.4018/978-1-4666-1773-5.ch015

Russo, M. R. (2014). Emergency Management Professional Development: Linking Information Communication Technology and Social Communication Skills to Enhance a Sense of Community and Social Justice in the 21st Century. In I. Management Association (Ed.), Crisis Management: Concepts, Methodologies, Tools and Applications (pp. 651-665). Hershey, PA: Information Science Reference. doi: doi:10.4018/978-1-4666-4707-7.ch031

Sajeva, S. (2011). Towards a Conceptual Knowledge Management System Based on Systems Thinking and Sociotechnical Thinking. [IJSKD]. *International Journal of Sociotechnology and Knowledge Development*, *3*(3), 40–55. doi:10.4018/jskd.2011070103

Sajeva, S. (2013). Towards a Conceptual Knowledge Management System Based on Systems Thinking and Sociotechnical Thinking. In J. Abdelnour-Nocera (Ed.), *Knowledge and Technological Development Effects on Organizational and Social Structures* (pp. 115–130). Hershey, PA: Information Science Reference.

Saleeb, N., & Dafoulas, G. A. (2014). Assistive Technologies and Environmental Design Concepts for Blended Learning and Teaching for Disabilities within 3D Virtual Worlds and Learning Environments. In I. Management Association (Ed.), Assistive Technologies: Concepts, Methodologies, Tools, and Applications (pp. 1382-1404). Hershey, PA: Information Science Reference. doi: doi:10.4018/978-1-4666-4422-9.ch073

Salvini, P. (2012). Presence, Reciprocity and Robotic Mediations: The Case of Autonomous Social Robots. [IJT]. *International Journal of Technoethics*, *3*(2), 9–16. doi:10.4018/jte.2012040102

Samanta, I. (2013). The Impact of Virtual Community (Web 2.0) in the Economic, Social, and Political Environment of Traditional Society. In S. Saeed, M. Khan, & R. Ahmad (Eds.), *Business Strategies and Approaches for Effective Engineering Management* (pp. 262–274). Hershey, PA: Business Science Reference. doi:10.4018/978-1-4666-3658-3.ch016

Samanta, S. K., Woods, J., & Ghanbari, M. (2011). Automatic Language Translation: An Enhancement to the Mobile Messaging Services. [IJTHI]. *International Journal of Technology and Human Interaction*, *7*(1), 1–18. doi:10.4018/jthi.2011010101

Sarkar, N. I., Kuang, A. X., Nisar, K., & Amphawan, A. (2014). Hospital Environment Scenarios using WLAN over OPNET Simulation Tool. [IJICTHD]. *International Journal of Information Communication Technologies and Human Development*, *6*(1), 69–90. doi:10.4018/ijicthd.2014010104

Sarré, C. (2013). Technology-Mediated Tasks in English for Specific Purposes (ESP): Design, Implementation and Learner Perception. [IJCALLT]. *International Journal of Computer-Assisted Language Learning and Teaching*, *3*(2), 1–16. doi:10.4018/ijcallt.2013040101

Saykili, A., & Kumtepe, E. G. (2014). Facebook's Hidden Potential: Facebook as an Educational Support Tool in Foreign Language Education. In G. Mallia (Ed.), *The Social Classroom: Integrating Social Network Use in Education* (pp. 120–146). Hershey, PA: Information Science Reference.

Sayoud, H. (2011). Biometrics: An Overview on New Technologies and Ethic Problems. [IJT]. *International Journal of Technoethics*, *2*(1), 19–34. doi:10.4018/jte.2011010102

Scott, C. R., & Timmerman, C. E. (2014). Communicative Changes Associated with Repeated Use of Electronic Meeting Systems for Decision-Making Tasks. In E. Nikoi, & K. Boateng (Eds.), *Collaborative Communication Processes and Decision Making in Organizations* (pp. 1–24). Hershey, PA: Business Science Reference.

Scott, K. (2013). The Human-Robot Continuum of Self: Where the Other Ends and Another Begins. In R. Luppicini (Ed.), *Handbook of Research on Technoself: Identity in a Technological Society* (pp. 666–679). Hershey, PA: Information Science Reference.

Shasek, J. (2014). ExerLearning®: Movement, Fitness, Technology, and Learning. In J. Bishop (Ed.), *Gamification for Human Factors Integration: Social, Education, and Psychological Issues* (pp. 106–121). Hershey, PA: Information Science Reference. doi:10.4018/978-1-4666-5071-8. ch007

Shen, J., & Eder, L. B. (2011). An Examination of Factors Associated with User Acceptance of Social Shopping Websites. [IJTHI]. *International Journal of Technology and Human Interaction*, *7*(1), 19–36. doi:10.4018/jthi.2011010102

Shrestha, P. (2012). Teacher Professional Development Using Mobile Technologies in a Large-Scale Project: Lessons Learned from Bangladesh. [IJCALLT]. *International Journal of Computer-Assisted Language Learning and Teaching*, *2*(4), 34–49. doi:10.4018/ijcallt.2012100103

Silvana de Rosa, A., Fino, E., & Bocci, E. (2014). Addressing Healthcare On-Line Demand and Supply Relating to Mental Illness: Knowledge Sharing About Psychiatry and Psychoanalysis Through Social Networks in Italy and France. In A. Kapoor, & C. Kulshrestha (Eds.), *Dynamics of Competitive Advantage and Consumer Perception in Social Marketing* (pp. 16–55). Hershey, PA: Business Science Reference.

Smith, M., & Murray, J. (2014). Augmentative and Alternative Communication Devices: The Voices of Adult Users. In I. Management Association (Ed.), *Assistive Technologies: Concepts, Methodologies, Tools, and Applications* (pp. 991-1004). Hershey, PA: Information Science Reference. doi: doi:10.4018/978-1-4666-4422-9.ch050

Smith, P. A. (2013). Strengthening and Enriching Audit Practice: The Socio-Technical Relevance of "Decision Leaders". In J. Abdelnour-Nocera (Ed.), *Knowledge and Technological Development Effects on Organizational and Social Structures* (pp. 97–108). Hershey, PA: Information Science Reference.

So, J. C., & Lam, S. Y. (2014). Using Social Networks Communication Platform for Promoting Student-Initiated Holistic Development Among Students. [IJISSS]. *International Journal of Information Systems in the Service Sector*, *6*(1), 1–23. doi:10.4018/ijisss.2014010101

Söderström, S. (2014). Assistive ICT and Young Disabled Persons: Opportunities and Obstacles in Identity Negotiations. In I. Management Association (Ed.), *Assistive Technologies: Concepts, Methodologies, Tools, and Applications* (pp. 1084-1105). Hershey, PA: Information Science Reference. doi: doi:10.4018/978-1-4666-4422-9. ch056

Son, J., & Rossade, K. (2013). Finding Gems in Computer-Assisted Language Learning: Clues from GLoCALL 2011 and 2012 Papers. [IJCALLT]. *International Journal of Computer-Assisted Language Learning and Teaching, 3*(4), 1–8. doi:10.4018/ijcallt.2013100101

Sone, Y. (2013). Robot Double: Hiroshi Ishiguro's Reflexive Machines. In R. Luppicini (Ed.), *Handbook of Research on Technoself: Identity in a Technological Society* (pp. 680–702). Hershey, PA: Information Science Reference.

Spillane, M. (2014). Assistive Technology: A Tool for Inclusion. In I. Management Association (Ed.), Assistive Technologies: Concepts, Methodologies, Tools, and Applications (pp. 1-11). Hershey, PA: Information Science Reference. doi: doi:10.4018/978-1-4666-4422-9.ch001

Stahl, B. C., Heersmink, R., Goujon, P., Flick, C., van den Hoven, J., & Wakunuma, K. et al. (2012). Identifying the Ethics of Emerging Information and Communication Technologies: An Essay on Issues, Concepts and Method. In R. Luppicini (Ed.), *Ethical Impact of Technological Advancements and Applications in Society* (pp. 61–79). Hershey, PA: Information Science Reference. doi:10.4018/978-1-4666-1773-5.ch006

Stern, S. E., & Grounds, B. E. (2011). Cellular Telephones and Social Interactions: Evidence of Interpersonal Surveillance. [IJT]. *International Journal of Technoethics, 2*(1), 43–49. doi:10.4018/jte.2011010104

Stinson, J., & Gill, N. (2014). Internet-Based Chronic Disease Self-Management for Youth. In I. Management Association (Ed.), Assistive Technologies: Concepts, Methodologies, Tools, and Applications (pp. 224-245). Hershey, PA: Information Science Reference. doi: doi:10.4018/978-1-4666-4422-9.ch012

Stockwell, G. (2011). Online Approaches to Learning Vocabulary: Teacher-Centred or Learner-Centred? [IJCALLT]. *International Journal of Computer-Assisted Language Learning and Teaching, 1*(1), 33–44. doi:10.4018/ijcallt.2011010103

Stradella, E. (2012). Personal Liability and Human Free Will in the Background of Emerging Neuroethical Issues: Some Remarks Arising From Recent Case Law. [IJT]. *International Journal of Technoethics, 3*(2), 30–41. doi:10.4018/jte.2012040104

Stubbs, K., Casper, J., & Yanco, H. A. (2014). Designing Evaluations for K-12 Robotics Education Programs. In I. Management Association (Ed.), K-12 Education: Concepts, Methodologies, Tools, and Applications (pp. 1342-1364). Hershey, PA: Information Science Reference. doi: doi:10.4018/978-1-4666-4502-8.ch078

Suki, N. M., Ramayah, T., Ming, M. K., & Suki, N. M. (2011). Factors Enhancing Employed Job Seekers Intentions to Use Social Networking Sites as a Job Search Tool. [IJTHI]. *International Journal of Technology and Human Interaction, 7*(2), 38–54. doi:10.4018/jthi.2011040105

Sweeney, P., & Moore, C. (2012). Mobile Apps for Learning Vocabulary: Categories, Evaluation and Design Criteria for Teachers and Developers. [IJCALLT]. *International Journal of Computer-Assisted Language Learning and Teaching, 2*(4), 1–16. doi:10.4018/ijcallt.2012100101

Szeto, A. Y. (2014). Assistive Technology and Rehabilitation Engineering. In I. Management Association (Ed.), Assistive Technologies: Concepts, Methodologies, Tools, and Applications (pp. 277-331). Hershey, PA: Information Science Reference. doi: doi:10.4018/978-1-4666-4422-9.ch015

Tamim, R. (2014). Technology Integration in UAE Schools: Current Status and Way Forward. In I. Management Association (Ed.), K-12 Education: Concepts, Methodologies, Tools, and Applications (pp. 41-57). Hershey, PA: Information Science Reference. doi: doi:10.4018/978-1-4666-4502-8.ch004

Tan, R., Wang, S., Jiang, Y., Ishida, K., & Fujie, M. G. (2014). Motion Control of an Omni-Directional Walker for Walking Support. In I. Management Association (Ed.), Assistive Technologies: Concepts, Methodologies, Tools, and Applications (pp. 614-622). Hershey, PA: Information Science Reference. doi: doi:10.4018/978-1-4666-4422-9.ch029

Tankari, M. (2014). Cultural Orientation Differences and their Implications for Online Learning Satisfaction. In J. Keengwe, G. Schnellert, & K. Kungu (Eds.), *Cross-Cultural Online Learning in Higher Education and Corporate Training* (pp. 20–61). Hershey, PA: Information Science Reference. doi:10.4018/978-1-4666-5023-7.ch002

Tchangani, A. P. (2014). Bipolarity in Decision Analysis: A Way to Cope with Human Judgment. In A. Masegosa, P. Villacorta, C. Cruz-Corona, M. García-Cascales, M. Lamata, & J. Verdegay (Eds.), *Exploring Innovative and Successful Applications of Soft Computing* (pp. 216–244). Hershey, PA: Information Science Reference.

Tennyson, R. D. (2014). Computer Interventions for Children with Disabilities: Review of Research and Practice. In I. Management Association (Ed.), Assistive Technologies: Concepts, Methodologies, Tools, and Applications (pp. 841-864). Hershey, PA: Information Science Reference. doi: doi:10.4018/978-1-4666-4422-9.ch042

Terrell, S. S. (2011). Integrating Online Tools to Motivate Young English Language Learners to Practice English Outside the Classroom. [IJCALLT]. *International Journal of Computer-Assisted Language Learning and Teaching, 1*(2), 16–24. doi:10.4018/ijcallt.2011040102

Tiwary, U. S., & Siddiqui, T. J. (2014). Working Together with Computers: Towards a General Framework for Collaborative Human Computer Interaction. In I. Management Association (Ed.), Assistive Technologies: Concepts, Methodologies, Tools, and Applications (pp. 141-162). Hershey, PA: Information Science Reference. doi: doi:10.4018/978-1-4666-4422-9.ch008

Tomas, J., Lloret, J., Bri, D., & Sendra, S. (2014). Sensors and their Application for Disabled and Elderly People. In I. Management Association (Ed.), Assistive Technologies: Concepts, Methodologies, Tools, and Applications (pp. 357-376). Hershey, PA: Information Science Reference. doi: doi:10.4018/978-1-4666-4422-9.ch018

Tomasi, A. (2013). A Run for your [Techno]Self. In R. Luppicini (Ed.), Handbook of Research on Technoself: Identity in a Technological Society (pp. 123-136). Hershey, PA: Information Science Reference. doi: doi:10.4018/978-1-4666-2211-1.ch007

Tootell, H., & Freeman, A. (2014). The Applicability of Gaming Elements to Early Childhood Education. In J. Bishop (Ed.), *Gamification for Human Factors Integration: Social, Education, and Psychological Issues* (pp. 225–241). Hershey, PA: Information Science Reference. doi:10.4018/978-1-4666-5071-8.ch014

Tsai, C. (2011). How Much Can Computers and Internet Help?: A Long-Term Study of Web-Mediated Problem-Based Learning and Self-Regulated Learning. [IJTHI]. *International Journal of Technology and Human Interaction, 7*(1), 67–81. doi:10.4018/jthi.2011010105

Tsai, W. (2013). An Investigation on Undergraduate's Bio-Energy Engineering Education Program at the Taiwan Technical University. [IJTHI]. *International Journal of Technology and Human Interaction, 8*(3), 46–53. doi:10.4018/jthi.2012070105

Tsiakis, T. (2013). Using Social Media as a Concept and Tool for Teaching Marketing Information Systems. In M. Pătruţ, & B. Pătruţ (Eds.), *Social Media in Higher Education: Teaching in Web 2.0* (pp. 24–44). Hershey, PA: Information Science Reference. doi:10.4018/978-1-4666-2970-7.ch002

Tu, C., McIsaac, M. S., Sujo-Montes, L. E., & Armfield, S. (2014). Building Mobile Social Presence for U-Learning. In F. Neto (Ed.), *Technology Platform Innovations and Forthcoming Trends in Ubiquitous Learning* (pp. 77–93). Hershey, PA: Information Science Reference.

Valeria, N., Lu, M. V., & Theng, L. B. (2014). Collaborative Virtual Learning for Assisting Children with Cerebral Palsy. In I. Management Association (Ed.), Assistive Technologies: Concepts, Methodologies, Tools, and Applications (pp. 786-810). Hershey, PA: Information Science Reference. doi:doi:10.4018/978-1-4666-4422-9.ch040

Van Leuven, N., Newton, D., Leuenberger, D. Z., & Esteves, T. (2014). Reaching Citizen 2.0: How Government Uses Social Media to Send Public Messages during Times of Calm and Times of Crisis. In I. Management Association (Ed.), Crisis Management: Concepts, Methodologies, Tools and Applications (pp. 839-857). Hershey, PA: Information Science Reference. doi:doi:10.4018/978-1-4666-4707-7.ch041

Vargas-Hernández, J. G. (2013). International Student Collaboration and Experiential Exercise Projects as a Professional, Inter-Personal and Inter-Institutional Networking Platform. [IJTEM]. *International Journal of Technology and Educational Marketing*, 3(1), 28–47. doi:10.4018/ijtem.2013010103

Velicu, A., & Marinescu, V. (2013). Usage of Social Media by Children and Teenagers: Results of EU KIDS Online II. In M. Pătruţ, & B. Pătruţ (Eds.), *Social Media in Higher Education: Teaching in Web 2.0* (pp. 144–178). Hershey, PA: Information Science Reference. doi:10.4018/978-1-4666-2970-7.ch008

Vidaurre, C., Kübler, A., Tangermann, M., Müller, K., & Millán, J. D. (2014). Brain-Computer Interfaces and Visual Activity. In I. Management Association (Ed.), Assistive Technologies: Concepts, Methodologies, Tools, and Applications (pp. 1549-1570). Hershey, PA: Information Science Reference. doi:doi:10.4018/978-1-4666-4422-9.ch081

Viswanathan, R. (2012). Augmenting the Use of Mobile Devices in Language Classrooms. [IJCALLT]. *International Journal of Computer-Assisted Language Learning and Teaching*, 2(2), 45–60. doi:10.4018/ijcallt.2012040104

Wallgren, L. G., & Hanse, J. J. (2012). A Two-Wave Study of the Impact of Job Characteristics and Motivators on Perceived Stress among Information Technology (IT) Consultants. [IJTHI]. *International Journal of Technology and Human Interaction*, 8(4), 75–91. doi:10.4018/jthi.2012100105

Wang, H. (2014). A Guide to Assistive Technology for Teachers in Special Education. In I. Management Association (Ed.), Assistive Technologies: Concepts, Methodologies, Tools, and Applications (pp. 12-25). Hershey, PA: Information Science Reference. doi:doi:10.4018/978-1-4666-4422-9.ch002

Wang, S., Ku, C., & Chu, C. (2013). Sustainable Campus Project: Potential for Energy Conservation and Carbon Reduction Education in Taiwan. [IJTHI]. *International Journal of Technology and Human Interaction*, 8(3), 19–30. doi:10.4018/jthi.2012070103

Wang, Y., & Tian, J. (2013). Negotiation of Meaning in Multimodal Tandem Learning via Desktop Videoconferencing. [IJCALLT]. *International Journal of Computer-Assisted Language Learning and Teaching*, 3(2), 41–55. doi:10.4018/ijcallt.2013040103

Wareham, C. (2011). On the Moral Equality of Artificial Agents. [IJT]. *International Journal of Technoethics*, 2(1), 35–42. doi:10.4018/jte.2011010103

Warwick, K., & Gasson, M. N. (2014). Practical Experimentation with Human Implants. In M. Michael, & K. Michael (Eds.), *Uberveillance and the Social Implications of Microchip Implants: Emerging Technologies* (pp. 64–132). Hershey, PA: Information Science Reference.

Welch, K. C., Lahiri, U., Sarkar, N., Warren, Z., Stone, W., & Liu, C. (2014). Affect-Sensitive Computing and Autism. In I. Management Association (Ed.), Assistive Technologies: Concepts, Methodologies, Tools, and Applications (pp. 865-883). Hershey, PA: Information Science Reference. doi: doi:10.4018/978-1-4666-4422-9.ch043

Wessels, B., Dittrich, Y., Ekelin, A., & Eriksén, S. (2014). Creating Synergies between Participatory Design of E-Services and Collaborative Planning. In I. Management Association (Ed.), Assistive Technologies: Concepts, Methodologies, Tools, and Applications (pp. 163-179). Hershey, PA: Information Science Reference. doi: doi:10.4018/978-1-4666-4422-9.ch009

White, E. L. (2014). Technology-Based Literacy Approach for English Language Learners. In I. Management Association (Ed.), K-12 Education: Concepts, Methodologies, Tools, and Applications (pp. 723-740). Hershey, PA: Information Science Reference. doi: doi:10.4018/978-1-4666-4502-8.ch042

Whyte, K. P., List, M., Stone, J. V., Grooms, D., Gasteyer, S., & Thompson, P. B. et al. (2014). Uberveillance, Standards, and Anticipation: A Case Study on Nanobiosensors in U.S. Cattle. In M. Michael, & K. Michael (Eds.), *Uberveillance and the Social Implications of Microchip Implants: Emerging Technologies* (pp. 260–279). Hershey, PA: Information Science Reference.

Wilson, S., & Haslam, N. (2013). Reasoning about Human Enhancement: Towards a Folk Psychological Model of Human Nature and Human Identity. In R. Luppicini (Ed.), *Handbook of Research on Technoself: Identity in a Technological Society* (pp. 175–188). Hershey, PA: Information Science Reference.

Woodhead, R. (2012). What is Technology? [IJSKD]. *International Journal of Sociotechnology and Knowledge Development*, *4*(2), 1–13. doi:10.4018/jskd.2012040101

Woodley, C., & Dorrington, P. (2014). Facebook and the Societal Aspects of Formal Learning: Optional, Peripheral, or Essential. In G. Mallia (Ed.), *The Social Classroom: Integrating Social Network Use in Education* (pp. 269–291). Hershey, PA: Information Science Reference.

Yamazaki, T. (2014). Assistive Technologies in Smart Homes. In I. Management Association (Ed.), Assistive Technologies: Concepts, Methodologies, Tools, and Applications (pp. 663-678). Hershey, PA: Information Science Reference. doi: doi:10.4018/978-1-4666-4422-9.ch032

Yan, Z., Chen, Q., & Yu, C. (2013). The Science of Cell Phone Use: Its Past, Present, and Future. [IJCBPL]. *International Journal of Cyber Behavior, Psychology and Learning*, *3*(1), 7–18. doi:10.4018/ijcbpl.2013010102

Yang, Y., Wang, X., & Li, L. (2013). Use Mobile Devices to Wirelessly Operate Computers. [IJTHI]. *International Journal of Technology and Human Interaction*, *9*(1), 64–77. doi:10.4018/jthi.2013010105

Yartey, F. N., & Ha, L. (2013). Like, Share, Recommend: Smartphones as a Self-Broadcast and Self-Promotion Medium of College Students. [IJTHI]. *International Journal of Technology and Human Interaction*, 9(4), 20–40. doi:10.4018/ijthi.2013100102

Yaseen, S. G., & Al Omoush, K. S. (2013). Investigating the Engage in Electronic Societies via Facebook in the Arab World. [IJTHI]. *International Journal of Technology and Human Interaction*, 9(2), 20–38. doi:10.4018/jthi.2013040102

Yeo, B. (2012). Sustainable Economic Development and the Influence of Information Technologies: Dynamics of Knowledge Society Transformation. [IJSKD]. *International Journal of Sociotechnology and Knowledge Development*, 4(3), 54–55. doi:10.4018/jskd.2012070105

Yu, L., & Ureña, C. (2014). A Review of Current Approaches of Brain Computer Interfaces. In I. Management Association (Ed.), Assistive Technologies: Concepts, Methodologies, Tools, and Applications (pp. 1516-1534). Hershey, PA: Information Science Reference. doi: doi:10.4018/978-1-4666-4422-9.ch079

Zelenkauskaite, A. (2014). Analyzing Blending Social and Mass Media Audiences through the Lens of Computer-Mediated Discourse. In H. Lim, & F. Sudweeks (Eds.), *Innovative Methods and Technologies for Electronic Discourse Analysis* (pp. 304–326). Hershey, PA: Information Science Reference.

Compilation of References

10. USC § 890 (1994) (UCMJ Art 90).

10USC §980, 21 CFR §50.24.

10USCA §1107 (West).

45CFR §46.111(a)(2).

50USC §1541-1548.

Abraham, A., & Zuckerman, D. (2011). Adolescents, celebrity worship, and cosmetic surgery. *The Journal of Adolescent Health, 49*(5), 453–454. doi:10.1016/j.jadohealth.2011.08.014 PMID:22018558

Abramowitz, J. S., & Moore, E. L. (2007). An experimental analysis of hypochondriasis. *Behaviour Research and Therapy, 45*(3), 413–424. doi:10.1016/j.brat.2006.04.005 PMID:16769034

Academy of Medical Sciences. (2012, November). *Human enhancement and the future of work*. Royal Academy of Engineering and the Royal Society. Retrieved from http://www.britac.ac.uk/policy/Human-enhancement.cfm

Ackerman, B. (2013). Reviving democratic citizenship? *Politics & Society, 41*(2), 309–317. doi:10.1177/0032329213483103

Addis, D. R., & Tippett, L. J. (2008). The contributions of autobiographical memory to the content and continuity of identity: A social-cognitive neuroscience approach. In F. Sani (Ed.), *Self continuity: Individual and collective perspectives* (pp. 71–84). New York: Psychology Press.

Agar, N. (2004). *Liberal eugenics: In defence of human enhancement*. Malden, MA: Blackwell Publishing. doi:10.1002/9780470775004

Agar, N. (2012). On the irrationality of mind uploading: A reply to Neil Levy. *AI & Society, 27*(4), 431–436. doi:10.1007/s00146-011-0333-7

Agar, N. (2014). *Truly human enhancement*. Cambridge, MA: MIT Press. doi:10.7551/mitpress/9780262026635.001.0001

Agu, S. U., Okeke, V. O. S., & Idike, A. N. (2013). Voters apathy and revival of genuine political participation in Nigeria. *Journal of Educational and Social Research, 4*(3), 439–448.

Allers, M. A., & Kooreman, P. (2009). More evidence of the effects of voting technology on election outcomes. *Public Choice, 139*(1-2), 159–170. doi:10.1007/s11127-008-9386-7

Allhoff, F., Lin, P., Moor, J., & Weckert, J. (2009). *Ethics of human enhancement: 25 questions & answers*. U.S. National Science Foundation Report 2009.

Allhoff, F., Lin, P., Moor, J., & Weckert, J. (2010a). Ethics of human enhancement: 25 questions & answers. *Studies in Ethics, Law and Technology, 4*(4).

Allhoff, F., Lin, P., & Moore, D. (Eds.). (2010b). *What is nanotechnology and why does it matter? From science to ethics*. Hoboken, NJ: Wiley-Blackwell Publishing. doi:10.1002/9781444317992

Alotaibi, N. (2013). Media effects on voting behaviour. *European Scientific Journal, 9*(20), 1–11.

Alport, K., & Macintyre, C. (2007). Citizens to netizens: Grass-roots driven democracy and e-democracy in South Australia. *International Journal of Electronic Government Research, 3*(4), 38–57. doi:10.4018/jegr.2007100103

Alvarez, R. M., Hall, T. E., & Trechsel, A. H. (2009). Internet voting in comparative perspective: The case of Estonia. *PS: Political Science and Politics, 42*(3), 497–505.

Aman, M. M., & Jayroe, T. J. (2013). ICT, social media, and the Arab transition to democracy: From venting to acting. *Digest of Middle East Studies, 22*(2), 317–347.

American Psychiatric Association Board of Trustees. (2012). *American Psychiatric Association Board of Trustees Approves DSM-5*. Arlington, VA: American Psychiatric Association.

American Psychiatric Association. (2012). *Healthy minds, healthy lives: Sexual orientation*. Retrieved 28 November, 2012 from http://www.healthyminds.org/More-Info-For/GayLesbianBisexuals.aspx

Anderson, D. (2007). *Identity's strategy: Rhetorical selves in conversion*. Columbia, SC: University of South Carolina Press.

Anderson, D. A. (2012). Transnational Libel. *Virginia Journal of International Law Association, 53*, 71–98.

Annas, G. J., Andrews, L. B., & Isasi, R. M. (2002). Protecting the endangered human: Toward an international treaty prohibiting cloning and inheritable alterations. *American Journal of Law & Medicine, 28*(2&3), 151–178. PMID:12197461

Appel, A. W. (2011). Security seals on voting machines: A case study. *ACM Transactions on Information and System Security, 14*(2), 18–29. doi:10.1145/2019599.2019603

Aristotle, . (2012). *Aristotle's Nicomachean ethics* (R. C. Bartlett, Trans.). Chicago: University of Chicago Press.

Armocida, G. (2007). A.M. Fiamberti and 'psycosurgery'. *Medicina Nei Secoli, 19*, 457–474. PMID:18450027

Army, U. S. (2005). Military working dogs. *Field Manual No. 3-19.17*. Retrieved 28 November, 2012 from http://www.fas.org/irp/doddir/army/fm3-19-17.pdf

Arnhart, L. (2003). Human nature is here to stay. *New Atlantis (Washington, D.C.), 2*, 65–78.

Aubrey, J. S. (2007). The impact of sexually objectifying media exposure on negative body emotions and sexual self-perceptions: Investigating the mediating role of body self-consciousness. *Mass Communication & Society, 10*(1), 1–23. doi:10.1080/15205430709337002

Babcock, S. (2010, February 20). Plastic front creates poor perfection. *Spokesman Review*, p. v1.

Baertschi, B. (2009). Devenir un être humain accompli: Idéal ou cauchemar? In J.-N. Missa, & L. Perba (Eds.), *Enhancement Éthique et Philosophie de La Médecine D'amélioration* (Vol. l, pp. 79–95). Paris: Vrin.

Bailey, R. (2005). *Liberation biology: The scientific and moral case for the biotech revolution*. Amherst, NY: Prometheus Books.

Bainbridge, W. S., & Roco, M. C. (Eds.). (2005). *Managing Nano-Bio-Infocogno innovations: Converging technologies in society*. Springer. Retrieved from www.wtec.org/ConvergingTechnologies/3/NBIC3_report.pdf

Bainbridge, W. S. (2003). Massive questionnaires for personality capture. *Social Science Computer Review, 21*(3), 267–280. doi:10.1177/0894439303253973

Bain, P., Kashima, Y., & Haslam, N. (2006). Conceptual beliefs about human values and their implications: Human nature beliefs predict value importance, value trade-offs, and responses to value-laden rhetoric. *Journal of Personality and Social Psychology, 91*, 351–367. doi:10.1037/0022-3514.91.2.351 PMID:16881770

Baker, J. L. (2004). Choosing breast implant size: A matter of aesthetics. *Aesthetic Surgery Journal, 24*(6), 565–566. doi:10.1016/j.asj.2004.09.009 PMID:19336211

Baker, L. R. (2000). *Persons and bodies*. Cambridge, UK: Cambridge University Press. doi:10.1017/CBO9781139173124

Baker-Sperry, L., & Grauerholz, L. (2003). The pervasiveness and persistence of the feminine beauty ideal in children's fairy tales. *Gender & Society, 17*(5), 711–726. doi:10.1177/0891243203255605

Balkany, T., Hodges, A. V., & Goodman, K. W. (1996). Ethics of cochlear implantation in young children. *Otolaryngology - Head and Neck Surgery, 114*(6), 748–755. doi:10.1016/S0194-5998(96)70097-9 PMID:8643298

Balough Law Offices. (2013). *RFID chip in student badge does not infringe on religious freedom*. Retrieved from http://www.jdsupra.com/legalnews/rfid-chip-in-student-id-badge-does-not-i-55406/

Balzarotti, D., Banks, G., Cova, M., Felmetsger, V., Kemmerer, R. A., & Robertson, W. et al. (2010). An experience in testing the security of real-world electronic voting systems. *IEEE Transactions on Software Engineering, 33*(4), 453–473. doi:10.1109/TSE.2009.53

Banks, D. (1998). Neurotechnology. *Engineering Science and Education Journal, 7*(3), 135–144. doi:10.1049/esej:19980306

Barad, K. (2007). *Meeting the universe halfway: Quantum physics and the entanglement of matter and meaning.* Durham, NC: Duke University Press. doi:10.1215/9780822388128

Barber, N. (1995). The evolutionary psychology of physical attractiveness: Sexual selection and human morphology. *Ethology and Sociobiology*, *16*(5), 395–424. doi:10.1016/0162-3095(95)00068-2

Barkan, J. (2013). Plutocrats at work: How big philanthropy undermines democracy. *Social Research: An International Quarterly*, *80*(2), 635–652.

Battista, C. M. (2009). History, the Human, and the World Between. *Modern Fiction Studies*, *55*(2), 391–394. doi:10.1353/mfs.0.1610

Baudrillard, J. (1988). The ecstasy of communication. (B. Schutze & C. Schutze, Trans.). New York: Semiotext(e).

Baudrillard, J. (1994). *Simulacra and simulation* (S. F. Glaser, Trans.). Ann Arbor, MI: University of Michigan Press.

Baumann, L. (2012). Ethics in cosmetic dermatology. *Clinics in Dermatology*, *30*(5), 522–527. doi:10.1016/j.clindermatol.2011.06.023 PMID:22902224

Baumann, S. (2008). The moral underpinnings of beauty: A meaning-based explanation for light and dark complexions in advertising. *Poetics*, *36*(1), 2–23. doi:10.1016/j.poetic.2007.11.002

Bazzini, D., Curtin, L., Joslin, S., Regan, S., & Martz, D. (2010). Do animated Disney characters portray and promote the beauty-goodness stereotype? *Journal of Applied Social Psychology*, *40*(10), 2687–2709. doi:10.1111/j.1559-1816.2010.00676.x

BBC. (2004, September 9). Barcelona clubbers get chipped. *BBC News.* Retrieved from http://news.bbc.co.uk/2/hi/technology/3697940.stm

Bdubs 1975. (2013, January 9). Retrieved from http://usnews.nbcnews.com/_news/2013/01/09/16427652-texas-school-can-force-students-to-wear-locator-chips-judge-rules?pc=25&sp=0#discussion_nav

Beauchamp, T. L., & Childress, J. F. (2001). *Principles of biomedical ethics* (5th ed.). New York, NY: Oxford University Press.

Beckhusen, R. (2012). Report: Ukraine trains dolphins with friggin' pistols on their heads. *Wired Danger Room.* Retrieved 28 November, 2012, www.wired.com/dangerroom/2012/10/dolphins/

Bekafigo, M. A., & McBride, A. (2013). Who tweets about politics? Political participation of Twitter users during the 2011 gubernatorial elections. *Social Science Computer Review*, *31*(5), 625–643. doi:10.1177/0894439313490405

Bekker, M. H. J., Rademakers, J., Mouthaan, I., Neef, M. D., Huisman, W. M., Van Zandvoort, H., & Emans, A. (1996). Reconstructing hymens or constructing sexual inequality? Service provision to Islamic young women coping with the demand to be a virgin. *Journal of Community & Applied Social Psychology*, *6*(5), 329–334. doi:10.1002/(SICI)1099-1298(199612)6:5<329::AID-CASP383>3.0.CO;2-B

Bellah, R. N., Madsen, R., Sullivan, W. M., Swidler, A., & Tipton, S. M. (2007). *Habits of the heart: Individualism and commitment in American life.* University of California Press.

Bennett, S. (2013). Civility, social media and higher education: A virtual triangle. In A. Finley (Ed.), *Civic learning and teaching* (pp. 6–24). Washington, DC: Bringing Theory to Practice.

Berger, T. W., Chapin, J. K., Gerhardt, G. A., McFarland, D. J., Principe, J. C., Soussou, W. V., & Tresco, P. A. (2008). *Brain computer interfaces: An international assessment of research and development trends.* Springer Link. doi:10.1007/978-1-4020-8705-9

Berkelman, R., Halsey, N., & Resnik, D. (2010, August 2). *Presidential Commission for the Study of Bioethical Issues.* 10th Meeting, 8th sess.

Berlin, I. (1962). Does political theory still exist? In P. Laslett, & W. G. Runciman (Eds.), *Philosophy, Politics and Society.* Oxford, UK: Basil Blackwell.

Berman, L. (2010, February 3). Heidi Montag throws a curve at young girls, obsession with perfection reinforces women's needless body insecurities. *Chicago Sun Times*, p. C4, Berry, M. G., Cucchiara, V., & Davies, D. M. (2011). Breast augmentation: Part III—preoperative considerations and planning. *Journal of Plastic, Reconstructive & Aesthetic Surgery; JPRAS*, *64*(11), 1401–1409.

Bertrand, A. (1999). *Droit a la Vie Privée et Droit a L'Image*. Paris: Litec.

Beurrier, C., Bioulac, B., Audin, J., & Hammond, C. (2001). High-frequency stimulation produces a transient blockade of voltage-gated currents in subthalamic neurons. *Journal of Neurophysiology, 85*, 1351–1356. PMID:11287459

Bielsky, I., & Young, L. (2004, September 25). *Oxytocin, vasopressin, and social recognition in mammals*. D. O. Center for Behavioral Neuroscience, Producer. Retrieved December 1, 2012 from http://www.ncbi.nlm.nih.gov/pubmed/15374658

Bilton, N. (2013, December 22). Bitcoin: Betting on a coin with no realm. *New York Times*. Retrieved from http://bits.blogs.nytimes.com/2013/12/22/disruptions-betting-on-bitcoin/?emc=eta1&_r=1

Bimber, O. (2008). Total recall. *Computer, 41*(10), 32–33. doi:10.1109/MC.2008.438

Biological and Toxin Weapons Convention. (1972). Convention on the prohibition of the development, production and stock-piling of bacteriological (biological) and toxin weapons and on their destruction. *The Biological and Toxin Weapons Convention Website*. Retrieved 28 November, 2012 from http://www.unog.ch/80256EDD006B8954/%28httpAssets%29/C4048678A93B6934C1257188004848D0/$file/BWC-text-English.pdf

Bird, A., & Reese, E. (2008). Autobiographical memory in childhood and the development of a continuous self. In F. Sani (Ed.), *Self continuity: Individual and collective perspectives* (pp. 43–54). New York: Psychology Press.

Bitzer, L. (1968). The Rhetorical Situation. *Philosophy & Rhetoric, 1*(1), 3.

Black, E. (1970). The second persona. *The Quarterly Journal of Speech, 56*, 109–119. doi:10.1080/00335637009382992

Blackmore, S. (2007). *Imitation Makes Us Human*. Retrieved December 2, 2012 from http://www.susanblackmore.co.uk/chapters/human.pdf

Blackmore, S. (1999). *The meme machine*. Oxford University Press.

Blommaert, J. (2005). *Discourse: A critical introduction*. Cambridge, UK: Cambridge University Press. doi:10.1017/CBO9780511610295

Bluck, S. (2003). Autobiographical memory: Exploring its functions in everyday life. *Memory (Hove, England), 11*, 113–123. doi:10.1080/741938206 PMID:12820825

Bluck, S., & Alea, N. (2008). Remembering being me: The self continuity function of autobiographical memory in younger and older adults. In F. Sani (Ed.), *Self continuity: Individual and collective perspectives* (pp. 55–70). New York: Psychology Press.

Blum, V. L. (2005). Becoming the other woman: The psychic drama of cosmetic surgery. *Frontiers: A Journal of Women Studies, 26*(2), 104-131.

Blum, V. L. (2003). *Flesh wounds: The culture of cosmetic surgery*. Berkeley, CA: University of California Press.

Boenink, M., Swierstra, T., & Stemerding, D. (2010). Anticipating the Interaction between technology and morality: A scenario study of experimenting with humans in bionanotechnology. *Studies in Ethics, Law, and Technology, 4*(2), 1–38. doi:10.2202/1941-6008.1098

Bonte, P. (2013). Athletic enhancement, human nature and ethics. In J. Tolleneer, S. Sterckx, & P. Bonte (Eds.), *Threats and Opportunities of Doping Technologies* (Vol. 52, pp. 59–86). Springer.

Bordo, S. (1993). *Unbearable weight: Feminism, Western culture, and the body*. Berkeley, CA: University of California Press.

Bortolotti, L. (2009). Do we have an obligation to make smarter babies? In T. Takala, P. Herissone-Kelly, & S. Holm (Eds.), *Cutting Through the Surface: Philosophical Approaches to Bioethics*. Amsterdam, The Netherlands: Rodopi Press.

Bortolotti, L., & Harris, J. (2006). Disability, Enhancement and the Harm–Benefit Continuum. In J. R. Spencer, & A. Du Bois-Pedain (Eds.), *Freedom and Responsibility in Reproductive Choic* (pp. 31–49). Oxford, UK: Hart Publishers.

Bortolotti, L., & Nagasawa, Y. (2009). Immortality without boredom. *Ratio, 22*, 262–277. doi:10.1111/j.1467-9329.2009.00431.x

Bostrom, N. (2003). *The Transhumanist FAQ (version 2.1)*. Retrieved from http://www.transhumanism.org/resources/FAQv21.pdf

Bostrom, N. (2005). In defense of posthuman dignity. *Bioethics*, *19*(3). doi:10.1111/j.1467-8519.2005.00437.x PMID:16167401

Bostrom, N. (2008). Dignity and enhancement. In P. C. Bioethics, & A. Schulman (Eds.), *Human Dignity and Bioethics: Essays Commissioned by the President's Council on Bioethics* (pp. 173–206). Washington, DC: Academic Press.

Bostrom, N. (2008). Dignity and enhancement. In *Human dignity and bioethics: Essays commissioned by the President's Council on Bioethics* (pp. 173–207). Washington, DC: The President's Council on Bioethics.

Bostrom, N., & Roache, R. (2008). Ethical Issues in Human Enhancement. In J. Rysberg, T. Petersen, & C. Wolf (Eds.), *New Waves in Applied Ethics* (pp. 120–152). New York: Pelgrave Macmillan.

Bostrom, N., & Sandberg, A. (2009). The wisdom of nature: An evolutionary heuristic for human enhancement. In J. Savulescu, & N. Bostrom (Eds.), *Human Enhancement*. Oxford, UK: Oxford University Press.

boyd, d. (2010). Social network sites as networked publics. In Z. Z. Papacharissi (Ed.), *A networked self: Identity, community and culture on social network sites* (pp. 39-58). New York: Routledge.

boyd, d. (2014). *It's complicated: The social lives of networked teens*. New Haven, CT: Yale University Press.

Boyden, E. S., Zhang, F., Bamberg, E., Nagel, G., & Deisseroth, K. (2005). Millisecond-timescale, genetically targeted optical control of neural activity. *Nature Neuroscience*, *8*(9), 1263–1268. doi:10.1038/nn1525 PMID:16116447

Brandeis, J. (1928). U.S. Olmstead v United States, 277 US 478 (1928) (dissenting)

Brandeis, L., & Warren, S. (1890). The right to privacy. *Harvard Law Review*, *4*, 194–219.

Brey, P. (2000). Method in computer ethics: Towards a multi-level interdisciplinary approach. *Ethics and Information Technology*, *2*(2), 125–129. doi:10.1023/A:1010076000182

Brey, P. (2000). Theories of technology as extension of human faculties. In C. Mitcham (Ed.), *Metaphysics, epistemology, and technology*. Academic Press.

Brey, P. (2008). Human enhancement and personal identity. In J. Berg Olsen, E. Selinger, & S. Riis (Eds.), *New waves in philosophy of technology* (pp. 169–185). New York: Palgrave Macmillan.

Brey, P. A. E. (2012). Anticipating ethical issues in emerging IT. *Ethics and Information Technology*, *14*(4), 305–317. doi:10.1007/s10676-012-9293-y

Brickner, R. M. (1952). Brain of patient A after bilateral frontal lobectomy, status of frontal-lobe problem. *American Medical Association Archives of Neurology and Psychiatry*, *68*, 293–313. doi:10.1001/archneurpsyc.1952.02320210003001 PMID:14952067

Brown, K. (2006). An ethical obligation to our service members: Meaningful benefits for informed consent violations. *South Texas Law Review*, *47*(1), 919–947.

Bruner, J. (1990). *Acts of meaning*. Cambridge, MA: Harvard University Press.

Buchanan, A. (2008). Enhancement and the ethics of development. *Kennedy Institute of Ethics Journal*, *18*(1), 1–34. doi:10.1353/ken.0.0003 PMID:18561576

Buchanan, A. (2011a). *Better than human: The promise and perils of enhancing ourselves*. Oxford University Press.

Buchanan, A. (2011b). *Beyond humanity? The ethics of biomedical enhancement*. Oxford University Press. doi:10.1093/acprof:oso/9780199587810.001.0001

Buchanan, A., Brock, D. W., Daniels, N., & Wikler, D. (2001). *From chance to choice: Genetics and justice*. Cambridge University Press.

Burckhardt, G. (1981). Über rindenexcisionen, als beitrag zur operativen therapie der psychosen. *Allgemeine Zeitschrift für Psychiatrie*, *47*, 463–548.

Burke, K. (1966). *Language as symbolic action*. Berkeley, CA: University of California Press.

Burke, K. (1969). *A grammar of motives*. Berkeley, CA: University of California Press.

Burnam-Fink, M. (2011). The rise and decline of military human enhancement. *Science Progress*. Retrieved 28 November, 2012 from http://scienceprogress.org/2011/01/the-rise-and-decline-of-military-human-enhancement/

Buwalda, F. M., Bouman, T. K., & van Duijn, M. A. J. (2007). Psychoeducation for hypochondriasis: A comparison of a cognitive-behavioural approach and a problem-solving approach. *Behaviour Research and Therapy*, *45*(5), 887–899. doi:10.1016/j.brat.2006.08.004 PMID:17055449

Bygrave, L. A. (1998). Data protection pursuant to the right to privacy in human rights treaties. *International Journal of Law and Information Technology*, *6*, 247–284. doi:10.1093/ijlit/6.3.247

Bygrave, L. A. (2010). Privacy Protection in a Global Context – A Comparative Overview. *Scandinavian Studies in Law*, *47*, 321–348.

Cabrera, L. Y. (2011). Memory Enhancement: The Issues We Should Not Forget About. *Journal of Evolution and Technology*, *22*(1), 97–109.

Cade, J. F. J. (1949). Lithium salts in the treatment of psychotic excitement. *The Medical Journal of Australia*, *36*, 349–352. PMID:18142718

Caldwell, J., & Caldwell, J. (2005). Fatigue in military aviation: an overview of US military-approved pharmacological countermeasure. *Aviation, Space, and Environmental Medicine*, *76*(7), 39–51. PMID:15672985

Caldwell, J., Caldwell, J., Smythe, N., & Hall, K. (2000). A double-blind, placebo-controlled investigation of the efficacy of modafinil for sustaining the alertness and performance of aviators: A helicopter simulator study. *Psychopharmacology*, *150*(3), 272–282. doi:10.1007/s002130000450 PMID:10923755

Camargo, C. R., Faust, R., Merino, E., & Stefani, C. (2012). The technological obsolescence of the Brazilian ballot box. *Work (Reading, Mass.)*, *41*, 1185–1192. PMID:22316881

Camilli, D. (2010, April 24). Montag is a cheap, plastic pool float after surgery. *The Gazette (Montreal)*, p. E5.

Camporesi, S., & Bortolotti, L. (2008). Reproductive cloning in humans and therapeutic cloning in primates: Is the ethical debate catching up with the recent scientific advances? *Journal of Medical Ethics*, *34*(9), e15. doi:10.1136/jme.2007.023879 PMID:18757615

Canaday, M. (2001). US military integration of religious, ethnic, and racial minorities in the twentieth century. *The Palm Center*. Retrieved 28 November, 2012 from http://www.palmcenter.org/publications/dadt/u_s_military_integration_of_religious_ethnic_and_racial_minorities_in_the_twentieth_cen tury#_ftnref1

Cannon, L. (2014). *What is Transfigurism?* Mormon Transhumanist Association. Retrieved January 14, 2014 from http://transfigurism.org/

Cantor, J. (2005). Cosmetic dermatology and physicians' ethical obligations: More than just hope in a jar. *Seminars in Cutaneous Medicine and Surgery*, *24*(3), 155–160. doi:10.1016/j.sder.2005.04.005 PMID:16202953

Cantor, N. (2001). *In the wake of the plague: The black death and the world it made*. New York, NY: The Free Press.

Caplan, A. (2009). Good, better, or best? In N. Bostrom, & J. Savulescu (Eds.), *Human enhancement* (pp. 199–210). Oxford University Press.

Cartwright, R., & Cardozo, L. (2008). Cosmetic vulvovaginal surgery. *Obstetrics, Gynaecology and Reproductive Medicine*, *18*(10), 285–286. doi:10.1016/j.ogrm.2008.07.008

Cassidy, S. (2010, January 24). Teens, young adults cut into cosmetic-surgery statistics, defining beauty breast wishes parental pressure? For the sport of it males do it, too. *Sunday News*, p. G1.

Castells, M. (2010). *The rise of the network society* (2nd ed.). Oxford, UK: Blackwell Publishing Ltd.

Census, U. S. (2011). Section 10: National security and veterans affairs. *US Census Bureau*. Retrieved 28 November, 2012 from http://www.census.gov/prod/2011pubs/12statab/defense.pdf

Centre for the Study of Existential Risk, University of Cambridge . (n.d.). Retrieved January 14, 2014 from http://cser.org/

Chadwick, R. (2008). Therapy, enhancement and improvement. In B. Gordijn, & R. Chadwick (Eds.), *Medical enhancement and posthumanity* (pp. 25–37). Springer.

Chadwick, R. (2011). Enhancements: Improvements for whom? *Bioethics*, *25*(4), ii. doi:10.1111/j.1467-8519.2011.01899.x PMID:21480931

Chalmers, D., & Clark, A. (1998). The extended mind. *Analysis*, *58*(1), 7–19. doi:10.1093/analys/58.1.7

Chandler, M. J., & Lalonde, C. E. (1995). The problem of self-continuity in the context of rapid personal and cultural change. I A. Oosterwegel & R. A. Wicklund (Eds.), The self in European and American culture: Development and processes (pp. 45-63). Dordrecht, The Netherlands: Kluwer Academic.

Chan, J. K.-K., Jones, S. M., & Heywood, A. J. (2011). Body dysmorphia, self-mutilation and the reconstructive surgeon. *Journal of Plastic, Reconstructive & Aesthetic Surgery; JPRAS*, *64*(1), 4–8. doi:10.1016/j.bjps.2010.03.029 PMID:20392680

Charkin, S. (1978). *The mind stealers*. Boston: Houghton Mifflin Company.

Chauhan, N., Warner, J., & Adamson, P. A. (2010). Adolescent rhinoplasty: Challenges and psychosocial and clinical outcomes. *Aesthetic Plastic Surgery*, *34*, 510–516. doi:10.1007/s00266-010-9489-7 PMID:20333519

Chen, B. (2014, January 29). Tech attire: More beta than chic. *New York Times*. Retrieved from http://www.nytimes.com/2014/01/09/technology/tech-attire-more-beta-than-chic.html?_r=0

Choe, Y., Kwon, J., & Chung, J. R. (2012). Time, consciousness, and mind uploading. *International Journal of Machine Consciousness*, *4*(1), 257–274. doi:10.1142/S179384301240015X

Chomsky, N. (2013). *The Origins of Modern Science and Linguistics*. Geneva International Congress of Linguists. Retrieved January 15, 2014 from http://www.youtube.com/user/TheChomskyVideos

Chomsky, N. (1999). *Profit over people: Neoliberalism and global order*. New York: Seven Stories Press.

Chorost. (2011). *World wide mind: The coming integration of humanity, machines and the internet*. New York: Free Press.

Chou, M. (2013a). *Theorizing democide: Why and how democracies fail*. Basingstoke, UK: Palgrave Macmillan. doi:10.1057/9781137298690

Chou, M. (2013b). Democracy's not for me: The Lowy Institute polls on Gen Y and democracy. *Australian Journal of Political Science*, *48*(4). doi:10.1080/10361146.2013.841844

Cindoglu, D. (1997). Virginity tests and artificial virginity in modern Turkish medicine. *Women's Studies International Forum*, *20*(2), 253–261. doi:10.1016/S0277-5395(96)00096-9

Claes, S., Vereecke, E., Maes, M., Victor, J., Verdonk, P., & Bellemans, J. (2013). Anatomy of the anterolateral ligament of the knee. *Journal of Anatomy*, *223*(4), 321–328. doi:10.1111/joa.12087 PMID:23906341

Clark, A. (1998). Embodiment and the Philosophy of Mind. *Royal Institute of Philosophy*, *43*(Supplement), 35–51. doi:10.1017/S135824610000429X

Clark, A. (2008). *Supersizing the mind: Embodiment, action, and cognitive extension*. Oxford University Press. doi:10.1093/acprof:oso/9780195333213.001.0001

Clarke, J., Drake, L., Flatt, S., & Jebb, P. (2008). Physical perfection for sale. *Nursing Standard*, *23*(8), 26–27.

Clark, S. R. L. (2003). Non-personal minds. In A. O'Hear (Ed.), *Minds and persons* (pp. 185–209). Cambridge, UK: Cambridge University Press. doi:10.1017/CBO9780511550294.011

Clauss, R., & Nel, W. (2006). Drug induced arousal from the permanent vegetative state. *NeuroRehabilitation*, *21*, 23–28. PMID:16720934

Code, N. (1947).. . *British Medical Journal*, *1448*(1).

Coeckelbergh, M. (2010). Human development or human enhancement? A methodological reflection on capabilities and the evaluation of information technologies. *Ethics and Information Technology*, *13*(2), 81–92. doi:10.1007/s10676-010-9231-9

Coenen, C., Schuijff, M., Smits, M., Klaassen, P., Hennen, L., & Rader, M. et al. (2009). *Science and Technology Options Assessment: Human Enhancement Study*. Brussels: European Parliament.

Cohen Kadosh, R. (2013). Using transcranial electrical stimulation to enhance cognitive functions in the typical and atypical brain. *Translational Neuroscience*, *4*, 20–33. doi:10.2478/s13380-013-0104-7

Cohen, A. (2010). Proportionality in modern asymmetrical wars. *Jerusalem Center for Public Affairs.* Retrieved 28 November, 2012 from http://jcpa.org/text/proportionality.pdf

Coleman, G. (2009). Code is speech: Legal tinkering, expertise and protest among free and open source software developers. *Cultural Anthropology, 24*(3), 420–454. doi:10.1111/j.1548-1360.2009.01036.x

Comiskey, C. (2004). Cosmetic surgery in Paris in 1926: The case of the amputated leg. *Journal of Women's History, 16*(3), 30–54. doi:10.1353/jowh.2004.0059

Condon, R. (1949). *The Manchurian candidate.* London: Orion Books.

Connell, J. (2013). Contemporary medical tourism: Conceptualisation, culture and commodification. *Tourism Management, 34,* 1–13. doi:10.1016/j.tourman.2012.05.009

Connolly, C. (2008). US Safe Harbor - Fact or Fiction? *Privacy Laws and Business International, 96,* 26–27.

Connor, D. J. (2011). Questioning normal: Seeing children first and labels second. *School Talk: Between the Ideal and the Real World of Teaching, 16,* 1–3.

Consciousness. (n.d.). Retrieved November 29, 2012 from http://dictionary.reference.com/browse/consciousness

Convention, H. (1899). *International Humanitarian Law – Treaties & Documents.* Retrieved 28 November, 2012 from http://www.icrc.org/ihl.nsf/INTRO/150?OpenDocument

Cooke, J. (1876). *A life of General Robert E. Lee.* New York, NY: D. Appleton and Company.

Cook, R. J., & Dickens, B. M. (2009). Hymen reconstruction: Ethical and legal issues. *International Journal of Gynaecology and Obstetrics: the Official Organ of the International Federation of Gynaecology and Obstetrics, 107*(3), 266–269. doi:10.1016/j.ijgo.2009.07.032 PMID:19717149

Cooney, B. (2004). *Posthumanity: Thinking philosophically about the future.* Rowman & Littlefield.

Cornum, R., Caldwell, J., & Cornum, K. (1997). Stimulant use in extended flight operations. *Airpower Journal, 11*(1).

Cornwell, W., & Ricci, G. (Eds.). (2011). Human nature unbound: Why becoming cyborgs and taking drugs could make us more human. Values & Technology: Religion & Public Life 37, 65-92.

Cortese, F. (2013b). The hubris of Neoluddism. *H + Magazine.*

Cortese, F. (2013c). Three spectres of immortality: A talk from the Radical Life Extension Conference in Washington D.C. *H + Magazine.*

Cortese, F. (2013a). *Transhumanism, technology & science: To say it's impossible is to mock history itself.* Institute for Ethics & Emerging Technologies.

Cortese, F. (2013d). Heidegger and the existential utility of death. In H. Pellissier (Ed.), *Human destiny is to eliminate death: Essays, arguments & rants about immortalism.* Niagara Falls, NY: Center for Transhumanity.

Council of Europe. (1970). *Resolution 428 containing a declaration on mass communication media and human rights.* Retrieved from http://assembly.coe.int/main.asp?Link=/documents/adoptedtext/ta70/eres428.htm

Coupland, R., & Herby, P. (1999). Review of the legality of weapons: A new approach: The SirUS Project. *International Committee of the Red Cross: Resource Center.* Retrieved 28 November, 2012 from http://www.icrc.org/eng/resources/documents/misc/57jq36.htm

Couser, G. T. (2011). What disability studies has to offer medical education. *The Journal of Medical Humanities, 32*(1), 21–30. doi:10.1007/s10912-010-9125-1 PMID:21042839

Crichton, M. (1972). *The terminal man.* New York: Ballantine Books.

Crowley, S., & Hawhee, D. (2012). *Ancient rhetorics for contemporary students* (5th ed.). New York: Pearson/Longman.

Curato, N., & Niemeyer, S. (2013). Reaching out to overcome political apathy: Building participatory capacity through deliberative engagement. *Politics & Policy, 41*(3), 355–383.

Czernich, N. (2012). Broadband Internet and political participation: Evidence for Germany. *Kyklos: International Review for Social Sciences*, *65*(1), 31–52. doi:10.1111/j.1467-6435.2011.00526.x

Damasio, A. (1994). *Descartes' error: Emotion reason and the human brain*. New York: Grosset.

Daniels, N. (2000). Normal functioning and the treatment-enhancement distinction. *Cambridge Quarterly of Healthcare Ethics*, *9*(3), 309–322. doi:10.1017/S0963180100903037 PMID:10858880

Davis, D., & Vernon, M. L. (2002). Sculpting the body beautiful: Attachment style, neuroticism, and use of cosmetic surgeries. *Sex Roles*, *47*, 129–138. doi:10.1023/A:1021043021624

Dawkins, M. A. (2012). *Clearly invisible: Racial passing and the color of cultural identity*. Waco, TX: Baylor University Press.

Dawkins, M. A. (2013). *Eminem: The real Slim Shady*. Santa Barbara, CA: Praeger Press.

Dawkins, R. (1976). *The selfish gene*. New York: Oxford University Press.

de Andrade, D. D. (2010). On norms and bodies: Findings from field research on cosmetic surgery in Rio de Janeiro, Brazil. *Reproductive Health Matters*, *18*(35), 74–83. doi:10.1016/S0968-8080(10)35519-4 PMID:20541086

de Leon, J. (2013). Is psychiatry scientific? A letter to a 21st century psychiatry resident. *Psychiatry Investigation*, *10*, 205–217. doi:10.4306/pi.2013.10.3.205 PMID:24302942

De Ridder, D., Langguth, B., Plazier, M., & Menovsky, T. (2009). Moral Dysfunction: Theoretical Model and Potential Neurosurgical Treatments. In J. Verplaetse, & S. Vanneste (Eds.), *The moral brain* (pp. 155–184). New York: Springer. doi:10.1007/978-1-4020-6287-2_7

De Ridder, D., & Van de Heyning, P. (2007). The Darwinian plasticity hypothesis for tinnitus and pain. *Progress in Brain Research*, *166*, 55–60. doi:10.1016/S0079-6123(07)66005-1 PMID:17956771

De Ridder, D., Vanneste, S., Menovsky, T., & Langguth, B. (2012). Surgical brain modulation for tinnitus: The past, present and future. *Journal of Neurosurgical Sciences*, *56*, 323–340. PMID:23111293

De Roubaix, J. A. M. (2011). Beneficence, non-maleficence, distributive justice and respect for patient autonomy—Reconcilable ends in aesthetic surgery? *Journal of Plastic, Reconstructive & Aesthetic Surgery; JPRAS*, *64*(1), 11–16. doi:10.1016/j.bjps.2010.03.034 PMID:20457018

de Vreese, C. H. (2007). Digital renaissance: Young consumer and citizen? *The Annals of the American Academy of Political and Social Science*, *611*, 207–216. doi:10.1177/0002716206298521

Deaux, K. (1992). Personalizing identity and socializing self. In G. M. Breakwell (Ed.), *Social psychology of identity and the self concept* (pp. 9–33). London: Surrey University Press.

Declaration of Geneva. (1948). Retrieved 15 August, 2013 from http://www.genevadeclaration.org/fileadmin/docs/GD-Declaration-091020-EN.pdf

Declaration of Helsinki. (1964). *World Health Organization*. Retrieved 15 August, 2013 from http://www.who.int/bulletin/archives/79(4)373.pdf

DeGrazia, D. (2005). Enhancement technologies and human identity. *The Journal of Medicine and Philosophy*, *30*(3), 261–283. doi:10.1080/03605310590960166 PMID:16036459

Delay, J., Deniker, P., & Harl, J. M. (1952). Therapeutic use in psychiatry of phenothiazine of central elective action (4560 RP). Annales medico-psychologiques (Paris), 110, 112-117.

Delgado, J. (1969). *Toward a psychocivilized society*. New York: Harper and Row Publishers.

Delgado, J. M. R. (1968). Intracerebral radio stimulation and recording in completely free patients. *The Journal of Nervous and Mental Disease*, *147*, 329–340. doi:10.1097/00005053-196810000-00001 PMID:5683678

Demoulin, S., Leyens, J. P., Paladino, M. P., Rodriguez, R. T., Rodriguez, A. P., & Dovidio, J. F. (2004). Dimensions of uniquely and non-uniquely human emotions. *Cognition and Emotion*, *18*(1), 71–96. doi:10.1080/02699930244000444

Dennet, D. (1991). *Consciousness explained*. Boston, MA: Little, Brown and Company.

Dennis, C. (2004). Genetics: Deaf by design. *Nature*, *431*(7011), 894–896. doi:10.1038/431894a PMID:15496889

DePietro, P. (2013). *Transforming education with new media*. New York: Peter Lang.

Derakhshani, T. (2009, August 13). Sideshow: Low-key farewell to Hughes. *Philadelphia Inquirer*, p. E02.

Descartes, R. (1637). *A discourse on the method of correctly conducting one's reason and seeking truth in the sciences*. Oxford, UK: Oxford University Press.

Descola, P. (2009). Human natures. *Social Anthropology*, *17*, 145–157. doi:10.1111/j.1469-8676.2009.00063.x

Diamandis, P. H., & Kotler, S. (2012). *Abundance: The future is better than you think*. New York: Free Press.

Dickinson, B., & Ferrante, E. (2013, September 10). *The kiss: A short film shot through Google Glass*. Retrieved December 28, 2013, from http://www.youtube.com/watch?v=tPNAD-RanBI

Dietrich, D. (1997). Refashioning the techno-erotic woman: Gender and textuality in the cybercultural matrix. In S. Jones (Ed.), *Virtual culture: Identity and communication in cybersociety* (pp. 169–184). London: Sage Publications.

Dion, K., Berscheid, E., & Walster, E. (1972). What is beautiful is good. *Journal of Personality and Social Psychology*, *24*(3), 285–290. doi:10.1037/h0033731 PMID:4655540

Dixson, B., Grimshaw, G., Linklater, W., & Dixson, A. (2011). Eye-tracking of men's preferences for waist-to-hip ratio and breast size of women. *Archives of Sexual Behavior*, *40*(1), 43–50. doi:10.1007/s10508-009-9523-5 PMID:19688590

Doe v. Sullivan, 938 F.2d 1370, 1372-1374, 1381 (DC Cir. 1991).

Dohnt, H., & Tiggemann, M. (2006). Body image concerns in young girls: The role of peers and media prior to adolescence. *Journal of Youth and Adolescence*, *35*(2), 135–145. doi:10.1007/s10964-005-9020-7

Dolmage, J. T. (2013). *Disability rhetoric*. Syracuse, NY: Syracuse University Press.

Dotov, D. G., Nie, L., & Chemero, A. (2010). A Demonstration of the Transition from Ready-to-Hand to Unready-to-Hand. *PLoS ONE*, *5*(3), e9433. doi:10.1371/journal.pone.0009433 PMID:20231883

Du, B., Shan, A., Zhang, Y., Zhong, X., Chen, D., & Cai, K. (2014). Zolpidem arouses patients in vegetative state after brain injury: Qualitative evaluation and indications. *The American Journal of the Medical Sciences*, *347*(3), 178–182. doi:10.1097/MAJ.0b013e318287c79c PMID:23462249

Duckworth, E. (2006). Piaget rediscovered. *Journal of Research in Science Teaching*, *2*(3), 172–175. doi:10.1002/tea.3660020305

Dutton, W. H., Elberse, A., & Hale, M. (1999). A case study of a netizen's guide to elections. *Communications of the ACM*, *42*(12), 48. doi:10.1145/322796.322808

Dvorsky, G. (2006, July 29). *All Together Now: Developmental and Ethical Considerations for Biologically Uplifting Nonhuman Animals*. Retrieved January 4, 2014, from IEET Monograph Series: http://ieet.org/index.php/IEET/print/702

Dvorsky, G. (2012). Should we upgrade the intelligence of animals? *i09: Futurism*. Retrieved 28 November, 2012 from http://io9.com/5943832/should-we-upgrade-the-intelligence-of-animals

Dyens, O. (2001). *Metal and flesh: The evolution of man: Technology takes over*. Cambridge, MA: MIT Press.

Dyer, C. (2000). Surgeon amputated healthy legs. *British Medical Journal*,, 320–332. PMID:10657312

Dyson, F. J. (2012). History of science. Is science mostly driven by ideas or by tools? *Science*, *338*, 1426–1427. doi:10.1126/science.1232773 PMID:23239721

Eagly, A. H., Ashmore, R. D., Makhijani, M. G., & Longo, L. C. (1991). What is beautiful is good, but... A meta-analytic review of research on the physical attractiveness stereotype. *Psychological Bulletin*, *110*(1), 109–128. doi:10.1037/0033-2909.110.1.109

Earp, B. D., Sandberg, A., Kahane, G., & Savulescu, J. (2014). When is diminishment a form of enhancement? Rethinking the enhancement debate in biomedical ethics. *Frontiers in Systems Neuroscience*, *8*, 12. doi:10.3389/fnsys.2014.00012 PMID:24550792

Ekman, P. (1992). An argument for basic emotions. *Cognition and Emotion, 18,* 71–96.

Elgie, R., & Fauvelle-Aymar, C. (2012). Turnout under semipresidentialism: First- and Second-order elections to national-level institutions. *Comparative Political Studies, 45*(12), 1598–1623. doi:10.1177/0010414012463903

El-Hai, J. (2005). *The lobotomist.* Hoboken, NJ: John Wiley and Sons, Inc.

Elliot, C. (2003). *Better than well: American medicine meets the American dream.* New York: W.W. Norton & Company.

Engel, G. L. (1977). The need for a new medical model: A challenge for biomedicine. *Science, 196,* 129–136. doi:10.1126/science.847460 PMID:847460

Epstein, S. (1984). Controversial issues in emotion theory. *Review of Personality and Social Psychology, 5,* 64–88.

Ericksen, W. L., & Billick, S. B. (2012). Psychiatric issues in cosmetic plastic surgery. *The Psychiatric Quarterly, 83*(3), 343–352. doi:10.1007/s11126-012-9204-8 PMID:22252848

Erler, A. (2012). One man's authenticity is another man's betrayal: A reply to Levy. *Journal of Applied Philosophy,* (1). doi: doi:10.1111/j.1468-5930.2012.00562.x PMID:23576833

Esposito, R. (2012). *Third person.* Cambridge, UK: Polity.

European Parliament. (1995). *Directive 95/46/EC of the European Parliament and of the Council of 24 October 1995 on the protection of individuals with regard to the processing of personal data and on the free movement of such data, OJ L 281, 23 November 1995.* Author.

European Parliament. (2009). *Human enhancement study.* Science and Technology Options Assessment (STOA) Annual Report. Brussels: Belgium: European Parliament. Retrieved from https://www.itas.kit.edu/downloads/etag_coua09a.pdf

European Parliament. (2013). *Science and Technology Options Assessment Annual Report 2012.* Brussels, Belgium: European Parliament.

Falk, U., & Mohnhaupt, H. (2000). *Das Bürgerliche Gesetzbuch und seine Richter: Zur Reaktion der Rechtsprechung auf die Kodifikation des deutschen Privatrechts (1896-1914).* Frankfurt am Main: Vittorio Klostermann.

Farah, M. J. (2005). Neuroethics: The practical and the philosophical. *Trends in Cognitive Sciences, 9*(1), 34–40. doi:10.1016/j.tics.2004.12.001 PMID:15639439

Farrell, H. (2002). Negotiating Privacy Across Arenas: The EU-US Safe Harbor Discussions. In A. Windhoff-Héritier (Ed.), *Common Goods: Reinventing European and International Governance* (pp. 105–125). London: Rowman & Littlefield.

Faulkner, P., & Runde, J. (2012). On Sociomateriality. In P. M. Leonardi, B. A. Nardi, & J. Kallinikos (Eds.), *Materiality and Organizing: Social Interaction in a Technological World* (pp. 49–66). Oxford, UK: Oxford University Press. doi:10.1093/acprof:oso/9780199664054.003.0003

Fenn, E. (2002). *Pox Americana: The great smallpox epidemic of 1775-82.* New York, NY: Hill and Wang.

Ferguson, P. M., & Nusbaum, E. (2012). Disability studies: What is it and what difference does it make? *Research and Practice for Persons with Severe Disabilities, 37*(2), 70–80. doi:10.2511/027494812802573530

Fergus, T. A., & Valentiner, D. P. (2009). Reexamining the domain of hypochondriasis: Comparing the Illness Attitudes Scale to other approaches. *Journal of Anxiety Disorders, 23*(6), 760–766. doi:10.1016/j.janxdis.2009.02.016 PMID:19339156

Fernández-Armesto, F. (2004). *Humankind: A brief history.* Oxford, UK: Oxford University Press.

Fetz, E. E. (2007). Volitional control of neural activity: Implications for brain-computer interfaces. *The Journal of Physiology, 579*(3), 571–579. doi:10.1113/jphysiol.2006.127142 PMID:17234689

Fiamberti, M. (1950). Transorbital prefrontal leucotomy in psychosurgery. *Minerva Medica, 41,* 131–135. PMID:15438855

Figee, M., Luigjes, J., Smolders, R., Valencia-Alfonso, C. E., van Wingen, G., & de Kwaasteniet, B. et al. (2013). Deep brain stimulation restores frontostriatal network activity in obsessive-compulsive disorder. *Nature Neuroscience, 16,* 386–387. doi:10.1038/nn.3344 PMID:23434914

Finney, G. R. (2009). Normal pressure hydrocephalus. *International Review of Neurobiology, 84*, 263–281. doi:10.1016/S0074-7742(09)00414-0 PMID:19501723

Fitzpatrick, W., & Zwaziger, L. (2003). Defending against biochemical warfare: Ethical issues involving the coercive use of investigational drugs and biologics in the military. *Philosophy, Science & Law, 3*(1).

Fletcher, J. (1972). Indicators of personhood: A tentative profile. *The Hastings Center Report, 2*, 5. doi:10.2307/3561570 PMID:4679693

Foley, N. (2006, May 24). *The Stigma of Not Working.* Retrieved December 1, 2013, from http://www.ragged-edgemagazine.com/departments/closerlook/001095.html

Forester, E. (1909). *The Machine Stops.* Retrieved December 01, 2012 from http://archive.ncsa.illinois.edu/prajlich/forster.html

Foucault, M. (1985). *The history of sexuality: The use of pleasure* (R. Hurley, Trans.). New York, NY: Vintage Books.

Fountas, K. N., & Smith, J. R. (2007). Historical evolution of stereotactic amygdalotomy for the management of severe aggression. *Journal of Neurosurgery, 106*, 710–713. doi:10.3171/jns.2007.106.4.710 PMID:17432727

Foust, J. (2012, September 24). Ask the experts: Do targeted killings work? *Council on Foreign Relations.* Retrieved 28 November, 2012 from http://blogs.cfr.org/zenko/2012/09/24/ask-the-experts-do-targeted-killings-work/

Fox, M. V. (1983). Ancient Egyptian rhetoric. *Rhetorica, 1*, 9–22. doi:10.1525/rh.1983.1.1.9

Frederick, D. A., Peplau, A., & Lever, J. (2008). The Barbie mystique: Satisfaction with breast size and shape across the lifespan. *International Journal of Sexual Health, 20*(3), 200–211. doi:10.1080/19317610802240170

Freeman, W. (1957). Frontal lobotomy 1936-1956: A follow-up study of 3000 patients from one to twenty years. *The American Journal of Psychiatry, 113*, 877–886. PMID:13402981

Freeman, W., & Watts, J. W. (1952). Psychosurgery. *Progress in Neurology and Psychiatry, 7*, 374–384. PMID:13004057

French, S. (2003). *The code of the warrior: Exploring the values of warrior cultures, past and present.* New York, NY: Rowman and Littlefield Publishers.

Friere, P. (1970). *Pedagogy of the oppressed* (M. B. Ramos, Trans.). New York: Continuum Publishing Company.

Fukuyama, F. (2003). *Our posthuman future: Consequences of the biotechnology revolution.* Picador.

Fukuyama, F. (2006). *Beyond bioethics: A proposal for modernizing the regulation of human biotechnologies.* Washington, DC: School of Advanced International Studies, Johns Hopkins University.

Fumagalli, M., & Priori, A. (2012). Functional and clinical neuroanatomy of morality. *Brain, 135*, 2006–2021. doi:10.1093/brain/awr334 PMID:22334584

Furnham, A., & Swami, V. (2007). Perception of female buttocks and breast size in profile. *Social Behavior and Personality, 35*(1), 1–7. doi:10.2224/sbp.2007.35.1.1

Gabriel, R. (2013). *Between flesh and steel: A history of military medicine from the middle ages to the war in Afghanistan.* Washington, DC: Potomac Books.

Gagnier, C. (2011, August 11). The Competitive Privacy Marketplace: Regulators Competing on Privacy, Not the Companies. *Huffington Post.* Retrieved from http://www.huffingtonpost.com/christina-gagnier/the-competitive-privacy-m_b_1078820.html

Galliott, J. (Forthcoming). *Unmanned systems: Mapping the moral landscape.* Surrey, UK: Ashgate.

Galliott, J. (2012a). Uninhabited aerial vehicles and the asymmetry objection: A response to Strawser. *Journal of Military Ethics, 11*(1), 58–66. doi:10.1080/15027570.2012.683703

Galliott, J. (2012b). Closing with completeness: The asymmetric drone warfare debate. *Journal of Military Ethics, 11*(4), 353–356. doi:10.1080/15027570.2012.760245

Galliott, J. (2013). Who's to blame? In N. Michaud (Ed.), *Frankenstein and philosophy: The shocking truth.* Chicago, IL: Open Court Press.

Garcia, J. (2010, January 25). Obsessed with being perfect. *People, 73*, 80–88.

Garcia, T., & Sandler, R. (2008). Enhancing justice? *NanoEthics*, *2*(3), 277–287. doi:10.1007/s11569-008-0048-5

Garnham, B. (2013). Designing older rather than denying ageing: Problematizing anti-ageing discourse in relation to cosmetic surgery undertaken by older people. *Journal of Aging Studies*, *27*(1), 38–46. doi:10.1016/j.jaging.2012.11.001 PMID:23273555

Garreau, J. (2006). *Radical evolution: The science and peril of enhancing our minds, our bodies—and what it means to be human*. New York, NY: Random House.

Geelen, J. (2012). *The emerging neurotechnologies: Recent developments and policy implications*. Policy Horizons Canada.

Geneva Additional Protocol I. (1977). Retrieved 28 November, 2012 from http://www.icrc.org/ihl.nsf/INTRO/470?OpenDocument

GetMeOutAlive42. (2013, January 9). Retrieved from http://usnews.nbcnews.com/_news/2013/01/09/16427652-texas-school-can-force-students-to-wear-locator-chips-judge-rules?pc=25&sp=0#discussion_nav

Gibson, W. (1984). *Neuromancer*. New York: Ace.

Gibson, R. (2002). Elections online: Assessing Internet voting in light of the Arizona Democratic Primary. *Political Science Quarterly*, *116*(4), 561–583. doi:10.2307/798221

Gillett, G. (2008). *Subjectivity and being somebody: Human identity and neuroethics*. Exeter, UK: Imprint Academic.

Gillett, G. (2009). *The mind and its discontents* (2nd ed.). Oxford, UK: University Press. doi:10.1093/med/9780199237548.001.0001

Gillett, G., & Huang, J. (2013). What we owe the psychopath: A neuroethical analysis. *American Journal of Bioethics Neuroscience*, *4*, 3–9.

Gillett, G., & Tamatea, A. J. (2012). The warrior gene: Epigenetic considerations. *New Genetics & Society*, *31*, 41–53. doi:10.1080/14636778.2011.597982

Gillett, G., & Walker, S. (2012). The evolution of informed consent. *Journal of Law and Medicine*, *19*, 673–677. PMID:22908611

Gillin, J. (2010, August 26). Montag wants implants out. *St. Petersburg Times*, p. 2B.

Glannon, W. (2001). *Genes and future people: Philosophical issues in human genetics*. Cambridge, MA: Westview Press.

Glannon, W. (2002). Identity, prudential concern, and extended lives. *Bioethics*, *16*, 266–283. doi:10.1111/1467-8519.00285 PMID:12211249

Glannon, W. (2007). *Bioethics and the brain*. Oxford, UK: Oxford University Press.

Glenberg, A. M., & Kaschak, M. P. (2002). Grounding language in action. *Psychonomic Bulletin & Review*, *9*(3), 558–565. doi:10.3758/BF03196313 PMID:12412897

Glenn, C., & Carcasson, M. (2009). Rhetoric and pedagogy. In A. Lunsford (Ed.), *The SAGE handbook of rhetorical studies* (pp. 285–292). Thousand Oaks, CA: Sage Publications, Inc.

Goertzel, B. (2012). When should two minds be considered versions of one another? *International Journal of Machine Consciousness*, *4*(1), 177–185. doi:10.1142/S1793843012400094

Gonzalez, R. T. (2011). *Breakthrough: Electronic circuits that are integrated with your skin*. Retrieved from http://io9.com/5830071/breakthrough-electronic-circuits-that-are-integrated-into-your-skin

Google. (2013). *Privacy Policy*. Retrieved from http://www.google.com/policies/privacy

Gopnik, A. (2002, September 30). Bumping into mr. ravioli. *New York Journal*, 80-84.

Gottschall, J. (2012). *The storytelling animal*. New York: Houghton Mifflin Harcourt.

Grabenstein, J. (2006). *Immunization to protect the US armed forces: Heritage, current practice, prospects*. Retrieved 28 November, 2012 from http://www.vaccines.mil/documents/library/MilitaryImztn2005fulc.pdf

Graham, E. (1999). Cyborgs or goddesses? Becoming divine in a cyberfeminist age. *Information Communication and Society*, *2*(4), 419–438. doi:10.1080/136911899359484

Graham, E. L. (2002). *Representations of the post/human: Monsters, aliens, and others in popular culture.* New Brunswick, NJ: Rutgers University Press.

Graimann, B., Pfurtscheller, G., & Allinson, B. (2010). *Brain computer interfaces: Revolutionizing human-computer interaction.* Springer Link. doi:10.1007/978-3-642-02091-9

Gray, H. M., Gray, K., & Wegner, D. M. (2007). Dimensions of mind perception. *Science, 315,* 619. doi:10.1126/science.1134475 PMID:17272713

Gray, J. (1970). *The warriors: Reflections on men in battle.* New York, NY: Harper and Row.

Greely, H. (2005). Regulating human biological enhancements: Questionable justifications and international complications. *University of Technology Law Review, 7*(1), 87–110.

Greely, H., Sahakian, B., Harris, J., Kessler, R. C., Gazzaniga, M., Campbell, P., & Farah, M. J. (2008). Towards responsible use of cognitive-enhancing drugs by the healthy. *Nature, 456,* 702–705. doi:10.1038/456702a PMID:19060880

Greenberg, D. S. (1967). *The politics of pure science.* Chicago: The University of Chicago Press.

Greene, J. (2004). Article. *Philosophical Transactions of the Royal Society of London, Series B., 359,* 1776.

Greenfield, S. (2012, August 7). How digital culture is rewiring our brains. *The Sydney Morning Herald.* Retrieved from http://www.smh.com.au/federal-politics/society-and-culture/how-digital-culture-is-rewiring-our-brains-20120806-23q5p.html

Greenfield, S. (2008). *Id: The quest for meaning in the 21st century.* London: Hodder and Stoughton Ltd.

Greenleaf, G. (2014). Sheherezade and the 101 data privacy laws: Origins, significance and global trajectories. *Journal of Law, Information & Science.* Retrieved from http://papers.ssrn.com/sol3/papers.cfm?abstract_id=2280877

Greeven, A., van Balkom, A. J. L. M., van der Leeden, R., Merkelbach, J. W., van den Heuvel, O. A., & Spinhoven, P. (2009). Cognitive behavioral therapy versus paroxetine in the treatment of hypochondriasis: An 18-month naturalistic follow-up. *Journal of Behavior Therapy and Experimental Psychiatry, 40*(3), 487–496. doi:10.1016/j.jbtep.2009.06.005 PMID:19616195

Griswold, E. N. (1961). The Right to be Let Alone. *Northwestern University Law Review, 55,* 216–226.

Gronke, P., Galanes-Rosenbaum, E., Miller, P. A., & Toffey, D. (2008). Convenience voting. *Annual Review of Political Science, 11,* 437–455. doi:10.1146/annurev.polisci.11.053006.190912

Grossman, D. (1996). *On killing: The psychological cost of learning to kill in war and society.* Boston, MA: Little, Brown and Company.

Gruzelier, J., Egner, T., & Verson, D. (2006). Validating the efficacy of neurofeedback for optimizing performance. *Progress in Brain Research, 159,* 421–431. doi:10.1016/S0079-6123(06)59027-2 PMID:17071246

Guild, E., & Lesieur, G. (1998). *The European Court of Justice on The European Convention on Human Rights: Who Said What, When?* The Hague, The Netherlands: Martinus Nijhoff Publishers.

Gupta, S. (2012). Ethical and legal issues in aesthetic surgery. *Indian Journal of Plastic Surgery, 45*(3), 547–549. doi:10.4103/0970-0358.105973 PMID:23450235

Habermas, J. (2003). *The future of human nature.* Cambridge, UK: Polity.

Hadenius, A. (2001). *Institutions and democratic citizenship.* Oxford, UK: Oxford University Press. doi:10.1093/0199246661.001.0001

Haish, B. (2009). *The God theory: Universes, zero point fields and what's behind it all.* San Francisco, CA: Red Wheel/Weiser, LLC.

Hakim, S., & Adams, R. D. (1965). The special clinical problem of symptomatic hydrocephalus with normal cerebrospinal fluid pressure: Observations on cerebrospinal fluid hydrodynamics. *Journal of the Neurological Sciences, 2,* 307–327. doi:10.1016/0022-510X(65)90016-X PMID:5889177

Hale, K., & Brown, M. (2013). Adopting, adapting, and opting out: State response to federal voting system guidelines. *Publius, 43*(3), 428–451. doi:10.1093/publius/pjt016

Hampshire, S. (1991). Biology, machines, and humanity. In J. J. Sheehan, & M. Sosna (Eds.), *The boundaries of humanity: Humans, animals, machines* (pp. 253–256). Los Angeles, CA: University of California Press.

Han, X., Qian, X., Bernstein, J. G., Zhou, H. H., Franzesi, G. T., & Stern, P. et al. (2009). Millisecond-timescale optical control of neural dynamics in the nonhuman primate brain. *Neuron*, *62*(2), 191–198. doi:10.1016/j.neuron.2009.03.011 PMID:19409264

Haraway, D. J. (1991). *Simians, cyborgs, and women: The reinvention of nature*. New York: Routledge.

Harbisson, N. (2014). *Cyborg Foundation*. Retrieved January 14, 2014 from http://cyborgfoundation.com/

Hargreaves, D. A., & Tiggemann, M. (2009). Muscular ideal media images and men's body image: Social comparison processing and individual vulnerability. *Psychology of Men & Masculinity*, *10*(2), 109–119. doi:10.1037/a0014691

Hariz, M., Blomstedt, P., & Zrinco, L. (2013). Future of brain stimulation: New targets, new indications, new technology. *Movement Disorders*, *28*, 1784–1792. doi:10.1002/mds.25665 PMID:24123327

Harper, B., & Tiggemann, M. (2008). The effect of thin ideal media images on women's self-objectification, mood, and body image. *Sex Roles*, *58*(9), 649–657. doi:10.1007/s11199-007-9379-x

Harris, D. L., & Carr, A. T. (2001). The Derriford appearance scale (DAS59): A new psychometric scale for the evaluation of patients with disfigurements and aesthetic problems of appearance. *British Journal of Plastic Surgery*, *54*(3), 216–222. doi:10.1054/bjps.2001.3559 PMID:11254413

Harris, J. (2007). *Enhancing evolution: The ethical case for making better people*. Princeton, NJ: Princeton University Press.

Harris, M. (2005). Contemporary ghost stories: Cyberspace in fiction for children and young adults. *Children's Literature in Education*, *36*(2), 111–128. doi:10.1007/s10583-005-3500-y

Hart, L. (2003, January 17). Use of 'go pills' a matter of 'life and death,' Air Force avows. *Los Angeles Times*.

Haslam, N. (2006). Dehumanization: An integrative review. *Personality and Social Psychology Review*, *10*(3), 252–264. doi:10.1207/s15327957pspr1003_4 PMID:16859440

Haslam, N., & Bain, P. (2007). Humanizing the self: Moderators of the attribution of lesser humanness to others. *Personality and Social Psychology Bulletin*, *33*(1), 57–68. doi:10.1177/0146167206293191 PMID:17178930

Haslam, N., Bain, P., Douge, L., Lee, M., & Bastian, B. (2005). More human than you: Attributing humanness to self and others. *Journal of Personality and Social Psychology*, *89*(6), 937–950. doi:10.1037/0022-3514.89.6.937 PMID:16393026

Haslam, N., Bastian, B., & Bissett, M. (2004). Essentialist beliefs about personality and their implications. *Personality and Social Psychology Bulletin*, *30*(12), 1661–1673. doi:10.1177/0146167204271182 PMID:15536247

Haug, C. (2013). What happened to Dan Markingson? *Journal of the Norwegian Medical Association*, *133*, 2443–2444. PMID:24326485

Hauser, G. A. (2002). Rhetorical democracy and civic engagement. In G. A. Hauser, & A. Grim (Eds.), *Rhetorical democracy: Discursive practices of civic engagement* (pp. 1–14). Mahwah, NJ: Lawrence Erlbaum Associates.

Hauskeller, M. (2012). My brain, my mind, and I: Some philosophical assumptions of mind-uploading. *International Journal of Machine Consciousness*, *4*(1), 187–200. doi:10.1142/S1793843012400100

Heath, R. G. (1963). Intracranial direct stimulation in man. *Science*, *140*, 394–396. doi:10.1126/science.140.3565.394 PMID:13971228

Hebb, D. O., & Penfield, W. (1940). Human behavior after extensive bilateral removal from the frontal lobes. *Archives of Neurology and Psychiatry*, *44*, 421–438. doi:10.1001/archneurpsyc.1940.02280080181011

Heidegger, M. (1962). *Being and Time* (J. Macquarrie, & E. Robinson, Trans.). New York, NY: Harper & Row.

Heidegger, M. (1977). *The question concerning technology and other essays*. New York: Harper & Row.

Heidi says she'll get more done, Will do some maintenance. (2010, February 15). *Chicago Sun Times*, p. 31.

Heilinger, J.-C. (2010). *Anthropologie und ethik des enhancements. Humanprojekt/Interdisziplinare Anthropologie*. De Gruyter. doi:10.1515/9783110223705

Hennink-Kaminski, H., Reid, L. N., & King, K. W. (2010). The content of cosmetic surgery advertisements placed in large city magazines, 1985-2004. *Journal of Current Issues & Research in Advertising, 32*(2), 41–57. doi:10.1080/10641734.2010.10505284

Henry, M., Fishman, J., & Youngner, S. (2007). Propranolol and the prevention of post-traumatic stress disorder: Is it wrong to erase the sting of bad memories? *The American Journal of Bioethics, 7*(9), 12–20. doi:10.1080/15265160701518474 PMID:17849331

Henseler, H., Smith, J., Bowman, A., Khambay, B. S., Ju, X., Ayoub, A., & Ray, A. K. (2013). Subjective versus objective assessment of breast reconstruction. *Journal of Plastic, Reconstructive & Aesthetic Surgery; JPRAS, 66*(5), 634–639. doi:10.1016/j.bjps.2013.01.006 PMID:23402935

Hermes, J. (2006). Citizenship in the age of the Internet. *European Journal of Communication, 21*(3), 295–309. doi:10.1177/0267323106066634

Herrnson, P. S., Niemi, R. G., Hamner, M. J., Francia, P. L., Bederson, B. B., Conrad, F. G., & Traugott, M. W. (2008). Voters' evaluations of electronic voting systems: Results from a usability field study. *American Politics Research, 36*(4), 580–611. doi:10.1177/1532673X08316667

Hessel, A., Goodman, M., & Kotler, S. (2012). Hacking the President's DNA. *The Atlantic*. Retrieved 16 December, 2012 from http://www.theatlantic.com/magazine/archive/2012/11/hacking-the-presidentsdna/309147/

Hester, P., & Shea-Moore, M. (2003). Beak trimming egg-laying strains of chickens. *World's Poultry Science Journal, 59*(4), 458–474. doi:10.1079/WPS20030029

Heyes, C. J. (2007). Cosmetic surgery and the televisual makeover. *Feminist Media Studies, 7*(1), 17–32. doi:10.1080/14680770601103670

Hill, L., & Alport, K. (2007). Reconnecting Australia's politically excluded: Electronic pathways to electoral inclusion. *International Journal of Electronic Government Research, 3*(4), 1–19. doi:10.4018/jegr.2007100101

Hogle, L. F. (2005). Enhancement technologies and the body. *Annual Review of Anthropology, 34*, 695–716. doi:10.1146/annurev.anthro.33.070203.144020

Holliday, R., & Sanchez Taylor, J. (2006). Aesthetic surgery as false beauty. *Feminist Theory, 7*(2), 179–195. doi:10.1177/1464700106064418

Holm, S., & McNamee, M. (2011). Physical enhancement: What baseline, whose judgment? In J. Savulescu, R. ter Meulen, & G. Kahane (Eds.), *Enhancing human capacities*. West Sussex, UK: Wiley Blackwell.

Holtzheimer, P. E., Kelley, M. E., Gross, R. E., Filkowski, M. M., Garlow, S. J., & Barrocas, A. et al. (2012). Subcallosal cingulate deep brain stimulation for treatment-resistant unipolar and bipolar depression. *Archives of General Psychiatry, 69*, 150–158. doi:10.1001/archgenpsychiatry.2011.1456 PMID:22213770

Hope, D. A., & Mindell, J. A. (1994). Global social skill ratings: Measures of social behavior or physical attractiveness? *Behaviour Research and Therapy, 32*(4), 463–469. doi:10.1016/0005-7967(94)90011-6 PMID:8192645

Hughes, J. (2004). *Citizen cyborg: Why democratic societies must respond to the redesigned human of the future*. Cambridge, MA: Westview Press.

Hughlings-Jackson, J. (1887). Remarks on evolution and dissolution of the nervous system. *The British Journal of Psychiatry, 33*, 25–48. doi:10.1192/bjp.33.141.25

Human Rights Watch. (2012). *Losing humanity: The case against killer robots*. Retrieved 28 November, 2012 from http://www.hrw.org/reports/2012/11/1 9/losing-humanity-0

Hume, D. (1739). *A treatise of human nature*. Project Gutenberg eBook.

Hu, R., Eskandar, E., & Williams, Z. (2009). Role of deep brain stimulation in modulating memory formation and recall. *Neurosurgical Focus, 27*, E3. doi:10.3171/2009.4.FOCUS0975 PMID:19569891

Hurst, R. A. J. (2012). Negotiating femininity with and through mother-daughter and patient-surgeon relationships in cosmetic surgery narratives. *Women's Studies International Forum, 35*(6), 447–457. doi:10.1016/j.wsif.2012.09.008

Husted, B. (2009, August 14). Heidi 'n' seek: Playboy, hubby reveal a bit about her. *Denver Post*, p. B03.

Huxley, A. (1932). *Brave new world*. London: Chatto & Windus.

Huxley, A. (1954). *The doors of perception*. London: Thinking Ink.

Hyslop-Margison, E. J., & Sears, A. M. (2006). *Neo-Liberalism, globalization and human capital learning: Reclaiming education for democratic citizenship*. SpringerLink Books.

I wish I'd NEVER had plastic surgery: Heidi Montag reveals her regret as she unveils new bikini body after breast reduction. (2013, November 28). *MailOnline*. Retrieved December 27, 2013, from http://www.dailymail.co.uk/tvshowbiz/article-2514988/Heidi-Montag-talks-plastic-surgery-regrets-breast-reduction.html

Internal Revenue Service. (2014, March 25). Notice 2014-21. *IRS.Gov*. Retrieved from http://www.irs.gov/pub/irs-drop/n-14-21.pdf

International Atomic Energy Agency. (1970). Treaty on the non-proliferation of nuclear weapons. *IAEA Information Circular*. Retrieved 28 November, 2012 from http://www.iaea.org/Publications/Documents/Infcircs/Others/infcirc140.pdf

Isin, E. F., & Nielsen, G. M. (2008). *Acts of citizenship*. London, UK: Zed Books.

Jacobsen, E. (1986). The early history of psychotherapeutic drugs. *Psychopharmacology*, *89*, 138–144. doi:10.1007/BF00310617 PMID:2873606

Jacobson v. Commonwealth of Massachusetts, 197 US 11, 18-19, 34 (1905).

Jaslow, R. (2012, January 12). Internet addiction changes brain similar to cocaine: Study. *CBS News*. Retrieved from http://www.cbsnews.com/news/internet-addiction-changes-brain-similar-to-cocaine-study/

JASON. (2008). *Human Performance* (Report No. JSR-07-625, March). JASON.

JASON. (2010). *The $100 Genome: Implications for DoD* (Report No. JSR-10-100, December). JASON.

Jeffreys, S. (2005). *Beauty and misogyny: Harmful cultural practices in the West*. London: Routledge.

Jenkins, J., Shajahan, P. M., Lappin, J. M., & Ebmeier, K. P. (2002). Right and left prefrontal transcranial magnetic stimulation at 1 Hz does not affect mood in healthy volunteers. *BMC Psychiatry*, *2*, 1. doi:10.1186/1471-244X-2-1 PMID:11825340

Jerslev, A. (2006). The mediated body. *Nordicom Review*, *27*(2), 133–151.

Johnson, T. (2004). *What is 20/20 vision?* Retrieved 28 November, 2012 from http://www.uihealthcare.com/topics/medicaldepartments/ophthalmology/2020vision/index.html

Johnson, J. A., Strafella, A. P., & Zatorre, R. J. (2007). The role of the dorsolateral prefrontal cortex in divided attention: Two transcranial magnetic stimulation studies. *Journal of Cognitive Neuroscience*, *19*, 907–920. doi:10.1162/jocn.2007.19.6.907 PMID:17536962

Johnson, S. K., Podratz, K. E., Dipboye, R. L., & Gibbons, E. (2010). Physical attractiveness biases in ratings of employment suitability: Tracking down the beauty is beastly effect. *The Journal of Social Psychology*, *150*(3), 301–318. doi:10.1080/00224540903365414 PMID:20575336

Joiner, T. E. Jr. (2007). Aesthetic surgery in adolescents: A suggestion informed by adolescent psychology. *Aesthetic Surgery Journal*, *27*(4), 419–420. doi:10.1016/j.asj.2007.06.001 PMID:19341670

Jonas, W., O'Connor, F., Deuster, P., Peck, J., Shake, C., & Frost, S. (2010). Why Total Force Fitness? *Military Medicine*, *175*(8), 6–13. doi:10.7205/MILMED-D-10-00280

Jones, B. C., Little, A. C., Penton-Voak, I. S., Tiddeman, B. P., Burt, D. M., & Perrett, D. I. (2001). Facial symmetry and judgements of apparent health: Support for a good genes explanation of the attractiveness-symmetry relationship. *Evolution and Human Behavior*, *22*(6), 417–429. doi:10.1016/S1090-5138(01)00083-6

Jordan, J. (2004). The rhetorical limits of the plastic body. *The Quarterly Journal of Speech*, *90*(3), 327–358. doi:10.1080/0033563042000255543

Jothilakshmi, P. K., Salvi, N. R., Hayden, B. E., & Bose-Haider, B. (2009). Labial reduction in adolescent population—A case series study. *Journal of Pediatric and Adolescent Gynecology*, *22*(1), 53–55. doi:10.1016/j.jpag.2008.03.008 PMID:19241623

Judge Decides in Favor of NISD in SmartID Case Against Student. (2013, January 8). Retrieved from http://www.kens5.com/news/Judge-decides-in-favor-of-NISD-in-SmartID-case-against-student-186077712.html

Juengst, E. (1998). The meaning of enhancement. In E. Parens (Ed.), *Enhancing human traits: Ethical and social implications*. Washington, DC: Georgetown University Press.

Juengst, E. (2000). The ethics of enhancement. In T. Murray, & M. Mehlman (Eds.), *The encyclopedia of ethical, legal and policy issues in biotechnology*. Hoboken, NJ: John Wiley & Sons.

Justman, S. (1993). The abstract citizen. *Philosophy and Social Criticism*, *19*(3-4), 317–332. doi:10.1177/019145379301900307

Kaiser, T. (2013, August 28). *UW researcher moves another human's finger with his thoughts*. Retrieved from http://dailytech.com

Kamenetzky, B. (2013, July 18). Google Glass delivers a Sam Bradford view of St. Louis Rams practice. *Digital Trends*. Retrieved December 28, 2013 from http://www.digitaltrends.com/sports/st-louis-rams-experiment-with-google-glass/

Kaminsky, M. (Ed.). (1992). *Remembered lives: The work of ritual, storytelling, and growing older*. Ann Arbor, MI: Michigan University Press.

Kammel, K. (2006). The cost of virginity: Virginity tests and hymen reconstruction. *DePaul Health Law Institute Newsletter*, *2*(3), 3.

Kanazawa, S. (2011). Intelligence and physical attractiveness. *Intelligence*, *39*(1), 7–14. doi:10.1016/j.intell.2010.11.003

Kanazawa, S., & Kovar, J. L. (2004). Why beautiful people are more intelligent. *Intelligence*, *32*(3), 227–243. doi:10.1016/j.intell.2004.03.003

Kandela, P. (1996). Egypt's trade in hymen repair. *Lancet*, *347*(9015), 1615. doi:10.1016/S0140-6736(96)91096-X PMID:8667878

Kang, J. (1998). Information privacy in cyberspace transactions. *Stanford Law Review*, *50*(4), 1193–1295. doi:10.2307/1229286

Kass, L. (2003). Ageless bodies, happy souls: Biotechnology and the pursuit of perfection. *New Atlantis (Washington, D.C.)*, 9–28. PMID:15584192

Kass, L. (2004). *Life, liberty & the defense of dignity: The challenge for bioethics*. Encounter Books.

Kass, L. R. (2002). *Life, liberty, and the defense of dignity: The challenge for bioethics*. San Francisco, CA: Encounter Books.

Katy M. (2013, January 9). Retrieved from http://usnews.nbcnews.com/_news/2013/01/09/16427652-texas-school-can-force-students-to-wear-locator-chips-judge-rules?pc=25&sp=0#discussion_nav

Katz, G., Alvarez, R. M., Calvo, E., Escolar, M., & Pomares, J. (2011). Assessing the impact of alternative voting technologies on multi-party elections: Design features, heuristic processing and voter choice. *Political Behavior*, *33*(2), 247–270. doi:10.1007/s11109-010-9132-y

Katz, R. (2001). Friendly fire: The mandatory military anthrax vaccination program. *Duke Law Journal*, *50*(6), 1835–1865. doi:10.2307/1373049 PMID:11794357

Keane, J. (2013). *Democracy and media decadence*. Cambridge, UK: Cambridge University Press. doi:10.1017/CBO9781107300767

Kellett, S., Clarke, S., & McGill, P. (2008). Outcomes from psychological assessment regarding recommendations for cosmetic surgery. *Journal of Plastic, Reconstructive & Aesthetic Surgery; JPRAS*, *61*(5), 512–517. doi:10.1016/j.bjps.2007.08.025 PMID:18316256

Kelly, M. (2014). *Google developing contact lens device to help those with diabetes monitor blood glucose levels*. Retrieved from http://venturebeat.com/2014/01/16/google-contacts/

Kelly, K. (2010). *What technology wants*. New York: Penguin Group.

Kerpen, D. (2011). *Likeable social media: How to delight your customers, create an irresistible brand, and be generally amazing on Facebook (and other social networks)*. New York: McGraw Hill.

Kilkelly, U. (2003). *The Right to Respect for Private and Family Life: A guide to the Implementation of Article 8 of the European Convention on Human Rights 10–19*. Strasbourg: Council of Europe.

Knights, A. (2007). *Unconventional animals in the history of warfare*. Retrieved 28 November, 2012, from http://www. allempires.com/article/index.php?q=Unconventional_ Animals_in_the_History_of_Warf

Kohler, J. (1900). Ehre und Beleidigung. *Goltdammers Archiv für Deutsches Strafrecht, 47*, 1–48.

Kopelman, M. D., Wilson, B., & Baddeley, A. (1990). *The autobiographical memory interview*. Suffolk, UK: Thames Valley Test Company.

Krichmar, J., & Wagatsuma, H. (Eds.). (2011). *Neuromorphic and brain-based robots*. New York, NY: Cambridge University Press. doi:10.1017/CBO9780511994838

Kulesza, J. (2012). Walled Gardens of Privacy or Binding Corporate Rules? A Critical Look at International Protection of Online Privacy. *University of Arkansas at Little Rock Law Review, 3*, 747–765.

Kumar, S., & Ekta, W. (2011). Analysis of electronic voting system in various countries. *International Journal on Computer Science and Engineering, 3*(5), 1825–1830.

Kuner, C. (2009). An international legal framework for data protection: Issues and prospects. *Computer Law & Security Report, 25*, 309–327. doi:10.1016/j.clsr.2009.05.001

Kurzweil, R. (2014). Singularity University home page. *Singularity Education Group*. Retrieved January 14, 2014 from http://singularityu.org/

Kurzweil, R. (1999). *The age of spiritual machines: When computers exceed human intelligence*. New York, NY: The Penguin Group.

Lakoff, G., & Johnson, M. (1980). *Metaphors we live by*. Chicago, IL: University of Chicago Press.

Land, B. (2010). Current Department of Defense guidance for total force fitness. *Military Medicine, 175*(8), 3–5. doi:10.7205/MILMED-D-10-00138

Lane, H., & Bahan, B. (1998). Ethics of cochlear implantation in young children: A review and reply from a deaf-world perspective. *Otolaryngology - Head and Neck Surgery, 119*(4), 297–313. doi:10.1016/S0194-5998(98)70070-1 PMID:9781982

Langlois, F., & Ladouceur, R. (2004). Adaptation of a GAD treatment for hypochondriasis. *Cognitive and Behavioral Practice, 11*(4), 393–404. doi:10.1016/S1077-7229(04)80056-7

Lariscy, R. W., Tinkham, S. F., & Sweetser, K. D. (2011). Kids these days: Examining differences in political uses and gratifications, internet political participation, political information efficacy, and cynicism on the basis of age. *The American Behavioral Scientist, 55*(6), 749–764. doi:10.1177/0002764211398091

Larratt, S. (2002). *ModCon: The secret world of extreme body modification*. BMEbooks.

LaRue, F. (2011). *Report of the Special Rapporteur on the promotion and protection of the right to freedom of opinion and expression*. U.N. Doc A/HRC/17/27.

Lass, P., Sławek, J., & Sitek, E. (2012). Egas Moniz: A genius, unlucky looser [sic] or a Nobel committee error? *Neurologia i Neurochirurgia Polska, 46*, 96–103. doi:10.5114/ninp.2012.27452 PMID:22426769

Latour, B. (1999). *Pandora's Hope: Essays on the Reality of Science Studies*. Cambridge, MA: Harvard University Press.

Latour, B. (2003). The promise of constructivism. In D. Ihde, & E. Selinger (Eds.), *Chasing Technoscience: Matrix for Materiality*. Bloomington, IN: Indiana University Press.

Lawson, C. (2010). Technology and the extension of human capabilities. *Journal for the Theory of Social Behaviour, 40*(2), 207–223. doi:10.1111/j.1468-5914.2009.00428.x

Laxton, A. W., Lipsman, N., & Lozano, A. M. (2013). Deep brain stimulation for cognitive disorders. *Handbook of Clinical Neurology, 116*, 307–311. doi:10.1016/B978-0-444-53497-2.00025-5 PMID:24112904

Laxton, A. W., & Lozano, A. M. (2013). Deep brain stimulation for the treatment of Alzheimer disease and dementias. *World Neurosurgery, 80*(S28), e1–e8. doi:10.1016/j.wneu.2012.06.028 PMID:22722036

Le, Q., Ranzato, M., Monga, R., Devin, M., Chen, K., Corrado, G., et al. (2012). Building high-level features using large scale unsupervised learning. In *Proceedings of the 29th International Conference on Machine Learning*. Edinburgh, UK: Academic Press.

Leebron, D. (1991). The Right to Privacy's Place in the Intellectual History of Tort Law. *Case Western Reserve Law Review, 41*, 769–777.

Lehrer, J. (2012). The forgetting pill erases painful memories forever. *Wired, 20*(3).

Lester, P., McBride, S., Bliese, P., & Adler, A. (2011). Bringing science to bear: An empirical assessment of the comprehensive soldier fitness program. *The American Psychologist, 66*(1), 77–81. doi:10.1037/a0022083 PMID:21219052

Lever, A. (2010). Compulsory voting: A critical perspective. *British Journal of Political Science, 40*(4), 897–915. doi:10.1017/S0007123410000050

Levin, K. (2008). It is well that war is so terrible. *Civil War Memory*. Retrieved 28 November, 2012 from http://cwmemory.com/2008/09/08/it-is-well-that-war-is-so-terrible/

Levy, N. (2011). Enhancing authenticity. *Journal of Applied Philosophy, 28*(3), 308–318. doi:10.1111/j.1468-5930.2011.00532.x

Lewis, S. (2009). History of biowarfare. *NOVA*. Retrieved 28 November, 2012 from http://www.pbs.org/wgbh/nova/military/history-biowarfare.html

Leyens, J. P., Paladino, M. P., Rodriguez, R. T., Vaes, J., Demoulin, S., & Rodriguez, A. P. (2000). The emotional side of prejudice: The attribution of secondary emotions to ingroups and outgroups. *Personality and Social Psychology Review, 4*(2), 186–197. doi:10.1207/S15327957PSPR0402_06

Leyens, J. P., Rodriguez, R. T., Rodriguez, R. T., Gaunt, R., Paladino, P. M., Vaes, J., & Demoulin, S. (2001). Psychological essentialism and the attribution of uniquely human emotions to ingroups and outgroups. *European Journal of Social Psychology, 31*, 395–411. doi:10.1002/ejsp.50

Lilley, S. (2013). *Transhumanism and society: The social debate over human enhancement (SpringerBriefs in Philosophy)*. Springer. doi:10.1007/978-94-007-4981-8

Lin, P. (2011, December 15). Drone-ethics briefing: What a leading expert told the CIA. *The Atlantic*. Retrieved 28 November 2012 from http://www.theatlan tic.com/technology/archive/2011/12/drone-ethics-briefing-what-a-leading- robot-expert-told-the-cia/250060/

Lin, P. (2012a). More than human? The ethics of biologically enhancing soldiers. *The Atlantic*. Retrieved 28 November, 2012 from http://www.theatlantic.com/technology/archive/2012/02/more-than-human-the-ethics-of-biologically-enhancing-soldiers/253217

Lin, P. (2012b, April 30). Stand your cyberground law: A novel proposal for digital security. *The Atlantic*. Retrieved 28 November, 2012 from http://www.theatlantic.com/technology/archive/2012/04/stand-your-cyberground-law- a-novel-proposal-for-digital- security/256532/

Lin, P., Abney, K., & Bekey, G. (2008). *Autonomous military robotics: Risk, ethics, and design*. Retrieved 28 November, 2012 from http: //ethics.calpoly.edu/ONR_report.pdf

Lin, P., Allhoff, F., & Rowe, N. (2012, June 5). Is it possible to wage a just cyberwar? *The Atlantic*. Retrieved 28 November, 2012 from http://www.theatlan tic.com/technology/archive/2012/06/is-it-possible-to-wage-a-just- cyberwar/258106

Lin, P. (2010). Ethical blowback from emerging technologies. *Journal of Military Ethics, 9*(4), 313–331. doi:10.1080/15027570.2010.536401

Lin, P., Abney, K., & Bekey, G. (Eds.). (2012). *Robot ethics: The ethical and social implications of robotics*. Cambridge, MA: MIT Press.

Lin, P., Mehlman, M., & Abney, K. (2013). *Enhanced warfighters: Risk, ethics, and policy*. New York, NY: The Greenwall Foundation.

Lin, T. J. (2010). Evolution of cosmetics: Increased need for experimental clinical medicine. *Journal of Experimental & Clinical Medicine, 2*(2), 49–52. doi:10.1016/S1878-3317(10)60009-5

Lipsman, N., Mendelsohn, D., Taira, T., & Bernstein, M. (2011). The contemporary practice of psychiatric surgery: Results from a survey of North American functional neurosurgeons. *Stereotactic and Functional Neurosurgery, 89*(2), 103–110. doi:10.1159/000323545 PMID:21336006

Lipsman, N., Zener, R., & Bernstein, M. (2009). Personal identity, enhancement and neurosurgery: A qualitative study in applied neuroethics. *Bioethics, 23*(6), 375–383. doi:10.1111/j.1467-8519.2009.01729.x PMID:19527265

Little, V. (2010, October 1). Physical readiness training standards take shape. *The Bayonet*. Retrieved 28 November 2012 from http://www.ledger-enquirer.com/

Lock, M., & Scheper-Hughes, N. (1996). A critical-interpretive approach in medical anthropology: Rituals and routines of discipline and dissent. In C. F. Sargent, & T. M. Johnson (Eds.), *Handbook of medical anthropology: Contemporary theory and method* (pp. 41–70). Westport, CT: Greenwood Press.

Lorenzo, G. L., Biesanz, J. C., & Human, L. J. (2010). What is beautiful is good and more accurately understood: Physical attractiveness and accuracy in first impressions of personality. *Psychological Science*, *21*(12), 1777–1782. doi:10.1177/0956797610388048 PMID:21051521

LoTempio, S. (2011, March 3). *From Special to Substantial*. Retrieved December 1, 2013, from http://www.poynter.org/how-tos/newsgathering-storytelling/diversity-at-work/74234/from-special-to-substantial/

Loughnan, S., & Haslam, N. (2007). Animals and androids: Implicit associations between social categories and nonhumans. *Psychological Science*, *18*(2), 116–121. doi:10.1111/j.1467-9280.2007.01858.x PMID:17425529

Loughnan, S., Haslam, N., & Kashima, Y. (2009). Understanding the relationship between attribute-based and metaphor-based dehumanization. *Group Processes & Intergroup Relations*, *12*(6), 747–762. doi:10.1177/1368430209347726

Lovas, D. A., & Barsky, A. J. (2010). Mindfulness-based cognitive therapy for hypochondriasis, or severe health anxiety: A pilot study. *Journal of Anxiety Disorders*, *24*(8), 931–935. doi:10.1016/j.janxdis.2010.06.019 PMID:20650601

Low, S. M. (1994). Embodied metaphors: Nerves as lived experience. In T. J. Csordas (Ed.), *Embodiment and experience: The existential ground of culture and self* (pp. 139–162). New York: Cambridge University Press.

Lunceford, B. (2008). The body and the sacred in the digital age: Thoughts on posthuman sexuality. *Theology & Sexuality*, *15*(1), 77–96. doi:10.1558/tse.v15i1.77

Lunceford, B. (2009). Reconsidering technology adoption and resistance: Observations of a semi-luddite. *Explorations in Media Ecology*, *8*(1), 29–48.

Lunceford, B. (2010). Sex in the digital age: Media ecology and Megan's law. *Explorations in Media Ecology*, *9*(4), 239–244.

Lunceford, B. (2012). Posthuman visions: Creating the technologized body. *Explorations in Media Ecology*, *11*(1), 7–25. doi:10.1386/eme.11.1.7_1

Luo, W. (2013). Aching for the altered body: Beauty economy and Chinese women's consumption of cosmetic surgery. *Women's Studies International Forum*, *38*, 1–10. doi:10.1016/j.wsif.2013.01.013

Lytle, R. (2013, August 12). Behold: A digital bill of rights for the Internet, by the Internet. *Mashable*. Retrieved from http://mashable.com/2013/08/12/digital-bill-of-rights-crowdsource/

MacIntyre, A. (1999). *Dependent rational animals: Why human beings need the virtues*. Chicago: Open Court.

MacNair, R. (2002). *Perpetration-induced traumatic stress: The psychological consequences of killing*. London: Praeger Publishers.

Makridis, C. (2013). Converging Technologies: A Critical Analysis of Cognitive Enhancement for Public Policy Application. *Journal of Science and Engineering Ethics*, *19*(3), 1017–1038. doi:10.1007/s11948-012-9396-1 PMID:23065536

Malle, B. (1999). How people explain behavior: A new theoretical framework. *Personality and Social Psychology Review*, *3*(1), 23–48. doi:10.1207/s15327957pspr0301_2 PMID:15647146

Maltby, J., & Day, L. (2011). Celebrity worship and incidence of elective cosmetic surgery: Evidence of a link among young adults. *The Journal of Adolescent Health*, *49*(5), 483–489. doi:10.1016/j.jadohealth.2010.12.014 PMID:22018562

Mancini, P. (2010). New frontiers in political professionalism. *Political Communication*, *16*(3), 231–245. doi:10.1080/105846099198604

Manji, H. K., Drevets, W. C., & Charney, D. S. (2001). The cellular neurobiology of depression. *Nature Medicine*, *7*, 541–547. doi:10.1038/87865 PMID:11329053

Mann, S., & Niedzviecki, H. (2002). *Cyborg: Digital destiny and human possibilities in the age of the wearable computer.* Toronto, Canada: Doubleday Canada.

Marcus, D. K. (1999). The cognitive-behavioral model of hypochondriasis: Misinformation and triggers. *Journal of Psychosomatic Research, 47*(1), 79–91. doi:10.1016/S0022-3999(99)00008-2 PMID:10511423

Marcus, D. K., Gurley, J. R., Marchi, M. M., & Bauer, C. (2007). Cognitive and perceptual variables in hypochondriasis and health anxiety: A systematic review. *Clinical Psychology Review, 27*(2), 127–139. doi:10.1016/j.cpr.2006.09.003 PMID:17084495

Markey, C. N., & Markey, P. M. (2010). A correlational and experimental examination of reality television viewing and interest in cosmetic surgery. *Body Image, 7*(2), 165–171. doi:10.1016/j.bodyim.2009.10.006 PMID:20089464

Markus, H. R., & Nurius, P. (1986). Possible selves. *The American Psychologist, 41*(9), 954–969. doi:10.1037/0003-066X.41.9.954

Marshall, L., Molle, M., Hallschmid, M., & Born, J. (2004). Transcranial direct current stimulation during sleep improves declarative memory. *The Journal of Neuroscience, 24*, 9985–9992. doi:10.1523/JNEUROSCI.2725-04.2004 PMID:15525784

Martínez Lirola, M., & Chovanec, J. (2012). The dream of a perfect body come true: Multimodality in cosmetic surgery advertising. *Discourse & Society, 23*(5), 487–507. doi:10.1177/0957926512452970

Marwick, A. E. (2013). *Status update: Celebrity, publicity, and branding in the social media age.* New Haven, CT: Yale University Press.

Mayberg, H. S., Lozano, A. M., Voon, V., & McNeely, H. E. (2005). Deep brain stimulation for treatment-resistant depression. *Neuron, 45*, 651–660. doi:10.1016/j.neuron.2005.02.014 PMID:15748841

Mayer-Schönberger, V. (2011). *Delete: The Virtue of Forgetting in the Digital Age.* Oxford, UK: Oxford University Press.

McAdams, D. P. (1997). The case for unity in the (post) modern self: A modest proposal. In R. D. Ashmore, & L. Jussim (Eds.), *Self and identity: Fundamental issues* (pp. 46–77). New York: Oxford University Press.

McAdams, D. P. (2001). The psychology of life stories. *Review of General Psychology, 5*(2), 100–122. doi:10.1037/1089-2680.5.2.100

McKean, E. (2005). *The new Oxford American dictionary.* Oxford University Press, Inc.

McKibben, B. (2004). *Enough: Staying human in an engineered age.* St. Martin's Griffin.

Mcloughlin, I., & Dawson, P. (2003). The mutual shaping of technology and organisation. In D. Preece, & J. Laurila (Eds.), *Technological change and organizational action.* London, UK: Routledge.

McLuhan, M. (1994). *Understanding media: The extensions of man.* Cambridge, MA: MIT Press.

McLuhan, M., & McLuhan, E. (1988). *Laws of media: The new science.* Toronto, Canada: University of Toronto Press.

Meagher, R. (1988). Techné. *Perspecta, 24*, 159–164. doi:10.2307/1567132

Mehlman, M. (1999). How will we regulate genetic enhancement? *Wake Forest Law Review, 34*(3), 617–714. PMID:12664908

Mehlman, M. (2000). The law of above averages: Leveling the new genetic enhancement playing field. *Iowa Law Review, 85*, 517–593. PMID:11769760

Mehlman, M. (2003). *Wondergenes: Genetic enhancement and the future of society.* Bloomington, IN: Indiana University Press.

Mehlman, M. (2004). Cognition-enhancing drugs. *The Milbank Quarterly, 82*(3), 483–506. doi:10.1111/j.0887-378X.2004.00319.x PMID:15330974

Mehlman, M. (2009a). Biomedical enhancements: A new era. *Issues in Science and Technology, 25*(3), 59–69.

Mehlman, M. J. (2009). *The price of perfection: Individualism and society in the era of biomedical enhancement.* The Johns Hopkins University Press.

Mele, N. (2013). *The end of big: How the internet makes David the new Goliath.* New York: St. Martin's Press.

Meningaud, J.-P., Benadiba, L., Servant, J.-M., Herve, C., Bertrand, J.-C., & Pelicier, Y. (2003). Depression, anxiety and quality of life: Outcome 9 months after facial cosmetic surgery. *Journal of Cranio-Maxillo-Facial Surgery*, *31*(1), 46–50. doi:10.1016/S1010-5182(02)00159-2 PMID:12553927

Menuz, V. (2014). Why do we wish to be enhanced? In S. Bateman, J. Gayon, S. Allouche, J. Goffette, & M. Marzano (Eds.), *Human Enhancement: An interdisciplinary inquiry*. MacMillan.

Menuz, V., Hurlimann, T., & Godard, B. (2011). Is human enhancement also a personal matter? *Science and Engineering Ethics*. doi:doi:10.1007/s11948-011-9294-y PMID:21786000

Metzinger, T. (2010). *The ego tunnel*. New York: Basic Books.

Michigan Disabilty Rights Coalition. (n.d.). *Medical Model of Disabilty*. Retrieved December 1, 2013, from http://www.copower.org/models-of-disability/181-medical-model-of-disability.html

Millar, M. S. (1998). *Cracking the gender code: Who rules the wired world?* Toronto, Canada: Second Story Press.

Miller, R. (2014, March 15). Why we hate Google Glass—and all new tech. *TechCrunch*. Retrieved from http://techcrunch.com/2014/03/15/why-we-hate-google-glass-and-all-new-tech/

Mitchell, C. B. (2009). On human mioenhancements. *Ethics & Medicine: An International. Journal of Bioethics*, *25*(3).

Moniz, E. (1994). Prefrontal leucotomy in the treatment of mental disorders. *The American Journal of Psychiatry*, *151*, 236–239. PMID:8192205

Montag wouldn't recommend multiple plastic surgeries. (2012, August 3). *Breakingnews.ie*. Retrieved December 27, 2013, from http://www.breakingnews.ie/showbiz/montag-wouldnt-recommend-multiple-plastic-surgeries-561757.html

Montagu, A., & Matson, F. (1983). *The dehumanization of man*. New York: McGraw-Hill.

Montain, S., Carvey, C., & Stephens, M. (2010). Nutritional fitness. *Military Medicine*, *175*(8), 65–72. doi:10.7205/MILMED-D-10-00127 PMID:20108845

Montgomery, C. (2001). *A Hard Look at Invisible Disability*. Advocado Press. Retrieved December 1, 2013, from http://www.ragged-edge-mag.com/0301/0301ft1.htm

Montgomery, C. (2005, December 16). *Autistics Speak*. Retrieved December 1, 2013, from http://www.ragged-edgemagazine.com/departments/closerlook/000677.html

Moor, J. (2005). Why we need better ethics for emerging technologies. *Ethics and Information Technology*, *7*(3), 111–119. doi:10.1007/s10676-006-0008-0

Moreno, J. (2006). *Mind wars: Brain research and national defense*. Washington, DC: Dana Press.

Mossberger, K., Tolbert, C. J., & McNeal, R. S. (2007). *Digital citizenship: The internet, society and participation*. Cambridge, MA: MIT Press.

Motohashi, N., Yamaguchi, M., Fujii, T., & Kitahara, Y. (2013). Mood and cognitive function following repeated transcranial direct current stimulation in healthy volunteers: A preliminary report. *Neuroscience Research*, *77*, 64–69. doi:10.1016/j.neures.2013.06.001 PMID:23811267

Moynihan, D. P., & Lavertu, S. (2011). Cognitive biases in governing: Technology preferences in election administration. *Public Administration Review*, *72*(1), 68–77. doi:10.1111/j.1540-6210.2011.02478.x

mpa-4893349. (2013, January 9) Retrieved from http://usnews.nbcnews.com/_news/2013/01/09/16427652-texas-school-can-force-students-to-wear-locator-chips-judge-rules?pc=25&sp=0#discussion_nav

Munzer, S. R. (2011). Cosmetic surgery, racial identity, and aesthetics. *Configurations*, *19*(2), 243–286. doi:10.1353/con.2011.0012

Murphy, T. F. (2009). Choosing disabilities and enhancements in children: A choice too far? *Reproductive Biomedicine Online*, *18*(Supplement 1), 43–49. doi:10.1016/S1472-6483(10)60115-0 PMID:19281664

Murray, T. (2007). Enhancement. In B. Steinbock (Ed.), *The Oxford handbook of bioethics*. Oxford, UK: Oxford University Press.

Naam, R. (2005). *More than human*. New York, NY: Broadway Books.

Nakamoto, S. (2010). *Bitcoin: A Peer-to-Peer Electronic Cash System*. Retrieved from http://bitcoin.org/bitcoin.pdf

Nass, C., & Yen, C. (2010). *The man who lied to his laptop: What machines teach us about human relationships*. New York: Penguin Group USA, Inc.

Navy, U. S. (2012). *Marine Mammal Program*. Retrieved 28 November 2012 from http://www.public.navy.mil/spawar/Pacific/71500/Pages/default.aspx

Negroponte, N. (1995). *Being digital*. New York: Knopf.

Nelson, K. (2008). Self in time: Emergence within a community of minds. In F. Sani (Ed.), *Self continuity: Individual and collective perspectives* (pp. 13–26). New York: Psychology Press.

Nielsen, J. (2007). Danish perspective: Commentary on recommendations for the ethical use of pharmacological fatigue countermeasures in the US Military. *Aviation, Space, and Environmental Medicine, 78*(1), 134–135.

Nietzsche, F. W. (1978). *Thus spoke Zarathustra: A book for all and none* (W. Kaufmann, Trans.). New York: Penguin Books.

Nisbett, R. E., & Wilson, T. D. (1977). The halo effect: Evidence for unconscious alteration of judgments. *Journal of Personality and Social Psychology, 35*(4), 250–256. doi:10.1037/0022-3514.35.4.250

Northoff, G. (2006). Neuroscience of decision-making and informed consent: An investigation in neuroethics. *Journal of Medical Ethics, 32*, 70–73. doi:10.1136/jme.2005.011858 PMID:16446409

Northside ISD Smart Student ID Cards Student Locator Pilot . (n.d.). Retrieved from http://www.nisd.net/studentlocator/

Nussbaum, M. (2011). *Creating capabilities: The human development approach*. Cambridge, MA: Harvard University Press. doi:10.4159/harvard.9780674061200

O'Meara, R. (2012). Contemporary governance architecture regarding robotic technologies: An assessment. In P. Lin, K. Abney, & G. Bekey (Eds.), *Robot ethics: The ethical and social implications of robotics*. Cambridge, MA: MIT Press.

Oakley, J., & Dean, C. (Eds.). (2001). *Virtue ethics and professional roles*. Cambridge, UK: Cambridge University Press. doi:10.1017/CBO9780511487118

Olds, J., & Milner, P. (1954). Positive reinforcement produced by electrical stimulation of septal area and other regions of rat brain. *Journal of Comparative and Physiological Psychology, 47*, 419–427. doi:10.1037/h0058775 PMID:13233369

Oliver, A. (2013). *The Lowy Institute Poll 2013: Australia and the world*. Sydney: Lowy Institute for International Policy.

Olson, E. (1997). *The human animal*. New York: Oxford University Press.

Olsthoorn, P. (2010). *Military ethics and virtues*. New York, NY: Routledge.

Organization for Economic Cooperation and Development. (1980). *OECD Guidelines on the Protection of Privacy and Transborder Flows of Personal Data*. Retrieved from http://www.oecd.org/internet/ieconomy/oecdguidelinesontheprotectionofprivacyandtransborderflowsofpersonaldata.htm

Organization for Economic Cooperation and Development. (2013). *The 2013 OECD Privacy Guidelines*. Retrieved from http://www.oecd.org/sti/ieconomy/privacy.htm#newguidelines

Orlikowski, W. J. (2007). Sociomaterial Practices: Exploring Technology at Work. *Organization Studies, 28*(9), 1435–1448. doi:10.1177/0170840607081138

Otchere-Darko, G. A. (2010). Ghana's fragile elections: Consolidating African democracy through e-voting. *Georgetown Journal of International Affairs, 11*(2), 67–73.

Pakulski, J. (2013). Leadership trends in advanced democracies. *Social Compass, 7*(5), 366–376. doi:10.1111/soc4.12035

Palm, E., & Hansson, S. O. (2006). The case for ethical technology assessment (eTA). *Technological Forecasting and Social Change, 73*(5), 543–558. doi:10.1016/j.techfore.2005.06.002

Palmeri, J. (2006). Disability Studies, Cultural Analysis, and the Critical Practice of Technical Communication Pedagogy. *Technical Communication Quarterly, 15*(1), 49–65. doi:10.1207/s15427625tcq1501_5

Pappone, J. (2000, June 8). Resistance is futile: Becoming cyborgs inevitable, conference ponders advances in technology that blur lines between humans and machines. *The Ottawa Citizen*.

Parens, E. (1995). The goodness of fragility: On the prospect of genetic technologies aimed at the enhancement of human capacities. *Kennedy Institute of Ethics Journal*, *5*(2), 141–153. doi:10.1353/ken.0.0149 PMID:10143182

Parfit, D. (1984). *Reasons and persons*. Oxford, UK: Oxford University Press.

Pariser, E. (2011). *The filter bubble: What the Internet is hiding from you*. New York: Penguin Press.

Parker, J. (2003). Computing with DNA. *EMBO Reports*, *4*(1). doi:10.1038/sj.embor.embor719 PMID:12524509

Penenberg, A. L. (2009). *Viral loop: From Facebook to Twitter, how today's smartest businesses grow themselves*. New York: Hyperion Books.

Perry v. Wesely, No. NMCM 200001397, 2000 WL 1775249, at *3 (N-M. Ct. Crim. App. November 29, 2000).

Persaud, R. (2006). Does smarter mean happier? In J. Wilsdon, & P. Miller (Eds.), *Better humans? The politics of human enhancement and life extension*. London: Demos.

Peters, T. (2011). Transhumanism and the posthuman future: Will technological progress get us there? In G. Hansell, & W. Grassie (Eds.), *Transhumanism and its critics*. Philadelphia, PA: Metanexus Institute.

Pitts-Taylor, V. (2007). *Surgery junkies: Wellness and pathology in cosmetic culture*. New Brunswick, NJ: Rutgers University Press.

Plato. (n.d.). *The symposium*. Retrieved from http://www.gutenberg.org/ebooks/1600

Plaw, A. (2012, September 25). Drones save lives, American and otherwise. *New York Times*. Retrieved 28 November, 2012 from http://www.nytimes.com/roomfordebate/2012/09/25/do-drone-attacks-do-more-harm-than-good/drone-strikes-save-lives-american-and-other

Plazier, M., Joos, K., Vanneste, S., Ost, J., & De Ridder, D. (2012). Bifrontal and bioccipital transcranial direct current stimulation (tDCS) does not induce mood changes in healthy volunteers: A placebo controlled study. *Brain Stimulation*, *5*, 454–461. doi:10.1016/j.brs.2011.07.005 PMID:21962976

Plumwood, V. (2002). *Environmental culture: The ecological crisis of reason*. London: Routledge.

Plutarch. (2009). *Theseus*. Retrieved November 25, 2012, from http://classics.mit.edu/Plutarch/theseus.html

Polonijo, A. N., & Carpiano, R. M. (2008). Representations of cosmetic surgery and emotional health in women's magazines in Canada. *Women's Health Issues*, *18*(6), 463–470. doi:10.1016/j.whi.2008.07.004 PMID:19041597

Ponder v. Stone, 54 MJ 613, 614 (N-M. Ct. Crim. App. 2000).

Postman, N. (1993). *Technopoly: The surrender of culture to technology*. New York: Knopf.

Pratico, D., Yao, Y., Rokach, J., Mayo, M., Silverberg, G. G., & McGuire, D. (2004). Reduction of brain lipid peroxidation by CSF drainage in Alzheimer's disease patients. *Journal of Alzheimer's Disease*, *6*, 385–389. PMID:15345808

Prensky, M. (2001). Digital natives, digital immigrants. *Horizon*, *9*(5), 1–6. doi:10.1108/10748120110424816

President's Council on Bioethics. (2003). *Beyond therapy: Biotechnology and the pursuit of happiness*. Dana Press.

Pressman, J. D. (1998). *Last resort: Psychosurgery and the limits of medicine*. Cambridge, UK: Cambridge University Press.

Putnam, R. D. (2001). *Bowling alone: The collapse and revival of American community*. New York: Simon & Schuster.

Quintelier, E., & Theocharis, Y. (2012). Online political engagement, Facebook, and personality traits. *Social Science Computer Review*, *31*(3), 280–290. doi:10.1177/0894439312462802

Rabins, P., Appleby, B. S., Brandt, J., DeLong, M. R., Dunn, L. B., & Gabriëls, L. et al. (2009). Scientific and ethical issues related to deep brain stimulation for disorders of mood, behavior, and thought. *Archives of General Psychiatry*, *66*, 931–937. doi:10.1001/archgenpsychiatry.2009.113 PMID:19736349

Racine, E., & Forlini, C. (2009). Expectations regarding cognitive enhancement create substantial challenges. *Journal of Medical Ethics*, *35*, 469–470. doi:10.1136/jme.2009.030460 PMID:19644002

Radhakrishnan, R. (2008). *History, the human, and the world between*. Duke University Press. doi:10.1215/9780822389309

Rapeli, L. (2013). *The conception of citizen knowledge in democratic theory*. Basingstoke, UK: Palgrave Macmillan. doi:10.1057/9781137322869

Raz, M. (2008). Between the ego and the icepick: Psychosurgery, psychoanalysis and psychiatric discourse. *Bulletin of the History of Medicine*, *82*, 387–420. doi:10.1353/bhm.0.0038 PMID:18622073

Reicher, S. (2008). Making a past fit for the future: The political and ontological dimensions of historical continuity. In F. Sani (Ed.), *Self continuity: Individual and collective perspectives* (pp. 145–158). New York: Psychology Press.

Reynolds, A. (2009). The augmented breast. *Radiologic Technology*, *80*(3), 241M–259M. PMID:19153201

Ribble, M. (2013). Digital citizenship: Nine elements. *Digital Citizenship*. Retrieved from http://digitalcitizenship.net/Nine_Elements.html

Ribble, M., & Bailey, G. (2011). *Digital citizenship in schools* (2nd ed.). Eugene, OR: International Society for Technology in Education.

Riis, J., Simmons, J. P., & Goodwin, G. P. (2008). Preferences for enhancement pharmaceuticals: The reluctance to enhance fundamental traits. *The Journal of Consumer Research*, *35*, 495–508. doi:10.1086/588746

Rivest, R. L., Chaum, D., Preneel, B., Rubin, A., Saari, D. G., & Vora, P. L. (2009). Guest editorial special issue on electronic voting. *IEEE Transactions on Information Forensics and Security*, *4*(4), 593–596. doi:10.1109/TIFS.2009.2034721

Roberto, B. C. (2010). M – Cognocracy: Building participatory democracy through the electronic voting and mobile ICT. *Vision de Futuro*, *13* (1).

Robison, R. A., Taghva, A., Liu, C. Y., & Apuzzo, M. L. (2012). Surgery of the mind, mood and conscious state: An idea in evolution. *World Neurosurgery*, *77*, 662–686. doi:10.1016/j.wneu.2012.03.005 PMID:22446082

Roco, M. C., & Bainbridge, W. (Eds.). (2002). *Converging technologies for improving human performance: Nanotechnology, biotechnology, information technology and cognitive science*. Arlington, VA: NSF/Department of Commerce. Retrieved from www.wtec.org/ConvergingTechnologies/Report/NBIC_frontmatter.pdf

Rodriguez, R. T., Leyens, J. P., Rodriguez, A. P., Betancor Rodriguez, V., Quiles de Castillo, M. N., Demoulin, S., & Cortés, B. (2005). The lay distinction between primary and secondary emotions: A spontaneous categorization? *International Journal of Psychology*, *40*(2), 100–107. doi:10.1080/00207590444000221

Roduit, J. A. R., Baumann, H., & Heilinger, J-C. (forthcoming). *Evaluating human enhancements: The importance of ideals*.

Roduit, J. A. R., Baumann, H., & Heilinger, J.-C. (2013). Human enhancement and perfection. *Journal of Medical Ethics*. doi:10.1136/medethics-2012-100920 PMID:23436909

Rohrer, J. (2009). Black presidents, gay marriages, and Hawaiian sovereignty: Reimagining citizenship in the age of Obama. *American Studies (Lawrence, Kan.)*, *50*(3/4), 107–130.

Rohrer, T. (2006). The body in space: Embodiment, experientialism and linguistic conceptualization. In J. Zlatev, T. Ziemke, F. Roz, & R. Dirven (Eds.), *Body, language and mind* (Vol. 2). Berlin: Mouton de Gruyter.

Rome Statute of the International Criminal Court. (1998). *United Nations Treaty Website*. Retrieved 15 August, 2013 from http://untreaty.un.org/cod/icc/statute/99_corr/cstatute.htm

Rose, N., & Gallagher, P. (2012). *Human enhancement and the future of work*. The Royal Academy of Engineering, The Royal Society.

Royal Society. (2012). *Brain waves module 3: Neuroscience, conflict and security*. Retrieved 16 December, 2012 from http://royalsociety.org/policy/projects/brain-waves/conflict-security/

Roy, T., Springer, B., McNulty, V., & Butler, N. (2010). Physical fitness. *Military Medicine*, *175*(1), 14–20. doi:10.7205/MILMED-D-10-00058 PMID:20108837

Rozner, E. (1998). Haves, have-nots, and have-to-haves: Net effects of the digital divide. *Berkman Center for Internet & Society*. Retrieved 28 November, 2012 from http://cyber.law.harvard.edu/fallsem98/final_papers/Rozner.html

Rubin, C. T. (2006, Winter). The rhetoric of extinction. *New Atlantis (Washington, D.C.)*, 64–73.

Ruetzler, T., Taylor, J., Reynolds, D., Baker, W., & Killen, C. (2012). What is professional attire today? A conjoint analysis of personal presentation attributes. *International Journal of Hospitality Management*, 31(3), 937–943. doi:10.1016/j.ijhm.2011.11.001

Russell, C. (2013, December 3). The stars who regret going under the knife. *Irish Independent*, p. 36.

Russo, M., Arnett, V., Thomas, M., & Caldwell, J. (2008). Ethical use of cogniceuticals in the militaries of democratic nations. *The American Journal of Bioethics*, 8(2), 39–41. doi:10.1080/15265160802015016 PMID:18570076

Ryan, C. (2009)... *Amputating Healthy Limbs*, 86, 31–33.

Saharso, S. (2003). Feminist ethics, autonomy and the politics of multiculturalism. *Feminist Theory*, 4(2), 199–215. doi:10.1177/14647001030042007

Sample, I. (2004, July 3). Wired awake. *The Guardian*, p. S4.

Sanchez Taylor, J. (2012). Fake breasts and power: Gender, class and cosmetic surgery. *Women's Studies International Forum*, 35(6), 458–466. doi:10.1016/j.wsif.2012.09.003

Sandel, M. (2009). The case against perfection: What's wrong with designer children, bionic athletes, and genetic engineering. In J. Savulescu, & N. Bostrom (Eds.), *Human Enhancement*. Oxford, UK: Oxford University Press.

Sandel, M. J. (2007). *The case against perfection: Ethics in the age of genetic engineering*. Belknap Press of Harvard University Press.

Sandler, R., & Cafaro, P. (Eds.). (2005). *Environmental virtue ethics*. Lanham, MD: Rowman and Littlefield.

Sani, F. (2008). Introduction and overview. In F. Sani (Ed.), *Self continuity: Individual and collective perspectives* (pp. 1–12). New York: Psychology Press.

Sani, F., Bowe, M., & Herrera, M. (2008). Perceived collective continuity: Seeing groups as temporally enduring entities. In F. Sani (Ed.), *Self continuity: Individual and collective perspectives* (pp. 159–172). New York: Psychology Press.

Sarker, M. M. (2013). E-Voting experience in Bangladesh by using electronic voting machines (EVMS). *International Journal of Engineering Science and Technology*, 5(5).

Sarwer, D. B., & Crerand, C. E. (2004). Body image and cosmetic medical treatments. *Body Image*, 1(1), 99–111. doi:10.1016/S1740-1445(03)00003-2 PMID:18089144

Sassòli, M. (2003). Legitimate targets of attacks under international humanitarian law. *International Humanitarian Law Research Initiative*. Retrieved 28 November, 2012 from http://www.hpcrre search.org/sites/default/files/publications/Session1.pdf

Savulescu, J. (2003). Human-Animal transgenesis and chimeras might be an expression of our humanity. *The American Journal of Bioethics*, 3(3), 22–25. doi:10.1162/15265160360706462 PMID:14594475

Savulescu, J. (2005). New breeds of humans: The moral obligation to enhance. *Ethics. Law and Moral Philosophy of Reproductive Medicine*, 1(1), 36–39.

Savulescu, J. (2006). Justice, fairness, and enhancement. *Annals of the New York Academy of Sciences*, 1093, 321–338. doi:10.1196/annals.1382.021 PMID:17312266

Savulescu, J., & Bostrom, N. (Eds.). (2009). *Human enhancement*. Oxford, UK: Oxford University Press.

Savulescu, J., & Kahane, G. (2009). The moral obligation to create children with the best chance of the best life. *Bioethics*, 23, 274–290. doi:10.1111/j.1467-8519.2008.00687.x PMID:19076124

Scanlon, D. (2013). Specific Learning Disability and Its Newest Definition: Which Is Comprehensive? and Which Is Insufficient? *Journal of Learning Disabilities*, 46(1), 26–33. doi:10.1177/0022219412464342 PMID:23144061

Schaefer, G. O., Kahane, G., & Savulescu, J. (2013). Autonomy and enhancement. *Neuroethics*. doi:10.1007/s12152-013-9189-5

Schater, D. L., Addis, D. R., & Buckner, R. L. (2007). Remembering the past to imagine the future: The prospective brain. *Nature Reviews. Neuroscience*, *8*, 657–661. doi:10.1038/nrn2213 PMID:17700624

Schermer, M. (2008). On the argument that enhancement is cheating. *Journal of Medical Ethics*, *34*(2), 85–88. doi:10.1136/jme.2006.019646 PMID:18234944

Schiller, B. (2013). Eight new jobs people will have in 2025. *FastCo Exist*. Retrieved from http://www.fastcoexist.com/3015652/futurist-forum/8-new-jobs-people-will-have-in-2025

Schlaepfer, T., George, M., & Mayberg, H. (2010). WFSBP Guidelines on brain stimulation treatment in psychiatry. *The World Journal of Biological Psychiatry*, *11*, 2–18. doi:10.3109/15622970903170835 PMID:20146648

Schlesinger, R. (2003, January 4). Defense cites stimulants in 'friendly fire' case. *Boston Globe*, p. A3.

Schmitz-Luhn, B., Katzenmeier, C., & Woopen, C. (2012). Law and Ethics of Deep Brain Stimulation. *International Journal of Law and Psychiatry*, *35*, 130–136. doi:10.1016/j.ijlp.2011.12.007 PMID:22244083

Schramme, T. (2002). Natürlichkeit als wert. *Analyse & Kritik*, *2*, 249–271.

Schroeder, S. (2013, December 25). Edward Snowden's Christmas message and other news you need to know. *Mashable*. Retrieved from http://mashable.com/2013/12/25/edward-snowden-christmas-brief/

Scollon, R., & Scollon, S. W. (2004). *Nexus analysis: Discourse and the emerging internet*. New York: Routledge.

Selgelid, M. (2007). An argument against arguments for enhancement. *Studies in Ethics, Law, and Technology*, *1*.

Shachar, A. (2005). Religion, state, and the problems of gender: New modes of citizenship and governance in diverse societies. *McGill Law Journal. Revue de Droit de McGill*, *50*, 49–88.

Shachtman, N. (2007a). Be more than you can be. *Wired*, *15*(3).

Shachtman, N. (2007b, March 8). Supercharging soldiers' cells. *Wired*. Retrieved 28 November, 2012 from http://www.wired.com/dangerroom/2007/03/supercharging_s/

Shakespeare, T. (2006). The social model of disability. In L. Davis (Ed.), *The disability studies reader* (pp. 197–204). New York: Routledge.

Shamos, M., & Yasinsac, A. (2012). Realities of e-voting security. *IEEE Security & Privacy*, *10*(5), 16–17. doi:10.1109/MSP.2012.124

Shanker, T., & Duenwald, M. (2003, January 19). Threats and responses: bombing errors puts a spotlight on pilots' pills. *New York Times*, p. 1.

Sharkey, N. (2011). The automation and proliferation of military drones and the protection of civilians. *Law. Innovation and Technology*, *3*(2), 229–240. doi:10.5235/175799611798204914

Shaughnessy, L. (2012). One soldier, one year: $850,000 and rising. *CNN Security Clearance*. Retrieved 28 November, 2012 from http://security.blogs.cnn.com/2012/02/28/one-soldier-one-year- 850000 andrising/

Shay, J. (1994). *Achilles in Vietnam: Combat trauma and the undoing of character*. New York, NY: Simon and Schuster.

Shields, V. R., & Heinecken, D. (2001). *Measuring up: How advertising affects self-image*. Philadelphia, PA: University of Pennsylvania Press.

Shiozawa, P., Fregni, F., Bensenor, I. M., Lotufo, P. A., & Berlim, M. T., Daskalakis, … Brunoni, A. R. (2014). Transcranial direct current stimulation for major depression: An updated systematic review and meta-analysis. *The International Journal of Neuropsychopharmacology*, *8*, 1–10.

Simon, G. E., Gureje, O., & Fullerton, C. (2001). Course of hypochondriasis in an international primary care study. *General Hospital Psychiatry*, *23*(2), 51–55. doi:10.1016/S0163-8343(01)00115-3 PMID:11313070

Simons, B., & Jones, D. W. (2012). Internet voting is unachievable for the foreseeable future and therefore not inevitable. *Communications of the ACM*, *55*(10), 68–77. doi:10.1145/2347736.2347754

Simpson, D. (2004, July 2). US pilot defends attack in secret. *Toronto Star*, p. A01.

Singer, P. (2009, November 12). How to be all that you can be: A look at the Pentagon's five step plan for making Iron man real. *The Brookings Institution*. Retrieved 28 November, 2012, from http://www.brookings.edu/articles/2008 /0502_iron_man_singer.aspx

Singer, P. (2000). *Writings on an ethical life*. London: Fourth Estate.

Singer, P. (2009). *Wired for war: The robotics revolution and conflict in the 21st century*. New York, NY: The Penguin Press.

Skinner, B. F. (1969). *Contingencies of reinforcement*. Retrieved from http://en.wikiquote.org/wiki/Machine

Slatin, J. (2001). The art of ALT: Toward a more accessible web. *Computers and Composition*, *18*, 73–81. doi:10.1016/S8755-4615(00)00049-9

Slevec, J., & Tiggemann, M. (2010). Attitudes toward cosmetic surgery in middle-aged women: Body image, aging anxiety, and the media. *Psychology of Women Quarterly*, *34*(1), 65–74. doi:10.1111/j.1471-6402.2009.01542.x

Slote, M. (2011). *The impossibility of perfection: Aristotle, feminism and the complexities of ethics*. Oxford, UK: Oxford University Press. doi:10.1093/acprof:oso/9780199790821.003.0003

Small, G., & Vogan, G. (2008). IBrain. New York: Collins Living (Harper Collins).

Smirnova, M. H. (2012). A will to youth: The woman's anti-aging elixir. *Social Science & Medicine*, *75*(7), 1236–1243. doi:10.1016/j.socscimed.2012.02.061 PMID:22742924

Smith, J. E. (2006, January 8). *It's a Life, Not a Feel-Good Moment*. Retrieved December 1, 2013, from http://www.washingtonpost.com/wp-dyn/content/article/2006/01/06/AR2006010601485.html

Snyman, N., Egan, J. R., London, K., Howman-Giles, R., Gill, D., Gillis, J., & Scheinberg, A. (2010). Zolpidem for persistent vegetative state—A placebo-controlled trial in pediatrics. *Neuropediatrics*, *41*(5), 223–227. doi:10.1055/s-0030-1269893 PMID:21210338

Solvi, A. S., Foss, K., von Soest, T., Roald, H. E., Skolleborg, K. C., & Holte, A. (2010). Motivational factors and psychological processes in cosmetic breast augmentation surgery. *Journal of Plastic, Reconstructive & Aesthetic Surgery; JPRAS*, *63*(4), 673–680. doi:10.1016/j.bjps.2009.01.024 PMID:19268646

Somerville, M. (2006). *The ethical imagination: Journeys of the human spirit*. Melbourne, Australia: Melbourne University Press.

Sotala, K. (2012). Advantages of artificial intelligences, uploads, and digital minds. *International Journal of Machine Learning*, *4*(1), 275–291.

Sparacio, R. (2013, November 15). Technology and medicine: Applying Google Glass in the medical field. *Multibriefs*. Retrieved from http://exclusive.multibriefs.com/content/technology-and-medicine-applying-google-glass-in-the-medical-field

Sparrow, R. (2010). Better than men? Sex and the therapy/enhancement distinction. *Kennedy Institute of Ethics Journal*, *20*(2), 115–144. doi:10.1353/ken.0.0308 PMID:20653249

Sparrow, R. (2011). A not-so-new eugenics: Harris and Savulescu on human enhancement. *The Hastings Center Report*, *41*, 32–42. PMID:21329104

Sparrow, R. (2011). Liberalism and eugenics. *Australasian Journal of Philosophy*, *89*(3), 499–517. doi:10.1080/00048402.2010.484464

Spegele, R. D. (1971). Fiction and political theory. *Social Research*, *38*(1), 108–138.

Spielmans, G., & Parry, P. (2010). From evidence based medicine to marketing based medicine: Evidence from internal industry documents. *Journal of Bioethical Inquiry*, *7*, 13–30. doi:10.1007/s11673-010-9208-8

Spilson, S. V., Chung, K. C., Greenfield, M. L. V. H., & Walters, M. (2002). Are plastic surgery advertisements conforming to the ethical codes of the American society of plastic surgeons? *Plastic and Reconstructive Surgery*, *109*(3), 1181–1186. doi:10.1097/00006534-200203000-00063 PMID:11884856

St. Louis Post-Dispatch Editors. (2003, July 3). The court martial. *St. Louis Post-Dispatch*, p. C12.

Stahl, B. (2011). IT for a better future: how to integrate ethics, politics and innovation. *Journal of Information. Communication & Ethics in Society*, *9*(3), 140–156. doi:10.1108/14779961111167630

Stanford Encyclopedia of Philosophy. (2011). Sorites Paradox. *Stanford Encyclopedia of Philosophy*. Retrieved 28 November, 2012 from http://plato.stanford.edu/entries/sorites-paradox/

Steiner, N. D. (2010). Economic globalization and voter turnout in established democracies. *Electoral Studies*, *29*(3), 444–459. doi:10.1016/j.electstud.2010.04.007

Stelarc. (1984). An interview with Stelarc. In J. D. Paffrath & Stelarc (Eds.), *Obsolete body: Suspensions: Stelarc* (pp. 16-17). Davis, CA: J.P. Publications.

Sterman, M. B., & Egner, T. (2006). Foundation and practice of neurofeedback for the treatment of epilepsy. *Applied Psychophysiology and Biofeedback*, *31*, 21–35. doi:10.1007/s10484-006-9002-x PMID:16614940

Stern, M. J. (2013, May 6). You are already enhanced: Everyday technologies give us superpowers that would make our ancestors wonder if we're entirely human. *Slate*. Retrieved December 27, 2013, from http://www.slate.com/articles/health_and_science/superman/2013/05/history_of_human_enhancement_how_plastic_surgery_birth_control_aspirin_ivf.single.html

Stewart, C. (2010, February 14). Montag took wrong road with plastic surgeries. *Orange County Register*, p. K.

Stewart, C. III. (2011). Voting technologies. *Annual Review of Political Science*, *14*(1), 353–378. doi:10.1146/annurev.polisci.12.053007.145205

Stice, E., Spangler, D., & Agras, W. S. (2001). Exposure to media-portrayed thin-ideal images adversely affects vulnerable girls: A longitudinal experiment. *Journal of Social and Clinical Psychology*, *20*(3), 270–288. doi:10.1521/jscp.20.3.270.22309

STOA (European Parliament Scientific and Technological Options Assessment). (2010). *Making Perfect Life: Bioengineering (in) the 21st Century. Interim Study*. IP/A/STOA/FWC-2008-96/LOT6/SC1, Study by the European Technology Assessment Group. Retrieved from http://www.itas.kit.edu/downloads/etag_esua10a.pdf

Stone, A. R. (2004). Split subjects, not atoms, or, how I fell in love with my prosthesis. *Configurations*, *2*(1), 73–190.

Stromer-Galley, J. (2003). Voting and the public sphere: Conversations on internet voting. *PS: Political Science and Politics*, *36*(4), 727–731.

Student Support Service. (2008, December 19). *The social and medical model of disability*. University of Leicester. Retrieved December 1, 2013, from http://www2.le.ac.uk/offices/ssds/accessability/staff/accessabilitytutors/information-for-accessability-tutors/the-social-and-medical-model-of-disability

Students Rebel Against Tracking Chips. (2012, November 27). Retrieved from http://www.ksn.com/content/news/also/story/Students-rebel-against-tracking-chips/MwIl-w0lUf0Od2qb5s0oEQw.cspx

Sullivan, D. A. (2000). *Cosmetic surgery: The cutting edge of commercial medicine in America*. New Brunswick, NJ: Rutgers University Press.

Sun, Y., Tao, F.-B., Su, P.-Y., Mai, J.-C., Shi, H.-J., & Han, Y.-T. et al. (2012). National estimates of the pubertal milestones among urban and rural Chinese girls. *The Journal of Adolescent Health*, *51*(3), 279–284. doi:10.1016/j.jadohealth.2011.12.019 PMID:22921139

Susman, J. (1993). Disabilty, Stigma, and Deviance. *Social Science & Medicine*, *38*(1), 15–22. doi:10.1016/0277-9536(94)90295-X

Swami, V. (2009). Body appreciation, media influence, and weight status predict consideration of cosmetic surgery among female undergraduates. *Body Image*, *6*(4), 315–317. doi:10.1016/j.bodyim.2009.07.001 PMID:19656747

Swami, V., Campana, A. N. N. B., Ferreira, L., Barrett, S., Harris, A. S., & Tavares, M. C. G. C. F. (2011). The acceptance of cosmetic surgery scale: Initial examination of its factor structure and correlates among Brazilian adults. *Body Image*, *8*(2), 179–185. PMID:21354875

Swami, V., Taylor, R., & Carvalho, C. (2009). Acceptance of cosmetic surgery and celebrity worship: Evidence of associations among female undergraduates. *Personality and Individual Differences*, *47*(8), 869–872. doi:10.1016/j.paid.2009.07.006

Swan, L. S., & Ward, J. (2012). Digital immortality: Self or 0010110? *International Journal of Machine Consciousness*, *4*(1), 245–256. doi:10.1142/S1793843012400148

Swanton, C. (2003). *Virtue ethics: A pluralistic view*. Oxford, UK: Oxford University Press. doi:10.1093/0199253889.001.0001

Sweeney, L. (2002). k-anonymity: A Model For Protecting Privacy. *International Journal on Uncertainty. Fuzziness and Knowledge-Based Systems, 10*(5), 557–570. doi:10.1142/S0218488502001648

Taggart, F. (2012, October 29). Buddhist monk is world's happiest man. *Google News*. Retrieved August 16, 2013 from http://www.google.com/hostednews/afp/article/ALeqM5gPq3GZRQBAW-dbDc1E_Y9yKlQEfA?docId=CNG.6f253034ff18b21babb269b6f776f4d8.3c1

Taleporos, G., & McCabe, M. P. (2002). Body image and physical disability - Personal perspectives. *Social Science & Medicine, 54*(6), 971–980. doi:10.1016/S0277-9536(01)00069-7 PMID:11996029

Tan, D. S., & Nijholt, A. (2010). *Brain-computer interfaces: Applying our minds to human-computer interaction*. Springer Link. doi:10.1007/978-1-84996-272-8

Taylor, C. (2007). Cultures of democracy and citizen efficacy. *Public Culture, 19*(1), 117–150. doi:10.1215/08992363-2006-027

Taylor-Gooby, P. (2008). *Reframing social citizenship*. Oxford, UK: Oxford University Press. doi:10.1093/acprof:oso/9780199546701.001.0001

Tedstaff. (2008). *Stroke of insight: Jill Bolte Taylor on TED.com*. Retrieved from http://blog.ted.com/2008/03/12/jill_bolte_tayl/

Thayer, K. A. (2012). *Cyborg metapathography in Michael Chorost's Rebuilt: Introducing the cyborg patient as transhumanist rhetor*. (Unpublished doctoral dissertation). Rensselaer Polytechnic Institute, Troy, NY.

Thayer, K. A. (2013). Beyond cyborg metapathography in Michael Chrost's *Rebuilt* to *World Wide Mind*: Introducing morphos as a rhetorical concept in cyborgography. *Teknokultura, 10*(2).

The Belmont Report: Ethical Principles and Guidelines for the Protection of Human Subjects of Research. (1979). Report of the National Commission for the Protection of Human Subjects of Biomedical and Behavioral Research. Retrieved from http://www.hhs.gov/ohrp/humansubjects/guidance/belmont.html

Thibaut, A., Bruno, M. A., Ledoux, D., Demertzi, A., & Laureys, S. (2014). tDCS in patients with disorders of consciousness: Sham-controlled randomized double-blind study. *Neurology, 82*, 1112–1118. doi:10.1212/WNL.0000000000000260 PMID:24574549

Thompson, S. J. (2011, June). *Endless empowerment and existence: From virtual literacy to online permanence in presence*. Paper presented at the First International Forum on Media and Information Literacy. Fez, Morocco.

Thompson, P. (2008). The opposite of human enhancement: Nanotechnology and the blind chicken problem. *NanoEthics, 2*(3), 305–316. doi:10.1007/s11569-008-0052-9

Thonnard, M., Gosseries, O., Demertzi, A., Lugo, Z., Vanhaudenhuyse, A., & Bruno, M.-A. et al. (2013). Effect of zolpidem in chronic disorders of consciousness: A prospective open-label study. *Functional Neurology, 28*(4), 259–264. PMID:24598393

Tignol, J., Biraben-Gotzamanis, L., Martin-Guehl, C., Grabot, D., & Aouizerate, B. (2007). Body dysmorphic disorder and cosmetic surgery: Evolution of 24 subjects with a minimal defect in appearance 5 years after their request for cosmetic surgery. *European Psychiatry, 22*(8), 520–524. doi:10.1016/j.eurpsy.2007.05.003 PMID:17900876

Tolbert, C. J., & McNeal, R. S. (2003). Unravelling the effects of the internet on political participation? *Political Research Quarterly, 56*(2), 175–185. doi:10.1177/106591290305600206

Tulving, E. (1985). Memory and consciousness. *Canadian Psychology, 25*, 1–12. doi:10.1037/h0080017

Tunçalp, D., & Fagan, M. H. (2013). *Bodyware: Information Systems in the Age of the Augmented Body and the Enhanced Mind. Call for Papers*. Paper presented at IS Philosophy Track: Philosophy for a Hyperconnected World, 19th Americas Conference on Information Systems. Chicago, IL.

Turkle, S. (1991). Romantic reactions: Paradoxical responses to the computer presence. In J. J. Sheehan, & M. Sosna (Eds.), *The boundaries of humanity: Humans, animals, machines* (pp. 224–252). Los Angeles, CA: University of California Press.

Turkle, S. (1995). *Life on the screen: Identity in the age of the Internet*. New York: Simon & Schuster.

Turkle, S. (2011). *Alone together: Why we expect more from technology and less from each other*. New York: Basic Books.

UK Academy of Medical Sciences. (2012). *Human enhancement and the future of work*. Retrieved on 28 November, 2012, http://royalsociety.org/policy/projects/human-enhancement/workshop-report/

Unger, P. (1990). *Identity, consciousness, and value*. New York: Oxford University Press.

United Nations Human Rights Committee. (1988). *CCPR General Comment No. 16: Article 17 (Right to Privacy), The Right to Respect of Privacy, Family, Home and Correspondence, and Protection of Honour and Reputation*. Retrieved from http://www.refworld.org/docid/453883f922.html

United States v. Chadwell, 36 CMR 741 (1965).

United States v. New, 50 MJ 729, 739 (A. Ct.Crim. App. 1999).

US Department of Defense. (2012a). *Department of Defense Directive 1010.1 (originally 28 December 1984)*. Retrieved on 18 December from 2012, http://www.dtic.mil/whs/directives/corres/pdf/101001p.pdf

US Department of Defense. (2012b). *Department of Defense Directive 6200.2*. Retrieved 18 December 2012 from http://www.dtic.mil/whs/directiv es/corres/pdf/620002p.pdf

US Department of Health and Human Services. (2008). *Short stature: Criteria for determining disability in infants and children*. Agency for Healthcare Research and Quality. Retrieved 28 November 2012 from http://www.ncbi.nlm.nih.gov/books/NBK36847/

US Government, Manual for Court-Martial. Part IV-19, ¶ 14c(2)(a)(i) (2010).

Van Staden, C. W., & Kruger, C. (2003). Incapacity to give informed consent owing to mental disorder. *Journal of Medical Ethics*, 29, 41–43. doi:10.1136/jme.29.1.41 PMID:12569195

Vatz, R. E. (2009). The mythical status of situational rhetoric: Implications for rhetorical critics' relevance in the public arena. *The Review of Communication*, 1(9), 1–5. doi:10.1080/15358590802020798

Veale, D., Ellison, N., Werner, T. G., Dodhia, R., Serfaty, M. A., & Clarke, A. (2012). Development of a cosmetic procedure screening questionnaire (COPS) for body dysmorphic disorder. *Journal of Plastic, Reconstructive & Aesthetic Surgery; JPRAS*, 65(4), 530–532. doi:10.1016/j.bjps.2011.09.007 PMID:22000332

Velmans, M. (2009). How to define consciousness – and how not to define consciounsess. *Journal of Consciousness Studies*, 16(5), 139–156.

Vernon, D. J. (2005). Can neurofeedback training enhance performance? An evaluation of the evidence with implications for future research. *Applied Psychophysiology and Biofeedback*, 30, 347–364. doi:10.1007/s10484-005-8421-4 PMID:16385423

Vertovec, S. (1998). Multicultural policies and modes of citizenship in European studies. *International Social Science Journal*, 50(156), 187–199. doi:10.1111/1468-2451.00123

Viets, H. R. (1949). Report of the librarian. *The New England Journal of Medicine*, 240, 917–920. doi:10.1056/NEJM194906092402304

Visser, S., & Bouman, T. K. (2001). The treatment of hypochondriasis: Exposure plus response prevention vs cognitive therapy. *Behaviour Research and Therapy*, 39(4), 423–442. doi:10.1016/S0005-7967(00)00022-X PMID:11280341

von Soest, T., Kvalem, I. L., Roald, H. E., & Skolleborg, K. C. (2009). The effects of cosmetic surgery on body image, self-esteem, and psychological problems. *Journal of Plastic, Reconstructive & Aesthetic Surgery; JPRAS*, 62(10), 1238–1244. doi:10.1016/j.bjps.2007.12.093 PMID:18595791

von Soest, T., Kvalem, I. L., Skolleborg, K. C., & Roald, H. E. (2009). Cosmetic surgery and the relationship between appearance satisfaction and extraversion: Testing a transactional model of personality. *Journal of Research in Personality*, 43(6), 1017–1025. doi:10.1016/j.jrp.2009.07.001

Walker, M. (2002). *What is transhumanism? Why is a transhumanist? Humanity+ (World Transhumanist Association)*. Retrieved May 22, 2012 from http://www.transhumanism.org/index.php/th/more/298/

Walker, J., Vincent, N., Furer, P., Cox, B., & Kevin, K. (1999). Treatment preference in hypochondriasis. *Journal of Behavior Therapy and Experimental Psychiatry*, *30*(4), 251–258. doi:10.1016/S0005-7916(99)00027-0 PMID:10759322

Walker, R., & Ivanhoe, P. (Eds.). (2007). *Working virtue: Virtue ethics and contemporary moral problems*. Oxford, UK: Oxford University Press.

Wall, S. (2008). Perfectionsism in moral and political philosophy. In E. N. Zalta (Ed.), *The Stanford Encyclopedia of Philosophy*. Retrieved from http://plato.stanford.edu/archives/fall2008/entries/perfectionism-moral

Walters, S. (2010). Toward an Accessible Pedagogy: Dis/ability, Multimodality, and Universal Design in the Technical Communication Classroom. *Technical Communication Quarterly*, *19*(4), 427–454. doi:10.1080/10572252.2010.502090

Wang, S., Li, M., Wu, J., Kim, D.-H., Lu, N., & Su, Y. et al. (2012). Mechanics of Epidermal Electronics. *Journal of Applied Mechanics*, *79*, 1–6. doi:10.1115/1.4005963

Ward, C. (2010, April 14). From the girl next door to freaky fake & she's not done with the surgery yet, exclusive fame-hungry Heidi Montag. *The Mirror (Stafford, Tex.)*, 24–25.

Warwick, K. (2013). Cyborgs in space. *Acta Futura*, *6*, 25–35.

Wasserman, G., & Grabenstein, J. (2003). *Analysis of adverse events after anthrax immunization in US army medical personnel*. Retrieved 28 November, 2012 from http://www.dtic.mil/cgi-bin/GetTRDoc?AD=ADA495915

Weber, R. (2012). How Does Privacy Change in the Age of the Internet. In C. Fuchs, K. Boersma, A. Albrechtslund, & M. Sandoval (Eds.), *Internet and Surveillance, The Challenges of Web 2.0 and Social Media* (pp. 274–285). London: Routledge.

Weber, R. (2013). Transborder data transfers: Concepts, regulatory approaches and new legislative initiatives. *International Data Privacy Law*, *1*, 117–130. doi:10.1093/idpl/ipt001

Weck, F., Neng, J. M. B., Richtberg, S., & Stangier, U. (2012a). Dysfunctional beliefs about symptoms and illness in patients with hypochondriasis. *Psychosomatics*, *53*(2), 148–154. doi:10.1016/j.psym.2011.11.007 PMID:22424163

Weck, F., Neng, J. M. B., Richtberg, S., & Stangier, U. (2012b). The restrictive concept of good health in patients with hypochondriasis. *Journal of Anxiety Disorders*, *26*(8), 792–798. doi:10.1016/j.janxdis.2012.07.001 PMID:23023159

Weldemariam, K., Kemmerer, R. A., & Villafiorita, A. (2011). Formal analysis of an electronic voting system: An experience report. *Journal of Systems and Software*, *84*(10), 1618–1637. doi:10.1016/j.jss.2011.03.032

Whyte, J., & Myers, R. (2009). Incidence of clinically significant responses to zolpidem among patients with disorders of consciousness: A preliminary placebo controlled trial. *American Journal of Physical Medicine & Rehabilitation*, *88*(5), 410–418. doi:10.1097/PHM.0b013e3181a0e3a0 PMID:19620954

Wiggins, J. S., Wiggins, N., & Conger, J. C. (1968). Correlates of heterosexual somatic preference. *Journal of Personality and Social Psychology*, *10*(1), 82–90. doi:10.1037/h0026394 PMID:4386664

Wilson, S., & Haslam, N. (2009). Is the future more or less human? Differing views of humanness in the posthumanism debate. *Journal for the Theory of Social Behaviour*, *39*(2), 247–266. doi:10.1111/j.1468-5914.2009.00398.x

Wilson, S., & Haslam, N. (2012). Reasoning about human enhancement: Towards a folk psychological model of human nature and human identity. In R. Luppicini (Ed.), *Handbook of Research on technoself: Identity in a technological society* (pp. 175–188). Academic Press. doi:10.4018/978-1-4666-2211-1.ch010

Wilson, S., & Haslam, N. (2013). Humanness beliefs about behavior: An index and comparative human-nonhuman behavior judgments. *Behavior Research Methods*, *45*(2), 372–382. doi:10.3758/s13428-012-0252-7 PMID:22993128

Witte, J. C., & Mannon, S. E. (2010). *The internet and social inequalities*. New York: Routledge.

Witt, K., Kuhn, J., Timmermann, L., Zurowski, M., & Woopen, C. (2003). Deep brain stimulation and the search for identity. *Neuroethics, 6*, 499–511. doi:10.1007/s12152-011-9100-1 PMID:24273620

Wolfendale, J. (2008). Performance-enhancing technologies and moral responsibility in the military. *The American Journal of Bioethics, 8*(2), 28–38. doi:10.1080/15265160802014969 PMID:18570075

Wolff, J. (2009). Disability, status enhancement, personal enhancement and resource allocation. *Economics and Philosophy, 25*(1), 49–68. doi:10.1017/S0266267108002277

Wolf, N. (1991). *The beauty myth: How images of beauty are used against women*. New York, W.: Morrow.

World Economic Forum. (2013). *Report: Unlocking the Value of Personal Data: From Collection to Usage, February 2013*. Retrieved from http://www.weforum.org/issues/rethinking-personal-data

Wright, D., & de Hert, P. (n.d.). Privacy Impact Assessment. *Law, Governance and Technology Series, 28* (6).

Wright, D. (2011). A framework for the ethical impact assessment of information technology. *Ethics and Information Technology, 13*(3), 199–220. doi:10.1007/s10676-010-9242-6

Wyer, R. S. Jr, & Srull, T. K. (1989). *Memory and cognition in its social context*. Hillsdale, NJ: Erlbaum Associates.

Zdenek, S. (n.d.). *Accessible podcasting: College students on the margins in the new media classroom*. Retrieved December 1, 2013, from http://www.bgsu.edu/cconline/Ed_Welcome_Fall_09/compinfreewareintroduction.htm

Zickuhr, K. (2013, September 25). Who's not online and why: Pew Research Center internet and American life project. *Pew Research Center*. Retrieved from http://www.pewinternet.org/Press-Releases/2013/Offline-adults.aspx

Zimbardo, P. (2007). *The Lucifer effect: Understanding how good people turn evil*. New York: Random House.

Zuckerman, D., & Abraham, A. (2008). Teenagers and cosmetic surgery: Focus on breast augmentation and liposuction. *The Journal of Adolescent Health, 43*(4), 318–324. doi:10.1016/j.jadohealth.2008.04.018 PMID:18809128

Zwaan, R. A., & Kaschak, M. P. (2009). Language in the brain, body, and world. In P. Robbins, & M. Aydede (Eds.), *The Cambridge handbook of situated cognition*. Cambridge, UK: Cambridge University Press. doi:10.1017/CBO9780511816826.019

Zwang, G. (2011). Vulvar reconstruction: The exploitation of an ignorance. *Sexologies, 20*(2), 81–87. doi:10.1016/j.sexol.2010.10.003

Zylinska, J. (2010). Playing God, Playing Adam: The politics and ethics of enhancement. *Journal of Bioethical Inquiry, 7*(2), 149–161. doi:10.1007/s11673-010-9223-9

About the Contributors

Steven John Thompson, PhD, is on faculty at Johns Hopkins University in the Krieger School of Arts & Sciences Advanced Academic Programs in Washington, DC, and at University of Maryland University College. His teaches media courses in Introduction to the Digital Age, Mass Media Law, and Media and Society. Steve's expertise is in research and analysis of Internet technologies, especially as existential phenomena. In 1996, he published pioneering quantitative research on Internet addiction and dependency. Dr. Thompson's research focuses primarily on the psychosocial, political, and policy effects of digital media on global societies. He is active internationally as a scholar on issues of digital media literacy, rhetorics, cyber-age freedom of expression, digital liberties, and media iconics and iconetics as expressed through cybersemiotics. He blogs as The Rhetorist at w8r.com.

* * *

Keith Abney was educated at Emory University, Fuller Seminary, and the University of Notre Dame. His research interests include the ethics of autonomous military robots, the ethics of human enhancement, space ethics, and other topics in the ethics and metaethics of emerging technologies. He has served on a hospital bioethics board and in his spare time enjoys being an amateur winemaker. He is co-editor (with George Bekey and Patrick Lin) of the book *Robot Ethics* (MIT Press, 2011).

Holger Baumann is a postgraduate researcher within the Zurich University Research Priority Program for Ethics and scientific coordinator of its network "Human Dignity in Practical Contexts" since 2009. His doctoral dissertation was about the concept of personal autonomy, and he has published several articles in this and related areas. In his recent work and publications, Baumann tries to bring together and connect general debates about the concepts of autonomy and human dignity with more specific debates within applied ethics in which these concepts are used – for example, some of his current research focuses on questions about human enhancement, organ trade, assisted suicide, and about the proper treatment and education of children.

Dev Bose, PhD, is a Lecturer in the Department of English at Iowa State University. Bose holds a Doctorate in Rhetorics, Communication, and Information Design from Clemson University. His scholarship is in disability studies and multimodal composition research, and he is an active member of the Disability Studies Special Interest Group at the Conference of College Composition and Communication (CCCC), where he is helping to draft legislation for disability accommodations at CCCC conferences. Dr. Bose is a member of the Society for Disability Studies.

Michael Burnam-Fink is a PhD candidate at Arizona State University in Human and Social Dimensions of Science and Technology. His work spans the history of medicine, science, and technology studies, encouraging innovation in assistive technologies for people with disabilities and narrative foresight methodologies. He is particularly interested in the practices of human performance enhancement. Michael was a Breakthrough Generation Fellow with The Breakthrough Institute and is a fellow with the Alliance for Person-Centered Accessible Technologies, a National Science Foundation IGERT grant.

Franco Cortese is a research scientist at ELPIs Foundation for Indefinite Lifespans, a non-profit research organization founded by biomedical gerontologist Dr. Marios Kyriazis to study interventions for aging and age-related diseases. Cortese is also an affiliate scholar of the Institute for Ethics and Emerging Technologies, where he works to analyze the philosophical, ethical, and socioeconomic implications of emerging technologies. He is the recipient of the IEET's 2013 Editor's Choice Award, and works with Ria University Press, *The Journal of Bioelectronics and Nanotechnology*, The Seasteading Institute, Brighter Brains Institute, and The Millennium Project. Franco lives in Ontario, Canada.

Marcia Alesan Dawkins, PhD, is a technology-loving, diversity-oriented intellectual entrepreneur from New York City, and communication professor at USC Annenberg in Los Angeles. An award-winning author, speaker, and educator, Dawkins understands how technology, diversity, and creative storytelling are changing who we are and how we communicate.

Dirk De Ridder, MD, PhD, is the Neurological Foundation Professor of Neurosurgery at the Dunedin School of Medicine, University of Otago in New Zealand. He is founder and director of the BRAI²N (Brain Research consortium for Advanced, Innovative, and Interdisciplinary Neuromodulation). His main interest is the understanding and treatment of phantom perceptions (sound, pain), especially by use of functional imaging navigated non-invasive (TMS, tDCS, tACS, tRNS, LORETA neurofeedback) and invasive (implants) neuromodulation techniques. He has developed "burst" and "noise" stimulation as novel stimulation designs for implants, and is working on other stimulation designs. He has published 30 book chapters, co-edited the *Textbook of Tinnitus*, and has authored or co-authored more than 130 PubMed listed papers, of which 100 deal with phantom sound perception. He is reviewer for 55 journals.

Mary Helen Fagan, PhD, is an Associate Professor of Information Systems & Management in the College of Business and Technology, University of Texas at Tyler. Dr. Fagan teaches courses in Introduction to Management Information Systems, E-Commerce, and Database Information Systems. She received her MBA and PhD in Information Systems from the University of Texas at Arlington. Before Dr. Fagan pursued her PhD, she worked for Andersen Consulting, now known as Accenture, a division of Arthur Andersen, helping organizations implement a wide range of information systems. Her primary research interests are concerned with the adoption and diffusion of information technologies, with research in a variety of areas (e.g., pen-based computing, teaching courseware, and electronic health records). Her research has been published in many academic journals in her field.

Elizabeth Falck is an entrepreneur, designer, and researcher based in San Francisco. Falck completed a BS at the University of Wisconsin, where she studied with groundbreaking researchers in educational gaming at the Games Learning and Society Program. She later studied exponential technologies, AI, and human-centered design at Singularity University's Graduate Studies Program. She has worked as a user-experience designer, filmmaker, and human-centered design specialist. Falck has co-founded several companies and nonprofits, and has built partnerships with governments and Fortune 500 companies around the world, raising capital and leading program development for her current organization, The Coalition of Innovative Development, Education, and Action.

Shannon E. French is the Inamori Professor in Ethics, Director of the Inamori International Center for Ethics and Excellence, and Associate Professor in the Philosophy Department at Case Western Reserve University. She has a secondary appointment as a professor in the CWRU School of Law and is a Senior Associate at the Center for Strategic and International Studies in Washington, DC. Dr. French taught for 11 years as an Associate Professor of Philosophy at the United States Naval Academy, and served as Associate Chair of the Department of Leadership, Ethics, and Law. Dr. French received her PhD in Philosophy from Brown University. Her main area of research is military ethics. She is author of *The Code of the Warrior: Exploring Warrior Values, Past and Present*; editor-in-chief for the *International Journal of Ethical Leadership*; and an associate editor for the *Journal of Military Ethics* and the *Encyclopedia of Global Justice*.

Jean-Paul Gagnon, PhD, is a social and political philosopher specializing in democratic theory. He joined the Australian Catholic University in 2013 as a university postdoctoral research fellow, and is based in the National School of Arts (Melbourne). He co-edits the Berghahn (Oxford, New York) journal *Democratic Theory* and also co-edits the Palgrave Macmillan book series *The Theories, Concepts, and Practices of Democracy*. His research focuses on democratic theory – especially innovations in democracy, the philosophy of democracy and democratization, and comparative democracy studies.

Jai Galliott is a military ethicist at Macquarie University in Sydney, Australia. He served briefly as an officer of the Royal Australian Navy prior to entering academic and is Lead Editor of Ashgate's *Emerging Technologies, Ethics, and International Affairs* series. Galliott has published widely on the topic of emerging military technologies and is a member of the Consortium for Robotics and Unmanned Systems Education and Research (CRUSER), the Institute for Ethics and Emerging Technologies (IEET), and the Institute of Electrical and Electronics Engineers (IEEE).

Grant Gillett, MSc MB ChB(Auck) DPhil(Oxf) FRACS FRSNZ, is a neurosurgeon and Professor of Medical Ethics from the University of Otago Medical School, Dunedin Hospital, and Otago Bioethics Centre in New Zealand. Grant trained as a neurosurgeon in New Zealand and the United Kingdom, and holds a Doctorate in Philosophy from the University of Oxford. Grant brings a deep analytical understanding to questions at the intersection of clinical neuroscience and philosophy. Professor Gillett is the author of over 200 peer-reviewed public publications and 5 books, including *The Mind and its Discontents*. Grant's current research interests include bioethics (end of life care, complementary and alternative medicine, autonomy, the patient's journey), neuroethics (brain birth, brain death, PVS, and minimally conscious states, issues of free will identity and responsibility), philosophy of psychiatry (the nature of mental disorder, psychopathy, dissociative disorders), and post-structuralist philosophy (the patient's voice, post-colonialism, human subjectivity).

Reuben Johnson, LLB, BSc(Hons), MB ChB, DPhil, FRCS (Neuro.Surg), MRSNZ, is currently Senior Lecturer and Consultant Neurosurgeon at the University of Otago, New Zealand. Reuben trained in Glasgow, London, Cambridge, Oxford, and Melbourne. He is a molecular neurobiologist, having completed a DPhil in the Department of Human Anatomy and Genetics in Oxford. Reuben has a dual qualification in law with a LLB from the University of London. He completed a Fellowship in Minimally Invasive Spinal Surgery and Scoliosis Surgery in Italy with Prof. Massimo Balsano in Alto Vincentino, and a Fellowship in Endoscopic Pituitary Surgery with Simon Cudlip at the John Radcliffe in Oxford. Reuben is the author of numerous peer-reviewed articles on neurosurgery. He is author and editor of four books in surgery, including the best-selling *Landmark Papers in Neurosurgery* by Oxford University Press, which he authored and co-edited with Alex Green from Oxford.

Joanna Kulesza, PhD, specializes in international Internet law. She is the author of *International Internet Law* (Routledge 2012), four monographs on international and Internet law, and over 30 peer-reviewed articles in Polish and English. She has been an invited lecturer with the Oxford Internet Institute, Norwegian Research Center for Computers and Law, Westfälische Wilhelms Universität Münster, and Justus-Liebig-Universität Gießen. She was a post-doctoral researcher at the University of Cambridge and Ludwig-Maximilians-Universität München, as well as a scholar of the Robert Bosch Stiftung, Polish Ministry of Foreign Affairs, Internet Governance Project, and the Foundation for Polish Science. She worked for the European Parliament, Polish Ministry of Foreign Affairs, and the Council of Europe. She currently is the Membership Committee Chair of the Global Internet Governance Academic Network (GigaNet). She is an assistant professor of international law at the Faculty of Law and Administration, University of Lodz, Poland and just finished a monograph on international law principle of due diligence.

Alexander LaCroix is a litigator at Jones, Skelton, and Hochuli in Phoenix, Arizona. He graduated from the Sandra Day O'Connor College of Law in 2012, where he contributed to "Enhanced Warfighters: Risk, Ethics, and Policy" (The Greenwall Foundation, 2013), a funded report in the area of technology ethics. He has delivered keynotes and presentations on cognitive enhancement at Arizona State University and the University of Arizona.

Patrick Lin, PhD, is the director of the Ethics + Emerging Sciences Group at California Polytechnic State University, San Luis Obispo, where he is an associate philosophy professor. He holds appointments at Stanford's School of Engineering; Stanford Law School's Center for Internet and Society; Consortium for Emerging Technologies, Military Operations, and National Security; University of Notre Dame's Emerging Technologies of National Security and Intelligence; and Australia's Centre for Applied Philosophy and Public Ethics. Previously, he held positions at the U.S. Naval Academy and Dartmouth College. Dr. Lin has published extensively in technology ethics. Dr. Lin has delivered invited talks and briefings on emerging military technologies to policy, defense, intelligence, and scientific organizations internationally. He earned his BA from University of California Berkeley and PhD from University of California Santa Barbara.

Brett Lunceford, PhD, The Pennsylvania State University, is a rhetorician who focuses on the intersections between the body, sexuality, and technology. He is the author of the book *Naked Politics: Nudity, Political Action, and the Rhetoric of the Body*, and more than two dozen articles and book chapters. His work has appeared in such journals as *Communication Law Review*, *ETC: A Review of General Semantics*, *Explorations in Media Ecology*, *Journal of Contemporary Rhetoric*, *Review of Communication*, and *Theology & Sexuality*. He is the current editor of *Journal of Contemporary Rhetoric*, and serves as Technology Officer for the Media Ecology Association. And, for the record, he has not had any cosmetic surgery.

Vincent Menuz is a research associate at the Universities of Montreal (OMICS-ETHICS group) and Zürich (Institut für Biomedizinishe Ethik), as well as a biology teacher in Geneva (Collège Roussessau). After completing a PhD in biology at the University of Geneva (Switzerland) in 2008, he started a post-doctoral fellowship in bioethics in 2010 at the University of Montreal (Canada), mainly focused on ethical and social issues related to human enhancement. His current work targets both academic and lay audience. On the one hand, he explores the influence of the concept of death on the current effort to decelerate aging and extend life span. On the other hand, he presents the socio-ethical issues related to human enhancement to lay audiences. He is also a columnist for the *Huffington Post* (France) as well as co-founder, vice-president, and senior editor for *Neo*Humanitas, a Swiss think tank, whose objectives are to democratize discussions on the socio-ethical issues related to the modifications of individuals through technological interventions.

Maxwell J. Mehlman is Distinguished University Professor, Arthur E. Petersilge Professor of Law and Director of the Law-Medicine Center, Case Western Reserve University School of Law, and Professor of Biomedical Ethics, Case Western Reserve University School of Medicine. He received his JD from Yale Law School in 1975, and holds bachelor degrees from Reed College and from Oxford University, which he attended as a Rhodes Scholar. Professor Mehlman practiced law with Arnold & Porter in Washington, DC. His published works include *Access to the Genome: The Challenge to Equality* and, most recently, *Transhumanist Dreams and Dystopian Nightmares: The Promise and Peril of Genetic Engineering,* among others. He is the director of the Consortium on Emerging Technologies, Military Operations, and National Security, and was a principal investigator on an NIH-funded project to examine ethical, legal, and policy issues raised by the use of genomic science by the military.

Johann A. R. Roduit is a founding member of *Neo*Humanitas, a think-tank fostering discussions about future and emerging technologies. He is finishing a doctoral dissertation in "Biomedical Ethics and Law" at the Institute of Biomedical Ethics in the University of Zurich. Funded by the Swiss National Science Foundation, Johann's research looks at the role of the notion of perfection in the ethical debate about human enhancement. Since 2013, Johann has been the recipient of a research grant to take part in the "Academic Visitor Programme" of the Oxford Uehiro Centre for Practical Ethics. Johann's research interests include bioethics, transhumanism, virtue ethics, ethics of human cloning, human dignity, and philosophical anthropology. A regular columnist for the *Huffington Post* and other newspapers, Johann has published in different scientific journals. He is the cofounder and curator of TEDxMartigny. He works as a scientific program coordinator at the University of Zurich.

Seth Schuknecht practices in the areas of commercial litigation, intellectual property, and aviation, aerospace, and autonomous systems. Prior to law school, Schuknecht served as a Naval Aviator for nine years on active duty in the U.S. Navy. His various assignments included selection and service as an instructor pilot at every operational squadron he was assigned. Schuknecht holds a civilian Airline Transport Pilot (ATP) Certificate with type ratings in five different aircraft. He received his BA with merit from the United States Naval Academy and his JD, cum laude, from Arizona State University, Sandra Day O'Connor College of Law.

Kevin A. Thayer received his PhD in Communication and Rhetoric from Rensselaer Polytechnic Institute in 2012. His dissertation, "Cyborg Metapathography in Michael Chorost's *Rebuilt*: Introducing the Cyborg Patient as Transhumanist Rhetor," pioneered an area of rhetoric at the intersection of rhetoric of the body, the rhetoric of medicine, and rhetoric of the cyborg. In 2013, he published the essay "Beyond Cyborg Metapathography in Michael Chorost's *Rebuilt* to *World Wide Mind*: Introducing 'Morphos' as a Rhetorical Concept in Cyborgography" in a special edition of *Teknokultura* entitled, "Cyborgs, Power, and Art: Race, Gender, and Class." He is currently a Cyborg Narrative Researcher at Cyborg-X.com.

Deniz Tunçalp, PhD, is an Assistant Professor of Management at Istanbul Technical University, Turkey, and teaches courses in the Faculty of Management at the Department of Management Engineering on Management and Organizations and Organization Theory. Dr. Tunçalp received his PhD in Management from Sabancı University. He worked for Gartner Group, META Group, Turkcell Mobile, and in strategic consulting, product management, and marketing fields. His primary research interests include organizational responses to technological change and qualitative research methods. Dr. Tunçalp has studied organizational adaptation to technology in different organizational situations at different levels of analysis. His research has been published in a number of academic journals in his field, such as *Operations Research* and *Journal of Organizational Ethnography*.

Shannon Vallor, PhD, is Associate Professor of Philosophy at Santa Clara University in Silicon Valley, where she studies the ethics of emerging technologies. She is co-leader of an interdisciplinary NSF project on big data and geospatial privacy, and author of a forthcoming book, *21st Century Virtue*. In collaboration with SCU's Markkula Center for Applied Ethics and Princeton Computer Scientist Arvind Narayanan, she recently developed a free online teaching module on software engineering ethics, now used by 21 universities on 5 continents. She is President-Elect of the Society for Philosophy and Technology and a member of the research initiative on Emerging Technologies of National Security and Intelligence (ETNSI) hosted by the University of Notre Dame's Reilly Center for Science, Technology, and Values.

Samuel Wilson, PhD, is a Research Fellow at the Swinburne Leadership Institute at Swinburne University of Technology. He received his PhD in Social Psychology from the University of Melbourne. After spending a year as a Post-Doctoral Research Fellow at the Melbourne Sustainable Society Institute at the University of Melbourne, Samuel joined Monash University's School of Psychology and Psychiatry as Lecturer in Psychology for two years, before moving to his present role. His research has been published in a number of journals including the *British Journal of Social Psychology*, *Ecology, and Society*, and *Social Networks*, as well as in the *Handbook of Research on Technoself: Identity in a Technological Society*. His research examines folk beliefs about humanness, especially in the context of human enhancement, conceptions of humanness in the Anthropocene, and the causes and consequences of self-continuity, especially as it relates to sustainability transitions and leadership for the public good.

Index